COMPARATIVE POLITICS 97/98

Fifteenth Edition

(Cover: Houses of Parliament, London, England. Cover image © 1996 PhotoDisc, Inc.)

Editor

Christian Søe
California State University, Long Beach

Christian Søe was born in Denmark, studied in Canada and the United States, and received his doctoral degree in political science from the Free University in Berlin. He is a political science professor at California State University, Long Beach. Dr. Søe teaches a wide range of courses in comparative politics and contemporary political theory, and actively participates in professional symposiums in the United States and abroad. His research deals primarily with developments in contemporary German politics, and he has been a regular observer of party politics in that country, most recently during the campaign leading up to the 1994 election of a new Bundestag. At present Dr. Søe is observing the shifts in the balance of power within the German party system, with particular attention to its implications for the formation of new government coalitions and changes in policy directions. Three of his most recent publications are a biographical essay on Hans-Dietrich Genscher, Germany's foreign minister from 1974 to 1992, in *Political Leaders of Contemporary Western Europe;* a chapter on the Free Democratic Party in *Germany's New Politics;* and another chapter on the Danish-German relationship in *The Germans and Their Neighbors*. Dr. Søe is also coeditor of the latter two books. He has been editor of *Annual Editions: Comparative Politics* since its beginning in 1983.

Annual Editions
A Library of Information from the Public Press
Dushkin/McGraw·Hill
Sluice Dock, Guilford, Connecticut 06437

Visit us on the Internet—http://www.dushkin.com/

This map has been developed to give you a graphic picture of where the countries of the world are located, the relationship they have with their region and neighbors, and their positions relative to the superpowers and power blocs. We have focused on certain areas to more clearly illustrate these crowded regions.

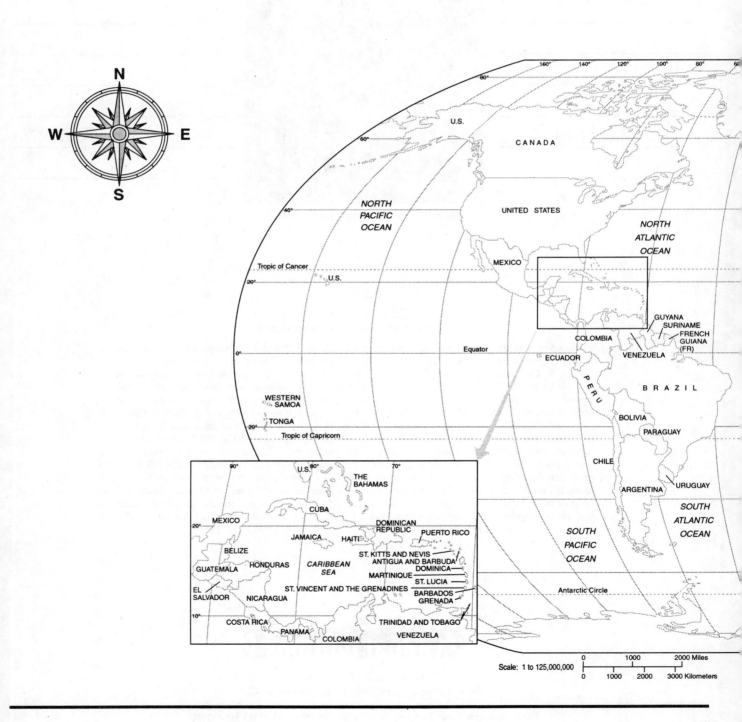

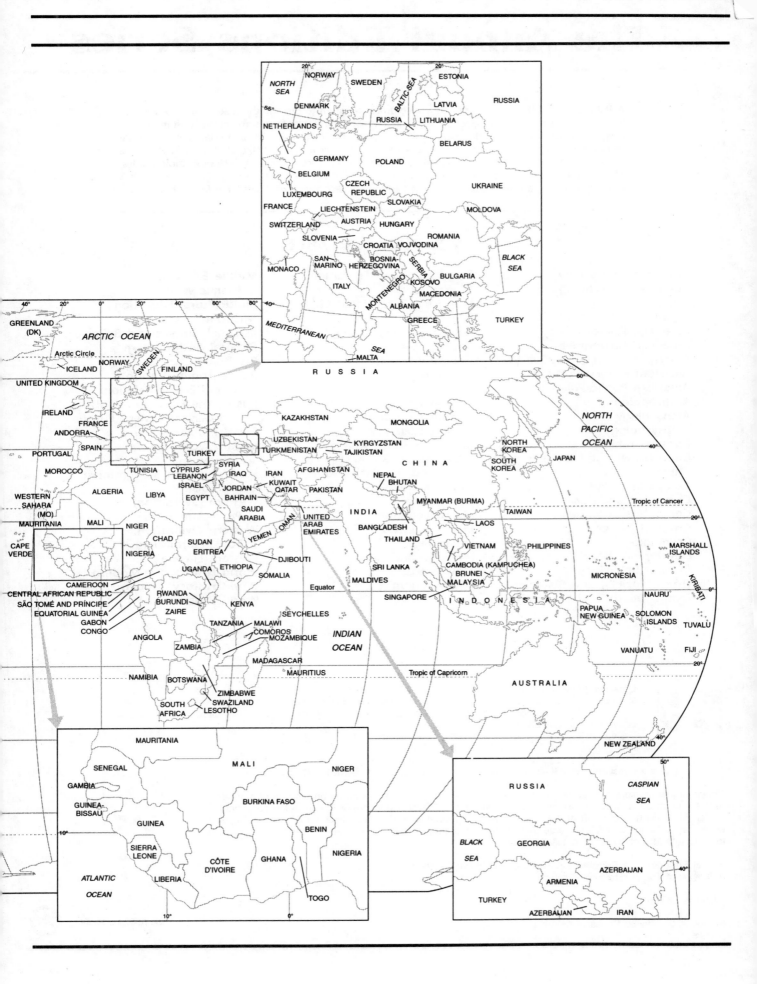

The Annual Editions Series

ANNUAL EDITIONS is a series of over 65 volumes designed to provide the reader with convenient, low-cost access to a wide range of current, carefully selected articles from some of the most important magazines, newspapers, and journals published today. ANNUAL EDITIONS are updated on an annual basis through a continuous monitoring of over 300 periodical sources. All ANNUAL EDITIONS have a number of features that are designed to make them particularly useful, including topic guides, annotated tables of contents, unit overviews, and indexes. For the teacher using ANNUAL EDITIONS in the classroom, an Instructor's Resource Guide with test questions is available for each volume.

VOLUMES AVAILABLE

Abnormal Psychology
Adolescent Psychology
Africa
Aging
American Foreign Policy
American Government
American History, Pre-Civil War
American History, Post-Civil War
American Public Policy
Anthropology
Archaeology
Biopsychology
Business Ethics
Child Growth and Development
China
Comparative Politics
Computers in Education
Computers in Society
Criminal Justice
Criminology
Developing World
Deviant Behavior
Drugs, Society, and Behavior
Dying, Death, and Bereavement

Early Childhood Education
Economics
Educating Exceptional Children
Education
Educational Psychology
Environment
Geography
Global Issues
Health
Human Development
Human Resources
Human Sexuality
India and South Asia
International Business
Japan and the Pacific Rim
Latin America
Life Management
Macroeconomics
Management
Marketing
Marriage and Family
Mass Media
Microeconomics

Middle East and the
   Islamic World
Multicultural Education
Nutrition
Personal Growth and Behavior
Physical Anthropology
Psychology
Public Administration
Race and Ethnic Relations
Russia, the Eurasian Republics,
   and Central/Eastern Europe
Social Problems
Social Psychology
Sociology
State and Local Government
Urban Society
Western Civilization,
   Pre-Reformation
Western Civilization,
   Post-Reformation
Western Europe
World History, Pre-Modern
World History, Modern
World Politics

Cataloging in Publication Data
Main entry under title: Annual Editions: Comparative Politics. 1997/98.
         1. World politics—Periodicals. 2. Politics, Practical—Periodicals. I. Søe, Christian,
comp. II. Title: Comparative Politics.
ISBN 0–697–37226–X   909'.05   83–647654

Fifteenth Edition

Printed in the United States of America

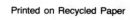

Editors/Advisory Board

To the Reader

In publishing ANNUAL EDITIONS we recognize the enormous role played by the magazines, newspapers, and journals of the *public press* in providing current, first-rate educational information in a broad spectrum of interest areas. Many of these articles are appropriate for students, researchers, and professionals seeking accurate, current material to help bridge the gap between principles and theories and the real world. These articles, however, become more useful for study when those of lasting value are carefully *collected, organized, indexed,* and *reproduced* in a *low-cost format,* which provides easy and permanent access when the material is needed. That is the role played by ANNUAL EDITIONS. Under the direction of each volume's *academic editor,* who is an expert in the subject area, and with the guidance of an *Advisory Board,* each year we seek to provide in each ANNUAL EDITION a current, well-balanced, carefully selected collection of the best of the public press for your study and enjoyment. We think that you will find this volume useful, and we hope that you will take a moment to let us know what you think.

This collection of readings brings together current articles that will help you understand the politics of foreign countries from a comparative perspective. Such a study not only opens up a fascinating world beyond our borders; it will also lead to greater insights into the American political process.

The articles in unit one cover the United Kingdom, Germany, France, Italy, and Japan in a serial manner. Each of these modern societies has developed its own political framework and agenda, and each has sought to find its own appropriate dynamic balance of continuity and change. Nevertheless, as the readings of unit two show, it is possible to point to some common denominators and make useful cross-national comparisons among these and other representative democracies. Unit three goes one step further by discussing the impact of two major changes that are rapidly transforming the political map of Europe. One of them is the irregular, sometimes halting, but nevertheless impressive growth of the European Union (EU). The other is the difficult political and economic reconstruction of Central and Eastern Europe after the collapse of this region's Communist regimes. The continuing political importance of Europe has been underscored by these two developments.

Unit four looks at developments in some of the developing countries, with articles on Mexico, sub-Saharan Africa and the Union of South Africa, China, and India. A careful reader will come away with a better understanding of the diversity of social and political conditions in these countries. Additional readings cover the newly industrialized countries of Eastern and Southeastern Asia—the small "dragons"—which have managed to generate a self-sustaining process of rapid economic modernization. Here the central question concerns the combination of factors which have made such a takeoff possible. Perhaps the answer will point toward a more promising strategy of development for other less-developed countries.

Unit five considers three major trends in contemporary politics from a comparative perspective. The "third wave" of democratization may already have crested, but it is nevertheless important in having changed the politics of many countries. The widespread shifts toward a greater reliance on markets, in place of centralized planning and heavy governmental regulation, is also of great significance. The move is frequently toward some form of a market-oriented mixed economy, and it should not be misunderstood for a sweeping victory of doctrinaire laissez-faire. Finally, the surge of what has been called "identity politics," with particular emphasis on exclusive cultural or ethnic group assertions, is a development that bears careful watching.

There has rarely been so interesting and important a time for the study of comparative politics as now. We have an increasingly clear view of how the political earthquake of 1989–1991 has altered the landscape with consequences for many years to come. The aftershocks continue to remind us that we are unlikely to ever experience a condition of political equilibrium. Even in a time of political transformation, however, there are important patterns of continuity as well as change. We must be careful to look for both as we seek to gain a comparative understanding of the politics of other countries and peoples as well as of our own condition.

This is the fifteenth edition of *Annual Editions: Comparative Politics.* It is a sobering reminder that the first edition appeared just as the Brezhnev era had come to a close in what was then the Soviet Union. Over the years, the new editions have tried to reflect the developments that eventually brought about the post–cold war world of today. In a similar way, this present edition tries to present information and analysis that will be useful in understanding today's political world and its role in setting the parameters for tomorrow's developments.

A special word of thanks goes to my own past and present students at Long Beach State University. They are wonderfully inquisitive and help keep me posted on matters that this anthology must address. Several of my past graduate students have come back to help gather material for this year's collection. I am particularly grateful to Susan B. Mason. She received her master's degree in political science several years ago, but continues to serve as a superb research assistant. Another graduate of our M.A. program, Erika Reinhardt, has provided me with some very useful articles from her own collection. My former student assistants, Linda Wohlman and Jon Nakagawa, cheered me on to the fifteenth edition before they went on to advanced studies in political science. Once again I also wish to thank three other students, Mike Petri, Rich Sherman, and Ali Taghavi, who have helped locate material included in this reader. Like the others named here, they first encountered this anthology as students in my comparative politics courses. It is a great joy to work with all these present and former students, whose enthusiasm for the project is contagious.

I am very grateful to members of the advisory board and Dushkin/McGraw-Hill as well as to the many readers who have made useful comments on past selections and suggested new ones. I ask you all to help me improve future editions by keeping me informed of your reactions and suggestions for change. Please complete and return the postage-paid article rating form in the back of the book.

Christian Søe
Editor

Contents

UNIT 1

Pluralist Democracies: Country Studies

Twenty-one selections examine the current state of politics in Western Europe, the United Kingdom, Germany, France, Italy, and Japan.

The concepts in bold italics are developed in the article. For further expansion please refer to the Topic Guide and the Index.

The concepts in bold italics are developed in the article. For further expansion please refer to the Topic Guide and the Index.

UNIT 2

Modern Pluralist Democracies: Factors in the Political Process

Twelve selections examine the
functioning of Western
European democracies with
regard to political ideas and
participation, ethnic politics, the
role of women in politics, and
the institutional framework of
representative government.

UNIT 3

Europe—West, Center, and East: The Politics of Integration, Transformation, and Disintegration

Ten selections examine the European continent: the European Union, Western European society, post-communist Central and Eastern Europe, and Russia and the other post-Soviet Republics.

UNIT 4

Political Diversity in the Developing World

Ten selections review the developing world's economic and political development in Latin America, Africa, China, India, and newly industrialized countries.

The concepts in bold italics are developed in the article. For further expansion please refer to the Topic Guide and the Index.

UNIT 5

Comparative Politics: Some Major Political Trends, Issues, and Prospects

Seven selections discuss the rise of democracy, how capitalism impacts on political development, and the political assertion of group identity in contemporary politics.

The concepts in bold italics are developed in the article. For further expansion please refer to the Topic Guide and the Index.

Selected World Wide Web Sites for Comparative Politics

(Some Web sites are continually changing their structure and content, so the information listed here may not always be available.—Ed.)

General International Relations Sites

CNN Online Page—http://www.cnn.com—U.S. 24-hour video news channel. News, updated every few hours, includes text, pictures, and film. Good external links.

Institute for Global Cooperation & Conflict (IGCC)—http://www-igcc.ucsd.edu/igcc/igccmenu.html (or gopher://irp-sserv26.ucsd.edu)—Text-only site includes books online and policy papers on Arms Control and Security, Asia-Pacific, Environment, Ethnic Conflict and Regional Relations etc.

International Network Information Center at University of Texas—http://inic.utexas.edu—Gateway has many pointers to international sites, organized into Asian, Latin American, Middle East, and Russian and East European subsections.

ISN International Relations and Security Network—http://www.isn.ethz.ch/—One-stop information for security and defense studies. Topics listed by categories: Traditional Dimensions of Security and New Dimensions of Security and Related Fields. Maintained by Center for Security Studies & Conflict Resolution.

Observatory/NASA site—http://observe.ivv.nasa.gov/—NASA's Observatorium site for Earth and space data uses satellite data and has excellent pictures of the Earth, planets, stars, and other cool stuff.

Political Science RESOURCES—http://www.keele.ac.uk:80/depts/po/psr.htm—Dynamic gateway to sources available via European addresses. Listed by country name. Include official government pages, official documents, speeches, elections, political events.

ReliefWeb—http://www.reliefweb.int—UN's Department of Humanitarian Affairs clearinghouse for international humanitarian emergencies. Has daily updates, including Reuters, VOA, PANA.

Social Science Information Gateway (SOSIG)—http://sosig.esrc.bris.ac.uk/—Project of the Economic and Social Research Council (ESRC). It catalogs 22 subjects and lists more European and developing-countries URL addresses than many U.S. sources.

U.S. Central Intelligence Agency Home Page—http://www.odci.gov/cia—Includes information about the CIA and its publications, 1995 World Fact Book, Fact Book on Intelligence, Handbook of International Economic Statistics, 1995, and CIA Maps.

World Wide Web Virtual Library: International Affairs Network Web—http://www.pitt.edu/~ian/resource/ipe.htm—Gateway to international affairs. Web links are BY TYPE and BY TOPIC.

Western Hemisphere

C-SPAN ONLINE—http://www.c-span.org/—See especially C-SPAN International on the Web for International Programming Highlights and archived C-Span programs.

DefenseLINK (U.S. government)—http://www.dtic.dla.mil/defenselink—Department of Defense's public affairs online service provides DoD news releases and other public affairs documents. Gateway to other DoD agencies (i.e., Secretary of Defense, Army, Navy, Air Force, Marine Corp).

Gallup Poll Organization—http://www.gallup.com/index.html—Most recent Gallup Polls and special reports, updates.

Mexico's Index—http://www.trace-sc.com/mexgov.htm—Mexican news, government, Web map, yellow pages, exchange rates, census data, and links for culture, history, politics.

PoliticsNow—http://www.politicsnow.com/—Major source for current U.S. political information. See Bookshelf, for historical documents, Almanac of American Politics, and Congressional References.

Statistics Canada—http://www.statcan.ca/welcome.html—Official Home Page of Statistics on Canada, in English and French. Site includes information on land, people, economy, government. Links to other Canadian Government sources.

The United States at the UN—http://www.undp.org/missions/usa/—Web site for U.S. Mission at UN: Fact Sheet, Economic and Social Issues, What America Gets at UN, What We Said at the UN in 1996, etc.

U.S. Department of State Home Page—http://www.state.gov/index.html—Organized by categories: Hot Topic (i.e., 1996 Country Reports on Human Rights Practices), Press Statements, Middle East Process, Environment. See also, http://www.state.gov/www/websites.html for U.S. missions abroad.

U.S. White House—http://www.whitehouse.gov/WH/Welcome.html—Information on President and Vice President and What's New. See especially, The Virtual Library and Briefing Room (today's releases).

The Former USSR

Politics-Russia, USSR & Eastern Europe—http://bib10.sub.su.se:80/sam/spruss.htm—Text-only information about Russia, USSR, and Eastern Europe. Additional headings include Russian Economic Resource Center, Post-Soviet Study Resources.

Russian & East Europe Network Information Center, University of TX at Austin—http://reenic.utexas.edu/reenic.html—Web site with clickable directory for Russia, Ukraine, Asian Republics and countries in central Europe.

Russian Today—http://www.russiatoday.com/—Part of European Information Network. Includes Headline News, Resources, Government, Politics, Election Results, and Pressing Issues.

Strengthening Democractic Institutions (SDI) Project—http://ksgweb.harvard.edu/csia/sdi/Reports.htm—Information organized under SDI Web-based news, Russian Elections, Initiative on the Caucasus, Reports (titles not full text).

Europe

BOSNIA LINK (U.S. government)—http://www.dtic.mil/bosnia/index.html—U.S. Department of Defense special Web site of information related to Bosnia, including TACON newspaper serving Task Force Eagle.

Central Europe Online—http://www.centraleurope.com/—Daily updated information on Central European countries. Classified under headings such as News on the Web Today, Economic, Trade, Currencies, and Stocks.

Czech Republic Info—http://www.czech.cz:80/washington/general/general.htm—Official Web page of Czech Republic with information organized by categories such as Constitution, Institutions, and Political Parties.

EUROPA—http://europa.eu.int/—Information on the European Union's goals and policies, history, institutions, publications, statistics.

I*M-EUROPE—http://www2.echo.lu/home.html—I*M-EUROPE lists European Union (EU) Programmes and Activities, official texts, and news.

NATO—gopher://marvin.stc.nato.int:70/11/natodata—Official site of North Atlantic Treaty Association. Site includes information on members, current programs, policy statements, etc.

Political Economy

I-Trade International Trade Resources & Data Exchange—http://www.i-trade.com/—Monthly exchange-rate data, U.S. Document Export Market Information (GEMS), U.S. Global Trade Outlook, and World Fact Book 1995 statistical demographic and geographic data for 180+ countries, maps included. Full text and synopsis information data of NAFTA.

U.S. Agency for International Development—http://www.info.usaid.gov/—Information in headings: Democracy, Population, Health, Economic Growth, Development, Regions and Countries.

World Bank Home Page—www.worldbank.org/html/Welcome.html—News (i.e., press releases, summary of new projects, speeches), publications, topics in development, countries and regions. Links to other financial organizations, including IBRD, IDA, IFC, MIGA.

World Trade Organization (WTO)—www.wto.org—Topics include foundation of world trade systems, roots of WTO, data on textiles, intellectual property rights, legal frameworks, trade and environmental policies, recent agreements, etc.

Asia, Middle East, and Africa

Africa News Web site: Crisis in the Great Lakes Region—http:// www.africanews.org/greatlakes.html—Africa News Web site on Great Lakes (i.e., Rwanda, Burundi, Zaire, and Kenya, Tanzania, Uganda). Frequent updates plus good links to other sites. Can order e-mail updates on Zaire crisis from this source.

African Policy Information Center (APIC)—http://www.igc.apc. org/apic/index.shtml—Developed by Washington Office on Africa to widen policy debate in U.S. on African issues. Includes special topic briefs, regular reports and documents on African politics.

ArabNet Site Directory—http://www.arab.net/arabnet_contents.html—Web links to 22 Arab countries, ranging from Algeria through Yemen. Includes search engine. Each country Web page classifies information using a standardized system of categories.

ASEAN—http://www.asean.or.id/—Official site of the Association of South East Asian Nations (ASEAN) provides overview of Asian Web resources, Asian Summits, Economic and World Affairs, Publications, Political Foundations, Regional Cooperation.

Asia-Yahoo—http://www.yahoo.com/Regional/Regions/Asia/—Specialized Yahoo search site permits key-word search on Asian events, countries, or topics.

Chinese Society Home Page—http://members.aol.com/mehampton/chinasec.html—Information listed under: Chinese Military Links, Data Sources on Chinese Security Issues, Key Newspapers and New Services, and Key Scholarly Journals and Magazines. Several links to other security-related sites.

Fertile Crescent Home Page—http://leb.net/fchp/—Independent nonpartisan organization Web site making information available about the Fertile Crescent. Categories include Documents, General References, and Other Minorities. Information available by countries including Cyprus, Lebanon, Palestine, and Syria.

The Heritage Foundation Publications Library—http://www.heritage.org/heritage/library/index/g5.html—Contains full-text policy briefing papers on Middle East topics under Publication and Research Classification. (Note: Has briefing papers for topics related to other regions and defense issues).

India Index—http://www.ubcnet.or.jp:80/jin/ind_gen.html—Information about India (i.e., demographics) organized under specific categories such as Japan-Indian News, Politics, Economy.

India News Network (India-L)—http://www.coalliance.org:80/unitrec/ej000423.html—Web site with free daily news and discussion and links about India.

Information Office of State Council of People's Republic of China—http://www.cityu.edu.hk/HumanRights/index.htm—Official site of China's government contains policy statements by the government related to Human Rights.

Inside China Today—http://www.insidechina.com/—Part of European Information Network. Recent information on China organized under Headlines News, Government, and Related Sites, Mainland China, Hong Kong and Macao, and Taiwan.

Iraq's World Wide Web Site—http://www.liii.com/~hajeri/iraq. html—Web site maintained by a private individual. General information about Iraq includes U.S. State Department's Advisory, Pictures, CIA 1994 Fact Book, and good links.

Israel Information Service—http://www.yahoo.com/Regional/Countries/Israel/Government/—Official gopher site of Israel Foreign Ministry Information Services. Text-only information includes policy speeches, interviews with leaders, etc.

Japan Ministry of Foreign Affairs—http://www.mofa.go.jp/— "What's new" lists events, policy statements, press releases. Foreign Policy section has speeches; Foreign Policy Archive; information under Countries, Region, Friendship.

Japan Policy Research Institute (JPRI)—http://www.nmjc.org/jpri/—Headings include What's New (i.e., recent speeches and articles related to U.S.-Japan relationships) and Publications before 1996, etc.

Pana News Agency—http://www.africannews.org/PANA/—Has both free and for-fee information from and about Africa from Afri-

can sources, 36 correspondents in Africa, and working relationships with 48 national news agencies in Africa.

Regional Arab Information Technology Network (RAITNET)— http://www.ritsec.net/raitnet/—Information on 21 Arab countries, organized within categories such as Culture, Tourism, Health, Business, Environment, Education, Discussion Bulletin Boards. Free membership.

South African Government Index—http://www.polity.org.za/gnuindex.html—Official site includes links to government agencies. Provides information on structures of government and links to detailed documents.

South-East Asia Information—http://sunsite.nus.sg/asiasvc. html— Focuses on Brunei, Burma, Cambodia, Indonesia, Laos, Malaysia, Philippines, Singapore, Thailand, and Vietnam. Excellent gateway for country-specific research. Information on Internet Providers and Universities in Southeast Asia, links to Asia online services.

Weekly Mail & Guardian (Johannesburg)—http://www.mg.co.za/ mg/— Free electronic daily South African newspaper (see especially What's New on Web). Includes archive of back issues of newspapers that can be searched. Good links to other links related to Africa.

Arms and Proliferation

Arms Control and Disarmament Agency (ACDA)—http://www. acda.gov/—Information under Fact Sheets (i.e., weapons of mass destruction, conventional weapons, missile defense), Speeches, Treaties, Reports, and Historical Documents. Good links to related U.S. government agencies, international organizations involved in arms control.

Center for Non-Proliferation Studies (CNS)—http://cns.miis.edu/ srclist.html—Site includes CNS publications and recent reports, such as updated reports on Democratic People's Republic of Korea.

The High Energy Weapons Archive—http://193.210.10.42/hew/—Australian Web provides current and technical information on nuclear weapons issues, very good links to other relevant sites, including U.S. National Labs, Trinity Site, which focuses on historical information, especially reproductions of public domain documents.

Global Issues

Canadian Air Force and UN Peacekeeping—http://www.achq.dnd. ca/peacekpg/—Provides details of all peacekeeping operations which involved Canadian forces including maps, mandates, duration, logistic information, main bases, etc.

Index of Heritage Library—http://www.heritage.org/heritage/library/ index/(at "index" scroll to j4.html—See especially Publications Library for full-text briefing papers on terrorism.

Program on Peacekeeping Policy (POPP)—http://ralph.gmu.edu/ cfpa/peace/peace.html—Use of military, humanitarian, and political forces in the conduct of multinational peace operations explored. Site includes electronic journals and systematic data on missions, personnel, financial aspects, current strengths, fatalities of UN Peacekeeping.

United Nations Home Page—http://www.unicc.org/—Includes United Nation Web and gopher servers, all listed alphabetically. Offers: UNICC; Food and Agriculture Organization.

UN Department of Public Information Home Page—http://www. un.org/—Text-only information in English, French, and Spanish, including news updates, pictorial history, and description of UN departments.

UN Development Programme (UNDP)—http://www.undp.org/— Publications and current information on world poverty (see Poverty clock), Mission Statement, UN Development for Women.

UN Environmental Programme (UNEP)—http://www.unchs.unon. org/—Official site of UNEP. Information on UN environmental programs, 1996/97, products, services, events, search engine.

World Health Organization (WHO)—http://www.who.ch/—Maintained by WHO's headquarters in Geneva, Switzerland, uses Excite search engine to conduct key-word searches on health topics.

We highly recommend that you check out our Web site for expanded information and our other product lines. We are continually updating and adding links to our Web site in order to offer you the most usable and useful information that will support and expand the value of your *Annual Edition*. You can reach us at: *http://www.dushkin.com/*.

Topic Guide

This topic guide suggests how the selections in this book relate to topics of traditional concern to students and professionals involved with the study of comparative politics. It is useful for locating articles that relate to each other for reading and research. The guide is arranged alphabetically according to topic. Articles may, of course, treat topics that do not appear in the topic guide. In turn, entries in the topic guide do not necessarily constitute a comprehensive listing of all the contents of each selection.

TOPIC AREA	TREATED IN	TOPIC AREA	TREATED IN
Africa's Politics	48. Democracy, of a Sort, Sweeps Africa 49. Why Is Africa Eating Asia's Dust?	**Economics and Politics (continued)**	37. Rising Health Costs 38. Europe and the Underclass 39. Inequalities in Europe
Britain's Government and Politics	1. Politics of Power 3. Britain's 1997 General Election 4. Revamping Britain's Constitution 5. Blair on the Constitution 6. What Is Scotland's Future? 7. After the Talking Stopped 22. The Left's New Start 23. Guide to the West European Left 30. Parliament and Congress 31. Campaign and Party Finance 32. Electoral Reform 33. Presidents and Prime Ministers 34. An American Perspective 35. Politics of European Monetary Union 37. Rising Health Costs 38. Europe and the Underclass 39. Inequalities in Europe 40. The Return of the Habsburgs 54. Is the Third Wave Over? 55. Capitalism and Democracy 58. A Debate on Cultural Conflicts 59. The Myth of Global Ethnic Conflict		42. A Transition Leading to Tragedy 46. The Backlash in Latin America 47. Mexico: Uneasy, Uncertain, Unpredictable 49. Why Is Africa Eating Asia's Dust? 50. Deng Xiaoping, Architect of Modern China 51. India: Between Turmoil and Hope 52. Miracles beyond the Free Market 55. Capitalism and Democracy 56. For Democracy, the Next Revolution 60. Jihad vs. McWorld
		Elections and Parties	1. Politics of Power 2. Tony Blair and the New Left 3. Britain's 1997 General Election 8. Helmut Kohl: Extra Extra Large 9. United Germany 10. The Shadow of Weimar 13. Chirac and France 17. Italy's General Election of 1996 19. Italy at a Turning Point 20. Hashimoto's Headache 23. Guide to the West European Left 24. Europe's Far Right: Something Nasty 26. Cherchez la Femme 27. Women, Power, and Politics 29. What Democracy Is . . . and Is Not 31. Campaign and Party Finance 32. Electoral Reform 42. A Transition Leading to Tragedy 43. Can Russia Change? 47. Mexico: Uneasy, Uncertain, Unpredictable 48. Democracy, of a Sort, Sweeps Africa 51. India: Between Turmoil and Hope 54. Is the Third Wave Over?
China's Government and Politics	50. Deng Xiaoping, Architect of Modern China		
Developing Countries	44. Let's Abolish the Third World 45. The 'Third World' Is Dead, but Spirits Linger 46. The Backlash in Latin America 47. Mexico: Uneasy, Uncertain, Unpredictable 48. Democracy, of a Sort, Sweeps Africa 49. Why Is Africa Eating Asia's Dust? 50. Deng Xiaoping, Architect of Modern China 51. India: Between Turmoil and Hope 52. Miracles beyond the Free Market 53. Confucious Says: Go East, Young Man 54. Is the Third Wave Over? 56. For Democracy, the Next Revolution 57. Cultural Explanations 58. A Debate on Cultural Conflicts 59. Myth of Global Ethnic Conflict 60. Jihad vs. McWorld	**Ethnicity and Politics**	6. What Is Scotland's Future? 7. After the Talking Stopped 9. United Germany 13. Chirac and France 15. Is Le Pen Mightier than the Sword? 19. Italy at the Turning Point 24. Europe's Far Right: Something Nasty 25. The Impacts of Postwar Migration 34. An American Perspective 39. Inequalities in Europe 40. The Return of the Habsburgs 51. India: Between Turmoil and Hope 57. Cultural Explanations 58. A Debate on Cultural Conflicts 59. Myth of Global Ethnic Conflict 60. Jihad vs. McWorld
Economics and Politics	2. Tony Blair and the New Left 3. Britain's 1997 General Election 6. What Is Scotland's Future? 7. After the Talking Stopped 9. United Germany 11. Perspectives on the German Model 13. Chirac and France 14. For France, Sagging Self-Image and Esprit 19. Italy at a Turning Point 21. Reforming Japan: The Third Opening 22. The Left's New Start 25. The Impacts of Postwar Migration 28. Where Women's Work Is Job No. 1 35. Politics of European Monetary Union 36. Sweden: A Model in Crisis	**European Union [former European Community]**	2. Tony Blair and the New Left 3. Britain's 1997 General Election 4. Revamping Britain's Constitution 8. Helmut Kohl: Extra Extra Large 9. United Germany 11. Perspectives on the German Model 12. Germany's New Foreign Policy 13. Chirac and France 14. For France, Sagging Self-Image and Esprit 19. Italy at a Turning Point

Pluralist Democracies: Country Studies

- The United Kingdom (Articles 1–7)
- Germany (Articles 8–12)
- France (Articles 13–15)
- Italy (Articles 16–19)
- Japan (Articles 20–21)

The United Kingdom, Germany, France, and Italy rank among the most prominent industrial societies in Western Europe. Although their modern political histories vary considerably, they have all developed into pluralist democracies with diversified and active citizenries, well-organized and competitive party systems and interest groups, and representative forms of governments. Japan appears to be less pluralist as a society, but it occupies a similar position of primacy among the few representative democracies in Asia.

The articles in the first unit cover the political systems of Britain, France, Germany, Italy, and Japan. Each of these modern societies has developed its own set of governmental institutions, defined its own political agenda, and found its own dynamic balance of continuity and change. Nevertheless, as later readings will show more fully, it is possible to find some common denominators and make useful cross-national comparisons among these and other representative democracies. Moreover, the Western European countries all show the impact of three major developments that are transforming the political map of the continent: (1) the growth of the European Union, or EU, as the European Community (EC) has been officially known since November 1993; (2) the rise of new or intensified challenges to the established political order after the end of the cold war, often reflected in a reshuffling or weakening of the traditional party system; and (3) the spillover effects from the reconstruction efforts in the countries of Central and Eastern Europe after their recent exit from communist rule.

The continuing political importance of Europe has been underscored by these developments. The integration of the European Community has been a process spanning several decades. However, it accelerated markedly in the last half of the 1980s as a result of the passage and measured implementation of the Single European Act, which set as a goal the completion of a free market among the 12 EC-member countries by the end of 1992. The follow-up Maastricht Treaty, which was ratified by 1993, outlined a further advance by setting up the goal of achieving a common European monetary system and foreign policy before the end of the century. It is a remarkable example of long-term political planning and cooperation in place of more traditional conflict.

By contrast, there was little advance notice or planning connected with the upheaval that ended many decades of communist rule in Central and Eastern Europe between 1989 and 1991. In the center of the continent, the unification of Germany in 1990 epitomizes the tremendous upheaval which swept away much of the political order created by the cold war. Each of the former communist-ruled countries has embarked on a cumbersome path of reconstruction, involving the transition from a party-and-police state with a centrally planned economy to a pluralist democracy with a market-oriented economy. By now it is clear that this process will take longer, involve more setbacks, and produce more painful dislocations than anyone had imagined a few years ago.

In the Western democracies, the end of the cold war has been accompanied by political dislocations. The most frequently heard word used to describe the political mood of Western Europe is *"malaise,"* which suggests a widespread mood of unease, anxiety, and disaffection that shows up in opinion polls and elections. Some even speak of the onset of a new "Europessimism" that is fed by a combination of economic setbacks, sociocultural tensions, political scandals, and a revival of right-wing populist parties and movements.

It is important to pay attention to such forces of change and challenge, but we must not lose sight of some equally important but less dramatic aspects of politics. In the stable pluralist democracies of Western Europe, the political process is usually defined by a relatively mild blend of change and continuity.

The **United Kingdom** has long been regarded as a model of parliamentary government and majoritarian party politics. In the 1960s and 1970s, however, the country became better known for its chronic governing problems. Serious observers spoke about the spread of a British sickness—"Englanditis"—a condition characterized by such problems as economic stagnation, social malaise, political polarization, and a general incapacity of the elected government to deal effectively with such a situation of relative deterioration.

There were several attempts to give a macro-explanation of Britain's problems. Some political scientists defined the country's condition as one of "governmental overload." According to their diagnosis, the British government had become so entangled by socioeconomic entitlements that the country had reached the threshold of a condition of political paralysis or "ungovernability." In the United States, Professor Mancur Olson developed a more general but similar explanation of political sclerosis in advanced pluralist democracies like Britain, which he traced to the effects of a highly developed interest group system making excessive demands on governments.

A second explanation of the British governing crisis focused on the unusually sharp adversarial character of the country's party politics, symbolized by the parliamentary confrontation of government and opposition parties. This approach emphasized that Great Britain's famed Westminster Model of government by a single majority party was more polarizing and disruptive than the power-sharing coalitions found in some other parliamentary systems in Western Europe. Still other interpreters explained Great Britain's relative decline in terms of a socioeconomic and institutional inertia that prevented the country from keeping pace with its European neighbors. Two of the most commonly cited problems were rooted in Britain's heritage as a class-divided society and former colonial power. Compared to its more modern European neighbors, it was argued, the United Kingdom was hampered by a dysfunctional and outmoded social order at home and an equally costly and unproductive legacy of overcommitment in foreign affairs. The latter thesis was advanced in a more general way by the British-American historian, Paul Kennedy, in his widely discussed book on the rise and fall of the great powers.

As if to defy such pessimistic analyses, Great Britain by the mid–1980s began to pull ahead of other Western European countries in its annual economic growth. This apparent turnabout could be linked in part to the policies of Prime Minister Margaret Thatcher, who had come to power in May 1979 and had introduced a drastic change in economic and social direction for the country. She portrayed herself as a conviction politician, determined to introduce a strong dose of economic discipline by encouraging private enterprise and reducing the role of government, in marked contrast to what she dismissed as the consensus politics of her Labour and Conservative predecessors. Her radical rhetoric and somewhat less drastic policy changes spawned yet another debate about what came to be called the Thatcher Revolution and its social and political consequences.

Fundamentally, the disagreement was not only about how to achieve economic growth but also about the kind of polity and society Britain ought to be. Even among the observers who were impressed by an economic revival of Britain in the mid–1980s, there were many who were disturbed by some of the apparent social and political trade-offs. By the late 1980s, moreover, the pragmatic argument in favor of Thatcher's approach lost much of its force when the country seemed to have slipped back into stagflation, or sluggish economic performance coupled with fairly high inflation. Some critics are convinced that her policies contributed to an exacerbation of this new and severe recession. There are, however, inevitably some supporters who argue that Thatcher's policies are now bearing fruit as a more competitive Britain again heads toward economic recovery somewhat ahead of its European neighbors.

The concern about ungovernability, which had dominated earlier discussions about British politics, has not ceased, but it has broadened to include questions about the dislocating consequences of Thatcher's economic and social policies. During the last decade, the British debate has come to include additional concerns about conservative efforts to tighten central controls over education at all levels, introduction of cost controls in the popular National Health Service, privatization of electricity and water industries as well as its inroads upon what had long been considered established rights in such areas as local government powers and civil liberties.

In foreign affairs, Prime Minister Thatcher combined an assertive role for Britain in Europe and close cooperation with the United States under the leadership of Presidents Reagan and Bush. As a patriot and staunch defender of both market economics and national sovereignty, Thatcher distrusted the drive toward monetary and eventual political union in the European Union. She became known throughout the Continent for her unusually sharp attacks on tendencies toward undemocratic statism or technocratic socialism in Brussels. There were critics in her own party who regarded her European position as untenable because it isolated and thus deprived Great Britain of possible influence on questions of strategic planning for the EU's future.

For the mass electorate, however, nothing seems to have been so upsetting as the introduction of the community charge, a tax on each adult resident, which was to replace the local property tax or rates as a means of financing local public services. Although this so-called poll tax was very unpopular, Thatcher resisted all pressure to abandon the project before its full national implementation in early 1990. Not only did such a tax appear inequitable or regressive, as compared to one based on property values, but it also turned out to be set much higher by local governments than the national government had originally estimated.

The politically disastrous result was that, as a revenue measure, the poll tax was anything but neutral in its impact. It created an unexpectedly large proportion of immediate losers, that is, people who had to pay considerably more in local taxes than previously, while the immediate winners were people who had previously paid high property taxes. Not surprisingly, the national and local governments disagreed about who was responsible for the high poll tax bills, but the voters seemed to

have little difficulty in assigning blame to Margaret Thatcher and the Conservative Party as originators of the unpopular reform. Many voters were up in arms, and some observers correctly anticipated that the tax rebellion would undermine Thatcher's position in her own party and become her political Waterloo.

The feisty prime minister had weathered many political challenges, but she was now confronted with increasing speculation that the Tories might try to replace her with a more attractive leader before the next general election. The issue that triggered such a development was Thatcher's stepped-up attacks on closer European union during 1990, which led her deputy prime minister, Sir Geoffrey Howe, to resign on November 1, 1990. There followed a leadership challenge in the Conservative Party which ended with Thatcher's resignation in advance of an expected defeat by her own parliamentary party.

John Major, who was chosen by his fellow Conservative members of Parliament to be Thatcher's successor as prime minister and leader of the Conservative Party, had long been regarded as one of her closest cabinet supporters. He was thought to support her tough economic strategy, which she often described as "dry," but to prefer a more compassionate or "wet" social policy without indulging in the Tory tradition of welfare paternalism against which Margaret Thatcher had also railed. Not surprisingly, he abandoned the hated poll tax. His undramatic governing style was far less confrontational than that of his predecessor, and some nostalgic critics were quick to call him dull. In the Gulf War of 1991, Major continued Thatcher's policy of giving strong British support for firm, and ultimately military, measures against the government of Iraq, which had invaded and occupied oil-rich Kuwait. Unlike his predecessor after the Falkland Battle almost a decade earlier, however, he did not follow up on a quick and popular military victory by calling for general elections.

By the time of Thatcher's resignation, Labour appeared to be in a relatively good position to capitalize on the growing disenchantment with the Conservative government. The big political question had become whether Prime Minister Major could recapture some of the lost ground. Under its leader, Neil Kinnock, Labour had begun to move back toward its traditional center-left position, presenting itself as a politically moderate and socially caring reform party. Labour had a leading position in some opinion polls, and it won some impressive victories in by-elections to the House of Commons. In the shadow of the Gulf War, Labour was overtaken by the Conservatives in the polls, but its position improved again a few months later.

As the main opposition party, however, Labour was now troubled by a new version of the Social Democratic and Liberal alternatives that had fragmented the non-Conservative camp in the elections of 1983 and 1987. The two smaller parties, which had operated as an electoral coalition or "Alliance" in those years, had concluded that their organizational separation was a hindrance to the political breakthrough they hoped for. After the defeat of 1987, they joined together as the Social and Liberal Democrats (SLD) but soon became known simply as Liberal Democrats. Under the leadership of Paddy Ashdown, they have attempted to overcome the electoral system's bias against third parties by promoting themselves as a reasonable centrist alternative to the Conservatives on the right and the Labour Party on the left. Their strategic goal was to win the balance of power in a tightly fought election and then, as parliamentary majority-makers, to enter into a government coalition with one of the two big parties. One of their main demands would then be that the existing winner-take-all, or plurality, electoral system, based on single-member districts, be replaced by some form of proportional representation (PR) in multimember districts. Such a system, which is used widely in Western Europe, would almost surely guarantee the Liberal Democrats not only a relatively solid base in the House of Commons but also a pivotal role in a future process of coalition politics in Britain. Given their considerable electoral support, the Liberal Democrats would then enjoy a position comparable to or even better than that of their counterparts in Germany, the Free Democrats (FDP), which has been a junior member of governments in Bonn for decades.

The rise of this centrist "third force" in British electoral politics during the 1980s had been made possible by a temporary leftward trend of Labour and the rightward movement of the Conservatives a few years earlier. The challenge from the middle had a predictable result: The two main parties eventually sought to recenter themselves, as became evident in the general election called by Prime Minister Major for April 9, 1992. The timing seemed highly unattractive for the Conservatives as governing party, because Britain was still suffering from its worst recession in years. Normally, a British government chooses not to stay in office for a full five-year term. Instead, it prefers to dissolve the House of Commons at an earlier and politically convenient time. It will procrastinate, however, when the electoral outlook appears to be dismal. By the spring of 1992, there was hardly any time left for further delay, since an election had to come before the end of June under Britain's five-year limit. At the time, many observers expected either a slim Labour victory or, more likely, a so-called hung Parliament, in which no party would end up with a working majority. The latter result would have led either to a minority government, which could be expected to solve the impasse by calling an early new election, or to a coalition government that included the Liberal Democrats as the majority-making junior partner.

The outcome of the 1992 general election confounded all those who had expected a change in government by giving the Conservatives an unprecedented fourth consecutive term of office. Despite the recession, they garnered the same overall percentage of the vote (about 43 percent) as in 1987, while Labour increased its total share only slightly, from 32 to 35 percent. The Liberal Democrats received only 18 percent, about 6 percent less than the share that the Alliance had won in its two unsuccessful attempts to break the mold of the party system in 1983 and 1987. In the House of Commons, the electoral systems bias in favor of the front-runners showed up once again. The Conservatives lost 36 seats but ended up with 336 of the 651 members—a slim but sufficient working majority, unless a major issue should fragment the party or its majority should erode by attrition. In 1992, Labour increased its number of seats from 229 to 271—a net gain of 42, but far short of an opportunity to threaten the majority party. The Liberal Democrats ended up with 20 seats, down from 22. A few seats went to representatives of the small regional parties from Northern Ireland, Scotland, and Wales.

Since the 1992 election, John Major has run into considerable difficulties with a wing of his own party that follows Thatcher in opposing his European policy. It was only by threatening to dissolve parliament and to call a new election that Major brought the dissidents into line during a crucial vote on the Maastricht Treaty in the summer of 1993.

The Labour Party, with its newest leader, Tony Blair, has made some tremendous advances in the regular opinion polls. It has moved to a commanding lead over the government party and was widely expected to win the general election which has to be held by early May 1997. John Major's decision against an earlier election date reflected his awareness of the Conservatives' plight.

Should the Labour Party win the election, as expected, it will face some problems of its own. Behind its show of unity, the party is hampered by its own factional disputes. The major ideological and strategic cleavage runs between traditional socialists and more pragmatic modernizers, who wish to continue the centrist reform policies of Tony Blair. But the issue of Europe would also trouble the Labour Party if it were to take over the government. Only the Liberal Democrats seem to be united in their commitment to a more fully integrated Europe.

One of the most interesting issues in contemporary British politics is the demand for constitutional change. In the late 1980s, an *ad hoc* reform coalition launched Charter 88, which called for a written constitution with a bill of rights, proportional representation, and a redefinition and codification of other basic "rules of the game" in British politics. The chartists chose the tricentennial of Britain's Glorious Revolution of 1688 to launch their effort, which has kindled a broad discussion of citizenship in the country. By now, a number of different proposals to define a new British constitution have come forward. The growing importance of this issue is reflected in the fact that Conservatives have also entered the fray. While they do not offer yet another draft constitution, they have sought to appropriate and redefine the debate about citizenship rights against state bureaucracy. It is significant that Tony Blair has identified himself and his party with constitutional reform, with the notable exception of the electoral system that underpins the Westminster Model of government by the majority party. We should expect some significant institutional changes under a new Labour government.

One of the recurrent reform suggestions is to set up a special regional assembly for Scotland within the United Kingdom. This is an issue for which the Conservatives have shown much less concern than have Labour or the Liberal Democrats. The regional problems associated with Northern Ireland are far more divisive, but they now appear headed for a resolution acceptable to all sides.

Germany was united in 1990, when the eastern German Democratic Republic (GDR) was merged into the western Federal Republic of Germany. The two German states had been established in 1949, four years after the total defeat of the German Reich in the Second World War. During the next 40 years, their rival elites subscribed to the conflicting ideologies and interests of East and West in the cold war. East Germany comprised the territory of the former Soviet Occupation Zone of Germany, where the Communists exercised a power monopoly and established an economy based on central planning. In contrast, West Germany, which emerged from the former American, British, and French zones of postwar occupation, developed a pluralist democracy and a flourishing market economy. When the two states were getting ready to celebrate their fortieth anniversaries in 1989, no leading politician was on record as having foreseen that the division of Germany would end during the course of the following year.

Mass demonstrations in several East German cities and the westward flight of thousands of citizens caused the GDR government to make an increasing number of concessions in late 1989 and early 1990. The Berlin Wall ceased to be a hermetical seal after November 9, 1989, when East Germans began to stream over into West Berlin. Collectors and entrepreneurs soon broke pieces from the Wall to keep or sell as souvenirs, before public workers set about to remove the rest of this symbol of the cold war and of Germany's division. Under new leadership, the ruling Communists of East Germany introduced a form of power sharing with noncommunist groups and parties. It was agreed to seek democratic legitimation through a free election in March 1990, in the hope of reducing the westward flight of thousands of East Germans, which was resulting in devastating consequences for the economy.

Such popular demonstrations and the willingness of East Germans to "vote with their feet" had become possible by two major preconditions. First, the Soviet leader, Mikhail Gorbachev, had abandoned the so-called Brezhnev Doctrine, according to which the Soviets claimed the right of military intervention on behalf of the established communist regimes in Central and Eastern Europe. And second, the imposed communist regimes of these countries turned out to have lost their will and ability to hold onto power at any cost.

The East German Communists had only abandoned their claim to an exclusive control of power and positions, but by the time of the March 1990 election it was clear even to them that the pressure for national unification could no longer be stemmed. The issue was no longer whether the two German states would be joined together, but *how* and *when*. These questions were settled when an alliance of Christian Democrats, largely identified with and supported by Chancellor Kohl's party in West Germany, won a surprisingly decisive victory, with 48 percent of the vote throughout East Germany. It advocated a short, quick route to unification, beginning with an early monetary union in the summer and a political union by the fall of 1990. This also meant that the new noncommunist government in East Germany, headed by Lothar de Maizière (CDU), followed a shortcut route to merger with the Federal Republic, under Article 23 of the West German Basic Law. The Social Democrats won only 22 percent of the East German vote in March 1990. That amounted to a defeat for its alternative strategy for unification, which would have involved the protracted negotiation of a new German constitution, as envisaged by Article 146 of the Basic Law.

During the summer and fall of 1990, the governments of the two German states and the four former occupying powers completed their so-called two-plus-four negotiations that resulted in mutual agreement on the German unification process. A monetary union in July was followed by a political merger in October 1990. In advance of unification, Bonn was able to negotiate an agreement with Moscow in which the latter accepted the gradual withdrawal of Soviet troops from East Germany and the membership of the larger, united Germany in NATO, in return for considerable German economic support for the Soviet Union. The result was a major shift in both the domestic and international balance of power.

The moderately conservative Christian Democrats repeated their electoral success in the first Bundestag election in a re-united Germany, held in early December 1990. Their small coalition partner, the liberal Free Democrats, did unusually well (11 percent of the vote). The environmentalist Greens, on the other hand, failed to get the required minimum of 5 percent of the vote in western Germany and dropped out of the Bundestag for the next 4 years. Under a special provision for the 1990 election only, the two parts of united Germany were regarded as separate electoral regions as far as the 5 percent threshold was concerned. That made it possible for two small eastern parties to get a foothold in the Bundestag. One was a coalition of dissidents and environmentalists (Alliance 90/Greens); the other was the communist-descended Party of Democratic Socialism. The PDS won about 10 percent of the vote in the East by appealing to a number of groups that feared social displacement and ideological alienation in a market economy. Its voters

included many former privileged party members but also some rural workers and young people. Ironically, the communist-descended party was very weak among the bluecollar workers.

The election results of 1990 suggested that national unification could eventually modify the German party system significantly. By the time of the next national election, in October 1994, it became evident that a new east-west divide had emerged in German politics. This time, the far-left PDS was able to almost double its support and attract 20 percent of the vote in the East, where only one-fifth of Germany's total population lives. At the same time, the PDS won slightly less than 1 percent of the vote in the more populous West and thus fell below the famous "5 percent hurdle" established in Germany's electoral law as a minimum for a party to win proportional representation in the Bundestag. The PDS was nevertheless able to gain parliamentary entry, because it met an almost forgotten alternative requirement of winning at least three single-member districts. Thus the political descendants of the former ruling Communists are now represented in the Bundestag by 30 deputies, who like to present themselves as democratically sensitive far-left socialists.

Despite a widespread unification malaise in Germany, the conservative-liberal government headed by Chancellor Helmut Kohl won reelection in 1994. His Christian Democrats benefited from a widely discussed and perceived improvement in the German economy after the spring, winning 41.5 percent of the vote. His Free Democratic ally barely scraped through with 6.9 percent of the vote. Together, the two parties had a very slim majority of 10 seats more than the combined total of the three opposition parties, the SPD (36.4 percent), the Greens (7.3 percent), and the PDS (4.4 percent). In the upper house or Bundesrat, the SPD has a comfortable majority of the seats, based on their control of many state governments.

The articles on Germany include evaluations of Helmut Kohl, the veteran chancellor who has now served in office longer than any of his predecessors since Bismarck. In addition, there are articles that contain economic and political balance sheets on the challenges and accomplishments of national unification. The task of post-communist reconstruction in eastern Germany goes far beyond the transfer of institutions and capital from the West. The transition to pluralist democracy and a market economy also requires a social and cultural transformation. Moreover, there are new problems facing the larger and more powerful Germany on the international scene, as it seeks to deal with an ambiguous mixture of expectations and anxieties that this European giant arouses abroad. Not least, there is a growing awareness that the generous social welfare model of Germany may have become unsustainable in the long run, as the country faces stiff economic competition from abroad.

France must also cope with major political challenges within a rapidly changing Europe. The bicentennial of the French Revolution was duly celebrated in 1989. It served as an occasion for public ceremonies and a revival of historical-political debates about the costs and benefits of that great exercise in the radical transformation of a society. Ironically, however, by this time there was mounting evidence that the sharp ideological cleavages which marked French politics for so much of the past 2 centuries were losing significance. Instead, there was emerging a more pragmatic, pluralist form of accommodation in French public life.

This deradicalization and depolarization of political discourse is by no means complete in France. If the Communists have become weakened and ideologically confused, Le Pen's National Front on the extreme right can arouse populist support with its xenophobic rhetoric directed primarily against the country's many residents of Arab origin. The apparent electoral appeal of such invective has led some leaders of the establishment parties of the more moderate Right to voice carefully formulated reservations about the presence of so many immigrants. An entirely new and different political phenomenon for France is the appearance of two small Green parties, one more conservative and the other more socialist in orientation.

As widely expected, the Socialists suffered a major setback in the parliamentary elections of 1993. After the second round of voting, held a week after the first, it was clear that the conservative alliance of the center-right Giscardists (the Union pour la Démocratie Française, or UDF) and the neo-Gaullists (the Rassemblement pour la République, or RPR) had garnered about 40 percent of the popular vote. However, that gave them an overwhelming majority of nearly 80 percent of the seats in the 577-seat National Assembly.

The Socialists and their close allies were among the losers in this largest electoral landslide in French democratic history. Receiving less than 20 percent of the popular vote, or about one-half as much as 5 years earlier, they plummeted from their previous share of 282 seats in 1988 to only 70 seats. The Communists, with about half as many votes, were able to win 23 seats because much of their electoral support is concentrated in a few urban districts. With a similar share of the vote, the ultraright National Front won no seats at all. The environmental alliance was doubly disappointed, winning a smaller share of the vote than expected and capturing no seats either.

François Mitterrand's 7-year presidential term lasted until May 1995. After the parliamentary rout of the Socialists in March 1993, he had been faced with the question of whether to resign early from the presidency or, as under similar political circumstances in 1986, to begin another period of "cohabitation" with a conservative prime minister. Mitterrand opted for the latter solution, but he made sure to appoint a moderate Gaullist, Édouard Balladur, as the new prime minister. Balladur in turn appointed a new, compact government that included members from all main factions of the conservative alliance. For a time, Balladur enjoyed considerable popularity, and he decided to enter the presidential race in 1995 instead of leaving Jacques Chirac, a former prime minister, to be the only Gaullist candidate.

The presidential race in France tends to become highly individualized, and eventually the tough and outspoken Chirac pulled ahead of his more consensual and lackluster party colleague. In the first round of the presidential election, however, a plurality of the vote went to the main Socialist candidate, Lionel Jospin, a former education minister and party leader. In the run-off election two weeks later Chirac defeated Jospin and thus ended 14 years of Socialist control of the presidency. He appointed another Gaullist, Alain Juppé, as prime minister.

The articles in this section include evaluations of Jacques Chirac's political leadership as well as a political postmortem of François Mitterrand, who died in January 1996, less than a year after leaving office. Other articles give a perspective on what some observers insist on calling "the new France." In fact, contemporary French politics and society combine traits that reflect continuity with the past along with others that suggest considerable innovation. One recurrent theme among observers is the decline of the previously sharp ideological struggle between the Left and the Right. There may well be a sense of loss among some French intellectuals who still prefer the political battle to have apocalyptic implications. They will find it hard to accept that the grand struggle between Left and Right has been replaced by a more moderate and seemingly more mundane party politics of competition among groups that cluster near the center of the political spectrum.

In the end, French intellectuals may discover that what they have long regarded as a tedious political competition between those promising a "little more" or a "little less" can have considerable practical consequences in terms of "who gets what, when, and how." Moreover, such incremental politics need not be without dramatic conflict, since new issues, events, or leaders often emerge to sharpen the differences and increase the apparent stakes of politics. In the last months of 1995, for example, French politics suddenly took on a dramatic form and immediacy, when workers and students resorted to massive strikes and street demonstrations against a new austerity program introduced by the conservative government. The proposed cutbacks in social entitlements such as pension rights appeared to be sudden and drastic. They were difficult to explain to the public at large, and many observers saw the political confrontation in France as a major test for the welfare state or social market economy that is now being squeezed in the name of international competitiveness throughout Western Europe.

The loss of great ideological alternatives may help account for the mood of political *malaise* that many observers claim to discover in contemporary France. But the French search for political direction and identity in a changing Europe has another major origin as well. The sudden emergence of a larger and potentially more powerful Germany next door cannot but have a disquieting effect upon France. French elites now face the troubling question of redefining their country's role in a post–cold war world, in which the Soviet Union has lost in power and influence while Germany has gained in both.

In this new European setting, some observers have even suggested that we may expect a major new cleavage in French politics between those who favor a reassertion of the traditional French nation-state ideal—a kind of isolationist neo-Gaullism that can be found on both the Left and Right—and those who want the country to accept a new European order, in which the sovereignty of both the French and German nation-states would be diluted or contained by a network of international obligations within the larger European framework.

Italy is roughly comparable to France and Britain in population and economic output, but it has a different political tradition which includes a long period of fascist rule and a far more persistent element of north-south regionalism. The country became a republic after World War II and, using a system of proportional representation, developed a multiparty system in which the center-right Christian Democrats played a central role as the major coalition party. The Communists, as the second major party, were persistently excluded from government at the national level. They played a considerable role in local politics, however, and embarked relatively early on a nonrevolutionary path of seeking social reforms in a pluralist society. Under their recently adopted new name, Democratic Party of the Left (PDS), the former Communists essentially adopted social democratic reform positions. In 1993 and 1994, they experienced a political revival, as Italian voters abruptly turned away from the Christian Democrats and other corrupt establishment parties.

The corruption issue had come to the fore as the cold war ended. As middle class fears of Communism declined, many Italians were no longer willing to tolerate the self-serving manner in which the establishment parties and their leaders had prospered from all manners of side payments for political services and government contracts. Some vigorous prosecutors and judges played a major role in exposing the extent of what became known popularly as *tangentopoli* (kickback city) in public affairs. In the local and regional elections of 1993, voter protest benefited both the PDS and some regional leagues in the North that favored greater autonomy from Rome. A frantic political facelift by the Christian Democrats, who regrouped as the Popular Party, did not stem their losses. Their old center-Left and center-Right partners in corruption experienced similar setbacks.

In late March 1994, Italy held what was heralded at the time as the most important parliamentary elections in over 4 decades. Once again Italian voters demonstrated their disgust with the old government parties, but the end result provided at least as much confusion as previous contests. Using a new electoral system, in which three-quarters of the members of parliament are elected on a winner-take-all basis and the rest by proportional representation, they decimated the centrist alliance which included the former Christian Democrats. On the left, an alliance led by the PDS won 213 of the 630 seats in the Chamber of Deputies, compared to the 46 seats for the main centrist group. But it was the Freedom Alliance of the right that triumphed by winning 366 seats. It consisted of an incongruous coalition of three main groups, of which the strongest was the *Forza Italia* (Go Italy) movement, led by the media magnate, Silvio Berlusconi. The others were the fascist-descended National Alliance (formerly MSI), led by Gianfranco Fini, and the federalist Northern League, led by Umberto Bossi. Berlusconi, who campaigned against both corruption (the centrists) and communism (the PDS), had catapulted himself and his party to the front by a skillful use of the electronic media. He faced the difficult task of creating a government based on a fractious coalition, in which the leader of the regionalist Northern League showed contempt for the centralist ideology of the neo-fascists. Berlusconi's government lost its parliamentary majority when Bossi's Northern League finally pulled out of the coalition. A new caretaker government of technocrats, headed by the banker Lamberto Dini, took over the reins in January 1995. Dini then surprised observers by managing to generate sufficient parliamentary toleration to hold on for a full year.

In April 1996, however, Italy finally went to the polls in an attempt to find a more stable parliamentary base for a new government. Using the hybrid electoral system that had resulted in such confusion 2 years earlier, the Italians voters managed this time to select a winning team. The victors were the left-of-center Olive Tree coalition, in which the PDS under its new leader, Massimo D'Alema, is by far the strongest parliamentary party. However, the new prime minister, Romano Prodi, is a banker who comes from the moderate PPI. The new government has been dependent upon the support of the far-Left party of Refounded Communists for its majority, but it may replace this partner in favor of small Catholic parties on the center-Right. Meanwhile, Bossi's rhetoric has become more ardently secessionist than ever before. One of the articles reminds us of the important north-south divide that is far older, and perhaps also deeper, than Germany's more recent east-west divide. Italy remains a fascinating political laboratory.

Japan, the fifth country in this study of representative governments of industrial societies, has long fascinated students of comparative politics and society. After World War II, a representative democracy was installed in Japan under American supervision. This political system soon acquired indigenous Japanese characteristics that set it off from the other major democracies examined here.

For almost 4 decades, the Japanese parliamentary system was dominated by the Liberal Democratic Party, which, as the saying goes, is "neither liberal, nor democratic, nor a party." It is essentially a conservative political force, comprising several delicately balanced factions. These are often personal followerships identified and headed by political bosses who stake out factional claims to benefits of office. At periodic intervals, the LDP's parliamentary hegemony has been threatened, but it was always able to recover and retain power until 1993. In that year, it lost several important politicians who objected to the LDP's reluctance to introduce political reforms. As a result of these defections, the government lost its parliamentary majority. A vote of no-confidence was followed by early elections in July 1993 in which the LDP failed to recover its parliamentary majority for the first time in almost 4 decades. Seven different parties, which span the spectrum from conservative to socialist, thereupon formed what turned out to be a very fragile coalition government. Two prime ministers and several cabinet reshufflements later, the rump LDP had managed, by the summer of 1994, to return to the cabinet in coalition with its major former rival, the Socialists. The curious alliance was possible because of the basically pragmatic orientation adopted by the leadership of both major parties at this point in Japan's history. By December 1995, the LDP had recaptured the prime ministership as the result of winning a parliamentary majority for its candidate, Ryutaro Hashimoto. He became the country's eighth prime minister in 7 years and appointed a cabinet that seemed to be dominated by the old guard of Liberal Democrats. In the parliamentary election of October 1996, however, his party made an advance but failed to win a clear majority for his government because its two coalition partners were decimated, as one of the articles points out.

Observers differ about the significance of the political change in Japan. There is a growing belief, however, that the entrenched bureaucratic elites have lost some of their invincibility and may now become the targets of reform geared at opening up a society that seems overregulated and sometimes poorly regulated. A setback for the entrenched bureaucrats could lead to long-term shifts in Japan's balance of power that would be even more significant than the end of one-party hegemony in the country.

Looking Ahead: Challenge Questions

How has Tony Blair taken major steps to reform the image and program of his Labour Party? What are the main issues that seem to divide the Conservatives in the House of Commons? What are the reasons for the electoral weakening of the Liberal Democrats?

How has Chancellor Kohl managed to stay in power so long? What are some of the political problems facing the Social Democrats? Explain how the Greens are trying to become an alternative coalition party, also at the national level, to the vulnerable Free Democrats.

What are the signs that French politics have become more centrist or middle-of-the-road for the main political parties? Explain the conservative landslide in the parliamentary elections of March 1993.

Explain the recent shake-up in the Italian party system. Compare the outcome of the 1994 and 1996 parliamentary elections.

Explain the political outcome and significance of the 1993 and 1996 parliamentary elections in Japan. Why do some observers believe that the political changes are more apparent than real?

The politics of power

*New divides have opened up in British politics. Europe and the
constitution now dominate the debate*

Philip Stephens

History always has a future. Fresh unexpected upheavals chase each new consensus. So it is with British politics. During the past few years the fault line that defined the post-war political landscape has all but disappeared. There is now an unprecedented measure of agreement among the main parties on the primacy of the market over the state in promoting economic prosperity. But other, deep fissures have appeared. The old arguments were about economics. The new ones are about Britain's place in Europe and about the way it is governed.

The fevered nature of current political debate in part reflects the imminence of the general election. It is at most 11 months away. The prime minister's wafer-thin majority in the House of Commons might force an earlier contest. The odds now seem to be stacked heavily in favour of an end to 17 years of Conservative rule. Mr Tony Blair's Labour party has a massive lead in the opinion polls. Mr John Major's latest confrontation with his European partners over the ban on British beef exports serves to underscore the bitter feuding in the Conservative party over Europe.

Consider first, though, the new consensus. By the conventional yardsticks of the 1970s and 1980s, there is little to separate messrs Major and Blair. Mr Major, chosen six years ago to smooth the rougher edges of Thatcherism, is a pragmatist rather than an idelogue. The 43-year-old Mr Blair has set as his ambition the permanent return of his party to the centrist mainstream. In another era, one could imagine the two men finding themselves on the same side.

Thus the most eloquent testimony to the success of Margaret Thatcher's revolution is found in Mr Blair's prospectus. During most of its lifetime, Labour has denied the reality of the marketplace. No longer. Mr Blair is a social democrat not a socialist. In the question of economics he is better described as a small "c" con-

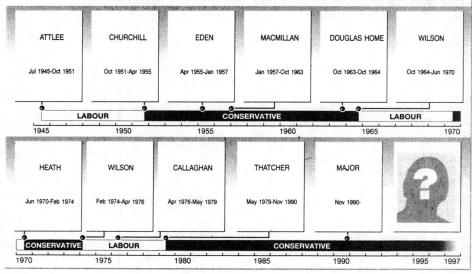

SWINGS AND BALANCES: POST-WAR POLITICAL BRITAIN

ATTLEE	CHURCHILL	EDEN	MACMILLAN	DOUGLAS HOME	WILSON
Jul 1945-Oct 1951	Oct 1951-Apr 1955	Apr 1955-Jan 1957	Jan 1957-Oct 1963	Oct 1963-Oct 1964	Oct 1964-Jun 1970

LABOUR — CONSERVATIVE — LABOUR
1945 · 1950 · 1955 · 1960 · 1965 · 1970

HEATH	WILSON	CALLAGHAN	THATCHER	MAJOR	
Jun 1970-Feb 1974	Feb 1974-Apr 1976	Apr 1976-May 1979	May 1979-Nov 1990	Nov 1990-	?

CONSERVATIVE — LABOUR — CONSERVATIVE
1970 · 1975 · 1980 · 1985 · 1990 · 1995 · 1997

servative. One of his first acts as leader was to strip his party's constitution of its emblematic commitment to state ownership. It now exalts instead the benefits of a "dynamic market economy". Mr Gordon Brown, the shadow chancellor, propounds an approach to fiscal policy and to inflation as tough as any.

There are Labour assurances also on tax. True, the (very) rich might be asked to pay more. But Mr Brown insists the middle classes can breathe easily. Labour has awoken from its redistributive dream. The ambition now is for a level playing field of opportunity. Mr Blair calls this "New Labour". Of course, there are still differences between right and left in their approach to the economic insecurity which has become the central preoccupation of the electorate. Technological advance, global competition and corporate down-sizing have turned upside down the comfortable assumptions of what the politicians call "Middle England". The middle classes have been robbed of the post-war certainties of life-

time employment of steadily rising prosperity. Mr Major's response is further deregulation and liberalisation, a flexible employment market, lower taxes and a smaller state. In this vision, competitiveness is all. Britain becomes an offshore haven for enterprise and investment on the edge of a sclerotic European continent. It is Hong Kong writ large, an economy in which the best security against change is the capacity to embrace it.

Mr Blair takes a different tack. Under-investment is the problem. The Conservatives are accused of fracturing the nation's social cohesion. Outside the economic mainstream, lies a growing underclass of badly educated, unemployed, underachievers. New Labour's answer is more investment and open, life-time, access to education and training, and thus to employment. Like Mr Bill Clinton, the US president, the Labour leader promises work to replace welfare.

Such issues will be fiercely debated before the election, no doubt with more heat than light. But it is political power—its distribution within Britain and the extent to which it should be shared with continental Europe—that will loom largest in the approach to the millennium. The nation has still to come to terms with its relative decline. Pragmatism pushes the politicians in the direction of Europe. Insecurity and pride tell them that Britain can stand apart. At home, an ancient, unwritten, constitution is creaking.

The politicians must decide how the nation is to be governed. They must establish a durable relationship with the rest of Europe. These are challenges which will not easily be met. The potential for agreement is often clearer across the old right/left divides than within the coalitions represented by the two main parties. A sensible outcome would fracture party allegiances.

Europe has dominated the political debate since sterling was driven from the exchange rate mechanism on that black Wednesday in September 1992. That event, alongside the protracted struggle that accompanied ratification of the Maastricht treaty, transformed the dynamics of Mr Major's government. The so-called beef war is just the latest episode in a sorry saga which has seen Britain drift further apart from Germany and France and the Conservative party fracture.

At this short distance, it seems incredible that the catalyst for Margaret Thatcher's fall in 1990 was her isolation in Europe. The deeply ingrained scepticism encapsulated in her Bruges speech is now commonplace in her party. Through the dark prism of resurgent Tory nationalism, the entity created at Maastricht seems a plot to subsume the nation in a German Europe. Mr Major and most, but not all, in his cabinet remain convinced that Britain's future lies firmly in the European Union. Politics as much as economics argues against isolation. So they have sought a compromise in which Britain holds to its present commitments but would stand aside from the next step on the road to integration.

A year or two ago such a stance might have preserved a veneer of unity.

But pro-European Conservatives are in retreat. The dispute over beef has demonstrated the capacity of sections of the Tory press to fan the flames of xenophobia. The Anglo-French financier Sir James Goldsmith, ready to spend £20m in his cause, demands a referendum on Britain's future in Europe. If Mr Major loses the election, his party will lurch further in the direction of the sceptics.

For Labour, the wheel has turned in the opposite direction. In the early 1980s it backed withdrawal. Now it pledges constructive engagement, an accommodation with, if not an enthusiastic embrace for, the ambitions of France and Germany. Mr Blair signals that a Labour government would probably not join a single currency in 1999, but it would do soon afterwards.

This all seems fair enough in opposition, but, alas, Mr Blair's party is not without its insecurities and its sceptics. For all his encouraging words about deeper co-operation, the Labour leader has shown himself wary of a national mood which still resents the replacement of empire by Europe. At the moment, the Labour sceptics are less influential than their Tory counterparts, but once in government they would secure leverage. To join, say, the single currency, Mr Blair would need the support of pro-European Conservatives. For all the recent hysteria, there remains a healthy pro-European majority in the House of Commons. But it is found across the parties, not within them.

Labour's ambitious plans for constitutional reform are similarly threatened by the strait-jacket of the two-party system. This programme, a pledge to reverse the creeping centralisation of power in the state, is the most radical in Mr Blair's prospectus. Put into practice, it would profoundly alter the way the nation is governed.

The concentration of political power in the Whitehall executive is the most damaging legacy of the Thatcher era. Accountability has been eroded. The Westminster parliament has never been so weak. Local democracy has been de-

prived of a significant voice. The regions are ruled from London. Appointed "quangos" have replaced elected officials. As in commerce, so in politics. A monopoly of power has corrupted the cause of efficient, responsive government.

Mr Blair proposes a new parliament in Scotland, an assembly in Wales, some restoration of the financial independence of local government and reform of parliament's second chamber, the House of Lords. An elected assembly for London and, over time, regional government elsewhere in England would follow.

Across the Channel, or the Atlantic, where political power has long been dispersed, these would seem modest, and somewhat ramshackle, aims. Devolution for Scotland is simply recognition of the distinct identity it retains within the UK. The alternative is the march of Scottish separatism.

This is an issue, though, over which common sense rarely prevails in Britain. Its constitution is a fragile edifice. Past attempts at reform invariably have been vexatious. The potential for agreement is stifled by party ties. Mr Blair is assured the support of the small, third, party, the Liberal Democrats. But the Tory leadership is implacably opposed to the dispersal of political power. Without a broader consensus, constitutional change might yet become for Mr Blair what Maastricht was for Mr Major.

There is an answer. The logical extension of the pluralist politics which Mr Blair promises is a more proportional voting system for the Westminister parliament. That would break the two-party system, creating coalitions across parties instead of within them. It would allow the emergence of strong alliances on Europe and on domestic political change. It would marginalise both Tory nationalists and the unreconstructed left, thereby entrenching the pro-European centre in British politics. In government, Mr Blair might find it hard to resist the temptation of building this new political consensus. So far, he has promised no more than a referendum on electoral reform. Events may well propel him much further.

Tony Blair and the New Left

Anne Applebaum

ANNE APPLEBAUM is a political columnist for London's Evening Standard.

A NEW DIRECTION FOR BRITAIN?

HE HAS been feted in Britain and abroad; denounced as the Stalin of the British left and hailed as its savior; profiled, interviewed, and investigated by the British press, the foreign press, and the tabloid press. But to my mind the phenomenon of Tony Blair, the man who became leader of the British Labour Party in the spring of 1994 and is now the leading contender to become Britain's next prime minister, is best illuminated by a conversation that took place in the lobby of the German parliament. A member of the Green Party was describing to me the impression Blair had made during his 1996 trip to Germany. Practically the whole of the Bundestag had heard him speak, she said: "What really excited us was this new idea of reinventing the left. Tony Blair is reinventing the left." I asked her what exactly that meant, the reinvention of the left. She winced slightly, and paused. "I don't remember any of the details, exactly," she replied, "but this reinvention of the left is very important."

It would be hard to find a better illustration of the feelings that Blair inspires. He undoubtedly interests people, in Britain and perhaps even more so in the rest of Europe. He even seems to many to be the harbinger of a whole new kind of European politics, a 21st-century politics: he himself speaks frequently of transcending left-right divisions, of leaving old ideas of party loyalty behind. In the three years he has been leader of Britain's opposition, he has galvanized his party, rejuvenated its supporters, and mounted the first serious challenge to the Tories since 1979, something that previous Labour reformers like Neil Kinnock and John Smith never managed. After losing four consecutive general elections over seventeen years, Labour could very well win the next one, which the current Conservative government must call by the end of May. Nevertheless, there are lingering doubts about the details: who is Tony Blair, what exactly would he do if he became prime minister, and what does it mean to reinvent the left in a post-Thatcherite Britain and a post-communist Europe?

The importance of that last question has frequently eluded American commentators who write about Blair. That is because unlike America's Democrats, the British Labour Party was genuinely socialist. Its members believed in a planned economy and nationalized industry, preferred state housing projects to private developments, and thought a "fair" society could be created with taxes as high as 90 percent of income. Many of them, including some of the party's leaders, still think that way. A member of the Labour Party's shadow cabinet once told me that the privatization of British industry in the 1980s was only a phase: "There are fashions for these things. At the moment, nationalization is out of fashion. Who knows, 20 years from now, it might come back in again." It is precisely because the Labour Party's belief in socialist economic solutions has long been so strong that any attempt to alter it must have an equal intellectual force. Since he became his party's leader—indeed, since long before he became its leader—Blair has tried to muster that intellectual force, both to exorcise Labour's socialist instincts and to replace them with something new.

Although he is frequently compared with Bill Clinton, Tony Blair's political position is different from Clinton's in that the first of his tasks—transforming his party—was a genuine struggle. Clinton easily reinvented the Democrats as a centrist party: they were centrists already. But Blair has had to reassure Conservative voters that the Labour Party is no longer "dangerous" to the British economy while simultaneously preserving his base among Labour socialists. He began by demonstrating that his personal break with socialism is complete. Writing in the *Daily Telegraph*, a newspaper historically linked to the Conservative Party, Blair declared that he admires Margaret Thatcher for her reinvention of the right nearly 15 years ago, an unthinkable

 Reprinted with permission from *Foreign Affairs*, March/April 1997, pp. 45-60. © 1997 by the Council on Foreign Relations, Inc.

sentiment for any previous Labour leader. During his first year in office Blair waged a surprisingly hard—fought campaign to rid the Labour constitution of its notorious "Clause 4," which proclaimed the goal of "securing for the workers by hand or by brain the full fruits of their industry, and the most equitable distribution thereof that may be possible, upon the basis of common ownership of the means of production, distribution, and exchange." Although he replaced it with a somewhat anodyne call for "a dynamic economy . . . a just society . . . an open democracy . . . a healthy environment," he made his point: the Labour Party has changed.

British tabloids describe Blair as "smarmy," and the label has stuck.

Still, when the history of Britain's Labour Party is written, the real break from socialism will probably be dated from January 20, 1997, the day that Gordon Brown, Labour's shadow chancellor of the exchequer, announced that a future Labour government would not raise personal income taxes during its first term in office—and would not increase public spending for its first two years in office. With that statement, which took most of the Labour Party by surprise, nearly two decades of Labour attacks on "Tory cuts" and the "unfair Tory tax system" fell by the wayside, along with more than four decades of socialist assumptions: Brown was telling not only the voters, but the nursing, teaching, and public sector unions who support the Labour Party that a Labour government's top priority would not be spending. Hardly surprising, then, that last year, when their own polling revealed that most voters do indeed believe Tony Blair is different from his predecessors, even Tories gave up trying to identify him with his party's socialist past. They instead invented a new slogan: "New Labour, New Danger."

Nevertheless, the more important part of Blair's mission—explaining what will replace socialism—remains unfulfilled. If opinion polls register opposition to the Tories, they also register quite a bit of confusion about what the Labour Party now believes. Worse, many people still think that Blair is untrustworthy or insincere, or that he stands for nothing at all. British tabloids describe him as "smarmy," and the label has stuck.

Some of this confusion would have arisen with any effort to change the left. On one hand, Blair

has discarded his party's belief in managed markets and nationalized industry, and even some aspects of the welfare state previously considered sacrosanct, including the absolute right to public housing; even his pledge to restrict spending would have been unthinkable in the past. On the other hand, he continues to reject British right-wing philosophies of individualism and what he describes as "unfettered" capitalism. What he is left with is a firm but ill-defined belief in the power of the state not only to regulate society but to improve it—albeit without spending any money. As Blair himself said in an article in the *Sunday Mirror* in 1994: "Labour's vision is of a Britain that is not just a collection of individuals but a society where a decent community backs up the efforts of individuals within it. That change can't come through market forces. It needs active government, local and national."

But "belief in the state" or in "active government" does not by itself provide enough definition to satisfy most voters, particularly those accustomed to the partisan gunfight that is British politics. To some, Blair's talk of community and society still sounds like the language of the old Labour Party. When he throws around words like "responsibility" and "entrepreneurship," on the other hand, he appears to others to have borrowed Tory language wholesale. The truth is that Blair and his colleagues have advocated a strikingly wide range of policies. Some grossly contradict one another, some complement one another, and some appear to have been floated simply to gauge public reaction before being discarded. On rare occasions one set of ideas appears to dominate and is hailed as the philosophy designated to replace socialism.

Over time, however, the dust has settled. It now seems as if it is precisely the contests and contrasts between policies and philosophies that define both "new Labour" and the reinvention of the left. There is no ideology or framework, or even a big idea. There is only a list of perceived problems—the damage that globalization supposedly inflicts on British communities, the need to reverse the "short-termist" instincts of British capitalism and transform corporate culture, the need for welfare reform, "modernization," and radical constitutional reform—and an elaborate rhetoric that describes a modest set of proposed solutions.

STAKING THE LEFT'S CLAIM

PERHAPS THE most interesting of those solutions is Blair's stakeholder economy. Blair first used the term "stakeholder" in a speech before an audience of businesspeople in Singapore in January 1996. He began by voicing his admiration for the achievements of the "Asian tigers," then said he wanted the same thing in Britain: "The creation of an economy where we are inventing and producing goods and services of quality needs the engagement of the whole country. It must be a matter of national purpose and national pride . . . The economics of the center and center-left today should be geared to the creation of the stakeholder economy which involves all our people, not a privileged few."

In Britain the speech was acclaimed by Blair's friends in the media as the philosophical breakthrough the Labour leader had been groping for. Andrew Marr, now editor of *The Independent,* wrote that Blair had started to "turn the intellectual tide." Not only had he found a credible new role for the state, but he was "able to distinguish new Labour's program from the Tories in ways that made sense." Stakeholding was hailed as Blair's new response to the shortcomings of free-market capitalism. Socialism was to be replaced by Asian-style corporatism—or, to put it differently, Anglo-Saxon free-market capitalism was to be replaced with something more controlled, more continental.

There was one small difficulty: the term "stakeholding" was not new. A number of left-leaning economists and journalists had used it before, and all of them leaped to take credit for Blair's Singapore speech. Many thought stakeholding implied reforming the composition of company boards and the laws governing them, a change that would ensure that the many different groups who have a stake in a company's operations—investors, workers, consumers, suppliers—are properly represented. The British journalist Will Hutton, whose best-selling book *The State We're In* contained a chapter entitled "A Stakeholder Economy," had called, for example, for state involvement in pension and investments, the incorporation of trade unions and banks into the constitution of a firm, and regulations forcing banks to make more long-term loans.

Stakeholding policies also have a price tag. Immediately after Blair's Singapore speech, the Tories issued a press release in which they claimed that his proposals would place more financial burdens on employers and businesses. People demanded an explanation of what exactly Blair meant by a stakeholder economy. Would he change corporate law? Would he change trade union law? As soon as the questions became penetrating, Blair backed off, claiming that his ideas were far more general. Since then he has been cautious about how he uses the word. In a speech that he delivered at a public meeting in Derby only ten days after the Singapore speech, the stakeholder economy was variously defined as "giving power to you, the individual," as "giving you the chances to get on and so help Brit-

ain get on too," and as "giving opportunities for all." No specific policies were mentioned.

Blair insists that he stands by the speech, but when pressed he confesses only to a belief that companies ought to be asked to do more, voluntarily, for their workers. The word "stakeholding" has also faded from his vocabulary. It was absent altogether from his speech at the Labour Party convention in October, traditionally the Labour leader's most important speech of the year.

CAUTIOUS OR VACUOUS?

THE "STAKEHOLDING" episode revealed a pattern in Blair's preelection politics: make strong proposals, allow them to be picked up and mulled over by the press, retreat if the criticism is too harsh. The charitable explanation for such behavior is that Blair fears his ideas will be twisted and exaggerated during the traditionally nasty campaign season leading up to the general election. Given that Labour has lost four elections running, the last thing he wants to do is frighten voters. The less charitable explanation is that Blair doesn't really know what he believes—or that he claims to believe different things at different times, depending on his audience.

The latter explanation has certainly been applied to another strand of Blairism, his tendency toward what Americans might recognize as communitarian thinking. Some might also call it paternalism; the unsympathetic would call it authoritarianism. Asked directly, Blair will agree that he is interested in communitarianism and has read communitarian writings, but shies away from plainly identifying himself with the philosophy—just as he shies away from plainly identifying himself with any philosophy. Nevertheless, he has employed the language of communitarianism in his speeches. "For myself," he said in a speech at Southwark Cathedral in January 1996, "I start from a simple belief that people are not separate economic actors competing in the marketplace of life. They are citizens of a community. We are social beings, nurtured in families and communities and human only because we develop the moral power of personal responsibility for ourselves and each other." What made that speech interesting was that Blair did not then continue (as his predecessors would have) by describing what the rich owe the poor, or what the state owes its citizens.

In fact, rather than talking about what the state can give to people, Blair adopts the kind of language that British conservatives normally use, speaking of duties and responsibilities that come with rights and rewards. In the same speech, Blair went on to say that "the key is to recognize that we owe a duty to more than self. Responsibility applies from top to bottom of society, from the responsibility to pay taxes to fund common services, to the responsibility of fathers to their children after a divorce, to the responsibility of people to respect the lives of their neighbors."

Blair is trying to signal a change of direction, a change of heart in his party.

That, at any rate, is the theory. In practice, this new emphasis on the needs and duties of community has resulted in a different Labour attitude toward law-and-order issues and some neighborhood and family topics that might once have seemed beneath the dignity of a national politician. Blair first hinted at a change of direction in the annual *Spectator* magazine lecture, which he delivered in March 1995, an address best described as his "noisy neighbors" speech. Announcing that "duty is the cornerstone of a decent society," he condemned noisy inhabitants of public housing developments, calling for their eviction or the confiscation of their stereos: "Families have the right to be housed but they do not have any right to terrorize those around them, be it with violence, racial abuse, or noise. If tenants do not fulfill their side of the bargain, the contract is broken." Using similar language, Blair has called for curfews for youths, penalties for parents who do not assure that their children attend school, and more homework. In these and other areas, he often sounds a great deal like Bill Clinton, who is also interested in communitarianism and curfews.

In fact, the two men advocate similar causes for similar reasons: both are trying to signal a change of direction, a change of heart in their respective parties. In the past, the Labour Party was not much interested in discussing the unpleasantness of life in Britain's deteriorating public housing developments and state schools, preferring to complain that there were not enough public housing developments and state schools to begin with. In the past, Labour leaders did not interest themselves in noise but in "social justice." In the past, the Labour Party concerned itself with the economic rights of the public, not people's duty to the community.

The noisy neighbors speech was also the first of several in which Blair found new uses for the state

in discouraging behavior that is not criminal, but antisocial. Early this year he caused a stir by suggesting that he rarely gave money to beggars, who, he implied, really ought not to be on the streets at all. Jack Straw, his shadow home secretary (in Britain, the home secretary is responsible for crime and immigration policy) is a vocal fan of New York City's crackdown on "squeegee men" and minor vandalism and has discussed the possibility of removing drunks from London parks. Straw has also issued a report on parenting, and muses aloud about the lack of information available to parents from government sources, especially compared with the wealth of information about driving cars.

Unlike stakeholding, these paternalist policies have stuck: his law-and-order speeches have probably been Blair's most popular and successful. The British public is already familiar with such ideas; the right wing of the Conservative Party and parts of the Tory press advocate similar ones. Coming from a Labour leader they seem fresh and original. But Blair's paternalism has not been wholly consistent. He does not always mention his communitarian policies in speeches to Labour audiences and certainly plays them down at party conferences, a habit that contributes to the impression that he is slippery. Pointing out that Blair's noisy neighbors speech was made to a largely Conservative audience, Craig Brown, a columnist for the *Daily Telegraph,* wondered how malleable the Labour leader might be: "What would he have yelled in a speech to the Noisy Neighbors Association Annual Dinner-Dance?"

TONY AND THE TOFFLERS

EVEN LESS clear is Blair's commitment to his third and closely related set of ideas. Blair's 1996 party convention speech may sound familiar to the American ear. He told his Labour audience that we live "in an era of extraordinary, revolutionary change. At work. At home. Through technology and the million marvels of modern science. The possibilities are exciting. But its challenge is clear. How do we create, in Britain, a new age of achievement in which all of the people, not just a few, can share?" The line was pure Blair—and pure Newt Gingrich. Along with the rhetoric of technological, social, and behavioral change come some distinctly Gingrichite inclinations, most notably a radically different approach to traditional entitlements, probably in the form of radical pension and welfare reform. Call it the neo-right-wing line of thinking in the Labour Party. If that sounds contradictory, it is. So contrary is this kind of thinking to the traditional views of the British Labour Party, in fact, that Blair rarely discusses such ideas in public. And so rarely does he discuss them in public that not everyone in British politics is convinced he really means it.

Though mocked by his Tory opponents and treated with suspicion by those who suspect he has no policies to match such language, Blair privately insists that this revolutionary rhetoric will produce revolutionary policy. At off-the-record meetings with journalists, he has insisted on the truly radical nature of his intentions, particularly regarding welfare and pension reform: "I want to be remembered as the prime minister who reforms the welfare state" is how he once put it. He often speaks about welfare reform in the same way he does law-and-order issues, emphasizing the need for people to work in partnership with the state rather than simply depending on it for handouts. As he told the businesspeople in Singapore, "The system will only flourish in its aims of promoting security and opportunity across the life cycle if it holds the commitment of the whole population, rich and poor."

Unfortunately, as was the case with stakeholding, Blair remains maddeningly vague about what exactly his radical reform of the welfare state might entail. Like the United States, Britain has a state pension system that will, in the next century, run out of money. Blair knows this, and is perfectly happy to concede that pensions will eventually have to be funded through private contributions (although he does not emphasize the point in public, presumably for fear of antagonizing traditional Labour voters). He has promised his party a "review" of pension policy, but has not said publicly what conclusions he believes it will draw. Even more radically, Blair has expressed admiration for Asian approaches to insurance like Singapore's Central Provident Fund, a system of compulsory personal insurance, and has praised the work of Frank Field, a Labour member of Parliament who advocates compulsory unemployment and pension insurance, possibly managed by private or semiprivate insurance funds.

Nevertheless, Blair's failure to provide many details on his plans for welfare and pension reform rankles many British political observers. When pressed, Labour politicians will claim—as Blair has—that they need to be in office before being certain which promises they can keep, or that they do not want to reveal too much detail before an election for fear of having their words manipulated by their Tory opponents. They may be right—frightening people about health care reform is easy and effective, as the Democrats' tactics in the 1996 U.S. elections revealed—but their refusal to give any detail has played, once again, into the suspicion that Blair is a man of profuse rhetoric and few ideas.

DEVOLVING FROM DOWNING STREET

A FINAL way in which Blair wants to use state institutions to new effect is by reorganizing the institutions themselves. The call for constitutional change is not new to British voters. The Labour Party has been talking about it for decades. Still, Blair's talk of constitutional change fits well with his rhetoric about economic and legal change: it is all part of the revolution needed to "modernize" Britain for the 21st century, to sweep the dust out of Britain's supposedly medieval political institutions.

Perhaps the most important and most controversial part of Labour's constitutional reform program is Blair's support for the devolution of power from London to other regional centers in the United Kingdom. Unlike the United States or the Federal Republic of Germany, the United Kingdom is not a federation. There are no regional governments to vie for power with the central government in the way that American states or German *Länder* do. Blair's proposals would reverse that tradition, with power devolving from London to a Scottish parliament, a Welsh assembly, and other regional English assemblies. He says he also wants to make changes to the British parliament, altering some rules of parliamentary procedure, adopting the European Convention on Human Rights into British law, signing a Freedom of Information Act, increasing the powers of local government, and eliminating the role of hereditary peers, who still sit in Britain's second chamber, the House of Lords, by right of birth. As if that were not enough, the Labour Party has also declared that it will hold a referendum on reform of the first-past-the-post British electoral system, presumably with the aim of replacing it with continental-style proportional representation.

At least on the surface, the logic behind constitutional reform is much the same as that behind Blair's other proposals. Describing the modern disillusionment with politics in a speech in February 1996 in honor of the late Labour leader John Smith, Blair put it this way: "The disaffection is because people feel no ownership, no stake in much of the political process. The citizen feels remote from power. He has issued the same almost revolutionary rhetoric about constitutional change that he has about economic change: "The reforms I have set out will transform our politics. They will redraw the boundary between what is done in the name of the people and the people themselves. They will create a new relationship between government and the people based on trust, freedom, choice, and responsibility."

Naturally, there are a few other reasons as well. Devolution of power from Westminster to Edinburgh might ease the pressure the Labour Party is beginning to feel in Scotland from the Scottish National Party, which advocates Scottish independence from Great Britain. Almost any change in the British electoral system would also give more power to the Liberal Democrats, Britain's third party, which wins many local elections and up to a quarter of the votes in national elections, but thanks to the current system holds very few seats in Parliament. Because the Liberal Democrats are now almost entirely in sympathy with Blair's Labour Party, almost any change in the voting system would make it difficult for the Tories to govern Britain again any time soon.

But over time Labour's constitutional reforms have been gradually played down. After the Tories pointed out that a Scottish parliament with powers of taxation would almost certainly result in higher taxes for Scotland (a "tartan tax," as it became known), and after some claimed that a Scottish parliament would mark the beginning of a process that would end in an independent Scotland, if not the dissolution of the United Kingdom, Blair backed away. Instead of creating a Scottish parliament, Blair said, he would hold a referendum in Scotland, on both whether to form such a parliament and whether it should have powers of taxation. His Scottish supporters interpreted this change of policy as a betrayal, but it was in fact consistent with Blair's de facto preelection strategy: propose a radical idea, listen to the criticism, retreat.

Nor has the Labour Party been particularly clear about the consequences and implications of some of the proposed changes. How would the delicate balance between the House of Commons and the decidedly inferior House of Lords be altered by the absence of hereditary peers? How would the Labour Party compensate English members of Parliament for the fact that their Scottish counterparts could vote on legislation affecting England, whereas they could not vote on legislation affecting Scotland? How would electoral reform change British politics—and, indeed, what kind of electoral reform might occur? As the general election approaches, these issues remain shrouded in mystery.

CLOSER TO EUROPE

LIKE CONSERVATIVE Prime Minister John Major, Blair has also been less than clear about another potentially enormous change: whether Britain should join a single European currency, possibly the largest constitutional and political issue Britain now faces. To be frank, his silence on the subject is probably politically wise. The Conservatives are tearing themselves apart over Europe. If the Labour Party says nothing whatsoever about the topic, it

will appear to have a much stronger, more consistent policy. But Blair's silence also masks strains within Labour. A solid group of about 50 Labour members of Parliament consistently opposes greater European integration, not so much out of concern for British sovereignty—as is the case with the Tories—but because of the strict budgetary and monetary criteria that members of the single currency will have to meet. Blair is eager to play down these strains and stress the enormous difference that having a Labour prime minister will make in Britain's difficult relationship with Europe. As always, his rhetoric emphasizes the revolutionary impact of Labour leadership in Europe. As he put it in his 1996 party convention speech, "Leading Britain into an age of achievement means Britain leading in Europe . . . for business and for Britain we will build a new relationship with Europe."

Blair's position on the single currency remains virtually identical to John Major's.

The Labour Party is certainly closer to the European mainstream than the Conservatives on some issues, notably the Social Chapter, the social legislation that all European countries except Britain have pledged to adopt. Falling in step with the rest of Europe, Blair has also agreed to adopt a minimum wage and says he will relinquish the British veto in certain areas of health and social legislation, pleasing other European countries that want to reduce veto power over European policy. But Blair vigorously denies any desire to relinquish the veto on defense and foreign policy issues, and claims he does not mind being "isolated" in Europe if it is in the British national interest. That, of course, is precisely the view that has got the Conservative Party into so much trouble in Europe.

In fact, on the single currency, Blair's position remains virtually identical to John Major's. The Labour Party promised only that the decision to enter a single currency would be made "after an election." After sustained media pressure, however, Blair, like Major, promised a national referendum on a single currency. Like Major, he claims that "our options on a single currency should remain open, to be determined according to our national interest." Privately, he describes himself as agnostic on the issue. He says he has no ideological commitment to the single currency but could be convinced of its merits—which is fair enough, except that if progress toward the single currency continues on schedule, and if the Labour Party wins the next election, Blair would have to decide almost immediately whether or not Britain joined European Monetary Union as part of its first wave. A referendum would have to be prepared, the economic criteria would have to be met, and bills on a wide range of issues—including one establishing the independence of the Bank of England—would have to be approved by the House of Commons. Embarking on such a venture would require enormous political will. But if Blair does not attempt it, Britain's relations with Europe will hardly be "radically" transformed. On the major issues the United Kingdom will simply stand, as it does now, in opposition to France and Germany. On the questions of European integration, as so many other issues, British voters will simply have to wait and see what Labour Party policy turns out to be.

VACILLATION AS VIRTUE

In the end, it is the fantastic gap between his almost messianic rhetoric and his actual policy proposals that most frustrates Blair watchers. Most have now resigned themselves to the assumption that there is no single ideology, that different strands run through the party's rhetoric, and that Labour Party policy will mold itself to fit the times. Nevertheless, Blair constantly seems to be promising something more. "Let us call our nation to its destiny," he said at the Labour Party convention in 1996. "Let us lead it to a new age of achievement and build for us, our children, and their children, a Britain united to win in the new millennium." In the same speech, he repeated the term "a new age of achievement" several times—much as Bill Clinton spoke of "a bridge to the 21st century"—and said Britain had only a few years to prepare for the next millennium: "A thousand days to prepare for a thousand years."

The combination of constitutional change, electoral change, welfare and pension reform, and modifications of corporate and criminal law that Blair sometimes prescribes would, for better or for worse, have a revolutionary impact on Britain. These measures would certainly win him allies and opponents across Europe's broad political spectrum, and might well change the traditional party structure in Britain, as Blair has suggested. The privatization of pensions alone would put him at risk of being unseated by a revolution in his own party—although it would also win him support among some conservatives.

But Blair's list of actual policy promises is tiny. He has made five election "pledges"—on classroom sizes, hospital waiting lists, youth training schemes, low inflation, and fast—track punishment of young offenders. He has promised not to raise personal income taxes. A few minor welfare reforms have been mentioned, and some of his constitutional commitments seem sincere. But while these are potentially important changes, none seem to merit the phrase "a thousand days to prepare for a thousand years." The gap between rhetoric and policy prescriptions has produced a peculiar result: weeks away from a British general election, some Labour members of Parliament tell me they still don't know what their party would actually do if elected.

Worse, if Blair does take office—which is not, at this writing, by any means guaranteed—it is not even clear that there will be much room to make sweeping changes. His ability to achieve anything will depend on the size of his majority in Parliament, the obstinacy of the socialist minority in his party, and the timetable for EMU. In the end, Tony Blair may find, like many political leaders in the industrialized world, that whatever his activist ambitions, his role is purely managerial: if taxes cannot be raised, if there are no wars to fight, and if there is no political will to dismantle the large entitlement programs, all that any modern political leader can do is alter the state at the edges.

Unfortunately for Tony Blair, it may also be the case that Britain is returning not to the political ideologies of the nineteenth century but to the apolitical system of the eighteenth, in which the point was not to articulate an ideology and then carry out a stated program but to win and maintain power. Britain may, in other words, be returning to a system in which candidates vie with one another to make the right noises in front of the right constituencies so as to keep or gain control of a state that remains, year in and year out, largely unchanged, one in which it hardly matters whether Tony Blair or John Major is in office. If such is the case, for the British left, which has waited 18 years to return to office; for the European left, which is hoping Tony Blair will lead a continentwide renewal; for Tony Blair's supporters, who have elected him after hearing his promises of revolutionary change; and for Tony Blair himself, who appears genuine in his belief that the state has the ability to make life better for its citizens, power may prove disappointing indeed.

Britain's 1997 General Election

Bland Blair, bland Britain

Anthony King

Anthony King: professor of government at Essex University; election commentator for the BBC and regular contributor to the *Daily Telegraph*.

British voters in 1997 will eject the Conservatives after 18 years and, without enthusiasm, elect a new government under Tony Blair. As a result, Britain will not find a new world role: it will finally cease looking for one. Mr Blair, born in 1953, will be Britain's first genuinely post-imperial prime minister.

Fortune should favour his early years. Britain's economy will grow in 1997 at a fast but sustainable rate, faster indeed than that of any other major European country. Living standards will rise; unemployment and inflation will stay low; foreign investment will pour in. It is even possible that the sour mood that has permeated British public life will lift. For all this, John Major will get little, if any, thanks.

What no one knows is whether the new government will also be a traditional "Labour government" with a stable majority in Parliament. Most voters despise the out-going Major administration; but many still distrust Labour—the party of high taxes, high prices and massed picket lines—and most respond blandly to Mr Blair's own blandness. The famous smile is already losing its gleam.

Combined fear and indifference could mean that Labour becomes the largest single parliamentary party but fails to win outright. That would suit Mr Blair nicely. Ever since becoming party leader in 1994, Mr Blair has been wooing Paddy Ashdown's Liberal Democrats. Nothing explicit. No hugs or kisses. But a steady aligning of policies together with a blanket refusal to engage in the kind of inter-party abuse that passes for political debate in Britain. Mr Ashdown happily reciprocates.

Why? Because both men know they may need each other. A minority Labour government, with a substantial block of Liberal Democrat MPS, would give the Liberal Democrats their first taste of power for a generation. It would also relieve Mr Blair of the need to bargain with the 30 or so "old Labour" MPS certain to be elected. With Labour in a minority, its left-wingers would know that over-frequent dissent could destroy the infant government.

The same effect, though without Mr Ashdown, would be achieved if millions of Britons on election day sighed, said with a single voice, "Oh, well, Labour couldn't do worse than the present lot," and proceeded to present Mr Blair with a victory of Canadian (remember Kim Campbell?) proportions.

But the most probable outcome in 1997 is also the one Mr Blair almost certainly fears most: Labour in power but with a small majority, like the one that has made John Major's life so wretched ever since 1992. Under those circumstances, the new prime minister would be vulnerable to endless left-wing raids on his person and policies. The old left is deeply alienated from Mr Blair's whole style. Mr Blair knows it. Another reason to be nice to Mr Ashdown.

Whatever the precise outcome, Mr Blair as prime minister will centralise his control over both party and government and be ultra-cautious, even hyper-cautious, in policy terms. The control will be needed to ensure the caution.

As a human being, Mr Blair is highly moral (closer to Jimmy Carter than Bill Clinton) and also extremely nervous (the wire holding him together is more brittle than most people suppose). As a politician, he is tactically adventurous; only he would have dared eliminate Clause 4, the old socialist clause, from Labour's constitution. But ideologically he hangs loose to the point where it is doubtful whether he hangs at all. He has never been in government. His socialism is of the strictly ethical variety. His aim is no more (but no less) than a more humane capitalism. Unless unbalanced by Labour's left, he will pursue orthodox economic policies, be tough with the unions and not seek to reverse privatisation. No wonder business likes him.

Not least, as the first serious British politician since the 18th century without a vision of Britain as a great world power, Mr Blair will be cautious on Europe. Pro-European by instinct, he nevertheless shares Mr Major's doubts about both a single European currency and the effect introducing the Maastricht social chapter might have on British jobs and investment.

Mr Blair's greatest single asset is that his outlook coincides almost exactly with the British people's. Personally he is not a close-to-the-people figure like Neil Kinnock or, in an earlier generation, Harold Wilson; but he addresses ordinary people's concerns in a language they can understand (and, when he slips into jargon, as he did in 1996 with "stakeholder society", he quickly drops it). Mr Blair is what political scientists call a "valence" politician. He emphasises agreement rather than disagreement, commonly desired ends rather than hotly disputed means. He adopts postures rather than policies. Only on constitutional issues, notably Scottish devolution, has Labour taken up distinctive policy positions; and, fortunately for Labour, most Scots want it and nobody else, except Mr Major, really cares.

Ironically, with the exception of Scotland, the present prime minister's instincts are also "valence" instincts. He is in fact a more genuine man of the people than his Labour rival. But he is weighed down—almost bent double—by Margaret Thatcher's policy inheritance, which he cannot disavow, and by the numerous and vociferous ideologues in the Conservative Party, who claim to be sceptical about Europe but lack scepticism about everything else.

Tony Blair, alone in British politics, carries no burdens from the past and has total freedom of manoeuvre. His party desperately wants him to win. If he is not installed, however precariously, in 10 Downing Street by May 1997, a near-miracle will have had to occur.

A Party Chief's Labors Are Not Lost on Tory Voters

WARREN HOGE

LONDON, Sept. 28—Blackpool, Britain, gaudy blue-collar resort on the Irish Sea, and the City of London, the country's august blue-suited center of financial activity, can be thought of as the two distant poles of a passage through British public life.

Tony Blair, the charismatic leader of the Labor Party, has just made the unlikely journey on the eve of the election season in a sure-footed manner that illustrates how profoundly he has reshaped his party and how that stands to benefit him in his pursuit of the job of prime minister.

John Major, 53, has held the post since November 1990. He must call an election by May, and the electioneering begins in earnest this coming week with the opening of the Labor Party conference.

A Victorian connection of amusement park arcades, seaside promenades and bed-and-breakfasts with pots of geraniums in the windows, Blackpool was created a century ago for the millworkers of the industrial north. It is where Labor will gather in the coming week, and it was the scene earlier this month of a speech by Mr. Blair to the annual Trades Union Congress.

In that appearance, Mr. Bair did not bring the unionists to their feet with the traditional impassioned chanting of the socialist mantra. Instead, he set them back in their seats with a crisp accounting of what they could not expect from a Labor government. He told them that the party, founded by and for the union movement, was no longer in the unions' "pockets"; that workers should curb their bent for calling strikes; that raises for the public sector, the only heavily unionized part of British industry, would have to be realistic, and that they should consider themselves the partner—not the enemy—of business.

They had to listen to an unaccustomedly confessional speech for such a partisan gathering, as Mr. Blair argued that Labor had gone "badly wrong" in recent decades. He kept referring to the party he heads as "New Labor" and said, "There is a process of evolution that is not about disowning our past, but about refusing to live in it."

"We are looking at new ways to resolve disputes in a new labor market where there is intense competition round the world," he said, adding, "You are not going to solve the problems of the 21st century with the debates of the 70's and 80's."

The grab bag of proposals that Labor leaders have traditionally toted to Blackpool was in Mr. Blair's grasp when he arrived days later in London for a speech to 600 bankers invited by the London Futures and Options Exchange. The setting was the Gothic Guildhall, built in 1430 and later decked out in pennants and crests and statuary from Britain's days of empire.

Saying he wanted British companies to be highly lucrative, Mr. Blair spoke as the head of a party founded on the notion that profits were the proceeds of exploitation, addressing a group dedicated to speculative capitalism.

He pledged to hold down the cost of capital, promised more independence for the Bank of England, said he would "adhere to strict rules" on borrowing and spending, called for tax breaks for small enterprises and concluded that the time had come for people to stop asking, "Which is the pro-business party?"

Newspapers reported the same day that Kenneth Clarke, the Chancellor of the Exchequer, had let slip his opinion that Labor was "not such a threat" as it had been to the national interest.

That gaffe undermined the Conservative party's active campaign to scare people away from Labor and rewarded the peregrinating Mr. Blair with just what he was seeking—growing acceptance of Labor as a mainstream alternative to the Conservatives.

Parties in France and Spain that once called themselves socialist have become believers in the free market once in power, but Mr. Blair has succeeded in recasting his party while still in opposition.

Youthful, telegenic, articulate, ingratiating in public and autocratic in private, Mr. Blair, 43, has centralized power over a party famous for suicidal feuding and has tried to broaden its appeal with his repositioning. So far it appears to be a winning strategy. A London Times poll on Friday showed Labor with 52 percent, Conservatives with 29 percent and Liberal Democrats with 14.

Internally, Mr. Blair has reined in left-wing members and aggressive trade unionists whose behavior in past elections scared away significant parts of the electorate. Labor has been out of power for the last 17 years and for all but 16 of the last 50 years.

Externally, he has attracted increasing support from members of the business and financial sector. In one dramatic case this month, a $1.5 million donation came from the insurance executive who is the owner of the Chelsea professional soccer team, which is well known as the favorite of Prime Minister Major.

There has been grumbling within the party about the changes Mr. Blair has wrought and some suspicion that they may stem more from the extensive focus-group research the campaign has done and the "spin doctors" on the party's public relations payroll than from real conviction.

Addressing these critics in The Guardian, a newspaper in which the defenders of Old Labor verities often air their complaints, Mr. Blair said, "I certainly don't believe that just because we are electable and winning new support, we are unprincipled."

Mr. Blair has provided himself some protection from the old loyalists by promoting the recruitment of new members, attracting money from individuals and thereby reducing the party's dependence on the unions. Party officials expect the percentage of total income coming from the unions, which was 77 a decade ago, to be 40 by next year.

More than a third of the party's members have joined since Mr. Blair became the leader in 1994. It has adopted one-person, one-vote decision making, abandoned a cherished clause of its charter that championed public ownership and nationalization, abandoned all references to a command economy and reversed its unilateralist defense and foreign policy postures.

But whether Mr. Blair's polished presentation of social democratic nostrums will provide as convincing an argument for making him leader of the country as it has for gaining him the dominance of his party remains to be seen.

Hoping that as Labor sheds its traditional colors, it might also be losing some traditional voters, the Conservatives took out full-page advertisements in major newspapers on Friday reading, "Trade Unionists, If Labor Don't Want You, We Do." Prime Minister Major also campaigned in the Thames Valley pointedly noting his humble origins in working-class Brixton and telling his listeners, "We will not abandon you."

In a cartoon in The Times of London last week, two men were pictured sitting atop ashcans filled with discarded initiatives from the Labor Party's past. One asks the other, "Is there anything left of Labor?"

The other answers, "The Tories are left of Labor."

It's Politics as Usual, but More American Than British

WARREN HOGE

LONDON, Nov. 9—The leading candidate is talkative and telegenic, he likes rock music, and his wife is a lawyer with a lucrative private practice. He promises a "covenant" with the public in a tub-thumping style that has been likened to revival-meeting preaching, and he has made a concerted election-year move to the middle, co-opting positions of the more conservative rival party.

The governing party is campaigning to gain the credit it feels it is due from voters in exchange for nearly four years of economic growth, and party leaders hope that this will impress voters more than the ongoing legislative investigations of "sleaze" in government.

Both parties vie to be identified as the champions of morality and family values, and the candidates are pressed to declare themselves on the issue of abortion.

To a degree that is provoking much comment and some dismay from Britons, the campaign for the British general election is following many of the trends and employing many of the techniques of the campaign that ended Tuesday in the United States.

Among the issues that John Major, the Conservative Prime Minister, and Tony Blair, the Labor Party leader, are debating are welfare reform, gun control, medical care, education and school safety, tax cuts, crime, drug use, and school dress codes. Of course, this is still Britain, so they are also debating whether or not the country should bring back caning as a punishment for delinquent students.

In the last week both parties have moved vigorously to respond to an appeal made by the widow of a London headmaster killed by a student—for an ethical renaissance. In one attempt to address that issue, the Government began discussing how to reduce the level of violence shown on television and in film.

Mr. Major must call an election by May and will probably wait until then, even though two recent deaths of Tory members have reduced his party's majority in Parliament to one seat. He can rely on the nine members of Parliament from the Ulster Unionist Party to keep the Conservatives in power even if he loses his majority, and he needs as much time as possible to overtake Mr. Blair, whose lead in the most recent Marketing and Research International poll is up to 28 points.

A campaign with well-worn phrases from public life in the United States.

Much is being made of the resonance of the American race in British politics. When Mr. Major and Mr. Blair interrupted their party conference speeches with confessional stories about youthful hard-knocks, commentators promptly termed the tactic "American style."

When they appeared on stage, kissing their wives at the festive conclusions of the party gatherings, comparisons were immediately made to the similar practice in the United States. "You never saw that kind of public cuddling at party conferences before," said Anthony King, a professor of government at the University of Essex.

Norma Major has in recent months emerged from the private, suburban housewife's life she has maintained as Britain's First Lady to give interviews and make public appearances. The Prime Minister has

called her his "secret weapon" in the race against Mr. Blair, whose wife, Cherie Booth, is a high-powered London lawyer with a sparkling academic background and roots in Labor's socialist past.

Well-worn phrases from American public life abound. Mr. Major told his party that "the buck stops here." Mr. Blair told his that "we have little to fear but fear itself."

When Mr. Major recently sought to characterize Mr. Blair's promises as untrustworthy, he compared him to Elmer Gantry, Sinclair Lewis's lapsed evangelist. When Mr. Blair accused Mr. Major of introducing class differences into the race, he called it "totally American-style negative campaigning." The people behind the candidates here are now being referred to as "spin doctors."

None of this is accidental. Both parties actively study the practices they are busy disparaging. Brian Mawhinney, the Conservative Party chairman, and Danny Finkelstein, the Tories' chief strategist, have been frequent visitors to Republican Party events in the United States, and Philip Gould, the Labor Party's director of polling, has just returned from Washington, where he hobnobbed with his counterparts in the Clinton campaign.

Another frequent trans-Atlantic traveler is Peter Mandelson, Mr. Blair's campaign manager and the man credited with crafting the reformed Labor Party, who has cited Mr. Clinton's moving the Democratic Party to the center as a model for his own strategy. He went to San

Diego to accompany George Stephanopoulos to the last Presidential debate, and the day after he returned to London, Mr. Blair proposed that there be televised debates between Mr. Major and himself.

Today Mr. Mandelson saluted Mr. Clinton's re-election as "tremendous vindication of his new democratic strategy." He said, "New Labor is building a similar coalition of support based on policies that appeal to the center and center left of British politics."

Robert M. Worcester, the American chairman of MORI who has lived here for 28 years, dated the Americanizing of British campaigning to Margaret Thatcher. "In the aftermath of Thatcher and her presidential style, British politics have become more presidential," he said.

Professor King, a Canadian who has been here 40 years, was dubious. "Every British election is described as more Presidential than the one before, and it's always untrue," he said. "One hundred years ago people were making judgments based on the personalities of Gladstone and Disraeli."

But if American notions of marketing political candidates haven't taken over the British political debate, how then to explain what The Financial Times, Britain's most serious newspaper, put on its front page Wednesday. The paper reported that as a result of a poll taken by Mr. Worcester's group showing that Mr. Blair's appeal to women voters was lagging, the candidate was changing his hairdo.

Revamping Britain's Constitution

The case for reform

**The British think something has gone wrong with their system of government.
This article, the first in a series, explains what may have to be done**

THE constitution is antiquated and anti-democratic. Britain's government is overcentralised and insufficiently accountable. Its citizens' basic freedoms are sorely in need of protection. So say many Britons. Others reply that Britain remains one of the world's most stable democracies, its ancient institutions widely admired and copied. Its unwritten constitution, a monument to pragmatism, is flexible enough to meet the demands of a changing society.

Britain is not the only country in which such an argument is taking place. One of the chief ironies of the end of the 20th century is that, as democracy takes new root in many parts of the ex-communist world and elsewhere, a growing number of ordinary voters in the older democracies of Europe and North America seem to be increasingly disenchanted with the way their political systems work. In the United States, Italy, France and Japan, to name but a few, there is deep disrespect for both politicians as a class and the current processes of politics.

It is particularly awkward for constitutional reformers in Britain that almost all of the changes they would like to make in the British system are already in place in one or other of these countries, without having saved them from their share of the general malaise. Nevertheless, the need for reform may be even greater in Britain than elsewhere, because Britain's constitutional arrangements are among the oldest and therefore, arguably, the most rusty of them all.

The Labour Party has promised a radical programme of constitutional reform, embracing a bill of rights, elected assemblies for Scotland and Wales, devolution of power to England's regions, more freedom for local government, reform of the House of Lords and a referendum on changing Britain's electoral system. The Conservatives have set their face against all of these changes as unnecessary, dangerous and a threat to the continued existence of the United Kingdom. Either Britain is poised on the brink of root-and-branch constitutional reform or, as so often in the past, it is about to embark on years of political dispute and learned verbiage which will, in the end, lead to little or nothing.

That may sound cynical. Campaigning groups such as Charter 88 (with over 60,000 signatories) have demonstrated a growing interest in changes to the way Britain is governed. A MORI opinion poll for the Joseph Rowntree Reform Trust, published in May, found 79% of respondents in favour of a written constitution, 79% wanting a bill of rights, 81% for a freedom-of-information act and 77% supporting the more frequent use of referendums. Innumerable polls have shown that nearly four in five Scottish voters want their own elected parliament in Edinburgh. The demotion of local government under the Tories, and the appointment of thousands of quangos to run bits of the public sector, appear to be widely resented. People hold members of Parliament in low esteem and regard many of the country's institutions with less and less respect; or so they tell the pollsters.

Yet translating such disaffection into actual reforms will be difficult. Past attempts to change overtly the way Britain is governed have failed miserably. In 1969 Labour's last attempt to reform the House of Lords, though supported by the Tory front bench, ran aground after an alliance of backbenchers from both sides of the House of Commons vehemently opposed it. In the 1970s the Labour government spent years, and enormous amounts of political capital, pushing devolution bills through the Commons, only to see their proposals fail in subsequent referendums to gain the required support of 40% of the Scottish and Welsh electorates. Indeed, the Welsh rejected the plan by a margin of four to one.

Why bother?

One obstacle to reform is the fact that most of the proposed changes are meant to reduce the power of central government, but can be pursued only by the party in power—which, naturally, finds the idea less than appealing. In this century constitutional reform has been, typically, far more attractive to oppositions than to governing parties. The Tories flirted with reform in the 1970s while out of power, when Lord Hailsham famously complained that Britain's constitutional arrangements were moving it towards an "elective dictatorship". A few years later, as Margaret Thatcher's first Lord Chancellor, he—and most other Tories—had lost their interest in radical reform.

If Labour wins the next general election, after nearly two decades in opposition, it may undergo a similar transformation, despite its current commitment to an ambitious agenda of constitutional change. Reducing its newly won power through reforms—which themselves are bound to be complicated and contentious—could soon seem less urgent than wielding that power to pursue its own policies on education, health, the economy and foreign affairs.

It is also far from clear whether the public's low regard for British institutions shows an appetite for real change or simply dislike of an unpopular Tory government that has been in office for too long. A set of fresh faces at the top may be enough to cheer up most voters. If it does, the demand for constitutional change may fade away.

The biggest obstacle to constitutional reform may indeed be the ingrained conservatism that runs through both main parties and the wider electorate. Most Britons seem wary of rapid change, suspicious of grand schemes of improvement and reluctant to abandon the tried and true for the uncertainties of the new. The case for constitutional reform is a powerful one. But all too often its advocates assume that the need for reform is obvious, and opposition to it merely self-interested. In fact, reformers confront, and need to refute, a "traditionalist" view which has always exercised a powerful grip on the popular imagination.

An intelligent traditionalist will point out that politicians and political institutions currently seem to be unpopular with voters throughout the industrialised world, not just in Britain. Despite the anomalies and inconsistencies in Britain's constitution, he would argue, the country is not obviously governed any worse than most other rich countries. Nor does it seem at all likely to tip into despotism.

Particular policies and governments may prove unpopular from time to time. But Britain's parliamentary system of government has weathered vast social changes without the upheavals seen in many countries that have written constitutions. Most other nations have been forced to adopt these after military defeat, revolution or political collapse. Britain is facing no such crisis. Small adjustments may have to be made occasionally, as in the past. But why overhaul a system which has taken more than 300 years to evolve, and whose accumulated wisdom has been admired and imitated throughout the world?

The trouble with this view is that it relies

on a misreading of Britain's own constitutional history. The key concepts pioneered by Britain which have so much influenced the growth of democracy elsewhere—the separation of the executive, legislative and judicial branches of government to provide institutional checks and balances, and the guarantee of fundamental rights protected from the encroachments of an overmighty government—were born of Parliament's battle to restrain the monarch in the 17th and 18th centuries; but they were never firmly established in Britain itself.

In 1765 Sir William Blackstone, the leading English legal authority at the time, wrote that the total union of the executive and legislative branches of government "would be productive of tyranny". Over the next century such a union is precisely what Britain achieved. The cabinet in effect assumed the executive role of the monarch. With the extension of the voting franchise to the middle and working classes and the rise of mass parties, the cabinet (and more particularly the prime minister) could stay in office only by exerting an iron discipline on its party supporters in the Commons, further concentrating power in its hands. By 1867 Walter Bagehot was praising the cabinet's control of nearly all government affairs, its "near complete fusion of the executive and legislative powers", as the "efficient secret" of the constitution.

When in 1885 Albert Venn Dicey came to write "The Law of the Constitution", the book that has most shaped debate on the subject, the British system of government not only bore little resemblance to the written democratic constitutions being adopted elsewhere; it barely made intellectual sense. In Dicey's view the British constitution was based on two fundamental principles: the absolute sovereignty of Parliament and the rule of law. There is an inherent contradiction in this description. A truly sovereign parliament would be unconstrained even by the law, which it would be free to change at any time. And this is precisely what British governments have done on many occasions when the law—even the common law built up over centuries by the courts—has stood in their way.

Use and abuse

Curiously, parliamentary sovereignty seemed too extreme a proposition even for Dicey, its greatest champion. A committed unionist, he was appalled at Gladstone's policy of Irish home rule and complained, quite correctly, that it was a fundamental constitutional change. But his doctrine of parliamentary sovereignty left no fundamental distinction between the handling of constitutional changes and of trivial changes to the highway code (there is still no such distinction today). So Dicey, remarkably, became the first to advocate the referendum in Britain as "the one available check on the recklessness of party leaders."

Since Dicey's day the doctrine of parliamentary sovereignty has bequeathed Britain a system of government which looks distinctly odd compared with those of other established democracies. After the powers of the House of Lords were drastically curtailed in 1911, parliamentary sovereignty came to rest solely with the Commons. And party discipline in the Commons has meant that, most of the time, real sovereignty has rested, in effect, with the cabinet.

In other words, the British people are invited every four or five years to choose one of two small committees of mostly professional politicians to run the government as they see fit, constrained only by what they think is politically possible, with almost no legal or institutional checks on what they can do. Voters are not directly consulted on any of the issues which come up in the intervening years, be they declarations of war or the regulation of dogs that bite too often. And then, at the next general election, they are again offered the choice between two small committees of politicians.

No party since 1935 has won more than 50% of the votes cast. And yet their minority victories have not stopped both Tory and Labour governments from claiming the right to steer the country abruptly in new directions. The Labour government of 1945 launched a massive nationalisation programme and created the welfare state after winning 48% of the votes cast. In the 1951 election the Labour government lost power to the Tories, a defeat widely seen as a decision by the voters to call a halt to further socialist measures, even though Labour's share of the votes cast actually rose from 46% in 1950 to 49% (exceeding that of the victorious Tories by a percentage point). And Mrs (now Lady) Thatcher launched her free-market counter-revolution after winning 44% of the vote in 1979 and only 42% and 43% in her two subsequent elections.

Such governments were, as the current system's proponents argue, strong ones. But strength and effectiveness are not the same thing. One result of "strong" governments may be to set policies swinging like a pendulum, as a new government indignantly reverses many of the old one's decisions. And the electoral system has recently been brutal to third parties, in effect disenfranchising millions of voters. In the 1983 and 1987 elections the Liberal-Social Democrat alliance received 25% and 23% of the votes respectively, but only 4% of seats in the Commons. In 1992 the Liberal Democrats received 18% of the votes, more than half of those cast for Labour, but only 3% of Commons seats, compared with Labour's 42% of seats.

In this system cabinet ministers, and the vast official bureaucracy over which they preside, have been the exclusive arbiters of what the public should know. British governments run by both main parties have been among the most secretive of all the western democracies, refusing to grant the

public, from whom they are supposed to derive their legitimacy, any legal right to information about, or held by, their government. Often the voters discover what the government has really been up to only when ministers leak information to discredit each other, or when some scandal or blunder forces it to divulge information to limit the damage to its own political prospects.

With no bill of rights to constrain them, both Labour and Tory governments have extended police powers, restricted press freedom, and sometimes suspended the ordinary workings of the criminal law. These moves, touching the basic freedoms of all citizens, have been impossible to challenge in British courts.

Last year the government severely restricted the right to silence in criminal trials—allowing judges and juries to draw adverse inferences from a defendant's refusal to testify—after little debate in the Commons. The measure is contained in a mere four sections of a giant 169-section law. Whatever the merits or demerits of this action it did, at a stroke, eliminate a right which had for centuries been thought a pillar of Britain's judicial system. This might have deserved a bit more debate, and some reference to the citizens whose rights were being so curtailed.

Down the Eurohole

Explicit constitutional reform to rein in the powers of government may have proved difficult in the past, but the lack of a codified constitution has allowed governments to innovate in ways which, in most other democratic countries, would be deemed to involve constitutional changes, and so subject to special procedures to win the consent of the electorate. Since 1979, for example, the Tories have drastically reduced the powers of local authorities.

And, when it comes to Europe, the enormous discretion in the hands of British governments has led to what can best be described as a giant constitutional cock-up. The Tory government which led Britain into the European Community in 1973 explicitly promised in a 1971 white paper that membership presented "no question of any erosion of essential national sovereignty" and that "our courts will continue to operate as they do at present". Any constitutional implications were also played down during Labour's referendum in 1975, and were brushed aside by the Thatcher and Major governments when they signed the Single European Act and the Maastricht treaty.

In fact, EU membership has blown a hole through the middle of Dicey's doctrine of parliamentary sovereignty. The Maastricht rebels are right about this. European Union law now takes precedence over laws passed at Westminster. After some hesitation, Britain's judges have concluded that, when an act of Parliament directly clashes with an EU directive or treaty, it is the EU law which must prevail, unless Parliament's law explicitly repudiates or violates the Treaty of Rome—which would probably lead to Britain's withdrawal from the EU.

Even an avid pro-European should feel uncomfortable that so momentous a change to the foundations of Britain's system of government was made without informing or consulting the British electorate. France and Germany, and other EU countries, made changes to their written constitutions to endorse the transfer of powers to the EU. Britain seems to have sleepwalked to the same destination. The electorate was never given any real choice in the matter. Even Tory ministers seem befuddled by the issue, continually complaining about the meddling of Brussels even though it is their governments that transferred powers to the EU.

Today government in Britain seems remote and unresponsive. Many services once managed locally—housing, hospitals and education—are now controlled from Westminster and administered by bureaucrats and political appointees. As centralisation has accelerated, the frustration of ordinary citizens has grown, expressed in open cynicism about the motives and behaviour of politicians and an increasingly visible indifference to politics itself.

Even the ministers running this overcentralised system often seem more like its prisoners than its beneficiaries. The Tories since 1979, like their predecessors, have

first accumulated power at the centre to push through specific changes, and then found that, to operate the immense government machine they have helped to expand, they needed to delegate some authority. But, without explicit constitutional guidelines, these efforts have foundered.

The creation of quangos and independent government agencies, instead of devolving managerial power as intended, has merely stuffed the public administration with political appointees, and has so tangled the lines of accountability that it is now almost impossible to pin the responsibility on anyone when something goes wrong. Too often ministers blame civil servants for implementing policies poorly even while civil servants blame ministers for thinking up bad policies in the first place.

The fiasco of the poll tax in 1990 can also, some say, be viewed as a constitutional failure. Intended to restore accountability, and taxation powers, to local government, the poll tax was widely seen as just the opposite: an attempt by an overmighty government to jam an unpopular change down the throats of the populace. This provoked a mass protest of delayed or non-payment by millions of normally law-abiding citizens. Though legally enacted, the poll tax was widely viewed as illegitimate.

More participators, fewer spectators

All the changes now proposed by reform-

ers—a written constitution, a bill of rights, devolved assemblies, proportional representation, an elected second chamber—are directed at a single goal: dispersing power through Britain's political system. Traditionalists are right to argue that Britain is not facing war, revolution or political collapse. But they are wrong to assume that it is only some wrenching crisis which justifies or makes possible constitutional change. Although few democratic nations have faced the kind of top-to-bottom changes now advocated by British reformers, many other countries (New Zealand is one example) have made significant constitutional changes without facing such a crisis.

Building a new British constitution will take years. Each addition or change will have to be debated and agreed upon. The eventual outcome will require more than the support of a single political party. And it may be that even these changes will not suffice; remember that many countries which already enjoy them are today angrily rebellious about the state of their politics.

The result, if this great effort does in the end succeed, will be a noisier, more rambunctious Britain. Getting new things done may then be more difficult than it has been in the past. But this does not defeat the case for reform. Indeed, it is the case for reform. The smooth exercise of silent power is the ideal of the autocrat, not the democrat.

Why Britain needs a bill of rights

Basic human and political rights in Britain enjoy no special legal protection, as they do in most other democratic countries. In our second article on constitutional reform, we argue that this should be changed

BRITAIN invented both the phrase "a bill of rights" and the concept of one. Yet today Britain is the only country in Western Europe which either has not incorporated the European Convention on Human Rights into its domestic laws or does not already have, like Ireland, a bill of rights which provides similar legally enforceable protections for the individual. Britain granted a bill of rights to Hong Kong in 1991 and the government has promised one for Northern Ireland as part of a new overall political settlement there. Opinion polls by MORI this year and in 1991 for the Joseph Rowntree Reform Trust found that 79% of respondents were in favour of a bill of rights for all of Britain. Labour and the Liberal Democrats now also back the idea.

Given such widespread public support, and Britain's anomalous position among democracies in not having a bill of rights, the argument for introducing one would seem to be an open-and-shut case. Yet it is not, and considerable opposition remains. John Major's government, like its Conserva-

tive and Labour predecessors, is hostile to the idea, as are many—on both the right and the left—who see it as a threat to the sovereignty of Parliament (founded on the 1689 Bill of Rights, which enumerated the rights of Parliament, not those of individuals).

An effective bill of rights would, indeed, be an infringement of parliamentary sovereignty; but this would be its principal attraction, not an argument against it. Bills of rights are designed to protect fundamental rights from the actions of transient majorities in the legislature in the longer-term interests of the citizenry as a whole. In most countries, none of the rights thus protected is exempt from revision or abolition by the electorate. But, because they are deemed fundamental, revision is made far more difficult than changes to an ordinary law, through special procedures that require more than simple majorities.

Individual liberties enjoy no such protection in Britain. Governments can eliminate a right, no matter how basic or how long-standing, in a single vote in the House

of Commons and have, on some occasions, used their extraordinary powers to do just that.

Traditionalists argue that, in practice, this matters not at all. British liberties, they say, have been better protected by Parliament and the common law built up over centuries by the courts than they would have been by any abstract listing of rights. They often accompany this argument with grandiose proclamations about Britain being a beacon of liberty in a turbulent and uncertain world.

Sadly, this is no longer true, if it ever was. One revealing test is Britain's record before the European Court of Human Rights in Strasbourg. The court has decided 37 cases against the United Kingdom, giving it one of the worst records of any of the 35 signatories to the European Convention. This means that actions in a wide range of areas which British courts, Parliament and successive governments had accepted as perfectly proper were rejected by the Strasbourg court as violations of basic rights.

This is a serious indictment of the state of civil liberties in Britain. The court is not staffed with starry-eyed idealists. In fact, the court's judges have tried to interpret the convention as narrowly as possible to avoid overruling elected governments. Nevertheless even this cautious court has found against the British government on issues that include telephone tapping, birching, discriminatory immigration rules, homosexuality, the law of contempt of court, the rights of prisoners and those accused of a crime, the rights of the mentally ill, press freedom, and sexual equality, among other issues—culminating in the celebrated ruling in September that the killing of three IRA terrorists on Gibraltar was unlawful. Often such findings have forced a revision of British laws.

Britain may not be about to lapse into despotism or tyranny, but that is not the immediate danger facing any established democracy. What British governments have repeatedly failed to do is to meet minimal standards of conduct when it comes to respecting the rights of individuals. It might be argued that the Strasbourg court is sufficient redress against such wrongs. But it is slow and costly. A British bill of rights would make redress easier and cheaper, and thus restore at least some popular respect for Britain's own system of justice.

A stronger objection to a bill of rights is that it is, in many ways, anti-democratic because it transfers power from elected representatives to unelected judges. It does do this, but such a transfer of power is not necessarily anti-democratic. Democracy itself, in all its myriad forms, derives its legitimacy from the consent of the governed, and that consent can only be given freely when certain basic rights—for example, freedom of speech, assembly and the press or the protection from arbitrary arrest—are respected.

British citizens have never had any positive, enforceable legal rights and still do not, except those awarded to them by specific statutes. Instead, liberty in Britain has been essentially negative: citizens have been traditionally free to do anything not specifically prohibited by law.

This may have seemed a reasonable proposition in the 19th century, when governments were tiny and there were far fewer laws. But since then the trickle of legislation has become a flood. The growth of the modern state in Britain, as elsewhere, has meant that government now intrudes into every nook and cranny of life, regulating everything from medical care to buildings to the terms on which employees can be hired or sacked. The purely private sphere has diminished greatly.

Trampling liberty for convenience

Today the view of liberty as merely the residue of activity not directly controlled or prohibited by governments is too weak a concept to protect individuals from the gradual erosion of rights and freedoms. Such rights are rarely assaulted directly by governments (though the British government's restrictions last year of an accused person's right to silence is one sorry example). Basic liberties are more commonly brushed aside or trampled by governments in a hurry to solve specific problems, or merely to do what is politically convenient.

When people complain (as thousands have, in the past few years) about over-zealous bureaucrats, especially those implementing European laws, their complaints often reflect this imbalance between official power and the individual's recourse against it. Meddling social workers, bullying police officers, autocratic planning officials and the like, even when they seem to act unreasonably, are often acting within the law, which frequently gives them wide discretion. Few people think "the government" is hostile to their liberties. And yet, at some time or other, almost everyone thinks "those little dictators" at the town hall, the Ministry of Agriculture or in Brussels commit outrages against both common sense and liberties—though few realise that such complaints make one of the strongest arguments for a bill of rights.

This is why even countries that, like Britain, have indisputably democratic governments have chosen belatedly to introduce a bill of rights. Canada enacted a new one in 1982. New Zealand adopted one in 1990.

It is undeniable that a bill of rights can hand a great deal of power to judges. Bills of rights, by their very nature, have to be written in broad terms. This leaves enormous scope for judicial interpretation. Not everyone concerned to enhance civil liberties in Britain is happy with that prospect.

One group of critics argues that Britain's judiciary—in the case of England and Wales selected by the Lord Chancellor, a member of the cabinet, from a small circle of top lawyers—has proven too biased towards the interests of governments, and too illiberal, to protect the rights of all citizens. Court rulings upholding police restrictions on the right of movement during the 1984-85 miners' strike; backing the broadcasting ban on Sinn Fein, the political wing of the IRA; and failing to lift the injunction against newspaper publication of the book "Spycatcher", have left a bitter taste for many.

Judges, argue such critics, may not always be better guarantors of rights than a democratically elected legislature. They point to the history of the American Supreme Court which, at various times, denied that freed slaves could become citizens and ruled that racial segregation was legal. And a bill of rights is no panacea against rights violations. Today Japan has an extensive bill of rights, which its citizens and courts largely ignore.

And yet, in the case of Britain, this seems unduly pessimistic. British judges have been constrained by the fact that they have no written constitution, or bill of rights, to guide them. In their absence, they have also had no explicit authority to strike down a law or action of government solely because it breached a basic human right. Indeed, the tradition has been that they should not do so. Given such a power, British judges would undoubtedly use it.

Handing more power over to judges would not necessarily guarantee more protections for the individual against the encroachments of government. A conservative judiciary might restrict freedoms, which is one reason why a more open selection procedure for British judges would be desirable if a bill of rights were established. And yet it seems likelier that even the current crop of judges would, like most of their modern counterparts abroad, produce a more liberal, rather than a more illiberal, interpretation of the law once given the chance to do so. Even within their current confines—deciding whether the government or public bodies have acted within the existing law—British judges have over the past 30 years created, for the first time, a useful body of administrative law to hold the exercise of government power in check.

Other critics, most within Westminster or Whitehall, argue just the opposite: that British judges would be all too keen to use their new powers. Once empowered to knock down laws, they say, judges cannot restrain themselves from acting as unelected legislators. They point, once again, to America's Supreme Court, which has created an immense body of case law far exceeding anything envisaged by the authors of the American constitution.

Even some advocates of a British bill of rights feel uncomfortable with the degree of power wielded by America's Supreme Court. Liberty, Britain's leading civil-liberties lobby group, favours an approach similar to that of Canada, which allows Canada's national parliament or provincial assemblies to bypass the courts by enacting laws that explicitly state that they are overriding the country's Charter of Rights.

In fact, any British bill of rights is likely to contain such a formal opt-out because, without a completely new written constitution defining the roles of Parliament and the courts, judges will have no independent legal authority to strike down acts of Parliament in any case. Bills seeking to incorporate the European Convention on Human Rights into British law recognise this fact by saying that judges will interpret the convention as prevailing over any act of Parliament—as they do now with European Union law—unless the act explicitly states that it intends to override the convention. The latest such bill, sponsored by Lord Lester, a Liberal Democrat peer, has passed the Lords, but is likely to be killed by the government in the Commons.

Such opt-outs should assuage fears that unrestrained judges would frustrate the concerted will of a large majority of the population. In practice, though, opt-outs are unlikely to be used very often. Passing a law which openly declares that it breaches the bill of rights is likely to prove unpalatable for most governments. The Canadian parliament has never passed a law overriding Canada's Charter of Rights, though two provincial assemblies have passed three such laws, one of which was knocked down by Canada's Supreme Court as too sweeping.

What's in, what's out?

Which specific rights should a bill of rights contain? There is, predictably, much debate on this subject even among those who favour the general idea. A minimum seems to be the rights enumerated in the European Convention, which the British government, after all, agreed to respect as long ago as 1951, when it ratified the document.

Incorporating the convention into British law, which Labour and the Liberal Democrats have promised to do, would be a big step. Though British citizens have had the right to pursue their cases under the convention at Strasbourg since 1966, doing so costs thousands of pounds in lawyers' fees, and cases are not heard for years. For most citizens it provides no realistic remedy against government abuse.

Incorporation would, in effect, give British citizens a bill of rights for the first time whose protections could be claimed in British courts. Judges might, of course, ignore its provisions, but this is unlikely. The Law Lords, Britain's most senior judges, united behind Lord Lester's bill for incorporating the convention into British law. In fact, incorporation could revolutionise British jurisprudence, not only empowering the Law Lords to overturn law that breach basic rights—unless they contain explicit provisions overriding the convention—but also obliging judges and juries to keep basic civil rights in mind when trying cases in the lower courts, and providing further grounds for appeal when they are breached.

But many supporters of a bill of rights want to go further. For one thing, the convention itself contains broad exceptions (not contained in the brief summary in our box). Some of these are sensible. Rights clash, and any list of rights will have to be interpreted by judges in the light of national security or threats to society. Even the cherished freedom of speech provision in America's bill of rights has not been interpreted as banning all obscenity laws or the prosecu-

tion of someone who stands up in a crowded cinema and shouts "fire".

But the repetition throughout the convention of phrases such as "subject only to such limitations as are prescribed by law and are necessary in a democratic society in the interests of public safety", sometimes followed by lists of more specific restrictions, seems to invite judges to focus on the exceptions, rather than the rights to be protected, and could be used to nullify the entire convention. Pruning the convention of such exceptions after incorporating it into British law would probably improve it.

Far more controversial is the idea of adding social and economic rights—such as a right to a job, education, medical care, welfare or protection of the environment— to the mostly civil and political rights contained in the convention. Labour wants, eventually, to do something like this, as do many others who are keen on the idea of a bill of rights. Such a move might be popular. Rowntree's most recent poll found that the favourite item suggested for a British bill of rights was the "right to hospital treatment on the National Health Service within a reasonable time", which was backed by 88% of those asked, giving it even more support than the right to a fair trial before a jury, backed by 82%.

Besides mere popularity, there is also a respectable argument for considering the inclusion of economic and social rights. It is difficult to enjoy your political and civil rights, or participate in a democracy, if you cannot feed or clothe yourself, obtain an education, or avoid dying from disease. And the line dividing the two types of rights can be fuzzy. For example, the right to equality, contained in both the 14th amendment to the American constitution and most other country's bills of rights, has been interpreted by judges in Europe as including equal pay for equal work for women, but having nothing to do with equal pay by American judges.

Moreover, rights can, over time, seem to shift between the two categories. When the right to bear arms was inserted into America's bill of rights in 1791, with the memories of the revolution against Britain still fresh, it seemed necessary for the maintenance of a free society, and so qualified as a political right. Today it seems more of a threat to such a society, and an obstacle to sensible gun control. No country drawing up a bill of rights today would consider such a provision a basic political right.

Nevertheless, some attempt to draw a line between the two categories of rights

should be made, and America's experience with the right to bear arms argues for confining a bill of rights to a minimal list of the political and civil rights essential to the functioning of a liberal democracy, such as those contained in the European Convention. Interpreting even these basic rights is problematic enough, and they can often clash, as they seem to do in the case of abortion (the right to life against the right to privacy) creating "hard" cases which will always leave some dissatisfied.

Remedies to economic and social deprivation should be sought elsewhere, through either political action or the courts using normal laws. Few people in Britain are so deprived of necessities that they cannot vote or participate, if they wish, in the democratic process. In a developed country like Britain, trying to turn access to economic resources into a matter of fundamental rights, giving them a higher status than the ordinary law, seems doomed. Such decisions usually have to be made as the result of a bargaining process between groups. Generally, this should be the stuff of everyday politics, not a subject for the courts.

In fact, the likeliest result of making a bill of rights too extensive, and including economic obligations on governments which courts cannot enforce, would be to undermine the entire concept of the bill of rights, and so weaken obstacles to breaches of the basic rights which it was originally designed to protect.

It is impossible to avoid the conclusion that any bill of rights, even if it contains only a minimal list of basic rights, will force Britain's judges to wade into the political arena. But the different objections to this that are hurled from both ends of the political spectrum—that judges are liable to usurp the role of legislators or to be too swayed by public opinion—miss the point, which is to place restraints in the path of governments. Interpreting how rights should be applied in the complex circumstances of a modern state, where the basic rights of different groups can sometimes clash, is bound to be controversial and rarely clear-cut. Reasonable men are bound to differ on such interpretations. And judges would be truly strange characters if they shared none of the views held by most of their fellow citizens.

A bill of rights cannot elevate contentious, political issues to an abstract plane beyond the reach of the rest of society. What it can do is to nurture a culture of liberty in a society which already recognises its value, and to create a judiciary which sees the protection of liberty as one of its primary tasks.

BLAIR ON THE CONSTITUTION

Democracy's second age

One of the biggest gaps between Britain's two main political parties concerns constitutional reform, where Labour is advocating far-reaching changes. Here Tony Blair, the party's leader, sets out his party's plans and defends them against the Tory charge that they would break up the United Kingdom.

BY INVITATION

WE ARE now in the Second Age of democracy. It is time to give it a second wind. After a long battle, the First Age established universal suffrage. This finally came to the United Kingdom, in 1928, when the vote was extended to all adult women.

Nearly 70 years later, however, Britain has changed radically. The attempt to change prevailing social and economic conditions (and the need to fight two world wars) hugely extended the scope of central government. In 1900, central government spending as a share of GDP amounted to 9.7%; in 1930 it was 13.0%. Today, it is over 42%—steady at that level since 1979.

In mid-century the majority of the country was self-consciously working class, and paid less than 10% of their income in tax. Today, the largest grouping is the middle class; the groups classified as "ABC1" by pollsters make up 52% of the electorate, and pay over 35% of their incomes in taxes. Even those in the bottom fifth of the income distribution pay almost 40%. So government now spends more public money and the majority of the population fund the expenditure.

These changes raise serious questions for democracy. Is it still supportable that the power to decide how these vast resources are spent should reside exclusively with a highly centralised national government? And do the more educated and wealthier citizens of today, albeit all of them with the vote, really have power over the system?

To make matters worse, some British institutions have not yet caught up even to 1928. They are actually pre-First Age. Think of the way Parliament works, sometimes seeming more private club than modern democratic forum; or the composition of the House of Lords; or constitutional conventions established in the 18th and 19th centuries.

The consequence of ignoring these questions is that politics becomes less respected, less accountable, more remote from people's lives. That is bad for Britain and bad for democracy.

Contrary to the Tory *canard,* constitutional reform is not an issue for the "chattering classes", irrelevant to most people. Properly done, it will go to the heart of public concerns. It is important not only for its own sake, but because it makes possible the attainment of other vital goals: a stronger economy, better transport, good schools and crime prevention.

Walter Bagehot, the great Victorian editor of *The Economist,* declared at the outset of his classic text "The English Constitution": "Every constitution must first gain authority, and then use authority." It must, he went on, "first win the confidence and loyalty of mankind, and then employ that homage in the work of government." These are wise words, and they summarise very well my approach to constitutional reform (or democratic renewal, as I prefer to call it).

Changing the way we govern, and not just changing our government, is no longer an optional extra for Britain. So

low is popular esteem for politicians and the system we operate that there is now little authority for us to use unless and until we first succeed in regaining it.

For three decades the standing of Britain's constitution has been declining. Barely a third of the people now declare themselves satisfied with their system of government. Parliament's very *raison dêtre* is to express and redress popular grievances. When it has itself become the focus of those grievances, it is obligated to act.

We do not need to exaggerate to make the case. Britain is not recovering from war-time defeat or social collapse, nor is it tainted by totalitarianism. We are not faced with the necessity of building a new constitution from scratch, as for example was post-war Germany.

Britain is, however, struggling to find its way after the collapse of the grand 20th century ideologies of left and right. These too often placed ends above means, grand projects of social or economic reconstruction above the democratic requirement for consent, self-government and respect for rights. The result has been 80 years since the first world war of a steady accretion of power to ministers.

New Labour's aim is a partnership between people and politicians based on trust, honesty and a realistic assessment on both sides as to what government can deliver.

The challenge facing us is that which confronted the Victorian reformers in the last century who, almost uniquely, gave

Britain democracy without revolution. It is to take a working constitution, respect its strengths, and adapt it to modern demands for clean and effective government while at the same time providing a greater democratic role for the people at large.

Labour's programme for democratic renewal is threefold: to strengthen the rights and obligations of citizens; to take decision-making closer to the people; and to improve the democratic credentials of Westminster.

Democracy can flourish only as part of a rich culture of rights respected and duties performed. Most of these rights and duties relate to community life beyond the sway of the politician or the ordinary scope of the courts. But the duty of the state's constitution to safeguard freedoms, and encourage the performance of duties, remains profound.

The British state presently does too little on these counts. Basic rights, to information, legal equality, due process and security of property, are too often flouted. And little attempt is made to encourage people to take more than a cursory part in their own governance. The idea that the people at large might play a greater political role is instinctively alarming to many in the elite for its implication of greater "direct democracy." It ought, instead, to be seen as critical to developing a richer notion of democratic citizenship.

Tory Bourbons

The case for a freedom of information act and the incorporation of the European Convention on Human Rights into British law is now generally agreed outside the Conservative Party and even by some within it. The onus must always be on public authorities to explain why citizens should not have access to information and not vice versa. Britain already has a *de facto* bill of rights through its ratification of the European Convention underpinned by a court in Strasbourg which delivers more hostile judgments against Britain than any other state. Only the strange mentality of the modern Tory Bourbons could think it satisfactory to force British citizens to go to France to enforce their rights because their own courts are incapable of doing so.

More information and guaranteed rights are only two means of achieving far broader democratic objectives. Greater use of referendums is another, to give citizens a veto over proposals to change their system of government, and to give legitimacy to the changes to which they do agree. Other democratic innovations, such as citizens' juries, are being piloted

with some success to assist decision-making in the NHS and local government. Informed public participation is the key, complementing not replacing established decision-making by elected representatives.

Most political decisions of concern to citizens affect their immediate locality. The revival of local government must be the prime means for achieving the second objective to taking government closer to the people. Local government's democratic voice needs strengthening, by establishing a closer engagement between local authorities and their electors. This is why I am so strongly attached to the principle of elected mayors for London and our leading cities—generating local chief executives with a direct mandate, able to mobilise their communities behind urban renewal as mayors across Europe and the United States do.

Strengthening the intermediate tier between London and the localities is also necessary. Here again our agenda is one of sensible, incremental change to meet modern democratic demands.

The Scottish Office was established as long ago as 1885 to provide a Scottish dimension to administration north of the border. But it is Westminster-controlled and Westminster-oriented. The Scottish people rightly insist on something more democratic, in the form of a Scottish parliament with legislative powers.

The Tories claim that this would threaten the unity of the United Kingdom, yet they rightly consider their proposals for devolved government in Northern Ireland as perfectly compatible with the union. Their opposition to our decentralisation plans ignores the wisdom of the ages, as well as concrete experience in other countries. As William Gladstone, the Victorian prime minister, said: "The concession of local self-government is not the way to sap or impair, but the way to strengthen and consolidate unity."

Precisely this rationale has led every other large European democracy, including France and Spain with centralising traditions as strong as Britain's, to create a regional tier between central government and local authorities. Spain, for example, has met regional aspirations of varying strengths by adopting a rolling programme of devolution, across a lengthy timespan, in line with the flow of popular sentiment.

We are proposing a similarly refined approach for the United Kingdom. Scotland with its distinct national, legal and cultural institutions is manifestly in a class of its own. Even the current secretary of state for Scotland, Michael Forsyth, concedes that once a Scottish parliament is established, it will be here

to stay. In their own separate ways, Wales and London also have powerful claims to—and their people want—their own authorities.

Across the rest of England, popular enthusiasm for a regional political voice varies greatly. Our policy reflects this, allowing greater regional government as people demand it. In the north-east and north-west demand for greater powers is strong. In other places, there is less demand. So be it.

Shaking up Westminster

Westminster has for too long insulated itself from change while imposing it on everyone else. Here again, Labour must settle some important unfinished business from a century ago, starting with the House of Lords. It delights and astonishes me that we are about to fight an election in which the Tories will be defending the right of ancestral dukes, marquesses, earls and barons to make the law in a modern democracy. And this in a society which John Major claims he wants to make "classless"!

Labour will remove the right of hereditary peers to sit and vote in the Lords and introduce a more open system for nominating life peers. We will consult widely about an appropriate second-stage reform, but we should be clear that removing the absurdity of the hereditary element will be a huge step forward in itself.

Effective democracy depends, above all, on the quality of the House of Commons. Electoral reform for the Commons has a totemic status among some of Britain's constitutional reformers. I appreciate the reasons for this, not least 17 years of "elective dictatorship" by Tory governments returned on minority votes, pushing through divisive and destructive policies such as the poll tax and rail privatisation, which is why I have confirmed John Smith's pledge to hold a referendum on the issue.

However, I personally remain unpersuaded that proportional representation would be beneficial for the Commons. It is not, as some claim, a simple question of moving from an "unfair" to a "fair" voting system. An electoral system must meet two democratic tests: it needs to reflect opinion, but it must also aggregate opinion without giving disproportionate influence to splinter groups. Aggregation is particularly important for a parliament whose job is to create and sustain a single, mainstream government.

Whatever the electoral system may be, something has to be done about the House of Commons itself, which, to more and more voters, seems arcane and ineffective, or worse. We need to improve the way we scrutinise and debate legislation, how MPs hold the executive to account, how we organise the legislative programme and how we deal with European legislation.

Opponents of reform

Opposition to Labour's plans for constitutional modernisation come from two camps. The first group are opponents of principle. They are against any tampering with Britain's "perfect" constitution. The second group are tactical opponents. Though not against reform, either they believe that it is a distraction from the "serious" business of reducing unemployment, improving education and such like, or they recoil from the parliamentary battles required to enact constitutional reforms.

The first camp, led by John Major, is intellectually barren. For Mr Major, whatever is is best, from hereditary peers to the unaccountable quangocracy. Nothing like this has been heard since the Duke of Wellington thundered in defence of pocket boroughs and electoral corruption in 1830.

Mr. Major's position is more extreme than that of his predecessors. Although the Tories opposed most of the big constitutional reforms of the past two centuries, no previous Tory leader since Wellington refused to countenance *any* democratic reform. Balfour favoured radical reform of the Lords as long ago as 1911. Even Lady Thatcher once proposed all-party talks on a bill of rights. Ted Heath and Alec Douglas-Home were once supporters of Scottish devolution. London's elected authority was established by a Tory government (in 1889), together with the national system of county councils.

In truth, as Mr Major's more sophisticated predecessors recognised, the undoubted strengths of the constriction are the fruit of deliberate reform in centuries past. Its growing weaknesses need to be tackled in the same way. Renovation, as any disciple of Edmund Burke knows, is a prime means of conservation.

The Tory opponents of change are also fatally inconsistent. They themselves have carried through far-reaching constitutional changes in the past 18 years, although in ways that have made Britain less democratic rather than more.

The balance of power between local and central government has radically shifted in favour of the latter. The Single European Act and the Maastricht treaty extended the powers of the EU. And the Major administration itself promises significant constitutional re-engineering, including an elected assembly in Northern Ireland (without any cut in the number of Northern Ireland MPs, or any brouhaha about a "West Belfast question").

Our unwritten constitution has its vices. But its virtue is that it does not require neat solutions. It can cope with the diversity of the United Kingdom, the specificities of its nations and regions. The union that makes up the UK is a partnership based on give and take to the benefit of all. By respecting the differences of tradition, culture and institutions, we strengthen the union rather than weaken it.

The more plausible critique of what we are proposing—and it is heard from some who count as supporters of New Labour—is that this programme is a distraction. Labour governments, they say, should be concerned with delivering jobs, growth and economic equality, not with airy-fairy notions such as democracy and participation.

This is historically unfounded. The role of left-of-centre parties around the world and down the ages has been to extend democratic power, while the right has struggled to reduce it.

But in any case economic reconstructions and democratic renovation are not alternatives. They go in tandem. To take a historical analogy, extending the vote to the middle and working classes was not an alternative to making Britain the workshop of the world in the last century. It was only by incorporating and empowering the people who made it such that their energies and skill could be fully harnessed to the task of modernisation.

Britain's constitutional exceptionalism would be tolerable if experience suggested it yielded social progress and economic success. The evidence points the other way.

Finally, there are those who argue that the path to constitutional reform is strewn with good intentions but failed plans. They remember the unsuccessful struggles of Harold Wilson's 1966–70 Labour government with House of Lords reform, and of Jim Callaghan's 1976–79 Labour government with devolution, and

are overcome by an understandable faintheartedness.

Constitutional change can, I accept, be a fraught endeavour. In the end it is a question of political will, parliamentary skill and eventually popular support.

And in this regard, history is a poor teacher. Times have changed. Constitutional issues are now at the heart of political debate. We gauge that constitutional conservatism is dying and that popular support for change is tangible and steadfast. As important, we are prepared this time to put that judgment to the test by laying our most important proposals to the test of popular endorsement through referendums. We will seek a specific mandate from the Scottish people for the creation of a parliament, and for its tax-varying powers. We will set up regional government only where people vote for it. We will give the people the ultimate say on the system by which they elect their representatives at Westminster. Despite the initial concern these commitments sparked within the Labour Party, I am convinced that they are essential to ensuring that constitutional reform does not run ahead of public opinion. That would be fatal to it.

Democratic renewal

In the late 1970s and early 1980s, there was a widespread perception that the right was "winning the argument" on the central economic issues of the day. Now the economic argument has changed, with labour advocating long-term investment—above all in education—reform of welfare and leadership by Britain in Europe.

If I am not mistaken, in the mid-1990s, another perception is taking hold: that the centre-left is "winning the argument" on constitutional matters. Mr Major in his bunker reminds me of those Labour diehards who went on arguing for nationalisation and statism long after their irrelevance was plain to the rest of the world.

We shall fight the general election *inter alia* on democratic renewal. More important still, with the support of the people we shall deliver what we promise on democratic renewal as an essential element in our project: the modernisation of Britain.

What is Scotland's future?

Anthony King

Foreigners seldom know what to call the country. "England" will clearly not do. It excludes Scotland and denies the separate identity of Wales. "Great Britain" (first used following the 1707 Act of Union between England and Scotland) is better but excludes Northern Ireland. The proper name (since the Irish republic seceded in 1921) has been "the United Kingdom of Great Britain and Northern Ireland". But who wants to say that?

There is just a chance that the name may have to change again. The Scots have long been a nation. Some of them now want to form a state—and almost all favour a degree of domestic self-rule that could lead to statehood. The British Conservatives in 1996 will set their faces against any move that could have that result.

The reality of Scottish nationhood is not questioned. The Scots have their own national football side, their own national dress, their own banknotes, their own newspapers, their own national drink (more Scotch is consumed per head in Scotland than anywhere else) and even their own national dish (though there is no export market for haggis). Above all, the Scots are a nation because they think they are. Surveys invariably find that most Scots feel themselves to be Scottish first and British second.

Nor can the claim to statehood be dismissed as absurd. With a population of 5.1m, Scotland has more people than Finland, Norway or Ireland. It attracts substantial inward investment and has a per capita GDP not substantially lower than England's. Outside the United Kingdom but inside the EU, Scotland could undoubtedly go it alone.

But should it? The Scottish National Party (SNP) says yes. It points to Scotland's pre-1707 history of independence, to Scots' undoubted sense of national identity and to the fact that since 1970 Scotland has been governed for 19 out of 25 years by a predominantly English political party enjoying the support of fewer than 40% (and latterly fewer than 30%) of Scottish electors. "Independence in Europe" is the SNP's current slogan.

But all the British parties say no to statehood. They draw attention to nearly 300 years of intimate English-Scottish association, to the comradeship of the two world wars (Scottish regiments still figure largely in the British army) and to the fact that separation would diminish the international standing of both countries. Not least, they point, like Quebec's federalists, to the job losses and loss of central government subsidies that would inevitably follow independence. "Scotland free", they say, "would be Scotland poor".

At this point, however, the British parties part company. The Conservatives, nowadays little reliant on Scottish votes, oppose any form of home rule. They insist that a Scottish government and administration would only create an expensive additional layer of bureaucracy. They also maintain that home rule would lead to statehood and independence.

Labour and the Liberal Democrats disagree. They insist that the Scots, being a nation, have a right to home rule and also that, granted home rule, the Scots would be more, rather than less, likely to want to remain within the United Kingdom.

All sides have now staked out their positions. Most Scots want home rule but shy away from complete independence. They will back Labour and the Liberal Democrats (and in some cases, *pour encourager les autres,* the SNP). But the real battle in 1996 will be for English hearts and minds. In the run-up to the next election, can the Tories persuade enough Englishmen that Scottish devolution means Scottish independence (and that that would be a bad thing)?

After the Talking Stopped

An IRA bomb in London underscores the dangers of a peace initiative

Fred Barbash
Washington Post Foreign Service

LONDON

There was no game plan for Northern Ireland, no secret deal, no honest broker and no shuttle diplomacy. The peace process that began 18 months ago—amid deeply conflicting emotions of hope and doubt—was grounded fundamentally on a blind faith that as long as the parties could be kept talking, violence might cease.

EUROPE

As it turned out, there was merit to this simple approach. For longer than anyone had envisaged, this reed-thin technique seemed to work. But there was a danger in it as well, the obverse side: What would happen when the conversation stopped, which is effectively what happened a few weeks ago?

The answer came Feb. 9 when the Irish Republican Army bombed London's largest office and residential development, killing two people and injuring dozens. The blast also dealt a potentially lethal blow to attempts to resolve Northern Ireland's generation of "troubles." On his visit here in December, President Clinton had hailed the peace process as an example to the world.

How did this symbol of hope so suddenly become, once again, a symbol of horror?

While blame for the bomb rests squarely with the IRA, responsibility for the lack of progress in the talks belongs to politicians on all sides both here and in Northern Ireland. The talking stopped because they placed hurdles in its way; the music died because the tune became "conditions" rather than concessions.

And that happened, most likely, because between the IRA cease-fire declaration on Aug. 31, 1994, and now, political conditions have changed. For different reasons, officials crucial to the talks have grown politically weaker rather than stronger. They reacted by becoming more rather than less intransigent. By the end, they backed themselves into corners from which they were unwilling or unable to escape.

Ingredients that have sustained other negotiations in other conflicts were absent: There was no outside third-party broker, who by virtue of trust or fear could "knock heads together." There was no equivalent of Serbian President Slobodan Milosevic, who could step in for his own reasons and call the shots for one party or the other. While many observe the tragic conflict in Northern Ireland, it presents no threat to global or regional stability and attracts only intermittent interest from the rest of the world. There is no oil in Ireland—north or south.

The troubles of Northern Ireland are rooted deep in history. Britain controlled Ireland for some 300 years, suppressing Catholicism and Irish nationalism by force. After years of conflict, it withdrew from the predominantly Catholic southern 26 counties in the 1920s but retained control of the majority Protestant six counties in the north of the island, now known as Northern Ireland.

■

THE PARTITION PRODUCED two opposing movements: Irish nationalism, or republicanism, which favors reunification with the republic to the south, and "unionism," or "loyalism," which seeks to keep the region as part of the United Kingdom. The former is composed largely of Catholics, who regard themselves as the victims of British and Protestant oppression; the latter is made up primarily of Protestants.

Both communities harbor violent paramilitary organizations that have wreaked havoc in the province for the past 25 years with reprisal attacks. Both also maintain aboveboard political parties.

The peace process that began 18 months ago was initiated largely by the British and Irish governments, with considerable help from John Hume, leader of Northern Ireland's nationalist Social Democratic and Labor Party, and Gerry Adams, president of Sinn Fein, the legal political wing of the IRA. Adams in particular managed to persuade the IRA to declare the cease-fire after convincing it that the nationalist movement had gotten nowhere using violence and other means might prove more productive.

Initially, there appeared to be some flexibility on all sides. Negotiating positions seemed to be just that—positions subject to negotiation.

British Prime Minister John Major put aside early demands that the IRA and Sinn Fein declare the cease-fire permanent as a precondition to the start of formal, high-level contacts between the British government and Sinn Fein. Major also put his name to a framework document with the government of Ireland that proposed some ideas once considered unthinkable in London, such as allowing the government in Dublin to have a formal, if limited, voice in the governance of Northern Ireland.

Unionist parties, while loathing that notion, seemed willing to talk about the document, which also contained a promise that the future of Northern Ireland would be determined by the consent of the majority. Sinn Fein, while opposing that idea, also appeared ready to proceed.

The process started to get bogged down about seven months ago, with Major's demand that before formal talks could start, the IRA had to begin decommissioning its arsenal of weapons and explosives. Sinn Fein refused, saying it had proved its commitment to the peace process and that decommissioning should be a subject for talks, not a precondition. Decommissioning, it said, was "surrender."

Months passed with no change on either side. The political situation did change, however. Major's Conservative Party saw its parliamentary majority dwindle to the point where it became more and more dependent on the support of the nine Northern Ireland unionists to keep control of Parliament.

The traditional leaders of Ulster unionism confronted two challenges: competition from fringe Protestant organizations in Northern Ireland capturing increasing television exposure by adopting more conciliatory positions on the peace process; and the resignation of James Molyneaux as longtime leader of the main unionist organization, the Ulster Unionist Party.

In his place, party members in September elected a more outspoken and younger member of Parliament, David Trimble, who ran on a platform urging less rather than more compromise in the peace process. The new leader also came forward with the party's own proposal to get the talks going: hold an election in Northern Ireland to let voters choose up sides.

No one budged, and talk of a crisis in the peace process replaced talk about the talks themselves. In November, Major and Irish Prime Minister John Bruton tried to restore momentum by appointing an international commission, headed by former U.S. Senate majority leader George Mitchell, to make recommendations on decommissioning so that negotiations on substantive political matters could begin independently of the weapons issue by the end of February.

Mitchell's panel recommended on Jan. 24 that Major drop his demand for weapons disposal as a precondition to talks, provided Sinn Fein and all other parties promised to use only peaceful means to advance their cause.

Major endorsed the report and said he would indeed drop that demand, but he then substituted a different condition: the proposal for an election in Northern Ireland originally proposed by Trimble.

Officials in Dublin were stunned. The nationalists were bound to reject the election idea, they said, because of the outnumbered Catholics' past disappointments at the polls in Northern Ireland.

The Dublin-London relationship reached a new low. Predictably, both Sinn Fein and the moderate Social Democratic and Labor Party, which has always opposed violence, angrily rejected Major's condition.

Most analysts say that was the watershed moment, a signal the talking could go no further. Officials in Dublin and London were holding emergency cabinet meetings, trying to find a way to keep the peace process alive. Bruton went on television Feb. 11 to advance his proposal for an effort similar to the U.S.-brokered Bosnian peace talks near Dayton, Ohio, in which Northern Ireland's political leaders would lock themselves in a building until they agree on something.

Ulster unionist spokesmen immediately rejected the idea.

Security forces here and in Belfast and Dublin have prepared themselves for the possibility of more violence.

HELMUT KOHL
Extra extra large

Is the enduring Helmut Kohl a statesman or just a politician?

THERE is something reassuring about a powerful German chancellor who, when he wakes up in the middle of the night, is thinking—by his own admission—about raiding the refrigerator, not re-arranging the world. Helmut Kohl is a leader who at first looked cloddishly ordinary and has grown extraordinary, all the while retaining a quality of solid averageness that invites popular trust.

On October 31st Mr Kohl will overtake Konrad Adenauer to become post-1945 Germany's longest-serving chancellor. The 14 years-and-one-month he will then have notched up exceeds the entire life-span of the Weimar Republic (1919-33), Germany's ill-starred first exercise in democracy. At summits, the German chancellor is shaking the hands of his third American president, fourth Russian leader and eighth Japanese prime minister. Since François Mitterrand's death in January, Mr Kohl has found himself grandly alone, despite chirpy pledges of common purpose from Jacques Chirac, at the head of the march for European political union. Another five years as chancellor—not out of the question, since he is a robust-seeming 66 years old—and he will outstrip Bismarck, the Iron Chancellor who held office in the second Reich for 19 years (without the regrettable necessity of seeking re-election).

In a democracy, Mr Kohl's popular durability is the more remarkable. That it has been Germany's democracy that has thrown up such longevity may be a partial explanation: the so-called "German model", by encouraging consensus among big social groups (workers, managers, parties and so forth), puts a premium on stability. But that is also true of Japan, say. Conceivably, Germans may be unusual in the way they respond to good leadership. At any rate, it is striking that, in Mr Kohl, Adenauer, and Willy Brandt, Germany has produced more post-war leaders with a claim to exceptional stature than any other western nation. In America, Truman and Ronald Reagan stand out for their personal impact on the world (Kennedy, perhaps); in France, De Gaulle and (perhaps) Mitterrand; in Britain, Margaret Thatcher.

Which raises two questions: How has Mr Kohl achieved the respect in which he is held? And, more important, what judgment should be passed about his achievements in office?

Letting Kohl be Kohl

The immediate explanation for the respect Mr Kohl commands is that he represents continuity and order after unification, an event that has brought Germans enough upheaval to last a lifetime. Yet that explanation is obviously partial. Mr Kohl had first to earn respect—and there was nothing predetermined about that.

After Mr Kohl lost the general election of 1976, Franz Josef Strauss, the bull-like premier of Bavaria, snorted: "Believe me, Helmut Kohl will never become chancellor. At the age of 90 he'll write his memoirs, 'Forty Years as Chancellor Candidate'." This was no doubt sour grapes from a man who himself lost the 1980 election but the comment also reflected a once-common tendency to dismiss Mr Kohl, a former premier of Rhineland-Palatinate, as a hick with little knowledge of the world who had over-reached himself when he secured the leadership of the Christian Democratic Union (CDU).

His first years as chancellor were inauspicious. He fell into the job in 1982 when the Free Democrats deserted their coalition with Helmut Schmidt's Social Democrats and switched to his CDU. Critics accused him of insensitive bumbling. Notoriously, he took a flummoxed Ronald Reagan on a visit to a German cemetery where some ss troops were buried. He likened poor Mikhail Gorbachev to Goebbels. Fellow politicians began to talk of him as a one-term chancellor.

Ordinary Germans, however, did not share the politicians' verdict. The fact that they have ensconced him in office suggests that he has made contact at some fundamental level: he has secured the average voter's confidence. He could not be ruffled. Soon he needed to go on slimming cures to combat an outsized appetite, a foible which rather appealed to his countrymen. It even helped that he came from (and has

kept a home in) Ludwigshafen, an industrial port on the middle Rhine which strikes everyone as just about the most averagely-German place imaginable.

German voters do not much go in for intellectual leaders and Mr Kohl makes no pretence to be one. He operates by instinct and like another non-intellectual, Ronald Reagan, exploits television with gusto. One of the great achievements of his cosy style is to make Germans feel content with themselves and their country—no small matter for a place with such a past. There is something apt about the choice of Mr Kohl's cardigan (size XXL) as an item on display in the Museum of History in Bonn.

This popular touch is the first of four features that have helped Mr Kohl consolidate his grip on German power and have forced his fellow politicians to reconsider their initial scepticism. The second is the transformation in his public skills on the world stage. No chancellor, it is often repeated, has learnt more in office. The tactlessness of the early years has all but gone. He has learned to speak the right language about Germany's past, which has helped foster warm relations not only with Poland and Russia but also with Israel and other nations which have most reason to fear Germany.

A third feature that has helped him is a lucky chance: a weak and fractious opposition. In the past four elections, the Social Democrats have run a series of almost sacrificially feeble candidates. In the 1994 election, the SDP candidate formed a troika with two of his party rivals at the last minute—hardly a sign of confidence. One of them has since staged a takeover as party boss. Mr Kohl has good taste in opponents.

The last feature that has given him such political dominance is his uninhibited approach to the exercise of power. Like Lyndon Johnson, Mr Kohl has the faculty that Germans call *Fingerspitzengefühl*, a fingertip feel for politics that enables him to know just where to apply pressure and where to give personal encouragement. His range of personal contacts is immense. And, while he is sometimes accused of being disengaged from policy issues, no one doubts his skills in party management. Like Adenauer, who once claimed he was 75% of the cabinet, Mr Kohl likes to command, using his imposing bulk and indefatigable self-confidence to dominate both his circle of advisers and his party.

Unlike Adenauer, he has few damaging critics. Karl Hugo Pruys, once his spokesman, recently his biographer, notes that he has no intimate friends. He is too consumed by politics for that. Politics, it seems, is his only passion (apart from food). Even opposition leaders confess admiration.

This may be good for him but not for his party. More than Adenauer, who founded the CDU, Mr Kohl embodies the party. He has led it for 23 years and has squashed first his rivals, then anyone who disagreed with him, such as Kurt Biedenkopf (now premier of Saxony). So absolute is his control of the CDU—at its annual conference in Hanover this week, 95.5% of delegates voted for him as party leader—that he is preventing it going through the process of renewal that could throw up the leader it will eventually need to replace him. He has made the CDU look like an assembly of yes-men.

The unification chancellor

So much for the 'how' of Helmut Kohl. The bigger questions concern the 'what': What has he done? What should one make of it?

Germany has changed enormously during his rule, not least in becoming one country instead of two. It has begun the difficult process of reforming its bloated welfare state and adapting its high-cost and specifically German system of doing business to the increasingly American ways of international competition. In diplomatic affairs, Germany has come out of its postwar shell. It has gone through the agony of allowing its soldiers to operate outside Germany and is now arming its peacekeepers in the Balkans to let them act as toughly, if need be, as other foreign forces. It feels sufficiently unburdened to press for a permanent seat on the United Nations security council. Of course, Germany has not overcome all its daunting post-war inhibitions: the self-questioning, the embarrassment about looking powerful, remains, often masked by the chancellor's personal self-confidence. Yet Germany dominates Europe in a manner it did not when Mr Kohl came to power.

Mr. Kohl has guided Germany calmly through all these changes, especially unification: it is hard to imagine any country handling an upheaval of that magnitude as smoothly as he, and Germany, did. All the same, there is no Kohlism; there are not even many coherent policies attached to his name. So should he be judged merely as a durable tactician on whose watch unification happened to occur? Or is he a statesman, able to look ahead and guide, even create, events to serve his purpose?

To answer the question, begin by considering Mr Kohl's record in the light of the two chancellors with whom many, perhaps most, Germans would compare him, Adenauer and Brandt. Adenauer's great achievement was to anchor his country securely in the West. To this end, he set unification aside. Stalin is said to have offered him East Germany back in exchange for German neutrality; Adenauer refused. His policies guaranteed closeness to America, a fundamental goal, and brought the famous reconciliation with De Gaulle's France which spurred what has become the European Union.

Brandt's great achievement concerned the eventual goal of unification. Getting there, he reasoned, meant going in the seemingly opposite direction of recognising communist East Germany. To this end, he used his stint as chancellor (1969-74) to advance *Ostpolitik*, a bold and intricate scheme to restore traditional German links with Eastern Europe and Russia that Hitler and communism had shattered. This helped reassure Russia that the intentions of its historic enemy were not aggressive.

Mr Kohl's great achievement has been to complete Brandt's aim of unification without compromising Adenauer's alliance with the West. At the outset of his chancellorship, Mr Kohl walked into a bitter east-west row over nuclear missiles. Controversially, he backed NATO plans to install cruise and Pershing missiles in West Germany. At great risk to his popularity (which was in any case shaky), Mr Kohl chose to emphasise Germany's commitment to the West and to the European Union (then Community) by ignoring the pacifist demands and neutralist temptations present in Germany. These amounted to a "Germany-first" belief that the country should go its own way; after all, supporters of this view asked, wouldn't neutrality relieve Germans of the pressures they bore?

That question returned with a vengeance when the prospect of unification drew near. In his newly-published account of that rousing time ("Helmut Kohl: I Wanted German Unity", Propylän, DM48), the chancellor relates how he supported his insistence on a unified Germany's westernness with a disarming line in folk-wisdom to win over Mr Gorbachev. Having sat the Soviet leader on a wall overlooking a moonlit Rhine in the chancellery gardens in Bonn, Mr Kohl softened him up thus:

> Look at that river flowing by, it symbolises history. There is nothing static about it. You can dam this river … technically it can be done. But then it will overflow its banks and find another way to reach the sea. So it is with German unity.

Soon afterwards, Mr Kohl had that unity, without paying the price of some form of disengagement from the West which the Soviet Union, and some Germans, had in mind. There are many doubts about the economic terms on which unification was achieved but none of the historic nature of the achievement itself. Mr Kohl reconciled unification with westernisation—an act of statesmanship.

Inches short of greatness

Teddy Roosevelt once said that even Lincoln would have been wasted had he lived during the relative calm of the early 20th-century. To be a great president, it is not enough to have great skills and a compelling vision; you also need great occasions.

Helmut Kohl has been able to measure himself by this yardstick. Unification was perhaps his greatest test but not the only one. Two others stand out: the challenges facing Germany's consensus system and Europe's unfinished business of economic and monetary union (EMU). All three tests suggest that while the chancellor is indeed capable of rising to the big occasion, he does so in a way that makes him fall short of the highest standards of statesmanship.

Mr Kohl's manner of dealing with the great issues is to establish a point of no return, march past it, and let "details" fall into place later. Squabbling over smaller matters, he tells himself, only creates enemies and problems. This helps him make the great leap in the first place. But it also means that he cannot—or does not—think through all the ramifications of the change.

Take unification. Here, the "details" are starting to qualify his achievement. Mr Kohl has been criticised for overruling the Bundesbank and deciding to exchange solid D-marks for East Germany's meagre Ost-marks at a rate of one-to-one. The reason he did this was to meet popular expectations in the East. But it does not require hindsight to see that this would make East-German businesses uncompetitive and increase the cost of modernising the ex-communist east—though few people expected the subsidy cost to rise to its current cumulative sum of over DM900 billion ($580 billion). Mr Kohl might also have freed up the east-German labour market and permitted more exemptions from the "social market" restrictions now hampering growth throughout Germany. Had he done so, the liberalisation now taking place painfully might have begun earlier.

This pattern—taking a bold decision then seeing some of the benefits eroded after the event—can be seen at work in the economic reforms launched this year (see pages 73 and 84 for examples). Having looked brave this autumn when pushing a first batch of welfare cuts through parliament, Mr Kohl is now shrinking from applying them in full. To take a small example: where full pay for sick leave is part of a labour contract, says the chancellor, it must stay—at least until the contract is renegotiated. This is vintage Kohl. Employers and unions are in a fog, but both sides have something to thank him for. He stands, above all, for consensus between government, managers and workers.

That system has proved successful in the past, as have high productivity and German exporting skills. They may no longer be so now, as competitiveness slides, tempting German firms to manufacture outside Germany where wages and other costs are lower, pushing up unemployment. Some people believe the end of "the German model" is nigh, barring an improbably strong economic surge—and even that would merely delay deep reform.

Is Mr Kohl the man to push that reform through? The evidence so far is against it: he enjoys power not conflict; he seems deeply committed to the consensus system; his now-abandoned promise to halve unemployment by 2000 had the ring of fantasy. It may be unfair to accuse Mr Kohl of adding to the problem through his concern to avoid conflict and keep winning votes. But it is fair to say that the chancellor, a historian not an economist by training, looks ill-at-ease in dealing with economic change.

As the "unification chancellor" Mr Kohl's reputation is secure. As an economic reformer, he is likely to go down (unless his zeal is renewed) as a man who took half his chances. But he himself wants to be judged by a European yardstick: as the man who pushed through EMU—a point of no return—and hence made inevitable some form of closer European Union able to prevent nationalist aggression from returning to the continent.

Chancellor for Europe?

With EMU still in the balance, it is obviously too early to make a judgment of Mr Kohl by this yardstick. But suppose EMU occurs. It would indeed be a triumph for the chancellor, upon whose unwavering support the whole plan has depended during the past uncertain year. But would Mr Kohl's broader, federating aim then be guaranteed? Not necessarily. For one thing, there is a short-run tension (which Mr Kohl has always denied) between the aims of EMU and EU expansion: the new members, when they join, will be members of a second class of Europeans who do not use the single currency. This is divisive, rather than inclusive.

For another thing, many Europeans, though few Germans, are less worried than Mr Kohl about the great threat of nationalism. That means Germany approaches Europe in a different way from most of its partners, France included. Mr Kohl's federating mission is, in a nutshell, to save Germany from itself. Other members of the European Union may dislike nationalism, but none (except perhaps for Italy) think it necessary to save themselves—or anything else—from the consequences of their own actions. Mr Kohl's project for EMU-driven integration is shaping up to be, like unification and welfare reform, a great leap forward—followed by years dealing with unforeseen consequences.

"Why does Germany, the most powerful state in Europe, appear bent on giving up voluntarily its newly won sovereign power?" Part of the answer, Peter Katzenstein argues, is that the "Germans have eliminated the concept of 'power' from their political vocabulary. They speak the language of 'political responsibility' instead."

United Germany in an Integrating Europe

PETER J. KATZENSTEIN

Revolutionary changes in global and European politics have reawakened old fears about Europe's domination by an unpredictable German giant. But these changes have also fueled new hopes for Germany and Europe as models of political pluralism in a more peaceful and prosperous world. In a different era, Thomas Mann distinguished between the specter of the "Germanization" of Europe and the vision of a "Europeanization" of Germany. It is a mistake to decide between these two views based on the extrapolation of fears from the past or hopes for the future. It is more useful to treat them as templates that may help us in discerning a more complicated pattern linking Germany and Europe.

German unification and European integration were indelibly linked in 1989 and 1990. German Chancellor Helmut Kohl's European partners gave their grudging, basic support for German unification in Strasbourg in December 1989. In return, Kohl agreed to back French President François Mitterrand's proposal to have the Intergovernmental Conference on the Economic and Monetary Union (EMU) start as early as December 1990 rather than at some later, unspecified date, as Germany had previously preferred. And, by March 1990, when it had become clear that pressure for Germany's early unification was building much more quickly than Kohl, Mitterrand, or most of Europe's other leaders

had expected, France predicated its support for an acceleration of the unification process on a German commitment to a second Intergovernmental Conference on political union that would encompass not only monetary and economic affairs but also foreign and security policy. This deal was approved politically by the European Council that met in Dublin in April 1990. It was then ratified in the Treaty on European Union, which amalgamated the proposals for economic and political union at Maastricht in December 1991. United Germany was thus to be embedded in an integrating Europe.

These diplomatic bargains point to two underlying questions. Why does Germany, the most powerful state in Europe, appear bent on giving up voluntarily its newly won sovereign power? And why have long-standing institutional inefficiencies not blocked advances in European integration? The answer to these two questions centers on a historic shift in the institutionalization of power in Germany and Europe, power that conventionally is measured in terms of material resources or bargaining strength.

The Germans have eliminated the concept of "power" from their political vocabulary. They speak the language of "political responsibility" instead. In his analysis of the taming of German power, Hans-Peter Schwarz has described a new forgetfulness of power that has replaced an old obsession with power.[1] Some observers view this rhetorical turn as little more than a cynical ploy in which the old wolf has put on new sheep's clothing; here it is regarded as an indication of a deeper transformation in the style and substance of German and European politics. The culture of restraint that characterizes German foreign policy and the conscious avoidance of assuming a high profile and a strong leadership role

---

PETER J. KATZENSTEIN *is Walter S. Carpenter, Jr., Professor of International Studies at Cornell University.*

---

[1]Hans-Peter Schwarz, *Die Gezähmten Deutschen: Von der Machtbessenheit zur Machtvergessenheit* (The Tamed Germans: From an Obsession with Power to an Obliviousness of Power) (Stuttgart: Deutsche Verlags-Anstalt, 1985).

From *Current History*, March 1997, pp. 116-123. Excerpted from *Tamed Power: Germany in Europe,* edited by Peter J. Katzenstein. © 1996 by Cornell University Press. Reprinted by permission.

in the European Union (EU) emanate from the same institutional source.

The German approach to power and the practices that sustain and reformulate it emphasize its "soft" institutional elements. Other views interpret German power differently. Some stress power as a form of domination from which actors can escape only by breaking the shackles that tie them down. Or they might stress contractual bargaining relationships in which the different parties gain, to different degrees, from making deals. Such views underline "hard" elements of power. In reality, soft and hard elements always blend. For example, in the summer of 1996, British tabloids stylized an English-German soccer match as a new "war," and the tabloids viewed Germany and Britain as the main protagonists in a diplomatic war over "beef derivatives" in the mad-cow disease saga. But, at the same time, the British and German foreign offices swapped officials as part of ongoing efforts to further European integration by exploring practical steps toward a unified European embassy.

The institutionalization of power is the most distinctive aspect of the relationship between Europe and Germany. Germany's willingness to give the smaller EU members disproportionate power is puzzling. Only by moving institutional power center stage can we hope to understand why Germany is willing to give up its new sovereign power or why institutional inefficiency has not stopped European integration. Because it takes the hard edges off hard power relations, the institutionalization of power matters. Over time institutions become actors themselves rather than mere constraints on other actors' preferences. They do so within particular normative contexts (of collective expectations for the proper behavior of actors with a given identity), or for specific collective identities (such as varying constructions of statehood). Norms and identities typically have two effects. They enable actors by constituting them and thus shaping their interests. But they also constrain actor preferences.

In recent decades European states, especially Germany, have acquired collective identities that are significantly more international than before. In this situation power is a variable quantity. Parents may act against their individual interests to further the family's interest. What may look irrational for them as individuals can be quite rational from the perspective of the family, with which they also identify. Similarly, both the individual member states and the EU family can simultaneously gain or lose power. "The term which captures most accurately the dominant character of the relationship between states and the region," concludes Paul Taylor, "is *symbiosis*. . . [T]here is no evidence to suggest that common arrangements could not be extended a very long way without necessarily posing any direct challenge to the sovereignty of states."[2] James Caporaso concurs when he argues that "regional integration is not a zero-sum process. . . Analysts should not have to choose between intergovernmentalism and international forms of political activity. Both logics operate in the European polity."[3] Nation-states are simultaneously "throwing out" functions to the supranational level and devolving responsibilities to subnational regions. In this view, power relations do not add to a fixed quantity that either resides in national states or gets transferred to a supranational center of decision making. This makes institutionalized power "soft" compared to other types of power.

Besides the internationalization of state identities, the softness of German power in Europe is also due to the institutional similarity of the EU and Germany. In both polities power is pooled, creating a European system of associated sovereignty and German semisovereignty. In both systems it is possible to exploit superior material resources and advantageous bargaining positions to exercise hard power. But such behavior is the exception, not the rule. As Elizabeth Pond argues, German interests are advanced not in balance-of-power clashes but in "tedious bureaucratic maneuvering in the confederation-plus of the EU and the confederation-minus of the transatlantic community."[4] Hence, what is distinctive about Germany is not its unintentional power, which, like all larger states, it possesses in good measure, but the fact that its political leaders exercise power only in multilateral, institutionally mediated systems (the EU, the Atlantic community, and broader international fora) that soften sovereign power.

SYMBOLS OF THE NEW EUROPE

In the fall of 1989, leading politicians such as Helmut Kohl, Oskar Lafontaine, Hans-Dietrich

[2]Paul Taylor, "The European Community and the State: Assumptions, Theories and Propositions," *Review of International Studies,* vol.17 (1991), p. 125.

[3]James A. Caporaso, "The European Union and Forms of State: Westphalian, Regulatory or Post-Modern?" *Journal of Common Market Studies,* vol. 34, no. 1 (March 1996), pp. 46–47.

[4]Elizabeth Pond, "Germany Finds Its Niche as a Regional Power," *The Washington Quarterly,* vol. 19, no. 1 (Winter 1996), p. 36.

Genscher, Mikhail Gorbachev, François Mitterrand, and James Baker tried to articulate new concepts—such as "unification through association" and a "common European home"—with which to describe the new political reality. Willy Brandt, Margaret Thatcher, and Henry Kissinger captured the changes with the more familiar political terminology of national unification and national power. Both sets of voices describe important aspects of reality. National power and state interests have not become irrelevant in Europe's new political context. But the Europeanization of that context has itself become important for how states like Germany conceive of their national interests and for how they pursue their political strategies. In a time of revolutionary change, the extension of a partly internationalized German state was in many German and European quarters accepted as a natural response.

In Germany, Europe, and more generally, state identities are primarily external; they describe the actions of governments in a society of states. National identities are internal; they describe the processes by which mass publics acquire, modify, and forget their collective identities. While national identities in Europe have probably not decreased recently, to date they have not posed an insurmountable barrier to European integration. The permissive consensus on European integration among national mass publics has been reinforced by the gradual growth of ambiguous and contested collective European identities that are beginning to complement national identities among some social strata. Cultural policy, language use, currency, citizenship, and anthems are ambiguous symbols of collective identity that mirror in the social sphere the intermingling of a "multiperspectival" polity with "multitiered" governance systems through which traditional state identities have been partly internationalized.

The institutional presence of Europe as a set of norms and a source of collective identity has been the subject of explicit political considerations. The Adonnino Committee, for example, debated a Europe more accessible to its citizens and in 1985 recommended, among other things, the extension of student exchanges and an all-Europe television channel. The Franco-German bicultural "arte" television channel, with an estimated budget of $150 million, has been broadcasting since 1991. Student exchanges have blossomed. Between 1995 and 1999 the EU is planning to spend about $2.5 billion on all types of educational programs. Student applications for the largest of these programs increased from 3,000 in 1987 and 1988 to 146,000 in 1994 and 1995.

In terms of language, however, Europe is not moving toward one standard, as Spain and France did in the eighteenth and nineteenth centuries. English is the lingua franca, state languages tenaciously defend their position in the educational systems of the EU members, and regional languages have made successful incursions into national language regimes.[5] A European living in southern England will be able to function effectively with one language; other Europeans will need command of their mother tongue and English; Europeans living in regions with their own distinctive languages, such as Catalonia or Scotland, will speak three languages. Europeans are institutionalizing a stable multiple language regime that they accept as natural and normal. But this regime is inefficient. States will retain separate state languages in a European and global language regime increasingly centered on English.

Much debated in the 1990s, the EMU also has an important symbolic dimension that touches Europe deeply. As with language, the outcome points to multiple collective identities. With German national identity closely linked to the deutsche mark, as is implied in the concept of mark-nationalism, the choice of a name and the look of a future European currency remained contested until late 1995. While the French favored sticking to the French-sounding ecu (identical in sound but not in orthography to the ECU, the European Currency Unit) that had been used in France several centuries earlier, Chancellor Kohl objected because this currency sounded in plain German too much like "cow" (or *Kuh*). For a while there was talk of calling the new currency the euro-franken or euro-franc, a concession to France and psychologically associated with a stable currency derived from both German history and present Swiss practice. Britain, however, vetoed the idea, dubbing the franken a "Frankenstein."

> *For a while there was talk of calling the new currency the euro-franken or euro-franc. . . Britain, however, vetoed the idea, dubbing the franken a "Frankenstein."*

[5]See David Laitin, "The Cultural Identities of a European State" (paper prepared for a conference on "European Identity and Its Intellectual Roots," Harvard University, May 1993, revised July 22, 1994).

The December 1995 EU summit meeting in Madrid agreed on a new name: the "euro." The look of the currency remains to be decided. The choice of euro leaves open the possibility of a hyphenated European-national currency, as in euro-pound, euro-franc, or euro-deutsche mark, and a design that will somehow integrate the blue colors of the European flag. The subdivision of the euro into cents foreshadows such a solution. Countries adopting the common currency will be permitted to put their own designs on one side of the coins. Such a combination of European and national symbols would be compelling not only for a transitional period but as a long-term solution for a polity in which citizens may retain some aspects of their national currencies in a future EMU. New automobile license plates in Europe are a daily reminder of what a euro coin might look like; national plates are now adorned with a blue strip on the left-hand side showing the European emblem, 12 golden stars against a blue background, and the national origin of the car.

The new EU passport, issued by all countries in identical format and red color but embossed with the names of the different member states, is another example of this practice. Arriving at European airports and forming longer and slower queues, travelers who are not citizens of an EU member state quickly notice that European citizenship is becoming a reality, however slowly, even though the Europeanization of border controls remains one of the most controversial aspects of the integration process in the 1990s. Social and economic rights that were once restricted to national citizens are gradually being extended to immigrants. And a European citizenship that is partly distinct from national citizenship has become a distinct possibility.

The adoption of the "Ode to Joy" from Beethoven's *Ninth Symphony* as Europe's anthem points in the same direction.[6] A well-known publicist for European unity in the interwar period, Count Coudenhove-Kalergie, had suggested the "Ode to Joy" as a possible anthem as early as 1949. Between 1952 and 1964, East and West Germany used the ode as their joint victory hymn at the Olympic Games. Overcoming a number of potential rivals, the ode gradually established itself as the most widely accepted European hymn, especially in local communities. Building on many unsolicited private suggestions, the Council of Europe made its first official plea for a European anthem in June 1971. The 1971 resolution recommended the tune of the "Ode to Joy," without the words, as Europe's anthem. The famous conductor Herbert von Karajan was commissioned to make the musical arrangements, which he provided in 1972 for orchestra and brass.

In 1986 the European Parliament took "formal note of the current practice concerning the European anthem" in the hope that it and other symbols would "strengthen the concept of European identity." Although the issue of language was not explicitly debated, the tune was condemned to be left without words, not so much because of the global rather than regional appeal of Schiller's verses but because of the simple, widely understood, and undebated fact that this was a German-language text. Reflecting on the ambiguities surrounding the adoption of this anthem, Caryl Clark concludes, "[H]ere was truly a bastard-child of the Enlightenment: a song without words; hope without a text. . . [A]t a basic level the Council of Europe acted out of ignorance, was seduced by commercialism, fell prey to an ideology which espoused the superiority of German music, and (unwittingly or not) succumbed to the powerful force exerted by the Beethoven myth itself."[7]

The wordlessness of the European anthem speaks volumes about the ambiguities created by the admixture of regional, national, European, and international elements that constitutes an evolving collective European identity. The weakness of pan-European media, multinational public discourse, and the European Parliament points to the fact that the European polity is not a democratic state-in-becoming that currently suffers from a democratic deficit. Its system of multilevel governance reflects primarily a transnational growth of public and private bureaucracies. This constrains the growth of a European collective identity and guarantees the persistence of strong national and subnational identities in an integrating Europe. Europe's collective identity has been carried by a permissive consensus among mass publics and by a strong commitment of political and social elites. Just as Beethoven continued to rework the ending to his *Ninth,* so too are European states continuously reworking a collective identity that now contains more international elements, in particular in Germany, than it has at any time in this century.

[6]This discussion follows Caryl Clark, "Confronting the Ninth: Beethoven's 'Ode' as European Anthem," ms., Music Department, University of Toronto.

[7]Clark, op. cit., pp. 13, 15.

GERMAN IDENTITY TODAY

Symbols of collective identity contain a mixture of national and international elements. In Britain and France traditional national and state identities are much stronger than in Germany, where collective identities have changed many times. In the decade preceding unification, for example, the Federal Republic was already commonly equated with Germany. German receptivity to ambiguous identities that incorporate new, internationalized forms is arguably greater than that of the British or the French. Klaus Goetz argues that "the Europeanisation of the German state makes the search for the national, as opposed to the European interest, a fruitless task. The national and the European interest have become fused to a degree which makes their separate consideration increasingly impossible."[8] The fact that Germany's Europeanization serves Germany's broad interests reinforces the important point that, far from undermining national interests, institutions are of critical importance in helping shape the conceptions of interests that inform policy in Germany and elsewhere.

Between 1949 and 1990, Germany's division and European integration were closely connected in a cold war setting. Within the context of the United States security guarantee for West Berlin, the Federal Republic, and Europe, West Germany's integration into Europe was, in Germany and in Europe, a calculated reaction to the disastrous consequences of Germany's bid for European and global supremacy in the first half of the twentieth century. The gradual fading of these memories and the sudden end of the cold war posed once again the issue of how a united Germany should relate to Europe. The answer, before and after 1989, was the same: through European integration.

Institutional politics in the EU mediates German power. Rare in contemporary Europe is what Simon

> *Germany's approach to European institutions since the 1960s has been based on a broad definition of European identity.*

Bulmer calls "deliberative" power, a direct international projection of German interest and power, as, for example, in the rules for the European Central Bank.[9] The Bundesbank's high interest rate policy soon after unification was instead an instance of "unintentional power" that had strong effects on Germany's neighbors. The economic consequences of German unification thus illustrate how Germany exercises power not so much strategically as by its sheer weight. Finally, what matters most often is Germany's "indirect institutional" power. In shaping the rules of the game Germany tends to mobilize a bias favoring its policy in the long term. Indirect power eventually translates into regulative power.

Indirect institutional effects derive partly from similarities. For example, multitiered governance arrangements are typical of the EU and Germany. To be sure, the European version of "cooperative federalism" resembles Germany's only superficially. The EU lacks an accretion of power at the top; the importance of legal institutions in the EU is due to the weakness, not the strength, of the state administration; the EU commands only a small fraction of the financial resources that are at the disposal of the German government; and the EU's Commission does not have access to a field system of administration. More important, enveloped by strong legal institutions, both the EU and Germany have multitiered governance arrangements that institutionalize consultative bargaining and consensual decision-making procedures between different centers that are jointly involved in deliberation, decision making, and implementation.

It is noteworthy, Jeffrey Anderson has argued, that German political elites embraced the European Community initially as a means of reestablishing Germany's national sovereignty.[10] Subsequently, Germany used its sovereign power to project onto its European partners a markedly different, internationalized state identity. The signing of the Maastricht treaty, however, may have been a high point of Germany's internationalization. This is illustrated by the increasing importance of the *Länder* for some policy issues and by the limits that the German Constitutional Court's 1993 judgment imposed on possible future constitutional reforms of the EU.

Since the mid-1960s, Germany's internationalist orientation has been reflected in its consistently strong support for successive enlargements of the

[8]Klaus Goetz, "Integration Policy in a Europeanized State: Germany and the Intergovernmental Conference," *Journal of European Public Policy*, vol. 3, no. 1 (1996), p. 40.

[9]Simon Bulmer, "Shaping the Rules? The Constitutive Politics of the European Union and German Power," in Peter J. Katzenstein, ed., *Tamed Power: Germany in Europe* (Ithaca, N.Y.: Cornell University Press, forthcoming 1997), chap. 2.

[10]Jeffrey Anderson, "Hard Interests, Soft Power, and Germany's Changing Role in Europe," in Katzenstein, op. cit., chap. 3.

EU. In the late 1950s and early 1960s, Chancellor Konrad Adenauer and Economics Minister Ludwig Erhard were still divided over the benefits of a "smaller" Europe, integrated around Germany and France, and a "larger" Europe more loosely structured to include Britain and most of the other European Free Trade Association members. But since then Germany has been a strong supporter of enlargement: British, Danish, and Irish accession in the 1970s; Spain, Portugal, and Greece in the 1980s; and the proposed eastern enlargement of the EU by the end of the 1990s. Put differently, in line with the internationalization of the identity of the German state after World War II, Germany's approach to European institutions since the 1960s has been based on a broad definition of European identity.

Unification has had noticeable effects on Germany's European policy. Underneath the "soft" power of institutional politics, newer, "hard" economic interests in the area of regulative politics express serious internal resource scarcities. These interests are beginning to supplant older, "hard" political interests that had aimed at the general stabilization of Germany's external environment.

Jeffrey Anderson notes that since 1992, the German government has tended to look much more closely at the bottom line, paying more attention to who gets what. This is not surprising. Germany is the largest net contributor to the EU budget, both in absolute and in per capita terms. While unification has made Germany drop from second to seventh in per capita income among EU members, its net contribution has increased from $6.3 billion in 1987 to $13.2 billion in 1992. It is estimated that it will rise to $18 billion by 1997. In 1993 and 1994, a German household with four members paid about $1,200 annually for the EU, more than the special solidarity tax levied after unification. By 1996 the leaders of all the major parties in Germany agreed that Germany's financial contribution to the EU amounted to about two-thirds of the EU's net income, while the German GDP made up only one-third of EU countries' total GDP; Germany's annual excess payment of about $9 billion, they said, would have to stop.

This shift reflects new conditions at home and abroad and increases the weight of short-term interests in German policy. The issue that is likely to reflect this new condition most clearly is the eastern enlargement of the EU. Germany favors enlargement more strongly than any of the other main EU powers. But for enlargement to work, the EU and

Germany will have to allocate additional funds. Considering Germany's budgetary and economic difficulties after unification, playing the role of Europe's paymaster will become increasingly difficult. Enlarging Europe to the east and paying off the southern European countries, which worry over a shift in the EU's funding priorities, will seriously test established patterns of conducting political business in Europe. German budgetary conditions thus are likely to dictate the pace and direction of Europe's future enlargement. This change in Germany's traditional stance will rob the European polity of a traditional shock absorber.

The Europeanization of Germany during the last 40 years has been furthered greatly by a transformation of the country's nationalist and neo-Nazi right. The dynamics of party competition in the Federal Republic, reinforced by the electoral strategy of the Christian Democratic Union/Christian Socialist Union, led in the 1950s to the gradual absorption of a traditional nationalist protest vote by refugees and former Nazis into a staunchly anti-Communist conservative camp that favored European integration. The revival of a neo-Nazi right in the mid-1960s was no more than a brief interlude. The alarming increase in the 1990s of neo-Nazi social movements, such as the skinheads, with their xenophobic and racist violence has had little resonance among the established political parties and major institutions in society. After Chancellor Kohl reacted to these attacks with a thunderous silence, they were countered by a largely spontaneous social movement and an eventual crackdown by the *Länder* governments.

Finally, it is a happy accident of German history that the party of postcommunism, the Party of Democratic Socialism, absorbs in the five new German states not only the votes of old Communists but also most of those who normally would vote for a protest party on the right. Thus, despite extraordinarily high unemployment rates and totally disorienting changes, a nationalist right has been unable to attract sizable popular support in the new eastern states of the Federal Republic. History, institutions, strategy, and luck have left Germany with an extreme right that is weak, if measured by the standards of other European states such as France, Belgium, and Italy. This has enhanced the trust of other European states in German politics and policies. And it has created space for an expansion of the international elements that have gradually become part of the identity of the German state. Hence, developments inside Germany and in

Europe have run parallel, not just in terms of government policy and market transactions, but also in terms of identity and political interests.

GERMANY'S NICHE

"Europe" stands not only for the institutionalization of human and democratic rights, but also for a substantive commitment to human welfare in capitalist markets. For this the Germans have coined the term "social market economy."

Nowhere has the power of this European identity been more evident than in Germany. The unification process illustrated that collective assertion had given way to individual entitlement. Sensing this momentous change, Chancellor Kohl did not promise Germans what the Bundesbank experts were telling him to expect: blood, sweat, and tears. Instead, he promised German voters business as usual: national unification without individual sacrifice. Combined with a firmly anchored welfare state identity, this nationalism of individual entitlement typifies not only Germany but all Western European states.

The process of a Europeanization of state identity has been considerably weaker in France and Britain than in Germany. British Prime Minister Margaret Thatcher's persistent public opposition and President Mitterrand's wavering covert opposition to German unification in 1989 are a reflection of this important fact. But it was France, not Germany or the smaller European democracies, that had accelerated the European integration process in the 1980s. Once it recognized that national strategies were becoming too costly, France turned toward Europe as the most promising way to defend a redefined, more international identity. Put bluntly, France became prepared to sacrifice a measure of control in Paris in expectation of gaining new instruments of control in Brussels. France thus has begun to follow Germany's postwar foreign policy strategy: seeking to regain national sovereignty through international integration. The end of the cold war and German unification reinforced Germany's traditional and France's newly found stance. Hence the Single European Act, the Maastricht treaty, and moves toward the creation of EMU were carried by a strong French-German consensus on the advantages that derive from a more international definition of state identities and interests.

In contrast to France, Britain's relationship to Europe has been more distant. Britain's traditional identity as a global power and a victor in World War II has made it harder to accept descent to the position of an important medium-sized state in Europe. Britain's special partnership with the United States retains a strong hold over British policy, reflected in adamant opposition to a common EU security and foreign policy. The Europeanization of British identity is also undercut by the traditional British role of playing one European state off against another from a position of splendid isolation. And British politicians are deeply committed to maintaining national sovereignty and protecting Parliament's role as the guarantor of British democracy. Furthermore, many of Britain's economic interests remain global (direct foreign investment and financial services), are totally separate from the EU (oil, which the EU imports and Britain exports), or are a source of profound financial and political irritation (agriculture). For many reasons Britain's relationship to Europe has remained awkward. In short, France has sought to strengthen existing state identities within a supranational framework. The United Kingdom's half-hearted commitment to Europe stems from the fact that Europe substitutes for the diminution of a global rather than the enhancement of a national role.

By contrast, Germany and some of the smaller European states have embraced Europe as a means of strengthening and projecting existing state identities. "[F]or many states," Brigid Laffan argues, "there has been a high degree of compatibility between the national project and European integration."[11] This difference in orientation is reflected in and reinforced by an internationalization of Germany's position in European and Atlantic institutions that is more far-reaching than France's or Britain's. France has become a strong supporter of European integration while taking a cautious attitude toward NATO and the role of the United States in European defense matters. Britain is deeply divided over the issue of European integration but remains an avid supporter of NATO. In contrast to Britain and France, Germany's position has been to further political integration in Europe, specifically by enhancing the power of the European Parliament and extending the principle of qualified majority voting. And Germany has not lacked fervor for NATO. As Ronald Asmus noted in the April 22, 1996, *International Herald Tribune,* the first post–cold war survey of the German elite showed that "today's German leaders are overwhelmingly

[11]Brigid Laffan, "The Politics of Identity and Political Order in Europe," *Journal of Common Market Studies,* vol. 34, no. 1 (March 1996), p. 87.

pro-European Union and pro-NATO, strongly favor enlargement to Eastern Europe, are sober about Russia's future, and are increasingly willing to deploy the German army under a NATO flag in 'out of area' missions to defend common Western interests."

German political controversies concern which international context to choose: the United Nations for peacekeeping operations, as the center-left prefers, or NATO for peace enforcement, as the center-right advocates. That the context for military action must be international is, however, beyond dispute in Germany. This is true neither of the unabashedly realist approach with which Britain seeks to defend its national sovereignty against an encroaching EU nor of the instrumental-institutionalist one with which France seeks to defend national interests with supranational instruments. Only Germany is a strong supporter of both the EU and NATO and appears ready to push ahead with a deepening institutionalization of Europe. Germany, writes Elizabeth Pond, "is thoroughly European in a way that none of its allies yet is. Germany is increasingly comfortable with its role as a medium-sized power. It no longer aspires either to be a big, cuddly Switzerland abstaining

---

12Pond, op. cit., p. 38.

from Europe, or [to gain] more global reach. It has found its niche."12

GERMANY INTERNATIONALIZED

Our initial question—will Germany dominate Europe or Europe Germany?—does not point simply to converging or crosscutting political processes that one can analyze solely in terms of material or bargaining power. The domination of one state by another and the coordination of conflicting objectives of different governments occur frequently in the European polity. But these interactions acquire different meanings in different historical and institutional contexts. And those contexts have changed greatly since 1945 as the identity of the German state has been internationalized.

Analyses that focus on the importance of material or bargaining power fail to recognize how institutions have softened the effects of German power in Europe. In brief, we need to think not of Germany *and* Europe but of Germany *in* Europe. Since the European polity offers a familiar political stage, it is highly improbable that German political elites will any time soon turn their backs on European institutions that have served so well the interests that motivate German policies at home and abroad. Germany in Europe is a political fact that will continue to define the international and national politics of the new Europe.

The shadow of Weimar

*German politics,
once reassuringly
boring, is
becoming less
predictable*

WEIMAR, in the east German *Land* of Thuringia, has taken a few knocks since the days of Goethe, Schiller and Mendelssohn, but its beautiful historic centre is now being expensively rebuilt in preparation for its turn as "European City of Culture" in 1999. These days, it prefers to dwell on its artistic rather than its political past. When in 1919 the German National Assembly moved to the city, away from the pressures of Berlin, to adopt a new constitution and found a republic, disaster soon followed. The "Weimar Republic" eventually disintegrated, its parties splintering to provide kindling for Hitler's Third Reich.

Mutterings of "Weimar" can occasionally be heard as Germany's post-*Wende* party landscape becomes ever more complex and less predictable. Since the second world war, west German politics had been remarkably straightforward; some would say downright boring. Power alternated between two big parties, the conservative Christian Democrats (together with their Bavarian arm, the Christian Social Union) and the left-leaning Social Democrats. Both share a commitment to a market economy softened by generous welfare programmes. The Free Democrats (liberals), habitually needed as a coalition partner, made sure that the left did not become too hostile to enterprise, and moderated the right's cultural conservatism. From time to time outrigger parties popped up, but they rarely won seats in the Bundestag (federal parliament), thanks to a rule—designed to prevent Weimar's fatal fragmentation—that requires any party to win at least 5% of the national vote before it gets any seats. Over the past decade or so the Greens have established themselves as a potential coalition partner. But on the surface, the big picture has remained much the same.

Even unification has not so far upset party allegiances. In the last federal elections before unity, in 1987, the ruling Christian Democrats and their Bavarian allies had won 44.3% of the votes in West Germany. In the first pan-German elections to the Bundestag, in 1990, that share dropped only marginally for Germany as a whole, and in the 1994 federal elections it slipped a little more, but the Christian Democrats still held on to power (see table 1). And even the latest polls suggest little change from the 1994 position, except that the Greens are doing somewhat better. Ask any German to tell you, honestly, whom he expects to win the next federal election in 1998, and he will say "Kohl" or, if the prospect does not please him, "*wieder der Dicke*" (the fat one again).

Last month Helmut Kohl, after 14 years in office, overtook Adenauer as the longest-serving postwar German chancellor, having survived mixed fortunes and plenty of banana skins with guile and near-perfect political pitch. His finest hour came in 1989 when, against all odds, he was presented with the opportunity to unify Germany and had the guts to grab it. Although the prize turned out to have more flaws than first suspected, that moment marked him out as a statesman rather than just another politician, and ensured his place in the history books. Despite the current disenchantment with unification, it also made him the best vote-catcher the Christian Democrats have got. After the 1994 election he hinted that he did not want to stand again in 1998, but he seems to have changed his mind, perhaps because he wants to add European unification to his shelf of trophies.

No eastern promise

For all Mr Kohl's electoral success, his party, like all the other western parties, lacks *Ostprofil* (a profile in the east). Moreover, its decision at the time of the *Wende* to take in the former GDR's Christian Democrat "block party", which had invariably done as the communists had told it, was widely criticised. But at least the Christian Democrats avoided the fate of the Social Democrats who, with few members and little organisation, managed to collect less than one-quarter of the vote in the east in the first post-unity elections.

The liberal Free Democrats started off well in the east in 1990 but were massacred there in 1994. Even for Germany as a whole, they are now, as so often before, too close for comfort to the 5% threshold below which political oblivion lurks. Dropping below it would mean losing their role in government and the handsome ministerial posts (including foreign affairs and economics) that come as part of the package. Their considerable consolation is that when their prospects have looked bleakest in the past, they have always been rescued by a sophisticated German electorate prepared to vote tactically in order to preserve them. Those voters might come to their aid again.

The Greens, founded in 1979, are younger than the mainstream parties. They, too, have had ups and downs since unification, but are now enjoying a renaissance. In the 1990 election they lost out heavily in both east and west, but in 1994 they recovered almost to their pre-unity level in west Germany, though their support in the east—after a merger in 1993 with the eastern Alliance 90 (B90)—remained thin. Their main handicap there is a climate in which jobs have become much more important than environmental scruples. They are beginning to heed that message. Since their pragmatists prevailed over their "fundamentalist" wing in the early 1990s, the Greens have shed their

Spot the difference German federal election results, % of votes cast 1

Party	1987*	1990 Eastern	1990 Western	1990 All Germany	1994 Eastern	1994 Western	1994 All Germany
CDU/CSU	44.3	41.8	44.3	43.8	38.5	42.1	41.5
SPD	37.0	24.3	35.7	33.5	31.5	37.5	36.4
FDP	9.1	12.9	10.6	11.0	3.5	7.7	6.9
Greens/B90	8.3	6.0	4.8	3.8	4.3	7.9	7.3
PDS	–	11.1	0.3	2.4	19.8	1.0	4.4
Others	1.3	3.9	4.3	5.5	2.4	3.8	3.5
% poll	84.3	74.5	78.6	77.8	72.6	80.5	79.0

Source: Bundeswahlleiter   *Western Germany only

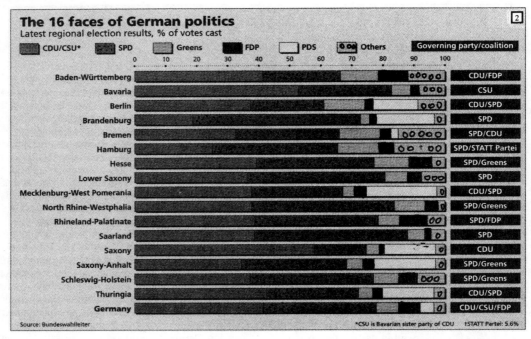

The 16 faces of German politics
Latest regional election results, % of votes cast

CDU/CSU* | SPD | Greens | FDP | PDS | Others | Governing party/coalition

	Governing party/coalition
Baden-Württemberg	CDU/FDP
Bavaria	CSU
Berlin	CDU/SPD
Brandenburg	SPD
Bremen	SPD/CDU
Hamburg	SPD/STATT Partei
Hesse	SPD/Greens
Lower Saxony	SPD
Mecklenburg-West Pomerania	CDU/SPD
North Rhine-Westphalia	SPD/Greens
Rhineland-Palatinate	SPD/FDP
Saarland	SPD
Saxony	CDU
Saxony-Anhalt	SPD/Greens
Schleswig-Holstein	SPD/Greens
Thuringia	CDU/SPD
Germany	CDU/CSU/FDP

Source: Bundeswahlleiter   *CSU is Bavarian sister party of CDU   †STATT Partei: 5.6%

loony-fringe image and become eligible as a coalition partner. They have already had plenty of experience in coalitions at local and regional levels, and are now looking for a federal "red-green" coalition after the next election. Even the Christian Democrats, it is thought, are eyeing the Greens as a possible future partner. Joschka Fischer, one of the party's parliamentary floor leaders, says it has "grown up".

The Party of Democratic Socialism (PDS), successor to the GDR's old communist party, has, by contrast, been radically downsized. From more than 2m in its monopoly days, the party's membership has shrunk to a mere 120,000. Most members are ageing leftovers from the communist party. But the PDS, known as the "Red Socks", is a rallying point for disgruntled and disadvantaged voters who in 1994 pushed up its share of the poll in the east to almost 20%. Although it still failed to clear the 5% hurdle nationally for lack of votes in the west, it bagged 30 seats in the Bundestag because it won a handful of eastern mandates outright.

The ideologists are now pondering the uses to which the party should put its new-found strength. Lothar Bisky, the party's smooth-talking parliamentary leader in its regional stronghold of Brandenburg, thinks that it should widen its appeal to win a couple of million voters in west Germany to lift it above the 5% limit. But what will its platform be? The party is still searching, he says. One model it is watching with interest is Britain's Labour Party (though the Social Democrats seem closer to sharing Labour's pink-tinged centrism). "We are not an ideological party, and we don't want the past back. But nor do we want a society where people have to use their elbows," says Mr Bisky.

Old-hand analysts reckon they have seen it all before. When west Germany's Refugee Party was founded in 1950, it attracted strong support from the millions of Germans who had moved in from further east. In the 1953 election it gained 27 seats in the Bundestag. But by 1957 its supporters were already being absorbed into mainstream German life, and by the early 1960s it was a spent force. Might the PDS go the same way? Possibly; but the worse the economy does in the east, the better it will be for the party.

Never the same again

Even if it does not, German politics is unlikely to return to its former idyllically predictable state. Even before unification, things were changing below the surface. Voters were getting fed up with the political process, and disenchanted with the way politicians looked after their own. They were becoming less loyal to the old parties and their ideologies, and more inclined to suit their own narrow interests. They took to changing their minds easily and often. Support for the old alignments was crumbling, and new alliances were emerging. Politicians were having to become more flexible, more prepared to strike compromises. Unification strengthened and hastened those trends.

Look away from federal politics for a moment to see how much has changed already. Chart 2 above shows the most recent election result and the political complexion of the regional government in each of the 16 *Länder*. This is where federal politicians traditionally cut their teeth. Ten years ago eight of the 11 West German *Länder* had single-party governments, and two had a coalition between one of the major parties and the Free Democrats. Now, out of the 16 all-German *Länder*, only five are governed by a single party, and in two of those, Brandenburg and Saxony, one-party rule is due to the extraordinary popularity of their respective premiers, Manfred Stolpe and Kurt Biedenkopf. The rest is a confusion of coalitions: four "red-green" ones between Social Democrats and Greens (one, in Saxony-Anhalt, made possible by the tacit support of the PDS); four "grand" ones between Christian and Social Democrats; and a handful of other permutations. Is that the sound of splintering in the air?

Perspectives on the German Model

Germany
Is the model broken?

Germany's social-market system—which has delivered enviable stability and prosperity for decades—is in worse shape than it looks

COUNTRIES around the world are seeking to reform their welfare states and deregulate their economies in the face of international competition. In most, success, where it has come, has been bought only at the cost of considerable social disruption. Last winter, France endured weeks of public-sector strikes and even riots in response to the government's plans to reduce public spending in line with the Maastricht criteria for economic and monetary union. In the 1980s, Britain faced even more turbulence (including a year-long miners' strike) as Margaret Thatcher's government pushed through deregulation and sharp public-spending cuts. Now, Germany is taking its biggest step yet down this road.

Helmut Kohl has proposed public spending cuts amounting to DM70 billion ($46 billion) next year alone, the scrapping of antiquated laws controlling the energy market and a modest liberalisation of the country's notoriously restrictive shopping hours. As thousands took to the streets in protest on May Day, the Chancellor must be hoping that the opposition will ebb away and that his country's much-admired consensus model of government—a system that encourages co-operation between parties, federal and local governments and trade unions and bosses—will enable Germany to reform itself smoothly, as it has done in the past.

Over the past five years, Germany has coped with the largest external shock any western country has faced for half a century: the incorporation, in a single blow, of 16m people with an average standard of living only one-fifth that of the rest of the country. Despite the gigantic bills of unification—in 1995 gross transfers to the former East Germany totalled DM200 billion—inflation was kept in check and GDP grew by an average of 1½ a year in 1991–95. This was slightly above the European average and more than Japan's growth.

But, though the model coped with unification well, that event still hit the system hard. On many measures, the economy has been lagging behind for a decade and a half: business productivity, for example, has grown by less than half the industrial-economy average since 1979; exporters have lost market share for nine of the past ten years. Now, according to the six big economic institutes, growth this year will be a mere 0.75%. Manifestly, considerable change has been possible within the existing model. Indeed, it was possible without the basic components of the system changing much. But what has happened is that unification has brought to the surface faults in the German model which were always there, but would otherwise have taken longer to become evident.

How it works

At the heart of Germany's distinctive "social-market economy" is a system called *Mitbestimmung* (or co-determination): by law, employees have half the seats on large companies' supervisory boards, the top governing bodies which hire and fire senior managers. This is part of a network of arrangements which both foster close ties between workers and managers and encourage a distinctive form of corporate governance: firms and banks own shares in each other, thus minimising the ownership-dispersing effects of stockmarkets and shareholders. The political counterparts to these economic arrangements are a highly decentralised federal system which gives extensive powers to 16 *Länder* (states) and a consensual form of politics in which decisions are taken—as far as possible—with the tacit support of the main parties, the Christian Democrats and Social Democrats.

Despite the shock of unification, the system survived virtually unscathed. The main parties' policies were closer after 1990 than they had been for many years. There was some tinkering with the arrangements that link workers and managers, but the workers' supervisory role remained untouched and most wage settlements were reached in the traditional manner—by agreement between established unions and bosses' organisations which applied not to individual firms but to whole industries. The federal arrangements underwent expansion, not reform: the new states were added to a largely unchanged federation.

To its supporters, the model does not merely allow change to occur; some argue that it helps reform to happen more smoothly, more predictably—and hence more effectively—than under adversarial systems. Because political parties eventually converge on one course of action, that course can be fixed more securely than in a confrontational country, such as Britain or America, where the possibility of policy reversal is greater. As a result, markets operate within a more stable framework.

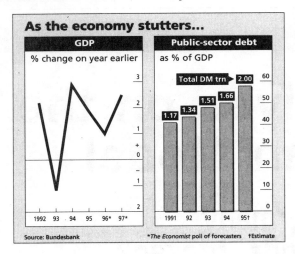

As the economy stutters...

GDP — % change on year earlier — 1992 93 94 95 96* 97*

Public-sector debt — as % of GDP — Total DM trn 2.00 — 1.17 (1991) 1.34 (92) 1.51 (93) 1.66 (94) (95†) — 60 50 40 30 20 10 0

Source: Bundesbank

*The Economist poll of forecasters †Estimate

So Mr. Kohl and his supporters are seeking to justify the government's new package by saying it is not an attack on the system, but a necessary measure to preserve it. "One cannot live beyond one's means", the chancellor told parliament. "If we do not act now, more jobs will disappear. Then welfare would be unfinanceable."

The reforms, as befits a consensual country, seek to spread the load evenly between the federal government, local governments and the social-security system. Some cuts threaten comfortable German ways and look a little like robbing the overfed of their third plum pudding; others affect the jobless and the sick. They include:
- A fall in unemployment benefits;
- A reduction of sick pay from 100% to 80% of basic wages;
- The limitation of state-subsidised cures at healthresorts—spas, beaches, moor and mountain retreats—to three weeks every four years instead of the present four weeks every three years;
- The postponment of a previously-agreed 10% raise in child benefit;
- A gradual rise in the retirement-age for women from 60 to 63 years starting next year, and for men from 63 to 65 from 2000;
- The removal from holiday pay of regular overtime earnings, hitherto included; and
- The removal of job-protection guarantees for firms with 10 or fewer employees.

When the government began this latest round of public-sector reform with a get-together of ministers, unions and bosses in January, Günter Rexrodt, the economy minister, said with pardonable pride that "there's bitter conflict over this sort of thing elsewhere, and here everyone gets together with the chancellor and we find the right direction." But the sheer size of the welfare reform suggests that, this time, something new is

happening. Far from smoothing the needed changes, the German model may be being tested to destruction by them.

Broken or chipped?

If implemented in full (admittedly a big if) these spending cuts would be equivalent to 2% of GDP next year. That is a huge sum, comparable to Margaret Thatcher's fiercest years. In contrast, the controversial "austerity" plan in France cuts public spending in real terms barely at all. Admittedly, welfare reform is not special to the German model: it is high on the agenda of other rich countries too. But because generous welfare payments help give everyone a stake in the system, and hence buttress consensus, it is hard to unravel the welfare state without affecting other parts of the consensual system too. Chancellor Kohl swears that he is determined to defend both—but the sheer scale of the welfare reform suggests that the cost of maintaining the wider system is rising to levels previously unheard of in Germany.

At least as important as the scale of the cuts is the manner of proposing them. Mr. Rexrodt's self-congratulatory comments came after a first meeting of ministers, unions and bosses. But by the time Mr. Kohl got round to unveiling the proposed reforms to parliament, negotiations with the unions had been broken off. The government nevertheless decided to stick its neck out and proposed the whole programme to parliament. Hence the outcry from Germany's powerful unions and from the Social Democratic opposition. "Socially obscene . . . merciless," they cried. "A declaration of war on social justice," said Oskar Lafontaine, the Social Democratic leader. Even within the governing coalition, half a dozen supporters, both Christian Democrats and liberal Free Democrats,

have balked at the plan. This is not the first time the government had gone out on a limb over an issue, but it is extremely rare for a step of this magnitude to be taken by the government alone.

So, paradoxically, in the name of preserving the model, the government has already dented two parts of it—the political-party consensus and the extensive welfare state. That alone might not be enough to make the whole system unravel. After all, there has been political conflict before, and the welfare state, which expanded hugely after the late 1960s, was not part of the original postwar model. The trouble is that the model has since developed in such a way that each part reinforces the others. Political consensus, for example, has been possible partly because, since the co-determination system helped defuse conflicts between managers and workers and the federal system lessened disputes involving regions and the centre, national parties were able to operate within a relatively narrow range of opinion. As a result, as one bit of the model goes awry, so could the rest.

Workers v managers

It is one element of the rest—the contract between capital and labour—that is now coming most under strain. Take the labour side first. Despite having increased productivity in 1992–94, German workers are not so much more productive than their fellows in Poland or Japan that they can justify the world's highest labour costs.

Some of the biggest companies are expanding their production abroad and the small and medium-sized companies that are Germany's manufacturing backbone are following suit, lured especially across the border in central Europe, where wages are around a tenth of domestic levels. This might not matter if new investment were flowing in. But foreign firms are also reluctant to set up in high-wage Germany, while local ones are investing mainly in labour-saving technology. Western Germany has shed more than 1m workers in the past four years; last year, the country invested DM37 billion more in direct investment abroad than foreigners invested in the country.

Germany's unemployment level—at over 4m, it has reached its highest since the frightening 1930s, though remaining far smaller as a percentage of the workforce—is something that affects the model directly, in a way that even the financing crisis of the welfare system does not. This is because the link between managers and workers lies at the root of the whole system. Already, union power is eroding because unions speak for a shrinking share of the population: in 1995 membership of the German Trade Union Federation dropped by 3.9% to 9.4m. In addition, if the labour laws are making workers too expensive and inflexible, and if they are preventing people being priced back into work, then something has gone wrong at the heart of the model. In that sense, unemployment is a measure of the model's failure.

Now employers are demanding not just pay restraint but fundamental changes to the collective-bargaining system, under which wages and conditions are set by industry associations on behalf of employers and by unions on behalf of workers. Most managers still accept the principle that basic labour contracts should be negotiated collectively. But they want these general agreements to specify little more than basic wages and working hours. Everything else would be negotiated between individual firms and their workers, who are usually more pliant than the trade unions that represent them. They would decide, for example, how to distribute work across the week. Firms also want permission to pay less than the basic agreed wage in times of hardship, demanding, in effect, an escape clause from the basic contract that would be almost unheard-of in western Germany.

Some companies are not waiting for new contracts. Daimler-Benz, Germany's biggest industrial conglomerate, has insisted on introducing Saturday working at some of its factories, even though its labour contract rules this out; its workers, desperate to stop Daimler from moving their jobs abroad, have agreed. Following the government's decision to chop sick pay from 100% of a worker's wages to 80%, employers are eager to redraft their own labour contracts along similar lines.

Moreover, managers are busily undoing some of the distinctive features of German corporate governance. Traditionally, German finance directors worried first about pleasing their banks and only second about delivering profits to shareholders. But now, with firms competing globally for capital as well as for markets and production sites, finance directors must measure the performance of their firms' shares against those of competitors worldwide. Shareholders no longer cool their heels while the chairman entertains his bankers; now they walk straight into the chairman's office. The fad for "shareholder value" is bring-

...labour pays the price

Unemployment — Trade union membership — Labour costs

Sources: Bundesbank; DGB; Morgan Stanley; EIU   *March

ing to Germany capitalist trappings that arouse resentment even in less egalitarian countries. Executives are starting to award themselves share options (the better to align their interests with those of shareholders); the stockmarket is booming; and companies are adopting new Anglo-American accounting standards that rip away the veils that once shrouded their profits.

In these circumstances, the new economic package represents a further and possibly decisive tilt in the balance of power between workers and managers. The government is proposing to let firms with ten employees or fewer sack workers easily (raising the threshold from five). Conceding business's long-standing argument that high taxes kill jobs, Mr. Kohl's fiscal package includes the abolition of a tax on capital and the reduction of one on profits, which finances mainly local governments. These cuts, admittedly, are to be financed by cutting tax breaks for depreciation (which could make investment even less attractive). But the government has made clear where its heart lies by proposing the abolition of a "wealth tax" on business.

System failure or system reform?

Despite the changes that are starting to transform the nature of Germany's contract between unions and labour, it would be wrong to assume that every component of the German model is now doomed to radical transformation. For one thing, other parts of the system have changed comparatively little. Despite the emergence of new parties such as the Greens and the former communists in the eastern states, the two larg-

est parties retain their traditional hold over electors' loyalty: the ruling Christian Democrats and the opposition Social Democrats continue to attract around 70% of all voters between them, roughly the same share as before unification. There is no sign of any sort of big political realignment.

For another, the government may well not command enough parliamentary support to ram its reform plans through over opposition from the SPD and from some of its own hesitating supporters. The coalition's majority in the lower house of parliament is only ten, while the SPD dominates the upper house (whose assent is required for some, though not all, of the reforms). It is a good bet that the government's proposed assault on the welfare state will be softened when it comes to a vote. In addition, one-third of the total spending cuts are supposed to come from a public-sector wage freeze—which the unions are unlikely to accept without a fight.

That said, it is clear that Germany's post-unification period is over and is giving way to change. Reform has begun and, at least in worker-manager relations, is likely to be deep. What remains in doubt is whether the changes will produce a new version of the model, better adapted to the next quarter-century, or whether the whole system will buckle under the strain of reform and end by producing in Germany a version of the Anglo-American model of capitalism, with its adversarial politics, and its red-in-tooth-and-claw economics. If the government and the companies have their way, the outcome is more likely to be a renewed, more flexible model. If the opponents of reform block real change, they risk the entire system unravelling.

★★★★★★★★★★★★★★★★★★★

The German Welfare Model That Still Is

Despite the Talk, Social Responsibility Remains This Country's Reigning Principle

Peter Ross Range and Robert Gerald Livingston

Peter Range is a freelance writer who has covered Germany. Robert Livingston, a former U.S. diplomat in Germany, is chief development officer at the American Institute for Contemporary German Studies at Johns Hopkins University.

AS AMERICA debates the fundamentals of its welfare state—Medicare, Aid to Families With Dependent Children, Social Security and health care—the example of Germany looms in the background.

Trashing the German economy, the world's third-largest, has become editorial blood sport. The New York Times op-ed page proclaims "The End of Germany's Economic Model"; Newsweek offers dire discourse on "the German disease"; and the Wall Street Journal calls Germany a "Failed Model." Washington Post columnist James K. Glassman, looking for a cudgel with which to fail the Clinton administration and this year's minimum wage hike, cavalierly dismissed the German model and all its works—national health care, guaranteed pensions, the uniquely successful vocational training system—as an outright "failure."

Is the German economic model, the so-called social market economy and its attendant welfare state, really dead?

Hardly. The political agenda of some commentators has edged out accurate reporting. True, Germany has been through a bad patch lately: double-digit unemployment, stagnant growth, lagging foreign investment, record bankruptcies. Germans are rightly worried about global competitiveness when wages and benefits make their manufacturing costs the highest in the world. And it's true that the German welfare state's generous benefits have outrun the economy's ability to pay for them and must be trimmed.

Those issues are being fought out in the parliament.

But reports of the imminent demise of the German system are not only premature—they are wrong. They ignore Germany's continuing high performance by most long-term indicators, its successful shouldering of the gigantic burden of absorbing East Germany, the solid and long-standing support it enjoys among Germans and the advantages it has brought not only to workers but to business.

Seen over time—the only reasonable way to judge comparative performance—Germany's economy is not in as bad shape as some argue. It certainly has not been seriously enough wounded to discredit the social market model that has guided Germany for the last 47 years.

Over the last decade, the German economy has performed as well as ours or better. Germany's real annual growth between 1986 and 1995 was 2.7 percent; that of the United States, 2.3 percent (over a 20-year period, the United States was marginally ahead). Germany's annual productivity gains over the past 10 years outpaced America's, 3.6 percent to 2.7. Still more striking was German superiority in the measure that truly counts in business—unit labor costs (the cost of labor per unit of output). Germany's grew by a mere 2 percent in the past decade, America's by 3 percent. Germany remains, by far, the world's leading exporter on a per capita basis—$4,950 in 1995. Germany's lead is unchallenged by America, with exports of only $2,240 per capita, or even by mighty Japan, with $3,530 per Japanese.

Still, Germany's recent mini-recession and swollen social costs have sparked a long-overdue national debate about reforming the system. Even though the latest indicators show that the downturn is already over and predict 2.6 percent growth in 1997, the long-standing consensus among labor, management and government, a pillar of the social market economy, is being tested by a $33 billion "savings package"—cutbacks in the welfare system—proposed by Chancellor Helmut Kohl. Kohl wants to knock total government spending down from 50 percent of gross domestic product to 46 percent, where it was in 1989, just before German unification.

These austerity measures were largely prompted by the huge and unexpected cost of unification, not the failure of the social welfare system. Since 1990, the German government has transferred more than $500 billion to formerly communist eastern Germany—more money in constant dollars that the United States transferred to all of Europe during the three years of the Marshall Plan. The costs of unification compounded the need for reform.

But reform is hardly rejection. "Restructuring, not destruction," is the name of the game, Kohl has announced. In fact, the changes Kohl envisions are laughably marginal by the standards of Ronald Reagan or Margaret Thatcher.

Under the proposed reforms, for instance, some workers would receive only 80 percent of their salaries, instead of 100 percent as is the case now, for the first six weeks of sick leave. Government insurance-paid visits to German's bucolic spas—where one takes the waters, breathes deeply and applies sulfurated mud to ailing body parts—would be reduced from four weeks every three years to three weeks every four years. The retirement age would be raised, after the turn of the century, from 63 to 65 for men and from 60 to 65 for women.

Workers in the smallest firms would lose job protection.

What Kohl is *not* doing is uprooting the social contract. Rather, he is seeking changes within the accepted framework of the German *soziale Marktwirtschaft*—best translated as a "socially responsible market economy." This is Germany's version of capitalism with a human face, a free market economy with a heavy emphasis on social equity.

The real key to understanding the German model is the word *sozial*. Germans use it to express a sense of society's underlying interconnectedness and mutual obligations. It is rooted not simply in the altruistic belief that the strong should help the weak, but in the self-interested conviction that the strong won't thrive if too many of the weak fall by the wayside.

Indeed, society's responsibility for all its citizens is built into Germany's legal definition of itself. "The Federal Republic is a democratic and socially responsible federal state," says the constitution's very first line after its bill of rights. The welfare of the society as a whole is con-sidered key to the success of the individual, not the other way around—communitarianism versus individualism on the American model.

This powerful ethic fosters consensus, relative equality of incomes and wealth, and social peace. Even Germany's most profit-minded industrialists believe this consensual approach is good for business. Jurgen Schrempp, the aggressive CEO of Daimler-Benz, Germany's largest conglomerate, made precisely this point in June to a New York audience of Wall Street fat cats. "The emphasis on social stability has paid off for us," he reported; " . . . the German system of a cooperative approach . . . based on consensus [has been] a guarantor of everybody's fast and steadily growing prosperity. . . . The German consensus system should under no circumstances be abandoned."

And it won't be. The recent experience of the powerful public employees' unions, representing 3.2 million workers, is a case in point. After throwing a few rhetorical tantrums over Kohl's proposed social welfare cuts, and calling out 350,000 demonstrators for a Sunday walkabout in Bonn to show a little muscle (no striking, please; we're Germans), the unions and the government sat down and did what they have always done: compromised in the interest of the commonweal.

The unions agreed to a mere 1.3 percent wage increase over the next 20 months, which is the functional equivalent of nothing since it's less than the rate of inflation. The Kohl government, in turn, backed off its plans to trim health insurance benefits right away and increase working hours. Consensus prevailed. The model worked.

Those who use Germany's current belt-tightening as proof of the blanket failure of the socially responsible market economy are grinding an ideological ax: the belief that the American model is the only one that works. They underestimate how committed most Germans—including Kohl's conservatives—are to their model. Worse, they mislead readers who deserve an accurate portrayal of how other countries cope with painful economic transitions.

✶✶✶✶✶✶✶✶✶✶✶✶✶✶✶✶✶✶

Bonn's principal policy headache

Labour in the east is more expensive than in much of the rest of the industrial world

Frederick Stüdemann

Six years after unification eastern Germany remains the principal policy headache for the Bonn government. Despite almost DM1,000bn of public money poured into eastern Germany since 1990, the region is still blighted with grave structural weaknesses.

Over the past year there has been a marked slowdown in the eastern economy. Government forecasts put growth this year at 3 per cent, down from 5.3 per cent in 1995 and 9.9 per cent in 1994. In the first quarter of this year growth actually fell, by 1.2 per cent, though this is seen as a result of a particularly harsh and long winter which af-fected the construction sector, the motor of economic recovery in the east.

Unemployment in the east is 15 per cent. If those people on government sponsored make-work schemes are taken into account then the proportion of people in the east without proper jobs rises to 25 per cent.

One of the main reasons for this bleak situation is the high cost of doing business in the east. In 1995 unit labour costs in the east were 31.2 per cent higher than those in western Germany. At the same time productivity in the east stood at only 55.2 per cent of that in the west.

Despite wages averaging 72.4 per cent of those in the west, labour in eastern Germany is now more expensive than in most of the rest of the industrial world. It is certainly considerably more expensive than labour in neighbouring Poland and the Czech Republic, countries which are attracting increasing numbers of German investors keen to escape high costs at home.

A further worry is that the Mittelstand, the swathe of small and medium-sized companies which in the west has typically been seen as the creator of economic success, has been slow to establish itself in the east.

According to the German chambers

of industry and commerce (DIHT) and the federation of German industry (BDI), two lobby groups which recently published a report on the Mittelstand in the east, companies in eastern Germany are hampered by inadequate equity levels, poor treatment from banks and late payment from the public sector.

A further concern was the small number of Mittelstand companies in the manufacturing sector. Of the 500,000 companies established since unification, only 14,000 are operating in the industrial sector.

These figures pinpoint one of the chief structural weaknesses of the eastern economy. According to government figures manufacturing accounts for 14 per cent of eastern German GDP, compared with 26.4 per cent in the west. This puts manufacturing below the construction sector which in the east accounts for 17.6 per cent of GDP.

The poor state of the eastern economy has prompted the government to accept that recovery in the east, to the point where it is self-sustaining, will take much longer than originally expected at the time of unification. And with that the need for public transfers to the east will remain for the foreseeable future. "We must prepare ourselves for a longer time-frame of around 15 years," says Johannes Ludewig, state secretary in the economics ministry and responsible for the eastern Länder.

But this poses an acute political problem for the government. Tightened budgets and rising unemployment across the country have dampened public support for the financing of recovery in the east.

Tax-payers pay a 7.5 per cent "solidarity surcharge" on their income tax for the east. Justifying this and measures such as the make-work schemes is increasingly difficult at a time when parts of western Germany, such as Bremen and Saarland, are also blighted with high unemployment.

Furthermore, the Bonn government must not only convince its own citizens of the need to continue subsidising the east. As the recent row over subsidies to an eastern German factory of the Volkswagen car group showed, Bonn must also argue the case with the European Union.

Such grumblings have not gone unnoticed in the east where the euphoria over the possibilities offered by unification has long evaporated. "Today, on both sides we think we know the quirks of each other very well. Yet who in the west knows that two-thirds of the people here feel themselves to be second-class citizens," says Eckhardt Rehberg, leader of the CDU in the state parliament in Mecklenburg-Pommerania, one of the poorest of the eastern Länder.

As such there has been a noticeable spread of nostalgia in the east. Whether this expresses itself in the choice of consumer products or in support for the reformed communist party, the Party of Democratic Socialism (PDS), the overall effect is the same: the wish to retain a sense of regional pride in a time of great upheaval and apparent steam-rolling by the west. "Our main problem is a mental one" says Rita Süssmuth, the president of the Bundestag, the parliament, and a westerner.

Overcoming this will not be a quick process. But there are areas where the government could have moved faster. Of the many federal agencies few have made the move east even though before the second world war many, such as the highest criminal court, were actually located there.

While this all makes for a gloomy picture, it would be wrong to overlook the very real benefits unification has brought to the east. Thanks to federal subsidies eastern Germany now boasts some of Europe's most modern infrastructure. Roads, motorways and regional transport systems have been overhauled. The telecommunications network, once a laughing stock, is now state of the art.

Such improvements have done much to remove the air of "wild frontier" from the east. Driving nowadays from west to east it is increasingly difficult to spot the former border which once divided the country.

This facelift operation is most apparent in Berlin where nearly all the important real estate and infrastructure development is taking place on the eastern side of the city. It is there where the mass of new office blocks, retail developments and hotels are being built. When the government arrives from Bonn—the move is forecast for sometime around 1999—it will spread itself largely in the centre of eastern Berlin.

Added to such concrete improvements come the benefits of no longer living under a dictatorship. In opinion polls the freedom of expression and the freedom to travel are regularly cited by easterners as the great benefits of unification.

GERMANY'S NEW FOREIGN POLICY

Looking Both East & West

Germany is a key foreign policy player in Europe today. Its aim is to repeat the brilliant post-World War II improvisation that brought prosperity and peace to Western Europe and do the same for Central Europe in the post-cold war world.

ELIZABETH POND

Elizabeth Pond is co-author of The German Question and Other German Questions, *published in the U.S. by St. Martin's (1995).*

Even more surprisingly, perhaps, both the German political class and representative allied governments in the United States, France, the Netherlands, and Poland basically approve of Bonn's chosen role.

At the beginning, everyone lamented, all the challenges came too soon, before the new Germany was ready for them. First, the Gulf War caught Bonn off guard within months of unification and added an unwelcome $10 billion bill to the $100 billion the western Germans began pouring annually into their new eastern half. For its part, the huge cost of resuscitating eastern Germany sucked German capital away from the rest of Europe, and along with the Bundesbank's insistence on suppressing inflationary pressure from so much liquidity helped worsen the whole continent's cyclical recession.

Simultaneously, Yugoslavia dissolved into war, and Bonn responded to the carnage and Europe's impotence by forcing its allies to recognize Croatia. Bonn's hope was that if the civil war became an inter-state war, this would legitimize outside involvement on behalf of the victims of expansionist Serbia.

The conjunction of the three issues dismayed a number of Germany's allies, however. Few went as far as Irish diplomat Conor Cruise O'Brien (and, by extension, German novelist Günter Grass) in initially fearing that German unifica-

tion could lead to a nasty "Fourth Reich." But many British and some French saw in the actions a new readiness to throw German weight around—or even to revive 19th century spheres of interest.

That was then, however. Now is now. With intervening cyclical growth, the Bundesbank's single-minded fight against inflation ceased to distress non-Germans quite so much (and despite today's record unemployment, the pendulum has not yet swung back fully). Then with Washington's re-engagement in the Yugoslav issue, Bonn was able to defer to American leadership and revert to a low profile in the Balkans.

Besides, in the meantime Germany's old taboo in sending the Bundeswehr outside NATO territory has been replaced by a consensus that it's more moral to stop local bullies by force than to condone them by peaceful inaction. Four thousand German soldiers are currently serving in NATO's Implementation Force (IFOR) in Bosnia and Croatia; allies' resentment of what was often seen before as German freeloading in security matters has correspondingly diminished.

European friends still complain about assertive Germans from time to time as their particular corns get stepped on. But fundamentally German foreign policy is now seen as benign, and the Germans are recognized as the continent's most post-national citizens and the staunchest proponents of European integration.

It might well be argued that united Germany's new policy, when cast against West Germany's pre-1990 policy, exhibits as much continuity as innovation. What clearly has changed a good deal, though, is Germany's authority in implementing this policy.

Thus, Germany's two top priorities remain the same: keeping the US engaged in Europe and pressing for greater European integration. Its two new additional goals—drawing the emerging democracies of Central Europe into the Western European clubs of prosperity and security and convincing Russia that its loss of empire does not shut it out from Europe—follow from the first.

The precept of keeping the US active in Europe is just the reverse of the estrangement that various commentators expected once the Soviet forces withdrew from Central Europe and Germany no longer needed Washington's nuclear guarantee against the Eurasian superpower. Yet it is plainly in Bonn's interest. At a psychological level, American involvement assures other Europeans that they will not be left alone with the powerful Germans. Conversely, it also assures the Germans that they will not be left alone with their sometimes parochial European friends.

More concretely, American leadership and hardware—in airlift, real-time intelligence, and the painstakingly constructed integrated military NATO command—are as needed as ever in a safer but less predictable post-cold war Europe.

Germans welcome a continued US lead in dealing with Yugoslavia and other tough problems that the Europeans have not been able to sufficiently resolve on their own.

Washington reciprocates the cordiality. A Democratic administration no longer uses the vocabulary of a Republican president in describing Germany as its "partner in leadership." Nonetheless, that phrase accurately describes the substance of its relationship with an ally that often shares America's foreign policy preferences, especially in enhancing stability in Central Europe and the former Soviet Union.

Germany's companion precept—for Chancellor Helmut Kohl this is an article of faith—is "deepening" the European Union while the present international fluidity still permits and before new rigidities set in. "This is the prime European mission for our entire generation," a senior German diplomat says in explaining the obsolescence of the lone-actor nation-state in an independent world. "We must create a new security and economic architecture for all of Europe. Such an historic chance doesn't come often. And if we fail for lack of a serious effort and give in to nationalism and protectionism, coming generations will never forgive us."

To accomplish this mission, Germany relies now as before on the driving force of its "alliance within the alliance" with France, despite the difficulties of French adjustment to the enhanced power of a fully sovereign, united Germany. The relationship was strained with the election of Gaullist Jacques Chirac as French president in 1995. Like his predecessor, however, Chirac ultimately concluded that he has no alternative; France could never influence a go-it-alone German giant, but it can have an impact if Germany is bound (as today's Germans wish to be bound) to an increasingly integrated Europe. Chirac therefore accepted the cost of painful domestic fiscal discipline today in order to achieve monetary union with Germany tomorrow. Unlike his predecessors, he also accepted the corollary—to the relief of the Germans—of the French rapprochement with NATO.

On the new precept of bringing Central Europe into the Western European community, Germany was virtually alone

in the early 1990s in saying that "deepening" of the European Community was not only compatible with "widening" it, but complementary. Admitting the new democracies as members would not paralyze the European Community, Bonn maintained, but would force it to make necessary changes in reducing national vetoes on common action and (in whispers) cutting exorbitant farm support.

Partly through sheer repetition from the nation that is still the paymaster of Europe—and from German cultivation of the European enthusiasts in the small Benelux countries—this view now prevails in the EU. A little noted sign of the acceptance of German leadership in the transformation of Europe and the EU has come in the recent full normalization of German-Dutch relations after decades of intimate economic cooperation but Dutch resentment of Germany from World War II.

Certainly in the East, Germany is viewed as the Central Europeans' window to the West. Bonn prodded its allies to issue a written promise of future membership for qualified Central European candidates and has pushed the opening of the European market to prospective members. Prior to membership, it has also gotten Central European heads of government admitted as regular observers at EU summits. And bilaterally, united Germany and Poland—the largest and economically most dynamic country in the region and the one that suffered the most dead proportionally in World War II—have finally copied French-German postwar reconciliation to establish exemplary relations.

Germany's fourth precept—avoiding making a pariah of Russia on the disastrous pattern of post World War I treatment of the Weimar Republic—might eventually engender quarrels with its allies as assessments diverge. So far it has not done so. Russian President Boris Yeltsin calls Kohl his best Western friend, and Kohl implicitly gave him a boost toward this summer's presidential election by visiting him in February. He also promoted Russia's recent admission to membership in the Council of Europe despite the country's tarnished human rights record in Chechnya.

Fully as important to Bonn as its allies' acceptance of German foreign policy is the domestic backing for this policy. Here too, a broad consensus reigns. After the Constitutional Court in 1994 conditionally sanctioned dispatch of the Bundeswehr outside the narrow NATO area, enough Social Democratic and Green members of the Bundestag approved the current Yugoslav operation to give Kohl a large parliamentary majority for German participation. And on what may be the most controversial element of policy, European Monetary Union, it appears that all the relevant politicians basically favor the step, despite widespread public opposition.

The full test of the still developing German foreign policy, of course, will be the outcome of the EU intergovernmental conference this year and next and of monetary union and admission of Central European members to both the EU and NATO in the early 21st century. Bonn must back its "soft power" or agenda-setting and steady persuasion along the infinite EU networks with enough of its political and economic clout to force decisions. Yet it must not exert so much pressure that it revives nightmares of that disastrous German past.

It is a self-imposed task that calls not only for Prussian principle, but also for French finesse.

"Legislative elections must take place by 1998 and, based on current trends, [President Jacques] Chirac could lose his majority in parliament. . . In the wings are politicians who have made distinctly anti-Maastricht and anti-EMU noises. Will Chirac try out 'another politics' to save his majority? Is there another politics?"

Chirac and France: Prisoners of the Past?

GEORGE ROSS

President Jacques Chirac's long body and tobacco-tuned voice are familiar, yet he has always been a puzzling man. Likable, with huge reserves of energy, Chirac enjoys chatting, eating, and drinking with ordinary people and is also a connoisseur of Asian art. As mayor of Paris from 1978 to 1995, he helped his city become the renewed jewel it is today. Yet he has never seemed to know his own political mind. His opponents would be less delicate, contending that he has never been sure of his principles.

As a young man in the early 1950s, Chirac was on the left. Then he moved right to become a protégé of President Georges Pompidou. Still later he became leader of the neo-Gaullist Rally for the Republic, and donned President Charles de Gaulle's statist regalia. He changed into a Reaganite costume for his first run for president in 1981. As prime minister under President François Mitterrand from 1986 to 1988, he was a privatizer and deregulator. But when he ran for the presidency for the third time in 1995, he campaigned as all things to all people. He pledged to cut taxes, spending, and the deficit, to get the French economy growing again, and to bring unemployment down and create new jobs. He also denounced the monetarism, austerity, and muddling through of Mitterrand's last years.

And in the midst of an effusion of punditry about Gaullism's "social democratic" side, he pursued a populist hunt for disgruntled socialist and communist voters, denouncing the "fracturing" of French social life. He was studiously vague, however, about France's commitment to European integration.

When questioned about the clashing ingredients in this soup, candidate Chirac most often responded that political will could overcome all obstacles. But the question in 1995 was the same as it had always been: Which Chirac was the real one?[1] Two years later, that question remains unanswered.

THE MITTERRAND LEGACY

The legacy of François Mitterrand's 14-year presidency fell heavily on his successor, especially in economic policy matters. After his election in 1981, Mitterrand briefly tried to build "social democracy in one country" through planning, extensive nationalizations, reforms to strengthen labor in the workplace, and mild demand stimulation. This package quickly brought painful consequences. By 1983, Mitterrand, faced with a choice between pulling back from the Exchange Rate Mechanism of the European Monetary System to continue the left's experiment or hewing to Europe, chose Europe.

When the dust from this had settled, it was evident that Mitterrand was proposing a new "grand strategy" of European integration as a substitute for abandoned leftism. Changes in French economic policy toward austerity brought new convergence among the larger member states of the European Union (EU) that made possible the move toward the "1992" program to complete the Single European Market. Mitterrand thought that France stood a

GEORGE ROSS *is Morris Hillquit Professor in Labor and Social Thought at Brandeis University, senior associate of the Minda de Gunzburg Center for European Studies at Harvard University, and chair of the Council for European Studies. His most recent book is* Jacques Delors and European Integration *(New York: Oxford University Press, 1995).*

[1]Whichever Chirac the 1995 vintage was, he was elected president on May 7 against Lionel Jospin, a Socialist, with 52.6 percent of the vote.

good chance of being able to shape new European integration to its own advantage. The Germans could not dominate, given their history. The Thatcherite British liked 1992 because it was deregulatory, but otherwise were profoundly anti-European. The French had ideas, a strong military position, and a skilled administrative elite. With luck and shrewdness, 1992 would create an upward spiral of new European integration with France in the lead.

Mitterrand hoped for large domestic payoffs from this. A French-led crusade for European integration could restore French "grandeur." Nationalist pride, plus the possibility that the single market program might stimulate economic growth and job creation, could consolidate a new, more "modern" coalition around the left. The "Europe option" also had hidden domestic dimensions. France's companies, labor unions, and technocratic leadership caste needed to be shocked out of old statist and corporatist reflexes. Pooling new sovereignty at the EU level allowed Mitterrand to claim "Europe made us do it" when unleashing painful reforms. He could further argue that since salvation for France lay in new European integration, France's interests were ultimately Europe's.

In fact, returns to France from renewed European integration have been much less than hoped. After a brief boomlet in the later 1980s, growth slowed, unemployment rose, young people could not find work (and those who worked tended to hold temporary jobs), income and wealth inequalities increased, social services came under increasing pressure, public sector workers suffered from a tough incomes policy, and wages stagnated.

The "Europe option" was responsible for much of this dismal record. Insisting that the franc should become as solid as the German mark cost jobs and discouraged investment. Behind the strong franc commitment lay movement toward Economic and Monetary Union (EMU), vigorously promoted by Mitterrand and agreed to by EU leaders at Maastricht in 1991.

The French had long advocated monetary union with a single currency and a Euro-level "economic government" to set broader economic goals. At Maastricht, however, the Germans were not eager to consent to the large sacrifices that these proposals implied (losing the mark, relinquishing control over European monetary policy) without eviscerating the "economic government" aspect, thus leaving central bankers, especially German ones, at center stage. The Germans also insisted on stringent "convergence criteria" for preparing EMU—very low inflation, interest rates, budget deficits, and debts plus currency stability. EMU thus would be committed primarily to strict price stability. The French, however, ended up caught in their own maneuvering. EMU, in French minds, was designed to wrest some monetary control away from the Bundesbank to allow Europe as a whole, and France in particular, to pursue more expansionary policies. Instead, EMU became a new device for the Germans to make everyone else followed their deflationary lead.

CHIRAC INAUGURATED BY THE STREETS OF PARIS

France was unhappy with the economic situation in 1995 and tended to blame European integration for its difficulties. This, plus the clear responsibility of the Socialists for the economic problems, dictated Chirac's populist promises about reflation, growth, and job creation, along with careful handling of European integration and EMU

Getting elected was easier than governing. The legacy of Mitterrand's "Europe option" was an albatross. The Maastricht EMU convergence criteria stretched out in front of Chirac well through the first half of his term. France's budget deficit was considerably out of line. A significant part of this deficit problem came from annual red ink in various social security accounts. Chirac had fudged these issues during the campaign, announcing repeatedly that "politics is not the art of the possible; it is the art of making possible what is necessary." But in power his choices were more difficult. Continuity dictated moving toward EMU, which France's technocratic elite wanted. Making France's economic life less arduous was what the people wanted, however. Continuing austerity and unemployment would be no more popular than welfare state cuts, although both seemed necessary for EMU. If Chirac slipped on these matters there were other, much less delicate "national populists" like Jean-Marie le Pen of the National Front waiting to capitalize.

Chirac's first months in 1995 were marked more by a buccaneering style in foreign policy than by biting economic policy bullets. Resuming nuclear testing in the South Pacific in time for the fiftieth anniversary of Hiroshima was an exemplary touch, even though it was tied to the modernization of French defense operations. Chirac then startled the usually staid Group of Seven meetings in Halifax, Canada with his direct, even indiscreet, way of speaking. And he concluded what had been a dismal French presidency of the EU Council of Ministers at the Cannes summit in June with loud complaints against Italian monetary policy. He also busied himself, rather more productively, promoting enhanced Western action on Bosnia (which, to Chirac's chagrin, United States President Bill Clinton cashed in on at Dayton). This frenzy of action was vintage Chirac, trying to establish himself as a worthy successor to de Gaulle.

While the new president paced world stages, he confided domestic policy to Prime Minister Alain Juppé. Juppé was a model French technocrat. Well-trained and highly skilled in the administrative arts, Juppé was heralded as a good choice. Juppé's real assignment, like that of all first prime ministers in a French presidential term, was to promote difficult policies and act as a lightning rod to protect Chirac—a lightning rod that could be removed when it came time to prepare for the 1998 legislative elections. Thus it was surprising that Juppé, amid multiple declarations about "reform," a "general mobilization against unemployment," and a "new Republican pact" to liberate France's *forces vives* made few extraordinary moves. Subsidized programs to soak up youth unemployment, new efforts to seduce employers to hire more workers, raising the minimum wage, and promises of tax cuts were all déjà vu, at best gentle attempts to prod economic recovery by pumping up consumption.

What was going on? First, Chirac could not turn to harsh new austerity measures immediately because he had run promising the opposite. He and his prime minister may also have believed that they could muddle through without major new cuts. The Germans would call the shots as EMU approached, and it was conceivable, given their eagerness for European integration, that they might soften the Maastricht criteria to make things easier for the French. Any such thoughts were dashed completely after Chirac met Chancellor Helmut Kohl at Baden-Baden at the end of October 1995. Kohl was firm: France was not to sabotage movement to EMU through policy laxness. Chirac was thus put on warning about EMU; some kind of policy shift for the Chirac administration was inevitable, because the easygoing economics of its first months jeopardized EMU.

The Juppé government's first strong reform proposal focused on the social security deficits. The Juppé plan was a complex document. Introduced in mid-November 1995, the plan proposed cost-

controlling changes in health care, taxing family allowances, and obliging everyone, including civil servants, to contribute a full 40 years to their pensions before retiring. There would also be a broadening of the "generalized social contribution," a special tax to pay for social programs introduced by the Socialists in 1991. The final item was a 0.5 percent supplement to the income tax for 13 years to pay off accumulated social security indebtedness (estimated at $60 billion). The Juppé plan was thus not "Thatcherite" at all. Rather than cutting programs substantially, it raised taxes to make streamlined existing programs solvent. Even if it was not Thatcherite, the plan contained plenty to anger different groups. A politically skilled government would have been able to cope with this but, as it turned out, Alain Juppé's technical skills were not accompanied by political savvy.

Juppé suffered from a classic technocratic blindness. He believed that he was wise enough to judge what was best for the French people. He further believed that the people should then see reason and have the good grace to accept this judgment. Juppé was insufficiently attuned to the deteriorating situation of French workers. Austerity, unemployment, political alienation, and the strong franc policy had produced frustration. Given this, the prime minister made about as many mistakes as he could, threatening vested interests on several fronts at once and uniting groups that otherwise had differing interests.

Chirac's first months in 1995 were marked more by a buccaneering style in foreign policy than by biting economic policy bullets.

French labor unions are often inept, and always divided, but with the prime minister's help in creating a coalition of different groups of angry workers and bringing usually feuding union organizations together, they were able to lead the largest strikes in recent French history against the Juppé plan. The fact that most of the strikers took to the streets to protect their own special privileges—retirement at the age of 50 for railroad engineers, for example, or early retirement and lower pension contributions for civil servants, deterred no one. It took nearly five weeks, until nearly Christmas, to get things back in order.

The strike was a shock for the Chirac presidency. In the words of the December 9, 1995, *Economist,* "strikers by the millions, riots in the street; the *évènements* in France. . .make the country look like a banana republic in which an isolated government is battling to impose IMF austerity on a hostile population." The prime minister, dividing and ruling by granting separate concessions to particular groups—doing what he should have done before he started the trouble—managed to separate the railroad workers from the civil servants, then some civil servants from others, to restore order. He also managed to preserve space to continue most of his plan. But the cost in terms of lost production and budget shortfalls in social security savings was large. The Juppé plan had projected a reduction in the social security deficit from $13 billion to $3.2 billion in 1996 and eliminating the deficit altogether for 1997. In fact, the 1996 deficit will be about $10 billion.

Perhaps more important, the price tag of the prime minister's clumsiness meant that France made much less progress toward meeting the EMU convergence criteria than it should have. The clock was ticking toward the moment when future members of EMU would be decided: the Madrid EU summit in December 1995 decided that monetary union would begin in 1999 and that membership would be decided in 1998 on the basis of 1997 results. The Chirac administration had probably made the situation worse in its first few months than it had been under Mitterrand.

JACQUES AND ALAIN IN THE TRENCHES

By early 1996 it was obvious that Chirac's pledge "to create 700,000 new jobs by the end of 1996" had been a vote-hunting fantasy. In fact, new jobs were being created at an even slower rate than they had earlier. Moreover, unemployment, which had declined a bit with recovery from the 1993 recession, had begun to rise again. Finally, economic growth had turned out much slower than projected, partly because of the strikes. Both president and prime minister paid dearly for the strikes. Chirac's and Juppé's opinion poll ratings dropped precipitously (by the end of 1996, Juppé was the most unpopular prime minister in French polling history). The first few months of the new administration had clarified at least one thing, however. Jacques Chirac, whose "Europeanism" had been in doubt, would take the steps needed to bring France toward EMU.

From the EMU point of view, the first months of the Chirac-Juppé stewardship had been negative. Much work remained to be done. The budget deficit had to be cut from 5 percent of GDP in 1995 to 3 percent by the end of 1997, requiring draconian budget cutting and making growth and job creation impossible. While Chirac and Juppé could

have raised taxes, they had already done so on social security and, moreover, the president had pledged to cut taxes. There were precious few other ways to save money without cutting back on public services and employment. Long-term debt also had to be reduced, with similar implications. All this had to be undertaken in a setting where the Chirac-Juppé tandem had lost public support and in which labor relations were a ticking bomb. That real terrorist bombs had begun to go off in the streets, the products of Corsican and North African groups, raised the level of tension even higher.

The "hot autumn" of 1996 that many predicted did not occur, and the 1997 budget that appeared in September 1996 was a stern affair whose main goal was to bring down the public sector deficit to Maastricht's 3 percent target. It froze public spending at 1995 levels (amounting to an actual 1 percent cut that would cost many public sector jobs). Skilled accounting also found money hidden in the social security system, despite the failure of the 1995 reform. The government's most creative bookkeeping, however, involved a one-time $8 billion charge off (lowering the deficit by 0.5 percent by itself) from the state takeover of some of France Télécom's pension funds, connected with the utility's imminent privatization. Juppé also pledged to continue social security reform and announced that certain benefits would henceforth be taxable. The final item was a promise to lower national taxes in 1997, although this was really a decentralization of taxation to lower jurisdictions. In general, the budget made it clear that if there was a creative "third way" or "other politics" between a retreat from European commitments and EMU as a forced march toward lower growth and higher unemployment, the Chirac presidency did not know what it was.

The administration also had other economic policy difficulties. It had been agreed since 1986 that much of France's immense public sector would be privatized. This was not only because of the privatization fad that swept the world in the 1980s, but also because highly centralized coordination looked like an ever larger liability with globalization. French privatization, however, has always been handicapped by the ambivalence of French elites about genuine market liberalism. France has had statist, centralizing perspectives on economic life—along with almost everything else—since Louis XIV mobilized luxury goods producers to compete with English capitalism. The French have done what comes most easily to them, learning to "talk the talk" but not to "walk the walk" of contemporary neoliberalism, and their privatizations have often been financial operations in which political elites have made completely sure that new managers in privatized firms were "sure," that is, members of the technocratic caste in good standing. Privatization continues to be fraught with complexity because of this.

DOWNSIZING DEFENSE

Privatization was connected with another difficult dimension of Chirac's brief: reconfiguring French security policy. The end of the cold war left France with a bloated defense budget and arms sector and defense strategies inappropriate to the new setting. The arms industries had to be shrunk. Arms exports were declining, the Americans were becoming even more competitive, and French defense budgets were to be cut. It made sense to have a European perspective on such matters, but the rest of Europe could not be counted on to cooperate on French terms. French arsenals had to be downsized quickly and large nationalized defense contractors had to be privatized.

Reforming the defense industry was tied to more general defense reforms. Here Chirac proceeded with skill, announcing extensive changes in French security policy on February 22, 1996. France, following General de Gaulle's lead, had spent vast amounts building its independent nuclear deterrent, at the cost of neglecting conventional forces beyond those needed to keep order in France's former colonies in Africa. Chirac did not propose to change this basic policy. The *force de frappe* would continue to exist, but weapons programs and strategic plans that made little post–cold war sense would be abandoned. In a context of decreasing spending in general, resources would be shifted to an ability to project significant numbers of well-trained, equipped and supported troops abroad. Because this change in focus implied a smaller, professionalized volunteer military, the president also proposed ending France's long tradition of conscription.

Chirac's most important proposals involved moving toward full participation in NATO. These ideas were not greeted with howls of betrayal from Gaullists, however, because Chirac intended to redesign, rather than abandon, the Gaullist quest for defense autonomy. Mitterrand had begun the shift, hoping to use the West European Union

Mitterrand's "Europe option"... had, by 1995, structured President Chirac's world.

(WEU) to create a degree of new defense autonomy from the United States after the cold war. The Maastricht negotiations and the years following them had demonstrated clearly that the Americans were not eager to cooperate. Chirac thus shifted focus from the WEU to building a genuine, relatively autonomous (and French-led, if possible) European pillar in NATO; to this end he proposed the reintegration of French forces into NATO's command structures. In exchange Chirac demanded that NATO's southern command be given to a European. The Clinton administration was skeptical and Chirac was stymied at the end of 1996. Recent discussions with Germany regarding the development of a "Europeanized" nuclear force indicate, however, that his determination is strong.

THE RELUCTANT EUROPEAN?

The overarching priority for the first months of the Chirac presidency remained EMU. Chirac had never been an enthusiastic European and his conversion to EMU was a pleasant surprise for other EU member states, especially Germany. It also happened in the nick of time, because energetic preparations had to be made for France to meet the Maastricht criteria. The diplomatic side of these preparations involved a different kind of game from the domestic one. Only close Franco-German collaboration would make EMU possible, and there were disagreements between the two countries on the issues. The first of these involved relationships between those eligible for EMU membership in 1999 and those who would not be. The Germans favored a "hard core" EMU that would marginalize the outs somewhat. The French wanted to constrain the outs onto a path toward eventual membership, and sooner rather than later. The issue was settled in a preliminary fashion at Verona in April 1996 and Florence in June 1996 by a decision in favor of an essentially French proposal for a new Exchange Rate Mechanism to link the ins and outs. The outs would be granted a reasonable exchange rate margin for fluctuation around the new currency, the euro, to deter speculation, but they would have to come closer to the euro's value as they approached membership.

The December 1996 Dublin European Council took up the next problem, which was finding arrangements to keep the outs from exploiting EMU by running large deficits and other free-riding tactics. But because Italy and Spain now appeared to be among EMU's early members, negotiating emphasis shifted toward the arrangements for moving to EMU itself. The French had always wanted an "economic government" to gain influence over German monetary policy. The Germans, in contrast, wanted to lock EMU members into an economic policy that reflected German monetary policy goals, a stance that partly reflected worries about the credibility of the new euro between 1999 and the finalization of EMU in 2002.

German resolve was strengthened by the prospect of Italian and Spanish EMU membership, which might well tarnish EMU credibility. Equally important was mistrust for the French themselves. Kohl had much less confidence in Chirac than in Mitterrand. At the same time, there were strong preferences among Chirac's own followers for an "other politics" that would grant France greater policy space. Chirac's presidential campaign had played to this and there was support for it across the French political spectrum.

The Germans had other ideas. Theo Waigel, the finance minister, proposed a new "stability pact" whose central feature was automatic financial sanctions on any EMU member failing to keep budget deficits below 3 percent of GDP. The pact would have emergency provisions for recessions and shocks, but its logic was something akin to a "balanced budget amendment." What Waigel and Kohl wanted, in effect, were new rules and regulations that would continue the stiff pre-EMU convergence criteria well into the life of EMU itself.

The French, speaking for almost everyone else (except the Dutch), strongly opposed this and asked that judgments be made on a case-by-case basis. Kohl and Chirac discussed the issues twice prior to the Dublin summit and failed to agree. It took tough negotiations at Dublin to get a deal. The obstinancy of both sides—which made one insider feel "lost somewhere between the Elysée and the Black Forest"—was driven by the mutual skepticism of French and German public opinion about EMU. The deal reached was not as hard-nosed as the Germans had wanted, but was much more demanding than anyone else desired; EMU members could get off the hook of sanctions if their GDP began to shrink seriously because of recession (a relatively rare event).

Jacques Chirac, either reluctant or recent European (no one knows for sure), won a few concessions from the Germans, but lost what really counted. The French, long enthusiastic Europeans but more reticent in recent years (polls today give

slightly more than 50 percent support for EMU), found themselves bound to a future where their freedom would be extremely limited. Monetary union seemed likely to happen, therefore, after a long period of uncertainty, and Chirac was responsible in important ways for this. But it would enjoin rigid price stability and budgetary rectitude. For France there was no escape, barring some miracle, from continued high unemployment, low growth, and slow but sure erosion of the welfare state. The French electorate was entitled to wonder what had happened since the spring of 1995 when they had elected a president pledged to promote exactly the contrary.

THE GHOSTS IN THE CLOSET

The scene after François Mitterrand's death in January 1996 dripped with symbolism. The first Socialist president of the Fifth Republic had dominated French life for 14 years. What was most striking about these January days was how much Mitterrand had been able to control his funeral from the tomb. Mitterrand as president had been opaque, manipulative, and not always successful, and in his last years he had been surrounded by scandal. Yet the funeral arrangements were an architecture Mitterrand had designed to show himself as the devoted son of an eternal rural France, with one set of funeral operations in Jarnac, the town where his family had resided. He also managed to capture his original Catholicism by staging another, quite royal, event in Paris's Notre Dame, replete with cardinals presiding and the angelic singing of Barbara Hendricks. For days French television devoted itself to extolling Mitterrand's wisdom, statesmanship, and patriotism. All this was an achievement for a consummate Parisian, a cynical and secularized man of the left and a notorious womanizer (incredibly, Mitterrand also managed to have his longtime mistress and illegitimate child included in the pomp and circumstance). Mitterrand had no desire to leave to others the task of making his place in history.

From Jacques Chirac's point of view, this symbolism must have been profoundly disagreeable, not only because there had never been any love lost between Chirac and his predecessor, but also because it transcended Mitterrand's funeral. Mitterrand had also staged the priorities of his successor. Mitterrand's "Europe option," the grand strategy for renewed European integration set out in the mid-1980s, had, by 1995, structured President Chirac's world. Whatever Chirac really desired to do after his election—and it has never been easy to know what Jacques Chirac has desired to do—he was obligated to carry out an agenda that programmed France's basic options beyond the millennium, indeed through the end of Chirac's seven-year term.

By the time Chirac finally won the presidency on his third attempt, the choices were stark. EMU had to be pursued or rejected. Rejecting EMU risked blocking new European integration, perhaps for decades during which Europe might well be passed over by history. In addition, the Franco-German "couple," the bedrock of European order during the second half of the twentieth century, would face divorce. Accepting EMU was the more likely choice. But since Maastricht the processes leading to EMU had slipped away from French control. EMU, rather than a set of instruments to "co-manage" European economic policy with the Germans, subordinated others, including the French, to German policy desires.

The Maastricht convergence criteria, to which Mitterrand had agreed for the years up to 1999, and the "stability pact" that Chirac agreed to for the years after 1999, were a corset of longer-term economic constraints, limiting France's ability to promote growth and employment and obliging it to trim social programs. Even if Chirac had desired to reject Maastricht, the costs of this course to his new administration were too great to contemplate. The new president thus fell into line, as Mitterrand had known he would. When Chirac had served as Mitterrand's prime minister in the first experience of left-right "cohabitation" in Fifth Republic history, Mitterrand had manipulated him, outmaneuvered him, and ultimately humiliated him electorally in 1988. In 1995 Mitterrand had once again outmaneuvered him, this time with even greater consequences.

To be sure, there were other matters for Chirac to take care of, in his own fashion. He could, and undoubtedly will, continue to privatize, and this may turn out to be important. Privatization is not the same from country to country, and when a statist and dirigiste culture privatizes it is unlikely to mean, at least in the first instance, "liberalization." Thus far privatization in France has largely meant transferring public assets to the private sec-tor to be controlled by the same caste of technocratic managers. Turning French companies into globally predatory lean and mean multinationals without regard for their national homes is unlikely to happen without a genuine "cultural revolution," something the French have avoided so far, perhaps for good reasons. Similar thoughts would apply to deregulation as well. What would France be without statism, either formal or informal? And who is to say today whether or not reconfigured statism will be a viable solution?

Chirac can also try to strut on the international stage, Gaullist style. He has already begun, sometimes in quite interesting ways. His efforts in Bosnia, in the Middle East, and in the redefinition of NATO have been flashy, but have not led to much. Bosnia and the Middle East have proved beyond his capacities to shape, while playing tough with the United States on NATO has run up against Americans resolved to maintain their hegemony. The profound reform of French security policies that he is undertaking may give his country new capacities. Then again, it may turn out to be an acknowledgment of France's inability to be a frontline player in the world. In a post–cold war world there seems even less room to be a Gaullist in foreign affairs than there was during the good old days of the general himself.

Legislative elections must take place by 1998 and, based on current trends, Chirac could lose his majority in parliament. Jacques Chirac is a changeable character, as has been noted. There are no obvious rabbits to pull out of hats to make the French less morose or anxious in the near future. Firing Juppé will solve few problems. The French will want credible promises that things will change for the better. In the wings are politicians who have made distinctly anti-Maastricht and anti-EMU noises. Will Chirac try out "another politics" to save his majority? Is there another politics? Ultimately, his situation is not that different from those of other European leaders. EMU is unlikely to generate popular support. European integration, to ordinary Europeans, appears to be a machine for austerity and high unemployment that EMU may extend well into the next millennium. The deep political issues involved in this will not go away.

For France, Sagging Self-Image and Esprit

ROGER COHEN

PARIS, Feb. 10—When Bernard Liautaud started Business Objects, a software company, he applied a simple formula that he naïvely thought might stir the imagination and shake the torpor of this country: dump French habits and do things the California way.

The results were spectacular. Founded in Paris in 1990 with $1 million of venture capital, the company was worth close to $1 billion by early last year.

From the French business world there oozed a collective gasp. Such rapid growth in a country where fortunes tend to build over generations was unprecedented. Intent on understanding the upstart who had so quickly created 600 jobs and such wealth, President Jacques Chirac invited Mr. Liautaud to Élysée Palace.

The 34-year-old multimillionaire's pitch last July to the French leader was, he said, simple—a summary of the Silicon Valley mantra he learned while a graduate student at Stanford and applied at his company. Promote a shareholding culture. Think global. Think marketing. Lower taxes.

The President listened. But no changes to France's heavily regulated economy followed. And when Business Objects' shares fell recently because of delays in a new software program, there were some smug "I told you so's" from the Paris establishment.

Where other countries have embraced the global entrepreneurship that drives Business Objects, France tends to see its economy and very identity threatened by innovation— a mood that provides a perfect feeding ground for peddlers of zenophobia like the National Front party.

France today is racked by doubt and introspection. There is a pervasive sense that not only jobs—but also power, wealth, ideas and national identity itself—are migrating, permanently and at disarming speed, to leave a vapid grandeur on the banks of the Seine. Rapid technological innovation, radical strategic shifts, the Internet and the global market have contributed to an optimistic mood in the United States, as measured by the ever-rising stock market, an increase in jobs and public opinion polls. But these same forces have cast an onimous cloud here.

The old cultural antagonism between France and America, rooted in the fact that both countries aspire to represent some universal model, has been brought to a new level by the American victory that a market- and Internet-driven revolution are seen to represent. There are now regular snipes at America's "velvet hegemony." Profiting from this somber mood, the racist, extreme-right

National Front party of Jean-Marie Le Pen has swept to a series of victories in municipal elections, including the southern town of Citrolles on Sunday. It has gained support precisely by attacking globalization— portrayed as the death of national culture—and the high unemployment said to stem from untrammeled market forces and immigration.

With left and right, socialism and conservatism increasingly indistinguishable, the National Front has successfully contended that is the only group with a distinct message.

"If we want to send the Arabs and Africans and Asians back to where they came from, it is not because we hate them, it is because they pollute our national identity and take our jobs," said Bruno Mégret, the deputy leader of the party and husband of the new Mayor of Vitrolles. "When we have power we will organize their return. We will stop renewing their residence cards, and we will force companies to pay a tax on foreign workers that will eventually lead to the foreigners losing their positions."

Such statements have a widening impact. Over a third of French people now say they sympathize with at least some of the National Front's ideas. Even a large city like Toulon has been won. The party's effectiveness appears to reflect the simmering frustration of a France that has lost its way.

As Pierre Birnbaum, a political scientist, put it, "Our problem is that we have not found the way to modernize while preserving our imagined community." In other words, how do you leap into the age of the Internet and remain French?

The Breakdown
An Uneasy Society Haunted by Ghosts

France is still rich and it enjoys an importance beyond its wealth. Its nuclear bomb, its permanent seat on the United Nations Security Council, its central place in European security, its hold on the world's imagination through its wines, its perfumes and its cheeses, and its universalist pretensions themselves—all this carries weight.

The country has many excellent companies; the Bourse rose 27 percent last year. As its leaders never tire of repeating in these dark days, France is the worlds' fourth-biggest industrial power.

But France has a stagnant economy—growth was slightly more than 1 percent over the past year. Its unemployment rate has swelled to 12.7 percent, more than double the rate in the United States.

France's corrosive anxiety is captured by a line from Rimbaud—"nos horreurs économiques" or "our economic horrors"—that is now widely used. The horror is not merely economic. Rather, the phrase captures the extraordinary collective agnst of a people seemingly convinced that, as the philosopher Alain Finkielkraut simply put it, "There is a crisis of the modern world."

That crisis, as lived in France, is about cultural and political identity. Market reform, the global panacea, tends to leave the French cold. A hankering for grandeur—some reconciliation of poetry and politics—remains.

In the gathering debate between advocates of the untrammeled global market and those who argue that it accentuates social injustice, France tends to identify with the critics of globalization. Indeed, it increasingly seems to equate its welfare state with its very identity.

The obsession with identity is particularly strong because France is on the verge of two historical steps that critics equate with an abandonment of sovereignty. It is scheduled to adopt a European currency, the Euro, by 1999, thus yielding control over much economic policy; and it has indicated that it will return to the integrated military command structure of NATO, thus abandoning the most potent symbol of the Gaullist "non" to Washington.

Both moves, however, appear vulnerable to the present mood. "The French are confronted by a lot of changes," said a senior adviser to Alain Juppé, the Prime Minister. "Are they prepared to accept them all? France disappearing into the Euro, disappearing into NATO, at the same time as we demand more mobility, harder work and sacrifice? An upheaval cannot be ruled out."

France does not look prerevolutionary. The country's manicured capital, impeccable roads, high-speed trains, glorious food, seductive scents and deep-rooted savoir-vivre provide a compelling image of wealth and tradition. But just as the golden statuary on the bridges of Paris distracts the eye from the homeless sleeping beneath the arches, so the moving beauty of France trends to mask what amounts to a kernel of despair.

In Pantin, just a couple of miles outside the gates of Paris, there is a housing development called Les Cortillières, most of whose 5,000 inhabitants are immigrants from Algeria, Morocco and West Africa. Into such places are emptied the human flotsam who cannot afford life in the showpiece capital.

Almost 40 percent of the population is unemployed. Graffiti hurl insults at Mr. Juppé and the police.

Life begins in the afternoon because, for many young people, there is no reason to rise early. Drug dealers hang around in doorways. At the Jean-Jaurès High School, repeated scrubbing has not quite effaced calls to join the ranks of militant Islamic groups that have carried out recent bomb attacks in Paris.

"Some of these kids have never seen the Eiffel Tower," said Boris Seguin, a teacher at the school. "They live on the margins of the city and the margins of society. If the French republican model stood for one thing, it was integration through education. So you see here how the model is threatened."

Mr. Seguin recently completed a dictionary translating the language spoken in Les Cortillières into standard French. A conversation with Sabah Benmimouna, a teenage French girl of Moroccan descent, reveals that a "lascar" is a guy and "fatal" is fantastic. Boys talk of a "passeport" for a condom, "kiffer" for loving and "dunker"—from basketball—for smashing somebody. Several of these expressions would not be widely understood in central Paris.

The spread of alienated suburbs matters particularly to the French because the revolution and the republic—and their universal resonance—were about the equal rights of citizens.

Indeed, the schoolteacher was the model republican figure, the person who instruction turned waves of Italian, Spanish, Portuguese, Polish and other immigrants into French citizens.

That system now appears to be cracking, and its decomposition is evident in the Tours suburb of La Rabaterie—a drab expanse of crumbling five-story apartment blocks that make the nearby chateaus of the Loire appear infinitely distant. La Rabaterie was built, like many poor suburbs, by North African immigrants in the boom years of the 1960's. France was in the midst of what is now nostalgically recalled as "les trentes glorieuses"—the 30 glorious postwar years.

La Rabaterie now houses the jobless children of those Algerian and Moroccan workers. Unemployed kids chant rap lyrics like "What are we waiting for to light the fire; What are we waiting for to no longer follow the rules of the game?"

Here, on Oct. 23, 1996, a 22-year-old Frenchman of Algerian descent, Mohammed Boucetta, was found in a coma with a bullet in his head. That led to a series of events that illustrated France's current malaise.

Anger among Mr. Boucetta's North African friends that no assailant was arrested exploded into rioting; the rioting was then apparently compounded when agents from the National Front sought to exploit the situation to gain votes.

The unrest started a week after Mr. Boucetta was found. Shop windows were smashed. More than 40 cars were burned. The chaos lasted for four nights.

After the first night, tracts distributed by the National Front began to appear. Some, emblazoned with the party's torch symbol, attributed the vandalism to the "immigration policies" of governments of the left and now of the right.

"With us, foreign delinquents will be sent back to their countries and French people will have priority for jobs," one said. Others contained such messages as: "Why do rats wear roller skates in Tours? To clean out the garbage cans faster than the Arabs." Or: "What do you do when you see an Arab on a mobylette? Run after it because it's yours." These were found beside the National Front tracts, but without the party's symbol.

To one of Mr. Boucetta's friends, Youssef Sana, who is 27 and the son of immigrants from Oran in northern Algeria, there is no doubt that his friend was a victim of racist violence. "We are at war here in the suburbs," Mr. Sana said. "And we, the children of Algerians, are already losers. It's apartheid; we don't even figure in the system."

"If Mohammed were a white French boy, the case would have been solved long ago."

More than three months later, the police say the Boucetta case remains a mystery. But Michel Mesmin, a local municipal official, said it now seemed clear that if the first night of violence was a spontaneous expression of outrage from the youth's friends, the others were mainly the work of what he called "provocateurs" from the National Front. "The only thing that is really clear from all this," he said, "is we are an increasingly uneasy society, haunted by specters."

The Paralysis
Out of Touch and
Out of Ideas

The unease appears to be linked partly to the rigidity of a highly centralized system. France's superb technocrats, who planned and managed the country's remarkable reconstruction after World War II, appear overtaken by the global economy, ill-adapted by their formal training to its challenges. Its labor unions, parading the rags of an exhausted socialist dream, often seem equally fossilized.

Its political class is widely seen as a group of cloned eggheads—Mr. Chirac, Mr. Juppé and the Foreign Minister, Hervé de Charette, all went to the same elite school—out of touch with a population that consistently gives the President and Prime Minister approval ratings in the 25-to-30 percent range.

At the same time, because socialism was long the source of idealism in France—the sustenance of left-bank intellectuals and a strong labor movement—and that idealism was simply exhausted by the 14-year rule of François Mitterrand that ended in 1995, the country has found itself suddenly bereft of any meaningful ideological debate.

A slogan of Mr. Mitterrand's second seven-year term was "Ni-Ni"—neither nationalization nor privatization. It translated into internal paralysis. It appears that it may now take the French left several years to fashion a new message for the electorate.

France suffers in this void. It is a country traditionally driven by politics rather than economics; to be deprived of a political dialectic is as painful as being deprived of wine. "We have no more clear political markers," said Christiane Laporte, a headmistress. "We feel lost."

This sense of loss is evident in France's reluctance to adopt the new. It is a society where fewer than 15 percent of homes have personal computers and fewer than 1 percent are connected to the Internet, figures well below not only the United States but also France's European neighbors.

Opening the new national library in December, Mr. Chirac discovered the computer "mouse" for the first time and gazed at it in wonder. Mr. Chirac has spoken dismissively of the Internet as "an Anglo-Saxon network," although he did meet with Bill Gates this month.

It is not surprising, then, that Mr. Liautaud and his partner Denis Payre of Business Objects are scarcely national celebrities, in the mode of a Mr. Gates. Outside business circles, or the world of computer nerds, few people have heard of them.

Yet the extraordinary success of their company, which makes a software that sifts data in order to further corporate decision-making, has thrown a sharp spotlight on many of France's problems.

"What I realized in America was that there is a technological revolution going on," Mr. Payre said. "Today, I look at France—our great conceptual thinkers and lousy doers, our brilliant engineers and lousy marketers, our risk-adverse culture that if you fail once it's all over—and I wonder if we're not simply going to miss out on tomorrow."

In 1982 France began offering people video terminals that were connected electronically to a phone line, allowing the transmission of text and simple images. The system, known as Minitel, gave the country the lead in the race toward the information society. But it was never effectively marketed outside France and never taken much further. Today it is outdated.

Business Objects sought to build on this lesson. Rather than concentrating on the French market, it immediately sought to expand worldwide. Rather than relying simply on a good product, it opted for aggressive marketing. And in the place of the security of a state-owned job, it presented employees with stock options that gave them a financial stake in the company's success.

At the other end of the spectrum from Mr. Liautaud stands Lawrence Bricogne. At 30 he is four years younger than the entrepreneur, he has a qualification in computer sciences from a technical school but he has not worked for almost a decade.

He has a small Paris apartment bought for him by his mother, a piano, a television, a personal computer and an answering machine. He recently sold his car. Every month, like about one million other French people, he collects what is known as the R.M.I.—the acronym for the "minimum revenue for insertion." It amounts to about $400; it is what the French state reserves for those not receiving any other unemployment benefits.

"The R.M.I. allows me not to work," Mr. Bricogne said. "It's bizarre; it's probably unhealthy. Without the R.M.I., I would have taken a job some time ago—a night watchman, or a kitchen job in a restaurant. Something menial." Many artists in Paris who once, like George Orwell, did such jobs to survive now collect the R.M.I. instead.

This Rmiste (pronounced air-MEEST), as people like him are known, considered his situation and then added: "But I still prefer the

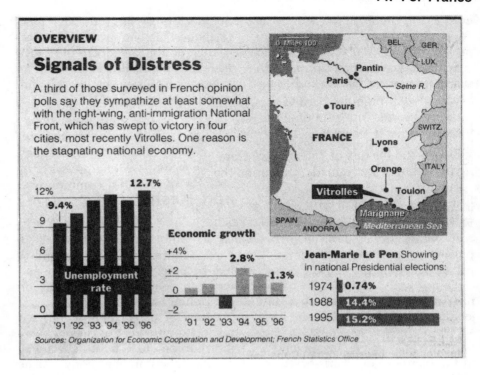

OVERVIEW

Signals of Distress

A third of those surveyed in French opinion polls say they sympathize at least somewhat with the right-wing, anti-immigration National Front, which has swept to victory in four cities, most recently Vitrolles. One reason is the stagnating national economy.

Unemployment rate: 9.4% ... 12.7%
12% 9 6 3 0 — '91 '92 '93 '94 '95 '96

Economic growth
+4% +2 0 −2 — 2.8% 1.3% — '91 '92 '93 '94 '95 '96

Jean-Marie Le Pen Showing in national Presidential elections:
1974 0.74%
1988 14.4%
1995 15.2%

Sources: Organization for Economic Cooperation and Development; French Statistics Office

French system to the American. Everybody envies us our social security."

The R.M.I. was introduced a decade ago. It was supposed to encourage the "insertion" into society of the jobless by committing people to prove they were looking, or training, for jobs. But Geneviève Monnot, who works with the unemployed at the Paris city administration, said only about 10 percent of Rmistes were certain to find jobs. "Many are now just too far from society," she said.

Mr. Chirac has recently tried to lay out a French "alternative" in which the energy of Mr. Liautaud and the solidarity that protects Mr. Bricogne are somehow married. Official calls for a more entrepreneurial spirit and streamlined state have been spiced with criticism of Anglo-Saxon "flexibility" in the workplace—deemed antisocial.

But this hodgepodge has fallen far short of the galvanizing message that French people habitually await from their leader in this, the most monarchical of republics.

It has left the country hurtling toward union with Europe even as a bloated state, overarching welfare, and cash-hemorrhaging state companies like Air France and the Crédit Lyonnais bank make the competitive demands of Europe and its German-dictated budget discipline hard to meet.

Since succeeding Mr. Mitterrand in mid-1995, Mr. Chirac has tried to battle the National Front by embarking on long-delayed reforms—of the army, the justice system, social security, pensions, state companies—that are designed to give the country new momentum and adjust it to the realities of the end of the millennium.

On a trip to Tokyo in December, Mr. Chirac spent his time hustling to sell everything from French apples to Airbus planes. For the man who personifies "La gloire de la France," it was a considerable step. Charles de Gaulle, who stood for a "certain idea of France," its civilizing mission and majesty, once dismissed the Japanese as transistor salesmen.

Times change. Gaullist grandeur no longer feeds the people. The numbers in France are not good; and capital and jobs, in the global village, are not much interested in a "certain idea of France."

France cannot afford its welfare state but is unwilling to abandon it. It has proved unable to create jobs even as the United States—for all its "downsizing"—has created over 10 million since 1993. But it is loath to ease the mandatory health and social security contributions that make hiring prohibitively expensive.

The minimum monthly wage here is about 5,000 francs, or $912, but after mandatory contributions for pensions, health coverage and unemployment benefits have been paid by employers and employees, it amounts to about 8,200 francs, or $1,518. Thus 36 percent of the wage cost comes from social insurance payments, compared with about 10 percent in America.

French and international companies, many of which can now shift jobs to Portugal or Indonesia, have shown a growing reluctance to hire, particularly as dismissing anyone is, in the words of one Paris-based international economist, "long, tedious and expensive."

The arithmetic of France's unrivaled social security net is also bleak. Already facing annual deficits of about $10 billion, the social security budget will face enormous pressure as the number of pensioners increases from 12 million to 17.3 million over the next two decades, while the active population scarcely grows, according to official forecasts.

Yet labor unions have recently suggested lowering the retirement age to 55 from 60, in line with a Government-sponsored settlement reached last year with striking truck drivers. They have also mounted a bitter attack on proposals to introduce American-style private pension funds, saying they will lead to a system "of every man for himself."

Similar resistance has met the beginnings of attempts to reform the cash-guzzling state that has inspired generations of French parents to dream of their offspring becoming

not doctors or lawyers but "fonctionnaires." Public spending here accounts for almost 60 percent of total national output, compared with an average of 40 percent in major industrialized countries.

The Crossroads
Sagging Energy and Hesitation

As its domestic woes have deepened, France's international policy has become more aggressive—and more strident in its aspersions on the United States.

Mr. Chirac has recently argued forcibly for the Euro as the only way for Europe to "fight effectively against American hegemony." As he has pressed—unsuccessfully—for French command of NATO's Mediterranean flank as a symbol of European emancipation from American military tutelage.

The impact of all this on French-American relations has been little short of poisonous. "They want an original foreign policy but they have recently gone a little overboard," said a senior American diplomat. "We have been through a trough, a very aggravated period."

France stands at a crossroads. Full NATO integration or the preservation of a uniquely French membership? Real market reform—privatization, private pension funds, a shareholding culture—or preservation of the highly centralized, state-heavy French welfare model? America as firm friend or threatening purveyor of an undifferentiated global culture? A European currently and a real commitment to building a federal United States of Europe or the temptations of the National Front's nationalism?

Hesitating before these choices, France quite palpably sags. To go to London or Berlin today is to feel how flat, how lacking in energy, Paris has become. The sense of living in a museum becomes almost tangible.

"We want to be an alternative, to show that if nobody resists America any more, at least we will," said the sociologist Jean Baudrillard. "The problem is that because we are not sure which model to embody, we tend to offer simply inertia."

What is left? Europe—and the extraordinary postwar French reconciliation with its old enemy, Germany. But this does not yet move the French as they want to be moved.

The yearning for some uplifting solution persists and makes France far less predictable than Germany or Britain, as the National Front's victory this weekend underscores. The country is deeply unrequited, susceptible to a political lurch. The republic was founded on ideas—"Liberty, Equality, Fraternity"—and the last two words retain a lingering resonance. Wealth, personal enrichment, is still considered a dubious measure of success.

Such views are unfashionable, feeble dikes to the global tide, but they are a deep part of French culture. Therein lies a profound problem: the distinctiveness of France no longer has much international resonance. Mr. Chirac said this month that France should be "exemplary," but candidates for its depressed example are hard to find.

"The ego is greedy, it needs to be nourished," said Marek Halter, a writer. "But the French ego is not being nourished these days. That is dangerous and that is why I feel that anything could happen."

Is Le Pen Mightier Than the Sword?

*Stock in France's popular hatemonger is rising and politicians
have no idea how to stop him*

Anne Swardson

Washington Post Foreign Service

PARIS

For more than a decade, mainstream French politicians on the left and on the right have struggled to figure out a way to deal with Jean-Marie Le Pen, the country's most popular hate-monger. Events of the last few weeks have demonstrated, analysts say, that every time the mainstream tries to squelch Le Pen and his xenophobic ideas, he just gets stronger.

His National Front party is more popular today than ever, and the other political parties are more flummoxed than ever about how to stop him. Le Pen is beginning to succeed in his effort to position himself as the only real alternative to the political establishment.

"We have made considerable progress," says Bruno Megret, general delegate of the National Front. "We have the capacity now to become a political party capable of rising to power. The tide is rising. It has not crossed the dike, but it is rising."

Le Pen's anti-immigration, anti-free-trade, law-and-order views garnered him 15 percent of the popular vote in the first round of last year's presidential election, and Front members last year were elected, and Front members last year were elected mayor in three French cities. Le Pen's support has increased since then.

Today, he is the politician of choice for one out of five workers, small-business owners and unemployed people. Fourteen percent of all French voters would cast their ballots for him today, according to polls, and somewhere between 30 percent and 50 percent of French people say they share some of Le Pen's views.

Le Pen also appears to be the favorite politician of animal-rights activist and former actress Brigitte Bardot.

In her recently published memoirs, Bardot wrote that Le Pen is "a charming and intelligent man who, like me, is revolted by certain things. On the terrifying surge of immigration, I share his views completely."

Those views: The 3 million or so legal and illegal residents of France who have come here from other countries, but are not citizens, should be deported immediately.

Other views: The lowering of world trade barriers should cease; such barriers should be strengthened in France; the European Union should be renegotiated to allow trade within Europe and raise high trade barriers against other countries; and American movies and other cultural products should be banned. Taxes should be reduced, defense spending increased and the death penalty reinstated.

The current round of controversy began early last month when Le Pen derided those who believe in the "absurd equality" of races.

The current round of controversy began early last month when Le Pen derided those who believe in the "absurd equality" of races. A week later, he said there was "evident inequality between the black race and the white race" because black athletes, he said, had performed better than whites during this summer's Olympic Games. He later said his point was that some civilizations were superior to others.

The response was clamorous. Le Pen—and political reaction to him—have been front-page news here for weeks. Justice Minister Jacques Toubon quickly announced he was preparing legislation to tighten laws against racism. Prime Minister Alain Juppe called Le Pen a "racist, antisemite and xenophobe." Le Pen snapped back that Juppe was a "criminal against humanity."

Ironically, Le Pen's political appeal is not so much among those who might believe races are unequal, a relatively small group. His supporters are those who say, as more and more do in economically troubled France these days, that immigrants are taking jobs and social benefits away from "real" French people and committing much of the crime.

"Every person who loses his job or his housing is a potential recruit for the National Front," says Mouloud Aounit, general secretary of the Movement Against Racism and for Friendship Between Peoples.

At the Front's national convention, one speaker after another emphasized the old-stock French nature of the movement. "When I walk the streets of my country I feel like a foreigner today," said one young speaker.

"The essential is not left or right, it's France. The rest is show business," said another, Samuel Marechal, Le Pen's son-in-law and head of the Front's youth wing.

Philip Breton, a municipal councilor and Front member, says Le Pen is just stating the truth. "What people feel is what Jean-Marie says," he says. "It is what people feel without wanting to say."

Many of Le Pen's positions concern issues on which the mainstream left and right are united in their opposition. The current Gaullist regime of President Jacques Chirac and the Socialist government under Francois Mitterrand that preceded it both favored open trade, European integration and military reform.

Recently the four major parties of the left—Socialists, Communists, Greens and an independent party—met and declared they would form a common front against Le Pen. And in regional elections two weeks ago, politicians from the left and right were quick to point out that Le Pen's candidates lost, in part, because voters from both ends of the political spectrum were united against National Front candidates.

In fact, analysts point out, that kind of voting puts Le Pen exactly where he wants to be.

Nothing makes the Front more appealing, they say, than the notion that it is the only party speaking against the political establishment and for the French people. The Front's campaign literature includes the slogan: "Neither left nor right. French."

Le Pen is a long way from gaining political power and probably never will. But his increasing strength not only has realigned the political landscape, it has influenced current government policies.

When French riot police in August stormed a church in which 300 immigrants from Africa had sought refuge to avoid deportation, officials were seeking to appeal to Le Pen voters.

And Le Pen has embarrassed the government, some say, into hasty action and bad legislation. The proposed anti-racism law, which will begin moving through the legislative process this month, allows judges to gauge intent when deciding whether speech or actions are racist.

Civil liberties groups fear Le Pen has pushed the government too far in restricting free expression.

"I think it's deplorable to pass a law in heat to respond to an event that has raised emotion. Laws of circumstance or exception are always bad laws," says Henri Leclerc, president of the League of the Rights of Man. "We must combat the ideas, not the man. It is his ideas that are dangerous."

Tocqueville in Italy

DAVID L. KIRP

MAKING DEMOCRACY WORK: Civic Traditions in Modern Italy. *By Robert Putnam. Princeton. 258 pp. $24.95.*

What makes a government responsive to the just wishes of its citizens? *Making Democracy Work* offers provocative and persuasive new ways to think about this ancient and pivotal political question. Political scientist Robert Putnam pays close attention to evidence—from historical accounts, personal narratives and survey data collected during a twenty-year experiment with local government—about how ordinary people's lives intersect with the power of the state. *Making Democracy Work* makes the past—a millennium's worth of the past—entirely relevant to today's headline stories. It takes up the classic chicken-and-egg puzzle of public life—does economic prosperity make *civitas* possible or is it the other way around?—and reaches conclusions that should prompt students of politics and economics alike to rethink their assumptions.

Seminal, epochal, path-breaking: All those overworked words apply to a book that, to make the point brazenly, is a *Democracy in America* for our times. But while Tocqueville drew his insights from a new nation famously experimenting

David L. Kirp is professor of public policy at the University of California, Irvine.

with representative government, Putnam has voyaged to Italy, perhaps the most unlikely place among Western nations to look for instruction in matters democratic. For nearly half a century in that country, coalition governments dominated by the Christian Democrats came and went with breathtaking speed, even as the very same politicians stayed on. And on— Amintore Fanfani, several times a prime minister and holder of innumerable Cabinet jobs into the 1980s, was a contemporary of Harry Truman. While the Christian Democrats were loved only by their families, they nonetheless regularly found their way back to Rome through the expedient of Communist-bashing. When the Socialists became a politically credible force, they too styled themselves as an alternative to the evils for which Communism stood. Always the Communists were in opposition.

In the aftershock of the end of the cold war, these arrangements started to collapse; keeping the Communists out of the government was no longer a rationale for ruling. Early in 1992, some brave Italian magistrates began poking around in the dustbins of national political life. While the investigations initially concentrated on petty misdeeds in Milan, the sweep of the corruption unearthed by Operation Clean Hands was stunning: Boatloads of politicians, Christian Democrats and Socialists alike, turned out to be on the payrolls of the biggest private and state companies, as well as the Mafia. This has proved too much to stomach, even in a

country where, as Sicilian novelist Giuseppe Tomasi di Lampedusa observed, everything must change so that nothing will change. Now there is a new government led by a banker with no discrediting political ties, a new electoral law and a new emphasis on regional rather than national authority.

It is in Italy's twenty regional governments, not in the Roman corridors of power, that Putnam and his colleagues have been nosing about for more than two decades (forever in the world of social science research, usually impatient for quick results). In 1970, barely a century after the country was first unified, the regions were granted new power to manage their affairs; and this taste of authority led, not surprisingly, to demands for more. Now these regions control as much as a third of the national budget, and their responsibilities include managing hospitals and health care, public safety, economic development, agriculture and housing.

Across Italy, the regional governments get more respect from the citizenry than do the overseers in Rome. Far more striking are the differences from one region to the next. In some places, public services are efficiently managed, with innovations ranging from family health clinics to environmental standards; officials are responsive and citizens are genuinely pleased. By contrast, other regional governments are cesspools, corrupt and exploitative, where personal connections rather than public priorities count for everything and the populace is grudging and resentful. What explains why the same form of government functions so well in some places, so badly in others? What makes democracy work?

None of the obvious explanations suffice. The formal administrative structures are almost identical from one region to another. Party politics or ideology isn't critical either, since Communists, Socialists and Christian Democrats can all handle or bungle the job. Social stability doesn't account for the performance of government, nor does the eucational level of the populace. Most surprising, economic modernization isn't the key either. Some "have not" regions actually do a better job of managing their public business than their economically better-off counterparts.

What's crucial, it turns out, is the "civic-ness" of regional life—voter turnout (not homages to patronage), newspaper readership and membership in associations ranging from sports clubs to **Lions Clubs, unions to choral societies— any kind of participation that "seems to depend less on** *who* **you are than on** *where* **you are."** Where people perceive a public world framed by exploitation, corruption, individual powerlessness, citizenship is stunted. In such places, civic life only confirms the wisdom of cynicism— everyone is expected to violate the rules and to do otherwise is foolish. Once **again, Tocqueville was right. "The most** democratic country in the world now," he wrote in *Democracy in America,* "is that **in which men have in our time carried to the highest perfection the art of pursuing in common the objects of common desires and have applied this new technique to the greatest number of purposes."**

Writing a quarter of a century ago, in *The Moral Basis of a Backward Society,* **political scientist Edward Banfield argued that "amoral familism"—"maximize the material, short-run advantage of the nuclear family; assume that all others will do likewise"—explained the failure of civic life in some regions of Italy. Putnam puts the community and its "stocks of social capital" first. The supply of mutual trust, civic involvement and reciprocity naturally grows, as "virtuous circles" take on a life of their own. By contrast, someone trapped in a world of distrust and exploitation is unlikely to survive by promoting collaboration, for "the strategy of 'never cooperate' is a stable equilibrium."**

That conclusion leads Putnam to search for the historic roots of the civic community, an inquiry that takes him all the way back to the twelfth century, when radically different political regimes first appeared in different regions of Italy. Autocratic rule, imposed in the South by Norman conquerers, became the regional norm, while unprecedented forms of self-government emerged in the very parts of the North where civic engagement and successful government presently prevail.

These successful communities, says Putnam, did not become civic because they were rich. On the contrary: The historical record strongly suggests that, over the past 150 years at least, they became rich because they were civic, even as feudal, fragmented regions have slipped deeper into backwardness. The mutual aid societies and choral groups of our times can be traced back to the guilds, religious fraternities and tower societies in the medieval communes of Northern Italy, while in parts of the South, as a nineteenth-century writer observed, "One feels too much the 'I' and too little the 'we.' "

This is an account of Italy, but its implications are global—and sobering. There are no quick fixes, no mass inoculations of social capital that will turn Bosnia into Bologna, no ready way to imprint P.T.A.s or AIDS services organizations (or, more pertinently, their underlying values) in the Slovak Republic or the old East Germany. Nor, closer to home, is it an easy matter to nurture the practice of civic life that Tocqueville praised but that seems imperiled in the daily news accounts—the chronicles of our own amoral familism—whether about the highways of Miami or the hopelessly homeless on the streets of Anytown, U.S.A. In this respect, *Making Democracy Work* is one of the saddest stories a social scientist has ever told.

Italy's General Election of 1996

Something New in Italy

MILAN

Italy has elected a left-of-centre government for the first time in 50 years. We analyse the results and then ask whether Italy's reds have really changed

A S ANY Italian will tell you, *Il Sorpasso*—"the overtaking"—is both a classic film from the 1960s and the Italian left's oldest, wildest dream: of zooming past the centre and right in a general election. In the republic's bumpy first half-century, the parties of the left have never managed to keep their jalopy on the road for long enough to make that dream come true. But this time, in an historic turnabout, the right's slick Ferrari skidded into the ditch—and the jalopy roared by, with the assorted passengers of the centre-left waving their Olive Tree symbol in delight.

Moreover, the result, though close, is pretty unambiguous. In a country that has turned political fudge into an art, it is big news that there were, for the most part, clear winners and losers. After three elections in the past four years, the centre-left now has a chance—no more than that, though—of staying behind the steering wheel for the next five years.

The chief driver is almost certain to be the plump and reassuring Romano Prodi, an economics professor who heads the Olive Tree coalition. But the horse-power will come from the biggest single party under the tree's branches, the ex-communists now calling themselves the Party of the Democratic Left (PDS), led by Massimo D'Alema.

All told, the Olive Tree won 157 seats in the 315-strong Senate and 284 in the lower

house. There it will need help from the Refounded (but unreformed) Communists, perhaps occasionally from the separatist Northern League. Both these parties—with 9% and 10%, respectively, of the vote in the nationwide party-list ballot, which accounts for a quarter of the total seats—were definitely winners, along with Mr D'Alema's social-democratic ex-communists, who won 21%. The League is now the largest party in the area north of the river Po, one of the richest bits of Europe.

The centre-right alliance known as the Freedom Alliance was the clear loser, although Forza Italia, the party invented only two years ago by the media mogul, Silvio Berlusconi, still got 21% of the party-list vote (roughly what it got two years ago, when it won). He now says he will lead the opposition. But some of his erstwhile allies say he should bow out, in favour of the hugely popular ex-magistrate, Antonio Di Pietro, the star of the "clean hands" investigation which was largely responsible for bringing down the corrupt old political system three years ago. Mr Di Pietro has never said publicly which party, if any, he supports. He did say after the election that the undecided voter had punished the arrogance of the centre-right.

The biggest loser of the lot is silver-tongued Gianfranco Fini, the leader of the post-fascist National Alliance, the other big

Tutti frutti
Seats in Chamber of Deputies

- Olive Tree 284
- Refounded Communists 35
- Northern League 59
- Freedom Alliance 246
- Others 6
- 630 seats

% of votes cast for parties in the 25% of seats elected by proportional representation	1996	1994
Refounded Communists	8.6	6.0
PDS	21.1	20.3
PPI/Prodi list	6.8	15.7*
Dini list	4.3	–
Greens	2.5	2.7
Other Olive Tree	0.1	5.3†
Northern League	10.1	8.4
CDU/CCD	5.8	–
Forza Italia	20.6	21.0
National Alliance	15.7	13.5
Other Freedom Alliance	1.9	3.5
Others	2.5	3.5

*PPI and Pact for Italy   †Under other names

chunk of the centre-right coalition. At one point last year, opinion polls said he was Italy's most popular politician, and during the campaign he seemed to have ousted Mr Berlusconi as the driving force of Italy's right. But his 16% was a setback. Many of his lieutenants lost their seats.

A victory for the left, then, or a rejection of the right? The answer is both. The centre-right looked more compact than the left, but its unity was flawed. Mr Berlusconi was no longer the "new man" who came from nowhere, in 1994, to wow the electorate with his promise to make Italy as successful as his business empire, but a failed former prime minister. His smoothness and perfectly tailored suits were a bit *déjà vu*, his conflicts of interest and difficulties in court unresolved, his hair suspiciously dark. The hostility of some right-wingers to the magistrates also frightened many middle-of-the-road voters ("This time," said one of Mr Berlusconi's friends, "We will take no prisoners if we win").

The votes that swung the election leftwards, however, were probably those that went to the caretaker prime minister and former central banker, Lamberto Dini, and his new party, Italian Renewal—another distinct, if modest, winner. His 4.3% lifted him over the threshold for earning seats on the party-list system and clinched victory for the centre-left.

In any event, the left, untypically, did several things right. Its patchwork of ex-communists, liberals, greens, the odd banker and the softer bits of the old Christian Democrats held together. Mr Prodi came over well—a bit worthy, but under-stated, good-humoured, sensible. Choosing him over Mr Berlusconi was rather like picking a homely black-and-white feature film over a glitzy Hollywood extravaganza.

The Olive Tree's pzazz came from Walter Veltroni, the coalition's number two, sometimes called "Italy's Baby Blair"—after the leader of Britain's Labour Party. A fan of the Kennedys and all things American (computers, button-down shirts and "Forrest Gump"), he won the votes of Italy's young.

The parties most likely to block the Olive Tree's path are the Northern League and the Refounded Communists. The League will demand—and probably get—a dollop of decentralisation as the price of its support. For a start, it may want Irene Pivetti, Lombardy's "Joan of Arc", to remain speaker of the lower house. The Communists may be keener in principle to keep the Olive Tree in power (they had an electoral pact during the campaign). But they may jib at backing the government if it tackles public services head-on or tries, as it may, to revamp a tax system that takes 53% out of the nation's wages and allows massive evasion by the self-employed.

The centre-left now seems to accept that the old system makes the poor, not the rich, the long-term losers. Mr Prodi promises fiscal rigour. He is also eager for Italy to rejoin the European exchange-rate mechanism as soon as possible, leading eventually to participation in Europe's planned single currency. Most businessmen seem sanguine about the right's defeat. Milan's stockmarket went up 5% the day after the election. The lira strengthened.

Parliament is due to meet on May 9th. Mr Prodi is expected to produce a cabinet list a few days later. There are early whispers that Mr Dini could take the foreign ministry, and Carlo Azeglio Ciampi, like Mr Dini, a central banker turned prime minister, may perhaps get the treasury. More intriguingly, Umberto Eco, author of the bestseller "The Name of the Rose", is being mooted as culture minister. Still more tantalising: Mr Di Pietro might be considered for the justice ministry—provided he is not persuaded to take on the job of reviving Italy's demoralised right. ∎

Senator for St James's

AMONG the olives whose tree triumphed on Sunday was an acorn. Tana de Zulueta, who has now entered the Italian Senate, has never carried a British passport, but her mother is English, she was educated in England and she was, until she became a candidate in this election, *The Economist*'s Rome correspondent. Her victory is our loss.

She is an improbable senator, first because she went into politics only last month and is not a member of any political party, merely of the Olive Tree coalition, a loose grouping of the centre-left. Second, she has only recently become an Italian, having been born in Colombia of a Spanish father; she is, however, married to an Italian and has lived in Italy for 20 years. Third, she fought a strongly conservative constituency in central Rome where a sitting right-wing candidate was considered well entrenched.

She was defeated. But the size of her vote—she lost by only 27 out of more than 136,000 valid ballots—was enough to secure her a seat in the Senate as one of the two members for the region, Lazio, chosen by proportional representation.

It is not unusual for journalists to go into politics. *The Economist*'s founder, James Wilson, became a member of Parliament in 1847 and later a government minister, even while nominally editing the newspaper. Other of our contributors have gone on to hold even higher political office. H.H. Asquith became prime minister of Britain and Garret FitzGerald held the same position in Ireland. Only one other correspondent was as illustrious: a certain Luigi Einaudi, who wrote for *The Economist* from Italy for nearly 40 years, sending his last report in 1946 while governor of the central bank. Later, from 1948 to 1955, he served as president of the republic.

Pinks and reds

ROME

THERE is a famous photograph of a balcony scene in Rome, taken on June 21st 1976. Enrico Berlinguer, the Italian Communist Party's leader, is waving and smiling above a sea of red flags on a warm summer night. His party has just won 34% of the nationwide vote, its best result ever and putting it only four percentage points behind the ruling Christian Democrats. Time to celebrate.

Last Sunday, on a balmy spring night, Massimo D'Alema, leader of the Democratic Party of the Left (PDS), the lineal descendant of Berlinguer's party, stood on the same balcony, smiling and waving. But this time the flags below were olive-green. All the outward symbols of communism have been junked, though a hammer-and-sickle still has a place on the party's logo. Mr D'Alema would be happy to scrap that too. And this time, though Mr D'Alema's ex-communists pulled in fewer votes than Berlinguer's more red-blooded (but far from Brezhnevite) version once did, their 21% makes them the single biggest party in parliament. They will be not just part of government but its very backbone. So the latest balcony scene was just as joyous.

Yet is Mr D'Alema a true descendant of Berlinguer? Berlinguer spent much of his political life edging away from Big Brother in Moscow, but Mr D'Alema has gone a lot further. He has expunged the word communist from his manifesto, adopting instead most of the attitudes and policies of the liberal centre-left.

Communism, however, is not dead. Fausto Bertinotti is the leader of the Refounded Communist party, the unreconstructed lot who declined to follow the majority's change of line and label in 1990. Last Sunday Mr. Bertinotti's diehards still persuaded 3,215,960 Italians to vote for them, against Mr. D'Alema's 7,897,044. Not bad for a busticated ideology.

The Refounded Communists are not actually part of the winning coalition, though they formed an electoral pact with it during the campaign and may often be needed to give it a majority in the lower house. Mr. D'Alema, however, says he has his own clear programme—and will not beg for Mr. Bertinotti's backing.

Mr D'Alema seems to be a genuine convert to an open economy, while Mr Bertinotti still rejects more privatisation and wants to bring back the *scala mobile*, the escalator that so disastrously linked wages to prices and thus fuelled Italian inflation.

★★★★★★★★★★★★

Italy Inches Toward Political Stability

Voters choose a Parliament from two opposing parties

Daniel Williams

Washington Post Foreign Service

ROME

Despite all the uncertainty and clutter, the April 21 national elections clearly have brought Italy closer to political stability. The results attracted attention mainly because they ushered in the first leftist government of the postwar era. But they also showed Italy is approaching something that approximates a two-party system.

There has long been wide agreement that to move such a process along, changes are needed in the way Italians vote. On election day, the voters themselves showed the way. They gravitated toward two main blocs, each representing fairly distinct and opposing ideas about where Italy should go in the next five years.

In doing so, they chose between contrasting personalities for prime minister: flamboyant Silvio Berlusconi, head of the rightist Freedom Alliance, and low-key Romano Prodi, leader of the center-left Olive Tree alliance.

They gave Prodi a majority backing in Parliament and a chance to take power without first having to make back-room deals.

Such wheeling and dealing was the way Italian politics used to work. Fractious parties were elected through a system that gave seats even to microscopic ones, and politicians built consensus on expanding patronage, sustained it by sending on pet projects of political allies and often greased the whole unwieldy system with corruption.

Deals were hatched after the elections, and voters who might have thought they were getting one set of leaders, with one set of policies, soon found they were getting something else. Governments rose and fell at the whim of small factions; the players stayed virtually the same over decades as waste and inefficiencies grew.

The evolving two-party or two-bloc system means essentially that deals must be worked out before the vote and electors get a clearer idea of what is coming. This election, which many observers predicted would mean nothing and result in a hung Parliament, produced both an air of impending change and a victor.

"Some may not think it wise, but Italy has entered the majority-rule system, in spite of defects" in the electoral rules, wrote editor Paolo Mieli of Corriere della Sera, Italy's big-gest-selling newspaper. "Or better yet, the citizen electors have entered into the spirit of that system."

The election has the second in two years, a sign of the old system's difficulties. Media conglomerate owner Berlusconi won the last vote, but his coalition collapsed in seven months. Much has been made of the fact that as a result of last week's vote, former Communists in the Democratic Party of the Left, the biggest branch of the Olive Tree, for the first time will share power. Some observers regard this as less important than the fact that power simply changed hands.

"For the first time in the history of our country, in two successive elections . . . opposing coalitions have won. [In 1994] the center-right, today, the center-left," wrote Norberto Bobbio, one of Italy's leading historians.

Still missing from the mix is a system that will increase the chances that a newly elected government can complete a full five-year term.

STILL MISSING FROM THE MIX IS A SYSTEM THAT will increase the chances that a newly elected government can complete a full five-year term. Because the Olive Tree depends on the votes of Marxists from the Communist Refoundation Party, few are giving it a chance to outlive the century.

The Olive Tree and the Communists made an alliance of convenience because of the unpredictability of a system in which 75 percent of the seats are won and lost based on head-to-head competition in voting districts, and the other 25 percent are doled out according to the percentage of the vote won by each party. Leaders of Olive Tree bet it would need the Communists, and they were right.

To avoid such future tangles, Massimo Dalema, the leader of the Democratic Party of the Left, wants to install a fully winner-take-all system in voting districts.

The Olive Tree–Communist tandem is not necessarily a good fit. The Olive tree wants to cut public spending and also to liberalize somewhat Italy's economy. The Communists want

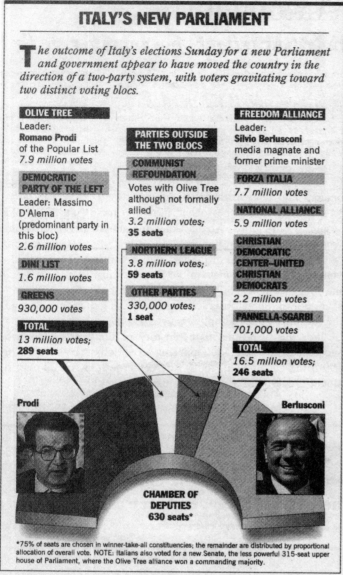

ITALY'S NEW PARLIAMENT

The outcome of Italy's elections Sunday for a new Parliament and government appear to have moved the country in the direction of a two-party system, with voters gravitating toward two distinct voting blocs.

OLIVE TREE

Leader:
Romano Prodi
of the Popular List
7.9 million votes

DEMOCRATIC PARTY OF THE LEFT
Leader: Massimo D'Alema
(predominant party in this bloc)
2.6 million votes

DINI LIST
1.6 million votes

GREENS
930,000 votes

TOTAL
13 million votes;
289 seats

PARTIES OUTSIDE THE TWO BLOCS

COMMUNIST REFOUNDATION
Votes with Olive Tree although not formally allied
3.2 million votes;
35 seats

NORTHERN LEAGUE
3.8 million votes;
59 seats

OTHER PARTIES
330,000 votes;
1 seat

FREEDOM ALLIANCE

Leader:
Silvio Berlusconi
media magnate and former prime minister

FORZA ITALIA
7.7 million votes

NATIONAL ALLIANCE
5.9 million votes

CHRISTIAN DEMOCRATIC CENTER–UNITED CHRISTIAN DEMOCRATS
2.2 million votes

PANNELLA-SGARBI
701,000 votes

TOTAL
16.5 million votes;
246 seats

Prodi

Berlusconi

**CHAMBER OF DEPUTIES
630 seats***

*75% of seats are chosen in winner-take-all constituencies; the remainder are distributed by proportional allocation of overall vote. NOTE: Italians also voted for a new Senate, the less powerful 315-seat upper house of Parliament, where the Olive Tree alliance won a commanding majority.

THE WASHINGTON POST

to protect the welfare state and reinstate the wage-inflation index under which salaries would automatically rise in lock step with prices.

Communist leader Fausto Bertinotti says his party will help give birth to the new Prodi government, without conditions, but then vote on a case-by-case basis. Despite these uncertain-ities, Prodi boasted last week that his government is immune from "any type of reversal" and predicted that it will last. He promises a cabinet by mid-May.

PRODI VOWS TO KEEP GOVERNMENT SPENDING stable, when measured against inflation. Budget cuts are to come from savings realized by reduced interest rates that he expects to follow declines in the inflation rate. If the formula works, Italy's currency will strengthen and the country will join a planned pan-European monetary union, if not right away, then "after a very short time," Prodi told reporters.

He outlines a parliamentary strategy of playing off the Communists against the regionalist Northern League, which is not part of his coalition but holds 59 seats in the lower house.

Northern League voters are mainly small-business people, and Prodi predicts the party would support him on fiscal issues. He also promises to institute sharp decentralization of govern-ment functions, a bow to the League.

The left wing of the Olive Tree faces the prospect of having to play an up front rather than an outsider role. For many years, the defunct Italian Communist Party influenced policy but never had to take direct responsibility for it. Its heirs in the Democratic Party of the Left supported the recent caretaker government of Prime Minister Lamberto Dini but again avoided direct responsibility.

The right wing faces the test of opposition. Berlusconi, who told reporters early in the campaign that he was not cut out for the opposition, changed his mind and will continue to lead his Freedom Alliance.

Farther to the right, Gianfranco Fini saw his image as a rising star of Italian politics punctured by the failure of his National Alliance faction to increase its share of the vote.

Last week's balloting was essentially split three ways. The Olive Tree and Communists won about 16.2 million votes, the Freedom Alliance 16.4 million in the key race for the lower house. Because one of Berlusconi's allies failed to make the cutoff for getting proportional seats, about 700,000 votes essentially were wasted.

The Northern League, which sometimes preaches autonomy and sometimes secession, won 3.7 million votes. If the League had allied with the Freedom Alliance, as in 1994, it is safe to say Berlusconi would have won.

Italy experiments with stability

Beppe Severgnini   MILAN

Beppe Severgnini: columnist for *Corriere della Sera* and Italy correspondent for *The Economist*; author of "Inglesi" (Rizzoli, 1990; Hodder & Stoughton, 1991) and "Un Italiano in America" (Rizzoli,1995).

Italy faces a rare and demanding challenge in 1997: normality. For the past ten years the country has been on a roller coaster: from the depths of *tangentopoli*, the series of scandals that swept the establishment, to the heights of *mani pulite*, the magistrates' attempt to clear the air; from the hopes raised by the "referendum movement" in 1993 to the disappointment of Silvio Berlusconi's aborted conservative crusade a year later.

Now the ride is over. The dizziness subsides. Terra firma, at last, is underfoot. Italy has a government, headed by an economist, Romano Prodi, and supported by the centre-left Olive Tree coalition. And the government has a target: to join EMU as soon as possible, even if France and Germany do not like the idea. And the target can be hit only by taking a number of specific measures—cutting the government's deficit, reducing inflation and nudging down public debt. This logical sequence is held together by an Italian rarity: 1997 will not be an election year. The Prodi government has four more years to go. This is a blessed relief for Italy, which cannot afford to transform its public life into a perpetual election campaign, as in the past five years. Many problems (state monopolies, pensions, the justice and fiscal systems, to name but a few) await a solution that only stability can provide.

The road to normality will not be smooth. The Prodi government needs the parliamentary votes of the unreformed Communists. Yet it also has to keep the support of cautious men such as former central bankers (and prime ministers), Carlo Azeglio Ciampi and Lamberto Dini. In 1997, Mr Prodi may be tempted to drop the Communists in favour of small Catholic parties on the centre-right.

The trade unions, though, will not like it and troubles can be expected on this front. The unions do not trust Mr Prodi, and they have already made it clear that reducing unemployment should be the priority, not commitments to Maastricht. Also, as the lira gains strength, exports—the driving power behind the Italian economy—will prove more difficult. And Italy will face an economic and financial squeeze: the 1997 budget includes spending cuts and tax increases for 62 trillion lire ($41 billion) including a controversial "tax for Europe". In these conditions, no serious attempt can be made to alleviate the oppressive fiscal burden, one of the highest in Europe.

The government will face even greater resistance as it tackles outdated labour legislation that prevents sacking civil servants and makes it virtually impossible in many areas of the private sector; or as it tries to dismantle bureaucratic nightmares that, for example, have transformed the postal service into a national joke. Mr Prodi knows what is needed: a robust injection of market disciplines, and the downsizing of the public sector. But it is far from sure that he will challenge the powerful lobbies that have sunk several governments in the past (despite the backing of Massimo D'Alema, leader of the Democratic Party of the left, a recent convert to European integration and the market).

1997 will almost certainly see a happy political event: the birth of an opposition. This would be another sign of incipient normality. Certainly there was no stable opposition in 1996—when the centre-right looked catatonic—nor in the 50 years before (communists and neofascists were either too extremist or too cosy with the government of the day). Who will lead this budding opposition? Mr Berlusconi says he will. But his coalition's electoral defeat, his own judicial problems and his desire—as a businessman—to get along with the government, have weakened his grip on Forza Italia, the party he invented (and paid for). Nonetheless, in the first-ever party congress, to be held in March 1997, he will seek a coronation.

United in its way

An effective government and a credible opposition are the only way Rome can show the rest of Italy that (some) things will change. The Northern League, the largest party north of the river Po after the 1996 general election, is unambiguously secessionist. Only bold and imaginative moves, though, will change the condition of the south, which falls behind the north and the centre in every statistic, bar those on crime (Lombardy's GNP per head is 131% of the EU's average, Calabria's is 60%). Unfortunately, change is not likely to come from the government. Grandiose statements and a certain southern touchiness will probably leave things as they are.

It is highly unlikely, nonetheless, that 1997 will see the end of a united Italy, born out of the Risorgimento in 1861. The year will just witness the erosion of an already eroded national sentiment. Expect many eyes to be on Umberto Bossi, the Northern League's autocratic leader; and secession, a taboo issue until recently, to be the most talked-about subject of 1997 in Milanese *salotti* (drawing rooms) together with the name of the new mayor, who will have the task of reviving a dispirited city. There, Italians might also start talking, once again, about the arts. As it is, nothing has replaced fashion, the art-form of the 1980s. Major exhibitions are rare, bookreading is among the lowest in Europe, Italian films do not fill cinemas, theatre is moribund and classical music—despite world-famous conductors—is ignored, unless it becomes the source of an argument (as often happens at La Scala). If Italians decide to do something about all this, after living on a diet of sport and television for most of the 1990s, there will be good reason to cheer.

"[Prime Minister Romano] Prodi must overcome the distrust of the state that has plagued Italy ever since Cavour and Garibaldi. . .unified the country little more than a century ago. This year may be decisive, the one in which the process of reform either succeeds or fails."

Italy at a Turning Point

Patrick McCarthy

As 1996 drew to a close, two views of Italy's political landscape suggested themselves. The optimistic view focused on a center-left government composed of competent men like Prime Minister Romano Prodi, who is a distinguished economist, and Treasury Minister Carlo Azeglio Ciampi, former president of the Bank of Italy, pushing through a budget that would cut the deficit to approximately 3 percent of GDP. This enabled Italy to rejoin the European Monetary System (EMS) and strengthened its chances of joining the group of European Union countries poised to fuse their currencies in a monetary union to be established in 1998. In the April 1996 elections, the government had won a majority of seats in the Senate, although in the Chamber of Deputies it was dependent on the votes of the far-left Communist Refoundation Party (RC). The process of change, which began in 1992 with the "Clean Hands" investigation into the organized corruption that had become a method of government, seemed to be moving forward.

This was the optimistic view, but there are not many optimists in Italy, and the pessimists have equally strong arguments. The core of the governing coalition is made up of Prodi's small Catholic party, the Italian People's Party, and the formerly Communist Democratic Party of the Left (PDS), which is Italy's largest party with 21 percent of the April 1996 vote. There are no doubts about the PDS's transformation into a reformist party, which is led efficiently by Massimo D'Alema. However, the Catholic Church is not enchanted by the alliance, and the two parties have different views on social issues like abortion. The fragility of the coalition is increased by its small right-wing component, Italian Renewal (RI), led by former Prime Minister Lamberto Dini, which abhors the dependence on the RC. Born of the group that decided to remain Communist when the PDS was formed in 1991, the Refoundation Party is not a group of nostalgic Stalinists. Nevertheless, it is a party of protest that resists public spending cuts and the privatization of Italy's still bloated public sector.

In short, Italy is still ruled by a weak coalition and the 1993 change in the electoral system, whereby three-quarters of the parliamentary seats were awarded by the British, winner-take-all method of voting, did not create a stable government. The pessimists could add that the uncovering in 1996 of a vast network of corruption rooted in the state-run railway system proved that the Clean Hands investigation had not achieved its goal. The opposition leader, Silvio Berlusconi of Forza Italia (Go Italy), faces several charges of tax fraud and bribery. In the meantime, on the very day when he was celebrating Italy's return to the EMS on November 25, Prodi discovered that the Rome magistrates were investigating him for the questionable sale of a public-sector firm during his period as head of the state holding company, the Institute for Industrial Reconstruction in 1993.

The legal system is itself under fire because the magistrates have acquired extensive power and are quarreling among themselves. Their disarray was exposed in early December when Antonio di Pietro, the investigating magistrate whose tenacious detective work helped spark the Clean Hands operation and whose rural manners and speech gave it popular legitimacy, was himself placed under investigation. With great ostentation his colleagues in the town of Brescia sent dozens of policemen to raid his

PATRICK MCCARTHY *teaches European studies at the Johns Hopkins University Bologna Center. His most recent book is* The Crisis of the Italian State *(New York: St. Martin's, 1995).*

office and homes in search of documents that would prove he had illegal dealings with the financier Pierfrancesco Pacini Battaglia, who was a leading actor in the railway scandal.

As yet the case against di Pietro looks flimsy (although there are mysterious episodes in his past) and only 6 percent of Italians believe he is guilty. He had switched jobs and until November he was minister of public works in the Prodi government. Then he suddenly resigned, proclaiming that he could no longer tolerate the attacks made against him. If he is indeed innocent of the Brescia charges, then it seems that some or all of the hordes of politicians, civil servants, and businessmen found guilty in the Clean Hands investigation are trying to destroy a symbol of justice while at the same time eliminating an enormously popular political rival.

The pessimistic view of the government's economic policy is that its success in cutting the deficit was achieved more by increasing taxes, including the creation of a special "tax for Europe," than by reducing government spending. Italy's pension system remains the most expensive in the European Union, or EU. The privatization program is moving slowly, while the reentry into the EMS was marred by the high value of the lira—990 to the German mark—which will create difficulties for Italian exporters. Italian businessmen are even forecasting that the 1997 deficit will be as high as 5 percent of GDP, which would rule out Italy's participation in monetary union.

Meanwhile, national unity is threatened by the electoral success of the Northern League, which has become the largest party in northern Italy, with 20.5 percent of the vote. The League's leader, Umberto Bossi, has adopted the policy of secession and talks of creating an independent state of Padania.

PADANIA: MYTH AND REALITY

Of this litany of woes, the issue of secession is the least understood outside Italy. There is indeed a problem, but it will not result in a Padania governed by the Northern League. There are two reasons for this. The first is that the League's real strength lies in the belt of smallish industrial towns that stretch below the Alps from Varese in the west to Treviso in the east. In the larger cities the League is weaker: when Bossi ran for Parliament in the rich, sophisticated center of Milan, he came in a poor third behind Berlusconi and the center-left candidate.

The second reason is that the League is a negative force, rather than a party of government. It grew in the late 1980s and early 1990s when the old

order was eroding. Bossi castigated immigrants, southern Italians, and the Rome bureaucrats, but this last target won him the most popularity. Bossi is a man of charisma and a mythmaker. But when he tells the tale of the medieval northern Italian cities that banded into a league to defeat the German Emperor Friedrich Barbarossa, all but his hardcore followers smile.

He gains broader support when he denounces Roman robbers and talks of decapitating the capital. Bossi personifies the Italian distrust of the state—which masks a burning need for the state. When he issues his invective, dressed in shabby pullovers and often without a tie, using the coarse language of the working-class bars of Milan, he convinces many people. They do not, however, wish to be ruled by him.

In the 1996 elections the League gained 30 percent of the vote in the Veneto region, which is the fastest-growing part of Italy. The hard-headed small entrepreneurs and workers who voted for Bossi were sending a message to the Rome government: they want more power for their local and regional authorities; from the central government they want less red tape, better infrastructure, and more job training. Theirs is a protest of people who are doing well but feel they are under-represented politically.

One answer to their demands is decentralization, which the center-left government is slowly undertaking. But moving power out of Rome will not in itself suffice. Rome must change too. In order to arbitrate among the various regions, it must not only become more efficient, but must gain the trust of its skeptical citizens.

A further complication is that almost any attempt by the state to reform society will be opposed by groups that, while proclaiming they want greater efficiency from Rome, profit from its laxity. One example is the tide of protest against the efforts made by recent governments to combat tax evasion. Since the self-employed find it easier to avoid paying taxes, governments have concentrated their enforcement efforts on this group. In turn this increases red tape and triggers protests like the shopkeepers' rally in Turin, which booed Prodi off the stage in March 1996. Continued reforms will almost certainly bring more noisy opposition.

LEARNING TO LOVE AUSTERITY AND THE MARKET

Disorder is all the more likely because the Prodi government, which is continuing the policies of all post-1992 governments (with the partial exception of Berlusconi's), is imposing austerity. Prodi justifies it by the need to meet the Maastricht treaty criteria for entry into Economic and Monetary Union (EMU). But he is also using Europe to convince Italians to make sacrifices they would not be willing to make in the name of their own country. In any event, the government's goal is to enable Italy to compete in the EU and to be part of the EU's attempt to compete in the global economy.

The Italian economy has many strengths. It is dynamic: between 1978 and 1996 annual growth averaged 2.3 percent in Italy, compared with 2.2 percent in Germany and 2 percent in France. Though Italy has few large companies, some of them—like Fiat or the Assicurazioni Generali—are the equals of car and insurance companies in other European countries. Italy's small companies outperform their counterparts in France or Britain. Often rooted in the family, able to adapt to changes of fashion in sectors like clothes and shoes, quick to seek new markets (as the Venetian firms have proved by their penetration of Central Europe), and present in sophisticated sectors like electronics, the small companies have taken full advantage of the devaluation of the lira in 1992.

The problem is that dynamism in the private sector and at the local level is not accompanied by organization and discipline at the national level. In 1994, Italy's public debt reached 120 percent of GDP, compared with 55 percent in Germany and 57 percent in France. Servicing the debt meant issuing government bonds at interest rates that reached 15 percent in 1992, and in quantities that left little room for the private sector in a restricted financial market.

Such debt was manageable only because, unlike the United States, Italy had a high savings rate that stood at 18 percent of national income in 1992. But in January 1996, spurred on by the risk-penalty factor, the yield on a 10-year government bond was 5 percentage points higher than the yield on a similar German bond and the difference between the prime rate in the two countries was roughly the same. As treasury minister, Ciampi has tried to promote a virtuous circle: cuts in the current deficit mean lower interest rates that in turn reduce the cost of servicing the debt. Moreover, Italy's entry into monetary union would eliminate the risk-penalty factor.

This is why the budget for 1997 has dominated recent politics. Passing the budget was tougher than expected because the government realized that EU countries like France, whose exports have suffered

[N]othing is less certain than the. . . survival of Prodi's government.

from the devalued lira, and Germany, where Chancellor Helmut Kohl has to convince a skeptical public and the austere Bundesbank that the euro, the proposed EU currency, will be as strong as the mark, were prepared to make few concessions to Italy over the Maastricht criteria. The budget is designed to save $41 billion and to reduce the deficit to 3 percent of GDP, as agreed at Maastricht. But, although the PDS appreciates the need for austerity, the RC opposed reductions in social spending, while the unions would not permit cuts in the overgenerous pension agreement that they brokered in 1995 with the Dini government. Prodi and Ciampi had few options other than to increase taxes and to raise $8 billion with a new "tax for Europe." This triggered a fresh conflict between the RC, which wanted to place much of the burden on the self-employed, and Dini's party, which sought to defend this group.

The center-right opposition parties pointed out that the new taxes were being imposed when unemployment was over 12 percent. Moreover, GDP had declined by 1.5 percent during the last three months and the *Economist* was forecasting a rise of only 0.8 percent for 1996 and 1.5 percent for 1997. In refusing to take countercyclical measures, the Italian government is following the example of other EU governments, such as the French. In doing so, it is doubling the risk of social disorder. The financial markets decided during the pre-budget debate to believe in the lira, but it is hard to imagine that Prodi's resolve will not be put to the test in the coming year. This list of obstacles does not take into account the viability of monetary union as a whole; the weaknesses of "Europe" are rarely discussed in Italy.

The other aspects of the government's economic policy continue the post-1992 reforms, while protecting the poorer segments of the population. Here the Catholics and the former Communists share the value of solidarity. Unemployment has been subsumed into the north-south question: the 12 percent figure hides the plight of many parts of the south, where unemployment stands at more than 20 percent. The government is trying to break with the old regime's practice of pouring money into schemes that enriched only its supporters. Prodi is concentrating on improving infrastructure, as demonstrated by a plan to develop the Sardinian railways, and on strengthening the private sector by helping the unemployed to start their own businesses.

Perhaps the most important innovation of the post-1992 period was a July 1993 agreement requiring employers and unions to negotiate wage agreements in the context of the projected inflation rate and other economic targets fixed by the government. The agreement replaces the old method of wage indexation, which is considered to have fostered inflation, and it also gives workers a role in economic decision making. However, the agreement does not specify what to do in the event that inflation rises beyond the rate that had been set. Because of this ambiguity, the July 1993 agreement has been put to a severe test by the metalworkers, whose contract came up for renewal in 1996. Their militant union talked of recovering the extra inflation in full; employers talked of giving much less, on the grounds that agreements at company level and merit increases had already refunded most of the money the workers had lost. The metalworkers want an additional $170 per month, whereas the employers are offering only an $80 increase. Minister of Labor Tiziano Treu is trying to negotiate a compromise that will save the July 1993 agreement.

Privatization, perceived as the way to relieve the burden on the overworked state and to strengthen the private sector, is continuing, but it is painfully slow. Like the RC, the right-wing National Alliance (AN), born of the neofascist Italian Social Movement (MSI), is unenthusiastic about the privatization process. The state managers have a vested interest in maintaining the present status of their companies, since they do not have to worry about shareholders. At the same time, financiers and industrialists seek to block their rivals from acquiring profitable firms. As a result of these machinations, Stet, the state telecommunications company—and a particularly desirable morsel—remains in public hands. Stet has, however, been placed directly under the control of the Treasury Ministry, which has promised to privatize it in the first half of this year.

The privatization of the state-owned oil, energy, and manufacturing conglomerate, Ente Nazionale Idrocarburi, begun by the Dini government, has continued. Most big banks are less concerned with privatization than with strengthening their position by forming alliances and taking over smaller banks. Almost all banks are overstaffed and may have to eliminate as much as 15 percent of their workforce. Southern banks, dogged by decades of Christian Democratic Party (DC) corruption, and in some cases—like Sicilcasse, the Sicilian savings bank—looted by organized crime, continue to struggle.

The banks, whose charter has been changed to allow them to hold shares in companies, are supposed to become players on an expanded stock market. The Stock Exchange Council, formed in 1993, is trying to bring more companies into the market. But Italians still worry that the privatized companies will end up in the hands of a small group of investors. Meanwhile, foreigners complain about the paucity of information provided by public companies and their shabby treatment of small shareholders. Italy must adapt to an instrument of modern capitalism that requires trust in other investors and in the organizations that run the stock market. But trust is in short supply.

THE PROCESS OF POLITICAL RENEWAL

The post-1992 period has reached a decisive moment. The process of change has penetrated many parts of Italian society. Resistance has been strong, whether it is expressed through violence, as in the Mafia's assassination of its most energetic enemies, the magistrates Giovanni Falcone and Paolo Borsellino in 1992, or in more diffuse forms, such as opposition to privatization.

Until the April 1996 elections, politics had lagged behind economic and social change, but now it has caught up by the creation of a government that has defined for itself five tasks. If successfully completed, these tasks will mark milestones on the road toward the refounding of the Italian state. Three have been discussed already: to set the state's finances on sound footing; to enter the EU's monetary union as a founding member; and to avoid secession in the north by decentralizing. This leads to the last two tasks, which are political. This is not to say that Italian life is shaped by politics, however. It may well be that the weaknesses—and successes—of the political system are determined by socioanthropological factors, such as the strength of the family, the lack of trust in people one does not know well, and the habit of forming clans. But these are factors that cannot be changed quickly. Wherever possible, Italy must try to turn such traits into strengths. Since trust is strongest in small communities, more power should be given to local government.

In the meantime, the political system must answer the demands emanating from Italian society and from Europe, which is also changing rapidly. The fourth task facing the Prodi government is, quite simply, to survive. Since 1992, no government has sent more than one budget through parliament; the center-left must be the first to do so. Political stability inspires confidence in the financial markets, as well as in the partners with which Italy bargains. Germany would be less difficult if it knew that Ciampi would still be treasury minister in three years' time.

Alas, nothing is less certain than the five-year survival of Prodi's government. A question mark hangs over Prodi himself: does he have the political skills to gain popular support for his project? Dini clearly sees himself not only as a past prime minister, but also one in the future. Although Dini's party, RI, received just over 4 percent of the vote, Prodi's Italian People's Party received less than 7 percent.

The plethora of small parties in the coalition has its roots in Italian history. The aim of the winner-take-all electoral system was to produce large parties. It may do so, but so far the parties unite for the elections and then bicker afterward. The center-right coalition broke up after eight months of government in 1994, and the strains in the center-left are apparent.

If the RI is too small, the PDS is, according to its rivals, too big and too influential. It is hard to follow this argument because, although the PDS is Italy's largest party, it usually receives far fewer votes than the British Labour Party and the French Socialists. Moreover, the PDS is loyally fighting the battle for austerity, although it surely knows the difficulty this will create with its working-class electorate. D'Alema has announced plans to merge the party with a segment of the old Italian Socialist Party, as well as with center-left independents. He is correct to think that 21 percent of the vote is too little rather than too much for the party that forms the pillar of the center-left.

In addition to backing austerity and the reentry into Europe, D'Alema is attempting to reach agreement with the center-right on institutional changes. They are designed to strengthen the executive but also to make Parliament work more efficiently and to redefine the relationship between political and legal authority. Berlusconi is hardly the ideal partner but D'Alema is right to try, because without stronger institutions Italy will be unable to make lasting economic reforms and bargain on equal terms within the EU.

The center-left's fragility is all the more unfortunate because the center-right suffers from handicaps that make it an implausible force of government. Forza Italia did well in the elections and held its share of the vote, 20.5 percent. But it remains too dependent on its leader, Silvio Berlusconi. Charismatic in the 1994 elections, he was no longer calm and self-confident in April 1996. Since then, his dazzling smile has often been switched off, and he makes wild statements that

Italy is no longer a democracy and that he is being persecuted by an unholy alliance of communists, Catholics, and judges.

Berlusconi's legal battles continue, while his conflict-of-interest problems have merely been veiled by his decision to launch his television holdings, Mediaset, on the stock market. In fact, he retains effective control of the company. He also maintains control over Forza Italia: its provincial coordinators are elected, but at the level above, the regional coordinators are not elected but are co-opted by the national officials. Berlusconi is not leading well, but as long as he remains, it will be hard for other leaders to emerge.

The second main component of the center-right is the National Alliance. As the neofascist MSI, it won some 4 to 5 percent of the vote from the postwar years until 1992. Its chance came when the Clean Hands investigation decimated the DC. The National Alliance—which had been, as the Italian Social Movement, both a fascist party that claimed Mussolini's legacy and a conservative party that competed with the DC—took over the Christian Democratic Party bastions in the south. In the 1994 elections, the National Alliance gained 13.5 percent of the vote, with peaks of 27.5 percent in Puglia and 27 percent in Rome, where the bureaucracy was seeking protection. Party leader Gianfranco Fini made speeches full of resounding banalities that convinced many voters that the National Alliance was harmless. In 1996 it was expected to make another leap forward, but its vote rose by only 2.2 percent.

Doubts about the National Alliance's commitment to democracy are probably misdirected. More realistic are doubts about the ability of its leaders to govern and the center-right conflict between Forza Italia's belief in the free market and the National Alliance's statism. Italy is thus weakened by an opposition that governed badly in 1994—when the lira plunged and the yield on government paper rose—and that has no convincing candidate for prime minister.

In early 1997, the center-left represents the only realistic government. Its fifth task is to give legitimacy to itself—especially to the PDS—and to the new political system. Further institutional reforms are needed, but they can be only part of the campaign to create a bond between citizen and state. Prodi must overcome the distrust of the state that has plagued Italy ever since Cavour and Garibaldi, who deeply distrusted each other, unified the country little more than a century ago. This year may be decisive, the one in which the process of reform either succeeds or fails.

Hashimoto's headache

TOKYO

THE one clear result of Japan's general election on October 20th is that it has solved nothing. Although the dominant Liberal Democratic Party (LDP) headed by Ryutaro Hashimoto, the prime minister, fell short of winning an absolute majority in the 500-seat lower house of the Diet, it nevertheless increased its strength from 211 to 239 members. Meanwhile, the challenge mounted by Ichiro Ozawa and his New Frontier Party (NFP) flopped miserably. Far from threatening the LDP's dominance, the main opposition party wound up with 156 seats, four fewer than it had before the election.

The irony is that, in clinching a bigger lead, Mr. Hashimoto has found that forming a new administration has suddenly become more difficult. The question this past week has been not just what political complexion Japan's new government will have, but how long it will last. Some are already beginning to suggest that another election could be needed within a year or so.

Mr. Hashimoto has two immediate problems. The first is the collapse of the LDP's two former coalition partners: the Social Democratic Party (SDP) and the smaller New Party Sakigake. Both were devastated in last Sunday's election; their combined strength plummeted to only 17 seats (see chart). The result is that, whereas Mr. Hashimoto could rely on a comfortable 40-seat majority over the opposition's combined strength before the election, the best he can muster now is a slender majority of five or six, even though his own party's strength rose.

The prime minister's other problem is that he cannot even bank on that slender majority. After flip-flopping a few times, the two surviving Sakigake members have now decided not to join his new government. They say they will co-operate with the LDP on administrative reforms, but from outside the cabinet.

Meanwhile, Takako Doi—the popular speaker of the house who was persuaded to rejoin the crumbling SDP on the eve of the election and lead its fight for survival—has threatened not to throw her party's lot in with the government. As with the pair of Sakigake survivors, Miss Doi has offered to support an LDP-led coalition on a case-by-case basis, but to keep her troops out of the cabinet.

There is no question that the SDP's fall from grace started when it compromised its socialist principles by joining forces with the conservative LDP to form a coalition government in 1994. Unlike the former SDP leader, Tomiichi Murayama, the redoubtable Miss Doi is not so easily seduced by the promise of power—and is determined not to let her party make such a near-fatal mistake twice. The SDP needs time, she says, to heal its wounds.

Others have learned much the same lesson about consorting with the LDP, and have been seeking likewise to distance themselves from the ruling party and its venal antics. The new Democratic Party of Japan, formed just weeks before the election by two Sakigake renegades, Yukio Hatoyama and Naoto Kan, has been even more reluctant to help Mr Hashimoto in his quest to form a government.

The fledgling Democratic Party did nowhere near as well last Sunday as expected, barely managing to keep its pre-election strength of 52 members. Pundits had predicted giddily that it would win at least 80 seats, making it a new focal point for liberal-minded forces within the Diet. But the Democrats confused the public by providing two figureheads, and by refusing to say whether they were standing unequivocally as an opposition party or as one that was prepared to work for reform from within a coalition government.

To his credit, Mr. Hatoyama has insisted all along that his new party—with its membership of young reformist politicians drawn largely from the ranks of the SDP and the Sakigake—should promote its legislative agenda from the opposition benches. But his colleague and co-founder, Mr. Kan, has continued to hint otherwise. Not surprisingly, it has been Mr. Kan whom the LDP leadership has been wooing assiduously this past week.

As health and welfare minister in the previous coalition government, Mr. Kan has made himself the most popular politician in Japan. He it was who rooted out the bureaucratic corruption within the health service that had allowed some 1,000 haemophiliacs to contract AIDS through the use of unheated blood products. The populist Mr. Kan let it be known that he would not be averse to another prominent cabinet post. But as Mr. Hashimoto's new coalition has begun

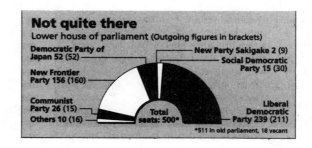

Not quite there
Lower house of parliament (Outgoing figures in brackets)

Democratic Party of Japan 52 (52)

New Frontier Party 156 (160)

Communist Party 26 (15)

Others 10 (16)

New Party Sakigake 2 (9)

Social Democratic Party 15 (30)

Liberal Democratic Party 239 (211)

Total seats: 500*

*511 in old parliament, 18 vacant

to look increasingly wobbly, joining the cabinet seems to have lost some of its appeal.

In desperation, the LDP bigwigs have started courting their bitter rivals (and former colleagues before the bust-up of 1993) in Mr. Ozawa's New Frontier Party. Dissidents within the NFP who have remained loyal to Morihiro Hosokawa and Tsutomu Hata, both former prime ministers, have been seething under Mr. Ozawa's dictatorial rule and have threatened to walk out of the party on several occasions. Mr. Hata's group, in particular, was on the verge of forming a party of its own several months ago but cancelled its plans when a general election appeared to be imminent.

Many of the NFP's younger members have also become distressed with the way the Soka Gakkai—a lay Buddhist organisation with deep pockets and an agenda of its own—has tightened its grip on their party. With roots in 8m households in Tokyo, Osaka and other big cities across Japan, the Soka Gakkai is by far the biggest vote-generator in the country. It is reckoned to be able to deliver an additional 20,000 votes (more than 10% of the total cast in a typical urban constituency) to any candidate it chooses to back. In Sunday's election, the Soka Gakkai backed more than 200 of the 235 candidates that the NFP fielded in single-seat constituencies. Those unhappy with religion's incursion into politics have been urging Mr Hata and Mr Hosokawa to wash their hands of the NFP and its Buddhist friends.

The LDP would be delighted if they did: between them, Mr Hata and Mr Hosokawa could be expected to bring anything up to 30 supporters with them if they defected and joined an LDP-led coalition. Such a move would provide Mr Hashimoto with the majority he is seeking in the upper as well as the lower house.

But the two senior NFP leaders are involved in a power struggle with Mr Ozawa, who half-heartedly offered to stand down after the party's poor showing. During the campaign, Mr Ozawa promised to slash taxes, instigate drastic administrative re-

Not the ASEAN way

EUROPE undoubtedly has a huge commercial and financial stake in East Asia. But when it comes to security matters, East Asian diplomats have long complained that Europeans punch well below their weight. Nowhere is this more evident than in the fledgling ASEAN Regional Forum (ARF), which groups together the seven South-East Asian countries with outsiders, including America, Japan, Russia, China—and the European Union (EU). Ever since the ARF opened for business in 1994, France and Britain have been campaigning for separate seats, an idea opposed by Eurocrats in Brussels, who want foreign policy to be pursued through the EU. This unseemly European row, watched by ASEAN governments with bemusement and embarrassment, has broken out anew, with a bizarre dispute over an ARF working-group to be held next month in Paris, and co-sponsored by France and Indonesia.

At the root of Europe's bickering is a real problem. Officially, Europe is represented at most ARF meetings by the European Commission and the troika of past, present and future presidents of the EU (the EU presidency rotates among members on a six-monthly basis). When that brings the French, the British or the Germans to the table, Europe can speak with a strong voice. When, as with the present troika of Italy, Ireland and the Netherlands, it brings smaller countries, or ones with less interest in Asian security, Europe has little to say. The commission, though happy to sit behind the Euro-

pean flag at ARF meetings, has no competence in defence. All of which, aside from a preference for national flags in security discussions, is what prompts Britain and France, both with real security interests in the region, to want their own seat.

The row is now moving from the arcane to the absurd. Though France is co-sponsoring next month's ARF working-group in Paris, the troika-and-commission-only rule means that no French diplomats may sit at the table. If any do manage to sneak in, they will have to sit at the back and keep their mouths shut. Britons cannot even do that, unless Britain can persuade the Irish government—current president of the EU and still standing on its troika dignity—to relent. Only if some of the troika seats go unfilled (a possibility, given the low priority accorded to Asian security issues by some of the governments concerned) can the organisers try to fill these at the last minute with other European "experts" (still no diplomats, please).

Supposedly informal, the working-group in Paris is only the second to be held in Europe. A meeting in December in Indonesia, co-sponsored by Germany, looks like suffering similar indignities. The Indonesian sponsors of both meetings, fed up with all the bureaucratic wrangling and rule books, may try to exclude the troika altogether, so as to get on with some real business.

The Paris working-group was organised to help tap Europe's experience in preventive diplomacy. Time for Europe's diplomats to practise what they preach.

forms and prop up the economy—and vowed to leave politics if he was prevented from honouring his pledges. But now the truculent Mr Ozawa, backed by the majority of his older colleagues in the NFP and their Soka Gakkai supporters, has decided

not to go without a fight. No love is lost between Mr Hashimoto and Mr Ozawa, but this is the one battle that the prime minister is praying his erstwhile rival in the LDP will win outright. The more disgruntled opposition MPs, the better for Mr Hashimoto.

Reforming Japan

The Third Opening

Ichiro Ozawa believes that Japan, for the third time in little over a century, needs radical reform. In this article, he explains why he finds the prospect exhilarating

NATIONS are nurtured by myths. Japan is no exception. If I mention the "third opening of Japan", most Japanese will immediately know what I mean, just as if I were citing the need for a new Magna Carta. Unless outsiders place what is happening in Japan today in the context of our history and our myths, they will find it difficult to understand the particular turning-point we are facing in our long evolution as a nation.

Our myths arise from the fact that we are a group of narrow islands off the coast of Asia, coming only sporadically into contact with our continental neighbours down through the years. We take comfort in our homogeneity, in our capacity to absorb influences from the mainland at our own pace, in timespans measured by centuries rather than decades. For us, much more than for Britain, "the jungle begins at Calais"—in our case, the Korea Strait. In essence, we see ourselves as a cosy village society where consensus is the norm and where we all live by unspoken rules to make life tolerable in a green but crowded land with few natural resources.

The first great challenge to these myths came in 1853, when Commodore Matthew Perry and his heavily armed "black ships" dropped anchor in Tokyo (then known as Edo) Bay, and sent a message from President Millard Fillmore demanding that Japan open its doors to trade with the world. Until then, the Tokugawa Shoguns who had ruled Japan since 1603 had imposed a near-total ban on travel into or out of the country, the single exception being the port of Nagasaki, in southern Japan, where Dutch and Chinese merchants were allowed to bring in their wares.

Ichiro Ozawa is the president of the New Frontier Party and leader of the Japanese opposition. A former secretary-general of the Liberal Democratic Party, Mr Ozawa left the LDP in 1993, precipitating the end of 38 years of conservative rule. He was the architect of the coalition that ruled Japan in 1993-94.

BY INVITATION

The Shogunate officials knew that their antiquated shore batteries were no match for Perry's cannons. They had no recourse but to give way, choosing to do so as little as they could. In so doing, they set in motion a nationwide debate between advocates of continued isolation and reformers who wanted to open up the country. The debate lasted 15 years—a period of great turmoil, ending only with the collapse of the Shogunate, the abolition of feudalism, and the establishment of a reform-minded central government under the direct rule of the Emperor Meiji. This series of events is known today as the first opening of Japan.

The Meiji era, which lasted for nearly half a century, was a heady time for Japan. The young reformers gathered around the emperor knew that for Japan's survival, they had to make drastic changes in the political, economic and social institutions of their country. One of the five pledges with which Meiji inaugurated his reign was to "seek knowledge throughout the world". His reformers created a modern army and navy, introduced capitalism, universal education, and a limited form of constitutional democracy, including the concept of equality under the law.

But the grafting of Western institutions and values on to traditional patterns of Japanese thought and behaviour was not achieved without great strain. The Meiji reformers were mostly bureaucrats and administrators, and, although they saw the need for elected parliaments, they preferred Bismarck to Gladstone—that is, they limited both the powers of parliament and the numbers of those able to vote for it. It was not until the early 1920s that Takashi Hara, the first commoner to become prime minister, introduced universal adult male suffrage. His reward was assassination. From the late 1920s, Japan became increasingly militaristic and authoritarian, embarking on adventures in China which led to confrontation with the United States and Britain and ended in disastrous defeat in the second world war.

Japan's surrender in 1945 and the sweeping reforms brought about during a six-year occupation by American forces under the command of General Douglas MacArthur constitute what many of us call the second opening of Japan. The second opening, like the first, began as a result of conflict with foreigners but continued differently because most of the changes took place under foreign duress. Yet the main planks of the occupation reforms embodied ideas and programmes begun in the Meiji period and were genuinely popular with voters: land reform, dissolution of the *zaibatsu* (giant financial and industrial trusts), freedom of speech and assembly, free trade unions and women's suffrage. A new constitution was drafted, including the famous article nine renouncing the right to go to war and banning the use of armed force. At least in form, Japan became a fully-fledged parliamentary democracy, with political power in the hands of the people's elected representatives.

Under the impetus of these reforms, and helped by the cold war which kept Japan firmly within America's orbit and under the protection of the US-Japan security treaty, our people concentrated single-mindedly on economic recovery and growth. With no natural resources to speak of beyond the education and talents of our citizens, we imported raw materials from all over the world and exported manufactured goods to all the world. By the late 1960s we had outstripped West Germany as the non-communist world's second largest economy, surpassed in size only by the United States.

Our political progress, however, did not keep pace with the explosive growth of our economy. Conservative political forces quickly came together to form the Liberal Democratic Party (LDP). But the opposition Socialists remained ideologically stuck in the rhetoric of the cold war, advocating the dissolution of the alliance with the United States and an unarmed neutrality that could only benefit the Soviet Union. Voters used the Socialists and other opposition parties to express dissatisfaction with the government of the day, but never in such numbers as to deprive the LDP of power. While we remained a parliamentary democracy in form, in practice the LDP was continuously in office, except for a brief period in 1947-48.

That long hold on power bred corruption, enhanced by the cosy village nature of Japanese society. Meanwhile, from outside Japan, and particularly from America and Europe, we began to hear increasingly shrill demands to open up our markets; outsiders also urged us to assume a diplomatic role in the international community commensurate with the size of our economy and its weight in the world.

The new frontier

To my mind, what these pressures building up inside and outside our country amount to is nothing less than a demand for the third opening of Japan—for changes as drastic and far-reaching as the ones brought about by the Meiji reformers and by the American occupation after 1945. That, indeed, is what my party, the New Frontier Party, stands for. If our programme succeeds, we will have brought about a revolution that will complete the work begun by the Meiji reformers more than 100 years ago. It will embody the most far-reaching changes that our country has ever known, and enable us to join the ranks of what I call the world's normal democratic states.

We have in Japan today the institutional forms of parliamentary government, but with a content rather different from what is regarded as normal in American or European democracies. Ours still reflects consensus politics and an isolationist mentality that excludes outsiders. The goal of the New Frontier Party is to break this mould and to bring about alternation in government between two political parties that will compete with each other on the basis of policy, not of factions or of personalities.

The Liberal Democrats' post-war monopoly of power was broken in July 1993, when Tsutomu Hata and I led a group of reform-minded colleagues to rebel against the party leadership and to establish a new party, the Japan Renewal Party. Together with other opposition parties, we won the general election that month and formed the Hosokawa coalition government. The following year, the Liberal Democrats made a deal with their sworn enemies, the Socialists, and returned to power. In reaction to this unholy alliance, all the main opposition parties except the Communists came together in December 1994 to establish the New Frontier Party.

Today, at least in form, we have the beginnings of a two-party system. On one side stands the government—a coalition of the LDP, the Socialists and the *Sakigake* or Harbingers, a minor party. The coalition was headed first by a Socialist, Tomiichi Murayama, and now by a Liberal Democrat, Ryutaro Hashimoto. Despite their differences in ideological outlook, the LDP and the Socialists are essentially status quo parties. They mouth the slogans of reform, but in fact they want to keep their vested interests.

The new agenda

By contrast, our party is dedicated to the cause of reform. We call for thoroughgoing changes in politics, in the economy, in education and in society. In politics, we have been partially successful in that, during our brief year in power, we changed the election system from one of multi-seat districts to one which has 300 single-seat constituencies and 200 seats to be voted for on a proportional-representation list. It is somewhat like the German system. Each voter will have two votes and can cast his ballot both for his local candidate and for the party of his choice.

The world has not yet recognised the revolutionary nature of this change because the first election under the new system has yet to be held. At the latest, however, the next general election must be held in July 1997. It could come much sooner—possibly this summer or autumn. It may not immediately bring about a permanent two-party system but, as voters become used to the system, minor parties will fade away. The Socialist Party, recently renamed the Social Democratic Party, will be the top candidate for extinction.

In each of the 300 single-seat constituencies, voters will have two clear points of view to choose between—that of the ruling coalition and that of the New Frontier Party. Many legislators, even those belonging to our party, are uncomfortable with this prospect. They want to build coalitions based on interests and personalities, as they have been doing till now, and are not sure that voters will respond to policy-based appeals. I am convinced, however, that the New Frontier Party must make this sort of appeal to the voters.

Lessons from Iwate

My own constituency in Iwate is largely rural but I have insisted that farmers, like other citizens, must face the fact of international competition and not simply hide behind protective barriers. My recipe for change brings pain to my constituents but so far I have managed to be re-elected with substantial majorities. I feel certain that, nationwide, voters will respond to political leadership if that leadership can provide a clear, compelling vision of the future and realistic steps to achieve it.

For us, there is no alternative to the third opening of Japan—to opening our markets wide to the international community, to chopping down the thicket of rules and regulations which are choking initiative, creativity and economic growth. I have no illusions about the difficulty of our task. Japan has been a regulated society for more than 1,000 years. We have a lot of people, little land, and few natural resources. For everyone to share in an economy of scarcity, there have to be regulations, and on the whole people have accepted these regulations. In modern times, the concept of fairness, of equality, has taken precedence over the concept of individual freedom. We are a society without vast gaps between rich and poor, management and workers. We would like to keep it so, but not at the cost of stifling personal freedom and individual initiative.

Despite my experience with voters in Iwate, I know that most Japanese still feel uncomfortable and disoriented by the prospect of living in a society with few regulations and where each person will have to be more self-reliant and take greater responsibility for his or her own actions. Nevertheless there is no other way for Japan to move into the 21st century and survive. What we are embarked upon is a revolutionary process, and it will not be completed in a day.

We want lean government at the centre, and more power devolved to local entities. At the moment, Japan has a highly centralised system with no clear division between the central and local governments. Ultimately we will have about 300 local authorities nationwide—small enough to be close to the voters, large enough to carry out effective government—to replace the present hodgepodge of prefectures, cities, towns and villages.

Educational reform may be the most important of the reforms we propose. Universal education was one of the great achievements of the Meiji reformers. Japan today is one of the world's most literate nations. But our education system remains stuck in the 19th century, emphasising rote learning and stuffing students with all sorts of relevant and irrelevant information. We need education that will foster self-reliance and creativity. Group values like fairness and equality are important, but the primary emphasis must be on allowing the individual to develop. Education is an area in which we may not see results for ten years or more. But we must begin now, for we are already far behind the leaders in this field.

Japan and the world

Internationally, I have long advocated a much more active and participatory stance in world affairs, with the proviso that we remain in close partnership with the United States.

Some Japanese argue that, with the cold war over and with America no longer as overwhelming a military and economic superpower as it used to be, we should form closer ties with Asia, perhaps even play the role of honest broker between China and the United States. I disagree. I hope that China, as its economy grows and its people prosper, will successfully make the transition from authoritarianism to democratic government. I also hope that China and Taiwan will settle their differences peacefully on the basis of their common recognition that Taiwan is part of China. But these are not yet foregone conclusions. North Korea is an even more troubling neighbour than China. Asia needs the American security presence, and the US-Japan security treaty provides the means for America not only to protect Japan but to remain involved with Asia. Furthermore, Japan's own past record in Asia is not forgotten. We will be accepted and considered nonthreatening by our Asian neighbours only to the extent that we retain a strong security relationship and economic partnership with the United States.

This does not mean that we will agree with America in all respects nor that we will fail to advance our own point of view. We may have as many disagreements with America as do Britain, France or Germany. But like them, our disagreements should always take place within the context of our basic alliance. Alliance with America is as essential for Japan as it is for Europe—perhaps more so, because in Asia we have nothing like NATO or the European Union.

We want a permanent seat on the United Nations Security Council, and pledge to play a leading role in the affairs of that body. The United Nations is far from perfect, but it is the only international forum we have, and we want to make it better. How can we do so unless we participate in all its activities, including peacekeeping? I have proposed that Japan establish a stand-by force, separate from the present Self Defence Force, that will be available for UN peacekeeping duties whenever called upon by the Security Council and the secretary general.

Our constitution forbids going to war as a sovereign right of the Japanese government, but I submit that it by no means forbids Japan from placing its forces under UN command for peacekeeping duties. In fact, the preamble of the constitution talks of preserving "our security and existence, trusting in the justice and faith of the peace-loving peoples of the world." How can we do so, how can we "occupy an honoured place in an international society striving for the preservation of peace, and the banishment of tyranny and slavery, oppression and intolerance," if we do not participate fully in UN peacekeeping?

Ultimately, the idea that underlies the third opening of Japan is the need to change society. We have to move from decisions by consensus, so called, into the essence of democracy, decision-making by the majority, with the minority accepting those decisions in the belief that today's minority will become tomorrow's majority. Our new election system is one means to this end, but I am under no illusions that we can reach our goal without repeated setbacks. Still, the 21st century is less than four years away, and it is urgent not only to get the process started but to make sure that it becomes irreversible.

Modern Pluralist Democracies: Factors in the Political Process

- Political Ideas, Movements, and Parties (Articles 22–24)
- The Ethnic Factor in Western European Politics (Article 25)
- Women and Politics (Articles 26–28)
- The Institutional Framework of Representative Government (Articles 29–33)

Observers of Western industrial societies frequently refer to the emergence of a *new politics* in these countries. They are not always very clear or in agreement about what is supposedly novel in the political process or why it is significant. Although no one would dispute that some major changes have taken place in these societies during the past quarter of a century, affecting both political attitudes and behavior, it is very difficult to establish clear and comparable patterns of transformation or to gauge their endurance and impact. Yet making sense of continuities and changes in political values and behavior must be one of the central tasks of a comparative study of government.

Since the early 1970s, political scientists have followed Ronald Inglehart and other careful observers who first noted a marked increase in what they called *postmaterial* values, especially among younger and more highly educated people in the skilled service and administrative occupations in Western Europe. Such voters showed less concern for the traditional *material* values of economic well-being and security, and instead stressed participatory and environmental concerns in politics as a way of improving democracy and the general quality of life. Studies of postmaterialism form a very important addition to our ongoing attempt to interpret and explain not only the so-called youth revolt but also some more lasting shifts in lifestyles and political priorities. It makes intuitive sense that such changes appear to be especially marked among those who grew up in the relative prosperity of Western Europe, after the austere period of reconstruction that followed World War II. In more recent years, however, there appears to have been a revival of material concerns among younger people, as economic prosperity and security seems less certain. There are also some indications that political reform activities evoke less interest and commitment than earlier.

None of this should be mistaken for a return to the political patterns of the past. Instead, we may be witnessing the emergence of a still somewhat incongruent new mix of material and postmaterial orientations, along with both old and new forms of political self-expression by the citizenry. Established political parties appear to be in somewhat of a quandary in redefining their positions, at a time when the traditional bonding of many voters to one or another party seems to have become weaker. Many observers speak about a widespread condition of political malaise in advanced industrial countries, suggesting that it shows up not only in opinion polls but also in a marked decline in voter participation and, on occasion, a propensity for voter revolt against the establishment parties and candidates. Without suggesting a simple cause-effect relationship, the British observer Martin Jacques has pointed to parallels between electoral malaise or dealignment and the vague rhetoric offered by many political activists and opinion leaders. He believes that the end of the cold war and the collapse of communism in Europe have created a situation that demands a reformulation of political and ideological alternatives. In that sense, he finds some paradigmatic significance in the great political shakeup of the Italian party system.

At this point, at least, it seems unlikely that Italy will set an example for many other democracies. Most established parties seem to have developed an ability to adjust to change, even as the balance of power within each party system shifts over time and occasional newcomers are admitted to the club. Each country's party system remains uniquely shaped by its political history, but there does seem to be some very general patterns of development. One frequently observed trend is toward a narrowing of the ideological distance between the moderate Left and Right in many European countries. It now often makes more sense to speak of the center-Left and center-Right respectively.

Despite such convergence, there are still some important ideological and practical differences between the two orientations. Thus the Right is usually far more ready to accept as inevitable the existence of social or economic inequalities along with the hiearchies they produce. It normally favors lower taxes and the promotion of market forces—with some very important exceptions intended to protect the nation as a whole (national defense) as well as certain favorite groups and values within it. In general, the Right sees the state as an instrument that should provide security, order, and protection of an established way of life. The Left, by contrast, emphasizes that government has an important task in promoting opportunities, delivering services, and reducing social inequities. On issues such as higher and more progressive taxation, high rates of unemployment, and inflation, there continue to be considerable differences between moderates of the Left and Right.

Even as the ideological distance between Left and Right narrows but remains important, there are also signs of some political differentiation within each camp. On the center-Right side of the party spectrum in European politics, economic neoliberals (who speak for business and industry) must be clearly distinguished from the social conservatives (who are more likely to advocate traditional values and authorities). European liberalism has its roots in a tradition that favors civil liberties and tolerance but that also emphasizes the importance of individual achievement and laissez-faire economics. For such European neoliberals, the state has an important but very limited role to play in providing an institutional framework within which individuals and social groups pursue their interests. Traditional conservatives, by contrast, emphasize the importance of social stability and continuity, and point to the social danger of disruptive change. They often value the strong state as an instrument of order, but many of them also show a paternalist appreciation for welfare state programs that will help keep "the social net" from tearing apart.

In British politics, Margaret Thatcher promoted elements from each of these traditions in what could be called her own mix of "business conservatism." The result is the peculiar tension between "drys" and "wets" within her own Conservative Party, even after she has ceased to be its leader. In France, on the other hand, the division between neoliberals and conservatives runs more clearly between the two major center-Right parties, the Giscardist UDF and the neo-Gaullist RPR, who are coalition partners in the present government. In Germany, the Free Democrats would most clearly represent the traditional liberal position, while some conservative elements can be found among the Christian Democrats.

There is something of a split identity also among the Christian Democrats, who until recently were one of the most successful political movements in Europe after World War II. Here idealists, who subscribe to the socially compassionate teachings of the Church, have found themselves losing influence to more efficiency-oriented technocrats or efficiency-oriented political managers. The latter seem to reflect little of the original ideals of personalism, solidarity, and subsidiarity that originally distinguished the Christian Democrats from both neoliberals and conservatives in post–war Europe. It remains to be seen whether political setbacks for the Christian Democrats in Italy will lead to more than a face-lift. Their new name of Popular Party seems unintentionally self-ironic and has done little to stem their recent electoral losses. In Germany, however, the Christian Democrats have managed to remain chancellor party despite some slippage in their electoral appeal.

On the Left, democratic socialists and ecologists stress that the sorry political, economic, and environmental record of Communist-ruled states in no way diminishes the validity of their own commitment to social justice and environmental protection in modern industrial society. For them, capitalism will continue to produce its own social problems and dissatisfactions. No matter how efficient capitalism may be, they argue, it will continue to result in inequities that require politically directed redress. Many on the Left, however, show a pragmatic acceptance of the modified market economy as an arena within which to promote their reformist goals. Social Democrats in Scandinavia and Germany have long been known to take such positions. In recent years, their colleagues in Britain and France have followed suit by abandoning some traditional symbols and goals, such as major programs of nationalization. The Socialists in Spain, who governed that new democracy after 1982, went furthest of all in adopting business-friendly policies before their loss of power in early 1996.

Some other Western European parties further to the left have also moved in the centrist direction in recent years. Two striking examples of this shift can be found among the Greens in Ger-many and the former Communist Party of Italy. The Greens are by no means an establishment party, but they have served as a pragmatic coalition partner with the Social Democrats in several state governments and have gained respect for their mixture of practical competence and idealism. The so-called realist faction (*Realos*) has clearly outmaneuvered its more radical rivals in the party's fundamentalist (*Fundi*) wing. The Italian communists have come even further toward a center-Left position. Years before they adopted the new name of Democratic Party of the Left (PDS), they had abandoned the Leninist revolutionary tradition and adopted reformist politics similar to those of social democratic parties elsewhere in Western Europe. Not every Italian communist went along, and a fundamentalist core broke away to set up a new far-Left party of Refounded Communists.

Both center-Left and center-Right moderates face a dual challenge from the populists on the Right—who often seek lower taxes, drastic cuts in the social budget, and a curtailment of immigration—and the neofascists on the ultra-Right. These two orientations on the Right can often be distinguished, as in Italy, where the populist Northern League and the neofascist-descended National Alliance represent positions that are polar opposites, on such key issues as government devolution (favored by the former, opposed by the latter). Sometimes a charismatic leader can speak to both orientations by appealing to their shared fears and resentments. That seems to be the case of Jörg Haider, whose Freedom Party has attracted over one-quarter of the vote in Austria's recent election. The electoral revival of the right-wing parties can be linked in considerable part to the anxieties and tensions that affect some socially and economically insecure groups in the lower middle class and some sectors of the working class.

Ultra-Right nationalist politicians and their parties typically eschew a complex explanation of the structural and cyclical problems that beset the European economies. Instead they simply blame external scapegoats, namely the many immigrants and refugees from Eastern Europe as well as from developing countries in northern Africa and elsewhere. The presence of the far-Right parties inevitably has an effect on both the balance of power and the political agendas that occupy the more centrist parties. Almost everywhere, for example, some of the established parties and politicians have been making symbolic concessions on the refugee issue in order to prevent it from becoming monopolized by extremists.

Women in politics is the concern of the third section in this unit. There continues to be a strong pattern of underrepresentation of women in positions of political and economic leadership practically everywhere. Yet there are some notable differences from country to country, as well as from party to party. Generally speaking, the parties of the Left have been readier to place women in positions of authority, although there are some remarkable exceptions, as the center-Right cases of Margaret Thatcher in Britain and Simone Weil in France illustrate.

On the whole, the system of proportional representation gives parties both a tool and an added incentive to place female candidates in positions where they will be elected. But here too, there can be exceptions, as in the case of France in 1986, when women did not benefit from the one-time use of proportional representation in the parliamentary elections. Clearly it is not enough to have a relatively simple means, such as proportional representation, for promoting women in politics; there must also be an organized *will* among decision makers to use the available tool for the purpose of such a clearly defined reform.

This is where a policy of affirmative action may be a chosen strategy. The Scandinavian countries best illustrate how breakthroughs may occur. There is a markedly higher representation of women in the parliaments of Denmark, Finland, Iceland, Norway, and Sweden, where the political center of gravity is somewhat to the Left and where proportional representation makes it possible to set up party lists that are more representative of the population as a whole. It is of some interest that Iceland has a special women's party with parliamentary representation, but it is more important that women are found in leading positions within most of the parties of this and the other Scandinavian countries. It usually does not take long for the more centrist or moderately conservative parties to adopt the new concern of gender equality, which may even move to the forefront; women have recently held the leadership of three of the main parties in Norway (the Social Democrats, the Center Party, and the Conservatives). Together they normally receive roughly two-thirds of the total popular vote. It is worth pointing out that in contrast to Margaret Thatcher, who included no women in her cabinet between 1979 and 1990, Norway's first female prime minister, Dr. Gro Harlem Brundtland, used that position to advance the number of women in ministerial positions (8 of 18 cabinet posts). The present Swedish government of Social Democrats, which took power in 1994, has an equal number of women and men in the cabinet.

In another widely reported sign of change, the relatively conservative Republic of Ireland has chosen Mary Robinson as its first female president. It is a largely ceremonial post, but it has a symbolic potential that Mary Robinson, an outspoken advocate of liberal reform in her country, is willing to use on behalf of social change. Perhaps most remarkable of all, the advancement of women into high political ranks has now also touched Switzerland, where women did not get the right to vote until 1971.

Altogether, there is undoubtedly a growing awareness of the pattern of gender discrimination in most Western countries. It seems likely that there will be a significant improvement in this situation over the course of the next decade if the pressure for reform is maintained. Such changes have already occurred in other areas where there used to be significant political differences between men and women. At one time, for example, there used to be a considerably lower voter turnout among women, but this gender gap has been practically eliminated in recent decades. Similarly the tendency for women to be somewhat more conservative in party and candidate preferences has given way to a more liberal disposition among younger women

in foreign and social policy preferences than among men. These are aggregate differences, of course, and it is important to remember that women, like men, do not represent a monolithic bloc in political attitudes and behavior but are divided by other interests and priorities. One generalization seems to hold, namely that there is much less inclination among women to support parties or candidates that have a decidedly "radical" image. Thus the vote for extreme right-wing parties in contemporary Europe tends to be considerably higher among male voters.

In any case, there are some very important policy questions that affect women more directly than men. Any statistical study of women in the paid labor force of Europe could supply conclusive evidence to support three widely shared impressions: (1) there has been a considerable increase in the number and relative proportion of women who take up paid jobs; (2) these jobs are more often unskilled and/or part-time than in the case of men's employment; and (3) women generally receive less pay and less social protection than men in similar positions. Such a study would also show that there are considerable differences among Western European countries in the relative position of their female workers, thereby offering support for the argument that political intervention in the form of appropriate legislation *can* do something to improve the employment status of women—not only by training them better for advancement in the labor market but also by changing the conditions of the workplace to eliminate both obvious and hidden disadvantages for women.

The socioeconomic status of women in other parts of the world is often far worse. According to the 1995 report of the UN Development Programme, there have been some rapid advances for women in the field of education and health opportunities, but the doors to economic opportunities are barely ajar. In the field of political leadership, the picture is more varied, as the UN report indicates, but women generally hold few positions of importance in national politics. To be sure, there have been some remarkable breakthroughs; for example, in South Africa women won 100 of the 400 seats in the first post-apartheid parliament in 1994.

The framework of government is the subject of the fourth section of this unit. Here the articles examine and compare a number of institutional arrangements: essential characteristics and elements of a pluralist democracy, two major systems of representative government, various rules governing campaign and party finance, different electoral systems, and the presidential and prime ministerial forms of executive.

The topic of pluralist democracy is a complex one, but Phillipe C. Schmitter and Terry Lynn Karl manage to present a very comprehensive discussion of the subject. Gregory Mahler focuses on the legislative-executive relationship of parliamentary and congressional systems, drawing mainly upon the British, Canadian, and American examples. He avoids the trap of idealizing any one way of organizing the functions of representative government. Arthur Gunlicks approaches the issue of campaign and party finance from an interesting angle and asks what

Americans might learn from the manner in which this problem is resolved in several other democracies. The article, "Electoral Reform: Good Government? Fairness? Or Vice Versa. Or Both?" examines the supposed advantages and disadvantages of different electoral systems, showing that proportional representation need not result in political instability or paralysis. Richard Rose compares the political executive in the United States, Great Britain, and France and finds that each system has its own constraints upon arbitrary rule that can easily become obstacles to prompt and decisive action.

Looking Ahead: Challenge Questions

How do you explain the apparent shifts toward the political center made by parties of the moderate Left and moderate Right in recent years? How do Social Democrats present themselves as reformers of capitalism? What are the main sources of electoral support for the far-Right political parties?

Why are women so poorly represented in parliaments and other positions of political leadership? How do institutional arrangements, such as elections systems, both help and hinder improvement in this situation? Which parties and countries tend to have a better record of female representation?

Would you agree with the inventory of democratic essentials as discussed by Schmitter and Karl? What do you regard as most and least important in their inventory? What are some major traits of a good constitution?

What are some of the major arguments made in favor of the parliamentary system of government? What are the main arguments against and in favor of proportional representation? What do you think the United States could learn from the manner in which other democracies handle campaign and party finance? What are some main differences among the executive structures in Great Britain, France, and the United States, and how important are they in shaping the governmental style and direction of each country?

The left's new start

A future for socialism

IN MUCH of Europe, left-wing politics is enjoying a revival. Scandinavian voters, who not long ago seemed to have abandoned their tradition of social democratic government, are putting left-of-centre parties into office again. Last month Hungary ditched its reformist pro-business government in favour of a "socialist" party made up of former communists; Social Democrats will do well in Germany's elections in October, opinion polls say; in Britain, the Labour Party trounced the Tories in recent local elections and stands a good chance of forming the next government; across the European Union, socialists expect to do well in elections to the European Parliament on June 9th and 12th. The revival is by no means universal—socialist parties are in trouble in Spain, France and Italy, to name just three—but it is nonetheless striking.

Just as striking is the fact that traditional ideas cannot claim the credit for the left's popularity. Today's socialist parties have all but abandoned many of their old policies. By the end of the 1980s most of Europe's left-of-centre parties already advocated (albeit grudgingly) slimmer government, lower taxes and privatisation—measures to which they were once bitterly opposed. Where parties called "socialist" are doing better, it is partly because they no longer espouse socialism.

This is a good thing. The left's traditional policies of widespread public ownership and punitive taxation only ever promised equality of disappointment. However, the realignment of the left is not as good a thing as it could be. Traditional socialists who ask why the left should seek power at all, if it is only to implement a soft-focus version of conservatism, ask a good question. For the sake of intelligent debate about public policy (ie, for the sake of good government) the left needs to do more than ditch the discredited policies of its past. It needs to develop a new programme that is not just economically literate, welcome though that would be, but distinctive as well.

Same means, different ends

In a variety of countries, attempts to do this are under way (see pages 17-19). Few of these efforts are promising, for a reason that is both revealing and dispiriting: most socialist modernisers remain instinctively hostile to market economics.

Some "market socialists" say, for instance, that capitalism would be all right as long as firms worked in a different way. They propose batteries of regulation to increase worker participation in management, to oblige firms to take a longer-term view, to make them more sensitive to the needs of their "stakeholders" (as opposed to the people who merely own them), and what not. Other modernisers see environmental questions as the niche for a new socialism. Still others emphasise the role of trade and industrial policies in maintaining some supposedly desirable mix of activities. The list goes on—each such policy justified by an elaborate appeal to the concept of "market failure". This idea remains the hallmark even of modernised socialism, central both to its substance and its presentation. The market alone cannot do this, cannot do that. State intervention—cleverer than before, but broadly based and, in its way, hardly less ambitious—remains the offered remedy.

Such thinking is profoundly misguided. In a sense market failure is pervasive. Competition is "imperfect", production and exchange involve externalities, the future is uncertain; for all these reasons, markets fail to allocate resources precisely as they would in the textbook world of basic economics. By the same test, there is much to be said for central planning. But this century's most important economic lesson is that, except in textbooks, government failure is broader, more damaging in economic terms and much more threatening to individual liberty than market failure.

The question is whether socialists can accept that truth whole-heartedly; rather than, as at present, half-heartedly, with

10,000 qualifications, or not at all. The answer may well be No. For many, "socialism" by definition cannot accept the market as the right framework for organising society. After all, socialism has a history. Its roots lie in an analysis of society that denies not merely the efficiency but also the moral content of free interaction among economic agents. If that analysis is bankrupt (and it is), what is there left for "socialism" to say?

Plenty, as it happens—with or without that label. The aims of socialism as a programme of social and economic reform, as opposed to the analysis of socialism as an intellectual discipline, have always been the source of its popular support. Goals such as reducing poverty, promoting equality of opportunity, and improving the quality of public services for all remain enormously appealing. In these aims, not in the arcane theories of economic planning, lies the reason why so many people for years invested in socialism their hopes for a happier and healthier society.

If those goals, as opposed to the ideological apparatus in which they were once couched, matter most to today's socialists, there is no reason why the left cannot be as vigorous in its enthusiasm for market economics as the right. If leftist parties could bring themselves to believe that the market is wonderful (not merely useful if kept in its place), that it has delivered the vast majority (not a privileged minority) of people in the West to material well-being which they would never have attained otherwise, that it must be trusted to co-ordinate the great bulk of society's activities, then they could be far more effective in pursuing their aims as social reformers.

These aims constitute an agenda that is not only distinctive but which also attacks the right at its weakest spot. In many countries (notably Britain), conservative governments have failed to reform welfare systems in such a way as to prevent, let alone reverse, increasing poverty. They have failed to invest adequately in the forms of education (notably nursery education, and basic training in literacy and numeracy) that do most to interrupt the transmission of failure from one generation to the next. They have failed to maintain the supply of some public services (such as public transport) to those who have no choice but to rely on them.

Left-of-centre parties account for this partly by saying that conservative governments, unlike them, are not chiefly concerned about the people who suffer as a result. By and large, this is true. But the policies that are needed in response do not call for a searching critique of the market economy. In the aggregate, the market provides the resources for effective action; case by case, moreover, it is often the only effective way to deliver help to the people who need it. The goals of defeating poverty, expanding economic opportunities for the less well-off, and improving the quality of public services will only in fact be achieved by people who can say the words "market" and "capitalism" without sneering.

Exploiting the market

In framing market-friendly policies with aims such as these in view, left-of-centre parties actually have two decisive advantages over their conservative counterparts. First, they can more readily attack certain sorts of privilege. In many countries in Europe and elsewhere, the fiercest opponents of change are those who have traditionally benefited from the restrictive practices established over the years by the middle-class professions: doctors, accountants, lawyers and so forth. The left may be—and certainly ought to be—less willing than the right to de-

fer to such interests. Second, the left's motives in reform are less in doubt. As a result, as "socialist" governments in Australia and New Zealand have shown, leftist reformers can often be more radical than right-of-centre governments in pursuit of efficiency, as well as in pursuit of equity.

This is especially true in management of the public sector. By getting better value for taxpayers' money, and by pruning subsidies to the better off, socialists can deliver more and better services to the people who need them.

Consider Britain's reforms of the National Health Service. By the end of the 1970s, the NHS had become a startlingly wasteful bureaucracy. The best that could be said for it was that it was comparatively cheap: Britain spent massively on health care, but less so than most other rich industrial countries. The service worked badly. Access to medicine and treatment was controlled by rationing; the system was slow and growing slower; standards of treatment and hospital accommodation compared poorly with those abroad.

The reforms undertaken by successive Conservative administrations—the attempt to introduce an "internal market", to ensure that resources were allocated according to the needs of users rather than the convenience of producers—made good sense. In principle, the changes were entirely consistent with the preservation of taxpayer-financed health care for all. In principle, they were capable of putting whatever resources the government devoted to the NHS to better use—meaning faster, better care, including for the least well-off. Voters remained intensely suspicious, however, not least because the government presented its plans as though saving money counted for more than improving the quality of the service. And the Labour Party vilified the reforms from the start, arguing that market economics has no place in the provision of health care.

If Labour wins power, it should think again. However much it plans to spend on health care, the intelligent use of market forces within the system would be its greatest ally in helping those who rely upon it. And because Labour would be trusted by the electorate to keep the NHS intact and free at the point of use, it could actually go further and faster than the Tories in improving the system.

The same goes for socialist parties in other countries, and for other forms of public investment. Adopt road-use pricing, for instance, and use the proceeds from that market-friendly policy to increase investment in railways and other forms of public transport. Introduce competition and market forces into education, by extending the freedom of parents to choose their children's schools, thus encouraging popular schools to grow and unpopular ones to shrink. In these and other areas, left-of-centre governments might still choose to spend more on public investment than conservative ones. That could make sense—but only if a framework (the market) was in place to ensure that the resources were well used.

Respect for market forces and incentives, together with a determination to help the unfortunate, can be expensive. A policy to equip the unemployed for work costs a lot: more, often, than it costs to keep failing industries afloat. However, measures that improve training opportunities for the unemployed make better sense than measures to defend a dying firm. They speed the creation of jobs in the right industries, promoting growth across the economy as a whole. Welfare reform is even more difficult than labour-market reform. It is costly and complicated to help the poor without worsening the poverty trap that is caused by the interaction of benefits and taxation. The remedy involves benefits that are better-targeted, but withdrawn more gradually as income rises, and minimal taxation at the bottom of the income scale. This costs money.

A left-of-centre party should nonetheless be ambitious in both these areas—making it all the more important to pare public spending of the kind that helps people who do not need to be helped. Here too, a left-of-centre government could be more daring than a conservative one. Acting as always in the name of equity and efficiency, it could make benefits to the elderly poor more generous, but reduce or eliminate benefits to the elderly not-poor; it could recover more of the costs of university education from the beneficiaries; it could narrow tax breaks and subsidies for the well-off; it could launch a vigorous assault on support (in the form of inflated prices and other sub-sidies) for farmers, thereby raising revenue for other purposes while cutting the cost of food.

A question of priorities

Much of this may seem unthinkable for Europe's socialists—like support for privatisation ten years ago. If so, it is because the character of the left, though altered and improved, needs to change further. Socialism must continue to define itself less in terms of means (we will manage the economy and civilise the market) and more in terms of priorities (we will help society's losers). The left should do this not merely to strengthen its elect-ability further, though that would be one result. It should do it mainly because, once in power, it would then be far more likely to change society, as it wants to, for the better.

Guide to the west European left

The left in western Europe is going through a difficult spell. If the Spanish Socialists are beaten this year, not one large country will have a left-of-centre government. **Paul Anderson** looks at what has gone wrong

Of course, as Tony Blair always reminds us, the next election in Britain is by no means in the bag for Labour. However desperate the plight of the ruling Conservatives might look today, it could be very different when the country goes to the polls.

All the same, it does look as if Labour is going to win the next election—its first general election success since October 1974. Elsewhere in western Europe, left parties are in a less happy position. The centre-left is in government in only one of the five biggest west European countries, Spain, and it is likely that Felipe González's Socialist government will be ousted on 3 March 1996. In Germany, the Social Democrats are way behind the centre-right government in the opinion polls—and the French Socialists are only just recovering from their defeat in the 1993 general election. Apart from Britain, Italy is the only country of the "big five" where the centre-left has a good chance of winning a general election in the near future.

In the smaller countries, the picture is brighter: indeed, at present every one has Socialists in government, whether as sole ruling party (Greece, Portugal, Sweden, Norway) or as part of a coalition (Netherlands, Belgium, Austria, Switzerland, Finland, Denmark, Ireland, Luxembourg). Each governing left party is different—but they also have much in common. Nearly all of them, particularly those in EU governments that are attempting to meet the Maastricht treaty criteria on economic and monetary union, have had to introduce tough (and unpopular) austerity budgets despite persistently high unemployment; and in

many cases the result has been the defection of Social Democrat and Socialist voters to parties of the far left and far right.

Will the same happen in Britain under a Blair Labour government? It is certainly likely to have to introduce unpopular measures of economic policy—but it is unclear whether disillusioned Labour voters will turn to the political extremes. The British electoral system has so far mitigated against the emergence of credible electoral parties of far left or far right. But if the electoral system is changed after Labour's promised referendum, our politics could take on a more continental hue.

Germany

If the German left sneezes, the rest of the west European left catches pneumonia. And the past 13 years have been less than glorious for the German Social Democratic Party (*Sozialdemokratische Partei Deutschlands*—SPD), the biggest of all Europe's social democratic parties.

After the liberal Free Democratic Party (*Freie Demokratische Partei*—FDP) abandoned SPD chancellor Helmut Schmidt's centre-left West German coalition government in 1982, the SPD went into opposition at federal level. It has remained there ever since, losing general elections to chancellor Helmut Kohl's centre-right ruling coalition in West Germany in 1983 and 1987 and in Germany as a whole in 1990 and 1994.

The SPD has been consistently outpolled in elections to the *Bundestag* (federal lower chamber) by the centre-right

Christian Democratic Union (*Christlich Demokratische Union*—CDU) and its Bavarian sister party, the Christian Social Union (*Christlich Soziale Union*—CSU). It has been unable to prise the FDP away from the CDU/CSU. Worse, it has been unable to stop the emergence and survival of the Greens (*Die Grünen*), who bounced back from a disastrous showing in the 1990 unification election to take 7.1 per cent in 1994 and are currently riding high in the opinion polls. Perhaps unsurprisingly, the SPD has spent much of the past decade engulfed by a crisis of confidence unprecedented since 1945.

It's not quite that the SPD thinks of itself as a natural party of government: before 1966, when it entered a "grand coalition" with the CDU/CSU, it had been excluded from federal government since the foundation of the *Bundesrepublik* in 1949. But the SPD was dominant in federal politics throughout the late 1960s and 1970s, and its regional power-base in the *Länder* (states) was formidable. (It remains so: a majority of *Länder* today have SPD-dominated governments, which gives the party a majority in the *Bundesrat*, the federal upper chamber.) It took the SPD several years to recuperate from the defection of the FDP and the emergence of the Greens as a serious electoral force in 1982-83—and the recovery was still incomplete when the party was subject to the even greater shock of unification.

The problem goes back to the last years of the Schmidt administration, which managed to alienate working-class voters with its austerity programme and the left with its enthusiasm for the stationing of new Nato intermediate-range nuclear

From *New Statesman & Society*, January 5, 1996, pp. 24-28. © 1996 by *New Statesman & Society*, a publication of Guardian News Service, Ltd. Reprinted by permission.

missiles in Germany. After the FDP jumped ship in 1982, the SPD spent several years desperately attempting to regain the support of both the working class and the largely middle-class protest movement against the missiles. It failed on both counts and lost ground to both the Greens and the ruling coalition in 1983 and again in 1987.

In the late 1980s, the SPD's fortunes improved, largely because of the thaw in the cold war. In the 1989 Euro-elections the SPD came within a whisker of overtaking the CDU/CSU share of the vote, and, with the charismatic radical Saarland premier, Oskar Lafontaine, as candidate for the chancellorship, the SPD seemed well placed to win the 1990 federal election. Then, however, the Berlin wall came down, and the party made the disastrous mistake of refusing to back immediate German unification—largely for economic reasons. In 1990, the party's vote was 33.5 per cent, its worst showing since the 1950s. In former East Germany it did particularly badly as the Party of Democratic Socialism (*Partei des Demokratischen Sozialismus*—PDS), the successor to the ruling East German communist party, split what there was of a left vote.

The SPD has still not recovered. After of the 1990 defeat, Lafontaine dropped out of the leadership, to be replaced by Schleswig-Holstein premier Björn Engholm; and after Engholm resigned in 1993 in the wake of a bizarre scandal, the post fell to Rhineland-Palatinate premier Rudolf Scharping. Scharping adopted a cautious strategy of wooing the centre and big business while shunning the idea of coalition with either the Greens or the PDS—and it didn't work. In the 1994 Euro-elections, the SPD took just 32.2 per cent of the vote, and later in the year it managed only 36.4 per cent in the federal election.

Remarkably, Scharping survived as leader after the defeat but, after a series of disastrous local and regional election results, he came under increasing criticism from within the SPD. At the time, it seemed that the main threat to his leadership came from Gerhard Schröder, the Lower Saxony premier. In fact, it was Lafontaine who dealt Scharping the fatal blow, at the November 1995 SPD conference in Mannheim. Lafontaine unexpectedly forced a vote on the party leadership, and won. The SPD, languishing in the opinion polls, immediately gained 5 per cent support.

Whether Lafontaine can keep up the momentum remains to be seen. His openness to dealing with the Greens and, more controversially, the PDS, which took 19.8 per cent of the east German

vote in the 1994 general election, could easily backfire with voters hostile to the old East Germany. If it doesn't, he is likely to be chosen as SPD candidate for the chancellorship in the 1998 general election. The first indication of his fortunes will be a set of *Land* elections in March 1996.

While the SPD has been in the doldrums, the Greens—now firmly in the hands of pragmatists—have been doing better than ever, taking more than 10 per cent of the vote in regional and local elections. Many observers reckon that they will replace the FDP as the party that either the SPD or the CDU/CSU must woo to form a federal government.

France

The 1980s saw the Socialist Party (*Parti Socialiste*—PS) dominate French politics as never before. After François Mitterrand won the presidency (at his third attempt) in April 1981, the PS, backed by the French Communist Party (*Parti Communiste Française*—PCF), won a landslide victory in elections for the National Assembly. Mitterrand, who appointed PCF ministers to his first government, tried to implement a radical Keynesian economic programme. He was forced to abandon it in 1982-83; the PCF quit the government in disgust at the ensuing austerity; and the right won the next legislative elections in March 1986—but the period of *cohabitation* between Mitterrand and the centre-right government of Jacques Chirac lasted only two years. In 1988, Mitterrand was returned for a second term, and the PS won the subsequent National Assembly election.

Today, all that seems ancient history. In 1993, the PS, led by former prime minister Michel Rocard, suffered a humiliating legislative election defeat, taking only 54 National Assembly seats to the right's 460. In 1994, it fared even worse in the Euro-elections—partly because of the intervention of the charismatic (but subsequently disgraced) Marseilles millionaire Bernard Tapie, whose centre-left *Energie Radicale* alliance took 12 per cent of the vote to the PS' 14.5 per cent. Last year, the PS candidate for the presidency, Lionel Jospin, a man chosen only because former European Commission president Jacques Delors refused to stand, was beaten by Chirac. Even though Jospin did better than expected, taking 23 per cent of the vote in the first round (more than any other candidate) and a creditable 47.4 per cent in the second, his defeat forced even PS loyalists to recognise that their party's hegemony had come to an end.

What went wrong? Both Mitterrand

and the PS became embroiled in a series of scandals in the early 1990s, and Mitterrand's manoeuvring to block Rocard's chances of succeeding him as president did major damage—most notably after he replaced Rocard as prime minister in 1991 with the incompetent Edith Cresson. But by far the most important factor behind the decline of the PS was Europe.

After it abandoned "Keynesianism in one country", the Mitterrand administration increasingly saw European integration as its flagship project. Along with former PS finance minister Delors, who took over the Commission in 1984, Mitterrand was one of the key figures behind the creation of the single European market; and the deal struck in Maastricht in 1991 on European economic and political union was essentially a Franco-German affair, with the French getting commitments to a single currency in return for concessions to the Germans on political union and independence for the European central bank. In preparation for the creation of a single currency, the value of the franc was tied to the Deutschmark in the exchange rate mechanism.

The problem was that Mitterrand had not foreseen German unification—or rather the hike in interest rates with which the Bundesbank decided to pay for it, which forced up French interest rates and unemployment. The popularity of the government slipped steadily through the early 1990s. In September 1992's referendum on Maastricht, called by Mitterrand after Denmark voted "no" to the treaty, the French voted "yes" by the narrowest of margins. Six months later came the National Assembly election debacle.

Not all the French left was tainted by Maastricht. The Eurosceptic PCF played a large part in the "no" referendum campaign. But it was in no position to benefit. Under the leadership of Georges Marchais, it had retreated into the hard-left ghetto after quitting government in 1984, and its slow but steady decline since the 1940s had turned into a collapse. The PCF had shunned the new social movements, closing off the possibility of renewal through an influx of middle-class environmentalists and feminists (which meant that, once the French Greens tired of the PS' attentions, they became resolutely hostile to the left), and its bone-headed Stalinism had destroyed its credibility among the intelligentsia. Meanwhile, disaffected working-class voters in its heartlands had turned increasingly to the far right. Even in defeat in 1993, the PS polled twice as many votes as the PCF.

So where does the French left go now? The PS has been thrashing about since 1993, first shifting left and then backing the centrist Jospin—now its leader and dominant figure—but there has been a partial recovery in its fortunes in recent months as the right-wing government's popularity has slumped. As for the PCF, Marchais' successor as general secretary, Robert Hue, seems to have at least slowed his party's decline. But it is unlikely that the left will benefit greatly from the wave of strikes and protests that swept France before Christmas (the PS has no real union link these days, and the PCF's union connections have been weakened). The PS and PCF are bereft of ideas and—Jospin apart—credible leaders. It looks as if it will be some time before the left returns to power.

Italy

Not for the first time, the left in Italy faces the possibility of making a breakthrough into government in the next few months—and the fear that it will be left out in the cold yet again.

The Party of the Democratic Left (*Partito Democratica della Sinistra*—PDS) and its centre-left allies are doing well in the opinion polls. If they manage to postpone a general election long enough to expand the centre-left alliance (and to legislate to ensure that former prime minister Silvio Berlusconi does not again use his television stations for political propaganda), there's a good chance of a centre-left coalition taking power in Italy later this year. If Berlusconi manages to force an election sooner rather than later, however, the centre-left is more likely to be disappointed yet again.

Many observers have a sense of *deja vu*. Two years ago, in the run-up to the March 1994 general election, there seemed to be a real prospect of a centre-left victory. The PDS, alone of the major parties, had survived more-or-less unscathed from the scandals that had wrecked Italy's political class in the early 1990s, and it looked well positioned to take advantage. Instead, the election resulted in a victory for Berlusconi's Forza Italia in alliance with the ex-fascist National Alliance (*Alleanza Nazionale*—AN) and the regionalist Northern League (*Lega Nord*).

The PDS took just 21 per cent of the vote in 1994 and failed to pick up support from among former voters for the disgraced Italian Socialist Party (*Partito Socialista Italiano*—PSI) as it had hoped. An even worse performance in the Euro-election in June led to the resignation of PDS leader Achille Ochetto and the appointment of his deputy, Massimo D'Alema, as his replacement. D'Alema was the choice of the party leadership but not the ordinary members (who were merely "consulted" about the decision), and he has been unable effectively to stamp his authority on the PDS. It was no surprise when, early last year, the PDS reluctantly accepted that Romano Prodi, a Catholic economist backed by the small centrist Popular Party (*Partito Popular Italiana*—PPI, the left wing of the former Christian Democrats) would lead the centre-left into the next election.

One effect of the PDS decision to back Prodi, however, was to sharpen divisions between the PDS and the hard-left *Rifondazione Comunista* grouping, founded in 1991 by those communists who objected to the creation of the PDS. Rifondazione took 6 per cent in the 1994 general election and has since performed well in local elections. It has opposed the austerity programme of the technocratic government of prime minister Lamberto Dini, appointed after the fall of Berlusconi a year ago and backed by the PDS, and it has recently capitalised on left-wing voters' disgust at the PDS' attempt to attract the Northern League to the centre-left alliance by backing League-sponsored anti-immigrant legislation.

How all this pans out in the next few months is impossible to predict with any certainty. Much depends on what Dini and Antonio Di Pietro, the magistrate who symbolises the anti-corruption drive of the early 1990s, do next. Di Pietro, who leans to the right, has declared his intention of going into politics—and is popular enough to sway large numbers of voters, even though he has himself been charged with corruption. Dini leans to the left. If both opt to back the centre-left, the PDS will be ecstatic; if only Dini does life will be sweet; but if the two join together to try to create a new centre-right bloc in competition with the centre-left, the PDS will be miserable.

Spain

Is the writing on the wall for Felipe González and his Spanish Socialist Workers' Party (*Partido Socialista Obrero Español*—PSOE)? Certainly their position has looked more and more precarious since they won the 1993 general election, their fourth win in a row since 1982. The PSOE, which relied from 1993 until late last year on the backing of Catalan nationalists, fared miserably in the 1994 Euro-elections, losing votes both to the right-wing Popular Party (*Partido Popular*—PP) and the communist-led United Left (*Izquierda Unida*—IU), and ever since has looked incapable of bouncing back in this year's general election, now fixed for 3 March.

One problem for the PSOE and González has been a string of corruption scandals, the most damaging of which is the long-running saga of GAL, a government-sponsored death-squad that murdered several Basque separatists in the mid-1980s. Another bugbear has been unemployment, which has increased to 24 per cent from 16 per cent in 1990. Yet another is the decreasing utility of the PSOE's accusations that the right is tainted with fascism—a ploy that made a crucial difference even in 1993. It is now more than 20 years since the death of Franco, and younger voters are uninterested in the right's antecedents. The PP is favourite to form the next government, possibly with Catalan nationalist support.

Of course, there are many who would question whether the PSOE is genuinely a party of the left: it has from the start of its period in office adopted a market-oriented economic philosophy closer to that of Margaret Thatcher than to the ideas of northern European social democratic parties.

This is one major reason for the survival (and recent success) of IU, which emerged out of the "no" campaign for the 1986 referendum on Nato membership, which was dominated by the Eurocommunist Spanish Communist Party (*Partido Comunista de España*—PCE). At the time, most commentators reckoned that nothing could stop the decline of PCE membership and support, but IU, led since 1988 by the popular PCE general secretary Julio Anguita, has proved the sceptics wrong. Its 13.5 per cent in the 1994 Euro-elections was better than the PCE got in its late-1970s heyday.

FURTHER READING

There is a vast literature on the left in western Europe. Some of the best recent titles are the following:

Stephen Padgett and William E Paterson: *A History of Social Democracy in Postwar Europe* (Longman, 1991)

Perry Anderson and Patrick Camiller (eds): *Mapping the West European Left* (Verso, 1994)

Richard Gillespie and William E. Paterson: *Rethinking Social Democracy in Western Europe* (Cass, 1993)

Dick Richardson and Chris Rootes (eds): *The Green Challenge* (Routledge, 1994)

Research by Paul Anderson, Andy Brown and Patrick Fitzgerald

Europe's far right

Something nasty in the woodshed

Millions of Europeans are voting for far-right parties. Is democracy under threat? Or is the far right becoming less far out?

BY CHRISTMAS, a militantly anti-immigrant party with Nazi echoes could be part of an Austrian government. Mussolini's successors might be back in an Italian coalition some time next year. In Russia, xenophobic nationalists could be riding high in parliament—and aiming for the presidency. Even in civilised France, a xenophobic populist won 15% of the vote in the first round of the presidential election and has seen the mayoralties of some famous cities drop into the hands of his *confrères*. Does this mean that the far right as we have known it is back?

The answer is a firm but uncomplacent No. First point: what the far right stands for has changed. Even if far-right parties in Austria and Italy do well, they are less frightening than most people recently thought, and far less so than their ancestors in the 1930s. Most would now accept that multi-party systems are the best form of democracy, that power should be won and held only by the ballot box, and that nobody is above the law. Some east Europeans (especially in Russia) may not pass that test of respectability. But fascism in its old west European clothing is dead. The main parties on the Italian, French and Austrian far-right have even junked most of the old state corporatism that characterised the 1930s.

A second qualification is that nowhere is there much chance of an extreme right-winger winning power untrammelled. Jörg Haider's Freedom Party, Austria, or Gianfranco Fini's National Alliance, in Italy, could win power only as junior partners in a coalition. Russia's Vladimir Zhirinovsky has been sliding down the polls (see chart). France's Jean-Marie Le Pen has virtually no chance even of sharing power nationally.

And consider the countries where the far right did once hold sway. In Germany, the Nazi-shadowing Republican Party has shrivelled to about 3% of the national vote. The Iberian far right has virtually vanished. In the smaller countries of western Europe, latest opinion polls and elections at various levels usually give the far right less than 10%.

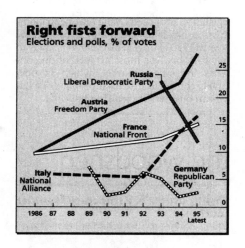

Right fists forward
Elections and polls, % of votes

Russia
Liberal Democratic Party

Austria
Freedom Party

France
National Front

Italy
National Alliance

Germany
Republican Party

1986 87 88 89 90 91 92 93 94 95 Latest

That is a far cry from the dark days of the 1930s. Despite the continuing existence of parties that are more or less fascist, the movement may have peaked. It is more worrying in eastern Europe than it is in the west. But even there, in a number of countries where leaders have handed out doses of unpleasant but necessary economic medicine, the threat is already diminishing or is likely to do so in the next few years. The appeal of the whackier sort of populist that burst forth from nowhere in the flush of post-communism to win big votes (Poland's Stanislaw Tyminski, for example, and Russia's Mr Zhirinovsky), is already fading as electorates become more sophisticated.

That is not to say the new ultra-right-wingers are unworrying. The latest one with a hope of power is Austria's Mr

Haider, whose Freedom Party may, according to some opinion polls, get nearly a third of the vote in a general election in December. The son of a high-ranking Nazi official, he has praised aspects of Hitler's rule. Once he thinks (often mistakenly) that he is out of earshot of the Viennese media, he tends to bash racial minorities, homosexuals and foreigners.

But he is able, sharp-witted and has learned not to rant, especially on television. Like Mr Fini in Italy, he has junked the old fascist corporatism in favour of the free market and recently chucked the pan-Germanism of old Austrian fascism. His hostility to the European Union goes down well in a country that is imposing austerity policies in an effort to meet the Maastricht criteria for economic and monetary union. Above all, he scores palpable hits against the corrupt, stagnant duopoly of the centre-left Social Democrats and centre-right People's Party, which have governed Austria as a shared fief virtually since 1945, dishing out jobs, contracts and even housing to its hitherto pliant constituents. Many Austrians think these parties deserve to lose.

That does not mean that Mr Haider deserves to win. The December election will be a three-way tussle, with the two long-ruling parties (which fell out over next year's budget) and Mr Haider's party all unlikely to win an outright majority. The question is whether Wolfgang Schüssel, the newish leader of the centre right could stomach teaming up with Mr Haider. So far, he has been studiously non-committal.

Look east, and tremble

In Italy, prospects are even muddier. Nobody knows when an election might happen or which parties will club together. A year ago, an opinion poll had Mr Fini as the country's most popular politician. The latest ones put his National Alliance in third place, with about a fifth of the vote, while the Democratic Party of the Left would get around a quarter and Silvio Berlusconi's Forza Italia something in-between. But, with Mr. Berlusconi due to stand trial on bribery charges, Mr Fini could press a claim to lead a right-wing coalition. And if the right does do well in Italy's next general election (anything could happen) then Mr Fini, like Mr Haider, would have a chance of power—even of becoming prime minister.

It is in the former Soviet block, where democracy has shallower roots, that the far right is more troubling. Ethnic turmoil, poverty, and the cynicism and corruption of voters and politicians, provide fertile ground for extremists of all kinds. In Slovakia, a populist prime minister, Vladimir Meciar, rails against gypsies and Hungarians, and retains power by allowing an even nastier far-right party to hold the defence and agriculture portfolios in his coalition. In Latvia, where Russians account for a

third of the population, a German-Latvian populist, who is appealing against a conviction in Germany for inciting racial hatred there, astonished pundits by nearly winning a recent general election. In Hungary, a more jocular populist, Jozsef Torgyan of the Independent Smallholders' Party, currently tops the opinion polls, by vilifying both the old communists and the new capitalists, stirring nationalist resentments, and praising God and "family values"—a rich recipe that goes down well across the whole of the old Soviet empire.

Even here, though, there are reasons for hope. Especially in ethnically homogeneous countries such as the Czech Republic and Poland, where the economy is improving, the far right is fading. Except for Latvia, the nationalist far right has shrunk in the rest of the Baltic area, and has dwindled in Belarus and Ukraine. If Hungary's so-far-sensible Socialists are tough enough on the economy, the appeal of Mr Torgyan's populist protest may well fizzle out by the time the next elections come round in 1998.

The biggest worry has been Russia, where the acrid Mr Zhirinovsky's 22% was the biggest vote for any party in the general election two years ago. But now that most Russian parties make nationalist noises, Mr Zhirinovsky seems to have faded too. The most popular party in Russia is the Communist Party and the biggest threat to democracy there comes from the left, not the right.

The trouble, though, is that the rhetoric of right and left is hard to distinguish. Nor, at either end of the spectrum, do parties comfortably pass the respectability test: their loyalty to democracy cannot be taken for granted. All the same, more moderate nationalists such as General Alexander Lebed—who is the most popular of Russian politicians—are less frightening than Mr Zhirinovsky. And there is still a good chance that politicians at the extremes will be outvoted by those nearer the centre. Give Russia another four years of moderation and even there the extremists should start to crumple.

The Impacts of Postwar Migration to Western Europe

Dr. Anthony M. Messina

Department of Political Science, Tufts University, Medford, Massachusetts

This essay identifies and analyzes the four most important impacts of postwar migration to Western Europe. First, early postwar immigration facilitated the rapid and sustained expansion of the domestic economy. Second, it eventually precipitated major changes in domestic immigration and citizenship regimes. Third, the influx of millions of immigrants, refugees, asylees, and migrant workers profoundly and permanently altered the social and cultural bases of West European societies. And finally, postwar immigration exacerbated the social tensions that helped to undermine the consensual foundations of the postwar political order. Professor Messina is the coeditor of Ethnic and Racial Minorities in Advanced Industrial Democracies *(1992) and the author of* Race and Party Competition in Britain *(1989), as well as numerous articles on the politics of ethnicity and immigration in Western Europe. He can be reached at the Department of Political Science, Tufts University, Medford, MA 02155.*

Before identifying and analyzing the most conspicuous impacts of post-World War II migration on the economies, societies, and politics of Western Europe, two facts are necessary to frame such an analysis. First, postwar migration to Western Europe did not unfold in a single, seamless pattern but, rather, in rolling waves, each wave precipitated by a unique set of stimuli and governed by its own peculiar internal logic. The first wave, which prevailed from the end of World War II until the early 1970s, was dominated by the mass movement of surplus workers from the Third World and Eastern Europe (Castles and Kosack 1973, 15–56). During the period of the great economic boom that swept across the western world from 1945 until 1969,

economic growth, an abundant labor supply, and productivity gains were strongly correlated in the industrial countries of Western Europe.

The second wave, whIch consists of the secondary migration of family members and the dependents of the original economic migrants, also began during the early postwar period but accelerated considerably when primary migration was severely curtailed by West European governments during the period of the first "oil shock" and the attendant economic recession of the early 1970s. This second migratory wave, having crested by the mid-1980s or so, has not ebbed entirely in Western Europe.

The third and latest great migration to Western Europe, originating during the early 1980s and persisting through the present, is mostly comprised of legitimate and illegitimate refugees and asylum seekers and illegal alien workers. The severe restrictions on legal immigration imposed by West European governments during the 1970s and the economic, social, and political convulsions associated with the East European revolutions of the late 1980s and early 1990s are the two major catalysts of this third migratory wave.

The second fact that should be considered about the postwar migration to Western Europe before analyzing its impacts is that, from its inception, it has been embedded in a larger cycle of global migration. That larger cycle, even some half century after it began, is far from exhausting itself (Castles 1989, 106–108). Indeed, Martin (1994) estimates that, worldwide, there are approximately 100 million persons residing outside their countries of citizenship. About half these persons, or 50 million immigrants, refugees, asylees, and migrant workers, live in the advanced industrial democracies, including at least 21 million in the countries of Western Europe. These expanding, predominantly nonwhite, populations currently account for as much as 4% of the total population of the United

Kingdom, 5% of The Netherlands, 6% of Austria and Sweden, 8% of France and Germany, and 16% of Switzerland.

How have the successive waves of postwar immigration affected Western Europe? The central argument of this essay is that few, if any, trends or phenomena affecting Western Europe as a whole since 1945 have been more transformative in their effects than the cumulative experience of postwar immigration. Postwar immigration has profoundly transformed Western Europe in four specific ways. First, early postwar immigration facilitated the rapid and sustained expansion of domestic economies, which fed the economic boom that enveloped all of Western Europe. Second, postwar migration to Western Europe eventually precipitated major changes in domestic immigration and citizenship regimes. Third, the influx of tens of millions of non-white immigrants, refugees, asylees, and migrant workers into Western European societies profoundly and permanently altered the social and cultural bases of these societies. And finally, postwar immigration exacerbated the intense social conflict that helped to undermine the consensual foundations of the postwar political order.

Immigration and the Postwar Economy

Although there is now substantial controversy about its current virtues and contributions to the economy (e.g., Coleman 1992; *The Economist* 1988), for a very long time a scholarly consensus prevailed concerning the effects of immigration on the domestic economies of Western Europe during the early to intermediate postwar period. Put simply, this consensus revolved around the view that postwar immigration was a necessary but insufficient factor in reviving the war-torn economies of Western Europe and, once they were revived, immigration helped to sustain domestic and regional economic expansion (Lamberts 1975). Postwar immigration was able to perform these vital functions primarily because it was so well attuned to the variable demands of the domestic economic market. To paraphrase Jones and Smith, postwar immigrants tended to enter the domestic economy during periods when, and settle in regions where, the shortage of native labor, for a variety of reasons, was most acute (1970, 132). Specifically, by satisfying the domestic demand for labor in the economy in a noninflationary to low inflationary manner (Jones and Smith 1970) during the early to intermediate postwar period, immigration "resolved recruitment bottlenecks, thus permitting profitable production and growth" (Fielding 1993, 16). Immigration is es-

pecially believed to have improved and sustained the health of the major economies of northwest Europe, including the Benelux countries, France, Switzerland, the United Kingdom, and the former West Germany.

Although there is widespread agreement that the economic impacts of postwar immigration were predominantly beneficial, there is also substantial consensus that immigration was not without its costs. According to some economists and political scientists, the primary economic fallout of postwar immigration was that it created a powerful incentive for West European industry not to rationalize its operations by introducing and adopting capital-intensive production methods (Freeman 1986, 55–56; Fielding 1993, 16). As Salowski states the problem:

> Instead of capital-deepening—the work-saving rationalization investment—we have capital-widening—that is, expanding investment. There is less substitution of capital for labor which would lead to an increase in work productivity. Old jobs with low productivity continue to be maintained (Salowski 1971, 22).

By propping up domestic firms that, without the use of foreign labor, would not have otherwise been competitive in the domestic and/or international marketplace, postwar immigration delayed the necessary restructuring and modernization of the macroeconomy. In this way, it is often argued, postwar immigration contributed to a long-term problem of low productivity and growth in the domestic West European economy.

This view of the negative economic dimensions of postwar immigration is not without its merits. Nevertheless, it is excessively critical and misleading on several scores. First, while the positive effects of postwar immigration on economic growth and short-term productivity were tangible and demonstrable, the assumed advantages of substituting capital for labor were largely speculative and unproven. As Korte (1985, 45) points out, in the 1960s the transition to qualitatively very different technologies was not seriously considered, nor would there have been sufficient capital or time available to accomplish it." Second, the view that immigration exacerbated more economic problems than it solved and, specifically, that it propped up declining and inefficient sectors of the economy, denies the benefits of an abundant labor supply for the whole economy, including that for firms with comparative cost advantages (Korte 1985, 45). These firms, too, benefitted from an adequate labor supply in expanding their operations during the great economic boom. And finally, early postwar immigration provided the more or less unparalleled benefits of being both highly flexible and self-regulating. In the British context, for example, Peach (1968) has demonstrated that, prior to the introduction of immigration controls, West Indian migration ebbed and flowed automatically in response to fluctuations in the British economy. Because of this self-regulating feature, early postwar immigration was much more efficient in satisfying the requirements of a rapidly expanding, full-employment economy than its economic critics have generally recognized. While these benefits could not be sustained forever, especially as immigrant workers began to settle more permanently in their adopted countries, they were nevertheless crucial and timely. In this sense, postwar immigration can be viewed as the necessary foundation upon which the spectacular growth and prosperity of postwar Europe was constructed (Kindelberger 1967).

The Transformation of Domestic Immigration and Citizenship Regimes

Regardless of its economic benefits, postwar immigration stimulated a great number and variety of social problems in its wake, most of which have been identified and extensively analyzed in what is now a vast literature that cuts across several major academic disciplines (e.g., Ireland 1994; Rex 1986; Richmond 1988). In a nutshell, these problems coalesce around the challenge of integrating the predominantly nonwhite, non-Western, and often non-Christian immigrant populations into the primarily white and nominally Christian societies of northwest Europe. In crudely responding to these challenges, West European governments from the mid-1960s forward adopted a two-pronged policy. First, they revised their immigration laws in order to make primary and sometimes secondary immigration more difficult. Many governments contended that by restricting immigration public authorities would be better able to cope with the problems affecting previously settled immigrants. And second, one by one West European governments altered their most important citizenship and nationality codes so as to accelerate the progress of integrating immigrants into their host societies. In some countries, as in Britain, citizenship and nationality laws were paradoxically made less inclusive in order to discourage the arrival of new immigrants already privileged with formal citizenship status. Successive British governments argued that restricting the access to citizenship of potential immigrants would facilitate the social acceptance of already settled immigrants by the native population (Messina 1989, 134–136). On the other hand, in other countries, such as the Netherlands, access

to citizenship was liberalized in order to encourage settled immigrants who held only foreign passports to apply for and adopt national citizenship. In Belgium, the Netherlands, Sweden, and elsewhere immigrants were eventually permitted to hold dual citizenship in the expectation that the extension of this privilege would stimulate greater numbers to apply for national citizenship.

Whether more inclusive or exclusive, immigration, citizenship, and nationality laws across contemporary Western Europe are not as they were before the onset of postwar immigration. As a direct result of the successive waves of migration to Western Europe, most states, by the mid-1990s, have recast their immigration, citizenship, and nationality laws and, in the process, redefined their identities as liberal polities (e.g., Soysal 1994; Hollifield 1992, 169–213).

The British experience is an extremely clear, if somewhat exaggerated, case in point. As a result of the passage of the 1948 British Nationality Act, which granted full British citizenship, including the right of unrestricted entry into Britain, to all citizens of the British Commonwealth, more than 200,000 Indian, Pakistani, and West Indian nationals migrated to Britain as workers or permanent settlers between 1955 and 1960. As greater numbers of foreign workers continued to arrive after 1960 under conditions of full employment and labor shortages, however, the British government responded to the influx and the social conflict it engendered by restricting new immigration through a series of legislative acts from 1962 through 1972.

The most important pieces of legislation in transforming British immigration, citizenship, and nationality law were the 1962 and 1968 Immigrants Acts and the 1971 Immigration Act. As a consequence of the 1962 Commonwealth Immigrants Act, the right of all further Commonwealth citizens to enter Britain without restriction was suddenly revoked and replaced with a labor voucher system divided into three tiers: "A" for immigrants with prearranged employment in Britain; "B" for immigrants with special skills in short supply; and "C" for all others, with preferential treatment for war veterans. As it developed, however, the 1962 Commonwealth Immigrants Act was only partially effective in slowing the expansion of the immigrant population. Although it substantially decreased primary migration to Britain, it inadvertently stimulated a wave of secondary immigration, as more than 100,000 dependents of foreign workers streamed into Britain between 1962 and 1965 in anticipation that further immigration controls would soon be imposed. Additional immigration restrictions were, in fact, implemented when the British government hastily passed the 1968 Commonwealth

Immigrants Act, which for the first time introduced the principle of patriality into British immigration and nationality law, a category that includes those persons with the automatic right of abode in the United Kingdom, including citizens of the Commonwealth and the U.K. born of or adopted by parents who had British citizenship by virtue of their own birth in the United Kingdom. The 1968 Act and the principle of patriality eventually provided the foundation for additional immigration controls legislated in the 1971 Immigration Act. By sharpening the distinction between the patrials and non-patrials, and by tearing down the barrier between the categories of aliens and Commonwealth citizens, the 1971 Immigration act eliminated all preferential treatment for the latter group (Freeman 1992, 26).

And finally, the 1983 British Nationality Act, by considerably diluting the long-observed principle of *ius soli*—citizenship conferred automatically on all persons born in the territory—in favor of the continental European practice of *ius sanguinis*—citizenship based on descent—rationalized postwar British nationality law and legitimized the 1962–80 wave of immigration restrictions. In so doing, the 1983 Act removed any doubt that the exceedingly liberal British immigration and citizenship regimes of the early postwar period, which were once originally defined by and embedded in the 1948 British Nationality Act, had now been completely discarded and replaced by new, less liberal regimes.

Few, if any, West European states to date have gone as far and as fast as Britain in altering their postwar immigration and citizenship regimes. Moreover, unlike Britain, most West European states have not enacted unambiguously illiberal change (de Rham 1990; Hammar 1985). Nevertheless, as Germany's alteration of its previously ultra-permissive asylum laws in 1993 and France's recent redefinition of its liberal citizenship rules vividly demonstrate, long-established immigration and citizenship regimes are in flux in Western Europe. Under the pressure of substantial mass migration to Western Europe during the postwar period, the concept and boundaries of national citizenship and the core rules that govern the flow of people in and out of the traditional nation-state have been, and continue to be, substantially altered.

The Sociocultural Transformation of West European Societies

In contrast to its economic impacts and its effects on contemporary immigration and citizenship regimes, effects that have been either invisible or largely tangential to the core concerns of ordinary citizens, the impact of postwar immigration on the immediate social and cultural environment in Western Europe has been highly transparent to mass publics and, in most countries, the subject of popular debate and concern. In the cultural realm in particular postwar immigration has done no less than undermine permanently the monocultural foundations of the traditional nation-state in Western Europe.

Strictly speaking, the traditional West European nation-state, of course, has never been monocultural. The ethnoregional and ethnoterritorial subcultures identified with the Walloons of Belgium, the Scottish and Welsh in Britain, Alsatians, Bretons, and Corsicans in France, and Basques, Catalans, and Galicians in Spain, for example, historically have not existed easily or without tension alongside the dominant sociocultural order of their larger respective societies (Esman 1977; Rudolph and Thompson 1989). Indeed, such differences have periodically fed considerable "traditional" ethnic conflict in these societies. Nevertheless, in contrast to these traditional subcultures that are, on the whole, compatible with the dominant sociocultural order of contemporary West European nation-states, the varied subcultures of the "new" ethnic and racial minorities in Western Europe are far more likely to engender problems.

The usual compromise reached is that the state concedes some of its policymaking authority in exchange for social harmony by allowing, for example, the new ethnic and racial minorities the right to found and operate religious schools or wear traditional headwear in public employment. However, with each compromise and concession the authority of the central state and government incrementally diminishes.

These problems are evident on several levels. First, the geographic concentration of the new ethnic and racial minorities in the major conurbations of

Western Europe and, within these cities, the most economically depressed areas has meant the American-style ghettoization of the minority groups themselves, as well as their social, cultural, and religious norms, and the estrangement of both from the larger, mainstream society. Immigrants and foreign citizens, for example, are disproportionately found in such major cities as Geneva, Frankfurt, and Brussels, where they comprise a quarter or more of the total population; London, Amsterdam, The Hague, Rotterdam, Munich, and Liège, where they are between 15 and 20% of all residents; and Paris, Cologne, and Hamburg, where they constitute more than 10% of the population. Geographic isolation has inhibited the process of accommodation of the new immigrant subcultures to the dominant national culture, which, in turn, has perpetuated further isolation and the defensive preservation and consolidation of the new subcultures.

Second, and most importantly, the entrance of millions of the new ethnic and racial minorities into the societies of Western Europe has challenged the state's promotion of the monocultural principle upon which the national identity has been historically constructed (Safran 1987). In this respect, the central states in Britain, France, Germany, the Netherlands, Norway, or Sweden cannot help but acknowledge that their respective societies are now multiethnic and increasingly multicultural. Once this reality is conceded, however, it is extremely difficult for the state to force the new minority groups to accept passively its traditional hegemonic authority in areas such as education or the delivery of public services (Ireland 1994, 90). The usual compromise reached is that the state concedes some of its policymaking authority in exchange for social harmony by allowing, for example, the new ethnic and racial minorities the right to found and operate religious schools or wear traditional headwear in public employment. However, with each compromise and concession the authority of the central state and government incrementally diminishes. Moreover, the argument of the new minorities that the state should be reconstructed and the dominant sociocultural order be redefined so as to reflect the new social realities of ethnic pluralism and multiculturalism inevitably strengthens.

Unaccustomed to challenges of this kind, both West European elites and mass publics are often motivated to respond by defending aggressively the dominant sociocultural order, a defense that, in many cases, soon degenerates into petty nationalism (Solomos 1992, 122–139). Whether manifested by a surge of electoral support for illiberal, neofascist parties or the state's repression of radical brands of Islam and other "subversive" faiths, elite and mass reactions to the new assault on the dominant sociocultural paradigm have been predictable, punitive, and pervasive across Western Europe. Whatever the elite or mass reaction, however, the fundamental realities associated with introduction of the new subcultures into West European societies cannot be conjured away. As even the briefest visit to any one of a score of Western Europe's major cities will soon reveal, the growing presence and assertiveness of black Britons, French Beurs, Dutch Muslims, and other ethnic minorities and their respective subcultures across Western Europe are permanently transforming the traditional sociocultural landscape.

Immigration and the Postwar Political Consensus

Of all the major impacts of postwar immigration, however, the most important, enduring, and disruptive has been its effects on the postwar political consensus, which, for the better part of three decades, informed and shaped public policy, defined the parameters of interparty competition, and largely reconciled the long-standing, entrenched antagonism between political Left and Right forces across Western Europe. The argument here is that the successive waves of immigration have melded together to undermine the consensual foundations of the dominant postwar political paradigm in Western Europe (Kesselman, Krieger, et al. 1987). Until its demise in the 1970s and early 1980s, this paradigm was defined by three key features. First, it meant that governments aggressively manipulated or regulated the macroeconomy in pursuing redistributive goals (Hall 1986). In every country in Western Europe the government redistributed wealth and income from the upper to the middle and lower classes, in part through the mechanisms of the rapidly-expanding, social welfare system. A second feature of the postwar political paradigm was the substantial political cooperation that existed among political parties aligned across the traditional ideological spectrum in Western Europe. With a few notable exceptions (e.g., Sartori 1966), the major political parties of Western Europe abandoned their traditional ideologies and allowed their policies to converge. And finally, the postwar political paradigm was defined by the "cooling" of ideological fervor among social and political actors associated with the old Left and Right. Trade unions and big business in particular found common cause in the progrowth strategies of economically interventionist governments, and the two often cooperated with one another in formal corporatist or tripartite arrangements (Shonfield 1974, 71–238).

What specific role did postwar immigration play in undermining consensual politics in Western Europe? Freeman argues that the mass migration of foreign workers eroded the political understanding upon which the postwar welfare state was originally established. His thesis is that mass migration reduced the political influence of those social strata that have traditionally been the strongest proponents of an extensive welfare state, thus precipitating the "Americanization of European welfare politics." Specifically, the postwar mass migration of foreign workers to Western Europe "diminished the power of organized labor by dividing the working class into national and immigrant camps, by easing the tight labor market conditions that would have enhanced labor's strategic resources, and by provoking a resurgence of right-wing and nativist political movements" (1986, 61). Moreover, he argues, "a little-noticed . . . consequence of the counter cyclical role of migrants is that by making high levels of unemployment tolerable, [they] . . . contributed to the establishment of a dangerous precedent: the smashing of the full-employment norm" that had been in effect in Western Europe from the conclusion of World War II until the 1970s (1986, 61).

Although Freeman's analysis sheds a great deal of light on the disruptive impact of immigration on the postwar political order in Western Europe, it both overstates and understates the issue. It overstates the impact of immigration in that it exaggerates the role of immigration in instigating conflict and dissension among the social forces that have historically supported a generous and comprehensive welfare system. Although such conflict did emerge and continues to unfold across Western Europe, it is largely a byproduct of revolutionary upheavals in the international political economy, changes that during the past 20 years or so have visited tremendous social turmoil and political conflict upon all the advanced industrial societies, including those with little experience of postwar immigration (e.g., Dinan 1994, 431–435). To be sure, postwar immigration *is* one component of the revolutionary changes that have incrementally exposed the domestic economy and national public policy to international influences. Also, postwar immigration has undoubtedly made the domestic response to the painful adjustments required to keep pace with these changes—including a contradiction in social-welfare spending, reduced government intervention in the economy, and abandonment of full employment policies—more intense and politically volatile. However, immigration is not the primary source of the social conflict and political upheaval as Freeman and others imply. Rather, postwar immigration has exacerbated social tensions and accelerated political conflict that, even in its absence, would inevitably have resulted from the increasing exposure of states and their citizens to the competitive pressures associated with the pervasive reach, some would say hegemony, of the new international political economy.

Freeman understates the impact of immigration on the postwar political order, however, in the sense that he underestimates the full scope of its political impact. In addition to its disruptive influence on the politics of the welfare state, postwar immigration has also disturbed established party systems and raised the ideological temperature of domestic politics as a whole (Messina 1990). Anti-immigrant sentiment, xenophobia, and blatant racism within the native working classes in Austria, Britain, France, Germany, the Netherlands, Switzerland, and elsewhere, for example, are polarizing politics and accelerating the flight of fragments of this class away from political parties of the traditional Left and toward the traditional and new Right (Betz 1990). Racist working class voters are defecting to the political Right because the Right has been more sympathetic than the Left to their views, and because the Left is fairly closely aligned politically, for ideological and electoral reasons, with the new ethnic and racial minorities. The defection of racist, working class voters threatens the Left's already declining electoral base and, in some countries, this trend promises to exclude parties of the Left from government indefinitely. The gradual political marginalization of the traditional Left, in turn, reinforces existing social trends that underpin a more conservative domestic politics.

Moreover, postwar immigration and the divisive politics and social conflict that it has exacerbated have aided the ascendancy, since the early 1980s, of what I have called in another context the "conservative project" (Messina 1990). At its core the conservative project is an ongoing campaign by conservative forces in Western Europe to discredit the Keynesian social-welfare consensus so as to facilitate the modernization of the economy through the restructuring of state and society. Across Western Europe the conservative project has inspired governments to abandon an interventionist approach to economic policymaking and to adopt more market-oriented economic strategies.

As a necessary and direct consequence of this project, consensual politics in Western Europe have eroded, ideological conflict has flared, and "economic sacrifice as apportioned by the market . . . [has fallen] disproportionally on those who lack the market power to protect themselves . . ." (Hall 1986, 283). Dissatisfaction and disillusion among the native "losers" of this project have been muted somewhat by the promotion of elites and the consumption by mass publics of a conservative political ideology emphasizing individualism, self-initiative, loyalty to the state, and the potential threat posed to the "nation" by internal enemies, including immigrants. At its most benign, this conservative ideology distracts native losers of the conservative project from focusing on the primary sources of their distress: government economic policy and disruptive changes in the new international political economy. At its most malignant, this ideology inflames latent tensions among the various races and classes. At every point between the two poles of distraction and conflict instigation the consolidation of the goals of the conservative project is facilitated.

The most important influence of postwar immigration on domestic politics, then, has been more subtle and indirect than transparent and straightforward. In helping to undermine the consensual foundations of the postwar political order, immigration has reinforced and accelerated conservative political and economic change in Western Europe.

Conclusions

Despite the cautionary note struck in the introduction, this essay has considered the three separate waves of postwar migration as more or less a single phenomenon for the purpose of analyzing their impacts on the economies, societies, and politics of Western Europe. At this point in the discussion it is appropriate to justify this approach.

First of all, with each wave hundreds of thousands of immigrants arrived in Western Europe with ethnicities, languages, religious practices, or cultural backgrounds that were less than completely compatible with those of their chosen host society.

Although a unique set of stimuli and a distinct logic precipitated each of the three migration waves, they share a number of common features. First of all, with each wave hundreds of thousands of immigrants arrived in Western Europe with ethnicities, languages, religious practices, or cultural backgrounds that were less than completely com-

patible with those of their chosen host society. Given this reality, it is unfortunate but hardly surprising that similar social and political stress have accompanied each wave of migration. Second, despite their different origins and logics, each successive wave has been perceived by West European publics as building upon the first. In this respect, the general public views the asylees and refugees of the 1990s to be as much, if not more, of an economic and cultural threat as the original economic migrants of the 1950s and 1960s.

Finally, and most importantly for the purpose of analyzing their collective impacts, it is appropriate to consider the three migration waves as a single phenomenon because virtually all migrants through time have shared the common condition of being primarily the objects of the economies, societies, and polities of Western Europe. Regardless of their national origins, formal citizenship status, or economic role, the migrants of each wave have historically been less than full participants in the domestic economy, society, and polity. Reluctantly accepted and sometimes strongly resented by large segments of the native population, the migrants themselves have often conspired in perpetuating their peripheral "object" status by refusing to acknowledge the permanency of their settlement in Western Europe (see e.g., Anwar 1979), thus isolating themselves from the larger society. As a result, anti-immigrant and xenophobic groups have found it easier than otherwise to depict both the new and longer-established immigrants as "intruders," whose presence can be banished through political will and initiative.

The marginalization of settled immigrants means that although the turmoil over immigration and immigrants ebbs and flows in the domestic context, it never dissipates, as both new and long established immigrants are convenient and frequent scapegoats for virtually all that can and does go wrong in the societies of Western Europe. The tremors associated with past migration waves continue to reverberate across Western Europe irrespective of the current levels of new immigration. New problems associated with the latest migration wave simply accumulate upon previous conflicts and difficulties.

Although there is evidence in some countries that immigrants, especially in long-established communities, are beginning to transcend their object status (Saggar 1992, 136–171), other evidence, including rising political sympathy and electoral support for illiberal, anti-immigrant parties, suggests the contrary. Whatever the future, it is fairly clear that conflict related to both the original and newer migration waves has not yet been, nor soon will be, resolved.

References

Anwar, Muhammad. 1979. *The Myth of Return.* London: Heinemann.

Betz, Hans-Georg. 1990. *Postmodern Politics in Germany.* New York: St. Martin's Press.

Castles, Stephen. 1989. *Migrant Workers and the Transformation of Western Societies.* Ithaca, NY: Cornell Studies in International Affairs. Western Societies Papers.

Castles, Stephen and Godula Kosack. 1973. *Immigrant workers and Class Structure in Western Europe.* London: Oxford University Press.

Coleman, David A. 1992. "Does Europe Need Immigrants? Population and Workforce Projections." *International Migration Review.* 26(2):413–459.

de Rham, Gérard. 1990. "Naturalization and the Politics of Citizenship Acquisition." In *The Political Rights of Migrant workers in Western Europe.* Zig Layton-Henry, ed. London: Sage.

Dinan, Desmond. 1994. *Ever Closer Union?* Boulder, CO: Lynne Rienner.

The Economist. 1988. December 3.

Esman, Milton, ed. 1977. *Ethnic Conflict in the Western world.* Ithaca, NY: Cornell University Press.

Fielding, Anthony. 1993. "Mass Migration and Economic Restructuring." In *Mass Migration in Europe: The Legacy and the Future.* Russell King, ed. London: Belhaven Press.

Freeman, Gary. 1986. "Migration and the Political Economy of the Welfare State." In *From Foreign Workers to Settlers?* Martin O. Heisler and Barbara Schmitter Heisler, eds. *The Annals.* 485:51–63.

——— 1992. "The Consequences of Immigration Policies for Immigrant States: A British and French Comparison." In *Ethnic and Racial Minorities in Advanced Industrial Democracies.* Anthony M. Messina, et al. eds. New York: Greenwood Press.

Hall, Peter. 1986. *Governing the Economy.* New York: Oxford University Press.

Hammar, Tonaas, ed. 1985. *European Immigration Policy: A Comparative Study.* Cambridge, England: Cambridge University Press.

Hollifield, James E 1992. *Immigrants, Markets, and States.* Cambridge, MA: Harvard University Press.

Ireland, Patrick. 1994. *The Policy Challenge of Ethnic Diversity.* Cambridge, MA: Harvard University Press.

Jones K. and A.D. Smith. 1970. *The Economic Impact of Commonwealth Immigration.* London: Cambridge University Press.

Kesselman, Mark and Joel Krieger, et al. 1987. *European Politics in Transition.* Lexington, MA: D.C. Heath.

Kindelberger, Charles. 1967. *Europe's Postwar Growth.* Cambridge, MA: Harvard University Press.

Korte, Herman. 1985. "Labor Migration and the Employment of Foreigners in the Federal Republic of Germany since 1950." In *Guests Come to Stay.* Rosemarie Rogers, ed. Boulder, CO: Westview Press.

Lamberts, Willi. 1975. "Die Bedeutung der Ausländer-beschäftigung für die Vermeidung struktureller Arbeitslosigkeit in der Bundesrepublik." *Mitteilungen des Rheinish-Westfälischen Instituts für Wirtschaftsforschung.* 26. Essen.

Martin, Philip L. 1994. "The Impacts of Immigration on Receiving Countries." Unpublished paper.

Messina, Anthony M. 1989. *Race and Party Competition in Britain.* Oxford: Oxford University Press.

——— 1990. "Political Impediments to the Resumption of Labour Migration to Western Europe." *West European Politics.* 13(1):31–46.

Peach, G. C. K. 1968. *West Indian Migration to Britain.* London: Oxford University Press.

Rex, John. 1986. *Race and Ethnicity.* Milton Keynes, United Kingdom: Open University Press.

Richmond, Anthony. 1988. *Immigration and Ethnic Conflict.* London: The Macmillan Press.

Rudolph Jr., Joseph and Robert J. Thompson, eds. 1989. *Ethnoterritorial Politics, Policy and the Western world.* Boulder, CO: Lynne Rienner.

Safran, William. 1987. "France as a Multiethnic Society: Is it Possible?" Unpublished paper.

Saggar, Shamit. 1992. *Race and Politics in Britain.* New York: Harvester Wheatsheaf.

Salowski, Heinz. 1971. "Gesamtwirtschaftliche Aspekte der Ausländerbeschäftigung." *Beiträge des Deutschen Iudustrieinstituts.* 9, 10/11. Cologne: Deutscher Industrieverlag.

Sartori, Giovanni. 1966. "European Political Parties: The Case of Polarized Pluralism." In *Political Parties and Political Development.* Joseph LaPalombara and Myron Weiner, eds. Princeton, NJ: Princeton University Press.

Shonfield, Andrew. 1974. *Modern Capitalism.* London: Oxford University Press.

Solomos, John. 1992. *Race and Racism in Contemporary Britain.* London: The Macmillan Press.

Soysal, Yasemin Nuhoglu. 1994. *Limits of Citizenship.* Chicago: Chicago University Press.

Cherchez la femme

PARIS

"**Y**OU love us as mothers [*mères*] or whores; why not as mayors [*maires*] or deputies?" read the banners of women protesting outside France's newly elected National Assembly three years ago. Of the 577 deputies, only 35 (6%) were women—exactly the same proportion, never surpassed, as when French women got the vote half a century earlier. Since then, the tally has dipped to 32, giving French women the smallest share of any parliament in the European Union.

Now the Socialists, who have only four women among their 63 deputies, have agreed that 30% of their candidates in the next parliamentary election, due in 1998, will be female. As many as 50 of the seats earmarked may be winnable. It is the first time that a French party has imposed a quota. Even among feminists, the policy is controversial: some consider it insulting because it implies that women cannot match men on merit. Others, including some Socialists, worry that quotas for other groups—Jews, homosexuals, Muslims—will now be sought.

Women have played a big part in French politics, though nearly always as éminences grises. France's Salic law, denying women succession to the throne, excluded them from wielding power directly. The 1789 revolution's "Declaration of the Rights of Man" enshrined "equality for all"—all men, that was. In 1848, "universal suffrage" gave the vote to men over 21; women had to wait nearly a century to win the same right.

Still, in the past two decades, women have fought their way into hitherto male bastions. You can find female generals, astronauts, trade-union leaders, gendarmes, football referees, judges, casino croupiers, bank presidents, members of the Académie Française, France's intellectual "holy of holies". Since 1992, there has even been a woman in the Constitutional Council. Women account for 46% of the workforce, mostly still in low-paid jobs. Women earn on average 20% less than men. But they also hold a third of senior professional posts (though only 5% of places on directors' boards). Girls now outnumber boys at university. The legalisation of contraception (in 1967) and abortion (in 1975) has let more women climb the working ladder.

But in politics the clamber up has stalled. As well as that less-than-6% score in parliament, women hold only 8% of mayoralties and, despite recent efforts, only 12% of ministries. True, Edith Cresson, an old flame of François Mitterrand, became France's first woman prime minister five years ago—and was such a flop (she says she was a victim of male prejudice) that she has probably hindered

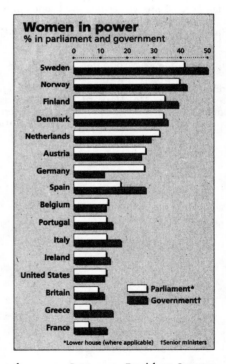

Women in power
% in parliament and government

the cause. Last year, President Jacques Chirac prodded the current prime minister, Alain Juppé, into putting a record 12 women (nearly a third of the total) into his first government. But within six months he had junked all but four, including the minister for women's rights, who headed a new government organisation to promote equality between the sexes.

Women, Power and Politics: The Norwegian Experience

Irene Garland

Irene Garland, a Norwegian social scientist, lives in London.

Three Scandinavian countries all have more than one third of women representatives in their national assemblies. In Norway the Prime Minister is a woman as are 9 out of 19 cabinet ministers as well as the leaders of 2 of the other political parties.

Commentators trying to explain this phenomenon have looked back through history and pointed to the independence of Norwegian women as far back as the Viking era, when they kept the homefires burning while their menfolk were away plundering. Others have referred to more recent times. Outstanding women, however, are to be found in most countries at some time or another. The reason for Norwegian women being so successful in gaining political power must therefore be found somewhere else. My belief is that the explanation is of a practical nature and is to be found in the post-war era.

Common to the three Scandinavian countries is a structure of progressive social democracy and election systems based on proportional representation. If one compares the number of women in parliaments across the world, one finds that proportional representation is the single most important element for women to gain entry into politics. However, it was the ability to use this system to their advantage, and the fact that a group of women managed to agree on a common course across party lines, that made it possible to break the mold of the male dominated political scene in Norway.

A SPECTACULAR BEGINNING

The year was 1967 and Brigit Wiik—editor, author, mother and leader of the Oslo Feminist Movement—recalls in her book a chance meeting between herself and Einar Gerhardsen on the street in Oslo. Einar Gerhardsen was a leader of the Labor Party and had been Prime Minister almost continuously since the war. He was, at the time, in opposition, having lost the previous election. With the local elections coming up he agreed to a quota for women on the Labor party lists. In doing so he saw an opportunity to activate a new group of voters for his party, and when his agreement was presented to the party in power, they felt compelled to do the same. With the two largest parties both agreeing to give a quota to women, representatives from The National Advisory Council for Women, The Working Women's Association and the Oslo Feminist Movement, formed a group to lead the campaign to get women into politics by harnessing the female vote. They used a professional PR firm to lead the campaign—a first in Norway. The result surprised everyone; there was a national increase in women representatives of 50%, and whereas there had been 179 local communities without women's representation prior to the election, afterwards the number was reduced to 79. Subsequent campaigns further increased the number of women in local government by 50%—except for 1975.

2. PLURALIST DEMOCRACIES: Women and Politics

WOMEN IN THE NATIONAL ASSEMBLY— THE STORTING

Though there was no campaign to elect women to the national assembly, there seems to have been a spill-over effect. Political parties were quick to recognize the advantage in gaining the female vote and soon extended the quota system to parliamentary elections.

Women's representation in parliament increased steadily from the 1969 election in parallel with what happened in the local elections.

WOMEN START WINNING THE ARGUMENTS

After the 1967 election the Central Bureau of Statistics started to separate voters by gender for the first time, and the 1970s saw an upsurge in research into the history of women's lives and living conditions. Young female researchers were for the first time given the opportunity and the funding to look into their own past, a hitherto ignored area of academic research, and much empirical data was collated during this decade. The history of women's lives ran to 18 volumes and a history of women writers to 3 volumes.

Once they gained entry into the corridors of power, women were increasingly taking up issues of importance to themselves and to the family. Such issues gained in importance by producing results at the ballot box. They could, therefore, not be ignored in party politics and as a result, became part of the overall political agenda.

Enabling policies such as the right to maternity leave and the ability to return to work after giving birth were important for women who wanted to have the choice between having a career and becoming a full-time housewife. With the increased number of women investing in higher education, going back to work was not only seen as a means of personal fulfillment, but became an economic necessity for those who needed to pay back their student loans. The availability of choice was also seen as central to the equality debate— why should men be able to have both a family and a career while women were forced to make a choice? The idea that there was such a thing as a "natural" place for a woman in the home despite qualifications or inclinations was rejected. If women were designed for domesticity by nature itself, then how could one explain the fact that women, given a chance, did very well in the outside world? The patriarchs were at a loss for an answer.

LAWS ARE CHANGED

The 1970s saw a number of typical feminist arguments being brought forward and legislation or common practices changed as a result. One such issue was the one over Miss and Mrs. Throughout the 1960s feminists had opposed the use of these titles and the alternative Ms. had not won approval. During the 1960s ardent feminists would reply to anyone asking if

they were Miss or Mrs. that it was none of their business whether they were married or not. These days no one would ask and such titles are not in general use.

Another issue was that of surnames upon marriage. Women regarded giving up their own names as losing their identities. The law on surnames has now changed so that couples can choose which name to use. Some prefer to keep their maiden name. Some couples take on her name after marriage instead of his,

---

THE INCREASE IN WOMEN'S REPRESENTATION

Local govern- ment elections	pre-1967	1967	1971	1975	1979
Women as a % of total	6.3	9.5	15	15	22.8
Parliamentary elections	1945–53	1969	1973	1977	1981
Women as a % of total	4.7	9.3	15	23.9	25.8

Maternity leave	2 weeks prior to confinement 30 weeks after confinement with full pay
Leave from work & the right to return	mothers have the right to a further year off work without pay
Paternity leave	fathers have the right to 2 weeks off work with pay, dependent on trade union agreement (applies to all civil servants)
Breast-feeding	mothers have their hours of work cut to accommodate breast-feeding
Children's illness	both parents have a right to 10 days off work with pay when a child under 12 is ill

	Born	Married	Chil- dren	Education
Gro H. Brundt- land Prime Minister (Labor)	1939	1960	4	Degree in med- icine; MA (Harvard)
Ase Kleveland Minister of Cul- tural Affairs (Labor)	1949	Co- habits	None	Part law degree; Studied music
Anne E. Lahn- stein Leader, Centre Party	1949	1975	3	Social worker
Kaci K. Five Leader, Conser- vative Party	1951	1972	2	Political Sci- ence degree

but many women prefer to attach their husbands' name to their own. The latter is the case with the three female party leaders. Children are no longer automatically given their fathers' surname—again it is subject to parental choice.

The debate on surnames formed part of a wider debate about the right to a separate identity for women after marriage. The argument was for women to be able to carry on with their own careers and not to take on the role of supporting player to that of their husbands. Marriage should not become synonymous with taking on the cooking, cleaning and entertaining in addition to their own jobs. Entertaining could equally well be done in a restaurant anyway. Men would have to grow up and stop relying on their wives taking over where their mothers had left off. Cooking and darning became part of every boy's curriculum at school—the emphasis was on enabling men to become self-sufficient.

This also extended to quotas being set for men in certain professions, such as nursing, which until then had been dominated by women.

WOMEN IN POWER TODAY

The quota system helped the Prime Minister, **Gro Harlem Brundtland,** on her way to power. When she became Prime Minister in 1981 for the first time, it was she who introduced the idea of 50/50 gender representation in the cabinet. Having formed her third government at the most recent election, she has taken with her a team of young and capable women. Mrs. Brundtland followed in her father's footsteps—he was a doctor and a cabinet minister—and has been involved in politics from an early age. She is known for her enormous capacity for work, and certainly her record of achievements bears witness to just this. In addition to working full time she has managed to raise a family of four children. Her first job was as a medical officer on the Oslo Board of Public Health. The first ministerial position came in 1974 when she was appointed Minister for the Environment. She was appointed leader of the Labor Party in 1981, the same year that she became Prime Minister at the age of 42, the youngest ever to hold this office.

Internationally she has served on The Palme Commission which published its report on "Common Security" in 1982. This was followed by her chairing the World Commission on Environment and Development whose report, "Our Common Future," was published in 1987. She has published many scientific papers and received numerous prizes in acknowledgement of her work in different fields.

The new leader of the Conservative Party, **Kaci Kullman Five,** also started in politics quite young. Her mother, an elegant looking lady in her 60s, is still active in the local conservative party in Baerum where Mrs. Five first started out. After serving as deputy leader locally, she joined the national party, and was elected

to parliament in 1981. Her first major office was as Deputy Secretary of State for commercial affairs in the Foreign Office in 1989. Having a degree in political science, she has served on the standing committees for foreign policy and constitutional affairs and on the finance committee. She has also published a book.

The third female party leader is **Anne Enger Lahnstein** of the rural Centre Party, who comes from a farming background. She headed the national action against free abortion in 1978–79, and was a member of the Nordic Council from 1979 on, but she did not enter parliament until 1985. She was head of the Oslo Centre Party from 1980–83. From 1983 on, she served as the deputy leader of the national party until she took over as its leader this year.

Ase Kleveland, the new Minister of Culture, differs from the others in that she has not gone through the rank and file of a party. She studied classical guitar and music theory for a number of years and during the '60s and '70s was one of Norway's best known popular singers. Ms. Kleveland won the Norwegian finals of the Eurovision Song Contest and later hosted the TV program for this contest the year it was held in Norway. She headed the Norwegian Musician's Union for a period and her most recent job was as a manager of the first amusement park in Norway. She was due to take over as Cultural Director for the Olympics to be held in Lillehammer in 1994 on the very day she was offered her cabinet post.

COMBINING CAREER AND FAMILY

Combining career with family commitments is no easy task, though office hours in Norway are short—9 to 4—giving more time for both parents to spend with their children. The smaller towns and communities constitute less danger to children which also makes it easier on working parents. Often though, it would seem that having a husband with flexible working arrangements such as a researcher or a journalist helps, and there is no doubt that joint efforts are necessary when both parents work. Fathers do take a much greater part in the up-bringing of their children and in the running of homes, than previously. This "new" role for fathers has now become the norm.

The Prime Minister's children are all grown up now and she is in fact a grandmother, but her husband's job as a researcher and writer no doubt being able to work from home when the need arose, must have been a help. Anne Lahnstein's children are in their teens, only Kaci Five has a young child (8 years old), and she said in an interview that she had to work very hard in order to make time for the family—something she viewed as important. Her husband is an editor and doubtless has to take his turn in looking after the children.

SOUR GRAPES?

It is perhaps inevitable that dissenting voices be heard when so many women reach such high positions in society. Recently a study has been published suggesting that men are leaving politics in Norway because, since it has become dominated by women, it is also becoming a low-paid occupation. Men, it is claimed, are opting for the better paid, higher status jobs in the private sector.

With increased internationalization, they argue, there are many constraints on national assemblies, and important decisions are being made elsewhere; Parliament is no longer the power house it used to be.

Research by Ms. Hege Skjeie from the Institute for Social Studies, disagrees with these conclusions. It is quite true that politicians whose wages are part of the civil service wage scale are lower than those received for the top jobs in the private sector and also that many professions dominated by women are badly paid. However, wages in the state sector have always been considered low relative to private industry, and this was the case before women started to take an interest in a career in politics. Ms. Skjeie's studies found that the men leaving politics did so because of age—they had all served for quite some time. Others had in fact lost their seats or been ousted from positions of leadership within their parties—some by women. There was certainly no difficulty in recruiting young men into

politics, and as regards the power and status associated with politics one could point to Ase Kleveland, Minister of Culture, who had the choice between politics and the Olympic Committee, and chose politics in spite of its uncertainties.

"I'M ON QUOTA—AND I LOVE IT!"

There can be no doubt that it was the quota system that made it possible for Norwegian women to enter politics in such a big way. The power that comes from parliament cannot be underestimated—it has given weight to arguments that had been previously ignored and as such has changed social attitudes of both sexes to the roles and rights of men and women alike. This change could not have taken place without political backing and without such backing, it would not have received such broad social acceptance. However, it is clear that when women work together across party lines, as was the case in Norway during the early days, that is when they achieve the most. Campaigning is also necessary as the experience of 1975 showed—no campaign, no increase in women's representation. The clock cannot be turned back, but even in Norway many women feel that there is no ground for complacency.

Where Women's Work Is Job No. 1

■ *A wave of female leadership in five Nordic nations has produced liberal day-care and parental-leave policies. But the bottom line on wages, equality is still a problem.*

MARY WILLIAMS WALSH

TIMES STAFF WRITER

STOCKHOLM—In the United States, for the first time, the wives of both major-party presidential candidates are women with careers and accomplishments of their own, each a grade-grinding graduate of an Ivy League law school. With 58.9% of women in the work force, Americans might be expected to applaud the end of the political-helpmate era.

But no. First Lady Hillary Rodham Clinton continues to be an object of suspicion and even loathing for some members of the press and public. And that gender discomfiture seems to extend generally to the political positions of power in Washington: No woman has served as president, vice president or leader of either chamber of Congress.

Here in Scandinavia, however, working women not only have been the prime minister's spouse, they've been the prime minister (in Norway). Women also hold key government and party-leadership jobs in all of the four main Nordic countries—Norway, Sweden, Denmark and Finland.

And Iceland, which also has a female head of state, and the numbers are even more striking: Among five nations, women lead nine of the 37 national political parties, hold three parliament speakerships and make up from a fourth (Iceland) to a half (Sweden) of Cabinet posts.

Such a wave of women in high places has left a mark on policy:

• Abortion, a hopelessly controversial barometer of a woman's freedom in the United States, is not only routinely accepted in all five Nordic countries—at least in the first three months of pregnancy—but it is also performed for free. No one would think of requiring a hus-band's permission. Contraception is also available free and without fuss.

• Legislation comparable to the United States' doomed Equal Rights Amendment was passed years ago in all five countries. (Iceland went first in 1976, after women there shut down the country with a one-day general strike.)

• Inexpensive institutional child care of high quality, provided by trained professionals, is widely available, with Sweden and Denmark boasting the most comprehensive systems. In Sweden, a day-care slot is guaranteed by law for every child older than 18 months, and care continues at after-school centers until children are 10. Family-values proponents take note: Sweden has not only one of the world's highest rates of female labor-force participation—79.5%—but also one of the highest birth rates in the Western industrialized world.

• Family-friendly parental-leave policies are popular in Scandinavia, with Swedish parents—mother or father, it doesn't matter which—free to take 64 weeks off their jobs after the birth of a baby, at 90% pay for the first year. Finnish parents have a legal right to a six-hour workday, and Danes are experimenting with a subsidized leave of up to one year, offered to all parents of children up to age 8.

One Swedish Cabinet minister, Margot Wallstrom, handles her cultural portfolio from her home, deep in rural pulp-and-paper country, 170 miles from the capital. There, Wallstrom tends her two small children and sends instructions to her Stockholf staff by fax and e-mail. The telecommunications cost to the Swedish taxpayer is $170,000 per year, but that is considered a small price to pay for the sending of a profound signal about family-friendly government.

Denmark, likewise, goes to special lengths to present a feminized face to the world, making sure that at least half of each year's recruitment of new diplomats are women.

Progress in the Home

Even in the home, far from the reach of government policy-making, Scandinavian women have made some strides. Norwegian equality laws make it impossible for a man to draw himself up imperiously as the sole representative of his wife or children, allowed to make all decisions for them. Substantially more Finnish women than a generation ago report feeling loved by somebody. Swedish men do more housework than they did in the 1960s—and fewer Swedish women with jobs and small children are telling researchers that they are exhausted every day. (The men report that they are more tired, however.)

Even a single mother has a tolerable deal in this part of the world, according to Anna-Lena Eriksson, a 37-year-old Swedish single mother who lost her job as a waitress two years ago. Eriksson even believes that it is time her government did something to help men.

Divorced fathers, she maintains, get the short end of the stick when it comes to Sweden's attractive array of apartment subsidies, enlightened judges and other low-hanging fruits of an advanced welfare state. She should know: As a single mother, she gets long-term unemployment benefits, special rental-support payments and a monthly "children's money" stipend that has been a mainstay of Swedish family life since 1938. Eriksson's brother, also divorced and a parent, gets less from the state, she says.

Status Report

How women are doing in various areas of Scandinavian society, according to gender breakdowns:

■ Politics: Except in Iceland, women fill about a third of the seats in national legislatures.

(percentage of parliament seats held by women)

Denmark	34%
Finland	39%
Iceland	24%
Norway	39%
Sweden	33%

■ Workplace prestige:

Women make up a substantial part of the labor force but hold few top positions in the private sector.

(women ages 20-64 in labor force)

Denmark	77%
Finland	74%
Iceland	83%
Norway	72%
Sweden	81%

(managing directors in the 100 largest private companies)

	Women	Men
Denmark	0	100
Finland	2	98
Iceland	3	97
Norway	0	100
Sweden	2	98

■ Type of work: Women tend to work in the services sector, men in other industries.

(percentage of women in community, social and personal services, which includes education and public health)

Denmark	67%
Finland	72%
Iceland	67%
Norway	64%
Sweden	72%

Women do a disproportionate share of cleanup work.

(percentage of cleaning people who are women)

Denmark	94%
Finland	95%
Iceland	93%
Norway	90%
Sweden	87%

Source: Nordic Council of Ministers

Los Angeles Times

"As a single parent, I get more as a woman," she says, drinking a warming cup of chicory in her small Stockholm kitchen while her 8-month-old son sleeps in the next room. "In Sweden, the mother is well protected."

'Political Will'

How did this state of affairs come to pass?

"I think it's a question of political will," says Mona Danielson, Sweden's assistant undersecretary for equality affairs. "It started when more and more women went out into the labor market in the beginning of the 1970s."

Sweden in those days much resembled the United States: More and more women were punching clocks, but decent child care was hard to find. So Swedish women began putting off motherhood. The birth rate collapsed, bottoming out at near-Depression-era levels in 1978.

Policy makers realized that if they did not do something, Sweden would face a labor shortage once the new "baby-bust" generation was grown up. And in high-tax Sweden, a labor shortage is a disaster because there are not enough revenue sources to finance the social-welfare benefits people have come to expect as the central pillars of the Swedish moral order.

Birgitta Dahl, now the parliament speaker, had just been elected when this was going on.

"She really had problems," recalls her spokeswoman, Louise Gerdemo Holmgren. On the nights when sessions ran late, Dahl had nowhere to send her children, and they ended up sitting in the hallway.

So Dahl became a sort of missionary for state-provided child care. At the end of the 1960s, there were abut 10,000 day-care slots in Sweden; by the end of the 1970s, there were 130,000. The number grew even more in the 1980s, and a law was entered on the books mandating institutional child care for all toddlers.

Today, thanks to Dahl and others like her, there is a sunny day-care center right in the Reksdagen, or Swedish parliament, where the deputies' children can play with blocks, paints, books and a computer, under the eye of supervisor Berit Welin. It's a far cry from sitting in the hallway, and even though Sweden is now under budgetary stress—and looking for such displays of public largess to rein in—Welin says her job is safe.

"This day-care center is one of the speaker's top priorities," she says with a confident smile. "I know that as long as she's sitting where she is, I'll be here."

While Sweden and Denmark were experimenting with day care, Norway went a wholly different route. Coming out of the 1960s, a time of manifest inequality between the sexes, Norway chose to promote the cause of working women not with universal child care but with energetically employed quota systems—something often rejected in the United States and elsewhere in Europe as belittling to women or unfair to men, or both.

Since 1972, Norwegian political parties have run special nominating campaigns to choose female candidates before every election. Quotas are part of life in higher education and can be found in the collective-bargaining agreements struck between civil service unions and the states and municipalities.

Also, under Norway's Equal Status Act of 1978, neither sex is supposed to hold less than 40% of the seats on any of the country's public committees, boards or councils.

Norway is not yet in complete compliance with its own statute: 36.4% of such posts are filled by women at the municipal level. But at the level of federal elected officials, women now hold 42% of the Cabinet posts and 39% of the seats in the Storting, or parliament.

Couple of Catches

Is there a catch to all this? In fact, there are a couple of big ones.

First, no matter how smoothly Nordic women have moved into the labor force in the past generation, they have tended to stay in the public sector, where they end up doing the same sort of jobs women have done at home down through the ages: nursing the sick, tending the very young, teaching the school-age, looking after the elderly. All of these are civil service jobs in the Nordic countries.

"On the labor market, most women have ended up with the most strenuous jobs, in the lowest-paid occupations,"

said Hanne Haavind, a professor of psychology at the University of Oslo.

In Norway, nearly half of all employed women work for the state, mainly in health care, social services, education or municipal government. Add that onto the additional 20% of Norwegian women who take up such traditional high-stress, low-security "women's jobs" such as shop clerk or waitress, and the picture is far less heartening than the undigested "labor-force participation" statistics might first suggest.

In Sweden, "we have a very male structure over the private labor market," says Bonnie Bergstroem, a former member of parliament who now runs a two-woman consulting firm. "Everybody knows everybody in Sweden"—the population is 8.9 million—"and especially in the private sector. They play golf together or go hunting together."

And it is difficult for an aspiring corporate woman to take part in these often-quite-literal stag parties, the Swedish equivalent of poker night in the United States. "Women can go [hunting], but I've noticed that very few do," Bergstroem says. "They have very special roles. They take care of the dogs."

Just 9% of the managerial jobs in Sweden's private-sector are held by women, compared to 45.7% in the U.S. In each Nordic country, a tiny number of the top executives in the 100 largest firms are women: two each in Finland and Sweden, three in Iceland and none in Norway or Denmark.

Another big catch to the Nordic way of doing things is that while the women may work as hard as men, and in nearly as great numbers, they still earn significantly less—just like their American counterparts. Although every Nordic

country has laws on the books making equal pay for comparable work a legal requirement, none has succeeded in eradicating the gender-based wage gap.

To help right things, Norway, Sweden and Finland have created equal-status commissioners or ombudsmen in their governments: independent monitors who can gather data, field specific complaints and rule on cases of discrimination directly or pass them to the courts.

Two years ago, Sweden's equality ombudsman ordered all employers to draw up and submit annual plans on how they will work toward pay equity.

'A Huge Job'

"Reviewing the plans is a huge job," Danielson says. "And the equality ombudsman has only 14 employees."

Still, Scandinavian feminists say their government ombudsmen have their uses.

"Women earn less than men," acknowledges Ingse Stabel, a Norwegian High Court judge who served as equal status ombudsman from 1988 to 1994. "But I remain fairly convinced that without the Equal Status Act, and without the enforcement apparatus we have at our disposal, the situation would have been far worse."

It all comes down to familiar old questions: What's better—a sedate but relatively limited life in a heavily regulated welfare state or a U.S.-style free-for-all in the dust and heat of unpoliced capitalism? Near-universal day care or more CEOs in heels?

Neither way, it seems, can offer both.

Walsh was recently on assignment in Stockholm.

WHAT DEMOCRACY IS . . . AND IS NOT

Philippe C. Schmitter & Terry Lynn Karl

Philippe C. Schmitter *is professor of political science and director of the Center for European Studies at Stanford University.* **Terry Lynn Karl** *is associate professor of political science and director of the Center for Latin American Studies at the same institution. The original, longer version of this essay was written at the request of the United States Agency for International Development, which is not responsible for its content.*

For some time, the word democracy has been circulating as a debased currency in the political marketplace. Politicians with a wide range of convictions and practices strove to appropriate the label and attach it to their actions. Scholars, conversely, hesitated to use it—without adding qualifying adjectives—because of the ambiguity that surrounds it. The distinguished American political theorist Robert Dahl even tried to introduce a new term, "polyarchy," in its stead in the (vain) hope of gaining a greater measure of conceptual precision. But for better or worse, we are "stuck" with democracy as the catchword of contemporary political discourse. It is the word that resonates in people's minds and springs from their lips as they struggle for freedom and a better way of life; it is the word whose meaning we must discern if it is to be of any use in guiding political analysis and practice.

The wave of transitions away from autocratic rule that began with Portugal's "Revolution of the Carnations" in 1974 and seems to have crested with the collapse of communist regimes across Eastern Europe in 1989 has produced a welcome convergence toward [a] common definition of democracy.[1] Everywhere there has been a silent abandonment of dubious adjectives like "popular," "guided," "bourgeois," and "formal" to modify "democracy." At the same time, a remarkable consensus has emerged concerning the minimal conditions that polities must meet in order to merit the prestigious appellation of "democratic." Moreover, a number of international organizations now monitor how well these standards are met; indeed, some countries even consider them when formulating foreign policy.[2]

WHAT DEMOCRACY IS

Let us begin by broadly defining democracy and the generic *concepts* that distinguish it as a unique system for organizing relations between rulers and the ruled. We will then briefly review *procedures*, the rules and arrangements that are needed if democracy is to endure. Finally, we will discuss two operative *principles* that make democracy work. They are not expressly included among the generic concepts or formal procedures, but the prospect for democracy is grim if their underlying conditioning effects are not present.

One of the major themes of this essay is that democracy does not consist of a single unique set of institutions. There are many types of democracy, and their diverse practices produce a similarly varied set of effects. The specific form democracy takes is contingent upon a country's socioeconomic conditions as well as its entrenched state structures and policy practices.

Modern political democracy is a system of governance in which rulers are held accountable for their actions in the public realm by citizens, acting indirectly through the competition and cooperation of their elected representatives.[3]

A *regime or system of governance* is an ensemble of patterns that determines the methods of access to the principal public offices; the characteristics of the actors admitted to or excluded from such access; the strategies that actors may use to gain access; and the rules that are followed in the making of publicly binding decisions. To work properly, the ensemble must be institutionalized—that is to say, the various patterns must be habitually known, practiced, and accepted by most, if not all, actors. Increasingly, the preferred mechanism of institutionalization is a written body of laws undergirded by a written constitution, though many enduring political norms can have an informal, prudential, or traditional basis.[4]

For the sake of economy and comparison, these forms, characteristics, and rules are usually bundled together and given a generic label. Democratic is one; others are autocratic, authoritarian, despotic, dictatorial, tyrannical, totalitarian, absolutist, traditional, monarchic, oligarchic, plutocratic, aristocratic, and sultanistic.[5] Each of these regime forms may in turn be broken down into subtypes.

Like all regimes, democracies depend upon the presence of *rulers*, persons who occupy specialized authority roles and can give legitimate commands to others. What distinguishes democratic rulers from nondemocratic ones are the norms that condition how the former come to power and the practices that hold them accountable for their actions.

The *public realm* encompasses the making of collective norms and choices that are binding on the society and backed by state coercion. Its content can vary a great deal across democracies, depending upon preexisting distinctions between the public and the private, state and society, legitimate coercion and voluntary exchange, and collective needs and individual preferences. The liberal conception of democracy advocates circumscribing the public realm as narrowly as possible, while the socialist or social-democratic approach would extend that realm through regulation, subsidization, and, in some cases, collective ownership of property. Neither is intrinsically more democratic than the other—just *differently* democratic. This implies that measures aimed at "developing the private sector" are no more democratic than those aimed at "developing the public sector." Both, if carried to extremes, could undermine the practice of democracy, the former by destroying the basis for satisfying collective needs and exercising legitimate authority; the latter by destroying the basis for satisfying individual preferences and controlling illegitimate government actions. Differences of opinion over the optimal mix of the two provide much of the substantive content of political conflict within established democracies.

"However central to democracy, elections occur intermittently and only allow citizens to choose between the highly aggregated alternatives offered by political parties . . ."

Citizens are the most distinctive element in democracies. All regimes have rulers and a public realm, but only to the extent that they are democratic do they have citizens. Historically, severe restrictions on citizenship were imposed in most emerging or partial democracies according to criteria of age, gender, class, race, literacy, property ownership, tax-paying status, and so on. Only a small part of the total population was eligible to vote or run for office. Only restricted social categories were allowed to form, join, or support political associations. After protracted struggle—in some cases involving violent domestic upheaval or international war—most of these restrictions were lifted. Today, the criteria for inclusion are fairly standard. All native-born adults are eligible, although somewhat higher age limits may still be imposed upon candidates for certain offices. Unlike the early American and European democracies of the nineteenth century, none of the recent democracies in south-

ern Europe, Latin America, Asia, or Eastern Europe has even attempted to impose formal restrictions on the franchise or eligibility to office. When it comes to informal restrictions on the effective exercise of citizenship rights, however, the story can be quite different. This explains the central importance (discussed below) of procedures.

Competition has not always been considered an essential defining condition of democracy. "Classic" democracies presumed decision making based on direct participation leading to consensus. The assembled citizenry was expected to agree on a common course of action after listening to the alternatives and weighing their respective merits and demerits. A tradition of hostility to "faction," and "particular interests" persists in democratic thought, but at least since *The Federalist Papers* it has become widely accepted that competition among factions is a necessary evil in democracies that operate on a more-than-local scale. Since, as James Madison argued, "the latent causes of faction are sown into the nature of man," and the possible remedies for "the mischief of faction" are worse than the disease, the best course is to recognize them and to attempt to control their effects.[6] Yet while democrats may agree on the inevitability of factions, they tend to disagree about the best forms and rules for governing factional competition. Indeed, differences over the preferred modes and boundaries of competition contribute most to distinguishing one subtype of democracy from another.

The most popular definition of democracy equates it with regular *elections*, fairly conducted and honestly counted. Some even consider the mere fact of elections—even ones from which specific parties or candidates are excluded, or in which substantial portions of the population cannot freely participate—as a sufficient condition for the existence of democracy. This fallacy has been called "electoralism" or "the faith that merely holding elections will channel political action into peaceful contests among elites and accord public legitimacy to the winners"—no matter how they are conducted or what else constrains those who win them.[7] However central to democracy, elections occur intermittently and only allow citizens to choose between the highly aggregated alternatives offered by political parties, which can, especially in the early stages of a democratic transition, proliferate in a bewildering variety. During the intervals between elections, citizens can seek to influence public policy through a wide variety of other intermediaries: interest associations, social movements, locality groupings, clientelistic arrangements, and so forth. *Modern democracy, in other words, offers a variety of competitive processes and channels for the expression of interests and values—associational as well as partisan, functional as well as territorial, collective as well as individual. All are integral to its practice.*

Another commonly accepted image of democracy identifies it with *majority rule*. Any governing body that makes decisions by combining the votes of more than half of those eligible and present is said to be democratic, whether that majority emerges within an electorate, a parliament, a committee, a city council, or a party caucus. For exceptional purposes (e.g., amending the constitution or expelling a member), "qualified majorities" of more than 50 percent may be required, but few would deny that democracy must involve some means of aggregating the equal preferences of individuals.

A problem arises, however, when *numbers* meet *intensities*. What happens when a properly assembled majority (especially a stable, self-perpetuating one) regularly makes decisions that harm some minority (especially a threatened cultural or ethnic group)? In these circumstances, successful democracies tend to qualify the central principle of majority rule in order to protect minority rights. Such qualifications can take the form of constitutional provisions that place certain matters beyond the reach of majorities (bills of rights); requirements for concurrent majorities in several different constituencies (confederalism); guarantees securing the autonomy of local or regional governments against the demands of the central authority (federalism); grand coalition governments that incorporate all parties (consociationalism); or the negotiation of social pacts between major social groups like business and labor (neocorporatism). The most common and effective way of protecting minorities, however, lies in the everyday operation of interest associations and social movements. These reflect (some would say, amplify) the different intensities of preference that exist in the population and bring them to bear on democratically elected decision makers. Another way of putting this intrinsic tension between numbers and intensities would be to say that "in modern democracies, votes may be counted, but influences alone are weighted."

Cooperation has always been a central feature of democracy. Actors must voluntarily make collective decisions binding on the polity as a whole. They must cooperate in order to compete. They must be capable of acting collectively through parties, associations, and movements in order to select candidates, articulate preferences, petition authorities, and influence policies.

But democracy's freedoms should also encourage citizens to deliberate among themselves, to discover their common needs, and to resolve their differences without relying on some supreme central authority. Classical democracy emphasized these qualities, and they are by no means extinct, despite repeated efforts by contemporary theorists to stress the analogy with behavior in the economic marketplace and to reduce all of democracy's operations to competitive interest maximization. Alexis de Tocqueville best described the importance of independent groups for democracy in his *Democracy in America*, a work which remains a major source of inspiration for all those who persist in viewing democracy as something more than a struggle for election and re-election among competing candidates.[8]

In contemporary political discourse, this phenomenon of cooperation and deliberation via autonomous group activity goes under the rubric of "civil society." The diverse units of social identity and interest, by remaining independent of the state (and perhaps even of parties), not only can restrain the arbitrary actions of rulers, but can also contribute to forming better citizens who are more aware of the preferences of others, more self-confident in their actions, and more civic-minded in their willingness to sacrifice for the common good. At its best, civil society provides an intermediate layer of governance between the individual and the state that is capable of resolving conflicts and controlling the behavior of members without public coercion. Rather than overloading decision makers with increased demands and making the system ungovernable,[9] a viable civil society can mitigate conflicts and improve the quality of citizenship—without relying exclusively on the privatism of the marketplace.

Representatives—whether directly or indirectly elected—do most of the real work in modern democracies. Most are professional politicians who orient their careers around the desire to fill key offices. It is doubtful that any democracy could survive without such people. The central question, therefore, is not whether or not there will be a political elite or even a professional political class, but how these representatives are chosen and then held accountable for their actions.

As noted above, there are many channels of representation in modern democracy. The electoral one, based on territorial constituencies, is the most visible and public. It culminates in a parliament or a presidency that is periodically accountable to the citizenry as a whole. Yet the sheer growth of government (in large part as a byproduct of popular demand) has increased the number, variety, and power of agencies charged with making public decisions and not subject to elections. Around these agencies there has developed a vast apparatus of specialized representation based largely on functional interests, not territorial constituencies. These interest associations, and not political parties, have become the primary expression of civil society in most stable democracies, supplemented by the more sporadic interventions of social movements.

The new and fragile democracies that have sprung up since 1974 must live in "compressed time." They will not resemble the European democracies of the nineteenth and early twentieth centuries, and they cannot expect to acquire the multiple channels of representation in gradual historical progression as did most of their predecessors. A bewildering array of parties, interests, and movements will all simultaneously seek political influence in them, creating challenges to the polity that did not exist in earlier processes of democratization.

PROCEDURES THAT MAKE DEMOCRACY POSSIBLE

The defining components of democracy are necessarily abstract, and may give rise to a considerable variety of institutions and subtypes of democracy. For democracy to thrive, however, specific procedural norms must be followed and civic rights must be respected. Any polity that fails to impose such restrictions upon itself, that fails to follow the "rule of law" with regard to its own procedures, should not be considered democratic. These procedures alone do not define democracy, but their presence is indispensable to its persistence. In essence, they are necessary but not sufficient conditions for its existence.

Robert Dahl has offered the most generally accepted listing of what he terms the "procedural minimal" conditions that must be present for modern political democracy (or as he puts it, "polyarchy") to exist:

1. Control over government decisions about policy is constitutionally vested in elected officials.
2. Elected officials are chosen in frequent and fairly conducted elections in which coercion is comparatively uncommon.
3. Practically all adults have the right to vote in the election of officials.
4. Practically all adults have the right to run for elective offices in the government. . . .
5. Citizens have a right to express themselves without the danger of severe punishment on political matters broadly defined. . . .
6. Citizens have a right to seek out alternative sources of information. Moreover, alternative sources of information exist and are protected by law.
7. . . . Citizens also have the right to form relatively independent associations or organizations, including independent political parties and interest groups.[10]

These seven conditions seem to capture the essence of procedural democracy for many theorists, but we propose to add two others. The first might be thought of as a further refinement of item (1), while the second might be called an implicit prior condition to all seven of the above.

8. Popularly elected officials must be able to exercise their constitutional powers without being subjected to overriding (albeit informal) opposition from unelected officials. Democracy is in jeopardy if military officers, entrenched civil servants, or state managers retain the capacity to act independently of elected civilians or even veto decisions made by the people's representatives. Without this additional caveat, the militarized polities of contemporary Central America, where civilian control over the military does not exist, might be classified by many scholars as democracies, just as they have been (with the exception of Sandinista Nicaragua) by U.S. policy makers. The caveat thus guards against what we earlier called "electoralism"—the tendency to focus on the holding of elections while ignoring other political realities.
9. The polity must be self-governing; it must be able to act independently of constraints imposed by some other overarching political system. Dahl and other contemporary democratic theorists probably took

this condition for granted since they referred to formally sovereign nation-states. However, with the development of blocs, alliances, spheres of influence, and a variety of "neocolonial" arrangements, the question of autonomy has been a salient one. Is a system really democratic if its elected officials are unable to make binding decisions without the approval of actors outside their territorial domain? This is significant even if the outsiders are relatively free to alter or even end the encompassing arrangement (as in Puerto Rico), but it becomes especially critical if neither condition obtains (as in the Baltic states).

PRINCIPLES THAT MAKE DEMOCRACY FEASIBLE

Lists of component processes and procedural norms help us to specify what democracy is, but they do not tell us much about how it actually functions. The simplest answer is "by the consent of the people"; the more complex one is "by the contingent consent of politicians acting under conditions of bounded uncertainty."

In a democracy, representatives must at least informally agree that those who win greater electoral support or influence over policy will not use their temporary superiority to bar the losers from taking office or exerting influence in the future, and that in exchange for this opportunity to keep competing for power and place, momentary losers will respect the winners' right to make binding decisions. Citizens are expected to obey the decisions ensuing from such a process of competition, provided its outcome remains contingent upon their collective preferences as expressed through fair and regular elections or open and repeated negotiations.

The challenge is not so much to find a set of goals that command widespread consensus as to find a set of rules that embody contingent consent. The precise shape of this "democratic bargain," to use Dahl's expression,[11] can vary a good deal from society to society. It depends on social cleavages and such subjective factors as mutual trust, the standard of fairness, and the willingness to compromise. It may even be compatible with a great deal of dissensus on substantive policy issues.

All democracies involve a degree of uncertainty about who will be elected and what policies they will pursue. Even in those polities where one party persists in winning elections or one policy is consistently implemented, the possibility of change through independent collective action still exists, as in Italy, Japan, and the Scandinavian social democracies. If it does not, the system is not democratic, as in Mexico, Senegal, or Indonesia.

But the uncertainty embedded in the core of all democracies is bounded. Not just any actor can get into the competition and raise any issue he or she pleases—there are previously established rules that must be respected. Not just any policy can be adopted—there are conditions that must be met. Democracy institutionalizes "normal," limited political uncertainty. These boundaries vary from country to country. Constitutional guarantees of property, privacy, expression, and other rights are a part of this, but the most effective boundaries are generated by competition among interest groups and cooperation within civil society. Whatever the rhetoric (and some polities appear to offer their citizens more dramatic alternatives than others), once the rules of contingent consent have been agreed upon, the actual variation is likely to stay within a predictable and generally accepted range.

This emphasis on operative guidelines contrasts with a highly persistent, but misleading theme in recent literature on democracy—namely, the emphasis upon "civic culture." The principles we have suggested here rest on rules of prudence, not on deeply ingrained habits of tolerance, moderation, mutual respect, fair play, readiness to compromise, or trust in public authorities. Waiting for such habits to sink deep and lasting roots implies a very slow process of regime consolidation—one that takes generations—and it would probably condemn most contemporary experiences *ex hypothesi* to failure. Our assertion is that contingent consent and bounded uncertainty can emerge from the interaction between antagonistic and mutually suspicious actors and that the far more benevolent and ingrained norms of a civic culture are better thought of as a *product* and not a producer of democracy.

HOW DEMOCRACIES DIFFER

Several concepts have been deliberately excluded from our generic definition of democracy, despite the fact that they have been frequently associated with it in both everyday practice and scholarly work. They are, nevertheless, especially important when it comes to distinguishing subtypes of democracy. Since no single set of actual institutions, practices, or values embodies democracy, polities moving away from authoritarian rule can mix different components to produce different democracies. It is important to recognize that these do not define points along a single continuum of improving performance, but a matrix of potential combinations that are *differently* democratic.

1. *Consensus:* All citizens may not agree on the substantive goals of political action or on the role of the state (although if they did, it would certainly make governing democracies much easier).
2. *Participation:* All citizens may not take an active and equal part in politics, although it must be legally possible for them to do so.
3. *Access:* Rulers may not weigh equally the preferences of all who come before them, although citizenship implies that individuals and groups should have an equal opportunity to express their preferences if they choose to do so.
4. *Responsiveness:* Rulers may not always follow the course of action preferred by the citizenry. But when

they deviate from such a policy, say on grounds of "reason of state" or "overriding national interest," they must ultimately be held accountable for their actions through regular and fair processes.
5. *Majority rule:* Positions may not be allocated or rules may not be decided solely on the basis of assembling the most votes, although deviations from this principle usually must be explicitly defended and previously approved.
6. *Parliamentary sovereignty:* The legislature may not be the only body that can make rules or even the one with final authority in deciding which laws are binding, although where executive, judicial, or other public bodies make that ultimate choice, they too must be accountable for their actions.
7. *Party government:* Rulers may not be nominated, promoted, and disciplined in their activities by well-organized and programmatically coherent political parties, although where they are not, it may prove more difficult to form an effective government.
8. *Pluralism:* The political process may not be based on a multiplicity of overlapping, voluntaristic, and autonomous private groups. However, where there are monopolies of representation, hierarchies of association, and obligatory memberships, it is likely that the interests involved will be more closely linked to the state and the separation between the public and private spheres of action will be much less distinct.
9. *Federalism:* The territorial division of authority may not involve multiple levels and local autonomies, least of all ones enshrined in a constitutional document, although some dispersal of power across territorial and/or functional units is characteristic of all democracies.
10. *Presidentialism:* The chief executive officer may not be a single person and he or she may not be directly elected by the citizenry as a whole, although some concentration of authority is present in all democracies, even if it is exercised collectively and only held indirectly accountable to the electorate.
11. *Checks and Balances:* It is not necessary that the different branches of government be systematically pitted against one another, although governments by assembly, by executive concentrations, by judicial command, or even by dictatorial fiat (as in time of war) must be ultimately accountable to the citizenry as a whole.

While each of the above has been named as an essential component of democracy, they should instead be seen either as indicators of this or that type of democracy, or else as useful standards for evaluating the performance of particular regimes. To include them as part of the generic definition of democracy itself would be to mistake the American polity for the universal model of democratic governance. Indeed, the parliamentary, consociational, unitary, corporatist, and concentrated arrangements of continental Europe may have some unique virtues for guiding polities through the uncertain transition from autocratic to democratic rule.[12]

WHAT DEMOCRACY IS NOT

We have attempted to convey the general meaning of modern democracy without identifying it with some particular set of rules and institutions or restricting it to some specific culture or level of development. We have also argued that it cannot be reduced to the regular holding of elections or equated with a particular notion of the role of the state, but we have not said much more about what democracy is not or about what democracy may not be capable of producing.

There is an understandable temptation to load too many expectations on this concept and to imagine that by attaining democracy, a society will have resolved all of its political, social, economic, administrative, and cultural problems. Unfortunately, "all good things do not necessarily go together."

First, democracies are not necessarily more efficient economically than other forms of government. Their rates of aggregate growth, savings, and investment may be no better than those of nondemocracies. This is especially likely during the transition, when propertied groups and administrative elites may respond to real or imagined threats to the "rights" they enjoyed under authoritarian rule by initiating capital flight, disinvestment, or sabotage. In time, depending upon the type of democracy, benevolent long-term effects upon income distribution, aggregate demand, education, productivity, and creativity may eventually combine to improve economic and social performance, but it is certainly too much to expect that these improvements will occur immediately—much less that they will be defining characteristics of democratization.

Second, democracies are not necessarily more efficient administratively. Their capacity to make decisions may even be slower than that of the regimes they replace, if only because more actors must be consulted. The costs of getting things done may be higher, if only because "payoffs" have to be made to a wider and more resourceful set of clients (although one should never underestimate the degree of corruption to be found within autocracies). Popular satisfaction with the new democratic government's performance may not even seem greater, if only because necessary compromises often please no one completely, and because the losers are free to complain.

Third, democracies are not likely to appear more orderly, consensual, stable, or governable than the autocracies they replace. This is partly a byproduct of democratic freedom of expression, but it is also a reflection of the likelihood of continuing disagreement over new rules and institutions. These products of imposition or compromise are often initially quite ambiguous in nature and uncertain in effect until actors have learned how to use them. What is more, they come in the aftermath of serious struggles motivated by high ideals. Groups and individuals with recently acquired autonomy will test certain rules, protest against the actions of certain institutions, and insist on renegotiating their part of the bargain. Thus the presence of antisystem parties should be neither surprising nor seen as a failure of democratic consolidation. What counts is whether such parties are willing, however reluctantly, to play by the general rules of bounded uncertainty and contingent consent.

Governability is a challenge for all regimes, not just democratic ones. Given the political exhaustion and loss of legitimacy that have befallen autocracies from sultanistic Paraguay to totalitarian Albania, it may seem that only democracies can now be expected to govern effectively and legitimately. Experience has shown, however, that democracies too can lose the ability to govern. Mass publics can become disenchanted with their performance. Even more threatening is the temptation for leaders to fiddle with procedures and ultimately undermine the principles of contingent consent and bounded uncertainty. Perhaps the most critical moment comes once the politicians begin to settle into the more predictable roles and relations of a consolidated democracy. Many will find their expectations frustrated; some will discover that the new rules of competition put them at a disadvantage; a few may even feel that their vital interests are threatened by popular majorities.

" . . . democracies will have more open societies and polities than the autocracies they replace, but not necessarily more open economies."

Finally, democracies will have more open societies and polities than the autocracies they replace, but not necessarily more open economies. Many of today's most successful and well-established democracies have historically resorted to protectionism and closed borders, and have relied extensively upon public institutions to promote economic development. While the long-term compatibility between democracy and capitalism does not seem to be in doubt, despite their continuous tension, it is not clear whether the promotion of such liberal economic goals as the right of individuals to own property and retain profits, the clearing function of markets, the private settlement of disputes, the freedom to produce without government regulation, or the privatization of state-owned enterprises necessarily furthers the consolidation of democracy. After all, democracies do need to levy taxes and regulate certain transactions, especially where private monopolies and oligopolies exist. Citizens or their representatives may decide that it is desirable to protect the rights of collectivities from encroachment by individuals, especially propertied ones, and they may choose to set aside certain forms of property for public or cooperative ownership. In short, notions of economic liberty that are currently put forward in neoliberal economic models are not synonymous with political freedom—and may even impede it.

Democratization will not necessarily bring in its wake economic growth, social peace, administrative efficiency, political harmony, free markets, or "the end of ideology." Least of all will it bring about "the end of history." No doubt some of these qualities could make the consolidation of democracy easier, but they are neither prerequisites for it nor immediate products of it. Instead, what we should be hoping for is the emergence of political institutions that can peacefully compete to form governments and influence public policy, that can channel social and economic conflicts through regular procedures, and that have sufficient linkages to civil society to represent their constituencies and commit them to collective courses of action. Some types of democracies, especially in developing countries, have been unable to fulfill this promise, perhaps due to the circumstances of their transition from authoritarian rule.[13] The democratic wager is that such a regime, once established, will not only persist by reproducing itself within its initial confining conditions, but will eventually expand beyond them.[14] Unlike authoritarian regimes, democracies have the capacity to modify their rules and institutions consensually in response to changing circumstances. They may not immediately produce all the goods mentioned above, but they stand a better chance of eventually doing so than do autocracies.

NOTES

1. For a comparative analysis of the recent regime changes in southern Europe and Latin America, see Guillermo O'Donnell, Philippe C. Schmitter, and Laurence Whitehead, eds., *Transitions from Authoritarian Rule*, 4 vols. (Baltimore: Johns Hopkins University Press, 1986). For another compilation that adopts a more structural approach see Larry Diamond, Juan Linz, and Seymour Martin Lipset, eds., *Democracy in Developing Countries*, vols. 2, 3, and 4 (Boulder, Colo.: Lynne Rienner, 1989).

2. Numerous attempts have been made to codify and quantify the existence of democracy across political systems. The best known is probably Freedom House's *Freedom in the World: Political Rights and Civil Liberties*, published since 1973 by Greenwood Press and since 1988 by University Press of America. Also see Charles Humana, *World Human Rights Guide* (New York: Facts on File, 1986).

3. The definition most commonly used by American social scientists is that of Joseph Schumpeter: "that institutional arrangement for arriving at political decisions in which individuals acquire the power to decide by means of a competitive struggle for the people's vote." *Capitalism, Socialism, and Democracy* (London: George Allen and Unwin, 1943), 269. We accept certain aspects of the classical procedural approach to modern democracy, but differ primarily in our emphasis on the accountability of rulers to citizens and the relevance of mechanisms of competition other than elections.

4. Not only do some countries practice a stable form of democracy without a formal constitution (e.g., Great Britain and Israel), but even more countries have constitutions and legal codes that offer no guarantee of reliable practice. On paper, Stalin's 1936 constitution for the USSR was a virtual model of democratic rights and entitlements.

5. For the most valiant attempt to make some sense out of this thicket of distinctions, see Juan Linz, "Totalitarian and Authoritarian Regimes" in *Handbook of Political Science*, eds. Fred I. Greenstein and Nelson W. Polsby (Reading Mass.: Addison Wesley, 1975), 175–411.

6. "Publius" (Alexander Hamilton, John Jay, and James Madison), *The Federalist Papers* (New York: Anchor Books, 1961). The quote is from Number 10.

7. See Terry Karl, "Imposing Consent? Electoralism versus Democratization in El Salvador," in *Elections and Democratization in Latin America, 1980-1985*, eds. Paul Drake and Eduardo Silva (San Diego: Center for Iberian and Latin American Studies, Center for US/Mexican Studies, University of California, San Diego, 1986), 9–36.

8. Alexis de Tocqueville, *Democracy in America*, 2 vols. (New York: Vintage Books, 1945).

9. This fear of overloaded government and the imminent collapse of democracy is well reflected in the work of Samuel P. Huntington during the 1970s. See especially Michel Crozier, Samuel P. Huntington, and Joji Watanuki, *The Crisis of Democracy* (New York: New York University Press, 1975). For Huntington's (revised) thoughts about the prospects for democracy, see his "Will More Countries Become Democratic?," *Political Science Quarterly* 99 (Summer 1984): 193–218.

10. Robert Dahl, *Dilemmas of Pluralist Democracy* (New Haven: Yale University Press, 1982), 11.

11. Robert Dahl, *After the Revolution: Authority in a Good Society* (New Haven: Yale University Press, 1970).

12. See Juan Linz, "The Perils of Presidentialism," *Journal of Democracy* 1 (Winter 1990): 51–69, and the ensuing discussion by Donald Horowitz, Seymour Martin Lipset, and Juan Linz in *Journal of Democracy* 1 (Fall 1990): 73–91.

13. Terry Lynn Karl, "Dilemmas of Democratization in Latin America," *Comparative Politics* 23 (October 1990): 1–23.

14. Otto Kirchheimer, "Confining Conditions and Revolutionary Breakthroughs," *American Political Science Review* 59 (1965): 964–974.

Parliament and Congress:

Is the Grass Greener on the other side?

Gregory S. Mahler

Gregory Mahler is chair of the Political Science Department at the University of Mississippi.

Aristotle long ago observed that man is a "political animal." He could have added that man, by his very nature, notes the political status of his neighbours and, very often, perceives their lot as being superior to his own. The old saying "the grass is greener on the other side of the fence" can be applied to politics and political structures as well as to other, more material, dimensions of the contemporary world.

Legislators are not immune from the very human tendency to see how others of their lot exist in their respective settings, and, sometimes, to look longingly at these other settings. When legislators do look around to see the conditions under which their peers operate in other countries, they occasionally decide they prefer the alternative legislative settings to their own.

Features which legislators admire or envy in the settings of their colleagues include such things as: the characteristics of political parties (their numbers, or degrees of party discipline), legislative committee systems, staff and services available to help legislators in their tasks, office facilities, libraries, and salaries. This essay will develop the "grass is greener" theme in relation to a dimension of the legislative world which is regularly a topic of conversation when legislators from a number of different jurisdictions meet: the ability or inability of legislatures to check and control the executive.

The Decline of Parliament

The theme of the "decline of parliament" has a long and well-studied history.[1] It generally refers to the gradual flow of true legislative power away from the legislative body in the direction of the executive. The executive does the real law-making — by actually drafting most legislation — and the legislature takes a more "passive" role by simply approving executive proposals.

Legislators are very concerned about their duties and powers and over the years have jealously guarded them when they have appeared to be threatened. In Canada (and indeed most parliamentary democracies in the world today), the majority of challenges to legislative power which develop no longer come from the ceremonial executive (the Crown), but from the political executive, the government of the day.

It can be argued that the ability to direct and influence public policy, is a "zero sum game" (i.e. there is only room for a limited amount of power and influence to be exercised in the political world and a growth in the relative power of the political executive must be at the expense of the power of the legislature). It follows, then, that if the legislature is concerned about maintaining its powers, concerned about protecting its powers from being diminished, it must be concerned about every attempt by the political executive to expand its powers.

Others contend that real "legislative power" cannot, and probably never did reside in the legislature. There was no "Golden Age" of Parliament. The true legislative role of parliament today is not (and in the past was not) to create legislation, but to scrutinize and ratify legislation introduced by the Government of the day. Although an occasional exception to this pattern of behavior may exist (with private members' bills, for example), the general rule is clear: the legislature today does not actively initiate legislation as its primary *raison d'être*.

Although parliamentarians may not be major initiators of legislation, studies have indicated a wide range of other functions.[2] Certainly one major role of the legislature is the "oversight" role, criticizing and checking the powers of the executive. The ultimate extension of this power is the ability of the legislature to terminate the term of office of the executive through a "no confidence" vote. Another role of the legislature involves communication and representation of constituency concerns. Yet another function involves the debating function, articulating the concerns of the public of the day.

Professor James Mallory has indicated the need to "be

From *Canadian Parliamentary Review*, Winter 1985/86, pp. 19-21. Reprinted by permission of the Committees and Parliamentary Associations Branch of the House of Commons in Ottawa, Ontario.

realistic about the role of Parliament in the Westminster system."[3] He cites Bernard Crick's classic work, *The Reform of Parliament:* "... the phrase 'Parliamentary control,' and talk about the 'decline of parliamentary control,' should not mislead anyone into asking for a situation in which governments can have their legislation changed or defeated, or their life terminated... Control means influence, not direct power; advice, not command; criticism, not obstruction; scrutiny, not initiation; and publicity, not secrecy."[4]

The fact that parliament may not be paramount in the creation and processing of legislation is no reason to condemn all aspects of parliamentary institutions. Nor should parliamentarians be convinced that legislative life is perfect in the presidential-congressional system. In fact, some American legislators look to their parliamentary brethren and sigh with envy at the attractiveness of certain aspects of parliamentary institutions.

Desirability of a Congressional Model for Canada?

Many Canadian parliamentarians and students of parliament look upon presidential-congressional institutions of the United States as possessing the answers to most of their problems. The grass is sometimes seen as being greener on the other side of the border. The concepts of fixed legislative terms, less party discipline, and a greater general emphasis on the role and importance of individual legislators (which implies more office space and staff for individual legislators, among other things) are seen as standards to which Canadian legislators should aspire.

A perceived strength of the American congressional system is that legislators do not automatically "rubber stamp" approve executive proposals. They consider the president's suggestions, but feel free to make substitutions or modifications to the proposal, or even to reject it completely. Party discipline is relatively weak; there are regularly Republican legislators opposing a Republican president (and Democratic legislators supporting him), and vice versa. Against the need for discipline congressmen argue that their first duty is to either (a) their constituency, or (b) what is "right", rather than simply to party leaders telling them how to behave in the legislature. For example, in 1976 Jimmy Carter was elected President with large majorities of Democrats in both houses of Congress. One of Carter's major concerns was energy policy. He introduced legislative proposals (that is, he had congressional supporters introduce legislation, since the American president cannot introduce legislation on his own) dealing with energy policy, calling his proposals "the moral equivalent of war." In his speeches and public appearances he did everything he could to muster support for "his" legislation. Two years later when "his" legislation finally emerged from the legislative process, it could hardly be recognized as the proposals submitted in such emotional terms two years earlier.

The experience of President Carter was certainly not unique. Any number of examples of such incidents of legislative-executive non-cooperation can be cited in recent American political history, ranging from President Wilson's unsuccessful efforts to get the United States to join the League of Nations, through Ronald Reagan's contemporary battles with Congress over the size of the federal budget. The Carter experience was somewhat unusual by virtue of the fact that the same political party controlled both the executive and legislative branches of government, and cooperation still was not forthcoming. There have been many more examples of non-cooperation when one party has controlled the White House and another party has controlled one or both houses of Congress.

✳This lack of party discipline ostensibly enables the individual legislators to be concerned about the special concerns of their constituencies. This, they say, is more important than simply having to follow the orders of the party whip in the legislature. It is not any more unusual to find a Republican legislator from a farm state voting against a specific agricultural proposal of President Reagan on the grounds that the legislation in question is not good for his/her constituency, than to find Democratic legislators from the southwestern states who voted against President Carter's water policy proposals on the grounds that the proposals were not good for their constituencies.

Congressional legislators know that they have fixed terms in office — the President is simply not able to bring about early elections — and they know that as long as they can keep their constituencies happy there is no need to be terribly concerned about opposing the President, even if he is the leader of their party. It may be nice to have the President on your side, but if you have a strong base of support "back home" you can survive without his help.

Are there any benefits to the public interest in the absence of party discipline? The major argument is that the legislature will independently consider the executive's proposals, rather than simply accepting the executive's ideas passively. This, it is claimed, allows for a multiplicity of interests, concerns, and perspectives to be represented in the legislature, and ostensibly results in "better" legislation.

In summary, American legislative institutions promote the role of the individual legislator. The fixed term gives legislators the security necessary for the performance of the functions they feel are important. The (relative) lack of party discipline enables legislators to act on the issues about which they are concerned. In terms of the various legislative functions mentioned above, congressmen appear to spend a great deal of their time in what has been termed the legislative aspect of the job: drafting legislation, debating, proposing amendments, and voting (on a more or less independent basis).

While many parliamentarians are impressed by the ability of individual American legislator to act on their own volition it is ironic that many congressional legislators look longingly at the legislative power relationships of their parliamentary bretheren. The grass, apparently, is greener on the *other* side of the border, too.

Desirability of a Parliamentary Model

The "decline of congressional power" is as popular a topic of conversation in Washington as "the decline of parliamentary power" in Ottawa or London. Over the last several decades American legislators have sensed that a great deal of legislative power has slipped from their collective grasp.[5] Many have decried this tendency and tried to stop, or reverse this flow of power away from the legislative branch and toward the executive.

One of the major themes in the writings of these congressional activists is an admiration for the parliamentary model's (perceived) power over the executive. Many American legislators see the president's veto power, combined with his fixed term in office, as a real flaw in the "balance of powers" of the system, leading to an inexorable increase in executive power at the expense of the legislature. They look at a number of parliamentary structures which they see as promoting democratic political behavior and increased executive responsibility to the legislature, including the ability to force the resignation of the executive through a non-confidence vote. The regular "question period" format which insures some degree of public executive accountability is also perceived as being very attractive .

Critics of the congressional system do not confine their criticism only to the growth of executive power. There are many who feel there is too much freedom in the congressional arena. To paraphrase the words of Bernard Crick cited earlier, advising has sometimes turned into issuing commands; and criticism has sometimes turned into obstruction. This is not to suggest that congressional legislators would support giving up their ability to initiate legislation, to amend executive proposals, or to vote in a manner which they (individually) deem proper. This does suggest, however, that even congressional legislators see that independence is a two-sided coin: one side involves individual legislative autonomy and input into the legislative process; the other side involves the incompatibility of complete independence with a British style of "Responsible Government".

In 1948 Hubert Humphrey, then mayor of Minneapolis, delivered an address at the nomination convention of the Democratic Party. In his comments he appealed for a "more responsible" two party system in the United States, a system with sufficient party discipline to have *meaningful* party labels, and to allow party platforms to become public policy.[6] Little progress has been made over the last thirty-seven years in this regard. In the abstract the concept of a *meaningful* two party system may be attractive; American legislators have not been as attracted to the necessary corollary of the concept: decreased legislative independence and increased party discipline.

While American Senators and Representatives are very jealous of executive encroachments upon their powers, there is some recognition that on occasion — usually depending upon individual legislators' views about the desirability of specific pieces of legislation — executive leadership, and perhaps party discipline, can serve a valuable function. Congressional legislators are, at times which correspond to their policy preferences, envious of parliamentary governnments' abilities to carry their programs into law because MPs elected under their party labels will act consistent with party whips' directions. They would be loath to give up their perceived high degrees of legislative freedom but many of them realize the cost of this freedom in this era of pressing social problems and complex legislation. Parliamentary style government is simply not possible without party discipline.

A Democratic Congressman supporting President Carter's energy policy proposals might have longed for an effective three-line whip to help to pass the energy policies in question. An opponent of those policy proposals would have argued, to the contrary, that the frustration of the president's proposals was a good illustration of the wisdom of the legislature tempering the error-ridden policy proposals of the president. Similarly, many conservative Republican supporters of President Reagan have condemned the ability of the Democratic House of Representatives to frustrate his economic policies. Opponents of those policies have argued, again, that the House of Representatives is

doing an important job of representing public opinion and is exercising a valuable and important check on the misguided policies of the executive.

Some Concluding Observations

The parliamentary model has its strengths as well as its weaknesses. The individual legislator in a parliamentary system does not have as active a role in the actual legislative process as does his American counterparts, but it is not at all hard to imagine instances in which the emphasis on individual autonomy in the congressional system can be counterproductive because it delays much-needed legislative programs.

The problem, ultimately, is one of balance. Is it possible to have a responsible party system in the context of parliamentary democracy which can deliver on its promises to the public, and also to have a high degree of individual legislative autonomy in the legislative arena?

It is hard to imagine how those two concepts could coexist. The congressional and parliamentary models of legislative behavior have placed their respective emphases on two different priorities. The parliamentary model, with its responsible party system and its corresponding party discipline in the legislature, emphasizes efficient policy delivery, and the ability of an elected government to deliver on its promises. The congressional model, with its lack of party discipline and its emphasis on individual legislative autonomy, placed more emphasis on what can be called "consensual politics": it may take much more time for executive proposals to find their way into law, but (the argument goes) there is greater likelihood that what does, ultimately, emerge as law will be acceptable to a greater number of people than if government proposals were "automatically" approved by a pre-existing majority in the legislature acting "under the whip".

We cannot say that one type of legislature is "more effective" than the other. Each maximizes effectiveness in different aspects of the legislative function. Legislators in the congressional system, because of their greater legislative autonomy and weaker party discipline, are more effective at actually legislating than they are at exercising ultimate control over the executive. Legislators in the parliamentary system, although they may play more of a "ratifying" role in regard to legislation, do get legislation passed promptly; they also have an ultimate power over the life of the government of the day.

The appropriateness of both models must also be evaluated in light of the different history, political culture and objectives of the societies in which they operate. Perhaps the grass is just as green on both sides of the fence.

Notes

[1]There is substantial literature devoted to the general topic of "the decline of legislatures." Among the many sources which could be referred to in this area would be included the work of Gerhard Loewenberg. *Modern Parliaments: Change or Decline?* Chicago: Atherton. 1971; Gerhard Loewenberg and Samuel Patterson,

Comparing Legislatures, Boston: Little, Brown, 1979; or Samuel Patterson and John Wahlke, eds., *Comparative Legislative Behavior: Frontiers of Research*, New York: John Wiley, 1972.

[2]A very common topic in studies of legislative behavior has to do with the various functions legislatures may be said to perform for the societies of which they are a part. For a discussion of the many functions attributed to legislatures in political science literature, see Gregory Mahler, *Comparative Politics: An Institutional and Cross-National Approach* (Cambridge, Ma.: Schenkman, 1983, pp. 56-61.

[3]J. R. Mallory, "Can Parliament Control the Regulatory Process?"

Canadian Parliamentary Review Vol. 6 (no. 3, 1983) p. 6.

[4]Bernard Crick, *The Reform of Parliament*, London, 1968, p. 80.

[5]One very well written discussion of the decline of American congressional power in relation to the power of the president can be found in Ronald Moe, ed., *Congress and the President*, Pacific Palisades, Calif.: Goodyear Publishing Co., 1971.

[6]Subsequently a special report was published by the Committee on Political Parties of the American Political Science Association dealing with this problem. See "Toward a More Responsible Two-Party System," *American Political Science Review* Vol. 44 (no. 3, 1950), special supplement.

Campaign and Party Finance: What Americans Might Learn from Abroad

Arthur B. Gunlicks

University of Richmond

When the Clinton Administration took office in January 1993 with a Democratic-controlled Congress, many Americans were hoping that the long-standing "gridlock" between the Congress and President would finally be broken on a wide variety of issues, not the least of which was a reform of campaign finance laws and practices. Ross Perot had raised the issue during the presidential campaign, and Democratic-passed reform legislation which had been vetoed by President Bush now seemed to have a good chance of being revived, perhaps modified, passed, and signed by the new President.

It was not to be. Democratic House leaders gave President Clinton's campaign reform proposals of May 7, 1993, a lukewarm reaction, and Senator Robert Dole threatened to use the filibuster to block congressional action. Reform is a risky business for both parties, and what looks good from the perspective of political scientists or even the White House may not be very appealing to politicians in the trenches who worry that would-be challengers might actually have a fighting chance. In any case, the Democrats in the Senate and House could not agree on a compromise bill, and by the time they finally did in the fall of 1994 their efforts were defeated by the inability to end a Republican filibuster in the Senate.

After the Republican takeover of both the Senate and House following the 1994 midterm elections, any serious hope for political finance reform was dead. First, because the Republican "Contract with America" set entirely different priorities, and, second, because "gridlock" had returned and there was little hope that the Republican-dominated Congress and the Democratic President could agree on reform measures. Certainly any proposals calling for federal subsidies or tax expenditures would have no chance in a Republican Congress determined to reduce drastically federal expenditures and the federal deficit. Still, Ross Perot continued to talk about political finance reform, and House Speaker Newt Gingrich and President Clinton agreed informally in early summer 1995 to work

together to promote campaign finance reform. In fact, not much has happened since then, although the issue refuses to go away.

It is easy and very tempting to argue that we should look at what other Western democracies do and adopt some of their practices. One of the difficulties we face, however, lies in the uniqueness of our political system, which raises questions about the relevance of foreign experiences. First, we have to focus on the party system. Our politics are candidate-oriented. In most democracies, they are more party-oriented. Many of us may regret this fact and even devote some energy and effort toward strengthening American parties, but the probability of a major change seems slight. The party orientation found elsewhere has an effect on political financing. Indeed, the concept of "political finance" is likely to mean candidate and campaign financing in the United States and party financing in other democracies. Therefore, it is not surprising that the administration backed away from the idea of funneling public funds to the parties.

Second, our institutions are different. Virtually all countries that we might look to for comparison are parliamentary democracies. France may have a semi-presidential system, but its parliamentary features still distinguish it from the United States. Most democracies are unitary states. Canada, Australia, Germany, Switzerland and Austria are federal states, but they differ in significant respects from the United States in their division of powers as well as in population and/or size of territory. They are also parliamentary democracies.

Third, we have a political culture which is not very conducive to government assistance to political parties. Anti-party and anti-government sentiments in the United States have deep roots, and reform proposals that might cost taxpayers money and bring about more government involvement must overcome serious obstacles. It may be that public financing is not very popular in other countries, either, but the fact remains that it is widespread abroad and not here.

It is clear that the kind of massive public funding of parties found, for example, in Germany, Austria, and Sweden has little prospect of being implemented in the United States. The generously funded party foundations which perform a number of useful tasks in Germany and Austria also are unlikely ever to gain majority support in Congress. Public funding on this scale would be unacceptable for very practical budgetary reasons, let alone the different American party system and political culture.

What, then, are some foreign practices that might be deserving of some careful consideration in spite of the odds against their passage? It should be possible to convince the public—and then Congress—that television and radio stations must provide a certain amount of free media time, a common practice in almost every other democracy. The Clinton Administration's proposal to provide congressional candidates vouchers to pay for television, printing and postage if they agree to adhere to spending limits is a step in the right direction, but it differs significantly from other democracies where free time is provided to the parties rather than individual candidates. Free billboard and poster space for political advertisements might also be offered by local governments, as is common in Europe. There can be no question, however, that the focus on individual candidates in this country makes free television time and billboard space more complicated to administer. It would probably be very difficult to convince Americans to ban altogether the purchase of media time by individual candidates, as is done in Canada, Britain and the European Continent.

In order to reduce the influence of the widely disliked PACs, which are not found abroad, one can make a strong case for limiting the amounts they may give individual candidates. Thus it is not surprising that the Clinton Administration has moved at least modestly in this direction. But placing limits on PACs raises the question of where the necessary campaign money is to come from besides wealthy candidates, their supporters, and other private interests. Some European countries, e.g., Germany, provide generous tax deductions for donations to political parties. The very modest deductions that were available in the United States were eliminated in the 1986 tax reforms. Surely small donations of up to at least $250 should be encouraged through tax deductions and/or public matching funds for candidates who have demonstrated that they enjoy minimal political support. Contributions to political parties should be promoted, and parties should be encouraged to assume more responsibility for financing the campaigns of their candidates. Perhaps "soft money" *to the parties* could be better regulated rather than banned, as appears to be a goal of the Clinton proposals.

We do, of course, have a $3 federal tax check-off to pay for *presidential* campaigns and national political conventions, but only a small percentage (15–18 percent) of taxpayers actually check the appropriate boxes even though it costs them nothing. A few states also have tax check-offs for helping to finance certain candidates or parties, while another handful of states have tax add-ons, where the taxpayer actually increases his or her tax liability by giving up a small portion of the refund due. As a result, only about one percent of state taxpayers participate in tax add-on schemes. In other words, the amount of public political financing that exists in the United States, except for presidential races, is minimal.

To level the playing field even more, Congress could again try to impose limits on individual spending by candidates in the hope that the Supreme Court might reconsider its decision in *Buckley v. Valeo.* The British and Canadians have limited expenditures by individual candidates without, at last check, weakening freedom of speech in any notable way. The British also require candidate approval of what we call "independent expenditures," which has hardly led to a serious undermining of free speech.

Some reformers have argued that tightening the regulation of parties and candidates, such as improved disclosure and reporting procedures, would "clean up" problems of political finance. Aside from the suspicion that such proposals reflect the "puritan" streak in American political culture, it is difficult to see how these measures would deal effectively with the funding problems we face.

If large amounts of money are being spent by individual candidates, PACs and special interests in general, and there is understandable public dissatisfaction with this state of affairs, it seems apparent that alternate sources of financing must be found. Placing ceilings on expenditures is probably not a very effective solution. Tightening regulations will not produce more private donations. The dilemmas—and there are several—are that alternatives seem to be very expensive, and there is the problem of increasing dependency on the state. This dependency may lead to a separation of the party from the grassroots, as appears to be happening in Germany and several other countries, especially Italy, which voted *recently* in a referendum to end public subsidies for the parties.

American parties are a very long way from becoming dependent on the state for their finances. Indeed, by international comparison we rank low on the dependency scale, especially if one excludes the presidential campaigns. Were we to adopt free media time, free billboard space, tax deductions for small donations to parties and candidates, or modest public subsidies for legislative candidates, all of which are practices common in numerous other democracies, we would not solve all of our current problems. But it seems difficult to believe that the conditions of political financing in the United States would not benefit from the adoption of some of these measures.

Arthur B. Gunlicks is the editor of *Comparative Party and Campaign Finance in Europe and North America,* published by Westview Press.

ELECTORAL REFORM

Good government? Fairness?
Or vice versa. Or both

Italians want to junk proportional representation. Others could usefully adopt it. Which electoral system is best? The arguments are many. So are the answers

BRITAIN elects its House of Commons by the simplest possible system: single-member constituencies in which the front-runner wins, even if he has under 50% of the votes. In 1983, 7.8m votes, a quarter of the total, went to the "third party", the Alliance. It got 23 seats. The Labour Party got 8.5m votes—and 209 seats. No wonder half of all Britons say they would like a fairer system.

Italy uses systems of proportional representation (PR) that are elaborately fair. It has also had 52 governments, mostly coalitions, since 1945, all dominated by the Christian Democrats. Italian government is famously inept, its parties—not only the Christian Democrats—infamously corrupt. No wonder Italians have just voted massively to adopt the British system for three-quarters of their Senate seats; the Chamber of Deputies will probably go much the same way.

These two countries exemplify—in parody—the arguments about electoral reform. Britain's "first past the post" system (FPTP) nearly always produces a single-party government with an overall, and solid, Commons majority. Unless that party itself is split—as now, over the Maastricht treaty—the government can override all opposition. The result, given a decisive prime minister, should always be decisive government.

In contrast, look at Italy, Israel or Poland. Their PR is as fair as it comes. Umpteen parties, even tiny ones with 1-2% of the national vote, can win seats. With 3% or 4%,

they can make or break policies and governments, as Israel's religious parties notoriously have done. It sounds like a recipe for feeble government, with the tail—as the enemies of PR put it—wagging the dog.

The choice looks clear: good government or fair representation? In fact, not so. British governments have often been feeble; Israel's often decisive, even fierce. Italy's governments are unstable and inept; not so Germany's, although the Bundestag they rest on is shaped by PR. True, it keeps out small parties. Yet most post-1949 German governments have had a "tail", the Free Democrats (FDP).

As for the corruption now disgusting Italy's voters, its cause, arguably, is too long tenure of office, not the electoral system. Japan has no formal PR, but its ever-ruling Liberal Democrats are hardly clean. True, PR at times prevents complete clear-outs of government; but the parties that stay in office, despite swings among voters, are usually small, as in Germany (Italy is a special case; its large Communist party was not acceptable as an alternative in government to the Christian Democrats).

Corruption anyway springs more from the climate of society—and state control of the economy—than from any parliamentary arrangements. Most government in India (an FPTP country) is corrupt within weeks of taking office. The African minister

who is not, by British standards, corrupt, is acting very oddly indeed by African ones (or indeed by British ones of the 18th century: not to help one's friends—and oneself—is, like elective democracy, a recent, North European curiosity of human behaviour).

So FPTP offers no monopoly, or even guarantee, of good government. But neither does PR of fairness. Americans fret about many aspects of their political system, but not its fairness between parties; and—given that no third party exists—its results are decently proportional. Still not fair, maybe. All Americans have one vote, but of wildly different values: Alaska's 400,000 voters elect two senators, as do California's 23m. Yet why is that so? Because the founding fathers chose so. And few Americans are bothered by this either.

That is a reminder that fairness has many faces. As much as a party, the voter may want a given person to speak for him. FPTP allows for this. He may want one kind of person. Women hold few seats: in the late 1980s, about 30% in the Nordic PR countries, 5-20% in many others whose parties, in filling the party lists used in PR, take little, if any, note of this; and 5-15% in FPTP countries. Even fewer members come from poor, ethnic minorities. A few constitutions (India's, eg) reserve seats for them. Some American electoral boundaries are drawn to help them. Mostly, they must rely on accidents of geography, notably inner-city concentration.

Nor is the voter picking only his representative. He votes for certain policies, and—save in presidential systems—for a government; a serious one, not a bunch of clowns. A PR system could be as fair as Snow White in reflecting party support, and yet, at times, frustrate all these hopes. Would the result fairly represent the electorate?

It depends who, where and for what

America offers another reminder: that neither fairness nor effectiveness exists *in vacuo*. They depend on their context.

An elected body may spring from long democratic tradition or little, from a multicultural society or a homogeneous one. It may be national or local. It may be part of a two-house set-up (America gets territorial fairness in its Senate, demographic from the House). It may provide a government, as do European parliaments, or just legislate and oversee one, as in America. It may be mainly a sounding-board, like the 12-nation parliament of the European Community. And what is "right" here, or for one function, may be wrong there, or for another.

Britain offers an example. Its local government cries out for PR, since the national demography to which parties adapt is not reproduced locally. Voting in 1991 left 15 of 36 English "metropolitan" districts with councils that were 80%-plus Labour (nine of them 90%-plus). Of 296 "non-met"—less urban—councils, 31 had no Labour members, 35 no Liberal Democrats. Point made? Yet it proves nothing about the Commons.

With so many ifs and buts, it is easy to say if it ain't broke don't even think of fixing it. Who would today invent Britain's House of Lords, a jumble of hereditary peers, bishops and judges, plus assorted notables (or party hacks) picked by successive prime ministers? Yet, in its way, it works. If it can survive—and reforming it is a barely an issue in Britain—maybe anything can, even should.

Should? A wise country leaves well, or even only moderately well, alone. After Holland's PR elections, it can take months even to form a government. Yet few Dutchmen worry, any more than Americans do about Alaska. But when a majority (Italy) or a large minority (Britain) feels grossly ill-served or ill-treated, it is time to think again.

Beside Italy, Poland has recently opted for change. Its infant post-Communist democracy chose extreme PR, and in its late-1991 elections paid the price. In all, 67 "parties" fought; the best-placed won only 13% of the vote, and the legislature now includes 29—often shifting—groups. A new electoral law, though it too is PR-based, will limit such follies.

New Zealand, now using FPTP, may go the other way. A referendum last September backed a switch to PR (mainly, as in Italy, to punish politicians). Even Britain's Labour Party is looking at PR, if less because of Liberal complaints than of its own fears that FPTP—which in the past served it well—may leave its Tory rivals for ever running solid one-party governments on 40% of the vote.

Britain's love of FPTP is criticised beyond its borders, because, except in Northern Ireland, it elects members to the European Parliament by this system. So the Tory-Labour balance swings wildly, while large Euro-constituencies crush other national parties. In 1984, the Alliance won 18.5% of the Euro-vote, but no seats; ditto the Greens in 1989, with 14.5%. The result distorts not just British representation but the make-up of the whole parliament.

France's recent elections aroused worries about its two-round voting. This was de Gaulle's substitute for the instabilities of PR, only briefly replaced by PR again in the mid-1980s. Its results can be fair enough. Not this year. Right-wing parties, with 39% of the vote, took 80% of the seats. The National Front, with 12½%, got none. Nasty as the Front is, many Frenchmen doubt that democracy should leave so many voters voiceless.

Pros and cons

Italians' dislike of PR far outruns French or British anxieties the other way. That is natural: they identify it with lousy government. And bad government both hits the whole nation and impinges visibly and constantly on daily life; the disfranchisement felt by third-party voters does neither. Yet worries about FPTP and related systems go deeper. It is representative democracy, not good government, that is the essence of "western" politics. *The Economist*, discussing these issues two years ago, wrote flatly that

> And since the perception of fairness is the acid test for democracy—the very basis of its legitimacy—the unfairness argument overrules all others.

There is a more pragmatic reason. Politicians can, and in Europe mostly do, provide decent government with PR. Unless, as in America, history has dumped third parties, FPTP cannot, except by chance, and normally does not provide fair representation. Human wit can get round the faults of PR; it cannot—except in drawing electoral boundaries—act on the crude mechanics of FPTP.

Yet any shift toward PR must, if possible, avoid its faults in advance. Its critics list many, not all as solid as they sound:

• **Too complicated.** Nonsense. What some think the best system, the single transferable vote, is indeed complex. But the Irish can work it, so why not others?

• **Too many small parties.** That depends how far fairness is pushed. A threshold can hold numbers down: Germany's fierce 5% one has usually kept the Bundestag to just four parties, rarely five. Is it acceptable to exclude 4.9% of opinion—or, as recently in Eastern Europe, several times 4.9%? FPTP too can let in many small parties, if (but only if) each has a regional base.

• **Too many weak coalitions.** Coalitions, yes. Weak, maybe. PR produces both.

• **Too much power for small "pivotal" parties.** Germany's FDP is often cited. In 1982 it quit a coalition with the SDP and joined the CDU. Undemocratic? Six months later the policy shift that the FDP had sought was endorsed by the voters. The "tail-and-dog" case too is weak. On minor issues dear to them, small parties may get their way (as in Israel). On big issues, in politics as in physics, small bodies can only influence large ones, not rule them. West German unification-seeking softness toward Russia in 1989 is cited. That began with the FDP foreign minister; but it was backed by Chancellor Kohl.

• **Policy decided in inter-party haggling after an election, not by voters during it.** Often true, shamefully so in Italy, though its smoke-shrouded deals were more about posts than policy. But the idea that it is "unfair" for those who backed the biggest party in a coalition to see its policy then diluted is bogus: in politics as in marriage, if you cannot win outright, you must compromise.

• **Too much power for party bosses.** In party-list systems, that is nearly always true. But STV lets voters choose among a party's candidates; so does Japan's simple system. Any coalition adds to the power of party machines in government—and (notoriously in Italy, notedly in Germany) in patronage and appointment to public bodies, not least state television. One can argue whether or not one-party patronage, as in Britain, is even worse. A better answer is open under any system: less patronage.

• **Weak links between a member and his constituents.** This is true of PR using large electoral districts, not in the ones of 3-5 members used in Ireland (and Japan). Members of the Irish Dail feel pressure, they say, to look after constituents, because their support may slip away not only to rival parties but to other members of their own. British critics fear such a member may care only for a section of his constituents. That may happen; PR supporters, in reply, praise the voter's freedom to choose which member he turns to. Districts of 5-7 members, as in most of Belgium, Spain or France in its PR days, allow both PR and acceptable member/voter links.

Many answers

For countries seeking less PR, the considerations, curiously, are much the same, since not even the angry Italians want the pure milk of FPTP. For them too the trick is to find a balance between proportionality and the faults voters feel in their form of PR. They too must remember the many faces of fairness, and ask, in each case, what function the elected body serves, what they want to achieve (punishing politicians, however deservedly, is an inappropriate answer) and is it worth the upheaval? Only zealots think one solution fits every case.

Presidents and Prime Ministers

Richard Rose

Richard Rose is professor of public policy at the University of Strathclyde in Glasgow, Scotland. An American, he has lived in Great Britain for many years and has been studying problems of political leadership in America and Europe for three decades. His books include Presidents and Prime Ministers; Managing Presidential Objectives; Understanding Big Government; *and* The Post-Modern Presidency: The World Closes in on the White House.

The need to give direction to government is universal and persisting. Every country, from Egypt of the pharoahs to contemporary democracies, must maintain political institutions that enable a small group of politicians to make authoritative decisions that are binding on the whole of society. Within every system, one office is of first importance, whether it is called president, prime minister, führer, or dux.

There are diverse ways of organizing the direction of government, not only between democracies and authoritarian regimes, but also among democracies. Switzerland stands at one extreme, with collective direction provided by a federal council whose president rotates from year to year. At the other extreme are countries that claim to centralize authority, under a British-style parliamentary system or in an American or French presidential system, in which one person is directly elected to the supreme office of state.

To what extent are the differences in the formal attributes of office a reflection of substantive differences in how authority is exercised? To what extent do the imperatives of office—the need for electoral support, dependence upon civil servants for advice, and vulnerability to events—impose common responses in practice? Comparing the different methods of giving direction to government in the United States (presidential), Great Britain (prime ministerial and Cabinet), and France (presidential and prime ministerial) can help us understand whether other countries do it—that is, choose a national leader—in a way that is better.

To make comparisons requires concepts that can identify the common elements in different offices. Three concepts organize the comparisons I make: the career that leads to the top; the institutions and powers of government; and the scope for variation within a country, whether arising from events or personalities.

Career Leading to the Top

By definition, a president or prime minister is unrepresentative by being the occupant of a unique office. The diversity of outlooks and skills that can be attributed to white, university-educated males is inadequate to predict how people with the same social characteristics—a Carter or an Eisenhower; a Wilson or a Heath—will perform in office. Nor is it helpful to consider the recruitment of national leaders deductively, as a management consultant or personnel officer would, first identifying the skills required for the job and then evaluating candidates on the basis of a priori requirements. National leaders are not recruited by examination; they are self-selected, individuals whose driving ambitions, personal attributes, and, not least, good fortune, combine to win the highest public office.

To understand what leaders can do in office we need to compare the skills acquired in getting to the top with the skills required once there. The tasks that a president or prime minister must undertake are few but central: sustaining popular support through responsiveness to the electorate, and being effective in government. Success in office encourages electoral popularity, and electoral popularity is an asset in wielding influence within government.

The previous careers of presidents and prime ministers are significant, insofar as experience affects what they do in office—and what they do well. A politician who had spent many years concentrating upon campaigning to win popularity may continue to cultivate popularity in office. By contrast, a politician experienced in dealing with the problems of government from within may be better at dealing effectively with international and domestic problems.

Two relevant criteria for comparing the careers of national leaders are: previous experience of government, and previous experience of party and mass electoral politics. American presidents are outstanding in their experience of campaigning for mass support, whereas French presidents are outstanding for their prior knowledge of government from the inside. British prime ministers usually combine experience in both fields.

Thirteen of the fourteen Americans who have been nominated for president of the United States by the Democratic or Republican parties since 1945 had prior experience in running for major office, whether at the congressional, gubernatorial or presidential level. Campaigning for office makes a politician conscious of his or her need for popular approval. It also cultivates skill in dealing with the mass media. No American will be elected president who has not learned how to campaign across the continent, effectively and incessantly. Since selection as a presidential candidate is dependent upon winning primaries, a president must run twice: first to win the party nomination and then to win the White House. The effort required is shown by the fact that in 1985, three years before the presidential election, one Republican hopeful campaigned in twenty-four states, and a Democratic hopeful in thirty. Immediately after the 1986 congressional elections ended, the media started featuring stories about the 1988 campaign.

Campaigning is different from governing. Forcing ambitious politicians to concentrate upon crossing and re-crossing America reduces the time available for learning about problems in Washington and the rest of the world. The typical postwar president has had no experience working within the executive branch. The way in which the federal government deals with foreign policy, or with problems of the economy is known, if at all, from the vantage point of a spectator. A president is likely to have had relatively brief experience in Congress. As John F. Kennedy's career illustrates, Congress is not treated as a

---

Looking presidential is not the same as acting like a president.

---

means of preparing to govern; it is a launching pad for a presidential campaign. The last three presidential elections have been won by individuals who could boast of having no experience in Washington. Jimmy Carter and Ronald Reagan were state governors, experienced at a job that gives no experience in foreign affairs or economic management.

A president who is experienced in campaigning can be expected to continue cultivating the media and seeking a high standing in the opinion polls. Ronald Reagan illustrates this approach. A president may even use campaigning as a substitute for coming to grips with government; Jimmy Carter abandoned Washington for the campaign trail when confronted with mid-term difficulties in 1978. But public relations expertise is only half the job; looking presidential is not the same as acting like a president.

A British prime minister, by contrast, enters office after decades in the House of Commons and years as a Cabinet minister. The average postwar prime minister had spent thirty-two years in Parliament before entering 10 Downing Street. Of that period, thirteen years had been spent as a Cabinet minister. Moreover, the prime minister has normally held the important policy posts of foreign secretary, chancellor of the exchequer or both. The average prime

minister has spent eight years in ministerial office, learning to handle foreign and/or economic problems. By contrast with the United States, no prime minister has had postwar experience in state or local government, and by contrast with France, none has been a civil servant since World War II.

The campaign experience of a British prime minister is very much affected by the centrality that politicians give Parliament. A politician seeks to make a mark in debate there. Even in an era of mass media, the elitist doctrine holds that success in the House of Commons produces positive evaluation by journalists and invitations to appear on television, where a politician can establish an image with the national electorate. Whereas an American presidential hopeful has a bottom-up strategy, concentrating upon winning votes in early primaries in Iowa and New Hampshire as a means of securing media attention, a British politician has a top-down approach, starting to campaign in Parliament.

Party is the surrogate for public opinion among British politicians, and with good reason. Success in the Commons is evaluated by a politician's party colleagues. Election to the party leadership is also determined by party colleagues. To become prime minister a politician does not need to win an election; he or she only needs to be elected party leader when the party has a parliamentary majority. Jim Callaghan and Sir Alec Douglas-Home each entered Downing Street this way and lost office in the first general election fought as prime minister.

The lesser importance of the mass electorate to British party leaders is illustrated by the fact that the average popularity rating of a prime minister is usually less than that of an American president. The monthly Gallup poll rating often shows the prime minister approved by less than half the electorate and trailing behind one or more leaders of the opposition.

In the Fifth French Republic, presidents and prime ministers have differed from American presidents, being very experienced in government, and relatively inexperienced in campaigning with the mass electorate. Only one president, François Mitterrand, has followed the British practice of making a political career based on Parliament. Since he was on the opposition side for the first two decades of the Fifth Republic, his experience of the problems of office was like that of a British opposition member of Parliament, and different from that of a minister. Giscard d'Estaing began as a high-flying civil servant and Charles de Gaulle, like Dwight Eisenhower, was schooled in bureaucratic infighting as a career soldier.

When nine different French prime ministers are examined, the significance of a civil service background becomes clear. Every prime minister except for Pierre Mauroy has been a civil servant first. It has been exceptional for a French prime minister to spend decades in Parliament before attaining that office. An Englishman would be surprised that a Raymond Barre or a Couve de Murville had not sat there before becoming prime minister. An American would be even more surprised by the experience that French leaders have had in the ministries as high civil servants, and particularly in dealing with foreign and economic affairs.

The traditional style of French campaigning is plebiscitary. One feature of this is that campaigning need not be incessant. Louis Napoleon is said to have compared elections with baptism: something it is necessary to do—but to do only once. The seven-year fixed term of the French president, about double the statutory life of many national leaders, is in the tradition of infrequent consultation with the electorate.

The French tradition of leadership is also ambivalent; a plebiscite is, after all, a mass mobilization. The weakness of parties, most notably on the Right, which has provided three of the four presidents of the Fifth Republic, encourages a personalistic style of campaigning. The use of the two-ballot method for the popular election of a president further encourages candidates to compete against each other as individuals, just as candidates for the presidential nomination compete against fellow-partisans in a primary. The persistence of divisions between Left and Right ensures any candidate successful in entering the second ballot a substantial bloc of votes, with or without a party endorsement.

On the two central criteria of political leadership, the relationship with the mass electorate, and knowledge of government, there are cross-national contrasts in the typical career. A British or French leader is likely to know far more about government than an American president, but an American politician is likely to be far more experienced in campaigning to win popular approval and elections.

Less for the President to Govern

Journalistic and historical accounts of government often focus on the person and office of the national leader. The American president is deemed to be very powerful because of the immense military force that he can command by comparison to a national leader in Great Britain or France. The power to drop a hydrogen bomb is frequently cited as a measure of the awesome power of an American president; but it is misleading, for no president has ever dropped a hydrogen bomb, and no president has used atomic weapons in more than forty years. Therefore, we must ask: What does an American president (and his European counterparts) do when not dropping a hydrogen bomb?

In an era of big government, a national leader is more a chief than an executive, for no individual can superintend, let alone carry out, the manifold tasks of government. A national leader does not need to make major choices about what government ought to do; he inherits a set of institutions that are committed—by law, by organization, by the professionalism of public employees, and by the expectations of voters—to appropriate a large amount of the country's resources in order to produce the program outputs of big government.

Whereas political leadership is readily personalized,

government is intrinsically impersonal. It consists of collective actions by organizations that operate according to impersonal laws. Even when providing benefits to individuals, such as education, health care, or pensions, the scale of a ministry or a large regional or local government is such as to make the institution appear impersonal.

Contemporary Western political systems are first of all governed by the rule of law rather than personal will. When government did few things and actions could be derived from prerogative powers, such as a declaration of war, there was more scope for the initiative of leaders. Today, the characteristic activities of government, accounting for most public expenditure and personnel, are statutory entitlements to benefits of the welfare state. They cannot be overturned by wish or will, as their tacit acceptance by such "antigovernment" politicians as Margaret Thatcher and Ronald Reagan demonstrates. Instead of the leader dominating government, government determines much that is done in the leader's name.

In a very real sense, the so-called power of a national leader depends upon actions that his government takes, whether or not this is desired by the leader. Instead of comparing the constitutional powers of leaders, we should compare the resources that are mobilized by the government for which a national leader is nominally responsible. The conventional measure of the size of government is public expenditure as a proportion of the gross national product. By this criterion, French or British government is more powerful than American government. Organization for Economic Cooperation and Development (OECD) statistics show that in 1984 French public expenditure accounted for 49 percent of the national product, British for 45 percent, and American for 37 percent. When attention is directed at central government, as distinct from all levels of government, the contrast is further emphasized. British and French central government collect almost two-fifths of the national product in tax revenue, whereas the American federal government collects only one-fifth.

When a national leader leads, others are meant to follow. The legitimacy of authority means that public employees should do what elected officials direct. In an era of big government, there are far more public employees at hand than in an era when the glory of the state was symbolized by a small number of people clustering around a royal court. Statistics of public employment again show British and French government as much more powerful than American government. Public employment in France accounts for 33 percent of all persons who work, more than Britain, with 31 percent. In the United States, public employment is much less, 18 percent.

The capacity of a national leader to direct public employees is much affected by whether or not such officials are actually employed by central government. France is most centralized, having three times as many public employees working in ministries as in regional or local government. If public enterprises are also reckoned as part of central government, France is even more centralized. In the United States and Great Britain, by contrast, the actual delivery of public services such as education and health is usually shipped out to lower tiers of a federal government, or to a complex of local and functional authorities. Delivering the everyday services of government is deemed beneath the dignity of national leaders in Great Britain. In the United States, central government is deemed too remote to be trusted with such programs as education or police powers.

When size of government is the measure, an American president appears weaker than a French or British leader. By international standards, the United States has a not so big government, for its claim on the national product and the national labor force is below the OECD average. Ronald Reagan is an extreme example of a president who is "antigovernment," but he is not the only example. In the past two decades, the United States has not lagged behind Europe in developing and expanding welfare state institutions that make government big. It has chosen to follow a different route, diverging from the European model of a mixed economy welfare state. Today, the president has very few large-scale program responsibilities, albeit they remain significant: defense and diplomacy, social security, and funding the federal deficit.

By contrast, even an "antigovernment" prime minister such as Margaret Thatcher finds herself presiding over a government that claims more than two-fifths of the national product in public expenditure. Ministers must answer, collectively and individually in the House of Commons, for all that is done under the authority of an Act of Parliament. In France, the division between president and prime minister makes it easier for the president of the republic to avoid direct entanglement in low status issues of service delivery, but the centralization of government necessarily involves the prime minister and his colleagues.

When attention is turned to the politics of government as distinct from public policies, all leaders have one thing in common, they are engaged in political management, balancing the interplay of forces within government, major economic interests, and public opinion generally. It is no derogation of a national leader's position to say that it has an important symbolic dimension, imposing a unifying and persuasive theme upon what government does. The theme may be relatively clear-cut, as in much of Margaret Thatcher's rhetoric. Or it may be vague and symbolic, as in much of the rhetoric of Charles de Gaulle. The comparative success of Ronald Reagan, an expert in manipulating vague symbols, as against Jimmy Carter, whose technocratic biases were far stronger than his presentational skills, is a reminder of the importance of a national political leader being able to communicate successfully to the nation.

In the United States and France, the president is both head of government and head of state. The latter role makes him president of all the people, just as the former role limits his representative character to governing in the name of a majority (but normally, less than 60 percent) of the voters. A British prime minister does not have the symbolic obligation to represent the country as a whole; the queen does that.

The institutions of government affect how political management is undertaken. The separate election of the president and the legislature in the United States and France create a situation of nominal independence, and bargaining from separate electoral bases. By contrast, the British prime minister is chosen by virtue of being leader of the largest party in the House of Commons. Management of Parliament is thus made much easier by the fact that the British prime minister can normally be assured of a majority of votes there.

An American president has a far more difficult task in managing government than do British and French counterparts. Congress really does determine whether bills become laws, by contrast to the executive domination of law and decree-making in Europe. Congressional powers of appropriation provide a basis for a roving scrutiny of what the executive branch does. There is hardly any bureau that is free from congressional scrutiny, and in many congressional influence may be as strong as presidential influence. By contrast, a French president has significant decree powers and most of the budget can be promulgated. A British prime minister can also invoke the Official Secrets Act and the doctrine of collective responsibility to insulate the effective (that is, the executive) side of government from the representative (that is, Parliament).

Party politics and electoral outcomes, which cannot be prescribed in a democratic constitution, affect the extent to which political management must be invested in persuasion. If management is defined as making an organization serve one's purpose, then Harry Truman gave the classic definition of management as persuasion: "I sit here all day trying to persuade people to do the things they ought to have sense enough to do without my persuading them. That's all the powers of the President amount to." Because both Democratic and Republican parties are loose coalitions, any president will have to invest much effort in persuading fellow partisans, rather than whipping them into line. Given different electoral bases, congressmen may vote their district, rather than their party label. When president and Congress are of opposite parties, then strong party ties weaken the president.

In Great Britain, party competition and election outcomes are expected to produce an absolute majority in the House of Commons for a single party. Given that the prime minister, as party leader, stands and falls with members of Parliament in votes in Parliament and at a general election, a high degree of party discipline is attainable. Given that the Conservative and Labor parties are themselves coalitions of differing factions and tendencies, party management is no easy task. But it is far easier than interparty management, a necessary condition of coalition government, including Continental European governments.

The Fifth Republic demonstrates that important constitutional features are contingent upon election outcomes. Inherent in the constitution of the Fifth Republic is a certain ambiguity about the relationship between president and prime minister. Each president has desired to make his office preeminent. The first three presidents had no difficulty in doing that, for they could rely upon the support of a majority of members of the National Assembly. Cooperation could not be coerced, but it could be relied upon to keep the prime minister subordinate.

Since the election of François Mitterrand in 1981, party has become an independent variable. Because the president's election in 1981 was paralleled by the election of a Left majority in the assembly, Mitterrand could adopt what J.E.S. Hayward describes in *Governing France* as a "Gaulist conception of his office." But after the victory of the Right in the 1986 Assembly election resulted in a non-Socialist being imposed as premier, Jacques Chirac, the president has had to accept a change of position, symbolized by the ambivalent term *cohabitation*.

Whether the criterion is government's size or the authority of the national leader vis-à-vis other politicians, the conclusion is the same: the political leaders of Great Britain and France can exercise more power than the president of the United States. The American presidency is a relatively weak office. America's population, economy, and military are not good measures of the power of the White House. Imagine what one would say if American institutions were transplanted, more or less wholesale, to some small European democracy. We would not think that such a country had a strong leader.

While differing notably in the separate election of a French president as against a parliamentary election of a British prime minister, both offices centralize authority within a state that is itself a major institution of society. As long as a French president has a majority in the National Assembly, then this office can have most influence within government, for ministers are unambiguously subordinate to the president. The linkage of a British prime minister's position with a parliamentary majority means that as long as a single party has a majority, a British politician is protected against the risks of cohabitation à la française or à la americaine.

Variations within Nations

An office sets parameters within which politicians can act, but the more or less formal stipulation of the rules and resources of an office cannot determine exactly what is done. Within these limits, the individual performance of a president or prime minister can be important. Events too are significant; everyday crises tend to frustrate any attempt to plan ahead, and major crises—a war or domestic disaster—can shift the parameters, reducing a politician's scope for action (for example, Watergate) or expanding it (for example, the mass mobilization that Churchill could lead after Dunkirk).

In the abstract language of social science, we can say that the actions of a national leader reflect the interaction of the powers of office, of events, and of personality. But

in concrete situations, there is always an inclination to emphasize one or another of these terms. For purposes of exposition, I treat the significance of events and personality separately: each is but one variable in a multivariate outcome.

Social scientists and constitutional lawyers are inherently generalizers, whereas critical events are unique. For example, a study of the British prime ministership that ignored what could be done in wartime would omit an example of powers temporarily stretched to new limits. Similarly, a study of Winston Churchill's capacities must recognize that his personality prevented him from achieving the nation's highest office—until the debacle of 1940 thrust office upon him.

In the postwar era, the American presidency has been especially prone to shock events. Unpredictable and nonrecurring events of importance include the outbreak of the Korean War in 1950, the assassination of President Kennedy in 1963, American involvement in the Vietnam War in the late 1960s, and the Watergate scandal, which led to President Nixon's resignation in 1974. One of the reasons for the positive popularity of Ronald Reagan has been that no disastrous event occurred in his presidency—at least until Irangate broke in November 1986.

The creation of the Fifth French Republic followed after events in Vietnam and in Algeria that undermined the authority and legitimacy of the government of the Fourth Republic. The events of May 1968 had a far greater impact in Paris than in any other European country. Whereas in 1958 events helped to create a republic with a president given substantial powers, in 1968 events were intended to reduce the authority of the state.

Great Britain has had relatively uneventful postwar government. Many causes of momentary excitement, such as the 1963 Profumo scandal that embarrassed

---

The French tradition of leadership is ambivalent.

Harold Macmillan, were trivial. The 1956 Suez war, which forced the resignation of Anthony Eden, did not lead to subsequent changes in the practice of the prime ministership, even though it was arguably a gross abuse of power vis-à-vis Cabinet colleagues and Parliament. The 1982 Falklands war called forth a mood of self-congratulation rather than a cry for institutional reform. The electoral boost it gave the prime minister was significant, but not eventful for the office.

The miner's strike, leading to a national three-day working week in the last days of the administration of Edward Heath in 1974, was perceived as a challenge to the authority of government. The prime minister called a general election seeking a popular mandate for his conduct of industrial relations. The mandate was withheld; so too was an endorsement of strikers. Characteristically, the events produced a reaction in favor of conciliation, for which Harold Wilson was particularly well suited at that stage of his career. Since 1979 the Thatcher administration has demonstrated that trade unions are not invincible. Hence, the 1974 crisis now appears as an aberration, rather than a critical conjuncture.

While personal factors are often extraneous to government, each individual incumbent has some scope for choice. Within a set of constraints imposed by office and events, a politician can choose what kind of a leader he or she would like to be. Such choices have political consequences. "Do what you can" is a prudential rule that is often overlooked in discussing what a president or prime minister does. The winnowing process by which one individual reaches the highest political office not only allows for variety, but sometimes invites it, for a challenger for office may win votes by being different from an incumbent.

Campaigning for office makes a politician conscious of a need for popular approval.

A president has a multiplicity of roles and a multiplicity of obligations. Many—as commander in chief of the armed forces, delivering a State of the Union message to Congress, and presenting a budget—are requirements of the office; but the capacity to do well in particular roles varies with the individual. For example, Lyndon Johnson was a superb manager of congressional relations, but had little or no feel for foreign affairs. By contrast, John F. Kennedy was interested in foreign affairs and defense and initially had little interest in domestic problems. Ronald Reagan is good at talking to people, whereas Jimmy Carter and Richard Nixon preferred to deal with problems on paper. Dwight D. Eisenhower brought to the office a national reputation as a hero that he protected by making unclear public statements. By contrast, Gerald Ford's public relations skills, while acceptable in a congressman, were inadequate to the demands of the contemporary presidency.

In Great Britain, Margaret Thatcher is atypical in her desire to govern, as well as preside over government. She applies her energy and intelligence to problems of government—and to telling her colleagues what to do about them. The fact that she wants to be *the* decision-maker for British government excites resentment among civil servants and Cabinet colleagues. This is not only a reaction

to her forceful personality, but also an expression of surprise: other prime ministers did not want to be the chief decision-maker in government. In the case of an aging Winston Churchill from 1951-55, this could be explained on grounds of ill health. In the case of Anthony Eden, it could be explained by an ignorance of domestic politics.

The interesting prime ministers are those who chose not to be interventionists across a range of government activities. Both Harold Macmillan and Clement Attlee brought to Downing Street great experience of British government. But Attlee was ready to be simply a chairman of a Cabinet in which other ministers were capable and decisive. Macmillan chose to intervene very selectively on issues that he thought important and to leave others to get on with most matters. Labor leader Neil Kinnock, if he became prime minister, would adopt a noninterventionist role. This would be welcomed in reaction to Thatcher's dominating approach. It would be necessary because Kinnock knows very little about the problems and practice of British government. Unique among party leaders of the past half-century, he has never held office in government.

In France, the role of a president varies with personality. De Gaulle approached the presidency with a distinctive concept of the state as well as of politics. By contrast, Mitterrand draws upon his experience of many decades of being a parliamentarian and a republican. Pompidou was distinctive in playing two roles, first prime minister under de Gaulle, and subsequently president.

Differences between French prime ministers may in part reflect contrasting relationships with a president. As a member of a party different from the president, Chirac has partisan and personal incentives to be more assertive than does a prime minister of the same party. Premiers who enter office via the Assembly or local politics, like Chaban-Delmas and Mauroy, are likely to have different priorities than a premier who was first a technocrat, such as Raymond Barre.

Fluctuations in Leaders

The fluctuating effect upon leaders of multiple influences is shown by the monthly ratings of the popularity of presidents and prime ministers. If formal powers of office were all, then the popularity rating of each incumbent should be much the same. This is not the case. If the personal characteristics of a politician were all-important, then differences would occur between leaders, but each leader would receive a consistent rating during his or her term of office. In fact, the popularity of a national leader tends to go up and down during a term of office. Since personality is held constant, these fluctuations cannot be explained as a function of personal qualities. Since there is no consistent decline in popularity, the movement cannot be explained as a consequence of impossible expectations causing the public to turn against whoever initially wins its votes.

The most reasonable explanation of these fluctuations in popularity is that they are caused by events. They may be shock events, such as the threat of military action, or scandal in the leader's office. Alternatively, changes may reflect the accumulation of seemingly small events, most notably those that are reflected in the state of the economy, such as growth, unemployment, and inflation rates. A politician may not be responsible for such trends, but he or she expects to lose popularity when things appear to be going badly and to regain popularity when things are going well.

Through the decades, cyclical fluctuations can reflect an underlying long-term secular trend. In Europe a major secular trend is the declining national importance of international affairs. In the United States events in Iran or Central America remain of as much (or more) significance than events within the United States. In a multipolar world a president is involved in and more vulnerable to events in many places. By contrast, leaders of France and Great Britain have an influence limited to a continental scale, in a world in which international relations has become intercontinental. This shift is not necessarily a loss for heads of government in the European Community. In a world summit meeting, only one nation, the United States, has been first. Japan may seek to exercise political influence matching its growing economic power. The smaller scale of the European Community nations with narrower economic interests create conditions for frequent contact and useful meetings in the European arena which may bring them marginal advantages in world summit meetings too.

If the power of a national leader is measured, as Robert A. Dahl suggests in *Who Governs?*, by the capacity that such an individual has to influence events in the desired direction, then all national leaders are subject to seeing their power eroded as each nation becomes more dependent upon the joint product of the open international economy. This is as true of debtor nations such as the United States has become, as of nations with a positive trade balance. It is true of economies with a record of persisting growth, such as Germany, and of slow growth economies such as Great Britain.

A powerful national leader is very desirable only if one believes that the *Führerprinzip* is the most important principle in politics. The constitutions and politics of Western industrial nations reject this assumption. Each political system is full of constraints upon arbitrary rule, and sometimes of checks and balances that are obstacles to prompt, clear-cut decisions.

The balance between effective leadership and responsiveness varies among the United States, Great Britain, and France. A portion of that variation is organic, being prescribed in a national constitution. This is most evident in a comparison of the United States and Great Britain, but constitutions are variables, as the history of postwar France demonstrates. Many of the most important determinants of what a national leader does are a reflection of changing political circumstances, of trends and shock events, and of the aspirations and shortcomings of the individual in office.

Europe—West, Center, and East: The Politics of Integration, Transformation, and Disintegration

- The European Union: From EC to EU (Articles 34 and 35)
- Revamping the Welfare State (Articles 36–39)
- Post–Communist Central and Eastern Europe (Article 40)
- Russia and the Other Post-Soviet Republics (Articles 41–43)

Most of the articles in this unit are in some way linked to one or the other of two major developments that have fundamentally altered the political map of Europe in recent years. The first of these major changes is the long-term movement toward supranational integration of many Western European states within the institutional framework of the European Community (EC), which officially became the European Union (EU) on November 1, 1993. Here the development has primarily been one by which sovereign states give up some of their traditional independence, especially in matters dealing with economic and (to a lesser degree) monetary policy. Some important decisions that used to be taken by national governments in Paris, Rome, Bonn, Dublin, and Copenhagen have become the province of EU representatives in Brussels. To be sure, the trend toward integration is neither automatic nor irreversible, as recent events have underlined. Nevertheless, the process continues to be very important in shaping the politics of Western Europe.

One important indication of the EU's continuing attractiveness is that other countries seek to join. Austria and two Scandinavian countries (Sweden and Finland) became the newest EU members in 1995, after their entry had been approved in national referendums in each country. In the case of another Scandinavian country, Norway, the voters decided against membership for a second time in recent history. In Norway, there is a deep split between supporters and opponents, with an overwhelming resistance to membership coming from farmers and fishers as well as from many women. A similar but weaker gender split is noticeable in the other Scandinavian countries, including Denmark, which has been a member since 1973. It appears that many Scandinavian women fear losing some of their social rights inside a European Union in which gender equality has not yet reached the level of their own countries.

The second major challenge to the established European state system is of a more disruptive nature. It consists of the disintegration brought about by the sudden collapse of Communist rule in Central and Eastern Europe at the end of the 1980s. Here states, nations, and nationalities have broken away from an imposed system of central control, and now assert their independence from the previous ruling group and its ideology. In their attempts to construct a new order for themselves, the post-Communist countries are encountering enormous difficulties. Their transition from one-party rule to pluralist democracy

and from centrally planned state socialism to a market-based economy has turned out to be much rougher than had been anticipated. The resulting destabilization has had an enormous impact in the western part of the continent as well. There is already considerable evidence that many people have a nostalgia for the basic material security and orderliness provided by the communist welfare states of the past. Communist-descended parties have responded by abandoning much of their Leninist political baggage and engaging in the competitive bidding for votes with promises of social fairness and security. In Poland and elsewhere, such parties have recently gained political leverage, but, by contrast with the recent past, they must now operate in a pluralist political setting and have adopted different strategies and goals than in the past.

A closer look at the countries of Western Europe reveals that they have their own internal problems, even if in a far less acute form than their counterparts to the East. Their relative prosperity rests on a base built up during the prolonged postwar economic boom of the 1950s and 1960s. By political choice, a considerable portion of their affluence was channeled toward the public sector and was used to develop a relatively generous systems of social services and social insurance. Between the early 1970s and the mid-1980s, however, Western industrial societies were beset by economic disruptions that brought an end to the long period of rapidly growing prosperity. The last half of the 1980s marked some improvement in the economic situation throughout most of Western Europe, partly as a result of some favorably timed positive trade balances with the United States. In the early 1990s, however, economic recession gripped these countries once again. It is becoming clear that there are more fundamental reasons why they no longer can take increasing affluence for granted in a more competitive global economy. Almost every one of them is today beset by economic problems that appear to be structural in origin, rather than just cyclical and therefore passing. In other words, it will take much more than an upturn in the business cycle to galvanize these economies.

The earlier economic shock that first interrupted the prolonged postwar boom had come in the wake of sharp rises in the cost of energy, linked to successive hikes in the price of oil imposed by the Organization of Petroleum Exporting Countries (OPEC) after 1973. In the 1980s, OPEC lost its organizational bite as its members began to compete against each other by raising production and lowering prices rather than abiding by the opposite practices in the manner of a well-functioning cartel agreement. The exploitation of new oil and gas fields in the North Sea and elsewhere also helped alleviate the energy situation, at least for the present. The resulting improvement for the consumers of oil and gas helped the Western European economies recover, but as a whole they did not rebound to their earlier high growth rates. The short Persian Gulf War did not seriously hamper the flow of Middle East oil in 1991, but it once again underscored the vulnerability of Europe to external interruptions in its energy supply.

Because of their heavy dependence on international trade, Western European economies are especially vulnerable to the kind of global recessionary tendencies that we have encountered during the past few years. Another important challenge to these affluent countries is found in a trend that is sometimes dubbed economic globalization. In particular, they face stiff competition from the new industrial countries (NICs) of East and South Asia, where productivity is sometimes higher and labor costs remain much lower. The emerging Asian factor probably contributed to the increased tempo of the European drive for economic integration in the late 1980s. Some observers have warned of a protectionist reaction, in which major trading blocs in Europe, North America, and Eastern Asia could replace the relatively free system of international trade established in the post-1945 period.

A related issue is how the increase in international trade within and outside the European Union will affect the established social market economies of continental Europe. The economic gains derived from international competition could have a positive consequence by providing a better base for consolidating and invigorating the social welfare systems. However, a different scenario seems to be starting that will result in a drastic pruning and reduction in social services, carried out in the name of efficiency and international competitiveness. The social problems that have resulted in Europe's growing underclass are presented in the essay "Europe and the Underclass: The Slippery Slope." Moreover, the corporatist and welfare state arrangements that have served these countries so well for so long now face other demographic and economic challenges as well. The debate about the best policy response to such problems will probably continue to agitate Western Europeans for years to come. It seems clear, however, that the famous Swedish Model is also being drastically revamped in the name of affordability.

In the mid–1980s, there was widespread talk of a malaise or "Europessimism" that had beset these countries. Thereafter the mood appeared to become more upbeat, and for a while some observers even detected a swing toward what they labeled "Europhoria." It is advisable to add some salt to such easy generalizations about swings in the public mood, but by now there seems once again to be a more sober, even pessimistic, spirit abroad in Western Europe. Observers plausibly link this latest shift in mood to the economic and social problems associated with the prolonged recessionary developments described above as well as with the dislocations that have accompanied the end of the cold war.

The demise of the Soviet bloc removed one major external challenge but replaced it with a set of others. The countries of Western Europe were simply unprepared for the chaotic conditions left behind by the former Communist regimes to the East. They are now affected by the fierce competition for scarce capital, as these Eastern Europe countries seek to attract investments that will build them new and modern economic infrastructures. At the same time, the daily poverty and disorder of life in Eastern Europe have encouraged a migration to the relatively affluent societies of the West.

Those who attempt the big move to the "Golden West" resemble in many ways the immigrants who have been attracted to the United States in the past and present. The major point of difference is that many Western Europeans are unwilling to accept what they regard as a flood of unwanted strangers. The newcomers are widely portrayed and perceived as outsiders, whose presence will further drain the generous welfare systems and threaten not only economic security but also the established way of life. Such anxieties are the stuff of sociocultural tensions and conflicts. One serious political consequence has been the emergence of anti-immigrant populism on the far Right. In response, the governments in several countries have changed their laws on citizenship, asylum, and immigration.

There can be no doubt that the issues of immigration and cultural tensions in Western Europe will occupy a central place on the political agenda in the coming years. Some of the established parties have already made symbolic and substantive accommodations to appease protesting voters, for fear of otherwise losing them to extremist ultra-Right movements. But it is important to remember that there are also groups which resist such compromises and instead oppose the xenophobic elements in their own societies. Some enlightened political leaders and commentators seek to promote the reasonable perspective that migrants could turn out to be an important asset rather than a liability. This argument may concede that the foreign influx also involves some social cost in the short run, at least during a recessionary period, but it emphasizes that the newcomers can be a very important human resource that will contribute to mid- and long-term economic prosperity. Quite apart from any such economic considerations, of course, the migrants and asylum-seekers have become an important test of liberal democratic tolerance on the Continent.

Prudent observers had long warned about a premature celebration of "Europe 1992," which really referred to the abolition on restrictions in the flow of goods, capital, services, and labor by January 1, 1993, under the EC's Single European Act (SEA), adopted and ratified a few years earlier. They suggested that the slogan served to cover up some remaining problems and some newly emerging obstacles to the full integration of the European Community. The skeptics seemed at least partly vindicated by the setbacks that have followed the new and supposedly decisive "leap" forward taken in the summit meeting of EC leaders at the Dutch town of Maastricht in December 1991. The Maastricht Treaty went beyond the SEA in delineating additional steps toward supranational integration during the last half of the 1990s. It envisaged a common European monetary system and a federal European Reserve Bank as well as common policies on immigration, environmental protection, external security, and foreign affairs.

In 3 of the then-12 member countries—Denmark, Ireland, and France—ratification of the Maastricht Treaty was tied to the outcome of national referendums. In the first of these expressions of the popular will, Danish voters in June 1992 decided by a very slim majority of less than 2 percent to reject the treaty. A huge Irish majority in favor of the treaty was followed by a very slim French approval as well. The negative Danish vote seemed to have had the effect of legitimating and releasing many pent-up reservations and second thoughts in other member countries, not least Germany. But in May 1993, Danish voters approved a modified version of agreement, pruned down with special "opt-out" provisions that met Denmark's particular reservations. Some weeks later British Prime Minister John Major was able to hammer together a fragile parliamentary majority for the treaty in the House of Commons. Here too, however, the agreement was a customized version of the treaty designed to meet British reservations. The last formal hurdle to the Maastricht Treaty was passed in Germany, where the Constitutional Court turned down a legal challenge based on an alleged violation of national sovereignty. But the difficult ratification process has revealed widespread political resistance which continues to hamper the course toward a federal union.

As several of the articles in this section point out, the European Union has effectively reached a crossroads. The European nation-state has turned out to have more holding power than some federalists had expected, especially in a time of economic setbacks and perceived threats to the social order. The absence of a quick and coherent Western European response to the violent ethnic conflict in the former Yugoslavia has added a further reason for doubt concerning the EU's imminent progression toward an elementary form of political federation. For these and other reasons, the present seems to be a time for new thought and debate about the EU's further goals and its route for reaching them, as Tony Judt and other commentators point out.

While much academic and political ink has been spilled on the problems of a transition from a market economy to state socialism, we have little theory or practice to guide Central and Eastern European countries that are trying to move in the opposite direction. The question of what would be the best strategy for restructuring the economies of the former Communist countries is far more than an interesting theoretical issue, for its answer could have important policy consequences. Some academics believe that a quick transition to a market economy is a preferable course, indeed the only responsible one, even though such an approach will be very disruptive and painful in the short run. They argue that such a "shock therapy" or "big bang" approach will release human energies and bring economic growth more quickly and efficiently. At the same time, these supporters of a "tough love" approach warn that compassionate half-way measures will not only bring stagnation but could end up making the economic plight of these countries even worse than at present.

Other policy strategists have come out in favor of a more gradual approach to economic reconstruction in these countries. They warn that the neo-classical economists, who would introduce a full-scale market economy by fiat, not only ignore the market system's cultural and historical preconditions but also underestimate the social pain and turmoil which are likely to accompany the big transition. In effect, these critics contend that the strategy of shock therapy has brought plenty of shock but very little therapy. Such gradualists therefore recommend pragmatic strategies of incremental change, accompanied by a rhetoric of lower expectations, as the politically more prudent course of action.

After a few years we may have some better insights into the relative merits of each argument. A pluralist society, however, rarely permits itself to become a social laboratory for controlled experiments of this kind. Instead, it seems likely that political factors will promote a "mix" of the two approaches as the most acceptable and practical policy outcome. Moreover, decision makers must often learn on the job. They cannot afford to become inflexible and dogmatic in these matters in which the human stakes are so high.

A similar debate about the best strategy for economic reconstruction has been carried out in the former Soviet Union during the past few years. In some ways, it could be argued that Mikhail Gorbachev, the last Soviet head of government (1985 to 1991), failed to opt clearly for one or the other approach to economic reform. He seems not only to have been ambivalent about the means but about the ends of his *perestroika*, or restructuring, of the centrally planned economy. In the eyes of some born-again Soviet marketeers, he remained far too socialist, while communist hard-liners never forgave him for dismantling a system in which they had enjoyed at least a modicum of security and privilege. In his article, George Kennan discusses these and other aspects of Gorbachev's important years in office.

More than anything else, however, the Achilles' heel of the now defunct Soviet Union turned out to be its multiethnic character. Gorbachev was not alone in underestimating the potential centrifugal tendencies of a country that was based on an ideological and political redefinition of the old Russian Empire. Many of the non-Russian minorities were ethnic majorities within their own territory, and this made it possible for them to long for greater autonomy or even national independence in a way that the scattered ethnic groups of the United States do not.

Gorbachev appears to have regarded his own policies of *glasnost*, or openness, and *democratization* as essential accompaniments of perestroika in his modernization program. He seems to have understood (or become convinced) that a highly developed industrial economy needs a freer flow of information along with a more decentralized system of decision making if its component parts are to be efficient, flexible and capable of self-correction. In that sense, a market economy has some integral feedback traits that make it incompatible with the traditional Soviet model of a centrally directed, authoritarian command economy.

But glasnost and democratization were clearly incompatible with a repressive political system of one-party rule as well. They served Gorbachev as instruments that weakened the grip of the communist hard-liners and at the same time rallied behind him some reform groups, including many intellectuals and journalists. Within a remarkably short time after he came to power in 1985, a vigorous new press emerged in the Soviet Union headed by journalists who were eager to ferret out misdeeds and to report on political reality as they observed it. A similar development took place in the history profession, where scholars used the new spirit of openness to report in grim detail about past atrocities of the Soviet system that had previously been covered up or dismissed as bourgeois lies. There was an inevitable irony to the new truthfulness. Even as it served to discredit much of the past, along with any reactionary attempts to restore "the good old days," it also brought into question the foundations of the Soviet system and the leading role of the Communist Party. Yet Gorbachev had clearly sought to modernize and reform the system, not to bring it down.

Most important of all, glasnost and democratization gave those ethnic minorities in the Soviet Union, which had a territorial identity, an opportunity to demand autonomy or even independence. The first national assertions came from the Baltic peoples in Estonia, Latvia, and Lithuania, who had been forced back under Russian rule in 1940, after some 2 decades of national independence. Very soon other nationalities, including the Georgians and Armenians, expressed similar demands through the political channels that had been opened to them. The death knell for the Soviet Union sounded in 1991, when the Ukrainians, who constituted the second largest national group in the Soviet Union after the Russians, made similar demands for independence.

In a very real sense, then, Gorbachev's political reforms ended up as a mortal threat not only to the continued leadership role by the Communist Party but also to the continued existence of the Soviet Union itself. Gorbachev seems to have understood neither of these ultimately fatal consequences of his reform attempts until quite late in the day. This explains why he could set in motion forces that would ultimately destroy what he had hoped to make more attractive and productive. In August 1991 Communist hard-liners attempted a coup against the reformer and his reforms, but they acted far too late and were too poorly organized to succeed. In fact, the would-be coup d'état became instead a coup de grace for the Soviet Communists and, in the end, the Soviet Union as well. Somewhat reluctantly, Gorbachev declared the party illegal soon after he returned to office. The coup was defeated by a popular resistance led by Russian president Boris Yeltsin, who had broken with communism earlier and, as it seemed, far more decisively.

After his formal restoration to power following the abortive coup, Gorbachev had become politically dependent on Yeltsin and was increasingly seen as a transitional figure. His days as Soviet president were numbered, as the Soviet Union ceased to exist a week before the end of 1991. It was formally replaced by the Commonwealth of Independent States (CIS), a very loose union which lacks a sufficient institutional framework to keep it together. Almost from the outset, the CIS seemed destined to be a loosely structured transitional device. It could serve a practical purpose for the former Soviet republics while they negotiate what to do with the economic, military, and other institutional leftovers of the old system and develop new and useful links to each other. Understandably, some political leaders want to find a way to restore a stronger union among these new states.

There is an undeniable gloomy, hangover atmosphere in many of the accounts of post-communist and post-Soviet Europe. It seems clear that much will become worse before it will become better in the economic and social life of these countries. The political consequences could be very important, for social frustrations can now be freely articulated and represented in the political process. Here the transition from one-party rule to pluralist democratic forms resembles the economic passage to a market economy in being neither easy nor automatic. A turn to some form of authoritarian nationalist populism cannot be ruled out in several countries, including Russia. Former communists with leadership skills are likely to play a major role in the process in countries like Poland and the Ukraine. They sometimes cooperate with ultra-Right nationalists, with whom they share the dream of a strong state.

Specialists on the former Soviet Union disagree considerably in their assessments of the current situation and what brought it about. One of the hotly debated issues concerned President Yeltsin's decision in September 1993 to use a preemptive strike to break a deadlock between his government and a majority in the Russian parliament. When a majority of the legislators, who had been elected over 2 years earlier, persisted in blocking some of his major economic reforms, Yeltsin simply dissolved parliament and called new elections for December 1993.

The electoral result was a political boomerang for Yeltsin. It resulted in a major setback for the forces that backed rapid and thoroughgoing market reforms. The new parliament, based on a two-ballot system of elections, was highly fragmented, but nationalists and former communists occupied pivotal positions in the Duma. Henceforth President Yeltsin played a more subdued role than previously and the new government pursued far more cautious reform policies than previously. The military in-

vasion of Chechnya, a breakaway Caucasian republic located within the Russian federation, did not give Yeltsin a quick and easy victory, which might have reversed his slide into political unpopularity among Russians. Nor could it stem the surge of authoritarian and nationalist political expression, which also thrived as a reflex to crime and social disorder. But neither the ultra-Right nor the former Communists, who resisted far-reaching market reforms, seem eager to return to the tradition of a centrally planned economy. In that limited sense, at least, the extensive Soviet chapter of Russian history appears finally to have been closed, even though the experience will continue, at times, to disturb the pattern of the country's future development.

New parliamentary elections in December 1995 provided a further setback for the democratic and economic reformers in Russia. However, it was far less their rivals' strength than their own disunity and rivalry, both before and after the election, that weakened their parliamentary position. Together, the reformers received close to a quarter of the vote, slightly more than the Communists, led by Gennady Zyuganov, and twice as much as the far-Right nationalists in Vladimir Zhirinovsky's Liberal Democratic Party. Under the Russian electoral law, however, the Communists received 35 percent of the seats in the new Duma. Observers of Russian politics differed in their assessments of this development, but all agreed that it left the cause of political and economic reform in considerable disarray. During the spring of 1996, Russian political leaders had their eyes fixed on the presidential elections of June, in which the incumbent Boris Yeltsin faced the toughest political challenge of his career. As expected, he did not win a clear majority in the first vote, but he did defeat Zyuganov with relative ease in a runoff election. David Remnick gives an informed and balanced account of the presidential election and of some later developments in Russia, where ill health has added seriously to Yeltsin's governing problems. In another article, Stephen Cohen provides a more pessimistic assessment of the country's present condition.

Looking Ahead: Challenge Questions

What are the major obstacles to the emergence of a more unified Europe? What differentiates the optimists and the skeptics as they assess the outlook for greater integration? What are the major institutional characteristics of the European Union, and why is there a widespread call for reform?

What is the evidence that the economic problems of Western Europe are not just cyclical but also structural in origin? What has been the impact of economic stagnation on the social services provided by the welfare state?

What are the main problems facing the newly elected governments in Eastern and Central Europe? How well are they doing in coping with the transition to political pluralism and a market economy?

Was Gorbachev mistaken in believing that the Soviet Union could be reformed without being dissolved? How have the recent parliamentary and presidential elections set back the cause of political and economic reform in Russia? What explains the electoral support received by the Communists and the nationalists?

An American Perspective on the European Experiment

★★★★★★★★★★★★★★★★★★★★★

The Untied States of Europe

■ Cultural differences, myths and rivalries are stymieing the quest for a continental union. Diversity—Latin verve! British pragmatism!—once was seen as strength. But now it is proving divisive.

TYLER MARSHALL

Times Staff Writer

Heaven is where the police are British, the chefs French, the mechanics German, the lovers Italian and it's all organized by the Swiss.

Hell is where the police are German, the chefs British, the mechanics French, the lovers Swiss and it's all organized by the Italians.

—An oft-told European joke

MAASTRICHT, Netherlands—For decades, those struggling to build a united Europe saw the Continent's rich cultural diversity as an asset in fulfilling their dream.

They noted how a Latin flair for the grand gesture helped generate such unifying symbols as the single lavender-colored passport now issued by all 15 European Union countries. And how British pragmatism helped streamline and decentralize the Union's formidable bureaucracy.

"Europe's strength is in its diversity" argued Richard Hill, a British-born specialist on cross-cultural dynamics who lives in Brussels.

Others are no longer so sure.

Efforts are moving ahead to strengthen the Union, and member states are beginning to hitch their economic fate to a common currency and mull revolutionary political steps such as adopting a single foreign and security policy. But the enormous differences in culture, values and outlook that have separated the nations of Europe for centuries now loom as a large impediment to deeper unity.

Although governments of several EU members devote resources to smoothing relations among linguistic or cultural groups within their countries, the issue of bridging these far greater divisions across the Union is largely ignored.

While in the United States diversity is a gut issue that triggers constant, often heated, public discourse and action, in Europe the architects of integration have hardly addressed the subject.

Stereotypes Thrive

Amid this inaction, raw national stereotypes continue to thrive, cropping up in jokes, offhand comments and easy banter.

As for the once conventional wisdom that Western Europe's economic and political convergence over the decades would gradually erode many of the differences, it simply hasn't happened.

"There was the belief that the Common Market, the European Union and [the goal of] unification would lead to a common culture, but it apparently doesn't work that way," said Niels G. Noorderhaven, director of the Institute for Research on Intercultural Cooperation, which is based in this picture-book Dutch town where the treaty on European political and economic unity was signed more than four years ago.

Today, Noorderhaven is only one of many who believe the experiment of forming a united Europe will probably fall well short of a "United States of Europe"—in part because of deep and fundamental divisions.

He and others go so far as to argue that there is evidence to suggest the opposite is happening—that cultural differences in Europe may be hardening.

"When you start talking about pulling down political boundaries or becoming part of a greater whole, people have a desire to want to preserve what is unique about themselves," noted Ralf Dahrendorf, the respected German-born social scientist who is now a British lord and head of Oxford University's St. Antony's College. "It's not surprising."

It's also unsettling, because history has proved that convictions of such uniqueness among people in Europe can, with only a little tension, quickly lead to friction and tragedy—as the recent Balkan conflict has underscored.

Some experts argue that either the notion of European diversity or the goal of integration must give.

Divided by History

Dutch academic Geert Hostede, who studied European cultural differences for U.S. computer giant International Business Machines Corp. in the 1970s and later emerged as one of the leading experts in the field, has argued that Europeans remain inevitably divided by their history.

"Countries have remained separate precisely because there existed fundamental differences in thinking and feeling between them," he said in a 1993 farewell lecture at the University of Limburg here. "Why do you think the Belgians revolted against the Dutch in 1830? The border between Belgium and the Netherlands revives the border between the Roman Empire and the barbaric Germanic tribes . . . in about 4 AD."

Hofstede said he found no other instance in the world in which two neighboring countries had so much in common yet still showed such differences in what he termed "their mental programming."

"The inheritance of the Roman Empire survives in the minds of the populations of the Latin countries," he said. "The Germanic countries never knew the same centralization of power, nor a universal system of laws, implying greater equality and tolerance for uncertainty."

Schooling Differs

Relationships between the individual and authority diverge at an early age among Europeans, according to Noorderhaven, with elementary school teachers in northern countries such as the Netherlands and Scandinavia having far less "distance" between themselves and their pupils than their counterparts in Mediterranean countries.

Dutch children, for example, are schooled to keep low profiles and taught that being first at something isn't necessarily a virtue. The message prepares them for life in one of the globe's most egalitarian societies.

At home and in school, children in Mediterranean countries such as Greece and Italy tend to be nurtured as special, unique (and, implicitly, superior) individuals.

In Britain, it's acceptable to finish first—but only if one can do it without seeming to work harder in the process.

For those nurturing the ideal of a united Europe, such diverse values carry important implications. "These cultural differences go very deep, and they aren't just about culture," Dahrendorf said. "Attitudes to the economy and to the state are fundamentally different in different countries."

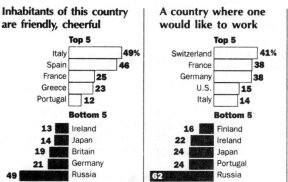

What Europeans Think of Others

The study was based on face-to-face interviews with 1,000 people in each country. Each person was shown a list of countries and for each item was asked to choose three countries for which that item was most applicable and three countries for which the item was least applicable. The numbers below show the percentage of people who named each country.

Inhabitants of this country are friendly, cheerful

Top 5
Italy	49%
Spain	46
France	25
Greece	23
Portugal	12

Bottom 5
13	Ireland
14	Japan
19	Britain
21	Germany
49	Russia

A country where one would like to work

Top 5
Switzerland	41%
France	38
Germany	38
U.S.	15
Italy	14

Bottom 5
16	Finland
22	Ireland
24	Japan
24	Portugal
62	Russia

"Made in this country" is a good label

Top 5
Germany	66%
Switzerland	43
France	40
Japan	36
U.S.	33

Bottom 5
22	Ireland
23	Spain
38	Greece
42	Portugal
60	Russia

Source: International Research Associates

Los Angeles Times

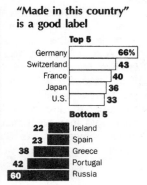

He described the tough anti-inflation criteria for monetary union written into the Maastricht Treaty as "German culture put into an international treaty," but he questioned how nations such as Italy or Britain, which have no such allergy to inflation, can settle into such a system. "In Britain, there is a feeling that a bit of inflation may not be such a bad thing."

In business, cross-border mergers in Europe historically have a high failure rate, usually because of "culture blindness."

Richard Branson, the British-based entrepreneur, in 1995 gave up a four-year attempt to face down recalcitrant German trade unions and closed his Virgin Megastore music, book and video outlet in Frankfurt, in part because German employees refused to wear T-shirts with the Virgin logo. Since trade union power in Britain was crushed in the early 1980s by then-Prime Minister Margaret Thatcher, such confrontations are a rarity in Britain.

At the political level, countries such as Britain and Denmark, with long traditions of relatively non-intrusive government but respect for law, have tended to resist proposals for new regulations from the EU's executive, the European Commission, in Brussels. Yet they have the best record of implementing those regulations once they are agreed upon.

On the other hand, Belgium—where bureaucracy is oppressive and evading laws and regulations is a national sport—ranks among the quickest to propose new EU rules yet has the worst record in the Union for implementing adopted legislation.

The relative importance of rules and regulations in European countries is sometimes easy to spot. Contrast the picture of the German woman unwilling to cross an empty road until the red light turns green with the Italian taxi driver in Naples who looks on red lights as little more than a suggestion to slow, views stop signs with disdain and considers a right turn from the left lane as a logical, routine maneuver.

Just why the unprecedented mobility of Europeans over the past 40 years—plus close economic and political cooperation—has not been a greater cultural leveler is unclear.

Few Lessons on Unity

But the absence of any moves toward common educational standards or school curricula are cited as one key reason. That children of all ages in EU member states are taught little about the Union, its origins or goals may be another factor, social scientists suggest. That only 3% of EU citizens reside outside their native countries also helps answer why even the crudest national stereotypes remain powerful:

• An American recalled being trapped on a Paris-Brussels express train, already hours late and going nowhere fast, and watching three Britons in the same car come to a slow boil over their plight and eventually spill out their prejudices. "The French and the Belgians don't know how to run anything," one said. "What they need is some good German control."

• At a seminar of former world leaders in Colorado Springs, Colo., last fall, Thatcher, the former British prime minister, commented that she remained apprehensive about reunified Germany despite the country's four decades of model democracy. "Her natural character is to dominate," she said of Germany. "There's something in this that I still fear."

• And polls conducted by the French Tourism Ministry about travelers' complaints seemed to tell more about visitors than about France: Germans said they found the French undisciplined, Belgians said they were nice but wrapped up in themselves, the Swiss said they weren't clean enough, and the British described them as quarrelsome and chauvinistic.

Many argue that, with Europe's cultural differences so deeply ingrained, the best that advocates of greater unity can hope for is broader understanding of what they face.

Taboo Subject

But social scientists such as Noorderhaven note that within the EU's formidable bureaucracy of 20,000, not one official studies the impact of the Continent's cultural diversity. "It's more or less a taboo within the European Commission that these differences might have an impact," he said. "Perhaps they see it as a threat to the idea of unification. But if you try to deny them, then the trouble really begins."

He cites a highly successful student exchange program that underwrites foreign studies for 150,000 high school and university students as the best EU weapon to foster awareness of diversity.

"It's a chance to study material with a European dimension," he said. "People also really get exposed to life in another culture, and, through that experience, they become aware of their own values and prejudices. This is the best-spent money in the European Union."

✮✮✮✮✮✮✮✮✮✮✮✮✮✮✮✮✮✮✮

European Unity Hinges on Factors Great and Small

TYLER MARSHALL

TIMES STAFF WRITER

FOURON-LE-COMPTE, Belgium— Jose Happart is a hard-nosed politician whose career has thrived on linguistic tensions.

In a nation that binds Dutch-speaking Flemings and French-speaking Walloons in an uneasy marriage, Happart is a Walloon agitator convinced that history betrayed his people, that Flemings are aggressors and that Belgium is doomed as a nation-state.

Those views helped catapult the 49-year-old farmer into the European Parliament two years ago with more votes than any other Belgian member.

"I'm a symbol of Wallonia," he said with a shrug, explaining his popularity.

Eighty miles to the east in Bonn, in a large corner office, German Chancellor Helmut Kohl towers above such disputes and impatiently wills Europeans toward the dream of greater unity that has become his big mission.

"The question of European unity is a question of war and peace in the 21st century," he said.

War or Peace

Two leaders. Two views. Two choices for Europe on the eve of the new millennium. Can Europeans make the leap of faith needed to transcend the past and enter a new age not filled with blood and war? Or will they succumb again to the call of tribal loyalty and be dragged by the weight of history back into confrontation and conflict?

Does Europe's future lie in Brussels or in Bosnia?

For Americans, the answers are more than academic.

A stable, more unified Europe constitutes a vital ingredient for the United States' prosperity and provides an important partner in world affairs.

The 15 countries of the European Union and the United Sates are bound together by the world's largest economic tie—three-quarters of a trillion dollars in direct investment and annual trade that translates into millions of jobs on both sides of the Atlantic.

Europeans may rankle at American attempts to strangle Cuba, Libya and Iran with trade boycotts, but perhaps more than anyone they share the United States' values and view of the world.

At the World Trade Organization meeting in December in Singapore, for example, it will be the EU that is expected to join with the United States to confront Asia to end child labor, stop slavery and offer such basics as the right to join a trade union.

Renewed conflict in Europe would inevitably involve the United States. The graves of 9,000 American war dead in a sprawling cemetery six miles east of here underscore the price of this alternative.

Many insist that Europe's fate lies in such stark "either/or" terms. The drive toward European unity is on a bicycle, they say. If you stop, you fall off.

It's not an easy ride.

Over the next decade, the EU states are committed to giving up sovereignty in such politically touchy areas as currency, foreign affairs, defense and law enforcement and opening their arms to new, less affluent members, mainly to the east.

At the same time, they must cut back popular welfare state benefits that have helped preserve social peace during the post-World War II era and also shoulder more of the burden for their own defense.

"Few countries in the world or international organizations face the number of daunting challenges the European Union and its 15 member states must confront in such a short period of time," summed up Stuart Eizenstat, the U.S. undersecretary of commerce for international trade, who until earlier this year was the U.S. ambassador to the EU.

The quest for a common currency, seen as the glue needed to hold the EU together over the long haul, has become a kind of death-defying tightrope walk as member states wobble uncertainly toward their self-imposed deadline of January 1999.

Austerity budgets needed to prepare for the currency union have already brought rioters into the streets of Paris and more than 300,000 Germans to Bonn in the country's largest street protest since World War II.

In Belgium, the Parliament has given Prime Minister Jean-Luc Dehaene the power to rule by decree to reduce public debt and contain budget deficits.

With more cuts inevitable, political analysts predict a hot autumn on the streets of Western Europe. Last month, angry union officials representing French teachers announced plans for a campaign of protests and a possible strike over government plans to reduce jobs in education for the first time since the early 1980s.

Despite such pressure, the will to push ahead among key European leaders remains strong, and global currency markets continue to bet that monetary union will occur.

Eastward Expansion

Enlarging the EU eastward, the ultimate step in erasing the Continent's old East-West divide, is also planned to start around the end of the century. It will probably be no easier and less popular than the run-up to monetary union.

Even the most economicaly advanced of the post-Soviet democracies, such as Poland, Hungary and the Czech Republic, will be drains on community coffers during their early years of membership. And because it is financially impossible to extend the EU's huge farm subsidies to new eastern members, the EU's single biggest handout—one equal to a whopping $15,400 annually for every full-time farm worker in the union—must either be slashed drastically or eliminated completely as part of the enlargement process.

But the cost of not enlarging eastward could be even greater, as Czech President Vaclav Havel reminded the European Parliament meeting in Strasbourg, France, as long ago as March 1994.

"If the future European order does not emerge from a broadening European Union . . . then it could well happen that . . . this future will fall into the hands of a cast of fools, fanatics, populists and demagogues, waiting for their chance to promote the worst European traditions," he warned.

The success or failure of Europe's great experiment rests on myriad unknowns, such as the commitment of a new generation of leaders now assuming power that has never experienced Europe at war.

For much of the last decade, Kohl, who dug bodies from the rubble of his bombed-out church in Ludwigshafen as a 15-year-old, the late French President Francois Mitterand, once a prisoner of war of the Germans, and others from their generation pushed forward the dream of a unified Europe.

The new standard-bearers of European unity and the collective political will of their generation to make the tough choices needed to keep going forward remain a giant question mark.

Lure of Demagogues

Equally uncertain is the lure of demagogues and local populists in a Europe where state benefits are cut, unemployment rises to new post-World War II highs and prosperity gradually begins to erode. The Continent's record in resisting the call to tribal loyalty is not good, and the tragedy of the former Yugoslav federation shows how quickly the grudges of history can explode when politicians start searching for scapegoats instead of solutions.

For Austrian Freedomist leader Joerg Haider or the president of France's National Front, Jean-Marie Le Pen, the target is foreigners; for Italy's Umberto Bossi, the Northern League secessionist, the enemy is the lagging Italian south and corrupt government in Rome. In Belgium, Happart talks of Flemish cultural aggression and claims that the country's very creation in 1830 was an Anglo-Prussian plot to contain French power.

For him, life's defining experience was not the convulsion of war but the forced closure of his town's French-speaking school by the Flemish government 20 years ago.

Even Europe's most respected leaders occasionally try to score cheap points by playing to volatile public emotions, as did German Finance Minister Theo Waigel earlier this year when he addressed a gathering of former Sudeten Germans and demanded a Czech "word of regret" for the expulsion of Germans 50 years ago.

Waigel's comments won calculated applause from his audience but drew a caustic response from Czech Prime Minister Vaclav Klaus, who suggested that Germans should discuss World War II in low whispers.

The role of Germany and the behavior of its leaders are a pivotal factor in Europe's future. More than half a century after the Nazi collapse, Germany still brings the jitters to its neighbors.

A controversial study of the Holocaust by Harvard sociologist Daniel Goldhagen concludes that such horror could only have happened in Germany because only there would a people have cooperated so willingly.

But for half a century, the realities have mainly pointed elsewhere.

The former West Germany blossomed into a model and admired democracy, while those in the East engineered a spectacular and peaceful revolution against totalitarian rule. Today, it is a reunited Germany—whose currency and prosperity are the envy of its neighbors—that drives European unity forward and that has consistently taken the extra step to achieve compromise.

While pacifist instincts remain strong among Germans, they also have gradually begun to accept more responsibility for military security beyond their own frontiers.

After sitting out the 1991 Persian Gulf War, German forces joined the peace Implementation Force in the Balkans. Some complain that the Germans refuse to go beyond the fringes of the conflict (they operate only in Croatia), but the fact they are present at all is seen as a major psychological step.

Germany's ability to accept a carefully measured military role in keeping the peace and to continue walking a fine line in political and economic affairs—leading while pretending not to lead—will also determine much of the Continent's direction.

So too will the image of the European Union itself. In less than four decades, the modest six-nation plan to form a common market has grown into a union of 15 countries embarked on the greatest pooling of sovereignty between free and independent states since the American Revolution. Yet the EU inspires little public loyalty.

Few hearts in Europe beat faster at the sight of the Eu's blue and gold-starred banner.

Its accomplishments are taken for granted; its shortcomings and mistakes are the stuff of headlines.

'Guardians of Peace'

If the EU fails to inspire, if it falls short of embracing much of the Continent in an economic and political union, then Europe could well go the way of Havel's warning and fall prey to the fools, fanatics, populists and demagogues.

At one dramatic moment during his final speech to the European Parliament in January 1995, a frail and dying Mitterrand pushed aside his prepared remarks and spoke to the hushed house of more than 500 lawmakers, much as a father conveys wisdom to his children.

He reminisced about his time as a POW in Germany, the Germans he met there, the values and hopes he found they shared beneath the poison of nationalism.

"Nationalism is war," he said. "And war is not just the past, it is perhaps the future too. It is you who are the guardians of peace and security."

Marshall spent 20 years reporting from Europe, most recently as chief of The Times' Brussels Bureau. Beginning Oct. 1 [1996], he will write from Washington.

As Europe moves closer to fiscal union and a single currency, it confronts a spectrum of national anxieties and practical concerns. For now, James Dougherty argues, the prospects for union appear strong, but with a caveat: "Prediction is a perilous task. . .when the basic political and economic interests of 15 states are at stake."

The Politics of European Monetary Union

JAMES E. DOUGHERTY

In 1986, the 12 members of the European Community (EC) agreed to create a single internal market by the end of 1992 that would allow the free flow of people, goods, services, and capital. That goal has now been more than 90 percent achieved, although problems remain in several areas and some countries have not yet passed all the needed implementing legislation.

In December 1991 the EC members completed negotiations on the Maastricht treaty, which entered into force November 1, 1993. The Maastricht treaty provided for an "ever closer" political union, as well as an economic and monetary union, including a single currency, to be launched no later than January 1, 1999. Since 1993, however, there have been recurring debates about a "two-speed Europe," "variable geometry,"" and "unity à la carte" as one or more member states have claimed exemptions or postponements with regard to the social charter on workers' rights, passport-free borders, police, military defense (a problem for "neutrals"), and—most important—the common currency.

Does the single market need a common currency? British Prime Minister Margaret Thatcher flatly denied that it did; the American economist Robert Samuelson once called it a "loony scheme" that "would be hard to introduce and, if introduced, would create more problems than it solved." Advocates of federal unity insist that a single market is incompatible over the long haul with unpredictable and wide fluctuations in the exchange rates of national currencies. Arguments over whether monetary union necessarily implies eventual federal union continue.

JAMES E. DOUGHERTY *is an emeritus professor of political science and scholar-in-residence at St. Joseph's University. He is coauthor, with Robert L. Pfaltzgraff, Jr., of* Contending Theories of International Relations: A Comprehensive Survey, *4th ed. (New York: Longman, 1997).*

Germany and France, the twin pillars of the unity movement, have led the effort to achieve monetary stability in Europe. With strong support from Belgium, the Netherlands, Luxembourg, and Denmark, they established a European Monetary System (EMS) in 1979, with an Exchange Rate Mechanism (ERM) and an artificial European accounting unit for financial and commercial transactions known as the ECU (European Currency Unit). The ERM was designed to manage currencies and oblige members' central banks to support each other's currencies to keep them within prescribed ranges of fluctuation. The standard range was 2.25 percent, but Italy was allowed a 6 percent margin (as were Spain and Portugal when they entered the ERM in the 1980s). The ERM was supposed to be a preparation for Economic and Monetary Union (EMU)—a means of currency stabilization through the imposition of budgetary discipline on member governments. An unenthusiastic Thatcher government brought the pound sterling into the ERM in 1990—initially at the 6 percent margin. Greece, with its very weak drachma, has never qualified.

The ERM succeeded in keeping fluctuations in line for more than a decade, but during the French debate in September 1992 over ratifying the Maastricht treaty, Europe's currency markets were plunged into turmoil. Some blamed the crisis on speculators trying to profit from monetary volatility in a period of political uncertainty. Others blamed it on the unexpected costs of German reunification, the post–cold war decline in defense spending, and the massive influx of immigrants from the former Yugoslavia as well as from Eastern Europe into Germany, and immigrants from North Africa into France.

London pointed to Germany's tight money policy as a major contributor to Europe's recession and rising unemployment, suggesting that the inflation-allergic Germans were relying on high interest rates to spread the cost of rebuilding East Germany through Europe's financial markets. Bonn pointed back at Britain's failure to exercise greater fiscal discipline in a period of high inflation and to raise interest rates in time to prevent the pound's fall. Besides the factors mentioned earlier, both countries also shared responsibility for the misalignment in exchange rates. Speculators, as always, took advantage of a lucrative situation.

The ensuing financial turbulence knocked the British pound and the Italian lira out of the ERM in September 1992, and soon forced devaluations of the Spanish peseta, the Portuguese escudo, and the Irish punt at the height of the crisis. Still, French President François Mitterrand and German Chancellor Helmut Kohl bravely insisted that the EMU, replete with a European Central Bank (ECB) and a common currency, would be achieved no later than the 1999 deadline.

For a decade France had striven to maintain parity between the franc and the deutsche mark, but this became increasingly difficult in the summer of 1993. When in late July the Bundesbank refused to lower German interest rates, the franc began to fall precipitously and the French government proved powerless to halt the flow of capital toward the mark. EU finance ministers, in a desperate attempt to save the ERM from total collapse, agreed in early August 1993 to allow the franc and other ERM currencies (except for the mark and the Dutch guilder) to float within a margin of 15 percent. This was humiliating for France, but it was a welcome relief for other countries and eased pressure sufficiently to preserve the ERM.

For a time there were calls (including one from European Commission President Jacques Delors) for measures to curb speculators. These were rejected for fear that reimposition of capital controls would be a step backward in the single market and would create a monetary "Fortress Europe" against non-EC buyers of European currencies.

The wider band did make life more difficult for speculators. Moreover, the "softer" ERM did not,

contrary to pessimistic predictions, lead to competitive devaluation (which helps a country's trade by making its exports cheaper) or to plummeting interest rates. Instead, it gave Germany's ERM partners a chance to reduce interest rates slowly, while watching their currencies appreciate gradually against the mark because of more rapid growth and lower inflation than in Germany.

DEUTSCHE MARK ÜBER ALLES?

The Maastricht treaty went into effect on November 1, 1993. The new European Union's first important task was to start Stage II of EMU on January 1, 1994, and select a site for the European Monetary Institute (EMI), the forerunner of a future European Central Bank.[1] Germany's wish to locate it in Frankfurt was both natural and paradoxical. Frankfurt was a natural choice because of the deutsche mark's central fiscal role, but paradoxical because opinion polls showed the German public was increasingly doubtful about the merits of trading the mark for a common currency.

None of the last three presidents of the Bundesbank (Otto Pohl, Helmut Schlesinger, and Hans Tietmeyer) has been an ardent believer in a common currency. For financial and domestic political reasons they have been reluctant to abandon the deutsche mark as Europe's stabilizing reserve currency. Chancellor Kohl, however, has been determined to keep the promise he made when Germany was reunified: to make sure that Germany would be a "good European" for the indefinite future by remaining a model Western democracy anchored to a united and, if possible, federal Europe. As the continent's recognized power broker, Kohl succeeded in making Frankfurt the EMI site, thus assuring the Bundesbank that Germany will always play a strong role in a future ECB. Much will depend on whether he can still persuade the Germans to give up the mark, and whether he wins a fifth term as chancellor in 1998.

Another aspect of Stage II concerns the "convergence criteria" for entering the EMU. Who will be eligible to join? The Maastricht treaty criteria set these guidelines:

- Consumer price inflation that is not more than 1.5 percent above average inflation for the three members with the lowest inflation rates;

- A currency that has not experienced severe fluctuations for at least two years;

- An average long-term interest rate not more

---

[1]Stage I, which began on July 1, 1990, was a four-year effort to stabilize currencies, eliminate restrictions on capital movements, and define criteria for economic convergence. Stage II is the current preparatory period in which EMU institutions are being developed and governments move their economies toward convergence. In Stage III the European Central Bank will become operative and exchange rates for the currencies of qualified members will be irrevocably fixed.

than 2 percent higher than those of the three best-performing member states;

- Annual budget deficits not exceeding 3 percent of GDP or declining toward that point;

- A ratio of government debt to GDP not exceeding 60 percent, or one approaching that point at a satisfactory pace.

These criteria are interrelated and subject to interpretation. In the last three years, all member states (including the three admitted in 1995—Austria, Sweden, and Finland) have fallen short, most significantly on deficits and debts (the exception has been Luxembourg). Even France and Germany have been and still are above the allowed limits on inflation and deficits. Portugal, the Netherlands, Italy, Belgium, and Ireland have had debts amounting to more than 60 percent of GDP, and only Ireland, Denmark, and Luxembourg have kept inflation within the 3 percent boundaries fixed by "Maastricht orthodoxy." Greece's economy is in the worst shape, and cannot be expected to qualify until at least the early twenty-first century.

THREE OPTIONS

European leaders have had difficulty deciding which of three courses they should pursue to fulfill the Maastricht treaty guidelines, and seem at times to be pursuing all three simultaneously. The first and easiest option is to perfect the single internal market and postpone EMU until Europe recovers fully from its recession and the EU-wide unemployment rate of nearly 12 percent. Monetary policy poses fewer hurdles to the completion of a single market than continuing disagreement or lack of enforcement regarding the social charter, worker mobility, harmonization of value-added taxes (VAT), government procurement contracts, national safety and health standards, intellectual property, company law, frontiers without passport controls, and other nonfiscal issues. Kohl, however, has expressed fear that the loss of momentum toward integration will lead not only to an economic standstill but to a resurgence of national particularism and the gradual weakening and eventual dissolution of the EU.

The second option is to loosen the qualifying criteria so that virtually all members (with the exception of Greece) would be eligible to join EMU in the "first wave," scheduled to begin in 1999. Both Bundesbank president Hans Tietmeyer and German Finance Minister Theo Waigel have adamantly opposed such proposals. They want even stricter criteria than those embodied in the Maastricht treaty, including budget deficits of no more than 1.5 percent of GDP in times of growth so that the long-term average will not rise above 3 percent during recessions. They also advocate penalties for delinquents. Waigel undoubtedly wants to assure the German people that the "euro" (the name he proposed for the common currency and the Madrid European Council approved in December 1995) will be as strong and stable as the mark.

German government officials have said that the timetable and the entry criteria for EMU must be adhered to, but that any conflict between the two should not be resolved by diluting the criteria. For them, postponement would be the preferable alternative. The Germans do not wish to loosen the criteria even for themselves, lest others demand leniency.

Through most of 1996, Germany and France appeared firmly committed to a third option: a "two-speed" Europe in which they, along with perhaps five or six other members, would form the advance guard of EMU and allow others a few years to catch up. The governments of Chancellor Kohl and President Jacques Chirac of France have launched austerity programs (reduced public spending, higher taxes or postponed tax breaks, wage freezes or changes in work rules, cuts in sick pay and other benefits) that have proved highly unpopular with taxpayers, entitlement program recipients, and trade unions (French truck drivers went on a paralyzing two-week strike in November 1996, forcing the government to reassess its budgetary plans). Nevertheless, several other states are using similar measures to put their economies in shape for EMU.

The Organization for Economic Cooperation and Development (OECD) and the IMF have warned that a sudden rush by several countries to meet simultaneously the convergence criteria by the end of 1997 could lead to deflation, increase the EU's already swollen unemployment rolls, and push Europe back from a fragile growth curve to a serious recession.

PROS AND CONS

Optimists predict that establishing EMU on schedule will boost Europe's self-confidence and reinvigorate economic growth. Besides facilitating internal trade through cost cuts in cross-border transactions, EMU promises to stabilize the euro by eliminating competitive devaluations, to attract foreign investment, and to enhance Europe's position in global financial markets when the euro becomes a reserve currency comparable to the dollar and the yen. Moreover, it will enable the EU to expand eastward in the new century, thereby strengthening the commitment of the former communist states to democracy and the market. The advocates of EMU also concur with Kohl's judgment: failure to meet the Maastricht monetary goals would mark a major setback for the unity movement and could lead to the eventual unraveling of the single market and revive the kind of nationalist policies that all too readily end in conflict.

Among the pessimists, British "Euroskeptics" are at the forefront—but certainly not alone—in advancing three arguments. The first is that several EU members cannot meet the convergence criteria by 1999; thus if EMU occurs it will split Europe into first- and second-class members and may even impose burdens on trade in the single market. Second, as transition deadlines approach, speculators cannot be prevented from disturbing currency markets (as they did in 1992 and 1993), except by imposing illiberal controls on capital movements. Finally, as the IMF and the OECD have warned, EMU-driven austerity programs will depress the sluggish growth rate throughout Europe and increase unemployment.

THE EMU TIMETABLE

The European Commission has ruled out a "big bang" approach under which the euro would suddenly replace national currencies, deciding in June 1995 to make the transition over four years. A critical decision will be made in the spring of 1998, when the emi will identify those countries that fulfill the Maastricht treaty convergence criteria. This process has already generated a good deal of controversy over how the criteria are to be interpreted and what kind of statistical data should be used. Depending on how many and which countries qualify, the 15 EU heads of governments will then decide whether to proceed with the establishment of the EMU by the January 1, 1999, deadline. By that date, assuming an affirmative decision in the spring of 1998, the European Monetary Institute will have become the European Central Bank, and the conversion rates irrevocably locking national currencies to the euro will be set. Locking conversion rates will curb speculation in EMU member currencies. After January 1, 1999, the ECB will

Although monetary union has significant economic implications for all EU members, in the final analysis it will be a matter of the highest politics. . .

determine monetary policy for all EMU member states' central banks, whose heads will compose the ECB's governing council. The ECB's main function will be to allocate the money supply for each member state and to maintain price stability by controlling interest rates in a system whose varying rates of growth, unemployment, inflation, and budget deficits will require adjustments by the ECB from time to time.

For a three-year period, however, the euro will exist as a unit of currency account; only in 2002 will the euro take physical form as actual cash notes and coins. From January 1, 1999, to December 31, 2001, it will be possible to conduct financial transactions in euros (issuing bonds, entering contracts, transferring funds, quoting prices) because the permanent conversion rates will have been fixed. All cash transactions will be carried out in national notes and coins.

The three-year waiting period is required in order to mint the new coins (1, 2, 5, 10, and 50 cents, as well as 1 and 2 euros) and to print seven notes (5, 10, 20, 50, 100, 200, and 500 euros). The coins will have a "European" design on one side and a national design on the other. The notes will carry generic Union designs (windows, gateways, arches and bridges of seven different ages from classical to modern) on one side, and a small space (perhaps 20 percent) will be reserved on the reverse for a national symbol. Each note will have its own distinctive size and dominant color for ease of recognition. Existing national currencies will cease to be legal tender within EMU member states six months after the euro is placed in circulation on January 1, 2002. (Some want the transition period drastically reduced from six months—even to one day—to limit confusion and speculation.) Union members that remain outside EMU will be free to operate within the Exchange Rate Mechanism's 15 percent margin of fluctuation or within a lower negotiated band.

CHARTER MEMBERS?

In November 1996, the European Commission optimistically forecast that 12 of the Union's 15 members might be able to meet the Maastricht criteria in 1997 if the criteria could be flexibly interpreted in a few cases, especially with respect to national debts above 60 percent of GDP. The three nonqualifiers are those outside the ERM: Britain,

Sweden, and Greece. The failure of Britain and Sweden to qualify under the Maastricht criteria results from internal dissent over certain aspects of EU membership, rather than the current state of their economies. Sweden, which voted by a narrow margin of 52 percent to join the union in 1994, is deeply split over the single currency. Prime Minister Goran Persson is in favor, but his own Social Democratic Party insists on a vote in the Rikstag. Greece, as noted earlier, cannot possibly qualify for several years. Britain and Denmark, having reserved the right to opt out of the common currency, are not expected to be candidates for "first-wave" entry. Since there is majority support for EMU in their business communities and substantial political opposition to it, both countries will put membership to a referendum.

Although British Labour Party leader Tony Blair at times appears more pro-EU than Conservative Prime Minister John Major, Blair's party still houses a strong anti-European wing, and today is no less divided than the Conservatives over EMU because it may pursue "capitalist" policies harmful to unions, in spite of its "social charter" for workers, which the Conservatives oppose. Both Major and Blair have been criticized for skirting the single currency issue in the run-up to the parliamentary elections—which must be held by May 1997 and may occur even earlier, now that there is no majority in Parliament. Both leaders promise a popular vote if and when the government should decide to enter EMU. No matter which party wins, it may by then be too late to prepare for first-wave entry.

Among the southern tier countries, the governments of Italy, Spain, and Portugal have made it a matter of political prestige and national honor to be part of the first wave, despite the doubts of the IMF, President Chirac, and many economists.

Italian Prime Minister Romano Prodi has pursued a course of belt-tightening that has led to protest strikes. He improved Italy's fiscal credibility by bringing the lira back into the ERM in November 1996 after an absence of more than four years, but Italy (whose debt is more than 120 percent of GDP) is not certain to qualify unless the criteria are interpreted generously.

If EMU begins on schedule, the most likely charter members will be Germany, France, Belgium, the Netherlands, Luxembourg, Ireland, Finland, and perhaps Austria.[2] Italy, Spain, and Portugal are less likely, but they cannot be ruled out. As noted, Britain, Denmark, and Sweden have yet to decide whether to join. Finally, neither Germany nor France, the indispensable players, can yet be certain of fulfilling the criteria by the end of 1997.

RECENT HURDLES ON THE EURO TRACK

Several practical problems to monetary union became apparent during the second half of 1996. The first was an acrimonious argument about a European "stability pact." Germany had consistently tried to reassure a skeptical public that the euro will be as solid as the mark. However, when Italy, Spain, and Portugal announced strenuous efforts to meet the Maastricht criteria in 1997, the Bonn government and the Bundesbank became more worried than ever. German Finance Minister Waigel reiterated a two-year-old proposal to toughen the criteria by making the budget deficit limit of 3 percent the maximum "worst case" in bad times, urging governments to aim for 1.5 percent during good times. He demanded a stability pact to ensure sustained fiscal discipline after EMU begins, and insisted that any member exceeding the 3 percent deficit level for more than six months face stiff penalties.

Most Union finance ministers considered Bonn's terms too severe, depriving a government of fiscal discretion when faced with an economic downturn. They wanted temporary exemptions from penalties to be granted under "exceptional circumstances" such as recession or natural disaster. A compromise was reached at the December 1996 Dublin summit. States running excessive budget deficits will be given a 10-month warning and must deposit from 0.2 to 0.5 percent of GDP with the European Commission; this amount will become a fine if the deficit has not been removed in two years. If a state experiences a natural disaster or if its GDP falls 2 percent in a year, it will be automatically exempt from penalties; in case of a fall between 2 and .75 percent, EU ministers may consider the entire record and impose penalties at their discretion; below .75 percent, penalties will be automatic. Waigel seemed satisfied with the compromise.

The cost of converting to the single currency is the second hurdle that must be overcome. Obviously, those who depend on currency exchange for income will lose a considerable sum. Banks, multinationals,

---

[2]The Austrian schilling is in the ERM, but Austria's future attitude became a question mark after its October 1996 elections to the European Parliament. The rightist anti-European Freedom Party, which campaigned against the austerity budget the government put in place to prepare for EMU, proved almost as strong as the pro-EMU ruling Social Democrats.

and domestic businesses that import or export must retrain their employees and prepare for double pricing and tax accounting for a period as long as three and a half years. Vending machines, pay telephones, cash registers, and taxi and parking meters must be replaced or modified. The most expensive and technically difficult challenge will be changes to computer systems involved in banking, finance, and commercial transactions. The millions of dollars this conversion will cost are a risky investment for a future event fraught with uncertainty. Systems experts have warned that there may be computer chaos and a severe shortage of software expertise needed to handle such a complex transition.

The third hurdle is working out rules to govern relations between EMU "insiders" and "outsiders." EU states that remain outside the single currency have been concerned about discriminatory policies. For the sake of controlling monetary policy and confining EMU benefits to members who have paid for them, Germany and France in mid-1996 proposed limiting the access of banks in nonmember countries to the euro payments and settlement system known as Target. British and Danish bankers worried about remaining competitive if their access to euros was restricted by their nonmember status, through, for example, differential costs of transactions or length of trading hours. Alarmists noted that any limits on Britain's ability to convert pounds to euros might cause the City of London to forfeit to Frankfurt its position as Europe's financial capital; some banks even considered relocating to Frankfurt. British officials hinted at legal action against any new burden imposed on the single market's freedom of capital movement. Fears were calmed somewhat when Europe's leading banks supported a December 1996 plan to provide an alternate euro payments clearing mechanism through the ECU Banking Association, which will continue to serve non-single-currency members in a revamped ERM system.

The final and perhaps most serious hurdle is potential controversy over interpreting the Maastricht convergence criteria. Here the debate is between reasonable "flexibility" and deceptive "fudging." Germany suspects some states have already resorted to "creative accounting" to make their 1997 budget deficits fit the criteria. France, for example, will count as national income a windfall in the form of a future pension liability payment from a partially privatized Télécom amounting to 0.5 percent of GDP. Italy plans to collect a Eurotax surcharge that will later be rebated. These are one-time gains, however.

Furthermore, budget statistics for 1997, which are crucial for determining eligibility, will probably lead to wrangling between the EMI and national finance ministers; EU countries use differing methods to measure inflation, deficits, and debts.

THE STAKES

As 1997 began, EMU appeared to be on track. Most EU governments were anxious to be in the first wave; only a few preferred to wait and see. A large majority of economists and politicians expected monetary union to happen. Companies were conducting seminars; supermarkets were holding "euro teach-ins" for consumers; and makers of cash and vending machines were anticipating handsome profits. The OECD was forecasting a two-year period of modest economic growth.

Prediction is a perilous task, however, when the basic political and economic interests of 15 states are at stake. Public moods are volatile, and elections in several countries before the end of 1998 could usher in new leaders, ruling parties, and national policies. And key personalities may pursue different goals for a variety of motives. Kohl and Chirac both seek a single currency, but for different reasons: Kohl as a means to create closer political unity, Chirac to gain leverage over the Bundesbank while concurring with Major on the undesirability of federal union. Although monetary union has significant economic implications for all EU members, in the final analysis it will be a matter of the highest politics: the national sovereignty, identity, and independence so dear to Chirac and Major versus Kohl's Euro-idealism, aimed at solidifying one of the world's most war-prone regions into a lasting zone of peace.

Sweden: A Model Crisis

After World War II Sweden appeared to be the very model of a successful welfare state. In recent years, however, the country has suffered from acute social, economic and political problems. A prominent foreign observer of Sweden attempts to place the crisis of the Swedish Model in historical perspective.

Joseph B. Board

Joseph B. Board, Ph.D. in Political Science, is Robert Porter Patterson Professor of Government at Union College, Schenectady, New York. He has written on Sweden and been a visiting professor at Lund and Umeå Universities.

Crisis. Formerly an unfamiliar word in the Swedish political lexicon, it is far more commonly encountered nowadays. The Swedish public sector, a national success story in the 1950's and 60's, has fallen into a persistent state of crisis, which smoulders on even if it does not burst into flame, and from which no immediate escape is readily apparent. Unemployment, at 13%, is extremely high by Swedish standards. The national debt is close to 100% of GDP, and the annual budget deficit is running at 11% of GDP (the average for major industrial countries is 4%). There are strong political differences between the formerly inseparable trade unions and Social Democrats; the combined strength of two old parade horses like the Liberals and the Center party barely equals that of a surging Left Party (formerly the Communists). The refractory problems of public finance and declining political consensus are exacerbated by

ethnic tensions at home, a hesitant and ambivalent decision to join the European Union, and contentious debate over the meaning of Swedish neutrality. A divided government and society have not yet come to grips with the real questions, which are not peculiar to Sweden, and which are essentially more political than economic: how large should government be, and what is its proper role in society?

The rise of the Swedish Model

In 1870, Sweden was a poor, backward, inward-looking, socially and politically undemocratic country on the outer rim of Europe. One hundred years later, by 1970, Sweden was as affluent, per capita, and as democratic as any nation in the world. A socially laggard Sweden modernized itself more quickly and thoroughly than any nation in the world, with the possible exception of Japan.

By the 1950's, this developmental spurt had culminated in the so-called Swedish Model, a term never subject to precise definition. Sweden became world-renowned as the prime example of a prosperous, democratic welfare state, its wealth created by a vigorous private sector, but distributed in accordance with an egalitarian vision of social justice. Beatified by apologists for the Welfare State, demonized by its enemies, the Model was widely touted as a superior alternative to autocratic socialism or to socially deficient liberalism; its political system was based on the bedrock of a broad consensus shared by all the major political parties but orchestrated by a dominant Social Democratic Party. In short order the Swedes created a complex system which rested on a large and powerful public sector, a high level of civic trust, a closed circle of private interest groups involved in public decision-making, a belief in social engineering, egalitarian distribution of the national income, voluntary labor peace (the so-called spirit of Saltsjöbaden), and low unemployment—altogether a heady mixture of democracy, prosperity, and social security.

The decline of the Swedish Model

By the early 1990's, it was becoming clear that the Swedish Model no longer accurately described a country plagued with high unemployment, strikes, declining consensus, ethnic tensions, persistent problems of public finance, uncertain about its place in the wider world or the future direction of public policy at home. A number of analysts, professional and amateur, foreign and domestic, responded with a flourish of attempts to explain what had caused the deterioration in the Swedish Model. The safe, sure, and predictable Sweden that one had come to expect with almost boring regularity had vanished in a cloud of malaise and a crisis of confidence.

Actually the changes had begun much earlier, probably in the early 1970's. The successful operation of the Swedish Model had depended on a number of factors, some domestic, others international, and when these began to change, it was inevitable that the Model would have to respond.

It should be emphasized that while the Swedish Model is widely associated with the Social Democrats and their trade-union allies, it was ultimately a creation of the non-socialist parties as well. One major condition on which the entire accomplishment rested was the presence of a highly stable party system in which the Social Democrats were the only party large enough to set and realize such an ambitious agenda. Following on the heels of a succession of weak governments in the 1920's and early 1930's, the Social Democrats were in power, alone or in coalition with a much weaker partner, for the entire period between 1932 and 1976, a world record for democratically sustained continuity. The first minor challenges to their pre-eminence came in the 1960's from amorphous New

Left movements. Later, in the 1970's, their ideological hegemony was weakened somewhat by the rise of the Center Party, and later by the Greens, over the issues of nuclear power and other ecological concerns.

The more serious challenge to Social Democratic hegemony came, however, from the Right. In the parliamentary elections of 1976, the non-socialist parties—Center, Liberals and Moderates—wrested power from its long accustomed holders, and despite problems in holding together their uneasy coalition, won re-election in 1979. The Social Democrats regained office in 1982, and remained there until 1991. However, during the 1980's the Moderate Party and its private-sector supporters introduced a vigorous infusion of neo-liberal ideology into the Swedish public debate, challenging the near monopoly of democratic socialist and social-liberal ideas that had provided the context of public debate throughout most of the post WW II era.

By the 90's, even when the Social Democrats recaptured power in 1994, things were clearly not the same. No longer did they enjoy the commanding heights of their hey-day, and this made it difficult for them to provide an agenda for a renewal of the Swedish Model, even if they had possessed one. The Social Democrats ended up victims of their own success. During their long tenure in power, the very class distinctions on which their movement had been founded had all but disappeared. Sweden had become a predominantly middle-class country; the Social Democrats had become more and more a white-collar party, and the earlier close association with the trade unions had become increasingly strained.

Some foundations of the Swedish Model

The Swedish Model, furthermore, was dependent on a spirit of compromise and mutual restraint prevailing between the labor movement (unions and Social Democrats) on the one hand and the large corporations and interest groups of Swedish industry on the other. This harmonious spirit was based on the awareness by all sides that a small Sweden could survive in a large and competitive world only if all could pull together. Swedish industry, whose role in producing the national wealth available to be distributed by the welfare state has been persistently underestimated by social scientists, perceived itself from the early 1970's in an increasingly disadvantageous position within the Swedish policy-making process. By the 1980's it had begun to fear for its very existence; high taxation, the enormous growth of the public sector, and fears of creeping nationalization prompted by the wage-earner funds and other new departures proposed by Labor caused it to launch a vigorous neo-liberal counterattack on the fundamental assumptions of continued governmental growth.

The Swedish Model, at least in its idealized form, presumed the existence of a society with an unusual degree of ethnic and religious homogeneity, its highly organized system of interest groups led by elites—political, economic, and social—and a rather docile citizenry disposed to follow its leaders. Today, the population is much less homogeneous. The heavy postwar immigration of workers, mostly from Europe, followed by a later influx of asylum-seekers, frequently of non-European origin, has created problems of assimilation and brought to the surface a latent xenophobia in Swedish society.

The loss of elite control was a serious one in a system based on peak-level corporative bargaining between the leaders of the government, political parties, trade unions, business organizations and the other major players in national policy-making. It is obviously easier to maintain control over events if the circle of decision-makers is a limited one. Some slippage could have been detected by an astute observer as early as the late 1960's, with demands originating among the young New Left for less bureaucracy and more grass-roots democracy. Although these pressures were contained and co-opted, a wave of labor unrest, most notably the LKAB strike in the iron mines of Kiruna at the decade's end, provided eloquent testimony to a serious decline in the ability of the Swedish Model to contain and channel social conflict.

There were other signs of similar decay, including the appearance of issues, i.e. nuclear power, and later EU membership, which from their inception could not be comfortably accommodated within the existing party system, but required the unusual expedient of referendums to reconcile the electoral contradictions.

The success of the Greens in obtaining seats in the Riksdag (Parliament) in the 1988 election (the first new party to do so in 70 years), and the rise of an openly populist party, New Democracy, in 1991, however fleeting its electoral success, are further signs of electoral decomposition.

Finally, and perhaps most importantly, the Swedish Model

presumed the existence of a domestic arena within which Swedish decision-makers, while obviously not totally impervious to world movements and trends, nevertheless were in a position to control the main outlines of Swedish domestic policy.

This situation has been utterly transformed in the past two or three decades. The gobalization of the economy, the arrival of larger European groupings such as the EU, and the global communications revolution have forever ended the illusion that the so-called sovereign State—much less one the size of Sweden—was any longer in complete control over its own political destinies. The cruel reality is that the room for internal political maneuver has been drastically reduced by global influences such as currency fluctuations, international business cycles, capital flows, the fax machine and the Internet, the Eurocrats in Brussels, and even by those semi-sovereign companies which evaluate the credit-worthiness of entire countries.

Sic transit gloria Sueciae?

When the awareness of Swedish difficulties began to sink in, journalists and social scientists alike struggled to find explanations for this change in national fortunes.The more perceptive scholars, alert to the nuances of what seemed to have been a stable and permanent system, were understandably bewildered. Critics of the Swedish Welfare State rushed in like scavengers at a long-deferred feast to explain all the Trouble in Paradise. The weakness in this analysis was, however, that Sweden had never been a paradise in the first place. Much of the popular publicity about Sweden had described, not a Model of reality but a romantic image, one which in fact obscured many of the real accomplishments of the Swedes.

Without in any way detracting from the efficacy of conscious efforts to attain the extraordinary combination of prosperity and security that were the hallmarks of the Swedish Model at its height, one is nevertheless compelled to conclude that much of that success was a happy accident. Neutral Sweden emerged from WW II with its industrial plant intact, its exports in demand, equipped with a skilled work force, a highly organized and homogeneous society, and a political system dominated by one large party which combined pragmatic good sense with fiscal responsibility, and strong government with a highly developed social conscience. Under these favorable conditions, including a period of vigorous economic growth of between 3 and 5% annually from the the late 40's through the 60's, the private sector could grow, welfare could expand, and there seemed to be no ceiling to the success of the Swedish Model.

Actually, the Swedish Model might better have been called the Swedish Image, one which served not only the needs of model-builders but also promoted the interests of Swedes and their foreign admirers alike. Liberals, would-be Social Democrats, and reformers of all persuasions in countries like America, could from Marquis Childs on, point to Sweden as a confirming case for the cause of democratic social reform. For Swedes it provided a powerful image, even a kind of marketing device with which to maximize their country's political and economic influence throughout the world. It is in fact illuminating to read today the descriptions of Sweden commonly encountered during the period of the Model's ascendancy. One is struck by the degree to which these accounts are not only congruent, but practically identical, whether they originated with politicians, business interests, civil servants, or scholars.

Swedes were also able, to a considerable extent, to view their foreign and domestic situation in idealistic, non-cynical terms. There is in Swedish history (as in American) a long tradition of exceptionalism, the incorporation into the national ethos of an unshakeable conviction that the country, unlike most others, has been blessed by Providence with a special mission. Having renounced Great Power ambitions in the 18th century (and it should be remembered that 17th century Sweden was in fact a genuine major power), the Swedes were able in the 20th century to transform their smallness into goodness, and replace the more conventional forms of national chauvinism with a kind of "Welfare Patriotism" or "moral imperialism."

Once the Swedish Model began to show signs of wear and tear, the government made efforts at repair. Most of the attempts were temporizing improvisations, aimed at keeping the wolf as far from the national door as long as possible. Devaluations of the krona, expansion of public-sector employment, and crisis packages negotiated by the politicians did not, however, really reduce the budget deficits, the growing national debt, and the rising unemployment. It is in fact a tribute to the strength of the Swedish system that it could be maintained for so long before it became apparent that the problems were profound, structural, and to some extent shared by most European countries. Neither the socialists nor the non-socialists had any sure-fire solutions.

Half-good may not be half-bad

In spite of the bewilderment, occasioned by these near-tectonic shifts in the Swedish political landscape, there is a bright positive side to all this change. Much of the malaise which observers began to detect during the 80's and 90's was nothing more than the harvest of the exaggerated expectations which had long grown around the Swedish Model; as a general rule, the greater the expectations, the deeper the disillusionment.

One reason why Sweden was becoming a more confusing place to interpret, for Swedes and foreign observers alike, is that it was—like most advanced industrial countries—rapidly becoming a much more heterogeneous pluralistic society. In its ethnic composition, the media, public debate, cuisine, religion (only a few years ago, who would have believed that by 1995 there would be in Sweden an estimated quarter of a million ethnic Moslems?) Sweden has become a country of greater, and admirable, variety. Small wonder it was that politics inevitably became less predictable as the society became less uniform and conformist. New political parties formed and re-formed, new political journals, such as *Moderna Tider* (Modern Times), provided a more cosmopolitan tone to public debate and even television was utterly transformed, for better or worse, with the advent of advertising and cable/satellite transmission.

It is especially apparent to the outside observer that Sweden has become less inward-looking, more vital, complex, politically nuanced, less Manichaean in the way the choices are posed—in short, the country has become more like other countries that long ago lost perfectionist ambitions. Sweden has become less perfect, but at the same time more human and more interesting. The ambivalent and changeable Swedish attitudes towards EU membership are illustrative. Having approved membership by only a 5% margin in the November 1994 referendum, the electorate was almost immediately seized by doubts, and only one half-year later, the opinion polls revealed a large majority against membership.

The Swedish Model was grounded philosophically in the paramount ideals of the 18th century Enlightenment: rationality, progress, social ameliorism, secularism—ultimately in the belief that one could attain social perfection through the wise use of concentrated political resources. It is not, however, totally unhealthy to learn that there are limits to perfection, that total control and predictability are impossible, and that even enlightened government can become overloaded. In short, what Sweden has been discovering is the contingent, fallible, unscientific, irrational, downright messy side of social and political life.

Even if the Swedish Model is clearly no longer what it once was, this does not mean that important components of it have not survived the buffeting of recent years. There is still a core of agreement on ethical and aesthetic matters, a remarkably durable set of attitudes towards Nature and Society, notions of order and propriety, an abhorrence of extremes, and a widely shared sense of social compassion. Even in the political realm there is agreement on fundamental principles of human rights, respect for law, democracy, parliamentary government, constitutionalism, honesty in government, and there is still immense support in Sweden for the main lines of a welfare state. There is a Civil Service of uncommonly high competence ready to implement the products of the policy-makers.

Confusion, maybe; paralysis, no

Confusion caused by the unexpected setbacks of the Swedish Model has not resulted in paralysis. While the government has yet to develop a new vision of how State and Society should relate to each other, there has begun a tentative, cautious step-by-step down-sizing of the public sector. Some cuts have already been made in areas like unemployment compensation, day care, parental leave and health care. These reductions have predictably been criticized by some as too small, and by others as too great, depending on whose ox is being gored. But the public as well as the politicians have gradually become aware that serious change is un-avoidable, even if there is no sizeable body of opinion in favor of dismantling the welfare state.

Swedes have by necessity been a resourceful people. From earliest times, their beautiful but demanding natural environment has compelled them to develop coping skills. More than most peoples they are well situated to deal with the new kind of internationalized and pluralized world that is emerging. They have strong ties with other Nordic countries, the Baltic, Western Europe, the United States, and the Third World. They have shown a remarkable penchant for invention, a capacity for social and industrial organization, and—like the Japanese—a supple willingness to borrow and transform to their own purposes the discoveries of other nations. The increased prominence of women in the Riksdag and the Cabinet, the already global mindset of Swedish industry, the renewed public debate over the place of government at all levels, from neighborhood to globe, are only a few of the hopeful signs of adaptation.

Swedish skills will be severely tested in the immediate years ahead, in a world of constantly evolving challenges, where it will be extraordinarily difficult for any country to maintain strong governments which can make long-term policies and provide stable expectations for their citizens. The swollen Swedish public sector, the largest in a democratic industrial country, as well as the monumental national debt and budget deficits are the products of a country that lived for a long time beyond its means, and they will not disappear without painful adjustments.

The Golden Age in perspective

Actually the period from the 1930's to the 1970's—the Golden Age of the Swedish Model—may have constituted an exception in modern Sweden. The weak and changing governments that characterized the earlier decades of the 20th century may well be the most likely types encountered in the forseeable future, an unenviable series of holding actions complicated by the public's lack of confidence in politicians and political solutions. It is a time of difficult choices, rendered more complicated by the natural inclination of a public to have it both ways—egalitarian social programs and fiscal discipline, low taxes and extensive benefits. It is one thing to distribute the benefits of growth another to distribute the burdens of a contracting economy.

Even if the celebrated Golden Age was part accident,

and only partly the intentional result of policy, the story of what the Swedes did with their windfall after the Depression and WW II is in the main a good one, a tale of cooperation between Capital, Labor, and Government to care for the disadvantaged, all within a democratic framework. It was certainly not an opportunity disfigured by greed, narrow selfishness, or pettiness. There is scant prospect for a return to the Golden Age, or to the unbridled Capitalism that preceded it, and the choices confronting any Swedish government, whether of the Left or Right, will be difficult. There remains a lot of hard bargaining over the proper balance between the public and private sectors before the Swedes are out of the woods, but this is what politics is all about, and for the enterprise ahead Sweden—for all its present burdens—has a better point of departure than most.

The author alone is responsible for the opinions expressed in this article.

Rising Health Costs Threaten Generous Benefits in Europe

CRAIG R. WHITNEY

PARIS, Aug. 5—Dr. Philippe Perez, a general practitioner in the Paris suburb of Thiais, used to think nothing of prescribing $500 worth of medicated salve a month for patients with painful herpes infection, because they would be almost completely reimbursed by the French national health insurance system.

But the state-run insurance fund, under Government orders to cut its huge deficit, is now threatening to take high drug costs out of the fees it pays to doctors if they write too many prescriptions. So Dr. Perez explains the problem to his patients, and some of them now pay for the medicine out of their own pockets instead of putting in claims.

Peter König, a retired post office employee in Bonn, has found that German doctors, too, are becoming more reluctant to prescribe remedies like cough medicine that used to go on the insurance bill. Television in Bonn, he says, is now full of advertising pitches to get people to buy over-the-counter remedies that used to be reimbursable by insurance.

In Britain, more than half of the general practitioners in the National Health Service now have budgets they cannot overspend for patients' medicines and hospital care, forcing them to think twice or bargain hard with hospitals and surgeons about the cost.

The high level of health care offered by the welfare states of Western Europe was long the envy of much of the rest of the world, but they can no longer afford the vast amounts required to pay for unlimited benefits.

So in country after country, administrators are turning to the same kinds of market-oriented cost-control measures used by managed care companies and health maintenance organizations in the United States, and raising many of the same ethical concerns.

The techniques include measures like encouraging hospitals to compete with each other in offering value for money, pressing doctors to follow the most cost-effective treatment methods and to order expensive tests only when necessary, and using computers to monitor their compliance.

Just like Americans, Europeans are being forced to think about what comprehensive medical care costs, something that never worried them before.

Britain
Tories Introducing
Dose of Competition

The debate, and the pressures to hold down costs, are most intense in

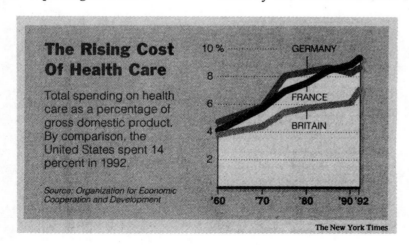

The Rising Cost Of Health Care

Total spending on health care as a percentage of gross domestic product. By comparison, the United States spent 14 percent in 1992.

Source: Organization for Economic Cooperation and Development

GERMANY
FRANCE
BRITAIN

10 %
8
6
4
2

'60   '70   '80   '90 '92

The New York Times

Britain, where the Government provides all health care, at a total cost of $61.8 billion this year.

British Conservative governments have been cutting taxes since the late 1980's. The state is still providing more money for Health Service, but is also putting it under tremendous pressure to squeeze as much as it can out of every penny.

Since the early 1990's, the Conservatives have been introducing the idea of competition into the system, giving hospitals and doctors' practices limited control of their funds and urging doctors to shop for the best hospital service they can find.

In a sense, many general practitioners have formed what amount to independent health maintenance organizations that then negotiate contracts with hospitals and surgeons, much the way American H.M.O.'s do.

The system now involves about 433 such hospital "trusts" and about half the general practitioners in the country, and they are rapidly changing the way health care is provided in Britain, both for better and worse.

Dr. James N. Johnson, a vascular surgeon at a district hospital in Cheshire, took a dim view of one recent experience.

"There was a practice of four G.P.'s who wanted a contract that would let them come in on ward rounds with the specialists and tell us when we could discharge patients," Dr. Johnson said.

"They clearly saw this as a way of controlling their hospital admissions costs," Dr. Johnson said. "We told them to get lost, and they took their business to another place."

While a health maintenance organization might use the money saved to increase profits, British doctors who administer their own budgets can spend it only on equipment or other services, like drugs.

But since British general practitioners usually own their practices and can sell before retirement, critics of the Government's measures say there is a built-in temptation for doctors to scrimp at the expense of

their patients' welfare to build up nest eggs.

Hospitals, under a Government-imposed mandate to perform 2.25 percent more services a year without an increase in their budgets, often do it, critics say, by closing wards and multiplying services on the ones left open.

According to figures supplied by the opposition Labor Party and not disputed by the Government, 50,000 nursing jobs and 60,000 beds have disappeared since 1990, while there has been an increase of 20,000 senior managers in the Health Service.

Henry McLeish, a Labor Member of Parliament, said, "The Tories tried to turn it into a business; we want to make it a public service again."

But about all Labor plans to do to change things if it wins the next election is to take the $1.15 billion it costs to administer the Government-imposed changes and put it into other ways of improving care, like reducing the number of people on waiting lists for routine operations. The party is no longer proposing big increases in Health Service spending as it did in the last election in 1992.

"Private polls show that most people are happy with the care they get," Mr. McLeish said. "There's no sense of a crisis."

Dr. Johnson, the vascular surgeon, said there would always be pressures to keep health costs from rising as fast as new technology and science allow. "Basically, the only choices are rationing care or raising taxes," he said, "but neither political party has the courage to say it."

France
Pressure to Cut Cost of Drugs

The French authorities are determined not to limit health care benefits, but they are circumscribing the freedoms both doctors and patients used to enjoy to make use of them.

French doctors are not state employees, and their bills are only 70 percent reimbursed by the health insurance the Government requires virtually everybody to subscribe to. Over the years, the deductible was raised to encourage people to think twice before going to the doctor, but gradually almost everybody—83 percent of the population—has gone out and acquired supplementary health insurance to cover the gap.

As a result, most French people felt free to go to the doctor as often as they wanted without worrying about the cost. But costs are constantly rising, and the health insurance system has not broken even since the early 1990's. It was nearly $8 billion in the red last year, and is expected to fall about $6.5 billion short this year.

With France facing a 1997 deadline to cut deficits to qualify for a common European currency, something had to give.

So starting this year, the Government will impose limits for the first time on patients' freedom to bypass general practitioners and consult specialists directly, and it is putting heavy pressure on doctors to cut back on the amount and cost of the medicines they prescribe.

The Government also decreed this year that the pharmaceuticals industry had to pay $500 million to the health insurance fund this year as a partly tax-deductible "contribution" in exchange for all the money it made off the system.

According to the Organization of Economic Cooperation and Development, France spends twice as much, as a percentage of total health spending, on medicine as the United States.

And it is easy to see how, judging by the experience of Véronique de Rivoire, a Parisian mother of three small children. She visits her pediatrician in Paris at least 10 times a year, she says, and every time she leaves his office, she has at least three prescriptions.

"National insurance pays 65 percent of the cost of the medicine, and my husband's supplementary plan reimburses the rest, so I don't think about the money," she said.

Gérard Rameix, director of the national sickness fund, said, "We had a system based on full employment, with seemingly unlimited resources, that made people think health care was basically free."

This year Prime Minister Alain Juppé ordered that doctors' total expenditures and the value of the medicines they prescribe should rise no faster than inflation, by 2.1 percent.

The results so far show that he might as well have decreed that the Seine flow backward. Costs went up by 6.1 percent in the first five months of the year, and they would have to sink for the rest of the year to meet the target.

One way to get them down would be for the Government to forbid any increase next year in the reimbursements doctors get from the insurance system, and it has threatened to do that. It has also introduced lists of treatments and medicines thought to be most cost-effective. Deviations from the recommendations have to be justified by doctors if health insurance officials check up on them.

Dr. Perez, in Thiais, said: "I don't want to prescribe more medicine than necessary, but I have some patients with AIDS, which requires a lot of very expensive prescriptions. I can save on those bills by sending them to a hospital instead of giving them ambulatory treatment, but that means, if they were still working, that they have to stop and lose their jobs. Is that really in their best interest?

"I wonder how long patients will continue to trust doctors they know have a financial interest in saving money," Dr. Perez said.

To bring tighter management into the National Fund for Sickness Insurance, which covers 81 percent of the population, the Government will begin this fall to issue computer health-care cards to all patients, recording the treatments they receive, the medicines prescribed and bought, and all the other financial

details the system never worried about when money was no object.

Mr. Rameix, the fund's director, said: "Our aim is to train our people to manage, rather than just to pay. The main hope is to be able to make sufficient savings by making care more efficient, while not reducing benefits, but our plan could be too little too late."

Germany
Government Seeks Reduced Costs

Some of the French measures may have been inspired by what has happened in Germany, where the Government has pushed the health insurance system even farther in the direction of managed care.

"Our system is like a big H.M.O.," said Dr. Gunnar Griesewell of the German Health Ministry in Bonn.

There are 850 "sickness funds" covering the 92 percent of the German population legally required to join them. All are state-regulated non-profit organizations that are supposed to break even.

The system was $4.7 billion in the red last year, and the funds want to raise premiums. But the national average is already close to 13 percent of gross salary, with employers and employees each paying half.

If premiums do not rise, the cost of claims will have to go down, and the Government is pressing doctors and hospitals to lower them.

The sickness funds negotiate fee-reimbursement schedules with regional associations of doctors taking part in the plans, as most do. For the last three years the Government has kept the funds from increasing their rates faster than wages grew.

The Government also decreed that doctors should cut back on the amount of money spent on prescriptions by prescribing generic medicine whenever possible, and by prescribing less medicine in general.

If they exceed the target, the Government ruled, the excess would come out of the pool that pays their claim fees. And last year the excess was about $1 billion.

Such steps promise to be difficult, for the political consensus on how to pay for health care, pensions and most of the rest of the German welfare state broke down this summer after Chancellor Helmut Kohl tried to make $33 billion in pubic spending cuts over the objections of the Social Democratic opposition, which controls the upper house of Parliament.

Part of the deficit-cutting plan is a 75-cent increase in the small co-payment that patients now make on prescriptions—$1.50 to about $5 per prescription—with the rest of the cost paid by health insurance. Even the 75-cent plan has been blocked so far, along with more ambitious proposals to cut health care costs.

The pressures on doctors look likely to continue to increase.

Dr. Joachim Maurer, a general practitioner with a busy practice in Bonn, said he got a computer printout from his regional doctors' association every three months, showing the total cost of all the medicines he had prescribed.

If it exceeds the average for doctors with his type of practice, he gets a warning letter, and if he still exceeds the average after that, he risks taking a cut in his fee reimbursements, which insurance funds pay to the regional doctors' associations.

He uses a thick book of guideline medicine reimbursement prices that tells him exactly how much the sickness funds will pay for thousands of different kinds of medicine. The guidelines have stimulated tremendous growth in the production of cheap generic drugs by German companies, something that worries the pharmaceutical giants.

Thomas Postina, a spokesman for the pharmacy industry in Frankfurt, said, "The Government simply decided at the end of 1992 that doctors should prescribe no more than 25 billion marks worth of medicine."

That amount is the equivalent of about $17 billion.

The limit was effective for a while: the value of prescriptions went from $18 billion in 1992 to $14.7 billion in 1993. But now it is rising again.

The Government would also like to reduce the number of practicing doctors, and even the head of the doctors' biggest lobbying association says there are now too many—about 267,000.

"We get reimbursements from the sickness funds, through the regional doctors' association, according to a point system," Dr. Maurer said. "A house call, for instance, is 400 points. At the beginning of the year, the association estimated that 400 points would be worth 40 marks ($27). But there are too many doctors performing too many services, and since the money pool is finite, it looks as if

400 points will actually be worth only about 24 marks ($16) this year."

"Even a washing machine repairman doesn't make house calls for less than 60 marks ($40) an hour," he observed, but there is a way out—the private health insurance market.

"I am allowed to charge 83.90 marks ($56) for a house call from a private patient," he said. "I pay my bills with my sickness fund business, but I need private patients to survive."

Private insurance covers only 8 percent of the population—people with incomes over the maximum for signing up with a sickness fund.

Franz Knieps, an official of a group of sickness funds with 30 million subscribers, said that ultimately the system would have to find ways to give patients an economic interest in lowering health care costs.

"We could negotiate contracts with groups of doctors, and we're hoping to do that in Frankfurt, for instance, and give people a reduction in premiums in exchange for lower rates negotiated with doctors," he said. "Right now the law bars us from doing that."

The Government would also like sickness funds to reduce their premiums by four-tenths of 1 percent next Jan. 1. But as things now stand, Mr. Knieps said, most of them would have to raise the premiums again on Jan. 2 to break even, as the Government requires them to do.

"It's always the little people who end up paying," said Henriette Dörr, a civil servant in Bonn, convinced that the Government or the health insurance fund will be taking even more out of her paycheck next year.

EUROPE AND THE UNDERCLASS

The slippery slope

ROTTERDAM

As yet, Western Europe does not have an urban underclass to compare with that of the United States. But the growth of long-term unemployment seems to be dragging it inexorably in that direction

IN ROTTERDAM'S vast harbour, a million containers a year are loaded and unloaded. Giant cranes poke towards the sky. Dry docks and oil refineries stretch to the horizon. But for all the gigantism of the harbour—the big ships, big machines, big statistics—there is something missing. People. The modernisation that began in the 1970s has meant that the burly types who used to do the heavy work have been mechanised out of their jobs. It is possible to cruise around Europe's busiest port on an average day and see only a handful of workers.

The decline of port employment, combined with a collapse of the Dutch textile industry, means that Rotterdam, a hardworking city where, it is said, shirts are sold with the sleeves already rolled up, has an unemployment rate of more than 20%. Of the 50,000 jobless, 32,000 have been unemployed for more than a year, and many for more than three years. Even this has come against a background of economic recovery. The finance and retail industries expanded in Rotterdam in the 1980s, yet unemployment still tripled. Few longshoremen were ready to become financial analysts.

In poor parts of the city where unemployment has become almost the norm, crime, drug abuse and one-parent families are increasingly common. The uneven concentration of unemployment—35% of Turks and 42% of Moroccans in Holland are unemployed, compared with 7% of ethnic Dutch—has provided fertile ground for political extremism. "People feel rejected. They don't participate in the social process. It's kind of a time bomb," says Jaap Timmer, a Dutch social scientist.

Lumped together

Such conditions are far from unique to Rotterdam. In cities across Western Europe—such as Frankfurt and Berlin, Lyons and Paris, Amsterdam and Utrecht, Naples and Dublin, Liverpool and Manchester—the shadowed lives of the urban poor are getting darker. Does Europe have an underclass to compare with that of America? Not yet. But the situation is deteriorating in ways that cause the question to be posed more often and more plausibly. And there are no ready solutions in view.

In America, the term "underclass" entered common usage in the 1970s and was a cliché, albeit a controversial one, by the end of the 1980s. It came to connote ghetto populations that were overwhelmingly black, isolated, unemployed, welfare-dependent, poorly educated and with disrupted family patterns. The origins of the underclass lay somewhere in a mix of racial inequality, middle-class black flight from the cities, public-housing policy and the loss of industrial jobs. As the underclass grew more entrenched, so too did a perception that those who peopled it were fundamentally different from other Americans—a universe of teenage moms, crack addicts, drop-outs and criminals.

When America was discerning the early outlines of its underclass in the 1970s, Europe had no poverty debate to speak of. There were some poor people in Europe's cities, certainly, but it was assumed they would not stay that way for very long; the welfare state, that most generous of European inventions, would help them to help themselves. Two decades on, that confi-

dence seems tragically misplaced. Even the richest European countries are seeing new, intractable and growing problems among troubled urban populations. Hamburg, Europe's richest city measured by income per head, had by 1990 Germany's highest proportion of millionaires—and its highest proportion of people on social welfare. Unemployment was 40% higher than the national average. A third of industrial jobs had disappeared in the past 15 years.

"You could use the old Marxist concept of a *lumpenproletariat*", says Pierre Bourdieu, a professor at the Collège de France in Paris. "That describes more exactly the kind of people below the level they need to be at in order to behave rationally, to be able to master the future. The main thing is, there are many, many poor people. When you have many, you have a sort of destruction of solidarity. Nobody can help the others."

Unlike in America, where the fundamental urban tension is that of race, the fundamental tension pulling at the social fabric of Europe's cities is that caused by long-term unemployment. But the effect, in both cases, is one of polarisation and marginalisation. The question is whether Europe's cities are now in the process of producing their distinctive brand of "underclass", different in its origins from that of America but equally damning to those that it claims.

For every new job of aerobics instructor or government clerk created in Europe in the past few decades, at least one older job, probably an industrial one, has disappeared. Blue-collar workers have suffered the most. People who are unskilled, uneducated or merely thick have little chance of finding even a toehold in the workforce. Job shifts are a natural part of economic progress: no surprise that there are far fewer blacksmiths and chimney sweeps, for example, than a century ago. The disappearance of some kinds of jobs would not be an issue if new jobs were springing up to absorb those affected. The problem is they are not. More than 40% of the 17m unemployed in the European Union have been out of work for at least a year; a third have never worked at all. In the United States, which creates and destroys jobs with a verve Europe gawps at, only 11% of the unemployed have been looking for work for more than a year.

But if Europe's unemployment is not fundamentally a racial issue—the majority of poor or unemployed people in any European country are indigenous whites—minorities and first- and second-generation migrants often have a particularly tough time. Large numbers of North Africans came to France, Turks to Germany, Surinamese to Holland, Cape Verdeans to Portugal and West Indians to Britain 20 or 30 years ago to do dirty work that Europeans spurned. When those jobs disappeared in the 1980s and 1990s, they and their children were often ill-equipped to adapt.

Coming to no good

Historically, immigration has been a positive economic force around the world. America absorbed large immigrant surges in the late 19th century and in the 1980s; its wide-open economy put to good use the commitment and hard work of those who made the effort to get in. But Europe does not have the same tradition of openness and individual enterprise, and new arrivals can find these more structured societies tough to crack. Generous social benefits may also blunt the sense of urgency that drives many immigrants in America.

Over time, these later immigrants to Europe, or their children, or their children's children, will probably make themselves at home as other immigrants have done before them. But the shorter-term outlook is so troubling because economic conditions are so straitened. In the former West Berlin, the number of unemployed foreigners nearly doubled between 1989 and 1993, while the unemployment rate for ethnic Germans rose by less than a third.

Unemployment exacerbates geographical divides as easily as it does racial ones. Mr Bourdieu evokes a street in the town of St Marcellin, central France: on one side are nice little single-family dwellings where working families live, on the other are big ugly buildings into which the poorest are stuffed. He speaks of a "translation of economic division into spatial division." People on the wrong side of the line start to cut themselves off from society, sometimes in minor but telling ways. In Holland, disproportionate numbers of the long-term unem-

ployed opt for unlisted telephone numbers; in Ireland they attend church less often.

In Europe as in America, when middle-class people start deserting a district and leaving it to the poor, the process feeds on its own momentum. The only people willing to move in become those with nowhere else to go. Private commerce shrinks or retreats. Long-term unemployment and economic segregation become mutually aggravating. Theft and violence rise as frustrated youths turn to crime and drugs. Because non-working men are less marriageable, illegitimacy rates rise (see chart, next page); the proliferation of one-parent families creates a new hard core of dependency. Public order can easily become fragile. Examples of such places can be found across Europe. Many Frankfurters will name Gallusviertel and Gutleutviertel as areas to avoid; residents of Griesheim, says Michael Wegener of the University of Dortmund in a report to the European Commission, "view their neighbourhood as a ghetto—the Bronx in Frankfurt." Some taxi drivers in Manchester refuse to take fares to Moss Side, an area of high unemployment notorious nationally for its incidence of violent crime.

Overlapping concentrations of urban decay and immigrant communities also provide an easy target for racists and political extremists. In Dreux, near Paris, five youths recently fired shots at a group of North Africans. Racist political parties have struck a chord in distressed neighbourhoods in France, Belgium, Germany, Hol-

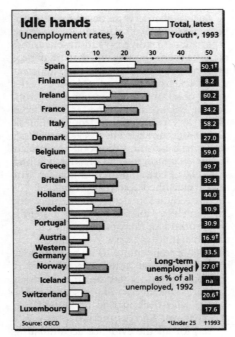

Idle hands
Unemployment rates, %

	Total, latest	Youth*, 1993
Spain		50.1†
Finland		8.2
Ireland		60.2
France		34.2
Italy		58.2
Denmark		27.0
Belgium		59.0
Greece		49.7
Britain		35.4
Holland		44.0
Sweden		10.9
Portugal		30.9
Austria		16.9†
Western Germany		33.5
Norway		27.0†
Iceland		na
Switzerland		20.6†
Luxembourg		17.6

Long-term unemployed as % of all unemployed, 1992

Source: OECD   *Under 25 †1993

land, Italy and Britain. The technique is simple: blame foreigners (preferably non-white ones) for economic problems, call for them to be kicked out, and collect the votes. In Sossenheim in western Frankfurt, ex-

tremist parties won 20% of the vote, the highest in the city. They have made similar breakthroughs in Rotterdam's Nieuwe Westen and in the East End of London.

A theory of relativity

Still, in important ways, Europe's poor are better off than America's. In the American perception, the underclass is threatening because those who compose it are believed to be different—a perception often reinforced by racial prejudice. Europe has managed to avoid this extreme degree of marginalisation, although there are hints of it in some British political attitudes and in the way some of France's wilder *banlieusards* are regarded. The continuing willingness of the mainstream of society to go on identifying with its poorest members (and vice-versa), and the preservation of a generally superior physical environment, is still sufficient to deny Europe anything classifiable as a full-blown underclass.

Europe's poor are less segregated than America's; their streets are cleaner and safer; and they are more likely to have access to medical care. Schools do not have gun detectors. In Wilhelmsburg, one of the poorest parts of Hamburg, there are boutiques, banks and grocery shops, even a travel agency and a Mormon church—the sort of institutions that have trouble keeping a foothold in America's ghettos. Public telephones work, and the modest three-storey brick council flats are in good shape. Even the dodgier bits of Manchester, London or Brussels look positively serene compared with America's urban war zones.

In another contrast with America, the living standards of Europe's poor have risen in absolute terms over the past couple of decades, even if differentials with those of Europe's rich have widened. The Policy Studies Institute, an independent British think-tank, found that infant mortality rates declined throughout Britain between 1977 and 1990 because people were generally better off, better fed and better cared-for*. Older Germans can remember being rationed to 700 calories a day after the war. Today, 96% of German households dependent on social-welfare benefits have a colour television, 89% have a washing machine and 52% have a car.

The reassurance communicated by such statistics may be misleading, however. Colour televisions cannot make people feel useful, or feel that they matter to the community in which they live; and these are the fault-lines along which Europe's social foundation is cracking. "I now hear constantly the question: Are we going to become like Los Angeles?" says Michael Parkinson of the European Institute for Urban Affairs at John Moores University in Liver-

....
* "Urban Trends 1". Edited by Peter Wilmott and Robert Hutchison. Policy Studies Institute, London, 1992

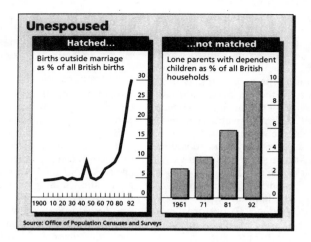

Unespoused

Hatched...

Births outside marriage as % of all British births

1900 10 20 30 40 50 60 70 80 92

...not matched

Lone parents with dependent children as % of all British households

1961 71 81 92

Source: Office of Population Censuses and Surveys

pool. "Crime, drugs, poverty, unemployment, social exclusion, segregation . . . People are beginning to raise the spectre of the ghetto in the [American] sense."

Many of Europe's young adults may never work, or work only occasionally, and are going to pass their frustration and isolation on to their children. Even when Europe's economies are doing as well as most were in the late 1980s, they have ceased to create the kinds of jobs needed to absorb the long-term unemployed. "Roughly, until the 1970s, the expansion of the economy translated into improvements at the bottom of the class structure," says Loïc Wacquant, a scholar at the Russell Sage Foundation, a New York think-tank, who has compared urban poverty in the United States and Europe. "Now when the economy goes into a downward spiral, neighbourhoods of exclusion get worse. But when it goes into an upward progression, they don't join in."

A system stalled

An absence of work promotes a growth in dependency among those who lose the energy to keep plugging away for an opening or for a chance to upgrade their skills. But there is, too, a kind of considered, calculated dependency practised by those who devote their energies to "working the system" as an end in itself. When four Dutch sociologists interviewed hundreds of people in three Dutch cities, they found that about 55% of the long-term unemployed in their sample had stopped looking for work[†]. More than half of this group had quit because they had found "other activities to give meaning to their lives: hobbies, volun-

---

[†] "Cultures of Unemployment: A Comparative Look at Long-Term Unemployment and Urban Poverty". By Godfried Engbersen, Kees Schuyt, Jaap Timmer and Frans Van Waarden, foreword by William Julius Wilson. Westview Press, Boulder, Colorado, and Oxford, England, 1993

tary work, studying, or working in the informal economy." Such findings seem to bear out the contention of an American sociologist, Charles Murray, that some people will, given the chance, make a rational economic choice to live on social welfare. The Dutch researchers concluded that Holland, with its generous, multifarious benefits, had produced "a group of enterprising and calculating unemployed people . . . the strategically operating welfare client." Across Europe, this kind of willful semi-poverty can be seen evolving into something entrenched, even socially acceptable. The mayor of Roubaix in northern France, for example, has complained publicly that too many residents prefer to collect their basic welfare payments rather than to seek work.

Such is the perverse destiny of a European model of a welfare state, devised in the expectation of universal full-time employment for men. The idea was that lots of people would pay into the system and far fewer would take money out of it. Most benefits would be administered through the payroll. But the balance has swung far away from those early expectations. The number of people receiving benefits has kept growing, while the proportion of people in work in European Union countries has been falling since 1960. The European Commission, in a report published last year, estimated Europe's needy at 52m poor, 17m unemployed, 3m homeless. Holland has only four full-time workers for every three people on full-time benefits. In western Germany, the number of recipients of social benefits doubled in the 1980s. "The worst scenario is people not feeling responsible for each other," says Radboud Engbersen, a social worker who lives in one of Rotterdam's poorer areas. "And yes, this is happening."

Yet, for all the evidence accumulating around them, many of Europe's academics

and politicians have still to drop the presumption that poverty and unemployment can best be addressed by, in effect, subsidising the poor and unemployed. The French prime minister, Edouard Balladur, gave a warning earlier this year of the risks of "social explosion" if France's 1.4m hard-core poor stayed that way. But the French poverty debate centres on purported solutions such as work-sharing, guaranteed incomes, liberation from employment and enhanced social benefits: ideas that are at best illusory, at worst dangerous. Europe cannot afford to spend any more than it does on welfare and other social programmes. In many instances, it cannot afford what it is spending already. In headier days Frankfurt spent 11% of its budget on culture; now it is DM8.5 billion ($5.4 billion) in debt and fighting off bankruptcy.

If Europe is to reverse the drift towards an underclass of American finality, the answer must lie in creating more jobs rather than in helping people to get by without them. Unfortunately, job-creation is something for which Europe seems to have lost the knack. The public sector, provider of millions of jobs over the past 30 years, is stretched to the limit; and the private sector seems incapable of filling the gap. As the European Commission's 1994 white paper on employment acknowledged, European industrial policy has concentrated "too much on the rents and positions established in traditional industries."

In effect, Europe has priced much of its labour force out of employment, compensating it with welfare payments. Only a thoroughgoing reversal of that strategy can do much to get Europe's unemployed off the park bench and back into work. Encouraging the kind of dynamic economy in which lots of jobs are created will mean hacking away at policies that have long operated in favour of rigid work rules, high social costs, subsidies and protectionism; and that may mean things getting worse for the poor before they can get better.

For years, Europeans sniffed at America's frisky but cruel economy. The New World opted for high risk and high reward, and left its losers to be pushed far from the economic and social mainstream. The Old World favoured a stabler, more secure economic order in which the losers would be looked after. Seen in those terms, the trade-off was a defensible one. But the terms were not what they seemed. As even prosperous cities like Hamburg, Rotterdam and Paris can testify, the European model has proved insecure and unsustainable. In Europe, too, there are millions in danger of slipping beyond the point of no return.

Inequalities in Europe: Affirmative Laissez Faire

Richard W. Stevenson

LONDON, Nov. 25 – As a Nigerian-born chef working in Britain, Richard Olufeko has encountered plenty of workplace discrimination, including being demoted and then dismissed two years ago from a London restaurant in what a Government equal-opportunity board later ruled was an act of blatant racism.

But when it comes to redressing discrimination, Mr. Olufeko is wary of American-style affirmative action plans, where jobs can be seen to go to people because of their race or sex. Although he has some reservations, he broadly supports Britain's system, which outlaws employment discrimination generally, but bars the use of quotas or any preference programs to help end bias in hiring and promotion.

"It's important to have a certain number of black people in a workplace to provide representation and encouragement," Mr. Olufeko said. "But we have to be careful here. When you try to force people to do something, it often backfires."

Affirmative action is not yet as hotly debated in Europe as it is in the United States. But as their populations become more racially and ethnically diverse, and as women demand greater economic opportunities, many European countries are being forced to deal more directly with employment discrimination.

And while they are still grappling with how to address the issue, there is a growing consensus among governments, employers, unions and groups representing minorities and women that the American model of aggressive affirmative action creates more problems than it solves.

The European approach, which has generally involved governments' financing training programs, encouraging employers to step up recruitment and taking legal action in discrimination cases, has yielded some successes. The successes have come mostly in increasing the proportion of women hired by national and local governments. But progress in changing employment patterns in corporate Europe has been much slower, and little effort has been directed at increasing minority opportunities in either the public or private sector.

"The mentality is such that if you want to make progress toward equality you have to adopt means that are acceptable to people," said Catherine Comtet-Simpson, a lawyer with the International Labor Organization in Geneva. "If you engage in discrimination to find remedies to discrimination, it would not be accepted. In the U.S. it was accepted, and perhaps it went too far."

People who study employment discrimination say that women in Europe are badly underrepresented outside of traditional female jobs like those of cashier, nurse and teacher, and that the underrepresentation is particularly acute in the upper ranks of big corporations.

Women in Europe are also paid substantially less on the average than men for the same work. The International Labor Organization said the disparity ranges from 20 percent to 50 percent depending on job category and country. In France the average differential is 30 percent, the group said.

About 85 percent of the 53,000 employees of Marks & Spencer, the British retailer, are women. But none of the company's top 17 executives and only two of its 32 divisional directors are women. The company said the proportion of women in its senior executive ranks is increasing.

In Britain, men and women from racial and ethnic minorities are twice as likely as white people to be unemployed, although officials said job discrimination is just one reason for the disparity. In London, where members of minority groups constitute roughly 20 percent of the population, the Metropolitan Police force is 97.3 percent white, although the department said applications from nonwhites are increasing as it steps up recruitment efforts.

Even where Europe does have programs that give preference to women and minorities, they are coming under intense legal scrutiny.

In October the European Court of Justice, which applies the legal directives adopted by the European

Union to cases in the member nations, struck down a program in the German city of Bremen that required municipal agencies to give preference to women over men in job categories where women were underrepresented, assuming the women had at least equal qualifications.

Even the victims of discrimination are reluctant to adopt American policies.

The court held that the program violated a 1976 European Union directive that requires equal treatment for men and women in employment, even though the directive provided for exceptions in cases where a measure was intended to remove existing inequalities.

In its ruling, the court said, "Rules which guarantee women absolute and unconditional priority for appointment or promotion go beyond promoting equal opportunities and overstep the limits of the exception."

Lawyers and government officials said it was still unclear how broad a precedent the ruling set.

But people who study employment discrimination in Europe said the ruling fits into what has become the predominant approach to the issue.

European labor experts said there are many differences between discrimination problems in Europe and those in the United States. For one thing, affirmative action programs in the United States were developed largely in response to longstanding patterns of discrimination against a large black population. In European nations other than Britain, the issue has so far been framed primarily in terms of sex, in part because minority populations are relatively small.

Most European countries have outlawed employment discrimination on the basis of sex, but only Britain has a statute extending equal opportunity to race. Even in Britain, however, employers are not required to monitor the racial composition of their work forces. Most employers believe that asking job applicants or employees their race could be construed as discriminatory.

For the most part, efforts in Europe to bring equal opportunity to private industry center on providing education and training programs to women and minorities to help them compete for jobs. In many countries, government has taken more of an advocacy role when it comes to filling jobs in the public sector, often through programs intended to recruit more women.

In the Netherlands, Ms. Comtet-Simpson said, a government program raised the number of women in certain categories of civil service positions to more than 25 percent in 1994, from about 1.3 percent in 1990, although there was little change in the higher-ranking positions.

The European systems generally allow a job-seeker to bring legal action against employers when he or she feels that a job or promotion has been denied because of discrimination. In the last several years the penalties that can be levied on employers who are found to have discriminated have been increased, giving the laws some financial bite for the first time.

In Germany, a 1980 anti-discrimination law limited financial compensation so strictly that it became known as the stamp law, because the biggest awards available to women barely covered the cost of mailing the necessary documents.

The legislation was changed in 1985 to allow maximum compensation of one month's pay. Last year the limit was increased to three months' pay, said Peter Hanau, director of the Research Institute for Social Law at the University of Cologne.

Even with the increased compensation, relatively few women take legal action because it is so hard to prove discrimination, Mr. Hanau said.

Indeed, even while they shy away from quotas, strict monitoring and other features of American affirmative action programs, Europeans involved in the field acknowledge that their less aggressive and less confrontational approach is working much more slowly.

"The evidence indicates slow progress, but it has to be seen in the context of what is happening overall in society," said Herman Ouseley, the chairman of Britain's Commission for Racial Equality.

"While it is painfully slow and allows discrimination to continue, we are able to move race relations in a more productive way than in the States," he said.

Experts said that in the current climate in Western Europe it would be hard to generate additional support for programs to promote the hiring of more women and minorities—much less to impose job quotas or other preference programs. Unemployment is stubbornly high. And immigration is on the rise in France and Germany, among other countries, bringing growing support for right-wing nationalist political parties.

The return of the Habsburgs

THE railway stations, you soon notice, are invariably yellow. The opera houses are all built by the same pair of architects. In cafés, the day's papers from far and wide hang on the wall with wooden slats up their middle. If you are lucky enough to receive flowers, count them and you are likely to find 11 or 13, not a round dozen. Central Europe has a certain harmony that goes deeper than the dilapidation bequeathed by communist times; deeper even than anguish over what Russia will get up to next. Yet it derives from something that Central Europeans seem curiously reluctant to recognise: theirs are the lands of the old Habsburg empire. Now those Central Europeans stand at the head of a queue of former eastern block nations that want to join the European Union. To be sure, they owe this front place to their own brave efforts at economic renewal. They also owe it to pedigree.

They are the Hungarians, the Czechs, the Slovaks, the Slovenes and, particularly, the Poles, more numerous than the others put together. Grant generous historical licence in the Poles' case. Only a quarter or so of modern Poland was part of the Habsburg monarchy's Austro-Hungarian realm that disappeared from the map in 1918. With that proviso, the Central European nations hold common credentials for entering the EU: they will be not so much joining Western Europe as coming home to it.

Bronislaw Geremek, an early hero of Poland's Solidarity movement, traces their western roots 1,000 years back—to a time when medieval German kings launched the Holy Roman Empire (headed, in due course, by the Habsburgs) and set about Christianising nearby Slavs by the sword. Those Slavs and the Hungarians went into the Roman Catholic church; Slavs to the east of them landed in the Orthodox church. This is the line between the western traditions of Rome and the eastern traditions of Byzantium.

Today's Central Europeans are very precise about where the boundaries lie. They object to the title "East Europeans", which they bore through the cold war. Eastern Europe, they say, lies to their east. It is Russia, Ukraine, Romania and Bulgaria that look to the Black Sea. The Central Europeans look to the Mediterranean or to northern waters, at a pinch to the Atlantic. Some talk, rather less precisely, of the "vodka line", separating beer and wine drinkers in Central Europe from those who prefer harder stuff further east; or of the "secret police line", separating those who fully dismantled their old security services when communism collapsed in 1990 from those who did rather less.

Through Renaissance, Enlightenment and balance-of-power wars, Central Europeans have undergone the western experience. The administrative and education systems they have today are rooted in Habsburg tradition. That is what still strikes Otto von Habsburg, heir to a vanished realm to which he has given up all claim. Mr von Habsburg, a German member of the European Parliament, instead works hard pressing the Central Europeans' claim to membership of the EU. His family's aura still has some of its glow. He spends a lot of time in Central Europe these days, having been banned under communism, and there is not a taxi driver who will not wave aside his money when he tries to pay his fare.

Joze Mencinger, who was economics minister of Slovenia when it broke free from chaotic Yugoslavia, is convinced that if Central Europe is now in better shape than its neighbours to the east, it is because it was helped through the communist period by whatever remained of Habsburg method, whereas East Europeans were left to their own devices. "That is the sole reason I can find for the difference," Mr Mencinger concludes.

As Central Europe turns west again, it is already beginning to look the part it wants to play. Its great cities, starting with Prague and Budapest, feel western once more. But stop for a moment. The Habsburg spirit was as quarrelsome as it was liberal; and quarrelsomeness is the trait most common to Central Europeans as they elbow their way to their western destination. Instead of co-operating with each other, they compete. Harmony is not helped by mutual distrust left behind by Comecon, the former Soviet trading block. They squabble as they chase exports to the EU to earn hard currency, and as they compete for foreign investment.

The Czech Republic, top of the economic class, can hardly resist showing off. Unlike its rivals, it has so far made a point of not formally requesting membership of the EU (a conceit it plans to drop before the year is out). It irritates its neighbours by frequently pointing out that its capital, Prague, lies west of Vienna. Hungary, the best performer in the years immediately following the fall of communism, and still the strongest magnet for foreign in-

The countries of Central Europe, unavoidably detained for a while, are clamouring to join the European Union. When they do, it will be a homecoming, says David Lawday

vestors, wants the EU to admit candidates on individual merits, not as a group. Quirky Slovakia, anxious to assert its identity, annoys the Czech Republic by reinterpreting customs agreements they made when separating in 1993. Little Slovenia, having divorced itself from its erratic Balkan neighbours, is now involved in a spat with Italy going straight back to Habsburg times. Giant Poland, facing one of the largest tasks of economic renewal, thinks all the applicants should enter Europe at the same time. Yet the co-operation it favours seems to go no further than freer trade among Central Europeans. Since their mutual trade is dwarfed by their vastly increased trade with Europe, that adds up to very little.

All individualists now

Central Europeans simply do not want to be regarded as a block any more. They have quietly dropped the name "Visegrad group", the title that stuck to four of them after their leaders got together in 1991 in Visegrad, Hungary, to consider life after communism. Membership of Comecon and of the Warsaw Pact, its military counterpart, has made them sick of working in political harness. Besides, they now fear that if they were to show up in Brussels as a political team, Europe might tell them that they had no pressing need to join the union. So they will not publicly admit to aiming for simultaneous entry (although privately they will admit that this is the likely outcome).

Helmut Kohl, the German chancellor, has promised Poland that it will be in the EU—and, for

Austro-Hungarian empire in 1914
00.0 Population, million, 1993
0 Km 200
Source: World Bank

Imperial handful

THE man who gave the Habsburg empire its identity in its later stages was Emperor Franz Joseph, who reigned from 1848 to 1916. Patriarchal yet liberal, this monarch managed to retain the affections of Central Europeans beyond the grave and to this day. He did not live to see his empire expire, predeceasing it by a couple of years. At the time it all came to an end in 1918, his successor, Charles I, bore the following string of titles:

"Emperor of Austria and King of Hungary; King of Bohemia, Dalmatia, Croatia, Slavonia, Galicia, Lodomeria and Illyria; King of Jerusalem, Grand Duke of Tuscany and Cracow; Duke of Lorraine, of Salzburg, Steyr, Carinthia, Krain and Bukovina; Grand Prince of Siebenbürgen; Margrave of Moravia; Duke of Upper and Lower Silesia, of Modena, Parma, Piacenza, of Auschwitz and Zator, of Friuli, Ragusa and Zara; Count of Habsburg and Tyrol, of Kyburg, Gorizia and Gradisca; Prince of Trento and Bressanone; Margrave of Upper and Lower Lusatia, and of Istria; Count of Bregenz; Lord of Trieste; Grand Voivod of the Voivodinate of Serbia etc, etc."

(from "Requiem Pour Un Empire Defunt", by François Fejto)

that matter, NATO too—before the decade is out. Mr Kohl has strong German reasons for promoting Polish membership, but he would not expose himself to charges of favouritism by backing Poland alone. His promise can be taken to extend to Central Europe as a whole. Just bluster? After all, no westerner would seriously propose extending the EU eastwards purely for economic benefit. With almost 70m people, ex-communist Central Europe is an inviting new market, but a poor one: living standards are a third of the EU's average.

Granted, no one who has recently been to lively Budapest would give credence to statistics suggesting that life in Hungary is five times humbler than life in Austria, a boat ride up the Danube. But the statistics cannot be ignored. Central Europe is strapped for cash; few of the various, sometimes ingenious, schemes used to privatise its economies have been accomplished with real money. And bureaucratic torpor, a chronic ailment left over from communist times, contrives to put off would-be investors. As in Russia, from which most of Central Europe is desperate to dissociate itself, red tape puts a brake on almost everything.

Count to three

Bringing Central Europe into the EU is essentially a political decision. Put aside miserly debate about the cost; consider the political imperatives. The European club requires members to meet three basic conditions: they must be European; they must be market-oriented; and they must be democratic. Thanks to geography, the new Central Europe has always met the first condition; it now meets the second; and, for the moment, its problems with the third are confined to a few areas of doubt. On the other hand the region is congenitally jittery, and during this century in particular its genius has been spent on sheer survival. The last thing the EU needs is an unhinged neighbour at its side. The stability and peace of mind which Central Europe hopes to secure by re-joining Western Europe surely promises as much benefit to those opening the door as to those coming through it.

There are those in Brussels who claim that all the countries formerly under Soviet sway in Europe are in the same boat; and certainly the EU has no business discouraging easterners or indulging in favouritism. But enlargement to the east has to start somewhere, and to maintain that there are no differences is hypocritical. The Baltic states, for all the economic progress they have made, still carry heavy baggage from their spell within the Soviet Union, including large Russian minorities. Romania and Bulgaria remain economically backward, as does Ukraine. Their time may come, but this survey will argue that for now the EU should concentrate on admitting the five states of Central Europe. They have a coherence which qualifies them for speedy integration. Since the decision to let them in is essentially political, not economic, there is no merit in delay: they should be in by the end of the decade.

The growing temptation in Brussels to seek an accountant's solution and send them off with partial membership at the lowest possible cost should be resisted. The Central Europeans will put up with all manner of transitional arrangements as long as it does not water down membership to the point where they feel it is no longer the real thing. Their simultaneous quest for membership of NATO, this survey will also argue, stands to create deeper insecurity even than the kind they suffer from now. Their priority must be integration with Western Europe to provide them with a better way of life and higher living standards. Membership of the EU is the basis of the kind of society they are already turning into.

Rich man, poor men

THE shadow over Central Europe is not only Russia's. Germany casts a bigger one, and for once the region is happy to see it there. Austria, the Habsburg power of old, is curiously shy about championing its kin, perhaps because it is small and itself new to the European Union. The role of sponsor falls to Germany; or rather, it is assumed by Germany as a duty. However, since worries about German domination are never far from the surface in this region, Germany tactfully refers to itself as the Central Europeans' "tutor" or "advocate". In the same vein, Germans refrain from talking about *Mitteleuropa*, a handy term but one fraught with history. It harks back to a time when the German Reich made precious little distinction between its economic and its military ambitions there. It is better for Germany not to overplay its new hand. After all, everyone knows that Berlin, its reinstated capital, is part of what one might call greater Central Europe—of which Berlin will in all probability emerge as the metropolis.

There are limits to Germany's leverage today. It still has its own eastern half to lick into capitalist shape. The former East Germany, which under communism was regarded as the most affluent in Eastern Europe, continues to have DM200 billion ($140 billion) a year of west German taxpayers' money poured into it—four times the likely annual cost to the EU of extending membership to the Central Europeans.

Clearly the new Germany has no spare cash to lavish on its eastern neighbours; nor would it ever contemplate providing support for them on anywhere near the scale it has done for eastern Germany. Just think: it has installed more new telephones in the east in three years than were plugged in there in the century from the invention of the telephone to the demise of East Germany. No one can stop Central Europeans dreaming that EU membership will bring them living standards like Germany's and Austria's. If ownership of consumer durables and cars is any guide, some of them are already better off than the poorest EU countries. But if they want to do better still, the help they must count on, Germany tells them, is the help they can give themselves.

Yet Germany is genuinely concerned about Poland and the others, and for good reasons. Integration of the Central Europeans meets a dual need: for stability on Germany's eastern border, and for new business opportunities. These two things matter to the whole of Europe, but to Germany more than others. Chancellor Kohl is not comfortable with the idea that Germany's eastern frontiers are also the EU's eastern frontiers. The government in Bonn shrinks from talking about a buffer, but that is what Poland-in-the-EU will be for Germany.

There may, however, be more to it than that. Poles think that Mr Kohl's willingness to bat for them reflects a deep desire to atone for the Nazi period. Germany made a point of asking for Polish "forgiveness", and got it. An agreement to fix the Oder-Neisse line as the immutable boundary between the two countries, belatedly signed in 1991, allayed the distrust between the two countries. The Poles are convinced that a united Europe has changed Germany for the better. The Czechs, who have an even longer border with Germany than does Poland, are of the same mind. To them, belonging to the same club as Germany is the best safeguard against German domination.

Germany's role as sponsor for Central Europe also arises naturally from its economic magnetism. This part of the world used to do the bulk of its trade with the communist east. In the space of five years

All Central European roads lead to Germany

How the West was won — Trade figures as % of total, 1994 — **1**

Source: IMF

the flow has been dramatically redirected. Well over half the region's trade is now done with Western Europe, and invariably Germany is the leading partner. Russia often comes lowish on the list, although it remains an important provider of energy. In foreign investment, too, it is most often the Germans who lead, with America and Italy in pursuit. Central European hotels can count on German businessmen to keep up their occupancy rate. At least informally, the D-mark zone has already expanded to embrace Central Europe. From Poland to Slovenia, ask anyone what their car is worth, and the answer is likely to come in D-marks.

It may seem odd, then, that the Poles, in particular, are not opening their arms wider towards German investors. At heart they fret that, as they privatise, German capital might buy them out. German industry complains about resistance to German buyers. Not so, says the government in Warsaw: it must be red tape regrettably holding things up. "It is the same for Americans and Japanese," says Andrzej Wroblewski, editor of *Nowa Europe*, a Warsaw business newspaper, "except that there may be some patriotic Polish bureaucrats who apply more red tape to Germans than to others."

Yet at the same time Poland bemoans a disappointingly slow rate of foreign investment. In Warsaw you will be told that the $4 billion or so of foreign capital invested in Poland since it turned democratic is roughly what the Germans are spending on doing up a single street in east Berlin, Friedrichstrasse. Hungary and the Czech Republic have indeed proved more attractive to German capital than Poland, mainly because they have been politically more stable.

Enduring memories

One relic from the past that complicates Germany's role as Central Europe's sponsor is the issue of stranded and expelled Germans: the Silesians left in Poland when that country was awarded a chunk of Hitler's Reich at the end of the second world war,

and those pushed out of the Sudetenland when the Czechs regained sovereignty after the war. Hungary, Slovakia and Slovenia have no borders with Germany, so mercifully they have no such problems. But even though the German government would prefer to leave well alone, sensitivities in the other two countries remain acute. In Poland, President Lech Walesa and the government are doubtful about the loyalty of more than 500,000 Poles of German extraction to whom Bonn, bound by Germany's federal constitution, will award German nationality on request. These folk live mainly in Upper Silesia near Poland's border with the Czech Republic. The idea of their having access to dual nationality does not go down well in Warsaw, despite the large sums in educational and social support that Germany pays to encourage Silesian Germans to stay in Poland.

The Sudeten Germans pose an even more difficult dilemma. At the end of the second world war an estimated 2.5m ethnic Germans were expelled from Czech lands. Most of them went to Bavaria, where they and their descendants continue to make loud claims on their former property. They are a pillar of support for Bavaria's ruling conservative party, which in turn is a pillar of Mr Kohl's government, which finds itself in a fix: it cannot ignore the Sudeten Germans, but nor can it seriously demand restitution from the Czechs. The Bonn government now hopes that early EU entry for Central Europe, with the freedom of movement that will eventually bring for its people, might just sort out both the Sudeten Germans and the Silesians.

Despite these problems, and despite Germany's (and everyone else's) reservations about Slovakia's fitness to enter the EU under its unpredictable prime minister, Vladimir Meciar, it is hard to avoid the impression that Germany has never enjoyed quite such good relations with all its neighbours—to east and west, to north and south—at the same time. If ever there was a time to hope that Germany will champion Europe's underdogs in a manner all Europeans can support, this is it.

A wobbly giant

Needs reassurance

A POOR neighbour is an expensive neighbour. That summarises Germany's view of Poland. Because Poland is big—a nation the size of Spain with close to 40m people that sits heavily atop Central Europe—the EU's enlargement to the east has to start with resurrecting Poland. The thing to remember about today's Poland (and Poles will not let you forget it) is that it has changed the world.

Back in 1980, when Soviet communism still stood on two legs, it was the Poles who started the workers' strikes and unrest that led to its collapse a decade later. Unfortunately, communism also took Poland to the edge of economic collapse. By the time its Central European neighbours had caught on to the revolution, Poland seemed done for.

Its answer was a painful course of shock therapy consisting chiefly of price liberalisation and privatisation. Helped by the Poles' strong entrepre-

neurial streak, this started to get the country back on its feet by 1992. Now Poland's economy is the healthiest in Central Europe, with 5% growth expected both this year and next. Already around 60% of gross national product comes from the private sector. Deutsche Bank, a level-headed German giant not known for its flights of fancy, has been moved to compare Poland with the Asian "tiger" economies. Inflation has come down by leaps and bounds, though at 20-30% it remains high. Unemployment too is falling after a sharp climb that went with the shock therapy. At about 12%, it is now roughly the same as in France and a great deal lower than in Spain.

But start looking west, and there is no hiding the fundamental imbalance. Polish living standards are less than a third of the West European average—and probably only a quarter of Germany's, even allowing for a thriving Polish black economy. An uncommonly large and poor agricultural population keeps Poland down. One-third of Poles make their living on the land, farming absurdly small patches.

In industry, too, dinosaurs abound in sectors such as steel, coal and shipbuilding which the state either cannot get off its hands or is reluctant to let go. Except for a short ribbon leading to Cracow in the south (the old Habsburg region), not a road in Poland comes close to western motorway standards. The main east-west highway linking Warsaw with Berlin and Moscow is a lethal two-way test of valour and brinkmanship. So although Poland is pressing ahead with the huge task of bringing its legislation into line with Europe's, it envisages a long period of transition to ease EU membership.

Here today, gone tomorrow

German investors might feel happier about the new Poland's stability if its governments lasted longer. Since 1990, they have changed every year. Ironically, now that former communists are back in control, the Polish government has acquired a more solid look that bodes well for continued reform. Josef Oleksy, the prime minister who took up the reins in March, is a skilful politician who, notwithstanding his communist credentials, firmly believes in modernisation along western lines. Lech Walesa, a somewhat tarnished hero these days, has been president from the start, underpinning reform but not stability.

There is, to put it mildly, minor cause for concern about democratic methods at the top in Poland. This has two sources, both of which touch Mr Walesa. The country is still operating under the so-called "small constitution", adapted from the communist model. This leaves presidential powers fairly loose, so power is to some extent up for grabs. Mr Walesa makes skilful use of the grey areas to get his own way. His glee at vetoing has increased since post-communists returned to government, since he owes what popularity he retains to his reputation as a communist-fighter. A definitive constitution is on its way, but the blockage between president and parliament could cause trouble with that too.

The other problem is the army. Army generals who in effect ran Poland for a time up to 1990 have been reluctant to submit to civilian control. Successive defence ministers might have had more success in asserting civilian authority had President Walesa sided with them instead of with the army, an institution he has wooed assiduously to underpin his personal authority.

Mr Walesa's co-warriors from the old Solidarity movement have deserted him. Many have also left Solidarity for the liberal Freedom Union, the main anti-left opposition party. Mr Walesa has no party behind him. Unfulfilled promises and the back-biting in his relations with parliament seemed, earlier this year, to have lost him favour with Poles, who see him as obstructive. Mr Walesa's place in Polish history is assured; his future as president less so. In a feverish presidential election now at its climax, the leader after a first round of voting on November 5th was Aleksander Kwasniewski, a moderate ex-communist with a lively campaign style. But liberals, devoted Catholics and others who had hoped to knock Mr Walesa out of second place, and so out of the second round, were disappointed. The communist-fighter did better than expected and looks, surprisingly, well-placed to emerge as winner from the run-off on November 19th.

Existential doubts

If one thing runs deeper in Poland than entrepreneurial drive, it is insecurity. Between 1772 and 1918, there was no state of Poland: it was split up between the Russian, Prussian and Habsburg empires. This has left the Poles with an identity problem that other Central Europeans do not share. With half their country having been run by Russia for so long, they ask themselves whether they are really as western as they like to think. They snatch comfort from the rather fanciful notion that the second-largest Polish country in the world is America, which they would happily join if they had the choice. The bulk of the roughly 10m Poles living abroad are in America.

Yet the most striking landmark in Warsaw today is Russian: a monumental piece of Stalin's mind. Stalin's Palace of Culture, a skyscraper office block, defines Warsaw just as the Eiffel Tower defines Paris. A lively Polish debate turns on whether to demolish the giant 1950s "birthday cake". Many consider it a blight on westward-looking Poland. An alternative to demolition might be to build around it (when there is money available) so that it does not stand out so much. But as Soviet memories fade, this neo-baroque whopper could well mellow, like the Eiffel Tower, into a well-loved tourist attraction.

Becoming resigned to Stalin's gift is not becoming resigned to insecurity. These days, that derives exclusively from fear of Russia, driven by Polish emotion rather than by Russian threat. It makes Poland desperately keen to join NATO as well as the EU. Indeed, Poles often see NATO as the better bet. For although fear of Russia is the root cause of their insecurity, practical fears over Europe ensue. Might southern Europe block their entry into the EU? Will the EU limit them to second-class membership? Will they be condemned to being half-Europeans? Such fears are commonplace in Warsaw. They are fears that only the EU can resolve. . . .

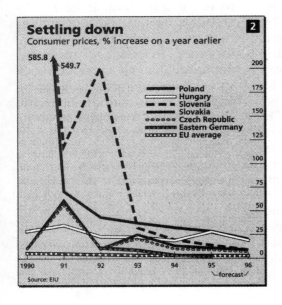

Settling down   **2**
Consumer prices, % increase on a year earlier

585.8
549.7

Poland
Hungary
Slovenia
Slovakia
Czech Republic
Eastern Germany
EU average

200
175
150
125
100
75
50
25
0

1990   91   92   93   94   95   96
forecast
Source: EIU

Witness to the Fall

George F. Kennan

Review of **Autopsy on an Empire: The American Ambassador's Account of the Collapse of the Soviet Union,** Jack F. Matlock, Jr. (Random House, 1995)

"Blest is the man who has visited
This world
in its fateful moments ..."
—F. I. Tyutchev (1803–1873)

Reviewing the history of international affairs in the modern era, which might be considered to extend from the middle of the seventeenth century to the present, I find it hard to think of any event more strange and startling, and at first glance more inexplicable, than the sudden and total disintegration and disappearance from the internal scene, primarily in the years 1987 through 1991, of the great power known successively as the Russian Empire and then the Soviet Union. History has recorded the decline and final collapse of a number of great empires of the past, and there has been no small number of scholarly and literary efforts to describe the circumstances and analyze the causes of these great developments. But in all these earlier instances the declines had been gradual, and the final collapses consisted normally only of prolonged and dismal trailings off of vitality into the realms of historical insignificance and ultimate oblivion. How then to explain the extreme abruptness, the sharp quick ending, and not least the rela-

tive bloodlessness with which the great Soviet Empire came to an end in the four years in question, bearing with it those attributes of the earlier Russian Empire which it had contrived to incorporate into itself?

These were the questions that preoccupied the author of *Autopsy on an Empire* as he looked back on his service as American ambassador in Russia from 1987 to 1991; and the book offers and explains the best answers he can give to them in retrospect. It did not, the author explains, fall within his intentions, as he undertook this task, to write a definitive history of the Soviet collapse. His focus was to be on those events that were germane to these fundamental questions. He tried to avoid involvement with matters that did not answer to that description. His task was plainly complicated by the fact that he was not only an observer of the course of events he describes but was from time to time actively and not insignificantly involved in them. Such involvement is normally not the best of recommendations for what might be called a book of political observation; but it must be said, to the author's credit, that he firmly resisted the temptation to be carried off into autobiography, and brought his own experiences into the picture only when they were indeed relevant to the inquiry at hand.

It is hard to think of anyone who would or could have been better prepared to conduct this inquiry than Jack Matlock. In his youth, he

plunged extensively into Russian studies as an undergraduate at Duke University and as a student at Columbia's Russian Institute. He then taught for a time at Dartmouth in the field of Russian history and culture. After entering the American Foreign Service, he had, among other assignments, served three times at the Moscow embassy in more junior (but not *very* junior) capacities before entering on his fourth and final tour of duty there as ambassador. He thus brought to his ambassadorial duties the advantages of extensive academic training, including a wide familiarity with Russian history and culture, an impressive fluency in the Russian language, and a thorough training in the situation and problems of the particular diplomatic mission he was now to head. And all these qualities found reflection in the book at hand.

This is, let it be said at once, a serious and in many respects masterful work, well-written, interesting throughout, unique in both concept and execution, and of high historical importance. As already noted, it could not, and does not, purport to be a definitive history of the Soviet collapse; the author specifically disclaims any such ambition. But it *is* unique as an answer to the problems it confronts. It will be a long time before it is overtaken by the more detached and specifically historical scholarly studies that must eventually follow. For the present the book may stand, therefore, for what it is:

a running and very useful account of the events of the decisive four-year period (1987–1991), as seen and commented upon by one who was not only uniquely prepared but also uniquely positioned for the task of understanding and judging them.

The body of the work leads the reader through the major developments of the period just mentioned, recording his reactions of the moment, and recounting, wherever justified, the circumstances of his involvement. Wider and more retrospective conclusions are reserved for the final chapter; but the narrative account—most of the book—is always enlivened by the author's immediate observations and reactions, sometimes as recorded in his personal diaries of the time.

The book concentrates strictly on the political aspects of the passing scene. The author was, of course, fully aware of what was happening in the economic and social realms: of the rapidly developing economic distress, of the nature and fate of the various reform programs, of the problems of inflation, corruption, and economic crime. He occasionally reminds the reader of this significant and essential background of the political life of the time. But he evidently considered that enough had been written, and was continuing to be written, on these subjects by other people, whereas the political aspect of the developing scene, particularly in its relation to the pending dissolution and disappearance of the Soviet Union, has lacked the sort of sustained portrayal and analysis that he was in a position to give it.

The period of Matlock's service as ambassador in Moscow, between 1987 and 1991, was very nearly coterminous with the ascendancy of Mikhail Sergeyevich Gorbachev, first in the Party and then in the government of the Soviet Union. When, in the first months of Matlock's service, Gorbachev began to make statements that pointed in the direction of a greater liberality in party and government, Matlock was initially skeptical. He recalled instances in both tsarist and Soviet history when statesmen (one of them, Khrushchev) who had started off with liberal impulses were eventually taken in hand by the reactionaries and forced to shift over to the hard line. But when it became evident, by the middle of 1987, that Gorbachev was not only serious in his liberal intentions but was consolidating his leadership and demonstrating the ability to carry the regime with him on a liberal course, things changed; Matlock was obliged to recognize that what his own government was now confronted with on the Soviet side was something new and highly interesting, with important implications not just for the nature of Soviet power but also for the improvement of Soviet-American relations. From that time on, until the dramatic events of 1991, Matlocks' hopes, and those of official Washington, centered on the person of Gorbachev, and were predicated on the success of the leadership he was assuming.

There were good reasons, rare to the point of uniqueness, for these hopes and expectations. Not only was Gorbachev continuing, as mentioned above, to master both Party and government, but he was steadily gaining the respect and confidence of other Western governments. He knew how to conduct himself in the international arena. He was well-educated, urbane, intelligent, and persuasive. He recognized the need for compromise in international problems. He was once said to have said that the other fellow's interests deserved your respect and were, in a sense, your own. He was, above all, sincere in the pursuit of the views he had put forward.

But with the advent of the 1990s it began to become evident that these positive qualities of Gorbachev were being disconcertingly overbalanced by negative ones. Some of these latter were personal. Matlock describes them very well in his book. Gorbachev, he says, was a very "private" person. He seemed to have no real friends—none, at least, in his Russian entourage. This meant in effect that he would never find himself surrounded by a circle of people upon whose loyalty he could depend and from whose advise he could profit. He was in general a bad listener, at least to Russians.[1] He preferred to lecture others on his own views rather than to inquire about theirs. He resented criticism, even when it was put forward with the utmost good will. He surrounded himself with second- and third-rate people, and not unsurprisingly found difficulty in keeping them in the positions they came to occupy. (Matlock might, I think, have added a reference to Gorbachev's habit of announcing decisions but failing to follow up on their execution.)

And the deficiencies, as Matlock saw them, were not only personal; they carried into the realms of political habit and choice, where Matlock found them increasingly disturbing. He deplored the swing to the right in Gorbachev's political behavior that began in 1990. He deplored the frequent vacillation between reform and reaction—between the liberals and the hardliners—and the obvious effort to appease the latter. Particularly disturbing in Matlocks' eyes was Gorbachev's uncertain and evasive conduct in relation to the unsuccessful attempt of Soviet military units to crack down on Lithuania by force of arms in January 1991. Increasingly, Matlock was obliged to recognize that Gorbachev was pursuing what were really self-defeating policies—policies that were bound to play into the hands of the unreconstructed right-wing extremists who were still clinging to powerful posi-

---

[1]Matlock quotes a senior Soviet official as saying to him about Gorbachev on one occasion: "He is closer to President Bush, Secretary Baker, and you than he is to any of us. You can have a franker conversation with him than we can. He really has no close friends here."

tions in certain parts of the governmental establishment. He feared, and again with good reason, that these elements would try first to use Gorbachev for their own purposes, with a view to eventually overthrowing and replacing him with one of their own number when they had got what they wanted out of him.

On one occasion in January 1991, when transmitting personally to Gorbachev a private message from President Bush warning that the use of violence against Lithuania and the other Baltic countries would be bound to damage Soviet-American relations, Matlock ventured to reinforce the President's warning by offering a few observations of his own about the difficulty he was having in understanding the direction Gorbachev's policies were taking. He did this with some trepidation, fearing that it would evoke only one of those explosions of anger of which Gorbachev was capable when some of his Russian associates tried to give him similar warnings. To Matlock's surprise Gorbachev, instead of blowing up, "thanked me for my candor" and replied seriously and quietly to the various reproaches involved. "Try to help your president understand," he said, "that we are on the brink of a civil war. As president, my main task is to prevent it." He might, he said, feel obliged to do things at times that would be hard for others to understand. ("We suffer from a low political culture," Matlock quotes him as saying.) He went on to defend his hard-line policy toward Lithuania. He described the difficulty he had in dealing with Yeltsin, who (in Matlock's words) "would make agreements, then renege, and he often promised more than he could deliver."

Matlock accepted the logic of these observations but his anxieties were not greatly assuaged. He felt that there were more dangers than Gorbachev seemed to realize in any attempt to collaborate with the hardliners in question.

In all of this, Matlock's fears were indeed vindicated by the further course of events. But after recounting these deficiencies in Gorbachev's statesmanship, he makes up for it with some very fine and thoughtful comments on the more positive sides of Gorbachev's career.

. . . Gorbachev's initiatives in 1988, 1989, and early 1990 made it possible for independent political forces to undermine and eventually destroy the Communist Party's monopoly on political power. His support for political openness and democratic changes was not always unqualified and was at times self-serving, but the fact remains that no fundamental change would have been possible as long as the Communist Party's grip on power remained. Unlike most of his colleagues in the Politburo, from 1988 Gorbachev usually backed democratic change rather than the Communist Party's narrow interests. When he failed to do so, it was to avoid being swept from power before he could implement his programs.

His judgment, of course, was not always above reproach, and many of his errors . . . were probably avoidable. But the fact remains that, despite his temporary alliance with the enemies of reform in the winter of 1990–1991, *he consistently refused to authorize the use of force to keep himself in power.* He was, in fact, the first Russian leader in history who used force not as a first but a last resort. As he pointed out in his Munich speech, all his predecessors who had come to power with visions of reform had abandoned the effort when they perceived threats to their own position. Gorbachev could have declared presidential rule at any one of several points in 1990 or 1991 and rallied the repressive forces in Soviet society to his side, but even though he may have come perilously close to doing so at times, in the end he refused to crush the embryonic democratic institutions and practices. For that service and for that precedent, Russia owes him a homage he has yet to receive. . . .

I am convinced that Russia will eventually regard Mikhail Gorbachev as the person who led it out of bondage. The fact that he

was unable to reach the Promised Land is secondary.

Nowhere did the negative features of Gorbachev's personality come more strikingly and unfortunately to the fore than in his relations with Yeltsin. The conflict between these two men is a unifying thread through the entirety of the book. It was not, of course, the sole reason for Gorbachev's ultimate failure. But it was a central, and perhaps the leading factor, in Matlocks' view. "The only real hope," he wrote, "that the Soviet Union could transform itself peacefully (or relatively peacefully) into a democratic state was that, before it was too late, Gorbachev and Yeltsin would realize they must cooperate." That they love each other was, of course, not to be expected. These were two very different men. They had come to prominence in different ways. Yeltsin would never have been a comfortable bedfellow for anyone in Russian politics. But politics (probably fortunately) does not require close personal friendship for useful collaboration.

And for the fact that they failed to collaborate Matlock puts the primary blame on Gorbachev. His behavior toward Yeltsin had not only been marked from the start by a bitter vindictiveness but was, as with other aspects of that behavior, ultimately self-defeating. Yeltsin, too, was of course not without blame for the unhappy relationship. His actions were uniformly designed, Matlock says, "to show Gorbachev in the worst possible light." Yeltsin knew "what psychological buttons to push to get a rise out of Gorbachev, and he was crafty in his timing." Gorbachev, for his part,

seemed never to grasp the obvious fact that it was his opposition to Yeltsin, more than any other factor, that made Yeltsin popular with the public. . . . But any politician who is misguided enough to humiliate and embitter a potential rival and then adopt tactics that enhance his rival's popularity is unlikely to possess the keen judgment required to lead a country through a difficult crisis.

At times, as the sensitive reader will observe, the Gorbachev–Yeltsin rivalry seemed to contain all the elements of a Shakespearean tragedy: the initial setting, the delineation of character and ambition, the mounting complication and discord, and finally, the open conflict and the tragic denouement. One feels sorry for the leading participants in this drama, but even more so for the innocent onlookers, who were also the victims: the Russian public.

And the issues of the conflict were more than personal. Behind it were differences of outlook and policy that were destined to play a crucial role in the final demise of the Gorbachev regime.

It was evidently the view of Gorbachev and a number of those around him that the restlessness and demands for independence among the non-Russian components of the Soviet empire flowed primarily from longstanding resentment of the harshness of the regime over all the years of Communist dominance. It was easy then to jump from this view to the expectation that the demands for complete independence could be largely disarmed by the liberalization of the Soviet Union generally. In a Soviet Union which understood the problems of these national minorities, it was argued, and which met them halfway in their desire for a greater degree of local autonomy, the idea of a total detachment from membership in the empire would lose its charms, and some sort of permanent *modus vivendi* between center and periphery could then be worked out.

Matlock, with all due sympathy for the feelings of the various nations that had been, as he put it, "trapped within the Soviet empire,"

seems to have shared much of this hope. "A voluntary union of limited powers, with democratic institutions and the checks and balances essential to an effective democracy, could have provided," he thought, "freedom and a framework for more effective economic development." Elaborations of his thinking on this subject in later parts of the work make it clear that what he had in mind at the time was not any modified version of Moscow's central authority over the nations in question, but rather a federative or confederative arrangement of some sort, giving the respective peoples the advantages of extensive domestic autonomy without breaking entirely the traditional tie to the Moscow center. ("Union" is the word used to denote such a solution throughout most of the book.)

But it soon became apparent, preferable as this alternative might have been, that the Baltic peoples and the leaders of the movement for an independent Ukraine were having none of it. Such was their resolve, their courage, and their persistence that by the middle of the 1990s their respective demands for total independence has been conceded by Moscow; and it was clear that there could thereafter be no turning back on this concession.

The recognition that this was so split opinions in the entourage of Gorbachev. Some believed that a rump "union," lacking these territories, would have poor chances of survival. It would be, they thought, too oddly constituted geographically. But Gorbachev clung to the belief that some sort of a federation or confederation would still be possible, and Matlock, if I read him correctly, had some sympathy with these increasingly faint hopes. Yeltsin, on the other hand, seems never to have entertained them. He evidently did not believe that a union of such dimensions could be successfully maintained, and one suspects that he did not greatly care. He had, as the future was to show, per-

sonal as well as more objective reasons for adopting this position.

By the outset of the year 1991 the political situation in Russia was beginning to heat up to dangerous levels. One of Gorbachev's finest and most able partners, Eduard Shevardnadze, had bowed out in the last weeks of 1990, with the intention of removing to his native Georgia. In January 1991 came the Lithuanian crisis. Then, in February, came Yeltsin's demand, put forward over national television, for Gorbachev's retirement from the presidency of the USSR. Although Gorbachev found support for his refusal to accept this demand, the break between him and Yeltsin was now irreparable.

This is not the place to describe the sad events of the remaining months of Gorbachev's political career. They included Yeltsin's brilliant chess move in securing the leadership of the long-moribund but now reviving Russian Republic (in theory only one of the constituent republics of the Soviet Union). They also included the crisis of August 1991, marked by the bizarre effort of a group of highly confused and partially inebriate reactionary personalities to stage a putsch against Gorbachev during his vacation in the Crimea. They ended with the almost incredible sleight of hand by which Yeltsin, at the end of December 1991, succeeded in putting an end to the Soviet Union itself as a member of the world community of sovereign states, and, by the same token, to Gorbachev's official position and (at least for some years) his active participation in political life.

By long prior understanding, Matlock's tour of duty as ambassador in Russia came to an end in August 1991, on the very eve of the putsch against Gorbachev. In completing his account, Matlock naturally covers, with his usual narrative verve, the dramatic final weeks before the denouement, even though he was no longer a close witness to them. They serve as fitting climax to much of the experience the book so richly describes. They complete, in fact, the answer to the question with which the book begins.

Yeltsin appeared only late in the day as a major factor in the events Matlock describes. Matlock knew him, of course, and talked with him on a number of occasions, but the most significant comments about him are reserved for the concluding chapter. Pointing to the differences of opinion among contemporaries about Yeltsin's political record, he goes on to say that Yeltsin and Gorbachev had contrasting personalities.

> Gorbachev was the more thoughtful, the more calculating, Yeltsin the more instinctive and impulsive. Gorbachev's formal education was superior; the country's premier university offered many advantages over the provincial construction institute Yeltsin attended. But both shared the professional experience of long and successful service in the Communist Party apparatus; both had made their names initially as provincial first secretaries.

And even here, Matlock, noted, there was a contrast. Gorbachev's family background was a modest one. He had been lucky to be able to study at Moscow University. His record there both as a student and as a Komsomol leader placed him "on the fast track for Party leadership." Yeltsin, on the other hand,

> ... did not benefit from such an initial advantage: he had to claw his way into the *nomenklatura* by wit and will—and liberal use of his elbows. As a consequence, the two viewed power differently: to Gorbachev it was his due, while to Yeltsin it was something to fight for and win.
>
> And fight he did. But he fought by the rules. His election campaigns and his tactics in parliament, up through his election as president of Russia in June 1991, would be considered normal in any democracy. Of course he attacked his opponents' vulnerabilities, took advantage of their

mistakes, and sometimes made campaign promises that he could not fulfill, but only people still wedded to the idea of a one-party dictatorship would find such practices abnormal.

It was Yeltsin's firm position, Matlock observes, that restrained Gorbachev from making the "tragic and bloody mistake" of authorizing the use of force in the Baltic states. In general, Yeltsin's support for the independence of the Baltic countries "required both political and physical courage, as did his immediate and unequivocal condemnation of the coup attempt in August." And Matlock credits him with preserving the possibility of further democratic development in Russia in the first months of 1991, "when that cause was under mortal threat."

On the other hand, Matlock points out, the way in which Yeltsin carried out his final political triumph undermined respect for the rule of law. In particular, when bringing Russia into the status of a new and independent state, he did so "without an unequivocal mandate from its citizens and with an unworkable constitution." These are of course very serious charges. But the verdict, in his view, is not yet in. Much will depend on the way the country will now develop. If things go well, Matlock thinks, Yeltsin's faults and mistakes will probably be largely forgiven.

> But if the country disintegrates further, drifts into a morass of crime and corruption, and is riven by demagogic appeals to revive the empire, he would be put down as a tragic Tsar Boris II, whose reign of questionable legitimacy brought on the Time of Troubles and of national shame.

There were of course deeper reasons, reaching back over all the decades of Communist power in Russia, for this sudden and miserable ending of the Soviet union. But it is evident that at the heart of the im-

mediate causes of the collapse there lay the inability of the Soviet regime to deal effectively with what was usually called "the national question" meaning the unhappiness of a number of the non-Russian national components of the union, and their demands for greater autonomy or independence.

Neither in his activity as ambassador nor in this composition of his book could Matlock be charged with any neglect of this problem. He had visited most of these outlying national entities. He had met their leaders, listened to their complaints, and taken full note of the many complexities of their respective situations. He did not underestimate the gravity of the problem.

But with all due respect and sometimes even admiration for the attentions he gave to this subject, I found myself wondering whether he fully recognized the intractability of the problem in question. There was from the very start—from Lenin's time—a basic incompatibility between the radical Marxist ideology of the Lenin variety and the demands of the small dependent peoples in Russia, as elsewhere, for self-government and independence in the name of national identity. Lenin was well aware of this incompatibility, but he found it politically expedient to retain within the confines of the Soviet Union those of the peoples in question that had been included in the tsarist empire, conceding to them the outward façades of their national identity while preserving for the Communist Party and the Soviet secret police the real levers of authority, and applying those levers with relentless and crushing severity.

So matters stood, generally speaking, over all the seven decades of Communist rule. But in the meantime, and particularly in the years following the Second world War, this arrangement was being increasingly undermined by developments both in Russia and elsewhere. The unrelenting harshness of Soviet rule was continuing to inflame among the subject peoples they very dissatisfactions it was designed to repress. Developments in the rest of the world—the Wilsonian doctrine of self-determination, the idealization of the nation-state, the disintegration of other great empires under anti-colonial pressures—were now becoming widely known within the Soviet Union, where they were stimulating and hardening the demands in the peripheral nations for separation and independence. And when there then occurred that general relaxation of Moscow's previously oppressive authority which marked the Gorbachev era, the demands for independence broke through with great violence, primarily among the peoples along the western and southwestern borders of the Soviet state; and it soon became evident that there was no stopping them, particularly in the Baltic region and Ukraine, other than by means that would have compromised the great process of change now overtaking the Russian heartland itself.

I would not like to be misunderstood. I have, personally, no enthusiasm for the concept of *one nation–one state* that has now been accepted, in the UN and elsewhere, as the basis for the emerging structure of international society. I have particularly deplored the absence of any formally recognized intermediate stages between total dependence as a national minority within the body of a larger and more powerful state, and an unlimited and often unreal independence as a full-fledged "sovereign" member of the international community. I can therefore have nothing but sympathy for the preference of Gorbachev and Matlock for the creation of just such an intermediate status to govern the relationship between center and periphery in the traditional Russian region. I can well see that in a number of instances (not in all) such a solution might have been preferable, in the interest of both parties,

to the total break that finally took place.

But in the confused interrelationships of the world community what is desirable is not always practicable; and I would suggest that if there was ever a possibility of creating such an intermediate status in the Russian realm, it was by the 1990s probably too late. The old rigidities had been maintained too long and could not now be easily bent. At the beginning of the 1990s neither the center nor the periphery was capable of the quality of statesmanship that would have been required to put forward, and to gain acceptance for, the sort of arrangement, whether of federation or confederation, that both Gorbachev and Matlock, each in his own way, would seem to have thought possible.

At the heart of this problem lay, in particular, the action of the Russian Republic in declaring, or at least dramatically reaffirming (no doubt under Yeltsin's prompting), in the spring of 1991, its own "sovereignty." It was not the first of the constituent Soviet republics to take this step. Some, headed by the Baltic states, had already done so; others were shortly to follow. For some of the others, this was only a pathetic gesture: a hasty self-association with the abuse of the work "sovereignty" that had by that time become a fad for ambitious political leaders of smaller political entities across the globe. But in the case of the Russian Republic, the gesture was far more serious. In the formal sense it ranked the Russian nation with the various other peripheral entities in the former Soviet Union, the status of which was now coming increasingly into question. For the Russian Republic to assume this position was to pose a mortal threat to the Soviet Union itself. For if the Russian national were to go ahead and declare its own full independence, or even if it were to become a member of some sort of a federal or confederal "union" on an equal basis with all the others, what, beyond the name, would be left of the Soviet Union?

It would have become an empty shell, without people, without territory, and with no more than a theoretical identity.

This specter hovered in the background of events over the entire year and a half before the final denouement. It would, I suspect, have thrust itself into the foreground at some point, even if Yeltsin had not deliberately propelled it in that direction. And when it did, it would in any case have posed an insoluble dilemma for everyone. For if Russia could not separate itself from the Soviet Union, neither would it, by 1991, have been able to find any other acceptable relationship to it.

The attention Matlock gave, as a diplomatic observer, to the spectacular dramas of the passing political scene was only the larger part of his activity in this ambassadorial position. Another part, scarcely less a claim on his time and energies, was composed of his responsibilities as the senior representative of the United States government to that of another great country in a very troubled time. One might have thought that his burden might, at least in the Reagan period, have been lighter than that borne by many other ambassadors; for he had served for several years as a member of the National Security Council staff before taking up these duties in Moscow, and in this capacity had been a senior advisor to President Reagan on Russian matters and plainly enjoyed the President's confidence. Although known in the Cold War period as a hard-liner (a charge he did not deny), he had, among other things, taken a prominent part in persuading Mr. Reagan to relax his attitude toward Russia in the final months of his presidency.

But George Bush, upon taking over as president in January 1989, had followed tradition in making a clean sweep of Reagan's advisors (Matlock being a rare exception), thus eliminating from the White House entourage just about everybody who knew or had learned anything about Russia. Matlock was then left to compete for the President's attention with more than a few Washington characters whose understanding of Russian matters was as small as his own was large. The result was that in several instances he was in disagreement with Washington attitudes and decisions, for example, over the forms that American aid to Russia might take, the degree to which Washington should commit its words and actions to the personal support of Gorbachev, and what attitude Washington should take toward Yeltsin while Gorbachev was still in office.

In trying to gain a hearing for his views on these and other issues, Matlock had it borne in upon him (though he probably knew it before) that in considering relations with another country, the last voice listened to in Washington (if listened to at all) by the bureaucracy and political establishment is normally that of the American ambassador on the spot. Had his views prevailed, there is reason to suppose that America's role in the fortunes of the Gorbachev regime would have been a somewhat more useful one, and the view of this country held by large sections of the Russian public would be less bitter, and marked by greater confidence. But Matlock bore this burden with a patience and understanding that few other ambassadors, myself included, would have been able to muster. And for this, too, he has no doubt to be given his fair share of credit.

There is one further aspect of Matlock's diplomatic activity as a representative of his own government and as the central go-between for that government and the Soviet one that must, after all, be mentioned here, for its omission would do Matlock a real disservice. This is the severity of the personal strains that his mission imposed upon him, and the strenuousness of the life that it required. One has to read the entire book in order to understand what these duties meant in interviews, travels, confusions, nocturnal instructions from Washington, contacts with Russian officials and other personalities, and support for prominent visiting American dignitaries. And all of this against the background of the myriad of minor harassments and complications which were inherent in the Russian life of his day and which only someone who had personally experienced them could understand.

That anyone could survive this life, as did Matlock, for an entire tour of duty of some four years' duration is itself a wonder. And this discussion may well be concluded by the observation that if there are still Americans who entertain the fond belief that the profession of diplomacy is somehow an idly luxurious one, they have only to read this book attentively in order to see how far from the truth such assumptions have been.

In the volume under review Matlock's account of his observations of the four-year-period of the disintegration of the Soviet Union is followed by an epilogue of some fifty-six pages addressed to the aftermath, in the period from 1992 to 1994, of the events to which the body of the book is devoted. This is a straightforward account, from a highly competent pen, of the developments of these later years. It is literature of a somewhat different order from the preceding account; and this is scarcely the place to discuss it in detail. Not everyone will be entirely in agreement, nor is this reviewer, with all of the analysis of the contemporary situation with which this epilogue concludes. But the principal two conclusions, concerning the possible future of Russia, deserve respectful attention, for they are the summary expression of a unique body of experience. They are as follows:

1. The Soviet system cannot be rebuilt. The circumstances that made it possible in the first place no longer prevail, and even at its height it was not competitive with free economies. Attempts to revert to the past, which may well occur, will fail and ultimately generate pressures to move ahead.

2. The Russian empire cannot be reassembled, even if the Russian people nurse an emotional attachment for an ill-understood past and are periodically victimized by demagogues. Only a healthy Russian economy could bear the cost, but the economy cannot be cured if Russia embarks on an imperialist course.

Were these judgments to be accepted as the point of departure for further discussion of the situation of Russia as of late 1995, the usefulness of that discussion might be significantly heightened.

A Transition Leading to Tragedy

■ *Russia: The U.S. extols 'reform,' but the former Soviet Union
is in a collapse of everything essential.*

STEPHEN F. COHEN

*Stephen F. Cohen is professor of politics
and Russian studies at Princeton University. His books include* Rethinking the Soviet Experience *(Oxford University Press).*

A terrible national tragedy has been unfolding in Russia in the 1990s, but we will hear little if anything about it in American commentary on this fifth anniversary of the end of the Soviet Union.

Instead, we will be told that Russia's "transition to a free-market economy and democracy" has progressed remarkably, despite some "bumps in the road." Evidence alleged to support that view will include massive privatization, emerging financial markets, low inflation, "stabilization," an impending economic "take-off," last summer's presidential election, a sitting Parliament and a "free press."

Few if any commentators will explain that Russia's new private sector is dominated by former but still intact Soviet monopolies seized by ex-communist officials who have become the core of a semicriminalized business class; that inflation is being held down by holding back salaries owned to tens of millions of needy workers and other employees; that a boom has been promised for years while the economy continues to plunge into a depression greater than America's in the 1930s; that President Boris Yeltsin's reelection campaign was one of the most corrupt in recent European history; that the Parliament has no real powers and the appellate court little independence from the presidency, and that neither Russia's market nor its national television is truly competitive or free but is substantially controlled by the same financial oligarchy whose representatives now sit in the Kremlin as chieftains of the Yeltsin regime.

In human terms, however, that is not the worst of it. For the great majority of families, Russia has not been in "transition" but in an endless collapse of everything essential to a decent existence—from real wages, welfare provisions and health care to birth rates and life expectancy; from industrial and agricultural production to higher education, science and traditional culture; from safety in the streets to prosecution of organized crime and thieving bureaucrats; from the still enormous military forces to the safeguarding of nuclear devices and materials. These are the realities underlying the "reforms" that most U.S. commentators still extol and seem to think are the only desirable kind.

Fragments of Russia's unprecedented, cruel and perilous collapse are reported in the U.S. mainstream media, but not the full dimensions of insider privatization, impoverishment, disintegration of the middle classes, corrosive consequences of the Chechen war or official corruption and mendacity. Why not? Why don't American commentators lament the plight of the Russian people as they did so persistently when they were the Soviet people? The United States has thousands of professed specialists on Russia. Why have so few tried to tell the full story of post-Soviet Russia? Indeed, why, despite incomparably greater access to information, do most reporters, pundits and scholars tell us less that is really essential about Russia today than they did when it was part of the Soviet Union?

There are, it seems, several reasons, all of them related to the American condition rather than to Russia's. As during the Cold War, most U.S. media and academic commentators think (or speak) within the parameters of Washington's policies toward Russia. Since 1991, Russia's purportedly successful transition and the U.S. "strategic" role in it have been the basic premise of White House and congressional policy.

American business people, big foundations and academics involved with Russia also have their own stake in the "transition." For the business community, it is the prospect of profits; for foundations, another frontier of endowed social engineering; for academia, a new paradigm ("transitionology") for securing funds, jobs and tenure. Confronted with the fact that the results of Russia's "transition" continue to worsen and not improve, most of its U.S. promoters still blame the "legacy of communism" rather than their own prescriptions or insist that robberbaron capitalism surely will reform itself there as it did here, even though the circumstances are fundamentally different.

More generally, Americans always have seen in Russia, for ideological and psychological reasons, primarily what they sought there. This time it is a happy outcome of the end of Soviet communism and of our "great victory" in the Cold War. How many of us who doubt that outcome, who think the world may be less safe because of what has happened in the former Soviet Union, who believe that ordinary Russians (even those denigrated "elderly" communists voters) have been made to suffer unduly and unjustly, who understand that there were less costly and more humane ways to reform Russia than Yeltsin's "shock" measures—how many of us wish to say such things publicly, knowing we will be accused of nostalgia for the Soviet Union or even of pro-communism? Crude McCarthyism has passed, but not the maligning of anyone who challenges mainstream orthodoxies about Soviet or post–Soviet Russia. And the presumed "transition to a free-market economy and democracy" is today's orthodoxy.

But does it even matter what Americans say about Russia today? Those of us who oppose the Clinton administration's missionary complicity in the "transition" and its insistence that Russia "stay the course" may wish the United States would say and intervene less. In one respect, however, U.S. commentary matters greatly. Eventually, today's Russian children will ask what America felt and said during these tragic times for their parents and grandparents, and they will shape their relations with our own children and grandchildren accordingly.

From the *Los Angeles Times*, December 13, 1996. Originally appeared in *The Nation*, December 30, 1995. © 1995 by The Nation Company, L.P. Reprinted by permission.

Can Russia Change?

David Remnick

DAVID REMNICK is a Staff Writer at *The New Yorker* and was the Moscow Correspondent for *The Washington Post* from 1988 to 1991.

THE DISAPPOINTMENT OF THE PRESENT

THERE WAS celebration in the State Department when Boris Yeltsin won re-election last July, but polls show that in Moscow and other Russian cities and towns there was no joy, only relief, a sense of having dodged a return to the past and the Communist Party. Political celebration, after all, usually welcomes a beginning, and the Yeltsin regime, everyone understood, was no beginning at all. Yeltsin had accomplished a great deal both as an outsider and as a president, but now, in his senescence, he represented the exhaustion of promise.

To prevail, Yeltsin had been willing to do anything, countenance anything, promise anything. Without regard for his collapsed budget, he doled out subsidies and election-year favors worth billions of dollars; he gave power to men he did not trust, like the maverick general Aleksandr Lebed; he was willing to hide from, and lie to, the press in the last weeks of the campaign, the better to obscure his serious illness.

Power in Russia is now adrift, unpredictable, and corrupt. Just three months after appointing Lebed head of the security council, Yeltsin fired him for repeated insubordination, instantly securing the general's position as martyr, peacemaker, and pretender to the presidency. On the night of his dismissal, Lebed giddily traipsed off to see a production of Aleksei Tolstoy's *Ivan the Terrible.* "I want to learn how to rule," he said.

In the new Russia, freedom has led to disappointment. If the triumph of 1991 seemed the triumph of liberal democrats unabashedly celebrating a market economy, human rights, and Western val-

ues, Yeltsin's victory in 1996 was distinguished by the rise of a new class of oligarchs. After the election, the bankers, media barons, and industrialists who had financed and in large measure run the campaign got the rewards they wanted: positions in the Kremlin, broadcasting and commercial licenses, and access to the national resource pile. Before 1991, these oligarchs had been involved mainly in fledgling small businesses—some legitimate, some not—and then, under the chaotic conditions of the post-Soviet world, they made their fortunes. Anatoly Chubais, who led Yeltsin's privatization and presidential campaigns, suddenly forgot his vow never to re-join the government and became chief of staff in the new administration, a position Yeltsin's bad health made all the mightier. Perhaps personifying the Kremlin's shamelessness, Chubais led the push to appoint one of the leading oligarchs, Boris Berezovsky, as deputy minister of security. The few Muscovites with enough patience left to care about Kremlin politics wondered what qualifications Berezovsky, who had made his fortune in the automobile business, brought to his new job.

The new oligarchs, both within and outside the Kremlin, see themselves as undeniably lucky, but worthy as well. They righteously insist that their fortunes will spawn a middle class, property rights, and democratic values. No matter that the Kremlin lets them acquire an industrial giant like the Norilsk nickel works for a thief's price; they claim to be building a new Russia, and rationalize the rest. Mikhail Smolensky, who runs Moscow's powerful Stolichnii Bank from his offices in the restored mansion of a nineteenth-century merchant, told me, "Look, unfortunately, the only lawyer in this country is the Kalashnikov. People mostly solve their problems in this way. In this country there is no respect for the law, no culture of law, no judicial system—it's just being created." In the meantime, bribery greases the wheels of commerce. Government officials, who issue licenses and permissions of all sorts, "practically have a price list hanging on the office wall," Smolensky said.

The new oligarchs are humiliating to Russians, not because they are wealthy but because so little of their wealth finds its way back into the Russian economy. According to Interpol and the Russian Interior Ministry, rich Russians have sent more than $300 billion to foreign banks, and much of that capital leaves the country illegally and untaxed. Yeltsin's Kremlin capitalism has so far failed to create a nation of shopkeepers—the British middle-class model. It has, however, spawned hundreds of thousands of *chelnoki*, or shuttle traders, young people who travel to and from countries like China, Turkey, and the United Arab Emirates carrying all manner of goods for sale. This sort of trade is probably only a crude, transitional form of capitalism, but it is also uncontrolled, untaxed, and mafia-ridden.

Under Yeltsin, power at the Kremlin has become almost as remote from the people it is supposed to serve as it was under the last communist general secretaries. In its arrogance, in its refusals to answer questions from the press, Yeltsin's Kremlin seems to believe that its duty to observe democratic practices ended with the elections. The Russian people, understandably, believe the government has much to answer for. The poverty rate is soaring. Life expectancy for men is plunging. The murder rate is twice as high as it is in the United States and many times higher than in European capitals to the west. According to Russian government statistics, by late 1995, 8,000 criminal gangs were operating in the county—proportionately as many as in Italy. The fastest-growing service industry in Russia is personal security. Hundreds of thousands of men and women now work for private businesses as armed security guards. The police are too few, and usually too corrupt, to do the job.

Though far better than in Soviet times, the press is still not free. State television, which is largely owned by the new oligarchs, is extremely cautious, even sycophantic, when it comes to Yeltsin. After acting like cheerleaders during the election campaign, some newspapers and magazines have once again become aggressive and critical, even probing impolitely into the state of Yeltsin's health. An investigation by *Itogi*, a Moscow magazine, forced Yeltsin to go public with his heart ailments, which in turn led him to agree to quintuple-bypass surgery last November. But there is still no institution—not the press, not parliament, certainly not the weak judiciary—with the authority to keep the Kremlin honest.

One of the most troubling deficiencies in modern Russia is the absence of moral authority. The country lacks the kind of ethical compass it lost when Andrei Sakharov died in 1989. Human rights groups like Memorial, in the forefront of the democratic reform movement under Mikhail Gorbachev, are now marginal. If Sakharov had a leading protégé, it was Sergei Kovalyov, a biologist who spent many years in prison under Brezhnev and later helped lead the human rights movement. One of Yeltsin's most promising gestures was his appointment of Kovalyov as commissioner of human rights, and one of the most depressing events of his reign was Kovalyov's resignation when he recognized that he could not convince the government to end the war in Chechnya. Kovalyov is hardly a presence in public life these days—he appears more often in *The New York Review of Books* than in *Izvestia*—and no one seems to have replaced him. Even the most liberal journalists seem uninterested in Kovalyov or anyone of his ilk. After years of talking about ideas and ideals, they are cynical, intent only on discussing economic interests; the worst sin is to seem naive, woolly, bookish—or hopeful.

"The quality of democracy depends heavily on the quality of the democrats," Kovalyov told me after the elections. "We have to wait for a critical mass of people with democratic principles to accumulate. It's like a nuclear explosion: the critical mass has to accrue. Without this, everything will be like it is now, always in fits and starts. Our era of romantic democracy is long over. We have finally fallen to earth."

THE DAMAGE OF RUSSIAN HISTORY

WHEN AND HOW will that critical mass accumulate? Russia should not be mistaken for a democratic state. Rather, it is a nascent state with some features of democracy and, alas, many features of oligarchy and authoritarianism. When and how will a more complete transformation of its political culture occur? Is Russia capable of building a stable democratic state, or is it forever doomed to follow a historical pattern in which long stretches of absolutism are briefly interrupted by fleeting periods of reform?

First, it pays to review the legacy—the damage—of history. Russia seems at times to have been organized to maximize the isolation of the people and, in modern times, to prevent the possibility of democratic capitalism. For example, the Russian Orthodox Church, for centuries the dominant institution in Russian life, was by nature deeply suspicious of, even hostile to, the outside world. After the fall of Constantinople in 1453, the church distanced itself from transnational creeds like Protestantism, Catholicism, Judaism, and Buddhism. Xenophobia pervaded both church and state. During the Soviet regime that xenophobia only intensified. Under the banner of communist internationalism, the Bolsheviks successfully kept the world at bay until the glasnost policy was instituted in the late 1980s.

Russian absolutism has proved unique in its endurance and intensity. In many regards the authority of the tsars exceeded that of nearly all other European monarchs. As Richard Pipes points out in the June 1996 *Commentary*,

> throughout Europe, even in countries living under absolutist regimes, it was considered a truism that kings ruled but did not own: a popular formula taken from the Roman philosopher Seneca that "unto kings belongs the power of all things and unto individual men, property." Violations of the principle were perceived as a hallmark of tyranny. This whole complex of ideas was foreign to Russia. The Muscovite crown treated the entire realm as its property and all secular landowners as the tsar's tenants-in-chief, who held their estate at his mercy on the condition of faithful service.

Tsarist absolutism was far more severe than the English variety because of its greater control of property. With the rise of the Bolshevik regime, property became, in the theoretical jargon of the period, the property of all, but in practice it remained the property of the sovereign—the Communist Party and its general secretary. And the communists were even less inclined to develop a culture of legality—of property rights, human rights, and independent courts—than the last of the Romanovs had been.

Likewise, under both the tsars and general secretaries, the government had only, in Gorbachev's rueful phrase, "the legitimacy of the bayonet." Violence and the threat of violence characterized nearly all of Russian political history. The two great breakthroughs—the fall of Nicholas II in February 1917 and the fall of Gorbachev as Communist Party leader in August 1991—came only after it was clear that both figures would refuse, or were incapable of, the slaughter necessary to prolong their regimes. Many Russian intellectuals today, including gulag survivors like the writer Lev Razgon, believe that the communist regime's policy of forced exile, imprisonment, and execution exacted a demographic, even genetic, toll on the Russian people's inherent capacity to create a democratic critical mass. "When one begins to tally up the millions of men and women, the best and the brightest of their day, who were killed or forced out of the country, then one begins to calculate how much moral and intellectual capacity we lost," Razgon told me. "Think of how many voices of understanding we lost, think of how many independent-minded people we lost, and how those voices were kept from

the ears of Soviet citizens. Yes, I am furious beyond words at Yeltsin for the war in Chechnya and for other mistakes. But we have to look at our capacities, the injuries this people has absorbed over time."

Finally, Russia will have to alter its intellectual approach to political life. Even though Gennady Zyuganov failed to carry the elections last year with his nationalist-Bolshevik ideology, he proved that maximalist ideas still resonate among a certain segment of the population. In 1957 Isaiah Berlin, writing in the October issue *of Foreign Affairs*, accurately described the traditional Russian yearning for all-embracing ideologies rooted in the anti-intellectual and eschatological style of the Russian Orthodox Church. As Berlin pointed out, the Russian revolutionaries of the nineteenth and twentieth centuries were obsessed not with liberal ideas, much less political and intellectual pluralism, but were instead given to a systemic cast of mind—and in the most extreme ways. They first absorbed German historicism in its Hegelian form, in which history obeyed scientific laws leading it in a determinate direction, and then the utopian prophecies of Saint-Simon and Fourier:

> Unlike the West, where such systems often languished and declined amid cynical indifference, in the Russian Empire they became fighting faiths, thriving on the opposition to them of contrary ideologies—mystical monarchism, Slavophile nostalgia, clericalism, and the like; and under absolutism, where ideas and daydreams are liable to become substitutes for action, ballooned out into fantastic shapes, dominating the lives of their devotees to a degree scarcely known elsewhere. To turn history or logic or one of the natural sciences—biology or sociology—into a theodicy; to seek, and affect to find, within them solutions to agonizing moral or religious doubts and perplexities; to transform them into secular theologies—all that is nothing new in human history; But the Russians indulged in this process on a heroic and desperate scale, and in the course of it brought forth what today is called the attitude of total commitment, at least of its modern form.

By the end of the process, Russian intellectuals—not least Lenin himself—derided the weakness, the unsystematic approach, of Western liberalism. For Lenin, Marxism provided a scientific explanation for human behavior. All he needed was the technological means of altering that behavior.

But while the Russian and Soviet leadership have been xenophobic, absolutist, violent, and extremist, there have always been signs of what the scholar Nicolai Petro, in his 1995 book *The Rebirth of Russian Democracy*, calls an "alternative political culture." If Russians today were to attempt to create a modern state purely from foreign models and experience, if there was nothing in Russian history to learn from, rely on, or take pride in, one could hardly expect much. But that is not the case. Perhaps Russia cannot rely, as the Founding Fathers did, on a legacy like English constitutionalism, but the soil of Russian history is still far from barren.

Even the briefest survey of alternative currents in Russian history must take note of the resistance to absolutism under Peter I and Catherine the Great or, in the nineteenth century, the Decembrist revolt against Nicholas I. While Nicholas was able to crush the Decembrists, their demands for greater civil and political authority did not fade; in fact, their demands became the banner of rebellion that persisted, in various forms and movements, until the February revolution of 1917. Alexander II's decree abolishing serfdom was followed by the establishment of local governing boards, or *zemstvos*, and out of that form of limited grassroots politics came more pressure on the tsar. In May 1905, after a long series of strikes, the Third Zemstvo Congress appealed to the tsar for a transition to constitutional government, and the tsar soon issued an edict accepting constitutional monarchy. The constitution published in 1906 guaranteed the inviolability of person, residence, and property, the right of assembly, freedom of religion, and freedom of the press—so long as the press was not criticizing the tsar.

Under Soviet rule, the Communist Party was far quicker to suppress signs of an alternative political culture than Nicholas II had been, but expressions of resistance and creativity endured. Under Krushchev, in the thaw years, a few artists and journalists began to reveal the alternative intellectual and artistic currents flowing under the thick ice of official culture, and beginning in the late 1960s one began to see the varied currents of political dissent: Sakharov and the Western-oriented human rights movement; "reform" socialists like Roy Medvedev; religious dissidents like Aleksandr Men and Gleb Yakunin, both Russian Orthodox priests; and traditionalist neo-Slavophile dissidents like Solzhenitsyn and the authors of *From Under the Rubble*.

Yeltsin's government has not been especially successful in articulating the nature of the new Russian state. But, however formless, the new state has made a series of symbolic overtures. By adopting the prerevolutionary tricolor and double-headed eagle as national emblems, the government has deliberately reached back to revive a sense of possibility from the past. Similarly, the mayor of Moscow, Yuri Luzhkov, has had restored and rebuilt dozens of churches and monuments destroyed during the Soviet period, including the enormous Cathedral of Christ the Savior on the banks of the Moscow River. There is also a revived interest in Ivan Ilyin, Nikolai Berdyayev, and other émigré philosophers who tried to describe Russian political and spiritual values. Academics are struggling to write new textbooks. Religious leaders are coping with the revival of the Russian Orthodox Church among a people with little religious education and only a sentimental attachment to their faith. These outcroppings are not mere kitsch or intellectual fashions but an attempt to reconnect Russians to their own history and the notion of national development that was shattered with the Bolshevik coup of 1917.

THE PROMISE OF RUSSIAN LIFE

ALTHOUGH DAILY life in Russia suffers from a painful economic, political, and social transition, the prospect over the coming years and decades is more promising than ever before. As former Deputy Prime Minister Yegor Gaidar has said, "Russia today is not a bad subject for long-term prognostication, and a very inappropriate subject for short-term analysis." There seems no reason why Russia cannot break with its absolutist past in much the way that Germany and Japan did after World War II.

Since the late 1980s, Russia has come a long way in this direction. The decades of confrontation with the West are over. Russia has withdrawn its talons, and except for the need to vent some nationalist rhetoric once in a great while, it offers little threat to the world. For all the handwringing by Henry Kissinger and other Russophobes, there is no imminent threat of renewed imperialism, even within the borders of the old Soviet Union. The danger of conflict between Russia and Ukraine over the Crimea or between Russia and Kazakstan over northern Kazakstan has greatly diminished in the last few years. After centuries of isolation, Russia seems ready to live not merely with the world but in it. The peril it poses is less a deliberate military threat than chaos and random events like the theft of "loose nukes." Russians are free to travel. They are free to consume as much foreign journalism, intellectual history, and popular culture as they desire. The authorities encourage foreign influence and business: more than 200,000 foreign citizens reside in Moscow, many times the number before 1990. Communication with the outside world is limited only by Russia's dismal international telephone system, and scholars and businesspeople have finessed that limitation with personal computers and electronic mail, which are rapidly becoming more widely available.

In the short term, most Russians cannot hope for much, especially from their politicians. If after his surgery Yeltsin's health does not improve dramatically, there will likely be an atmosphere of permanent crisis in Moscow. "I lived through the last days of Brezhnev, Andropov, and Chernenko, and I know how illness in power leads to danger," Mikhail Gorbachev told me shortly after the recent elections. "We survived back then thanks only to the inertia of the Soviet system. But Russia needs dynamic people in office and now, well . . ." Gorbachev has never been charitable to Yeltsin (nor Yeltsin, Gorbachev), but he was right.

The most important figures in the government will be Yeltsin's chief of staff, Chubais, the prime minister, Viktor Chernomyrdin, and Yeltsin's daughter, Tatyana Dyachenko. Such a government is likely to uphold a more or less friendly relationship with Washington and the West and to preside over a semicapitalist, semioligarchic economy. But unless the government begins to fight corruption, create a legal order, and strengthen the court system, the state will continue to be compared with the Latin American countries and the South Korea of the 1970s.

If Yeltsin dies sooner rather than later, his circle will either follow the letter of the constitution and hold presidential elections after three months, or it will find an excuse to avoid them. The latter choice would go a long way toward negating the limited progress made since 1991. Russia has yet to prove it can undergo a peaceful and orderly transfer of power—one of the most crucial tests in the development of a democracy. If the government does go forward with elections, the likely combatants would include Chernomyrdin, Luzhkov, Lebed, and Zyuganov.

Lebed's popularity is the highest of the four, but what kind of man he is and what sort of president he would be is unknown. He is considered flexible and educable by many Western visitors, but his is a flexibility born mainly of ignorance. Lebed is a military man, but unlike Colin Powell or Dwight Eisenhower—to say nothing of his hero, Charles de Gaulle—he has hardly any experience beyond the military. Lebed must be given credit for signing a peace treaty with the Chechens during his short tenure as security minister. He is also, by most accounts, a decent and honest man, which sets him apart from most who have set foot in the Kremlin. But he has displayed a willful, even outrageous, disregard for the president he was ostensibly serving. Aleksandr Lebed's first priority, so far, appears to be Aleksandr Lebed. It is discouraging that the most visible political alliance he formed after leaving the Kremlin was with Aleksandr Korzhakov, Yeltsin's crony and bodyguard before he was bounced from the government during the campaign. Korzhakov, for his part, has landed easily on his feet; he has decided to run for parliament from Lebed's home district, Tula, and should any old rivals threaten him, he has promised to release "incriminating evidence" against Yeltsin and his aides.

Lebed's potential rivals are more fixed in their views and political behavior, but they are not a promising lot. Zyuganov still has supporters, especially in the oldest and poorest sectors of the population, but he has little or no chance to win if he repeats the tactics and rhetoric of 1996. The communists would do well to jettison any traces of the past and adopt, as some are proposing, a new name for the party and younger faces to run it. A party of social democrats is inevitable in Russia, but not under Zyuganov.

Chernomyrdin represents a longed-for predictability abroad, but to Russians he represents the worst of Yeltsin's government: corruption, privilege, and an almost delusional disregard for the public. Chernomyrdin is also singularly inarticulate. The only way he could win the presidency would be to exploit the resources of the Kremlin and gain the support of the media to an even greater degree than Yeltsin did in 1996. As mayor, Luzhkov is extremely popular in Moscow—a kind of Russian Richard Daley—but he would have to cope with the traditional Russian tendency to be suspicious of political figures from the capital.

At this writing, the Kremlin depends on the heart tissue of one man and the conflicting economic and political interests of his would-be inheritors.

But not all depends on Yeltsin, or on Moscow. Russia is a far less centralized country than the Soviet Union was, for while Moscovite political life is rife with intrigue and gives off the whiff of authoritarian arrogance, it is also relatively weak. In Soviet times, regional party leaders looked to Moscow as if to Mecca. Now one decree after another is issued, but local authorities adopt what they like and ignore the rest. Development and progress are wildly different in the country's 89 regions, and much depends on the local political map. Beyond Moscow, in the most encouraging region, centered around Nizhny Novgorod, young, progressive politicians like Mayor Boris Nemtsov have made good on their promises to create "capitalism in one country." One of the biggest problems with the Soviet economy was its heavy militarization; Nizhny Novgorod, the third-largest city in the country, was one of the most militarized. Yet not only has the city managed, by privatizating, breaking up monopolies, and issuing bonds, to create thriving service and manufacturing sectors, it has also converted 90 percent of its collective farms to private ownership. Meanwhile, 500 miles down the Volga River, the communist-run city government of

Ulyanovsk, Lenin's hometown, has refused to participate in radical reform. Ulyanovsk's economy is a shambles. Unfortunately, too many Russian cities have followed the path of Ulyanovsk rather than Nizhny Novgorod.

Not all regions, however, can thrive simply by adopting the market reforms of Nizhny Novgorod. The coal-mining regions of western Siberia will continue to suffer for the same reasons the miners of many other countries have suffered: the mines are nearly exhausted and no alternative industry has developed. Most farming regions have resisted the difficult transformation to private enterprise, largely because of the vast amounts of capital needed for modern equipment and the inevitable reductions in the work force privatization entails. Agricultural areas like the Kuban or Gorbachev's home region of Stavropol have only suffered since 1991.

The mafia and tough moral questions also play a local role in deciding how or whether reform occurs. The mobster Vladimir "The Poodle" Podiatev controls the city of Khabarovsk to the extent that he has his own political party and television station. Chechnya will continue to gnaw at the attention, if not the conscience, of Moscow. Grozny, Chechnya's capital city, is in ruins, and the local authorities consider themselves victors; the rule of Islam, not the rule of Moscow, now prevails.

When describing Russia's situation and the country's prospects, analysts tend to grope for analogies with other countries and eras. The rise of oligarchy summons up Argentina, the power vacuum evokes Weimar Germany, the dominance of the mafia hints at postwar Italy, and the presidential constitution recalls de Gaulle's France of 1958. But while Russia's problems alarm the world on occasion, none of these analogies takes into account the country's possibilities.

Since 1991 Russia has broken dramatically with its absolutist past. The almost uniformly rosy predictions for China and the almost uniformly gloomy ones for Russia are hard to justify. Political reform is not the only advantage Russia has. Unlike China, where rural poverty and illiteracy still predominate, Russia is an increasingly urban nation with a literacy rate of 99 percent. Nearly 80 percent of the Russian economy is in private hands. Inflation, a feature of all formerly communist countries, dropped from a runaway 2,500 percent in 1992 to 130 percent in 1995. Russia's natural resources are unparalleled. In their perceptive 1996 book, *The Coming Russian Boom*, Richard Layard of the London School of Economics and John Parker, a former Moscow correspondent for *The Economist*, arm themselves with an array of impressive statistics allowing them to predict that by the year 2020 Rus-

sia "may well have outstripped countries like Poland, Hungary, Brazil and Mexico with China far behind."

Not least in Russia's list of advantages is that its citizens show every indication of refusing a return to the maximalism of communism or the xenophobia of hard-line nationalism. The idea of Russia's separate path of development is increasingly a losing proposition for communists and nationalists alike. The highly vulgarized versions of a national idea—Zyuganov's "National Bolshevism" or the various anti-Semitic, anti-Western platforms of figures like the extremist newspaper editor Aleksandr Prokhanov—have repelled most Russian voters, no matter how disappointed they are with Yeltsin. Anti-Semitism, for example, has no great political attraction, as many feared it would; even Lebed, who has his moments of nationalist resentment, has felt it necessary to apologize after making bigoted comments. He will not win as an extremist. Rather, he appeals to popular disgust with the corruption, violence, and general lack of integrity of the Yeltsin government.

Perhaps it is a legacy of the Cold War that so many American observers demand so much so soon from Russia. Russia is no longer an enemy or anything resembling one, yet Americans demand to know why, for example, there are no developed political parties in Russia, somehow failing to remember that it took the United States—with all its historical advantages, including its enlightened founders—more than 60 years of independence to develop its two party system, or that in France nearly all the parties have been vehicles for such less than flawless characters as François Mitterrand and Jacques Chirac. The drama of 1991 so accelerated Western notions of Russian history that our expectations became outlandish. Now that many of those expectations have been disappointed, deferred, and even betrayed, it seems we have gone back to expecting only the worst from Russia.

The most famous of all nineteenth-century visitors to Russia, the Marquis de Custine, ended his trip and his narrative by writing, "One needs to have lived in that solitude without tranquillity, that prison without leisure that is called Russia, to appreciate all the freedom enjoyed in other European countries, no matter what form of government they have chosen . . . It is always good to know that there exists a society in which no happiness is possible, because, by reason of his nature, man cannot be happy unless he is free." But that has changed. A new era has begun. Russia has entered the world, and everything, even freedom, even happiness, is possible.

Political Diversity in the Developing World

- Politics of Development (Articles 44 and 45)
- Latin America/Mexico (Articles 46 and 47)
- Africa (Articles 48 and 49)
- China (Article 50)
- India (Article 51)
- Newly Industrialized Countries (Articles 52–53)

Until recently, Third World was a widely used umbrella term for a disparate group of states that are now more frequently called the developing countries. Their most important shared characteristic may well be what these countries have *not* become—namely, relatively modern industrial societies. Otherwise they differ vastly from each other in terms of their past and present situations as well as their future prospects. The Third World designation has been used so variously and loosely that it is now dismissed by some critical observers as a category that produces more confusion than analytical precision or political insight. Such objections should at least make one cautious when speaking about a Third World. Perhaps the time has come to let go of the vague and slippery concept, as Charles Lane suggests in the first essay of this unit. But even he acknowledges that there are some commonalities among these countries that need conceptual recognition of some kind. Moreover, as Barbara Crosette next explains in her article, the lingering "spirit" of Third World oratory still retains some of its power.

Originally the term referred to countries—many of them recently freed former colonies—that had chosen to remain nonaligned in the cold war confrontation between the First World (Western bloc) and the Second World (Communist bloc). It was common to speak of "three worlds," but the categories of First World and Second World themselves never gained very wide usage. They make very little sense today in view of the collapse of Communist rule in Central and Eastern Europe, including Russia and the other former Soviet republics.

The Third World category still continues for some to be a handy, if imprecise and sometimes misleading, term of reference. It sometimes still carries the residual connotation of non-Western as well as non-Communist. Increasingly, however, the term is used to cover all largely nonindustrialized countries that are predominantly nonmodern in their economic and social infrastructures. In that sense, the remaining Communist-ruled countries would belong to the Third World category, with China and a few of its Asian neighbors as prime examples. In the same sense, Cuba is one of many Third World countries in Latin America, although it differs significantly from the others in (still) being Communist-ruled.

Most of the Third World nations also share the problems of poverty and, though now less frequently, rapid population growth. However, their comparative economic situation and potential for development can vary enormously, as can be illustrated by a simple alphabetical juxtaposition of countries such as Angola and the Argentines, Bangladesh and Brazil, or Chad and China, with their vastly different socioeconomic and political profiles. An additional term, Fourth World, has therefore been proposed to designate countries that are so desperately short of resources that they appear to have little or no prospect for self-sustained economic improvement. Adding to the terminological inflation and confusion, the Third World countries have often been referred to collectively as the "South" and contrasted with the largely industrialized "North." Most of them in fact are located in the southern latitudes of the planet—in Latin America, Africa, Asia, and the Middle East. But Greenland would also qualify for Third World status along with much of Russia and Siberia, while Australia or New Zealand clearly would not. South Africa would be a case of "uneven" or "combined" development, as would some Latin American countries in which we find significant enclaves of advanced modernity located within a larger context of premodern social and economic conditions.

It is very important to remember that the developing countries vary tremendously in their sociocultural and political characteristics. Some of them have representative systems of government, and a few of these, like India, even have an impressive record of stability. Many others are governed by authoritarian, often military-based regimes that often advocate an ideologically adorned strategy of rapid economic development. Closer examination will sometimes reveal that the avowed determination of leaders to improve their societies carries less substance than their determination to maintain and expand their own power and privilege. In any case, the strategies and politics of development or modernization in these countries vary greatly.

In recent years, market-oriented development has gained in favor in many countries that previously subscribed to some version of heavy state regulation or socialist planning of the economy. The renewed interest in markets resembles a strategic policy shift that has also occurred in former Communist-ruled nations and the more advanced industrial countries. It usually represents a pragmatic acceptance of a "mixed economy" rather than a doctrinaire espousal of laissez-faire capitalism. In other words, targeted state intervention continues to play a role in economic development, but it is no longer so pervasive or heavy-handed as often in the past. Above all, the belief in some form of Soviet-style centralized state planning has long since withered away.

In studying the attempts by developing countries to create institutions and policies that will promote their socioeconomic development, it is important not to leave out the international context. In the recent past, the political and intellectual leaders of these countries have often drawn upon some version of what is called *dependency theory* to explain their plight, often combining it with demands for special treatment or compensation from the industrial world. Dependency theory is itself an outgrowth of the Marxist or Leninist theory of imperialism, according to which advanced capitalist countries have established exploitative relationships with the weaker economic systems of the Third World. The focus of such theories has often been on alleged external reasons for a country's failure to generate self-sustained growth. They differ strikingly from explanations that give greater emphasis to a country's internal obstacles to development (whether sociocultural, political, environmental, or a combination of these). Such theoretical disagreements are not merely of academic interest. The theories themselves are likely to provide the intellectual basis for strikingly different policy conclusions and strategies for development. In other words, theory can have important consequences.

The debate has had some tangible consequences in recent years. It now appears that dependency theory in its simplest form has lost intellectual and political support. Instead of serving as an explanatory paradigm, it is now more frequently encountered as a part of more pluralist explanations of lagging development that recognize the diversity of both internal and external factors likely to affect economic development. There is much to be said for middle-range theory that pays greater attention to the contextual or situational aspects of each case of development. On the whole, multivariable explanations seem preferable to monocausal ones. Strategies of development that may work in one setting may come to naught in a different environment.

Sometimes called the Group of 77, but eventually consisting of some 120 countries, the developing states used to link themselves together in the United Nations to promote whatever interests they may have had in common. In their demand for a New International Economic Order, they focused on promoting changes designed to improve their relative commercial position vis-a-vis the affluent industrialized nations of the North. Their common front, however, turned out to be more rhetorical than real. It would be a mistake to assume that there must be a necessary identity of national interest among these countries or that they pursue complementary foreign policies.

Outside the United Nations, some of these same countries have tried to increase and control the price of industrially important primary exports through the building of cartel agreements among themselves. The result has sometimes been detrimental to other developing nations. The most successful of these cartels, the Organization of Petroleum Exporting Countries (OPEC), was established in 1973 and held sway for almost a decade. Its cohesion eventually eroded, resulting in drastic reductions in oil prices. While this latter development was welcomed in the oil-importing industrial world as well as in many developing countries, it left some oil-producing nations such as Mexico in economic disarray for a while. Moreover, the need to find outlets for the huge amounts of petrodollars, which had been deposited by some oil producers in Western banks during the period of cartel-induced high prices, led some financial institutions to make huge and often ill-considered loans to many developing nations. The frantic and often unsuccessful efforts to repay on schedule created new economic, social, and political dislocations, which hit particularly hard in Latin America during the 1980s. The memory of these recent economic and financial misadventures is likely to have some prudential influence on policy makers in the future.

The problems of poverty, hunger, and malnutrition in much of the developing world are socially and politically explosive. In their fear of revolution and their opposition to meaningful reform, the privileged classes often resort to brutal repression as a means to preserve a status quo favorable to themselves. In Latin America, this led to a politicalization of many lay persons and clergy of the Roman Catholic Church, who demanded social reform in the name of what was called *liberation theology*. For them, this variant of dependency theory filled a very practical ideological function by providing a relatively simple analytical as well as moral explanation of a complex reality. It also gave some strategic guidance for political activists who were determined to change this state of affairs. Their views on the inevitability of class struggle, and the need to take an active part in it, often clashed with the Vatican's outlook.

The collapse of communist rule in Europe has had a profound impact on the ideological explanation of the developing world's poverty and on the resulting strategies to overcome it. The Soviet model of modernization, which until recently fascinated many developing countries' leaders, now appears to have very little of practical value to offer these countries. The fact that even the communists who remain in power in China have been willing to experiment widely with market reforms, including the private profit motive, has added to the general discredit of the centrally planned economy. Perhaps even more important is the positive demonstration effect of some countries in Africa and Latin America that have pursued more market-oriented strategies of development. On the whole, they appear to have performed much better than some of their more statist neighbors with their highly regulated and protected economies. This realization may help explain the intellectual journey of someone like Michael Manley, the late prime minister of Jamaica, who broke away from the combination of dependency theory and socialist strategies that he had once defended vigorously. During the 1980s, Manley made an intellectual U-turn as he gained a new respect for market-oriented economic approaches, without abandoning his interest in using reform politics to promote the interests of the poor. More recently, Jorge G. Castañeda has called upon the Left in Latin America to abandon utopian goals and seek social reforms within "mixed" market economies.

Latin America illustrates the difficulty of establishing stable pluralist democracies in many parts of the developing world. Some authors have argued that its dominant political tradition is basically authoritarian and corporatist rather than competitively pluralist. They see the region's long tradition of centralized oligarchic governments, whether of the Left or Right, as the result of an authoritarian "unitary" bias in the political culture. From this perspective, there would seem to be little hope for a lasting pluralist development, and the current trend toward democratization in much of Latin America would appear unlikely to last. Today, however, the cultural explanation for the prevalence of authoritarian governments in Latin America seems to meet with far more skepticism than it did a few years ago. One simple reason is the fact that dictatorships in the region have serially been replaced by elected governments. Effective democratic governments in Spain and Portugal may also have set important examples for the Latin American countries. Finally, the negative social, economic, and political experience with authoritarian rulers may well be one of the strongest cards held by their democratic successors. But unless they also meet the pragmatic—Does it work?—test, by providing evidence of social and economic progress, the new democracies in Latin America could also be in trouble shortly. They may yet turn out to be short interludes between authoritarian regimes that always achieve a modicum of political and social order through repression.

In much of Latin America there has been a turn toward a greater emphasis on market economics, replacing the traditional commitment to strategies that favored statist interventions. An important example was the attempt by former president Carlos Salinas of Mexico to move his country toward a more competitive form of market enterprise. His modernization strategy included Mexico's entry into a North American Free Trade Agreement (NAFTA) with the United States and Canada. In a time of enormous socioeconomic dislocations, however, Salinas showed considerable reluctance to move from economic to political reform. Such a shift would have undermined the long-time hegemony of his own Institutional Revolutionary Party (PRI) and given new outlets for protest by self-perceived losers in the process. On the other hand, critics have argued that a market-oriented approach was too technocratic in its assumption that economic modernization could be accomplished without a basic change of the political system. During his last year in office, Salinas was confronted by an armed peasant rebellion in the southern province of Chiapas, which gave voice to the demand for land reform and economic redistribution. Mexican criticism of Salinas intensified after he left office in December 1994 and 3 months later sought political exile abroad. Since then, some top Mexican officials and their associates have been accused of having links to major drug traffickers with a sordid record of corruption and political assassination.

The successor to Salinas was elected in August 1994, in a competitive contest that was reported as not seriously distorted by fraud. The ruling party won with 51 percent of the vote. The PRI's first presidential candidate, Luis Donaldo Colosio, had been assassinated in the early part of the campaign. His place was taken by Ernesto Zedillo, an economist and former banker who fits the technocratic mold of recent Mexican leaders. He has continued the basic economic policies of Salinas, but he appears more willing to listen to demands for meaningful political reform as well. Shortly after he took office at the beginning of December 1994, however, the Mexican peso collapsed and brought the economy into disarray. A major factor was the country's huge trade deficit and the resultant loss of confidence in the peso. In early 1997, the Mexican government announced that it had payed back a huge relief loan provided by the United States, and overall economic prospects for the struggling country appeared to have improved somewhat. Yet it would be difficult to think of a more meaningful reference to Mexico than Denise Dresser's title, "Uneasy, Uncertain, Unpredictable." She points to many reasons for such an ambiguous assessment of our southern neighbor.

South Africa faces the monumental task of making democracy work in a multiracial society where the ruling white minority had never shared political or economic power with black Africans or Asian immigrants. A new transitional constitution was adopted in late 1993, followed by the first multiracial national elections in April 1994. Former president Frederik de Klerk seems destined to go into history as an important reformer, but his political work could not possibly please a broad cross section of South African society. His reforms were judged to have gone much too far and too fast by members of the privileged white minority, and they clearly did not go nearly far enough or quickly enough for many others who demanded measures that went far beyond formal racial equality.

Nelson Mandela, who succeeded de Klerk in the presidency, has an even more difficult historical task. He has some strong political cards in addition to his undisputed leadership qualities. He clearly represents the aspirations of a long-repressed majority, but he has managed to retain the respect of a large number of the white minority. It will be important that he continue to bridge the racial cleavages that otherwise threaten to ravage South African society. In the interim constitution, the reformers had sought political accommodation through an institutional form of power sharing. A new constitution, adopted in 1996, lays the foundation for creating simple majority-based governments that are bound to be dominated for now by the African National Congress, Mandela's political party. As Suzanne Daley points out, however, the new charter contains many guarantees of individual and group rights, and political prudence will recommend some form of meaningful interracial coalition-building in South Africa's policy-making process.

The continued task of finding workable forms of power-sharing will be only one of Mandela's many problems. In order for the democratic changes to have much meaning for the long-suppressed majority, it will be necessary to find policies that reduce the social and economic chasm separating the races. The politics of redistribution will be no simple or short-term task, and one may expect many conflicts in the future. Nevertheless, for the first time since the beginning of colonization, South Africa now offers some hope for a major improvement in interracial relations, and some sober optimists believe that a firm foundation has been laid that should ensure political stability also in the post-Mandela era.

China is the homeland of over a billion people, or more than one-fifth of the world's population. Here the reform Communists, who took power after Mao Zedong's death in 1976, began much earlier than their Soviet counterparts to steer the country toward a relatively decontrolled market economy. They also introduced some political relaxation, by ending Mao's recurrent ideological campaigns to mobilize the masses. In their place came a domestic tranquillity such as China had not known for over half a century. But the regime encountered a basic dilemma: it wished to maintain tight controls over politics and society while freeing the economy. When a new openness began to emerge in Chinese society, comparable in some ways to the pluralism encouraged more actively by Gorbachev's *glasnost* policy of openness in the Soviet Union, it ran into determined opposition among hard-line Communist leaders. The aging reform leader Deng Xiaoping presided over a bloody crackdown on student demonstrations in Beijing's Tiananmen Square in May 1989. The regime has refused to let up on its tight political controls of society, but it continues to loosen the economic controls in the areas or zones designated for such reforms. In recent years, China has experienced a remarkable economic surge with growth rates that appear unmatched elsewhere in the world. A still unanswered question is whether the emerging industrial society can long coexist with a repressive political system. It would be surprising if the succession in political leadership does not produce tensions and conflicts at the elite level. In early 1996, Beijing ordered large-scale military exercises in the coastal waters between the mainland and Taiwan. There was good reason to believe that these maneuvers were intended to direct national and international attention away from the succession crisis and toward the continuing Chinese claim to the island. In February 1997 Beijing announced the death of Deng Xiaoping, whose long illness had prevented his appearance in public for several years. Specialists in China differed in their analyses of the likely consequences of Deng's death, but they saw little likelihood of a major power struggle or destabilizing policy changes.

India is often referred to as a subcontinent. With its almost 900 million people, this country ranks second only to China in population and ahead of the continents of Latin America and Africa combined. India is deeply divided by ethnic, religious, and regional differences. In recent years, Hindu extremists have become politicized and now constitute a threat to the Muslim minority as well as the secular foundation of the state. For the

vast majority of the huge population, a life of material deprivation seems inescapable. However, some policy critics point to the possibility of relief if the country's struggling economy were freed from a long tradition of heavy-handed state interference. There have been some promising steps in that direction. The potential for political crisis nevertheless looms over the country. In 1992 the national elections were marred by the assassination of Rajiv Gandhi, the former prime minister and leader of the Congress Party. Prime Minister P. V. Narasimha Rao, the political veteran who took charge of a tenuous minority government after the election, soon followed in the steps of other reform governments in the developing world by adopting more market-oriented policies. Rao's Congress Party was badly defeated in the general election of May 1996 and is now in the parliamentary opposition, trying to heal its deep internal divisions. India's new coalition government includes 14 political parties and could hardly be more representative of the country's diversity. It has pledged to continue the market-oriented reforms but is necessarily hampered in promoting new policies by deadlock among its many different partners. Some observers believe that the real action in India now comes from a more dynamic economy that has been energized by the relaxation of the country's long tradition of heavy state regulation and protectionism. Other India watchers suggest that the accompanying social and economic dislocations could spark new political turmoil and ethnic strife. As always, this huge country bears careful watching.

The *Newly Industrialized Countries (NICs)* have received much attention as former Third World nations that are breaking out of the cycle of chronic poverty and low productivity. It is not fully clear what lessons we can draw from the impressive

records of the four or five "tigers," or "dragons"—Singapore, Hong Kong, South Korea, Taiwan, and possibly Thailand or Malaysia. Some observers have suggested that their combination of authoritarian politics and market economics have provided a successful mix of discipline and incentives that have made the economic takeoff possible. Others point to the presence of special cultural factors in these countries (such as strong family units and values that emphasize hard work, postponement of gratification, and respect for education) that supposedly encourage rational forms of economic behavior. It would also be possible to cite some geopolitical and historical advantages that helped the NICs accumulate investment capital at a critical phase. The subject is of great importance and it seems bound to become one of the main topics in the field of study we call the politics of development. These countries are of special interest as possible role models for economic development. They can also serve as examples of how authoritarian political and social traditions can be reformed in tandem with the development of a more affluent consumer society. The authors give a perspective on the new industrial countries by carefully reviewing the debate concerning the relative contributions made to their remarkable economic development by market forces, state intervention, and cultural and social factors.

Looking Ahead: Challenge Questions

Why is the term Third World of little analytical value? What have these developing countries in common, and how are they diverse? Is there any value in keeping the label, or should we scrap it? Why did some observers promote the usage of another term, the Fourth World?

How do explanations of Third World poverty and slow development differ in assigning responsibility for these conditions to external (foreign) and internal (domestic) factors? Why can theories of development be important factors in shaping strategies of modernization?

What is dependency theory, and why has it had so much appeal, especially in Latin America? How do you explain the current wave of market-oriented reforms? How did the widespread optimism about Mexico's economic development arise, and why did it come to such an abrupt end? Why is the PRI so resistant to political reform in Mexico?

Why do economic development and representative government run into such difficulties in most of Latin America and much of Africa? What are some of the major political, economic, and social problems that South Africa still has to face in overcoming the legacy of apartheid? What are the most important features of the new constitution?

How do you explain China's relative success in turning toward market reforms for the economy, as compared to the Soviet Union? Compare Mao and Deng in terms of their development strategies and ideological orientation. After Deng's death, what kind of political tension can we expect at the elite and mass levels of Chinese society?

How has India managed to maintain itself as a parliamentary democracy, given the many cleavages that divide this multiethnic society?

What can the new industrial countries of Asia teach us about the possibility of economic modernization and democratic reform?

LET'S ABOLISH THE THIRD WORLD

*It never made much sense, and it doesn't exist in practice.
So why not get rid of it in theory?*

Sometimes language lags history. Take the Third World. Did we ever have another name for the poor, unstable nations of the south? In fact, the Third World is a 1950s coinage, invented in Paris by French intellectuals looking for a way to lump together the newly independent former European colonies in Asia and Africa. They defined *le tiers monde* by what it wasn't: neither the First World (the West) nor the Second (the Soviet bloc). But now the cold war is over, and we are learning a new political lexicon, free of old standbys like "Soviet Union" that no longer refer to anything. It's a good time to get rid of the Third World, too.

The Third World should have been abolished long ago. From the very beginning, the concept swept vast differences of culture, religion and ethnicity under the rug. How much did El Salvador and Senegal really have in common? And what did either share with Bangladesh? One of the bloodiest wars since Vietnam took place between two Third World brothers, Iran and Iraq. Many former colonies remained closer to erstwhile European metropoles than to their fellow "new nations."

Nevertheless, the Third World grew. Intellectuals and politicians added a socioeconomic connotation to its original geopolitical meaning. It came to include all those exploited countries that could meet the unhappy standard set by Prime Minister Lee Kuan Yew of Singapore in 1969: "poor, strife-ridden, chaotic." (That was how Latin America got into the club.) There's a tendency now to repackage the Third World as the "South" in a global North-South, rich-poor division. To be

sure, in this sense the Third World does refer to something real: vast social problems—disease, hunger, bad housing—matched by a chronic inability to solve them. And relative deprivation does give poor nations some common interests: freer access to Western markets, for example.

But there are moral hazards in defining people by what they cannot do or what they do not have. If being Third World meant being poor, and if being poor meant being a perennial victim of the First and Second Worlds, why take responsibility for your own fate? From Cuba to Burma, Third Worldism became the refuge of scoundrels, the "progressive" finery in which despots draped their repression and economic mismanagement. Remember "African socialism" in Julius Nyerere's Tanzania? It left the country's economy a shambles. A good many Western intellectuals hailed it as a "homegrown" Third World ideology.

Paternalism is one characteristic Western response to a "victimized" Third World. Racism is another. To nativists such as France's Jean-Marie Le Pen or Patrick Buchanan, "Third World" is a code phrase for what they see as the inherent inferiority of tropical societies made up of dark-skinned people. Either way, the phrase Third World, so suggestive of some alien plant, abets stereotyping. "The Third World is a form of bloodless universality that robs individuals and societies of their particularity," wrote the late Trinidad-born novelist Shiva Naipaul. "To blandly subsume, say, Ethiopia, India, and Brazil under the one banner of Third Worldhood is as

absurd and as denigrating as the old assertion that all Chinese look alike."

Today, two new forces are finishing off the tattered Third World idea. The first is the West's victory in the cold war. There are no longer two competing "worlds" with which to contrast a "third." Leaders can't play one superpower off the other, or advertise their misguided policies as alternative to "equally inappropriate" communism and capitalism. The second is rapid growth in many once poor countries. The World Bank says developing countries will grow twice as fast in the '90s as the industrialized G-7. So much for the alleged immutability of "Third World" poverty—and for the notion that development must await a massive transfer of resources from north to south. No one would call the Singapore of Lee Kuan Yew poor, strife-ridden or chaotic: per capita GNP is more than $10,000, and its 1990 growth rate was 8 percent. South Korea, Taiwan and Hong Kong also have robust economies, and Thailand and Malaysia are moving up fast.

American steelmakers have recently lodged "dumping" complaints against half a dozen Asian and Latin American countries. Cheap wages explains much of these foreign steelmakers' success, but the U.S. industry's cry is still a backhanded compliment. "A nation without a manufacturing base is a nation heading toward Third World status," wrote presidential candidate Paul Tsongas. But Tsongas was using obsolete imagery to make his point: soon, bustling basic industries may be the *hallmark* of a "Third World" nation.

Patina of modernity: Nor can the Third World idea withstand revelations about what life was really like in the former "Second World." It was assumed that, whatever the U.S.S.R.'s political deformities, that country was at least modern enough to give the West a run for its money in science and technology. In fact, below a patina of modernity lay gross industrial inefficiency, environmental decay and ethnic strife. Nowadays, it's more common to hear conditions in the former Soviet Union itself described as "Third World," and Russia seeks aid from South

Korea. Elsewhere in Europe, Yugoslavia's inter-ethnic war is as bad as anything in Asia or Africa. The United States itself is pocked with "Third World" enclaves: groups with Bangladeshi life expectancies and Latin American infant-mortality rates.

A concept invoked to explain so many things probably can't explain very much at all. The ills that have come to be associated with the Third World are not confined to the southern half of this

planet. Nor are democracy and prosperity the exclusive prerogatives of the North. Unfair as international relations may be, over time, economic development and political stability come to countries that work, save and organize to achieve them. Decline and political disorder come to those who neglect education, public health—and freedom. The rules apply regardless of race, ethnicity, religion or climate. There's only one world.   CHARLES LANE

The 'Third World' Is Dead, but Spirits Linger

Indonesia saw a movement born, and now hosts its wake.

Barbara Crossette

Not more than 60 miles down the highway from the Indonesian hill town of Bogor, where President Clinton will take part this week in an economic summit of Asian-Pacific nations, is a genteel city that once symbolized everything the third world believed in and hoped for when it was young. The city is Bandung. There, another generation of world leaders—Nehru, Nasser, Nkrumah, Sukarno, Zhou Enlai—met at another summit, the 1955 Afro-Asian Conference, a gathering full of post-colonial promise, with dreams of self-sufficiency, solidarity among newly independent nations and commitment to an anti-super-power international policy that became known as nonalignment.

"Sisters and brothers!" President Sukarno of Indonesia told the delegates. "How terrifically dynamic is our time!"

The fraternal third world these founders envisioned is dead. The agenda for Bogor, where the heirs of the Bandung generation plan to talk mostly about economic liberalization, competition for foreign investment and free trade, is its obituary. The hollowness of the dream of Afro-Asian commonality is never so starkly evident as when Pacific Rim countries get together, a number of them boasting higher living standards than some European nations.

Nehru's India is barely on the horizon of this world; Nkrumah's Africa isn't even in the picture.

The "third world," a phrase first used by French journalists in the 1950's, was meant to describe those who were not part of the industrial world or the Communist bloc. The distinction has no more relevance now than the idea that developing nations automatically have much in common with each other. People speak of the "tigers" who form a class of their own, or a "fourth world" of the poorest countries. A "fifth world" might be found among proliferating populations of rootless refugees. And so on.

"We no longer have a coherent image of the third world," says Jean-Bernard Mérimée, France's chief delegate to the United Nations and a former Ambassador to India. "It is now composed of totally different elements. What do nations like Burkina Faso and Singapore have in common? Nothing, except a sort of lingering perception that they belong to something that had the tradition of opposing the West and the developed world." All that is left, the envoy said, are "remnants of the Bandung attitude" and memories of the fight against colonialism that once bonded emerging nations.

Bandung's oratory lives on, however, resurfacing regularly in the frustration of poor countries looking for easy explanations for develop-

ment shortcomings. The new "imperialists" now tend to be lending organizations like the World Bank and International Monetary Fund, which have tried to impose stringent fiscal regimes. The "neocolonial" tag has also been attached to donor nations asking questions about rights abuses, child labor, religious or sex discrimination and population policy. At the recent United Nations population conference in Cairo, some of the hottest buttons and bumper stickers proclaimed angrily, "No to Contraceptive Imperialism."

The days of Bandung were heady days of shared underdevelopment, before yawning material gaps between the richest and poorest of these nations began to widen. In Asia, Pakistani business leaders say ruefully that a few decades ago their nation was roughly on a par with South Korea and both had military governments. Both are now democracies, at least on paper, but South Koreans live a decade longer, earn 10 times as much and send 10 times as many children to college with less than half Pakistan's population. In Egypt, intellectuals recall how their country once exported skilled labor to other Arabic-speaking nations that now import a more educated work force, even for menial jobs, from Southeast Asia. In decades of building organizations—the Nonaligned Movement, the Group of 77—third world nations never devised effective mechanisms to help one another.

Ideologies, economic policies, cultural differences and the creation of superpower clienteles all played a part in widening fissures among developing countries. Different growth rates were not always predictable. Singapore's lack of natural resources did not prevent it from growing into an economic powerhouse. A sea of oil has not turned Nigeria into Texas or Mexico. Authoritarian policies contributed to the boom in some nations. Repression and corruption drained the life of others, or drove the dispossessed into violence.

Dirt Poor, With Tanks

What happened to the shared dreams of the third world is documented in the United Nations' Human Development Index. Looking at daily lives rather than macroeconomic figures, the index has for the last five years ranked more than 100 developing nations in education, access to basic services and conditions of women, among other topics. "What emerges is an arresting picture of unprece-dented human progress and unspeakable human misery, of humanity's advances on several fronts mixed with humanity's retreat on several others, of a breath-taking globalization of prosperity side by side with a depressing globalization of poverty," the 1994 report says.

This year, the index focuses on big military spenders. "Many nations have sacrificed human security in the search for more sophisticated arms," it says. "For example, India ordered 20 advanced MIG-29 fighters that could have provided basic education to all the 15 million girls now out of school. Nigeria bought 80 battle tanks from the United Kingdom at a cost that would have immunized all two million unimmunized children in that country while also providing family-planning services to nearly 17 million couples."

While the third world had divided itself into unequal streams of development well before the end of the cold war, developing nations hoped there would be peace dividends for them after the collapse of communism. They have been disappointed. Not only have sources of aid from the former Soviet bloc withered, as Cuba has discovered most painfully, but also the European nations reborn as democracies—now labeled "economies in transition"—have moved in to claim a lot of attention and scarce development funds.

What to do? Development experts say doing nothing about the Global South—the new term—will lead only to more ethnic wars, migrations from overpopulated regions and rapid depletion of natural resources. On the other hand, those "remnants of the Bandung attitude" that the French envoy identified do not want the industrialized world to get an opportunity to intervene in national policies as a condition of granting more aid.

"You get a certain feeling that on many issues—social policies, environmental policies, human rights—the developing countries get a feeling of interference," said Austria's United Nations delegate, Ernst Sucharipa. "We would not say this is true, though I can see why some countries would feel that way. We have to have an open discussion on issues of global consequence." The need for universal sisterhood and brotherhood is now no longer confined to the world of Bandung.

THE BACKLASH IN LATIN AMERICA

Gestures against reform

In dribs and drabs, a populist reaction is gathering pace against the bold free-market reforms of Latin America

BEFORE Eastern Europe, Latin America was the region that first saw the ascendancy of free-market democrats over authoritarian protectionists. In just a decade, well-educated, market-minded civilians arrived in power everywhere (bar Cuba), shoving aside the protectionists and brass-hats who had long run the place. In some countries radical free-marketeers have been in charge (Argentina, Mexico); others have been run by more gradualist reformers (Brazil, recently Chile). But everywhere, the direction of policy has been the same: to chop back the over-mighty state. And everywhere, the results have been similar: inflation is down; foreign investment is up; dictatorships are out.

Yet (as in much of Eastern Europe) the liberal ascendancy stopped short of triumph. And now a backlash is appearing. From the rugged sierras outside the Mexican resort of Acapulco, the People's Revolutionary Army (EPR) has been running a vicious bombing campaign in half a dozen states. Maximo Gomez, the priest of Atoyac de Alvarez, a scrubby town in rebel country, thinks that "90% support the guerrillas in their heart ... if the government does not act soon, this place will explode."

The rise of the EPR is a small but worrying part of wider regional reaction against the new generation of free-market reformers. The great expectations that accompanied their bold reforms have come crashing down. Unemployed and angry voters have looked to populists—only to find the easy solutions they proffered also disappear. The resulting disgust with all politics is coinciding with rising violence of all kinds, from guerrilla action to crime.

This rising discontent represents the greatest challenge yet faced by the continent's reformers. Chile's President Eduardo Frei seems to have got the message. Earlier this month, he got the annual summit meeting of Latin American and Iberian leaders to focus on "governability for efficient and participatory democracy". In plain English, rulers too are frustrated by the pace of reform. They are looking for new ways to encourage growth and speed up the delivery of its social benefits. Time does not seem to be on their side.

Given the sweeping nature of the reforms, that is hardly surprising. For decades, Latin America was mired in state controls, bouts of hyperinflation and slump. Hope dawned in the late 1980s, when a new generation of brash, foreign-educated leaders embraced the so-called "Washington consensus", a heady mix of privatisation, financial liberalisation and trade reform which sought to balance the books and end the power of a corrupt and paternalistic state.

Despite bumps along the way—most notably Mexico's currency and banking troubles of 1994-95—the gains are undeniable. One is the slaying of inflation, that most insidious of taxes on the poor, which fell from a regional mean of 196% in 1991 to just 19% last year. Fiscal discipline has slashed the average budget deficit by two-thirds, from 5.5% of GDP in 1988 to 1.8% in 1995.

Most impressive has been the embrace of freer trade. Protectionist barriers have tumbled unilaterally or as part of accords which doubled intra-regional exports to $32 billion in the five years to 1994. NAFTA, the North American Free-Trade Agreement, has linked Mexico with the giants to its north. In South America, Mercosur is edging Argentina, Uruguay, Paraguay and Brazil the same way. In December 1994, Latin leaders pushed the United States and Canada to agree to negotiate a Free-Trade Area of the Americas by 2005. The opening of the region's economies has spurred exports; they grew 6% a year during the early 1990s, up from 1.8% a year during the mid-1980s.

This first wave of reform was popular, as liberalisation boosted growth. Along came an expansion of credit and a flood of cheap imports, which pleased consumers, and propelled reformers such as Peru's Alberto Fujimori and Argentina's Carlos Menem to re-election.

But the reforms' popularity was based partly on unrealistic expectations. They were liked not because they laid a foundation for a far brighter future than had seemed possible during the "lost decade" of the 1980s. Rather, voters liked reform because it was accompanied by spurts of

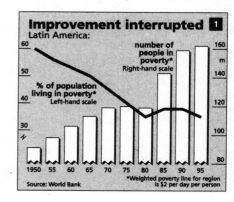

Improvement interrupted ⓵
Latin America:

number of people in poverty*
Right-hand scale

% of population living in poverty*
Left-hand scale

Source: World Bank

*Weighted poverty line for region is $2 per day per person

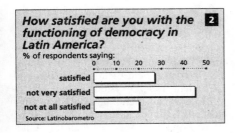

How satisfied are you with the functioning of democracy in Latin America?
% of respondents saying:

	0	10	20	30	40	50
satisfied						
not very satisfied						
not at all satisfied						

Source: Latinobarometro

growth. Alas, these boomlets were not "the pay-off for reform", as Ricardo Hausmann of the Inter-American Development Bank (IDB) argues. Rather, many of them were fuelled partly or largely by one-off inflows that resulted from the return of stability. In Mexico and Venezuela short-lived booms ended in banking crises; Brazil's boom escaped that, but not by much; Argentina's was killed by sudden monetary contraction after the Mexican crisis.

The fundamental economic outlook is favourable. But the poor cannot eat "fundamentals". What they see is that the region's traditionally wide gap between incomes is widening further. The reforms of the early 1990s did reduce the percentage in poverty, but population growth ensured that the absolute number soared (see chart 1 on previous page). Real wages have fallen. Unemployment in most countries is now higher than in 1990.

The reforms have not yet delivered the kind of sustained growth needed to wipe out poverty. True, the region's GDP grew 3.5% in 1991 after the reforms started. But growth fell to 0.8% last year after Mexico's crash. From about 3% this year, it may reach 4% next year.

Not bad, but it may not be enough. Many economists reckon growth of 6% will be needed to reduce poverty as populations continue to rise. A year ago, Shahid Burki, until recently the World Bank's top Latin America man, thought regional growth might reach 6% soon. No longer. In a candid and controversial assessment, he argued that the ripple effects of the Mexican crisis have exposed the fragility of banks from Mexico to Argentina. He worries that it will take another decade to achieve a stable growth rate of 6% or so. Will voters wait that long?

Abajo neoliberalismo!

The answer may be no. In recent months, the golden boys of reform—Messrs Menem and Fujimori—have seen their popularity plummet. Everywhere, polls show citizens have an exceptionally low opinion of politicians and parties (see chart 2).

What seems to be happening is that middle-class folk are joining the backlash of the poor. A remarkable revolt took place at a recent assembly of Mexico's ever-ruling Institutional Revolutionary Party (PRI). Furious that unpopular market reforms had resulted in electoral defeats, hardliners re-

belled. "Down with neo-liberalism!" rang the cries as they voted to stop privatisation and ban technocrats from high office. The public cheered the rebellion. Middle-class anger at cuts in utility and energy subsidies helped drive Venezuela's Carlos Andres Perez from office in 1993. And Nicaraguans were so disgusted with six years of IMF-encouraged reform that nearly 40% (on the official count) voted for the ex-Marxist Sandinists in the recent election. The Sandinists did not win the election, but the warning was plain.

This backlash may, however, bring disappointment and frustration. In Mexico, the reaction against reform was led by the dinosaurs of the PRI, who, if their record in office in the 1960s and 1970s is any guide, are more likely to stuff their pockets once in power than to help the poor.

In more pluralistic countries, the backlash is no more likely to lead to leftward policy shifts. By and large, the Latin left has failed in opposition. Alvaro Vargas Llosa, the son of Mario Vargas Llosa, a Peruvian writer and defeated presidential candidate in 1990, explains why in a controversial book, "The Idiot's Guide to Latin America". The left, he says, blames the CIA, multinational companies and the IMF for the region's woes. Leftist leaders have not come up with any coherent alternative to the prevailing free-market agenda.

Old-style populists are no better at defusing voters' discontent, though for a different reason. Venezuela's Rafael Caldera portrayed himself as an outsider who would end unpopular reforms; he won in 1993. In Ecuador, the populist to end all populists, Abdala Bucaram, swept into office last July with a campaign featuring rock CDs, strippers and pork-barrel politics. Yet in office both returned to their senses. Mr Caldera is now implementing IMF-style reforms, while Mr Bucaram has taken advice from Domingo Cavallo, the architect of Argentina's reforms. Presidents Menem and Fujimori both traversed a similar path.

Enter the caveman

The resulting victory of sound policies over populism is good news for the economy. It may give the policy reforms a little more time to work. But if so, the extra time may be bought at the expense of further political disillusion.

Guerrilla insurgencies, which many thought would subside with the Central American civil wars of the 1980s, are back. Colombia, where peace had seemed not far out of reach a year ago, has seen guerrillas unleash attacks of such fury that some compare the past few months to the early days of la violencia, the terrible civil war of the 1950s which claimed nearly 300,000 lives.

Colombia is the worst case but not the only one. Peru's Shining Path has shown, through recent horrific attacks, that the cap-

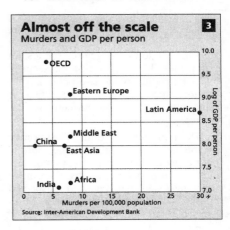

Almost off the scale
Murders and GDP per person

Source: Inter-American Development Bank

ture of Abimael Guzman, its mastermind, has not dealt it a death blow. Mexico has both the telegenic masked Zapatists and the EPR, the "cavemen of the left", as Denise Dresser, a Mexican political scientist calls them, roaming the countryside.

It is easy to dismiss this—as some officials do—as merely a tale of bandits in remote regions. Certainly, guerrilla violence is nothing like as bad as it was in the 1960s and 1970s. Nor are guerrillas any longer the proxy warriors of a cold war fought in Uncle Sam's backyard. Yet if their ideology does not amount to much, their willingness to resort to violence does. For guerrilla activity is just part of a much broader escalation of violence.

Nearly every city in Latin America is more dangerous today than it was ten years ago, before the reforms began. The region's murder rate, already six times the world average, is surging (see chart 3). Kidnappings are rife; half of all the world's abductions take place in Colombia, where rich and poor pay a combined total ransom of $100m a year to get their loved ones back.

The root causes of violence are complex, ranging from drug trafficking and consumption to income inequality, mega-cities without services, and corrupt police and courts. But, according to Luis Ratinoff of the IDB, discontent with the political order has contributed to the recent spurt in violence. He thinks that the demise of traditional purveyors of hope—from radical clergymen to Utopian parties and trade unions—means that those frustrated by the reforms may be more willing to resort to violence. Even in Mexico, traditionally one of the region's more peaceful countries, a poll by a daily newspaper, Reforma, showed that nearly a third of the population believes armed violence is justified.

Institutional breakdown

Contributing to this strain on the rule of law is the weakness of institutions. With few exceptions, courts are inefficient and corrupt; in many countries, policemen and former policemen engage in murder.

The spiral of violence has produced a

spiral of spending on private security, which often contributes to more crime, as private armies turn into paramilitary squads. All told, the region spends an astonishing 13-15% of GDP on security expenses (both private and public). That is more than total welfare spending. It represents a crippling burden on the economy.

The rich and the middle classes may be able to afford this for a while. But the poor cannot. They are turning to mob justice. In the past few months, there have been televised lynchings of suspected criminals by villagers in Ecuador, Mexico and Guatemala.

Frightened by the violence, governments are calling in the military. The army has been given special powers in chunks of Colombia. Several Mexican states have a heavy military presence. Over a dozen of Peru's departments have been under army rule for years. One of Mr Bucaram's first acts as president was to give the Ecuadorian army a role in public security.

One worry is that these armies may not be under full civilian control. In Chile, General Augusto Pinochet today cannot be sacked by the civilian president. In Venezuela, the soldiers who launched two bloody coup attempts in 1992 have been granted a pardon. In Paraguay, a seditious general nearly toppled the civilian government earlier this year. By and large, though, the threat is not (at least, not now) the old Latin American one of the *caudillo*, the army strongman. It is that, in dealing with security problems, too many armies think they can do more or less as they like.

Civilian rulers, in short, are failing to strike a balance between democracy and efficiency—and the answer, some people think, is to have less democracy. "Right or wrong," says Peter Hakim of Inter-American Dialogue, a think-tank, "the public blames democracy for the current outbreaks of criminal violence." Some technocrats are beginning to wonder whether too much democracy is a reason why reforms have been so slow to bear fruit.

In Peru and Argentina, presidents have got the constitution changed to allow themselves immediate re-election. The presidents of Brazil and Ecuador are thinking about following suit. There are arguments for this trend, which is anyway very different from the old military authoritarianism. Civilians are still in charge and are still submitting themselves to the test of electoral opinion. Nevertheless, in the context of widespread discontent, growing violence, and military rule in some areas, there are risks. The consequence may well be to shift attention away from the painstaking business of building up institutional democratic bulwarks (political parties, the courts, an accountable civil service) and towards the personalisation of power.

A Santiago consensus

If that danger is to be avoided, some policy shifts may well be needed. John Williamson, formerly of the Institute for International Economics, muses that a powerful president may be best for governability and growth. That is remarkable coming from the father of the Washington consensus, whose followers have tried to get the state out of almost everything. He now says: "Policy needs to shift from cutting back a state that had become bloated to strengthening a number of key state institutions whose efficient functioning is important for rapid and/or equitable growth." Call this policy shift the Santiago consensus:

• **Strengthen the state.** In their zeal to end the overbearing state, some reformers fear they went too far. Devolution of central power can allow local elites to derail reform. It is clear that tackling profligate state governors in Brazil and Argentina, or drug barons in Mexico or Colombia, requires a strong president.

• **Heighten supervision.** Privatisation and deregulation have sometimes ended in corruption or corporate crisis. Mr Williamson recommends the setting up of institutions similar to America's Securities and Exchange Commission to improve supervision. Many argue for independent central banks.

• **Bolster institutions.** Disregard for the law has made reform of the judiciary and police essential. Already, America's US AID is helping train new police forces in Haiti and El Salvador. The World Bank is helping overhaul Venezuela's secretive and inefficient judicial system.

• **Target social spending where it is most needed.** Latin America spends more of its GDP on social services than the Asian tigers, but lags behind in standards of primary education and basic public health. A main reason, suggests the IDB in its new annual report, is that social spending is run by centralised bureaucracies which are corrupt. It argues that local governments and non-governmental agencies should be permitted to provide social services.

Given the populist backlash, the authoritarian temptations and the economic obstacles ahead, can Latin America stick with market reforms and democracy? Paul Krugman, an eminent American economist, argued last year that the zeal for reform "may usefully be thought of as a sort of speculative bubble" and that Mexico's crisis marked the beginning of its deflation.

That may be too pessimistic. Latin American leaders, at any rate, seem determined to stay the course, if only because their room for manoeuvre is restricted both by financial markets and the glare of publicity (in Mexico, NAFTA and the American television spotlight it throws on the country was a big reason why the army did not try to crush the Zapatists).

In short, the most likely outcome of the strains and stresses of reform remains a long, hard slog towards stable growth. A shift towards new ways of maintaining a social safety net could help calm the violent backlash and recoup some of the support for reform free-marketeers once enjoyed. Even then, it will not be easy. Sebastian Edwards of the University of California, Los Angeles puts it this way: being a reformer in Latin America is rather like running up a down escalator: you have to keep running to stand still.

"As Mexico slouches from economic meltdown to recalcitrant recovery, several questions loom large in the minds of pundits and investors, Mexicans and foreigners alike: Will President Ernesto Zedillo maintain current economic policy or will he succumb to political pressures and electoral cycles? Will the social fabric unravel or will it withstand the brunt of 'adjustment fatigue'? And is the predicted demise of the PRI likely, or will the party display its traditional resilience?"

Mexico: Uneasy, Uncertain, Unpredictable

DENISE DRESSER

An indigenous uprising, political assassinations, kidnappings, and former President Carlos Salinas de Gortari's dramatic political demise have transformed Mexico into the country of uncertainty. Along with unprecedented political turbulence, Mexico has been wracked by a severe economic crisis, triggered by the December 1994 devaluation of the peso. Gross domestic product fell 10.5 percent in the first months of 1995, over a million people lost their jobs, and tens of thousands of businesses closed, broken by plummeting sales and unpayable debts. This combination of events has contributed to the rapid erosion of the Institutional Revolutionary Party's dominance, loosening the grip PRI has held since its inception in 1929 and opening new avenues of political change. Mexico has undoubtedly embarked on a transition from authoritarian rule, but the final outcome of this process remains unclear.

As Mexico slouches from economic meltdown to recalcitrant recovery, several questions loom large in the minds of pundits and investors, Mexicans and foreigners alike: Will President Ernesto Zedillo maintain current economic policy or will he succumb to political pressures and electoral cycles? Will the social fabric unravel or will it withstand the brunt of "adjustment fatigue"? And is the predicted demise of the PRI likely, or will the party display its traditional resilience?

THE INVISIBLE PRESIDENCY

Among the most significant political developments to occur in the postcrisis era has been the decline of presidential authority in Mexico. As head of a disciplined, loyal, and united PRI, and at the helm of a system devoid of checks and balances, the president had ruled supreme. However, political and economic turmoil have dismantled many of the sources and instruments of presidential power, including the PRI's unchallenged hegemony. As a result, the Mexican presidency has become much more constrained, and much less omnipotent. The demise of *presidencialismo* is partly the result of economic and political turbulence, but it is also the product of a deliberate decision by the current occupant of the presidential chair, Ernesto Zedillo, who has inaugurated a new presidential style.

Zedillo's immediate response to the political challenges created by the devaluation was to announce what he called the "modernization" of the Mexican presidency. Zedillo's intention has been to transform a historically activist and interventionist presidency into a neutral arbiter and enforcer of the rule of law. He has offered to reduce discretionary policymaking, promote a new federalist pact, decentralize power, and bring an end to the symbiotic relation-

DENISE DRESSER *is a professor of political science at the Instituto Tecnológico Autónomo de México (ITAM). She is the author of several articles on Mexico, including "Mexico: The Decline of Dominant-Party Rule," in Jorge I. Domínguez and Abraham F. Lowenthal, eds.,* Constructing Democratic Governance: Latin America and the Caribbean in the 1990s *(Baltimore: Johns Hopkins University Press, 1996), from which this essay draws.*

ship between the presidency and the PRI. Zedillo has argued that a presidential retreat will allow other institutions, such as the judiciary and Congress, to flourish. Zedillo also believes that the legitimacy provided by his relatively clean election has endowed him with a mandate to deepen economic reform, which means subsequent efforts to build popular consensus are not required.

The retrenchment of presidential authority under Zedillo has significant political implications. A leaner presidency is strengthening other political actors, including legislators and opposition party leaders, and contributing to the creation of a more accountable political system. However, Zedillo's seclusion has been criticized as an abdication of responsibility that is creating rather than solving problems. Members of traditional factions in the PRI are taking advantage of a perceived presidential weakness to strengthen their personal fiefdoms in states such as Guerrero, Tabasco, Yucatán, and Puebla. Hard-liners at the helm of several PRI-controlled governorships constantly oppose the president, question his decisions, and jeopardize the governability of their states.

In many geographic regions and in many economic activities, Mexico is still characterized by the existence of powerful *cacicazgos*. The country seems to be witnessing the growing "feudalization" of the PRI, with local power brokers governing their states as they see fit, often resorting to violence, fraud, and repression. To win the 1994 election, Zedillo allied himself with some of the more traditional power brokers within the PRI. As a result, he often appears to be constrained by political commitments and reluctant to push forward a significant political modernization agenda against traditional fiefdoms.

Zedillo's policy preference has been to restore financial stability, and during his first two years in office he has tended to discount—or ignore—the political and economic needs of the ruling party. Consequently, the president has been unable to elicit widespread support from prominent PRI members, and his efforts have repeatedly been blocked by unwilling groups within the political elite. The Zedillo team has frequently underestimated the ferocity of PRI resistance to policy initiatives such as the increase in the value-added tax (IVA) from 10 to 15 percent, the creation of a pension fund system, and the privatization of the petrochemical industry. Within the ranks of the PRI there is growing disaffection with Zedillo and the general thrust of eco-

nomic decision making. In March 1996, 250 PRI congressmen drafted an open letter to the president that called for a rethinking of his economic policies and an end to neoliberalism. During its last assembly in September, the PRI passed a resolution that bars technocrats who have never been elected to public office from running as PRI presidential candidates. Next year could witness the strengthening of groups that call for an unprecedented break with the president and a return to a more populist, center-left political stance.

Zedillo's term has been characterized by erratic policy maneuvers: the president announces a specific policy, is confronted with opposition from affected interests, and as a result, the initiative is abandoned. The president pledged to promote clean elections throughout his term, but then proceeded to support a fraudulently elected PRI governor in the state of Tabasco. Zedillo vowed to establish the "rule of law," and forced the governor of Guerrero to resign for his involvement in the June 1995 massacre of 17 peasants, only to subsequently exonerate him. Zedillo launched an attack against the Salinas family, only to later indefinitely postpone investigations into the Salinas' alleged involvement in corruption and assassination scandals. The president promised the inauguration of a "healthy distance" between the presidency and the party, only to recently name an unconditional supporter and traditional PRI hack, Roque Villanueva, as its new head.

[Mexico] seems to be witnessing the growing "feudalization" of the PRI. . .

These schizophrenic and often contradictory presidential decisions have undermined Zedillo's credibility as a democratic reformer. Given the dilemmas created by the weakening of dominant party rule, the presidency will be a key factor shaping the prospects and limits of the Mexican transition. In the past, Mexico had been unable to fully achieve democratic rule because of the unlimited power of the presidency; in the future, presidential strength will be required to undertake the critical task of institution-building and political control over antireform-minded groups. Zedillo will have to use the presidency to strengthen representative institutions that can order the country's political life and eventually act as counterweights to the presidency and the PRI. The real challenge for Zedillo throughout the remainder of his term will be to strike a balance between what he calls a "modern" presidency and what others perceive as an "invisible" presidency. He needs to decentralize power, but retain enough leadership to sanction and control members of the old guard who want to defend the prevalence of the PRI as a way of life in Mexico.

THE POWER OF THE BALLOT BOX

While PRI electoral victories were once the norm, and opposition parties occupied a symbolic and secondary role, the reverse is the case today. Competitive elections at the state and municipal level are changing the very nature and functioning of the political system. The PRI is no longer an unchallenged hegemonic party; in almost every area of the country it faces stiff electoral competition, and in all likelihood this trend will become more important.

The center-right opposition National Action Party (PAN) has become the primary beneficiary of the *"voto de castigo"* (punishment vote) against the PRI. As a result of the economic crisis, it is evolving into an electoral force to be reckoned with. PAN has gradually been able to extend its support beyond the confines of the urban middle class and garner a growing number of votes in the countryside. The party's next goal is to win the majority in Congress in 1997 and the presidency in 2000.

In the past PAN had not adopted a clear position on economic or social policy, partly because it did not need to. The party had traditionally been a loyal opposition with few chances of actually governing. That may change in 1997, when for the first time in its history PAN has a real opportunity to gain control of Congress and also win the election for mayor of Mexico City. As that possibility looms larger, PAN will be forced to clarify what its positions are on the exchange rate, monetary policy, inflation, social policy, and redistributive issues.

In the short term, PAN leaders will also have to decide whether they will continue to support the tacit center-right alliance struck with the government during the Salinas term, or whether the party should be less loyal and more of an opposition. The Zedillo term could witness the radicalization of intemperate sectors within PAN—possibly led by the charismatic governor of the state of Guanajuato, Vicente Fox—for whom the costs of perpetuating conciliatory tactics are outweighed by the benefits of a frontal attack against the Zedillo government. PAN would thus abandon its strategy of "concerted gradualism" in favor of a more "critical gradualism."[1]

One of the main concerns among longtime PAN leaders is the loss of the party's soul as the result of its spectacular electoral ascent. Ideologues in the party fear that the more confrontational political style displayed by a new breed of *panistas*, led by Fox, could undermine PAN's ideological backbone. Those advocating confrontation argue that PAN should worry about achieving power first and leave the defense of doctrinal purity for later. The traditionalists advocate a strategy baptized as "winning the government without losing the party" and argue that PAN should remain loyal to the socially conservative platform it has espoused since its inception. This unresolved struggle for definition has produced numerous public attacks among PAN leaders, and revealed a lack of internal unity that the party had been immune to in the past.

Meanwhile, the left has experienced a political renaissance under the leadership of a new party leader. Although Cuauhtémoc Cárdenas remains an important moral force within the Party of the Democratic Revolution (PRD), his political protégé, Andrés Manuel López Obrador, has emerged as a successful national figure. López Obrador heads a political current within the PRD that supports a hybrid incarnation of the party, known as " *partido-movimiento*" (party-movement), that seeks to combine organizational and institutional development with mass mobilizations and marches to protest electoral irregularities and government policies. Through popular demonstrations that pressure the government into negotiating on key issues—such as forcing the government oil monopoly PEMEX to invest in development projects in the state of Tabasco—López Obrador has inaugurated a tough but compromising strategy that is becoming the PRD's trademark. López Obrador's leadership has already produced good results for the party, including recent electoral inroads in the state of Mexico, where the PRD tripled its vote in November 1996.

The growing electoral clout of the opposition led the PRI to approve—without the support of opposition parties—an electoral reform that is far from "definitive." Although the 1994 presidential election was generally perceived as the cleanest in Mexico's history, the consensus among opposition parties was that many of the electoral system's structural imbalances prevailed. Among the main sources of contention stemming from that election were issues of campaign finance, unequal access to the media, the biased role of the Federal Electoral Institute, and many extralegal sources of government support for the ruling PRI.

On assuming office, Zedillo called for a "definitive" accord that would decidedly eliminate suspicion and recrimination from the electoral process.

---

[1]See René Delgado, "Elecciones: evolución o involución?" *Reforma*, May 27, 1995.

After two years of difficult negotiations, the main parties reached an agreement in November 1996. However, at the last minute, the PRI refused to budge on the issue of campaign financing and used its majority in Congress to push through a reform that continues to grant the dominant party privileged access to government funds. Although it is undeniable that the reform is a significant improvement on existing electoral legislation, its rejection by PAN and the PRD suggests that postelectoral conflict is far from over.

The political backlash created by the economic crisis has strengthened the prospects for a highly contested congressional race in July 1997, and the possibility of an opposition victory in the presidential election in 2000. Although the Mexican economy is limping toward recovery, the benefits of renewed economic growth have yet to translate into concrete benefits for the majority of the Mexican population. The PRI will therefore not be able to campaign on assurances of prosperity as it had in the past. Economic liberalization policies have cut to the core of traditional sources of party patronage, including political slush funds that oiled the party's clientelist machinery.

Tensions among contending groups in the PRI will undoubtedly escalate as the party heads into the midterm elections. PRI leaders believe the survival of the party's historic control over Congress—and seven governorships—will be at stake, and are currently devising strategies to assure PRI's predominance. More traditional factions, led by Minister of the Interior Emilio Chuayfett and a constellation of hard-line governors (from the states of Tabasco, Puebla, Yucatán, Veracruz, and Aguascalientes) are determined to ensure the PRI's staying power even if the use of patronage, intimidation, and electoral fraud is required.

Although the PRI faces increasingly strong competition, predictions of its impending demise may be exaggerated. The party has demonstrated a remarkable capacity to reinvent itself in the face of adverse circumstances, as it did during the 1994 presidential race. In many regions of the country the party's clientelist machine is deeply entrenched and will not be easily dislodged. The PRI also benefits from a divided opposition, which enables it to retain a relative majority of the vote. Among opposition leaders there is a growing perception that only a broad coalition front that unites the left and the right will have the capacity to remove the PRI from power.

However, PAN is reluctant to join forces with the left, since PAN leaders believe they can win Congress without the assistance of the PRD. The congressional elections will undoubtedly be a testing ground for this proposition. If PAN is unable to achieve a congressional victory, it might be willing to support the prospect of an opposition coalition in 2000.

BYPASSING THE BALLOT BOX

Economic malaise has created a much more volatile and much less loyal electorate for the PRI, and has opened up windows of opportunity for opposition parties on both the left and the right. However, whether parties will be able to bridge the chasm of distrust that currently separates them from an increasingly disaffected population is an open question. Economic decline could lead to widespread disillusionment with the existing political options offered by parties and to the strengthening of opposition movements working outside party channels.

While the party system has matured, parties and elections do not fully represent or encapsulate the demands of many social groups. As a result, parties are routinely eclipsed by other protagonists in civil society, including guerrilla groups and their sympathizers, nongovernmental organizations (NGOs), drug traffickers, the media, and groups of disaffected intellectuals. Although in the electoral sphere Mexican politics is becoming more institutionalized, and more actors are willing to play by the rules of the game, several key groups and individuals continue to operate at the margins of established politics.

The dramatic appearance of the guerrilla Popular Revolutionary Army (EPR) underscores the disaffection that looms large in the Mexican countryside, and the distance that separates modern, market-driven Mexico from its impoverished, rural counterpart. The EPR feeds on this anger and finds sympathy among millions of Mexicans who are bearing the brunt of a crisis brought on by mismanagement, corruption, and the hubris of an insulated technocratic elite. (A recent public opinion poll revealed that over a third of those surveyed justify the use of violence to combat injustice.) Although many Mexicans may not applaud the EPR, they support combating a government that fails to bridge the divide between the haves and the have-nots.

But poverty itself is not the only explanation for guerrilla insurgency. The EPR is active in the states

Zedillo's much-touted political reform has failed to reach. . .rural Mexico, where the worst aspects of authoritarian rule continue to thrive.

of southern Mexico—Chiapas, Oaxaca, Guerrero—that are saddled with exploitative politicians and corrupt caciques. Zedillo's much-touted political reform has failed to reach the hills and hamlets of rural Mexico, where the worst aspects of authoritarian rule continue to thrive.

The Zedillo government has attempted to discredit the EPR by arguing that it has no social base. This analysis is probably misguided and underestimates the EPR's influence. As with most guerrilla movements, the EPR's social base is fluid and largely invisible: members of the EPR are guerrillas one day and peasants the next. The EPR's mobility and capacity to maintain a presence in several states simultaneously underscores the generous endorsement it receives from rural communities in the form of food, shelter, and safe haven. This behind-the-scenes support allows the EPR to engage in the low-intensity guerrilla warfare that has become its trademark; the EPR attacks a military convoy or army base, then retreats into the hills and melts away into the jungle.

Just as the EPR has baffled analysts and investors, it has made life much more difficult for Mexico's other guerrilla incarnation: the Zapatista National Liberation Army (EZLN). In 1994 the Zapatistas captured the imagination of millions of Mexicans and became a fulcrum for greater political change. The mercurial and seductive Subcommandante Marcos garnered international media attention and public praise for focusing attention on the plight of the indigenous. But after two years of inconclusive peace talks and army encirclement, the EZLN's star appeared to be waning. Unable to extract any clear concessions from the government at the bargaining table, the EZLN seemed to be merely treading water.

The emergence of a more radical and more confrontational guerrilla organization has highlighted what many believe is the EZLN's perennial weakness: its incapacity (or unwillingness) to use weapons to advance its cause and pose a real military threat. By stealing part of his thunder, the EPR will undoubtedly force Marcos to toughen his stance toward the government. Marcos understands that the EPR is gaining ground—even in the Zapatista stronghold of Chiapas.

The EPR also poses important challenges to more politically sophisticated members of the Mexican left, including the leadership of the PRD. Conceived as a political voice and vehicle for impoverished Mexicans, the party must now deal with a guerrilla organization that rejects party politics. The EPR offers an immediate outlet for age-old grievances;

the PRD can provide only gradual political change through the ballot box. If the PRD distances itself from the guerrillas it will ostracize those who believe in the need for deep and dramatic reforms. If the PRD sides with the guerrillas, the party will once again be branded as an instigator of violence and lose its appeal among the conservative middle class. The PRD does not know whether to cater to the EPR—whose political ideology suggests that they are the cavemen of the left—or behave as a modern, institutional force that condemns violence in any incarnation. The situation is currently at a stalemate; an impasse in which the government has the upper hand in military if not moral terms. Popular sympathy for the EZLN and the EPR is widespread and could grow as the persistence of monumental income disparities becomes evident.

In addition to guerrilla groups, drug traffickers have become an increasingly destabilizing force in states such as Jalisco, Baja California Norte, Sinaloa, and Guerrero. During the Salinas term the Mexican government led an uneasy coexistence with drug traffickers, and in some cases even provided political protection for them. Drug cartels established ties with high-level government officials, state governors, and money-laundering corporations, and cajoled Mexican authorities to deal with them on the management of the United States–Mexico drug enforcement relationship. To shore up his credibility at home and abroad, Zedillo may break many of the unwritten rules that have governed relations between drugs and political power by arresting regional drug lords. If he does, violence and retribution could become an integral part of Mexico's political landscape á la Colombia.

Other actors, such as the debtors' movement known as El Barzón (The Yoke), and Manuel Camacho, the former mayor of Mexico City, constitute significant challenges given the unpredictable direction of their actions. El Barzón began as a union of indebted farmers in the western state of Jalisco, has captured news headlines with its protest marches and bank boycotts, and claims to have 4.5 million members in 300 groups affiliated across the country. The debtors' movement is a spontaneous, grass-roots uprising, now overwhelmingly middle class and with no apparent ties to political parties. El Barzón lost some momentum with Zedillo's $1 billion plan to restructure private debts, but if interest rates remain high and economic recovery is sluggish, El Barzón could gain renewed appeal.

As for Camacho, he has indicated that he intends to run for the presidency. The former mayor's strategy has been to sit at his doorstep and watch the corpses of his political enemies roll by. Camacho would like nothing better than to be the Mexican Fujimori, and he hopes that if economic recovery fails to materialize, Zedillo loses credibility, and the PRI is unable to reinvent itself, he can take advantage of the resultant political vacuum. As historian Lorenzo Meyer suggests, "Camacho sees himself as a de Gaulle figure, waiting for the call to come as the country's political situation deteriorates." Camacho might attempt to create a fourth political party, positioned at the center-left of the political spectrum, that would serve as a "catchall" option for those disaffected with the existing parties.

WHERE IS MEXICO HEADED?

In his efforts to decentralize power and depoliticize and shrink the authority of the executive, President Zedillo has disarticulated lines of control that had granted the political system its enviable stability. This presidential retreat may ultimately lead to a decentralization of power favorable to democratic evolution. But it has also empowered the leaders of authoritarian enclaves, who are taking advantage of the president's weakness to strengthen their fiefdoms. In the midst of a difficult transition, the critical issue has become how to sustain public confidence in the Zedillo team, given that there are no clear indications of the relatively quick success of the president's economic policies.

The only way the ruling technocracy can survive the current impasse is to channel discontent through the ballot box and hope that democracy becomes an effective containment policy. Throughout the rest of the Zedillo term Mexicans will vote their pocketbooks, and the PRI may lose a host of state elections. In the best case scenario, the deepening of economic reform will entail the inevitable unraveling of the PRI and the electoral ascent of PAN; in the worst case, electoral politics will be unable to contain social disaffection.

Zedillo has not developed a clear strategy to generate political consensus for economic adjustment. Maintaining the current course of economic policy, despite the long-term wisdom of doing so, could create governability problems in the short-term. Under Zedillo, Mexico's stricken economy will have to generate jobs for a labor force that is growing more than 3 percent a year. More than 40 percent of the Mexican population continues to live in poverty and real wages have declined to pre-1980 levels. Extreme inequalities in income and social well-being prevail among states and regions, and between urban and rural areas.

These disparities were accentuated in the first six months after the devaluation. In addition, the benefits of greater integration with the United States have been unevenly distributed within Mexico, deepening regional disparities between a prosperous north increasingly tied to the United States economy and a backward south (especially the states of Chiapas, Oaxaca, and Guerrero) plunged into agricultural stagnation. Mexico is becoming a "dual society" wherein a growing portion of the population does not enjoy the bounties of free trade and economic reform.

For the neoliberal experiment to survive, Mexico's leaders will need to broaden the coalition of beneficiaries of economic reform and lessen both economic and social polarization. As Jorge Castañeda pointed out in the July 1996 issue of *Foreign Affairs,* "as long as Mexico delays the changes that will bring prosperity to all, the country will remain stalled, divided between a minority whose lot depends on the United States and a majority periodically buffeted by economic and political crisis."

One lesson from 1994—Mexico's year of living dangerously—is already clear: widespread economic modernization in Mexico cannot survive and flourish without substantive political modernization. The lack of institutionalized mechanisms to generate consensus, scrutinize politicians, and create checks and balances may render Mexico's NAFTA-based growth strategy vulnerable to political and economic upheaval.

Mexico will not reap the benefits of free trade and renewed growth until and unless those benefits reach the dispossessed, and until and unless clean and fair elections reflect the popular will of the country's marginalized groups. As the Chiapas uprising underscored, NAFTA, fiscal discipline, surging exports, and external support are no longer sufficient to keep the "other" Mexico at bay. And as the devaluation revealed, even economic dream teams—when they operate without accountability —can and do make mistakes. Until and unless Mexico institutes reforms that ensure government accountability, electoral transparency, and the rule of law—the stuff of which democracy is made—Mexico's future will continue to be tumultuous and uncertain; a constant struggle between upward mobility and downward drift.

Democracy, of a Sort, Sweeps Africa

*Across the continent, countries are holding elections.
But they may or may not indicate true political freedom.*

Judith Matloff

Staff writer of The Christian Science
Monitor

JOHANNESBURG

Looking at an electoral map of Africa, one might think the continent was undergoing a rousing shift toward democracy.

More than a score of presidential, legislative, or local elections are set to take place this year and in 1997. Many of the votes involve more than one party for the first time in countries not known for allowing free choice.

But lining up to cast ballots does not necessarily mean freedom of speech or tolerance of dissent. On a continent of 52 nations and 800 million people, where opposition parties often lack funds, rulers control power with the gun, and ethnicity decides loyalties, these exercises in Western-style voting are often at best tepid moves toward more open political systems. At worst, they're farces, many political analysts say.

Take the example of the June 26 local elections in KwaZulu-Natal Province in South Africa, a country considered one of the continent's showcase democracies. Factional fighting between the two main parties led to assassinations of more than a half-dozen candidates. (One party had to drop leaflets by airplane into the enemy camp because its canvassers would have been killed on the spot.)

Armed supporters of the two main parties, the Inkatha Freedom party and

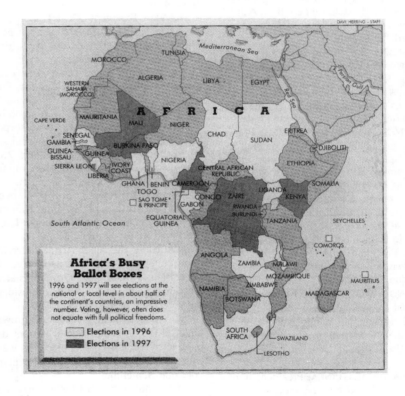

Africa's Busy Ballot Boxes

1996 and 1997 will see elections at the national or local level in about half of the continent's countries, an impressive number. Voting, however, often does not equate with full political freedoms.

☐ Elections in 1996
■ Elections in 1997

the African National Congress, often prevented rivals from entering each other's territory. "If Inkatha tries to come here, we'll shoot them," said a youth named Lucky, who had his gun handy, in an ANC-controlled area of KwaZulu-Natal.

Peter Miller, the provincial minister who oversaw the election, says problems like this are endemic across Africa. "One cannot talk about fully free and fair elections in Africa. The conditions aren't there," he says.

But Kingsley Amoako, head of the United Nations Economic Commission on Africa, based in Addis Ababa, Ethiopia, maintains that any election is better than none. "These elections, even if flawed, are a start," he says. "People are slowly getting used to the idea of pluralism, and change is gradually taking place."

Hopes had been high that political freedom would sweep Africa after the end of the cold war. No longer pawns of the United States–Soviet Union rivalry, Af-

Africa south of Sahara boasts dictators and wide political freedom

ANGOLA: First multiparty elections in 1992 declared free and fair, but ended in resumed civil war after UNITA rebel leader Jonas Savimbi rejected his defeat. Fighting continues.

BENIN: Benin has made a strong transition from dictatorship to pluralism. In elections earlier this year, Nicéphore Soglo was voted out of office after five years, and Mathieu Kerekow was reinstated.

BOTSWANA: Africa's most stable democracy, helped by relative prosperity.

BURKINA FASO: Superficially democratic, but there is widespread criticism of President Blaise Compaore's thwarting of political openness. General elections due in January-February 1997.

BURUNDI: Hutus and Tutsis fighting in Africa's bloodiest current conflict. A July coup installed Pierre Buyoya as self-proclaimed "president."

CAMEROON: President Paul Biya reelected in 1992. Municipal elections due in 1997.

CAPE VERDE ISLANDS: Multiparty elections brought opposition to power in 1991 after 16 years of one-party rule.

CENTRAL AFRICAN REPUBLIC: President Agne-Félix Patasse was elected in 1993. In May, France sent troops in to put down revolt by mutinous soldiers.

CHAD: President Idris Deby, who came to power in a December 1990 coup, won July 3 elections.

COMORO ISLANDS: Failed coup attempt in September 1995. French intervened. Presidential elections earlier this year went smoothly. Parliamentary elections due Oct. 6.

CONGO: Multiparty elections in 1993 thwarted by serious irregularities. Presidential election due in July-August 1997.

DJIBOUTI: French military presence. Cease-fire signed in December with Afar rebels.

EQUATORIAL GUINEA: President Teodoro Obiang said he won more than 90 percent of a February vote that was boycotted and called a farce by the opposition.

ETHIOPIA: Opposition boycotted May 1995 elections in which ruling EPRDF won more than 90 percent of parliamentary seats.

ERITREA: Africa's youngest state declared independence in 1993. No sign of elections yet.

GABON: Local elections due Sept. 28.

GAMBIA: Yahya Jammeh came to power in a bloodless military coup in 1994.

Presidential election is due in September, legislative elections in December.

GHANA: President Jerry Rawlings, who seized power in 1979 coup, was elected in 1992 to legitimize the government for international donors. Election set for December.

GUINEA: In January, soldiers held the capital; President Lansana Conte accuses them of trying to overthrow him.

GUINEA-BISSAU: President "Nino" Vieira, in power since 1980 coup, narrowly won the first multiparty election in August 1994.

IVORY COAST: October 1995 presidential elections were won by Henri Konan Bedie, whose government has shown little tolerance for opposition and press freedom.

KENYA: President Daniel arap Moi could declare elections this year or next. His government stymies the opposition, headed by Richard Leakey.

LESOTHO: A palace coup was overturned in 1994 following elections. Succession following King Moshoeshoe II, who died in January, has been smooth.

LIBERIA: Chaos. Regional peacekeepers unable to maintain order among militias.

MADAGASCAR: President Albert Zafy won elections last year after changing the Constitution to remove his premier.

MALAWI: Elections in 1994 overturned dictatorship of Hastings Kamuzu Banda and installed Bakili Muluzi. Local elections set for September.

MALI: One of French Africa's thriving democracies. Local elections due in November-December 1996, legislative elections in February 1997, and presidential elections in April 1997.

MAURITIUS: Strong economic growth undergirds this island state's vibrant democracy. December 1995 elections were considered free and fair. Parliamentary vote due September.

MOZAMBIQUE: FRELIMO party has ruled since independence from Portugal in 1975. Multiparty elections in 1994. The former rebel group RENAMO lacks funds to be a viable opposition.

NAMIBIA: SWAPO party, which has ruled since independence, is entrenched more firmly after 1994 elections. A de facto one-party state.

NIGER: Opposition criticized July 8 vote, saying Ibrahim Bare Mainassara held ill-prepared elections. Mainassara took power in Jan. 27 coup.

NIGERIA: Military dictatorship more entrenched after local elections earlier this year.

RWANDA: Still reeling from genocide of up to 1 million people in 1994.

SÃO TOMÉ AND PRÍNCIPE: Elections in 1991 brought pluralism to tiny island state. Government of president Miguel Trovoada was rocked by aborted coup attempt in August 1995. Trovoada reelected in July.

SENEGAL: A long multiparty tradition. Regional elections due in October-November.

SEYCHELLES: A tourist island state that boasts a representative government established by relatively open multiparty general elections in 1993 after 13 years of one-party rule.

SIERRA LEONE: Military coup in January did not prevent elections in February.

SOMALIA: No recognized government. Death of leading strongman Gen. Mohamed Farah Aideed adds to chaos.

SOUTH AFRICA: Africa's showcase democracy. Elections in April 1994 ended whites-only rule. Local elections held this year in KwaZulu-Natal Province came off peacefully.

SUDAN: Political parties were banned from March election, the first since 1989 coup that brought in Islamic fundamentalists. Civil war continues.

SWAZILAND: Africa's only absolute monarchy resists calls for democratic reforms.

TANZANIA: Opposition groups, particularly on Zanzibar island, claimed fraud during October 1995 elections.

TOGO: Held multiparty elections in 1994.

UGANDA: President Yoweri Museveni, in power for 10 years, won May election. Doesn't believe in sharing power with other parties, but his pragmatic economic policy has brought stability.

ZAIRE: Political and economic chaos under the rule of Mobutu Sese Seko. Elections promised for 1997.

ZAMBIA: Elections due in October. But President Frederick Chiluba has disqualified as candidates most opponents, including ex-President Kenneth Kaunda.

ZIMBABWE: President Robert Mugabe won an election in March. In power since 1980. His ZANU party has quashed opposition via intimidation and monopoly on campaign funds. ZANU holds 98 percent of parliamentary seats.

rican countries would be free to choose their political systems.

But the transition has been tough for many states accustomed to dictatorship or one-party rule after independence from colonialism in the 1960s and 1970s.

Some ill-prepared for balloting

According to Richard Cornwell, a political analyst at the Africa Institute, a think tank in Pretoria, South Africa, immense poverty means that those in power will try to hold onto it. Without power, he says, they have no guarantee of economic survival. The problem has been worsened by privatizing state industries, which employ many people, and austerity measures demanded by the World Bank and International Monetary Fund (IMF), which have strained the economies and put thousands of people out of work.

"The promise of a liberation [through elections] was false," Mr. Cornwell says.

Cornwell and others say that many times elections will be held in African countries to satisfy Western countries and institutions that give them aid. But the polls then become exercises with little substance. Donors such as the World Bank and IMF are sometimes more lenient toward abuses of civil liberties as long as their prescribed economic programs are adhered to, Cornwell says.

Often African countries are ill-prepared for truly democratic voting because of illiteracy, traditions of authoritarianism, corruption, and weak government institutions. In many African societies, the chief rules in a village. That pattern of authority often becomes reflected on the national level.

Weak government institutions are another problem. When Portugal exited Mozambique in 1975, there were only 30 university-educated people in the country. The nation has been struggling ever since with incompetent leadership, political analysts say.

In addition, Africans often vote along ethnic rather than ideological lines creating tensions for the losers, many Africa experts say. This especially happens when the winner takes all in elections, and there is no mechanism for power sharing with smaller parties.

This was apparent in Tanzania, where the mainly Muslim population of Zanzibar island claimed it was denied victory in fraudulent elections last year. "They don't [just] oppress us politically; they also want to suppress our culture," says a Zanzibar shopkeeper named Ali. The risk now is that ethnic nationalism and calls for secession could rise, diplomats say.

Africa watchers do see some encouraging signs, especially in southern Africa, perhaps the continent's most stable subregion because of its comparative wealth and higher education levels.

South Africa's 1994 multiracial general elections, which ended 300 years of white domination, were flawed. But they did bring about majority rule and a thriving opposition—helped in part by the country's economic strength and the political maturity of both the black and the white leadership that negotiated the transition from apartheid.

Likewise, Botswana, a tiny country that has consistently posted one of Africa's highest economic-growth rates, has been quietly enjoying what some analysts call Africa's purest democracy with a high level of political tolerance. Mauritius, another relatively affluent island state, also has a vibrant democracy. Both countries have pragmatic leadership.

Cape Verde, Guinea-Bissau, and Malawi held elections in recent years that were seen as largely free of irregularities. Sierra Leone has astounded observers by its relative calm since elections in February. The vote was held despite a civil war and a military coup the previous month. Many wonder if the chaos in next-door Liberia will spill over the border.

France nurtures democracies

France is involved militarily and economically in its former African colonies, mostly in West Africa. But its attempts to nurture multiparty democracy have been mixed. The Comoro Islands went to the polls this year after a history of coups. Benin held elections March 18 that returned a former dictator to power and surprised many with its fairness.

But each success story can be matched by a failures. Extreme poverty prompts social discontent. São Tomé and Príncipe held its first pluralistic elections a few years ago, but the lack of democratic traditions meant few were surprised by a coup attempt last year.

Some political analysts argue that Western models may not always apply to Africa. They point to Uganda, whose President Yoweri Museveni ruled against other parties taking part in elections earlier this year, claiming that the country was ill-prepared for Western-style pluralism after a long history of ethnic strife. Many observers said Mr. Museveni's election victory was the best solution for a country that has prospered under the stability of his rule.

Pat Keefer, an expert on Africa at the National Democratic Institute, a nongovernmental organization based in Washington, questions whether political liberalization can occur when poor countries are under the pressure of reforms prescribed by the World Bank and IMF.

She points to Zambia, where the popularity of President Frederick Chiluba was so eroded by austerity measures he imposed under IMF and World Bank guidance that he was nearly ousted by the opposition.

"Maybe you cannot do this economic restructuring and democratic development at the same time," Mrs. Keefer says.

Why Is Africa Eating Asia's Dust?

While one scrambles toward development, the other slips into despair

Keith B. Richburg

Washington Post Foreign Service

NAIROBI—Ugandan President Yoweri Museveni is a thoughtful, analytical man who often takes on a professorial tone when discussing Africa's myriad problems. So he seemed uncharacteristically at a loss when asked at a recent news conference: Why has African development lagged so far behind that of East Asia, a region that suffered from a somewhat similar set of obstacles?

After offering several well-explored explanations, he paused and admitted some hesitancy to go further. Finally, he said what seemed most on his mind: "The discipline of Asians compared to Africans." People from East Asian countries with scarce resources and large populations "may tend to be more disciplined than people who take life for granted," he said. Some Africans, he intoned, "have so much land that they don't know what to do with it."

It is an explanation heard time and again to a question that fascinates and perplexes anyone who has spent time in both Africa and East Asia. Why has East Asia over the past two decades become a model of economic success, while Africa, since independence, has seen largely failure—increasing poverty, hunger and economies propped up by foreign aid? Is it largely a matter of discipline, as Museveni suggests, or are other factors at work?

There was nothing innate in the peoples of East Asia and Africa that made this outcome inevitable. In 1957, Ghana—one of the bright hopes of black Africa—had a higher gross national product than South Korea, then emerging from a devastating war. Now South Korea is a newly industrialized country—one of the "four dragons" of Southeast Asia. Ghana, meanwhile, has actually slid backwards; its gross national product is lower than it was at independence. It is fair to ask, what happened?

For four years, from 1986 until late 1990, I traveled throughout Southeast Asia as a Washington Post correspondent, seeing firsthand the economic dynamism of a region that has been largely defined by its successful growth and development. Some countries—Singapore, Malaysia and Indonesia—emerged just as Africa did from under colonial tutelage. Singapore became independent as a tiny city-state, with no natural resources. Indonesia and Malaysia at independence were as divided, along ethnic, religious and linguistic lines, as many African countries are today. Thailand, which was never colonized, was a front-line state for the Indochina wars of the late 1960s and was beset by its own Communist insurgency.

Yet from these uncertain beginnings, Southeast Asian nations have prospered. Their average growth rates for the 1980s measured between 8 percent and 10 percent. They avoided the pitfall of heavy external debt through deft management of their economies. And they have successfully diversified away from reliance on single commodity exports, making them less vulnerable to world market price shocks.

There are, of course, examples in East Asia of non-prospering countries, such as Cambodia, Vietnam and Laos—all of which opted for a Communist path and were wracked by lengthy wars. And the Philippines—once the most prosperous country in East Asia—was ravaged by 20 years of authoritarian rule by Ferdinand Marcos.

Moving last year to sub-Saharan Africa, I found a continent in a dismal state of disrepair. From the statistics and the background briefings, one expects to find Africa underdeveloped; the surprise is discovering just how underdeveloped it is. Africa has most of the world's poorest nations. Its children are most likely to die before the age of 5. Its adults are least likely to live beyond the age 50. Africans are, on the whole, more malnourished, less educated and more likely to be afflicted by fatal diseases than any other people on earth.

Any Asia-Africa comparison must allow for many important differences. Although the two continents became independent at roughly the same time, they didn't begin the economic race at the same starting point. East Asian

ECONOMIC DISPARITY

A generation ago, Nigeria's gross national product and exports topped those of South Korea, Malaysia and Thailand. Today, however, Nigeria lags behind its Asian counterparts.

Nigeria is not atypical. In Ghana, Kenya, Tanzania and Zaire as well, per capita gross national product has declined over the past decade even as it has increased steadily in Asia's Little Dragons.

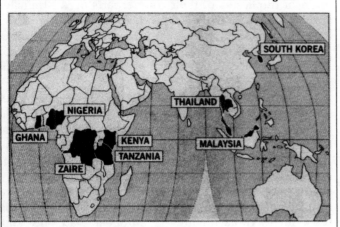

PER CAPITA GROSS NATIONAL PRODUCT
IN THOUSANDS OF U.S. DOLLARS

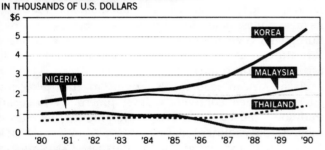

GROSS NATIONAL PRODUCT
IN BILLIONS OF U.S. DOLLARS

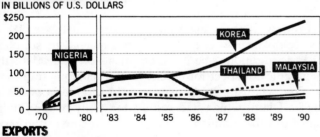

EXPORTS
IN BILLIONS OF U.S. DOLLARS

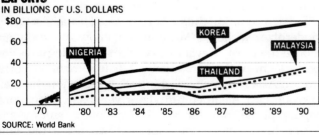

SOURCE: World Bank

push from the West. In the years since independence, they have received far more Western and Japanese investment. And East Asia, unlike Africa, did not have to spend its early post-colonial years recovering from the physical and psychological trauma associated with three centuries of slavery.

What follows is not a detailed statistical comparison; it is rather a set of interviews and impressions gathered by a reporter who has lived in both places. For the past seven months, I have lived in Kenya and traveled to seven other countries of this troubled continent. One, Somalia, has in fact ceased to be a functioning country, divided as it is between armed warring clans and now in a state of anarchy. Zaire and Malawi are reeling under repressive dictatorships—and in Zaire, years of corruption and neglect have brought the official economy to collapse. Ethiopia and Uganda are struggling to emerge from the shadow of decades of ethnic conflict and dictatorial repression that have driven the economies of both those countries into the ground.

Tanzania in many ways is the saddest, because it has enjoyed 30 years of peace and considerable foreign assistance, but its economy has been ravaged by years of socialist mismanagement. Dar es Salaam, its capital, is in a worse state of disrepair than Hanoi; the road system has collapsed, telephones do not work, electricity is sporadic, its store shelves are bare. Tanzania remains, by many estimates, the third-poorest place on earth.

Kenya and Nigeria, along with Ghana, represented hope in sub-Saharan Africa. But neither has realized its potential. Both have seen their economic advances canceled out by debilitating corruption. Nigeria has often been compared to Indonesia—big, diverse and oil-rich. But where Indonesia managed the oil boom of the 1970s successfully, and has begun to diversify away from its dependence on oil, Nigeria used the boom years to borrow heavily, creating a debt burden that today constrains government action. And Nigeria, unlike Indonesia, remains dependent on oil for 95 percent of its export earnings and 80 percent of its budget receipts.

These resource-rich African countries need not have emerged as basket cases. And Tanzania and Malawi have had ample opportunities to develop through foreign assistance.

Foreign reporters often are criticized for not reporting more "good news" from Africa. There seems a simple reason for that: So much of what happens here is so bad. In East Asia, the stories are largely about economic growth. But in Africa, the issues are more basic. Thirty years after independence, Africans are still trying to learn how to live together in civil societies and how to forge a sense of national identity inside the artificial boundaries of their nation-states.

The continent today is on the economic sidelines. It accounts for a mere pittance of the world's trade. Its share of world markets has fallen by half since the 1970s.

economies had a substantial head start; they had developed elaborate patterns of trade and development long before the European colonists arrived. The East Asians, in addition to starting out ahead, also have had a stronger

African trade accounts for less than 0.1 percent of North American imports.

How did Africa reach this current predicament? And what lessons, if any, does the East Asian success hold for this troubled region?

⚹ Africans themselves, when asked the questions, often point to a familiar list of reasons: the legacy of colonialism; the problem of having diverse ethnic groups within national boundaries; the long-running East–West conflict that constrained Africa's independent decision-making; small countries with fragmented markets; widespread corruption of Africa's ruling elite; and now, more recently, the lack of popular participation in governance. "There is absolutely no way you can achieve economic development without democracy," said Museveni.

Yet many of the East Asian nations also have had to contend with these problems. East Asia, more than Africa, became a playing field for the East–West rivalry. Some of East Asia's most economically successful countries—Thailand, Malaysia and Indonesia, for example— are notoriously corrupt. And precious few East Asian countries can be called democratic, as evidenced by the recent protests in Thailand against the military's continued domination of politics.

An answer, then, would seem to lie deeper. It may be found in the respective patterns of colonialism, in the economic choices pursued and in the differences in the post-independence leadership that emerged in East Asia and Africa. And, as Museveni suggests, it may also be a question of differing cultural traditions.

At a restaurant in Washington last year, a diplomat from the Embassy of Cameroon was explaining to a reporter the problem of Africa's black elite. Go to the cafes and the bistros, he said. See them in their European suits, reading the latest editions of European newspapers. The problem of African development, he said, is that the educated elite have never developed indigenous models, but instead have tried to transplant Europe to Africa.

It doesn't take long in Africa to see what the diplomat was talking about. Basil Davidson, a renowned British scholar on Africa, writes in his new book "The Black Man's Burden" how European colonialism in Africa set out to deny and eventually eliminate the continent's pre-colonial history. And in that, the Europeans found willing accomplices among Africa's European-oriented elite, the "modernizers," who were in constant conflict with Africa's "traditionalists," including the acknowledged tribal chiefs.

These modernizing Africans clung to the notion that anything traditional was by definition primitive. And it was this elite that came to the forefront of the independence movements and proceeded to impose European models on their new African states. Rather than seek to build on tradition, as the Confucianist societies of East Asia tried to do even in their revolutionary phases, the new Africans often sought to purge what was deepest and most authentic in their cultures.

That influence can still be seen today. Judges in Kenyan courts wear white wigs and speak in a flowery, archaic English that might be considered "quaint." Governmental institutions in the former British colonies—from parliaments to the "special branch" internal security forces— are near-duplicates of their counterparts at Westminster and Whitehall. Colonial governments in Africa were dictatorships backed up by a top-heavy bureaucracy. Independence seems to have substituted black autocrats for the old white colonial governors, with little thought of Africa's traditions.

The suppression of indigenous culture has been especially pronounced in the former French colonies of West Africa, which were treated as an overseas department of France, notes Pauline Baker, an Africa specialist with the Aspen Institute. "The French tried to have black Frenchmen," she says.

After traveling through East Africa, the late Shiva Naipaul concluded in his book "North of South" that the black man's contact with the European had only succeeded in destroying African culture. "Black Africa, with its gimcrack tyrannies, its field marshals and emperors, its false philosophies, its fabricated statehoods, returns to Europe its own features," he wrote, "but grotesquely caricatured—as they might be seen in one of those distorting funhouse mirrors."

Black African leaders also point to the deleterious effects on their continent's development, heritage and traditions caused by slavery. They note that slavery robbed the continent of its brightest and most able-bodied men and women for more than 300 years, and some leaders today are going so far as to demand "reparations" from the West.

Contrast that to East Asia. A common feature of Western colonialism was that it never managed to supplant historic traditions—be it the emphasis on education, the hierarchical respect for elders, or the religious traditions of Confucianism, Buddhism and, in Indonesia and Malaysia, Islam, which had come later. Only in the Philippines did the Spanish friars succeed in converting most of the population to Roman Catholicism.

Today, a common theme of East Asian leaders is how to modernize without Westernizing, how to pick and choose the most relevant of Western technology without losing sight of their traditions. A fear commonly voiced around Asia is that encroaching Westernization threatens to erode East Asian culture. Four years ago, Singapore's deputy prime minister, Lee Hsien Loong, summed up the challenge in an interview. "If we reach the point where we all become Americanized," he said, "then that's the end of Singapore."

After independence, many of the African countries became swayed by socialism, the ideology in vogue throughout Europe at the time. Theirs became an African variety, whether dubbed "humanism" as in Zambia, or *ujamaa* in Tanzania. But even in avowedly capitalist countries such as Kenya, the result became the same: government ownership of most enterprises, and a distrust of private-sector initiative and foreign investment.

Asia found another way. Theirs was a brand of state-centered capitalism that was neither completely free enterprise nor dogmatically Marxist. The state intervened in the economy, but in a positive way, supporting "winning" corporations and settling wage disputes. East Asia also had three wars fought on its soil—World War II, Korea and Vietnam—leading the United States to offer benign trading relations to secure stable partners in its fight against Communist expansion.

In a paper examining East Asian and African responses to the global debt crisis, World Bank economist Ishrat Husain detailed how from the mid-1970s, East Asian countries adopted "outward" development policies— meaning liberal trade with low tariff barriers to imports, and realistic exchange rates that enhanced exports. This outward orientation allowed the East Asians to diversify their imports while the international competition improved the efficiency of its producers.

Africa, on the other hand, pursued "inward" economic policies, throwing up trade restrictions and maintaining overvalued currencies.

Herman Cohen, the U.S. assistant secretary for African affairs, sees another reason East Asia has largely prospered. "They did all the right things—plus land reform," he says. By privatizing land holdings, East Asian countries saw agricultural production increase, Cohen says. In Africa, land was communally owned in traditional society and expropriated by the state after independence; prices for farm products typically have been set by state marketing boards.

In comparing East Asia and Africa, it has become fashionable among those who know both regions to say the key difference is that Africa has not produced a Lee Kuan Yew. As long-time prime minister of tiny Singapore, Lee has come to personify the idea of benevolent authoritarianism, a paternalistic ruler who brooked no dissent but nonetheless guided his city-state into the ranks of East Asia's "little dragons."

Africa has had its share of towering figures. But by contrast, some of the best known—such as Tanzania's Julius Nyerere and Zambia's Kenneth Kaunda—ran their countries' economies into the ground. Africa also has produced more than its share of dictators, tyrants and buffoons—such as Uganda's Idi Amin and Jean Bedel Bokassa, who declared himself emperor and his impoverished country the Central African Empire. Zaire's Mobutu Sese Seko and Malawi's H. Kamuzu Banda cling to power through repression. In between are a host of corrupt dictators and military men who seem more intent on padding their European bank accounts than improving the lot of their impoverished peoples.

To be sure, Asia is not without its corruption. In Thailand, corrupt military officers and unscrupulous politicians are involved in a host of illegal activities. But there is a difference between corruption Asian-style and its African equivalent. In Asia, the corruption has not been as debilitating to economic growth. In fact, corruption and growth seem to run parallel.

A Western economist in Nigeria, who lived previously in Indonesia, puts it this way: "In Indonesia, the president's daughter might get the contract to build the toll roads, but the roads do get built and they do facilitate traffic flow. . . . That sort of corruption is productive corruption as opposed to malignant corruption."

In Addis Ababa, an official of the Organization of African Unity, Mamadon Bah, was explaining to a visiting reporter the problem of bringing more democracy to the continent. "What we need in Africa these days is mainly discipline," he said, "but discipline from the top."

Any discussion of cultural differences between Asians and Africans by definition treads on explosive ground, since it feeds on past racist stereotypes of Asians as hardworking and Africans as lazy.

"People work like dogs in Kenya," says Makau wa Mutua, a Kenyan exile at the Harvard University law school's human rights program. "Nobody sits around waiting for mangos to drop from trees." Referring to Museveni's comments about discipline, Mutua recalls how Kenyan President Daniel arap Moi once visited Asia and similarly came back urging Kenyans to emulate the Asian example. "As a leader, one has to talk about discipline to get people to work harder," Mutua says. "That is the stereotype of the Asian machine, that people work so hard. But I think that's pure garbage."

Still, many other Africans agree with Museveni and the OAU official that cultural factors do play a role in development. They argue that lack of discipline among African leaders is a particular problem. For even the hardest-working African has difficulty building a solid life if his country's political leadership is corrupt and undisciplined.

Pauline Baker speaks of the "five bads" that she says help explain Africa's poor record of economic development: "bad luck, bad environment, bad policy, bad government and bad faith [by Western governments that failed to deliver on expected aid and investment]." Baker says that although cultural analysis has gone out of fashion among academics, it may be appropriate to add a sixth factor—"bad outlook."

As examples of the cultural factors that enrich African life but may limit economic development, Baker cites "the role of the extended family" and "the role of tradition." In Africa, she notes, "the real obligations are blood ties to the family or tribe, rather than national ties." The extended family provides a private welfare system that helps take care of people, but it also limits the development of a middle class. The lucky entrepreneur who makes a little money finds he is expected to house, feed and educate his cousins, nieces and nephews. He is pulled back, toward family and village. It is typical, says Baker, that the first thing a newly wealthy city dweller will do with his money is build a big house back in his village.

In most of the Southeast Asian countries, discipline has been imposed from the top. Singapore's People's Action Party under Lee Kuan Yew has been highly authoritarian, micro-managing people's lives to the point of prohibiting chewing gum, using financial incentives to encourage better-educated couples to have more children and launching nationwide campaigns to encourage people to smile more. Governments in Malaysia and Indonesia, trying to forge cohesion out of diverse populations, have force-fed their people a common language policy. In all the Southeast Asian countries except the Philippines, civil liberties are sacrificed as a necessary price of stability—something Asians call the "social contract" between rulers and the ruled.

These Asian regimes draw support from cultural traditions that foster order, hierarchy and stability. The Confucian tradition, for example, is widespread throughout East Asia. It encourages a disciplined work ethic and a stable, stratified political system; it also reinforces the Asian emphasis on education, which is prized in disciplined, authoritarian societies such as Korea and China almost as a secular religion.

Africa has had its share of authoritarian regimes. But far from fostering discipline, most of them have led to chaos. Dictators who tried to enforce unity and discipline—Ethiopia's Mengistu Haile Mariam and Somalia's Mohamed Siad Barre are just two examples—were overthrown last year in bloody revolutions; other African autocrats are teetering. The single feature of African autocracies seems to be their inability to impose their will on their populations.

Even when the military tries to impose political discipline from the top down, as in Nigeria, moral discipline remains lax among the top leaders—and corruption is widespread.

On the individual level, the question of discipline is more difficult to address. No one, for example, would say that the average farmer in Tanzania or Malawi works less than his Asian counterpart. People in hard-pressed Kinshasa, Zaire, survive only by their endurance—working several jobs, selling goods on the streets. In Uganda, government offices are largely empty during the daytime, because low-paid bureaucrats are out running private businesses. In Kenya, even when no milk was available on store shelves because of government price controls, farmers with cows were busy building their own networks of urban buyers. Together, this private sector activity accounts for a disciplined economic sector often overlooked in official statistics.

Lawrence Harrison, a retired Foreign Service officer who has written two books exploring cultural values in the developing world, says he has found Confucianism to be the key ingredient in East Asian development.

"Confucius imparts to his followers a strong sense of future, the importance of education, the importance of merit, the importance of saving for future generations," he says. "All of those things in an economic sense are things that you don't associate with the African culture."

But some African leaders are beginning to express similar themes in their own terms. As Museveni put it recently in Kampala, Uganda, this is the time "for the people of Africa to take their destiny in their own hands."

DENG XIAOPING, ARCHITECT OF MODERN CHINA, DIES AT 92

Part 1

Successors in Search of a New Mandate

PATRICK E. TYLER

For thousands of years, the Chinese have looked up to one over-arching authority—whether emperor or commissar—to rule them with the "mandate of heaven."

Deng Xiaoping's deteriorating health has long left him inactive and all but invisible, but his presence conferred a reassuring sense of order and direction on a fractious leadership struggling to sustain an economic miracle, to contend with an ambitious military and to extend China's influence in a suspicious world.

Now Mr. Deng, the last of China's revolutionary titans, has passed the mandate to a collective of younger men centered around Jiang Zemin, a 70-year-old power engineer turned party boss, and Prime Minister Li Peng, a tenacious political survivor best known to the world as the face of authoritarianism that crushed the pro-democracy uprising at Tiananmen Square in 1989.

These men hold the titles and the power, but it is not at all clear either can inherit the imperial authority

needed to unite China as it deals with new, divisive challenges.

Among them are pressures for greater economic liberalization and a more open debate of the past—and for greater attention to human rights and political liberty—the corrosive influence of corruption and China's delicate relations with Hong Kong and Taiwan.

Mr. Jiang's lack of stature in comparison to Mao and Mr. Deng has already consigned him to a life of political maneuver and compromise among the tangle of factions and families that dominates the hierarchy of the Chinese Communist Party. And it has forced him to an uneasy alliance with Mr. Li, who day to day wields the machinery of government and the management of China's foreign policy.

And, perhaps most importantly, Mr. Jiang's relative political weakness has forced him to accommodate the growing demands of the Chinese military for larger budgets and for a more bellicose posture toward Tai-

wan, the exile bastion of Chiang Kaishek where 21 million residents spend much of their time trying to come to terms with Beijing's demands for reunification.

The good news for Mr. Jiang in the seven years since Mr. Deng nudged him into place as General Secretary of the party in the aftermath of Tiananmen is that he has maneuvered so effectively that none of his potential rivals have been able to seriously fault his leadership. But he has always had the Gibraltar-size mantle of Mr. Deng's authority to fall back on. Now it is gone.

A new mandate of heaven now must be fashioned in China, and Mr. Deng's prodigious legacy of economic reform that delivered such a rising tide of prosperity for the Chinese cannot quite overcome one glaring omission: failure to provide a constitutional or legal framework for political succession.

Despite efforts to establish the rule of law, when it comes to picking a leader, the Chinese Communist

Party still resembles Mao's revolutionary tribe, where seniority in the party and ties to the military or to heroic events in the Communist past create the seating chart in the high councils of the party that must agree on a new leader.

That was the manner employed in selecting Jiang Zemin when the wreckage of Tiananmen forced Mr. Deng to abandon an earlier hand-picked heir, Zhao Ziyang.

The world saw it as Mr. Deng's decision—and his hand was certainly uppermost—but the selection of Mr. Jiang was carefully vetted among revolutionary elders, men whose names are scarcely known outside China, but whose seniority and contribution to the party always gave them a seat at Mr. Deng's table.

Some of them, like Chen Yun and Yao Yilin, have died. But a powerful constellation remains, among them Peng Zhen, the former Mayor of Beijing; Song Ping, an aged party ideologue; Bo Yibo; Song Renqiong; Wan Li, and Yang Shangkun. They are in their 80's and 90's, and none cuts the profile of Mr. Deng, but their power is as certain as it is invisible.

After lingering for so long, Mr. Deng could not have departed at a more sensitive moment—as the party prepares to celebrate the return of Hong Kong to Chinese sovereignty, one of Mr. Deng's greatest achievements, and as it also prepares for a major party congress to ratify the leadership lineup that will lead China into the next century.

This year's party congress will be the first at which Mr. Jiang stands alone, without Mr. Deng's support.

"As long as Deng was alive, Jiang's position was unassailable," said Kenneth Lieberthal, a professor of political science at the University of Michigan.

Mr. Deng's death opens up two key areas for political discussion that were off-limits while he was alive, in Mr. Lieberthal's view: criticism of Mr. Deng himself and a reappraisal of the 1989 crackdown.

"Jiang's position is still very strong," Mr. Lieberthal said. "But

having said that, with Deng now gone, those who wish to cut back Jiang's role can do so by criticizing Deng. They can say that Deng was a great man but that he made some mistakes. Since one of Deng's acts was to pick Jiang, it opens the door for critics of Jiang."

As a witness to the last party congress, in 1992, when Mr. Deng choreographed the resignations and promotions that enhanced Mr. Jiang's chances to consolidate his own position at the top of the party, Mr. Jiang understands how much he is now flying solo.

Liberalization or more repression? China's course is unclear.

The most difficult question he faces is what to do with Li Peng, who must step down a year from now after two consecutive five-year terms as Prime Minister.

With Mr. Deng gone, the Chinese will want to know whether Mr. Jiang has the ability to pull off a major reshaping of the party or whether his vision and authority will be challenged by some collection of opponents who, freed by Mr. Deng's death, will now make their move.

There is no shortage of challengers.

It was just five years ago that many Chinese looked to Yang Shangkun, now 90, as the man who would inherit Mr. Deng's role as paramount leader, leaving Mr. Jiang to run the party and Mr. Li to run the Government. But Mr. Yang, an old revolutionary like Mr. Deng, met his political demise in the summer of 1992 when he turned against the Deng leadership team of Mr. Jiang and Mr. Li.

A number of Chinese who lost their jobs or who went into exile af-

ter Tiananmen have harbored the hope that Mr. Yang would stage a political comeback after Mr. Deng's death and demand the rehabilitation of Zhao Ziyang, a former Prime Minister and party General Secretary, as the party's pre-eminent reformer.

Mr. Zhao was stripped of all of his titles after refusing to order a military assault on the student demonstrators in 1989, but he retains his party membership even as he lives out his days in a closely guarded courtyard home in central Beijing.

These political exiles and reformers in waiting see Mr. Zhao's rehabilitation as the key that would unlock a whole a series of possibilities for democratic reform and bring to an end the hard-line rule that has characterized the era of Mr. Jiang and Mr. Li.

Such bold steps would immediately reopen the question of the party's condemnation of the Tiananmen uprising as a "counterrevolutionary rebellion," a judgment that still divides Chinese society here and abroad.

Like no other event in modern Chinese history, the Tiananmen massacres, played out before a world television audience, changed a buoyant world view of emergent China and replaced it with a paradigm of the repressive state that jails its political and religious dissidents and traffics in nuclear technology and ballistic missiles to unstable parts of the world.

Some of the issues: economy, human rights and Hong Kong and Taiwan.

But the party may not be ready for such a wrenching and dangerous reevaluation, since it would immediately raise the issue of culpability for the hundreds, if not thousands, of deaths that occurred during the military crackdown in 1989.

It is hard for many Chinese to imagine that such a re-evaluation could occur while Li Peng is in power, which is also undoubtedly one of the reasons why Mr. Li so tenaciously holds on to power.

He is now fighting to stay on in a key role after he steps down next year as Prime Minister, and he needs

only look at South Korea's treatment of retired leaders who sent troops against unarmed students for his motivation to remain on the political stage. It is his best protection.

But Mr. Li has a host of enemies who would like to change the face of China's future by foreclosing his and resurrecting the earlier and more promising paradigm of China as a more open and tolerant society interested in democracy and political reform.

Mr. Deng, who fought so hard at the end of his life to resist any idea of revisiting the party's decision to send tanks and machine guns against the Tiananmen movement, may, in death, allow a new debate to finally begin.

It may take more time than many Chinese hope, but as Mr. Deng's daughter and biographer said in early 1995, reversing the verdict of Tiananmen "is for the people who come after" to debate.

Part 2

CHOSE CAPITALISM

Resilient Leader Kept a Firm Political Grip on His Country

SETH FAISON

BEIJING, Thursday, Feb. 20— Deng Xiaoping, one of the founding revolutionaries of Communist China and the architect of economic modernizations that transformed the world's most populous nation, died Wednesday night in Beijing. He was 92.

> *A wily pragmatist, China's paramount leader led the country to enormous economic growth.*

The official New China News Agency reported that Mr. Deng, who for the last 18 years was referred to as the paramount leader, died at 9:08 P.M., Beijing time (8:08 A.M. Eastern standard time). He suffered from Parkinson's disease, the agency said, and died from "complications of lung infections."

As the sun rose on Beijing this chilly morning, many residents learned the news on radio and television broadcasts before they set off for work and school, and the reaction of those on the street at dawn was restrained and, in some cases, nonchalant. It is part of Mr. Deng's legacy that ordinary people no longer hang on daily reminders of their leaders' every pronouncement.

Mr. Deng leaves behind his designated successor, Jiang Zemin, 70, China's President and general secretary of the Communist Party. He was chosen by Mr. Deng and other senior leaders in late June 1989, in the weeks after the crackdown on prodemocracy demonstrators near Tiananmen Square, one of the darkest episodes of Mr. Deng's legacy, and yet one in keeping with his deep-seated reliance on authoritarian measures.

Early today, Mr. Jiang was quickly named chairman of a funeral committee, made up of 459 leaders of China's Government, evidently formed

long in advance of last night's news. No announcement was made about the timing or scope of a funeral.

A wily pragmatist Mr. Deng led China to economic growth few Chinese had dreamed of, making the country much less prone to unrest than it might have been if Mr. Deng had died a few years earlier.

An unyielding authoritarian, he left behind a Communist Party that still has absolute political authority and crushes all dissent, even though its ideology has lost its legitimacy with most Chinese.

While many Chinese were prepared to some degree for Mr. Deng's death, it still leaves a void.

"I think for the steady development of our nation we can't be without him," said Yang Xiaoping, 39, a hotel attendant who was heading off to work in the early morning hours here. "I am not totally shocked. In earlier years when Mao died, we all thought it impossible, and were shocked, and could not accept it."

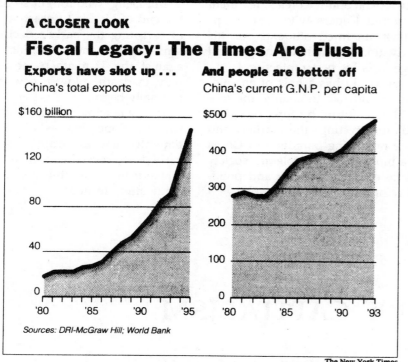

A CLOSER LOOK

Fiscal Legacy: The Times Are Flush

Exports have shot up . . .
China's total exports

And people are better off
China's current G.N.P. per capita

Sources: DRI-McGraw Hill; World Bank

The New York Times

Others were divided over the changes Mr. Deng helped unleash.

"In the past everyone was equal," said Gao Yilun, a 64-year-old retired worker who repairs bicycles by the road. "Now even college graduates can't get a job." But he added, almost reflexively, "It is not for us little people to talk about."

Mr. Deng was the last of a generation of leaders who shared the hardships of forging a revolution, proclaimed the People's Republic of China in 1949, and presided over decades of drastic political upheaval. The convulsions culminated in the Cultural Revolution, a movement that was initially endorsed by Mr. Deng but then toppled him as one of its chief victims. Only after he survived his political exile and brought the ideas of the market to a China founded on rejecting them did his policies help bring China a measure of prosperity and stability.

A charismatic, chain-smoking man who stood barely 5 feet tall, Mr. Deng was known for a personality as peppery as the cuisine of his native Sichuan province, and was given to punchy political pronouncements, like his well-known maxim for pragmatic economics: "It doesn't matter whether a cat is black or white, as long as it catches mice."

Mr. Deng formally retired from his last important post, chairman of China's central military commission, in 1989. Yet he continued to wield immeasurable influence, reserving final say in all important political matters for several years afterward, and finally relinquishing power only as he grew frail and disoriented.

In his final public appearance in February 1994, Mr. Deng was visibly weak, walking only with assistance and badly hard of hearing. Since then, while outsiders speculated about his steadily deteriorating health, Mr. Deng's slow retreat from political power allowed his successors to achieve an almost seamless transition.

Mr. Jiang, first seen as a transitional figure when he was named as Mr. Deng's heir apparent in 1989, has steadily asserted his authority in recent years, consolidating his influence over the military and China's enormous political bureaucracy.

Although Chinese long feared that Mr. Deng's death would leave the country prone to political chaos or even civil war, those worries receded noticeably in recent years. Mr.

Deng's gradual disappearance, coupled with steadily growing standards of living, seem to have lulled ordinary people and Beijing's political elite into the belief that China's leadership would proceed without a major change in direction.

Yet the danger of unrest always lurks at times of transition in China. It was the death of a lesser senior leader of China in April 1989, the former Communist Party chief Hu Yaobang that unleashed vast demonstrations for a more open and accountable political system, as prodemocracy students used Mr. Hu's memorial services as an opening to air their grievances.

Extraordinary political circumstances—a gaping split between Mr. Deng and the party chief at the time, Zhao Ziyang, once Mr. Deng's expected successor—allowed the demonstrations to swell. The crackdown that left hundreds dead on the streets and tarnished the image of China and Mr. Deng followed on June 4, 1989.

This year, public expressions of grief for Mr. Deng are likely to be closely guarded, and any attempt to organize independent memorial services is likely to be suppressed with force, if necessary.

Mr. Deng's death also comes at a political moment strikingly different from that of September 1976, when Mao Zedong died at the age of 82. At that time, there was a sharp division between political radicals led by Mao's widow, Jiang Qing, and moderates, led by Mr. Deng.

Mr. Deng was not able to seize power right away, though, and Mao was replaced by Hua Guofeng, a middle-of-the-road compromiser, who was eventually edged aside by Mr. Deng in December 1978.

While once analysts thought that the same disorder and jockeying for power that followed Mao's death would occur after Mr. Deng died, Mr. Deng's long illness gave Mr. Jiang time to establish himself.

"The transition has been in place probably for three years," said James Lilley, a former United States Ambassador to China. "Jiang Zemin is a Deng selection."

One of Mr. Deng's great achievements was to open China to the outside world, encouraging young Chinese to study overseas, urging foreign businesses to invest in China, and insuring that China joined the international community.

Mr. Deng oversaw the negotiations that led Britain to agree in 1984 to return its colony of Hong Kong to the sovereignty of China on July 1, 1997, and took many opportunities to proclaim that "one country, two systems" would guide a hands-off approach that would allow Hong Kong to preserve its capitalist economic system.

Mr. Deng often expressed his determination to visit Hong Kong for the handover, when meeting with visiting foreign leaders, some of whom were unsure whether to take him seriously. Not everyone expected him to live until 1997, and his death comes a little more than four months before one of the last colonies is handed back to China, an event that symbolized China's triumph over the humiliations that helped unleash the revolution Mr. Deng helped incite.

Mr. Deng's death comes at the beginning of a year of great political sensitivity in China. The handover of Hong Kong on July 1 will require careful attention of Beijing's leaders, and it will be followed a few months later by the Communist Party's 15th Party Congress.

Hong Kong, in addition to being closely watched for any rolling back of economic and political freedom, is widely seen as a test of Beijing's promises of autonomy, the same assurances it wants to extend to Taiwan some day.

Taiwan is one of the largest looming issues for Mr. Jiang, who brought China to a tense military standoff a year ago when President Lee Tenghui held Taiwan's first presidential election, and increasingly asserted diplomatic independence, to which Beijing's leaders strongly object.

The Communist Party's congress in October will endorse a political platform and anoint a leader.

China's official appraisal of Mr. Deng, issued by the New China News Agency in the hours after his death was announced, eulogized Mr. Deng in solemn tones.

"The death of Comrade Deng Xiaoping is an immeasurable loss to our Party, our army and the people of various ethnic groups throughout the country, and will certainly cause tremendous grief among the Chinese people," the official obituary said.

"We must conscientiously study Deng Xiaoping's theory of building socialism with Chinese characteristics, learn from Comrade Deng Xiaoping's revolutionary style and his scientific attitude and creative spirit in applying a Marxist stand, viewpoints and methods to studying new problems and solving new problems.

"Without Comrade Deng Xiaoping's theory, there would not be the new situation of reform and opening up in China today, and there would not be the bright future of China's socialist modernization."

The official obituary made no direct mention of the June 4 Tiananmen Square massacre, referring only to "the domestic and international political disturbances in the late 1980's and early 1990's.

The official appraisal did refer to Mr. Deng's trip to southern China in 1992, which was his last major political stand. Facing opposition to his view that China should fuel fast economic growth no matter the risks of inflation and social instability, Mr. Deng toured several cities in southern China and made a key speech in Shenzhen, the fast-growing, modern city that abuts Hong Kong, that became a political touchstone in national policy of fast growth.

That speech, in today's official description "profoundly answered many key questions for understanding, which had been perplexing and binding people's minds for a long time, especially the questions con-

cerning the relationship between socialism and market economy."

Huang Yasheng, a senior associate at the Carnegie Endowment for International Peace, argued that Mr. Deng's death would have less immediate effect on politics in China than might be expected, precisely because of the change that Mr. Deng helped engineer.

"Deng Xiaoping will mainly be remembered for his economic achievements, but people don't always realize that his enduring contribution also lies in politics," said Mr.

Huang. "He restored a sense of normalcy to China. One of the reasons that his death won't make much difference is that power is now shared among leaders and among different institutions. He made sure that the Great Leap Forward and the Cultural Revolution would not happen again."

One of the most durable leaders in China's long history passes from the scene.

Mr. Deng generally discouraged efforts to create a cult around himself, as his predecessor Mao had done. But then Mao was a man of considerable charisma and megalomania, and Mr. Deng was stronger at organizing and consensus-building.

As Mao remarked about Mr. Deng to Nikita S. Khrushchev, the Soviet leader, in 1957: "Do you see that little man over there? He is very intelligent and has a great future ahead of him."

Only in Mr. Deng's final years did the party authorities start to elevate "Deng Xiaoping Thought" to the level of national catechism.

In 1992, Mr. Deng said boldly that reform "must be insisted on for 100 years." He continued, "Whoever wants to change this will be overthrown."

Mr. Jiang, not known for the kind of political daring that characterized Mr. Deng's long career, nonetheless appropriated Mr. Deng's fast-growth policy and has benefited from it.

"He looks very secure," said Andrew Nathan, a professor of political science at Columbia University, referring to Mr. Jiang. "He has put a lot of his people in power. On the face of it, he is much more secure than Hua Guofeng was, but history says that there is no such thing as secure power in a system like this."

Mr. Hua's name, long forgotten by so many, appeared again today, way down toward the bottom of the list of the 479 members of Mr. Deng's funeral committee, a virtual who's who of China's political elite. Zhao Ziyang, the former party chief who unlike Mr. Hua did not go quietly, was not on the list.

The official appraisal of Mr. Deng concluded in traditional, Communist Party-style language:

"Under the strong leadership of the Party Central Committee with Comrade Jiang Zemin at the core, the whole party, the whole army and the people of various ethnic groups all over the country, holding high the banner of Deng Xiaoping's theory of building socialism with Chinese characteristics, firm and unshakable and full of confidence, will certainly be able to carry out the great cause of socialist reform, opening up and modernization drive pioneered by Comrade Deng Xiaoping and triumphantly reach our destination. Eternal Glory to Comrade Deng Xiaoping!"

> "The new regime that emerged after the general election this May is genuinely representative of the extraordinary diversity of the country.... Within its first few months in office this coalition has sought to address many of the vexing challenges that India faces in both domestic and foreign policy, including arresting the decline of political institutions, continuing the program of economic reform, decentralizing decision making, and improving strained relations with many of India's neighbors."

India: Between Turmoil and Hope

SUMIT GANGULY

When England withdrew from India in 1947, many British conservative spokesmen, most notably Winston Churchill, expressed little hope for the future of their former colony. The Tories were especially dubious about the survival of democratic institutions, which they falsely believed they had bequeathed to India. Many observers around the world also doubted that India would long remain a secular state. Today, however, on the eve of India's fiftieth year of independence, there is little question that democracy has survived in India. And despite the popularity of religiously based nationalist parties, secularism also survives, albeit in an attenuated form.

That said, India on the eve of its fiftieth year presents a mixed picture. The generation that governs is a far cry from the one that fought for and obtained the country's independence. Not since Jawaharlal Nehru was prime minister has India produced a national leader who could be considered a statesman of global stature. Corruption and cravenness are too often the hallmarks of modern-day Indian politicians. Nevertheless, the Indian polity appears to have an extraordinary capacity for social and political renewal. The Nehruvian and post-Nehruvian generations of leadership had predominantly upper-class and upper-caste roots. The new regime that emerged after the general election this May is genuinely representative of the extraordinary

ŠUMIT GANGULY *is a professor of political science at Hunter College and the Graduate School of the City University of New York. He is the author of* Kashmir: Between War and Peace *(Cambridge: Cambridge University Press, forthcoming) and coeditor with Ted Greenwood of* Mending Fences: Confidence and Security-Building Measures in South Asia *(Boulder, Colo.: Westview, 1996).*

diversity of the country and reflects its vast socio-economic and regional cleavages. Within its first few months in office this coalition has sought to address many of the vexing challenges that India faces in domestic and foreign policy, including arresting the decline of political institutions, continuing the program of economic reform, decentralizing decision making, and improving strained relations with many of India's neighbors.

THE ROOTS OF DISCONTENT

Despite the survival of democracy, India's political institutions have not progressed untarnished. Since the 1970s virtually every political institution in India has seen some decline. The once-dominant Congress Party is a shell of its former self; the prestigious Indian Administrative Service, successor to the colonial Indian Civil Service (commonly referred to as the "steel frame" of India), has been politicized; the judiciary has been subjected to parochial pressures; constitutional norms have been exploited for partisan purposes; and the army has repeatedly been used to quell civil disorders. Worse still, politicians of every hue have been implicated in (if not actually convicted of) every conceivable form of illegal activity.

Yet, for all its shortcomings, the Indian polity continues to function. Several factors provide grounds for optimism about India's future. The most compelling of these is the extraordinary growth of political mobilization. Ironically, the populist appeals and slogans of Prime Minister Indira Gandhi, the leader responsible for much of India's political decline, played a major role in this political awakening. India's institutional capacity proved inadequate to meet many of the expectations raised by her populist slogans (such as "*garibi hatao*"—literally, "abolish poverty"). Nevertheless, these slogans awakened India's hitherto disenfranchised electorate to the possibilities of social and economic uplift.

The experience of successive elections at municipal, local, and national levels coupled with growing literacy and media exposure also contributed to the increasing political sophistication of India's electorate. Even India's poor and lower-caste groups gradually came to understand the power of the ballot. Much to the dismay of the wielders of political power, India's dispossessed no longer chose to vote in predictable patterns. Unsurprisingly, virtually every political party, regardless of political coloration, came to rely on coercion to shape electoral outcomes. Such efforts were, for the most part, futile; thanks to India's feisty and open press and the vigor of its newly mobilized electorate, little could be done to force particular electoral outcomes.

THE POLITICAL AXIS SHIFTS

The outcomes of the eleventh general election, which was held between late April and early May 1996, reflect a number of profound sociopolitical shifts that have transformed the foundations of the Indian polity. One of these is the rise of a brand of muscular Indian nationalism with a strong majoritarian component. Consequently, it was no surprise that the xenophobic and jingoistic Bharatiya Janata Party emerged as the largest party in parliament. In conjunction with its allies, the BJP managed to secure 195 seats in the 545-seat body. The organizational and ideological disarray of the Congress Party led to an electoral debacle: the former ruling party came in second, with 141 seats. But the shift in the axis of political power in the country is best reflected in the success of a range of regional parties. A loose agglomeration of these parties of the center-left coalesced under the banner of the National Front-Left Front, and managed to corner third place in parliament, with a combined 120 seats.

During the election campaign the BJP had sought to soften its antisecular image and had also appropriated the "stability" card, an old Congress slogan. Like the Congress, the BJP argued that it alone was capable of providing "stable" governance. Furthermore, it had attempted to exploit the shortcomings of the economic liberalization program that the Congress government of Prime Minister Narasimha Rao had initiated in 1991. Specifically, the BJP focused on the misgivings of the Indian lower middle class, which has yet to benefit from the economic reform. Simultaneously, it pandered to the anxieties of medium-sized Indian businesses that fear the entry of foreign multinationals in a range of consumer goods industries.

The Congress Party, battered by allegations of corruption, resorted to various populist strategies to garner votes. In the 1995-1996 budget, for example, the government increased spending on the rural poor, avoided tackling the contentious issue of labor law reform, and refused to liberalize consumer goods imports further. Yet these gestures proved inadequate to prevent the Congress from losing many of its traditional bases of support. Muslims had already deserted the Congress in the wake of the party's failure to prevent the destruction of the Babri mosque by Hindu fanatics in December 1992 and its subsequent inability to protect Muslim communities in the riots that followed. Simultaneously, newly mobilized lower castes, who had once been staunch Congress supporters, left the party and turned to smaller caste-oriented parties, such as the Bahujan Samaj Party or the Samajwadi Party. These parties made explicitly caste-based appeals and successfully siphoned off a significant portion of the Congress vote in the populous states of northern India.

The lack of skilled party leadership and the end of the Gandhi family mystique also cost the Congress dearly. Prime Minister Rao's lackluster campaign style failed to inspire voters. Nor did his secretive and conniving political style, which had become his political conceit, serve him well. Furthermore, the Congress Party's organization was in acute disrepair, and Rao did little or nothing to revitalize its machinery. Most important, for idiosyncratic reasons, he entered into a dubious electoral alliance with J. Jayalalitha, the chief minister of the key state of Tamil Nadu. The combined effects of these choices proved devastating for the Congress.

COALITION RULE

The National Front-Left Front (NF-LF), which emerged to control the third largest bloc in parliament, cobbled together an unforeseen coalition of regionally based parties. This coalition was formed on the basis of the regional predominance of some of its members, such as the Communist Party of India-Marxist, which has long controlled the state of West Bengal. The NF-LF also attracted a significant share of the Muslim vote. According to an exit poll conducted by analysts from the New Delhi-based Center for the Study of Developing Societies, 48 percent of Muslim voters cast their ballots for the NF-LF coalition.

Following constitutional guidelines, President Shankar Dayal Sharma asked the BJP and its allies, on the basis of their parliamentary plurality, to form the government. The BJP's term in office was short lived; it proved unable to tempt any regional parties, or any faction of the Congress, to forge a working majority. On May 28, on the verge of losing a no-confidence vote, the BJP government resigned after only 12 days in office. With the Congress in disarray, the NF-LF cobbled together some 190 members and stepped forward to form a new government under the banner of the United Front. The Congress, until recently one of the principal adversaries of the NF-LF, agreed to support the coalition in parliament.

India's experience with coalition governments has been far from exemplary. However, despite the prognostications of many political pundits, there is considerable likelihood that this coalition of 14 center-left parties will survive, if only because of the weakness of its competition. The Congress, the party that not only brought India its independence but also ruled it for the better part of four decades, may well be in its death throes. It has not held internal elections in decades. Rao, the former prime minister and, until his recent resignation, the party's president, faces multiple charges of bribery and corruption. Apart from having ushered in the tumultuous process of economic liberalization and promoting a degree of economic growth, the Congress can claim few accomplishments. In the May election its share of the popular vote plummeted from an all-time high of 48.1 percent in 1984 to 31 percent. As a consequence of its weak organization, crippled leadership, and incoherent ideological vision, it is in no position to withdraw its support and thus bring down the present government. Only when the party manages to restore a degree of internal coherence will it abandon the United Front and seek a new mandate.

The BJP, which initially assumed office with considerable fanfare, has come to the harsh realization that its popularity may have reached its natural limit. No party of any consequence, apart from the predominantly Sikh, Punjab-based Akali Dal Party and former firebrand labor leader George Fernan-

The Congress, the party that not only brought India its independence but also ruled it for the better part of four decades, may well be in its death throes.

des, was prepared to forge a parliamentary coalition with the BJP. Admittedly, the unwillingness of many parties to make common cause with the BJP at the national level may have not stemmed from enlightened motives: most simply feared the future electoral wrath of the highly mobilized lower castes and Muslims. The BJP's ability to mount any substantial challenge to this government depends in considerable measure on the future of the Congress. If the Congress were to split apart, the BJP would be in a position to absorb a rump Congress and then seek to undermine the present regime.

The coalition's political fortunes improved slightly in light of the results of the state assembly elections in early October in the critical, populous north Indian state of Uttar Pradesh. Despite widespread expectations of a BJP victory, the voters returned a deeply divided verdict. None of the three major contestants in Uttar Pradesh—the alliance between Congress and the Bahujan Samaj Party representing socially disadvantaged groups, the state-level coalition formed by the BJP and Fernandes's Samata Party, or the low-caste Samajwadi Party—managed to win a clear-cut victory. Faced with this split electoral outcome, the central government in New Delhi chose to administer Uttar Pradesh at the federal level for a renewable six-month term.

Apart from the external challenges that the United Front confronts, it has to contend with questions of internal ideological and political coherence. A number of fissures exist in the ideological corpus of the front. The motley 14-party coalition includes communists, former members of the Congress, and various regional parties. Managing the diverse array of interests and constituency demands within the coalition will be no easy task for the 63-year-old prime minister, H. D. Deve Gowda, a politician from the southern state of Karnataka with no national political experience.

To its credit, the United Front did try to fashion a common platform just before assuming office. This "common minimum program" calls for growth with equity and promises to promote federalism, combat official corruption, dramatically increase foreign investment (except in consumer goods industries), improve infrastructure, maintain fiscal prudence, and expand social welfare spending. It calls for steps to restore normalcy to the insurgency-wracked state of Jammu and Kashmir, and in the foreign policy realm efforts to improve relations with India's neighbors. Some of the stated fiscal and economic goals are obviously contradictory, however; an expansion of spending on social welfare is at odds with the pursuit of macroeconomic stability and fiscal prudence.

Two issues already reveal the tensions within this alliance. Finance Minister P. Chidambaram, a Harvard-educated lawyer and a firm advocate of the economic reforms, generated the first controversy when he called for a 30 percent increase in the price of petroleum products in July to help reduce a gaping fiscal deficit. Faced with prompt and strident criticism from many of his left-leaning colleagues, he was forced to halve the proposed 30 percent hike in diesel prices.

Chidambaram also grappled with conflicting priorities when he presented his first budget in August. For example, the budget contained high fertilizer subsidies—a nod to the new prime minister's rural background and ties to the farming community. In fairness to the government, Chidambaram's budget does curtail capital expenditures. To offset the adverse impact of these cuts on the growth of infrastructure, the government is planning to set up an Infrastructure Development Finance Company. This company, which will receive its initial funding from the Reserve Bank of India, is designed to raise capital and lend it for infrastructural projects.

The budget also continues fitful reforms in trade and foreign investment. It lowers customs duties by about 8 percent, exempts excise rates on various consumer goods, and reduces barriers to imports of technology. No doubt with an eye toward making up some of the revenues lost due to tariff reductions, the budget imposes a 15 percent across-the-board minimum corporate tax. Of course, this tax has been greeted with considerable dismay in the corporate sector. The Mumbai (formerly Bombay) Stock Exchange registered the unequivocal disapproval of the corporate community by dropping an astonishing 248 points within three days of the budget's presentation.

The economic reform process may well be irreversible, but the contradictory ideological pulls within the NF-LF coalition will necessarily lead to uneven changes in economic policymaking. For example, despite its initial commitment to the reform of the insurance sector, the government has decided to move with caution in that area. More recently, Finance Minister Chidambaram faced a flurry of criticism from the leftist members of the coalition after he announced that the government planned to divest up to 74 percent of state-owned firms in noncore and nonstrategic sectors.

KASHMIR: CONFLICT UNENDING?

Apart from maintaining internal cohesion over economic and social policies, the government faces important challenges in other arenas as well. Two issues will likely preoccupy the NF-LF leadership in the immediate future: the search for peace in Jammu and Kashmir and India's opposition to the Comprehensive Test Ban Treaty (CTBT), now on the agenda of the United Nations.

Since 1990, an ethnoreligious insurgency in the northern state of Jammu and Kashmir has plagued the various governments attempting to suppress it. While the origins of this insurgency are indigenous, systematic Pakistani support for the insurgents has greatly escalated the level of violence and has sustained it over the last six years.[1]

In June 1996, as part of the eleventh general elections, the Indian government held elections for the Lok Sabha (lower house of the parliament) in Jammu and Kashmir for the first time since 1991. The electoral turnout was extraordinary: close to 65 percent of the eligible electorate voted. However, a number of Indian news organizations alleged that voters had been coerced to participate in some parts of the state. Although Indian government officials publicly denied that any coercion had taken place, they admitted privately that security forces may have prodded voters into showing up at the polls. Such encouragement, they argued, was necessary: without some boost from the security forces, the fear of reprisals from the insurgents would have discouraged many prospective voters from exercising their franchise.

Through much of September, elections for the state legislature were also held in Jammu and Kashmir. The turnout in the fourth and final round of this election was approximately 53 percent. Apart from a few sporadic incidents of violence, these elections were free of any taint. The normally critical Indian press praised the government for its safe and fair conduct of the state assembly elections.

The tasks that lie before Jammu and Kashmir's new National Conference government, led by Chief Minister Farooq Abdullah, are daunting. Even

---

[1] For a discussion of the origins of the insurgency in Kashmir, see Šumit Ganguly, "Political Mobilization and Institutional Decay: Explaining the Kashmir Insurgency," *International Security,* Fall 1996.

though large sections of the state's war-weary population took part in the election, important sources of dissent remain. The All-Party Hurriyat Conference (APHC), an agglomeration of political parties opposed to the government of India, remains unreconciled to the election results. The APHC boycotted the elections and actively campaigned against holding them. One of the first tasks before the government will be to try to entice the APHC to reenter the conventional political arena.

The other key challenge that confronts the government may be even more demanding. In an attempt to sow discord among the ranks of the insurgents, the Indian security forces have created a number of "counterinsurgent" groups. These organizations, composed of former insurgents, were trained, armed, and generously supported by the security forces. One of these organizations, the Jammu and Kashmir Awami League, led by Kukka Parrey, even contested the elections in May. However, they failed to win a single seat, which raises questions about their future role in the politics of Jammu and Kashmir. The government's most immediate and compelling task will be to disarm this 5,000-strong militia before its members return to the fold of the insurgents.

THE CTBT

The other security-related task on the plate of the United Front government will be to manage India's growing prominence on the international scene. India has long lobbied for a larger profile at the United Nations; this summer, it raised eyebrows by opposing the Comprehensive Test Ban Treaty (CTBT), an accord it had once championed.

India's interest in the CTBT is long-standing. On April 8, 1954, India introduced a resolution in the UN General Assembly calling for a suspension of all nuclear tests. The Indian proposal failed to generate any support from the three extant nuclear weapons states: the United States, the Soviet Union, and the United Kingdom. Over the next 30 years or so, the disarmament debate continued in a desultory fashion in the UN. The Partial Test Ban Treaty limiting underwater and atmospheric tests was signed in August 1963, but little progress was made toward a comprehensive test ban treaty.

It was not until September 1993, when the United States and India cosponsored a resolution in the General Assembly, that serious efforts for a comprehensive test ban were undertaken. The negotiations for the CTBT were begun in Geneva under the aegis of the UN Conference on Disarmament and

were proceeding apace when a number of seemingly unrelated forces impinged on India's negotiating stance. Multilaterally, much to the surprise and dismay of the Indian leadership, the United States and its allies carefully shepherded the extension of the nuclear Non-Proliferation Treaty (NPT) through the UN General Assembly. As part of its historical opposition to the NPT, India had chosen not to participate formally in the negotiations and consequently proved unable to influence the text of the treaty. Most uncomfortably for India, the United States sought and was able to obtain an unconditional and indefinite extension of the NPT. Of all the UN member states, only India, Pakistan, and Israel remained outside the NPT framework. The remarkable dexterity with which United States negotiators stage-managed the negotiations left India largely isolated.

India's lack of initiative on the NPT negotiations generated domestic criticism of its diplomacy on key issues relating to security and disarmament. The domestic critics of India's negotiating strategy on the NPT found further grist for their mill in November 1995 when the United States Congress, at the behest of the Clinton administration, passed the Brown amendment to the Foreign Assistance Act. The Brown amendment relaxed the Pressler amendment of 1990, which had prohibited all forms of military and economic assistance to Pakistan because of its pursuit of a clandestine nuclear weapons program. The Clinton administration's active support of the Brown amendment and the amendment's subsequent passage strengthened the hands of India's defense hawks, who, ever suspicious of United States motives in South Asia, saw the Brown amendment as a first step in the post–cold war renewal of United States-Pakistani military ties. Accordingly, many of them lobbied for a tougher Indian stance on the CTBT negotiations in Geneva.

Indian domestic politics also contributed to a hardening of its negotiating stance on the CTBT. As the eleventh general election approached, the Congress government of Prime Minister Narasimha Rao sought to outbid the BJP on a key national security issue, namely India's nuclear policy. In an attempt to gauge international reaction while simultaneously tackling the BJP challenge, the Indian government started work at the nuclear test site in Pokhran in the state of Rajasthan. Not unexpectedly, in December 1995 United States reconnaissance satellites discovered these preparations. The reaction of the United States and other key members of the international community was sharp and swift. After initial denials, the Ministry of External Affairs in New Delhi dismissed the United States claims as "speculative." The strong reaction of the international community to the possibility of a second Indian nuclear test (its first was in 1974) was not lost on India's political leadership. The Indian strategic community, in particular, realized that if the CTBT were passed, the pressures on India from the international community not to further develop its military nuclear capabilities would be overwhelming.

In the wake of these developments, the Indian diplomatic position at the UN Conference on Disarmament hardened. India's representative to the conference, Arundhati Ghose, renewed India's call for a time-bound plan for complete, worldwide nuclear disarmament. The nuclear weapons states ignored her pleas, dismissing them as political posturing meant largely for domestic consumption.

An Australian proposal eventually brought the treaty before the UN General Assembly on September 10, 1996, where it passed on a 158 to 3 vote. The only three states voting against the treaty were India, Libya, and Bhutan. Five states—Cuba, Lebanon, Mauritius, Syria, and Tanzania—abstained. India continues to maintain that the treaty is fundamentally flawed and that it will never accede to its terms. According to legal experts it is not entirely clear whether the treaty can enter into force without India's eventual acquiescence. Since India's rejection of the treaty was supported across the political spectrum at home, obtaining its accession will not be easy.

Despite the intransigent approach that the Indian diplomatic community has adopted toward the CTBT, the new government has already demonstrated a significant willingness to alter India's positions on other foreign policy issues. Most notably, the government has sought to continue strengthening India's economic relations with Southeast Asia. This effort follows India's elevation to full dialogue partnership with the Association of Southeast Asian Nations in 1995. India has also offered to renew negotiations with Pakistan after several years' hiatus. Pakistan, which is faced with a legion of domestic woes, has yet to respond meaningfully to the Indian offer. Finally, the new government has also shown a greater interest in addressing the concerns of another of India's neighbors, Bangladesh. During a visit to that country in September, Foreign Minister Inder Kumar Gujral expressed a willingness to address Bangladesh's long-standing complaints about inadequate access to various river waters.

NAVIGATING THE POLITICAL WATERS

The diplomacy and posture of this government on the CTBT negotiations is certainly debatable. However, on virtually every other front the government has made laudable efforts to tackle a range of problems that have long prevented India from surging ahead. The central challenge for the regime will be to cope with the demands of its extraordinarily diverse constituencies. Previous coalition governments have foundered on familiar shoals. In the brief period that it has been in office, members of the motley United Front coalition have shown a willingness to work together. It remains to be seen if they can continue to demonstrate similar political sagacity as the government moves to contend with more contentious issues at home and abroad.

Miracles beyond the free market

Michael Prowse

The biggest challenge for economists today is understanding the extraordinary success of east Asia. The region has nearly quadrupled per capita incomes in the past quarter of a century—a record unparalleled in economic history. On present trends it may begin to overtake much of the industrialised west early in the 21st century.

If its startling success could be replicated elsewhere, billions of people in developing and formerly communist countries could look forward to improved living standards. And the hope, eventually, of eliminating the scourge of grinding poverty would seem less quixotic.

Yet the region is as puzzling as three-dimensional chess. It has done far better than conventional theories predict, even allowing for such quantifiable pluses as macroeconomic stability, high rates of investment and a focus on exports. There is just no generally accepted explanation for its main distinguishing feature—supercharged rates of productivity growth.

The puzzle is deepened by the region's lack of homogeneity. The high-fliers are far from being carbon copies. At one extreme, Hong Kong has pursued a broadly free market approach; at the other, South Korea has intervened in just about every way conceivable. And the magic formula for growth has entirely eluded some countries in the region, such as the Philippines.

At the World Bank in Washington, an exhaustive analysis of the "Asia miracle" is nearing completion. Bank staff are distilling lessons from Japan, the four "tigers"—South Korea, Taiwan, Hong Kong and Singapore—and the so-called "cubs"—Malaysia, Thailand and Indonesia. They have also taken a look at the recent explosive growth in parts of southern China.

The study was undertaken partly at the instigation of Japan, the bank's second-largest shareholder, which has long wanted to play a bigger role in policy design. Japan has been critical of aspects of conventional World Bank/International Monetary Fund prescriptions and, justifiably, believes more attention should be paid to its own outstandingly successful development strategies—which formed a model for much of east Asia.

In 1991, Japan's Overseas Economic Co-operation Fund told the bank it was putting too much emphasis on deregulation and privatisation and made a case for selective import protection in developing countries and for the use of subsidised credits as a tool in industrial policy.

Mr John Page, a senior member of the bank's Asia miracle team, says the Japanese criticism struck a chord because the results of market-oriented reforms had often proved disappointing in developing economies. By cutting budget deficits, eliminating market distortions and shrinking government, client countries had stabilised their economies. But too often they had not achieved a virtuous cycle of rapid growth; they still lay "at the bottom of the league table relative to east Asia". The question became: "What now?"

The bank's benchmark for judging Asian policies is not an extreme free market philosophy, which would have the public sector shun responsibility for just about everything bar national defence. It is rather the less controversial "market friendly" strategy set out at length in the bank's 1991 World Development Report.

This clearly delineates the role of markets and the state. Development would be fastest, it claimed, when government concentrated on two jobs: maintaining macroeconomic stability through conservative fiscal and monetary policies; and investing in people through public education, training and healthcare programmes.

Beyond this, developing countries should rely on market forces. They should create as competitive as possible a regime in industry, commerce and the financial sector. And they should eliminate all barriers to trade and foreign investment. The core idea is that governments should focus on the things only they can do and leave everything else to markets.

It turns out that most of the Asian high-fliers have adopted a more permissive attitude to the role of government. Indeed, Mr Page argues that the success of the region can best be understood in terms of a "strategic growth" model that focuses more on what has to be done to achieve rapid growth than on who should do what.

On the strategic theory, development will be rapid provided countries find a way of: accumulating capital rapidly; allocating resources efficiently; and catching up technologically.

But there is no presumption that any of these functions should be reserved exclusively for the private sector. The miracle economies appear to have used a mixture of market incentives and state intervention in each of these areas:

• Accumulation. Gross domestic investment averages a startling 37 per cent of GDP in east Asia against an average of 26 per cent in developing countries as a whole. Yet this advantage was not won purely by adhering to the market-friendly approach.

The region has admittedly created a positive climate for business investment by pursuing conservative fiscal and monetary policies—inflation has averaged 9 per cent over the past 30 years, less than half the rate in other developing countries. The public sector has also invested effectively in people (enrollment in primary education far exceeds levels elsewhere, as does attention to vocational education), although it has not spent an atypical proportion of national income on social services.

But most of the Asian high-fliers have also interfered with market mechanisms.

They have limited the personal sector's ability to consume and heavily regulated the financial sector so as to ensure a predictable supply of low-cost capital for industry. Mechanisms for forcibly shifting resources from consumption to investment vary—Japan, South Korea and Taiwan, for example have maintained stringent controls on consumption and housing. The net effect, however, is the same everywhere: an abnormally high rate of savings.

• Efficient allocation of resources. Governments have striven to ensure that the most important market of all—that for labour—is flexible, if not fully competitive. Wages have largely reflected market supply and demand, partly because trade unions have been suppressed. Focusing hard on success in export markets has also imposed crucial competitive discipline and prevented domestic prices for industrial inputs moving far out of line with world markets.

Yet bank research indicates governments have also intervened vigorously. While less protectionist than the third world as a whole, few accepted western free-trade principles. Many have used import controls to protect strategic sectors (for example, quotas in South Korea, high tariffs in Thailand) and showered offsetting subsidies on export industries. At one time or another state-owned industries have played an important role in many of the economies, including South Korea, Taiwan, Indonesia, Singapore and Thailand. Many have not hesitated to direct the supply of credit to particular sectors. Both South Korea and Taiwan provided automatic credit for exporters in the early stages of development.

• Technological catch-up. The lesson again is that remarkable productivity growth only partly reflects market-oriented policies. Singapore, Malaysia, Thailand and, to some degree, Taiwan, have welcomed foreign investment. Early developers such as Japan and South Korea used other devices, such as licences letting them copy foreign technology. But unlike many other developing countries none tried to rely on home-grown technology.

However, all high-fliers intervened selectively to promote particular industries, with varying intensity and success. The process of trying to shift industrial output towards high-valued-added sectors is described by enthusiasts as "getting prices wrong in order to create dynamic comparative advantage".

South Korea provides a wealth of examples of aggressive and successful intervention. The government's most audacious move was perhaps to create from scratch a domestic steel industry despite foreign donor opposition and lack of private-sector enthusiasm. The state-run business went on to become the world's most efficient steel producer.

An internal bank memo sums up South Korea's record: "From the early 1960s, the government carefully planned and orchestrated the country's development. . . . [It] used the financial sector to steer credits to preferred sectors and promoted individual firms to achieve national objectives. . . . [It] socialised risk, created large conglomerates (chaebols), created state enterprises when necessary, and moulded a public-private partnership that rivalled Japan's."

Singapore provides another classic example of directed growth. When private sector companies failed to respond to opportunities identified by bureaucrats, state-owned or controlled groups were often pushed to the fore, the memo says. The bank has documented selective interventions throughout the region, even in supposedly free market Hong Kong.

The Asian example poses a dilemma for bodies such as the IMF and the World Bank, especially in former communist countries. Does it still make sense to advocate a form of "shock therapy"—the doctrine that deregulating and privatising everything as fast as possible is the optimum policy? Or should they recommend east Asia's slower, more interventionist path to economic maturity? It all depends on whether east Asia's deviations from orthodoxy can be replicated.

There are some grounds for caution. Mr Vinod Thomas, the bank's chief economist for east Asia and an architect of the market-friendly strategy, points out that government activism outside east Asia has produced dismal results. A distinction should also be drawn between the earlier "northern tier" of Asian high-fliers—Japan, South Korea and Taiwan—and the later "southern tier" of Malaysia, Thailand and Indonesia.

Until the 1980s, countries such as South Korea were able to promote exports and protect imports without provoking much criticism. But pressure for a more level playing field has since grown intense. Broadly speaking, the southern tier of later developers has pursued more market-oriented policies than the first wave of Asian stars. Indus-

trial interventions have also tended to be less successful. A bank memo describes Malaysia's efforts as "by and large a costly failure" and Thailand's as "largely ineffective".

Less tangible political and cultural factors may also be crucial. Most Asian high-fliers benefited from long periods of stable (if authoritarian) political rule. This encouraged long-term horizons. Public-sector bureaucracies have also tended to be more able and less corrupt than in most other third world countries. Governments were thus unusually well placed to implement development strategies.

Policymakers were also remarkably pragmatic; if a policy did not work it was rapidly dropped. South Korea, for example, went through several phases. It was relatively market-oriented in the early 1960s, became highly interventionist during the "heavy and chemical industries" drive of the 1970s, and then reverted to greater reliance on market forces in the mid-1980s. No region, it seems, has been less weighed down by ideology or more willing to seek advice from abroad.

The bank has only just begun the politically charged process of drawing conclusions from mountains of research papers. But senior officials believe the study may lead to a new paradigm for development in the 1990s. The evidence confirms that the miracle economies did indeed "do things differently". In many instances, "government played a big role, trade was not open and financial markets were repressed", concedes Mr Thomas.

"If we're right," says Mr Page, "the economic policy arsenal has many more weapons than we suspected." Mr Thomas agrees: the lesson from east Asia is that "you need a government guiding hand; you cannot just abdicate development to the private sector". He predicts that the bank will pay more attention to the role of institutions and to the potential for partnerships between the public and private sectors.

The most encouraging aspect of the Asian story, officials say, is that habits and institutions crucial for economic success were created rather than inherited. To raise the social standing of entrepreneurs, for example, South Korea had to overcome its Confucian traditions, which had glorified the scholar-bureaucrat. Singapore raised its savings rate from 1 per cent in 1965 to more than 40 per cent today. The implication is that sufficiently determined governments can work similar miracles in other places.

Confucius Says: Go East, Young Man

Many Asians now think their lives and values are superior to 'the American Way'

T. R. Reid

T. R. Reid, who just completed a five-year tour as The Washington Post's Tokyo bureau chief, is on leave from the paper while writing a book, "Confucius Lives Next Door."

The Asian leaders who gathered in Osaka for the annual Asian-Pacific Economic Cooperation (APEC) summit expressed pious regrets that Bill Clinton had to cancel his attendance at the last minute. At some level, though, they were probably delighted. The image of a U.S. president trapped in Washington by political chaos surrounding a red-ink budget can only strengthen the Asians' growing superiority complex toward the once-revered U.S.A.

Many Asian politicians, scholars and business leaders are proudly proclaiming these days that there is an ocean of difference in basic social values across the Pacific. They have decided that the Western, democratic, Judeo-Christian value structure, with its emphasis on the primacy of the individual—in short, "The American Way"—is fundamentally different from the Eastern, group-oriented, vaguely Confucian cultural pattern that is now proudly labeled "The Asian Way."

And it's not just that the values are different. Rather, these Asian Neo-Confucianists insist that their cultural values are better than ours.

"Many Western societies—including the United States—are doing some major things fundamentally wrong today, while a great number of East Asian societies are doing the same things right," argues Kishore Mahbubani, a Singaporean scholar and diplomat who has emerged as the Max Weber of this new "Confucian Ethic."

In an endless series of articles and lectures bearing titles like "The Dangers of Decadence" and "Go East, Young Man," the engaging and articulate Mahbubani tells his fellow Asians that "the American boat is sinking" and that a strong dose of Confucian values is needed to set things right. "If Americans were to try to begin learning from Asians, their nation would become a better place."

Even in Japan, most Westernized of the Asian nations, there is a movement to turn back East. "By following the insights of Confucianism," insists the Japanese academician Kichitaro Katsuta, "we can avoid the social catastrophe befalling the West, the result of centuries of individualism and egotism."

Americans, still patting themselves on the back for winning the Cold War, may not be ready just yet for another global ideological struggle over first principles. But an increasingly wealthy and confident East Asia is eager to engage us in a debate that raises direct challenges to cherished Western ideals.

Fueling the notion of "Asia Good, America Bad" is the palpable sense of social and economic well-being sweeping over East Asia. Overall, the Asian members of APEC have much higher economic growth rates than the Western democracies—coupled with much lower rates of unemployment, violent crime, drug use, broken homes, welfare dependency and other detritus of Euro-American society.

From Kuala Lumpur to Kawasaki, people cite the 1994 World Bank report that sought to predict which countries would be the richest on earth a quarter-century from now. In that ranking, four of the five wealthiest nations, and seven of the top 10, are Asian. The United States, the world's richest nation today, is projected in second place in the year 2020, between China and Japan.

Economic statistics can go up and down, of course—just ask Japan, yesterday's Asian Superman, now wallowing in extended recession. But Asia's current crop of Neo-Confucians look more at social indicators than economic statistics. "You Americans have this mantra about your high standard of living," Mahbubani told me once, soft-spoken and amiable even as he plunged the rhetorical dagger.

"And yes, if standard of living means the number of square feet in your home, or the number of channels on your TV,

America leads the world. But if standard of living means not being afraid to go outside that home after dark, or not worrying about what filth your children will see on all those TV channels, then our Asian societies have the higher standard."

That gets to the core of the Neo-Confucian case against Western democracy. The free nations of Europe and America are simply too free, the argument runs; they have gone too far to indulge individual freedom at the expense of society as a whole. When Asian leaders talk about American democracy, the names that come up are not Washington or Jefferson, but rather Tonya Harding, Howard Stern, the Menendez brothers and the Michigan Militia. "Democracies are only beginning to learn that too much freedom is dangerous," argues Mahathir Mohamad, prime minister of Malaysia, who is perhaps the most caustic critic of Western values among Asia's current political leadership.

"Whether the West admits it or not, David Koresh and the [Jim] Jones cult were the products of the Western form of democracy," Mahathir told an applauding audience in Tokyo this spring. "So also is the recent bombing in Oklahoma. The Michigan Militia corps has as yet done no real harm. But you can bet that sooner or later they will be using those guns which they democratically own."

There's an arrogant flavor to this kind of attack—not terribly surprising for people who have decided they are winners. "The growing realization among East Asians," Mahbubani says, "that they can do anything as well as, if not better than, other cultures has led to an explosion of confidence."

Most of today's Neo-Confucianists grew up in an Asia where Westerners were the colonial governors, the preachers, the teachers, the founders of great colleges and giant business enterprises. Now the Asian Way folks want to reverse the cultural flow.

Naturally, the Neo-Confucianists are encouraged to see Americans agreeing with them on some points.

When Mahathir complains that "Abolition of religious instruction in [public] schools . . . has resulted in a loss of direction," he is singing a chorus right out of Pat Robertson's hymn book. His criticism of the freedom to own guns resonates with a whole different group of Americans. Singapore strong-man Lee Kuan Yew likes to point out that when his island state subjected teenager Michael Fay to a whipping for the crime of vandalizing cars, opinion polls showed that most Americans supported the sentence.

One of the nicer ironies of the Neo-Confucian boom is that this whole "pan-Asian" movement borrows its most basic concept from Western thought. The very existence of a "Far East," a place called "Asia," is a modern Western invention, dreamed up by European geographers and traders.

If the geography underpinning the Neo-Confucian boom is a tad ambiguous, the same can be said for the basic philosophy. As with the ancient prophets of other cultures, Confucius and his ideas are open to a wide range of interpretations.

The great sage K'ung Fu-tzu (that Latinate name "Confucius" is another Western concoction) was appalled by the vice and corruption all about him in Chou dynasty China of the 5th century B.C. He taught that the remedy for broad social ills lay in individual dedication to basic virtues.

The Confucian virtues, as they are generally described nowadays, include thrift, hard work, honoring the family unit and obeying the law. There is also a deep commitment to education, to pass along these virtues and other necessary skills.

None of this sounds particularly alien to anybody who grew up in a Judeo-Christian Western society. As Michael Armacost, the president of the Brookings Institution, used to say during his tenure as ambassador to Japan, "Americans can't criticize people for working hard, saving a lot, investing in the future, educating rigorously. Those are things we've always prided ourselves on."

At at least two points in the Confucian Cannon, the master declares that the most important single guide to life can be found in the term shu. Confucius defines it this way: "Do not impose on others what you do not want done to yourself." To any veteran of Sunday school, of course, this is simply The Golden Rule.

In their contempt for Western ways, however, the Neo-Confucianists insist that the teachings of their ancient Chinese ancestor involve a unique set of values. Even that Confucian statement of The Golden Rule is "different in a subtle way," argues Katsuta, the Japanese academician. The Confucian Golden Rule is stated in the negative, he notes. "Confucius thus advocated tolerance, " Katsuta maintains. "The Christian rule encourages well-intentioned activism. But sometimes well-meaning people are importunate and self-righteous. . . . Western individualism leads to a clash of egos that will destroy tolerance."

Katsuta has Westerners in mind when he denounces intolerance and self-righteousness. In fact, though, the world capital of self-righteousness at the moment may well be the tidy, industrious and thoroughly intolerant city-state of Singapore, a place tightly controlled by Lee Kuan Yew's personal clique of self-styled Neo-Confucians.

Lee charges that Americans "have abandoned an ethical basis for society"—and he's not about to let the same thing happen on his island. Thus police keep watch from the rooftops of Singapore to catch people committing such crimes as littering or chewing gum. Parents of school children deemed to be overweight receive letters ordering them to change the family menus. The government tells people how much of their money to save.

And almost nobody complains about this—at least, not publicly. Quick to attack the problems they see in the West, the thin-skinned Singapore Confucianists go ballistic the minute anyone criticizes them. No media outlet circulating in Singapore would dare reproduce this article, for example; the sentence a few paragraphs up describing Lee as the nation's "strongman" would likely draw libel fines in the tens of thousands of dollars.

If this is The Asian Way, most people would probably be happy to do without it. But many Neo-Confucianists say Lee's Singapore is a gross perversion of the sage's teaching. These critics say that auto rats like Lee and Malaysia's Mahathir have appropriated Confucius as a high-minded rationale for maintaining personal power.

Confucianism need not necessarily involve the spic-and-span authoritarianism of Singapore. South Korea, a bulwark of Confucian learning to this day, is a noisy, dirty, rambunctious nation where people not only chew gum on the streets but do many more offensive things there as well. But Koreans furiously deny that they are less Asian than Lee Kuan Yew.

"Lee's view of Asian culture is not only unsupportable but also self-serving," charges Kim Dae Jung, the veteran South Korean politician who risked his life repeatedly opposing military dictators in his own country. Kim insists that dissent and democracy are cherished Confucian ideals, and that the master's teaching was a key element in South Korea's dramatic switch to democracy in 1987. In short, proponents of The Asian Way are hazy about which direction their Way is headed. In Asia, though, the most important point is that it is not The American Way. The Neo-Confucianists are convinced that their cultural pattern is preferable, and they want the whole world to know it.

"For the past several hundred years, the world has been dominated by Greek and Judeo-Christian ideas," Kim Dae Jung wrote recently. "Now it is time for the world to turn to . . . Asia for another revolution in ideas."

Comparative Politics: Some Major Political Trends, Issues, and Prospects

- The Democratic Trend: How Strong, Thorough, and Lasting? (Article 54)
- The Turn toward Markets: What Role for the State? (Articles 55 and 56)
- Ethnic and Cultural Conflict: The Political Assertion of Group Identities (Articles 57–60)

The articles in this unit deal with three major political trends or patterns of development that can be observed in much of the contemporary world. It is important at the outset to stress that, with the possible exception of Benjamin Barber, none of the authors predict some form of global convergence in which all political systems would become alike in major respects. On closer examination, even Barber turns out to argue that a strong tendency toward global homogenization is offset by a concurrent tendency toward intensified group differentiation and fragmentation.

Thus the trends or patterns discussed here are neither unidirectional nor universal. They are situationally defined, and therefore come in a great variety of forms. They may well turn out to be temporary and partly reversible. Moreover, they do not always reinforce one another but instead show considerable mutual tension. Indeed, their different forms of development are the very stuff of comparative politics, which seeks an informed understanding of the political dimension of social life by making careful comparisons across time and space.

After such cautionary preliminaries, we can proceed to identify three recent developments that singly and together have had a very important role in changing the political world in which we live. One is *the democratic revolution*, which has been sweeping much of the world. This refers to a widespread trend toward some form of *popular government* which often, but not always, takes the form of a search for representative, pluralist democracy in countries that were previously ruled by some form of authoritarian oligarchy or dictatorship.

Another trend, sometimes labeled *the capitalist revolution*, is the even more widespread shift toward some form of *market economy*. It includes a greater reliance on private enterprise and the profit motive, and involves a concurrent move away from heavy regulation, central planning, and state ownership. But this need not mean laissez-faire capitalism. The social market economy, found in much of Western Europe, allows a considerable role for the state in providing services, redistributing income, and setting overall societal goals. In some of the Asian Communist-ruled countries, above all China, we have become used to seeing self-proclaimed revolutionary socialists introduce a considerable degree of capitalist practices into their formerly planned economies. Some wags have suggested that it is time to speak of "Market-Leninists."

The third major trend could be called the *revival of ethnic or cultural politics*. This refers to a growing emphasis on some form of an *exclusive group identity* as the primary basis for political expression. In modern times, it has been common for a group to identify itself by its special ethnic, religious, linguistic, or other cultural traits and to make this identity the basis for a claim to rule by and for itself. The principle of national self-determination received the blessing of Woodrow Wilson, and it continues to have a democratic appeal, even though some critics warn against the potential dangers that may stem from fractious politics of ethnocracy. They detect a collectivist or antipluralist potential in this form of political expression, and point out that it can contribute to intolerance and conflicts among groups as well as between the group and the individual.

The articles in the first section cover democratization as the first of these trends, that is, the startling growth in the number of representative governments in recent years. Even if this development is likely to be reversed in some countries, we need to remember how remarkable it has been in the first place. Using very different criteria and data, skeptics on both right and left for a long time doubted whether representative government was sufficiently stable, efficient, accountable, attractive or, ultimately, legitimate to survive or spread in the modern world. It would be instructive to review their more recent discussion of the 1970s and early 1980s, not in order to refute the pessimists but to learn from their insights as well as their oversights.

Samuel Huntington's widely discussed thesis concerning a recent wave of democratization is usefully summarized and carried further by Larry Diamond. Huntington is one of the best-known observers of democratization, who in the past emphasized the existence of cultural, social, economic, and political obstacles to representative government in most of the world. Even before the collapse of the communist regimes in Europe, however, he had begun to identify a broad pattern of democratization that had started in the mid–1970s, when three dictatorships in southern Europe came to an end (in Greece, Portugal, and Spain). In the following decade, democratization spread to most of Latin America. Central and Eastern Europe then followed, and the trend has also reached some states in Eastern and Southern Asia as well as some parts of Africa, above all, South Africa.

In a widely adopted phrase, Huntington identified this trend as the "third wave" of democratization in modern history. The first wave was both slow and long in its reach. It began in the 1820s and lasted about one century, until 1926, a period during which first the United States and subsequently 28 other countries established governments based on a wide and eventually universal suffrage. In 1922, however, Mussolini's capture of power in Italy began a period of reversal that lasted until the early 1940s. During these 2 decades, the number of democracies fell from 29 to 12, as many became victims of dictatorial takeovers or military conquests.

A second wave of democratization started with the Allied victory in World War II and continued during the early postwar years of decolonization. This wave lasted until about 1962 and resulted in the conversion of about 2 dozen authoritarian systems into democracies or quasi-democracies, sometimes of very short duration. There followed a second reverse wave, lasting from 1962 to 1973. During this period, the number of democracies fell from 36 to 30 and the number of nondemocracies increased from 75 to 95 as various former colonies or fresh democracies fell under authoritarian or dictatorial rule. In the mid-1970s, then, the important "third wave" of democratization got its start.

At the beginning of the 1990s, Huntington counted about 60 democracies in the world, which roughly amounts to a doubling of their number in less than 2 decades. It is an impressive change, but he points out that the process is likely to be reversed once again in a number of the new and unstable democracies. The findings of Huntington and Diamond lend support to the conclusion that democracy's advance has been at best a "two steps forward, one step back" kind of process. The expectations associated with the coming of democracy are in some countries so high that disappointments are bound to follow. Already, the third wave democratic advances in such countries as the Sudan, Nigeria, Algeria, and Peru have been followed by authoritarian reversals. Haiti has gone through its own double wave. The prospects for democracy on that poverty-stricken Caribbean island do not seem bright, but there has been some positive news to report. In 1994 Jean-Bertrand Aristide could return to the presidential office for which he had been elected in 1991 and overthrown by a military coup in the same year. He stepped down at the end of his regular term in 1996, and Haiti has now experienced its first democratic succession in office. There are ominous signs of authoritarian revivals elsewhere in the world, including some parts of the former Soviet Union.

What are the general conditions that inhibit or encourage the spread and stabilization of democracy? Huntington and other scholars have identified some specific historical factors that appear to have contributed to the third wave. One important factor is the loss of legitimacy by both right- and left-wing authoritarian regimes, as they have become discredited by failures. Another factor is the expansion in some developing countries of an urban middle class that has a strong interest in representative government and constitutional rule. In Latin America, especially, the influence of a more liberal Catholic Church has been important. There have also been various forms of external influence by the United States and the European Community as they have tried to promote a human rights agenda. A different but crucial instance of external influence took the form of Mikhail Gorbachev's shift toward nonintervention by the Soviet Union in the late 1980s, when he abandoned the Brezhnev Doctrine's commitment to defend established Communist rulers in Eastern Europe and elsewhere against counterrevolution. Finally, there is the snowballing effect, in such countries as Spain and Poland, of a successful early transition to democracy, which has served as a model for other countries in similar circumstances. This has also been very important in Latin America.

Huntington's rule of thumb is that a democratic form of government can be considered to have become stable when a country has had at least two successive peaceful turnovers of power. Such a development may take a generation or longer to complete, even under fortunate circumstances. Many of the new democracies have little historical experience with a democratic way of life. Where there has been such an experience, it may have been spotty and not very positive. There may be important cultural or socioeconomic obstacles to democratization. Huntington, like most other observers, sees extreme poverty as a principal obstacle to successful democratization.

Both old and new democracies face dangers, as Larry Diamond points out. He analyzes the special problems that tend to dog the new democracies, including the difficulty of living up to the initial expectations entertained by their citizenry. Popular dissatisfaction normally focuses on a particular government in the established political systems, but where representative form of government is a new development there is a danger that the democratic system itself may become the target of criticism rather than a governing group that can be replaced.

Germany provides a valuable case study for testing some of these interpretations of democracy. After World War I, antidemocratic critics identified its Weimar Republic with international disaster, socioeconomic ruin, and political weakness and instability. After World War II, by contrast, the Federal Republic became increasingly credited with stability and prosperity. At first accepted passively, the fledgling West German state soon generated an increasing measure of pragmatic support from its citizenry, based on its widely perceived effectiveness. In time, the new republic also appeared to gain a deeper, more affective support from much of the population. A major question is how national reunification, with its accompanying wrenching changes and inevitable disappointments, will influence German attitudes toward representative government. In the new Eastern European states, in particular, reunification was linked to unrealistic expectations of almost immediate socioeconomic alignment with the prosperous West. How will eastern Germans react, as the new polity fails to deliver promptly and bountifully? Comparatively speaking, Germany is fortunate in having a stable set of institutions, a well-developed democratic culture in the Western states of the Federal Republic, and a solid economic structure. Unfortunately, many of the new democracies face dislocations that make them more comparable to the conditions of the Weimar Republic rather than the successful western German state after World War II.

The second section of this unit covers the trend toward capitalism or, more accurately, market economics. Here Gabriel Almond explores the connections between capitalism and democracy in an article that draws upon both theory and empirical studies. His systematic discussion shows that there are ways in which capitalism and democracy support each other, and ways in which they tend to undermine each other. Is it possible to have the best of both? Almond answers at length that there is a nonutopian manner in which capitalism and democracy can be reconciled, namely in democratic welfare capitalism.

Almond's discussion can be linked to a theme emphasized by some contemporary political economists. They point out that the economic competition between capitalism and socialism, in its Communist form of state ownership and centralized planning, has become a largely closed chapter in history. The central question is now which form of capitalism or market economy will be more successful? A similar argument has been made by the French theorist, Michel Albert, who also distinguishes between the British-American and the continental "Rhineland" models of capitalism. The former is more individualistic, antigovernmental, and is characterized by such traits as high employee turnovers and short-term profit maximizing. It differs considerably from what the Germans themselves like to call their "social market economy." The latter is more team-oriented, emphasizes cooperation between management and organized labor, and leaves a considerable role for government in the setting of general economic strategy, the training of an educated labor force, and the provision of social welfare services.

These different conceptions of capitalism can be linked to different histories. Both Britain and the United States experienced a head start in their industrial revolutions and felt no need for deliberate government efforts to encourage growth. By contrast, Germany and Japan both played the role of latecomers, who looked to government protection in their attempts to catch up. To be sure, governments were also swayed by military considerations to promote German and Japanese industrialization. But the emergence of social capitalism in other continental countries of Europe suggests that cultural rather than military factors played a major role in this development.

A crucial question is whether the relative prosperity and social security associated with this kind of mixed economy can be maintained in a time of technological breakthroughs and global competition. Ralf Dahrendorf addresses these questions in his article and, in his usual manner, provides a combination of thoughtful analysis and assessment.

The third section deals with the revival of the ethnic and cultural dimension in politics. Until recently, relatively few observers foresaw that this element would play such a divisive role in the contemporary world. There were forewarnings, such as the ethnonationalist stirrings in the late 1960s and early 1970s in peripheral areas of such countries as Britain, Canada, and Spain. It also lay behind many of the conflicts in the newly independent countries of the developing world. But most Western observers seem to have been poorly prepared for the task of anticipating or understanding the resurgence of politicized religious, ethnic, and other cultural forces. Many non-Westerners were taken by surprise as well. Mikhail Gorbachev, for example, grossly underestimated the centrifugal force of the nationality question in his own country.

The politicization of religion in many parts of the world falls into this development of a "politics of identity." In recent years, religious groups in parts of Latin America, Asia, the Middle East, sub-Saharan Africa, Asia, and Southern Europe have variously set out on the political road in the name of their faith. As Max Weber warned in a classic lecture shortly before his death, it can be dangerous to seek "the salvation of souls" along the path of politics. The coexistence of people of divergent faiths is possible only because religious conviction need not fully determine or direct a person's or a group's politics. Where absolute and fervent convictions take over, they make it difficult to compromise pragmatically and live harmoniously with people who believe differently. Pluralist democracy requires an element of

tolerance, which for many takes the form of a casual "live and let live" attitude rather than a well-intentioned but futile determination to make others conform to one's central beliefs.

There is an important debate among political scientists concerning the sources and scope of politics based on ethnic, religious, and cultural differences. Samuel Huntington argues forcefully that our most important and dangerous future conflicts will be based on clashes of civilizations. In his view, they will be far more difficult to resolve than those rooted in socioeconomic or even ideological differences. His critics, including the German Josef Joffe, argue that Huntington distorts the differences *among* civilizations and trivializes the differences *within* civilizations as sources of political conflict. Chandra Muzaffar, a Malaysian commentator, goes much further by contending that Huntington's thesis provides a rationalization for a Western policy goal of continual domination of the developing world. In a separate article, John R. Bowen argues forcefully that ethnic conflicts are in fact often the result of political choices made by elites. He offers evidence for what is, after all, a hopeful thesis, because it contains the conclusion that such conflicts could be avoided if other political choices were made.

In the final article, Benjamin Barber brings a broad perspective to the discussion of identity politics in the contemporary world. He sees two major tendencies that threaten democracy. One is the force of globalism, brought about by modern technology, communications, and commerce. Its logical end station is what he calls a "McWorld," in which human diversity, individuality, and meaningful identity are erased. The second tendency works in the opposite direction. It is the force of tribalism, which drives human beings to exacerbate their group differences, become intolerant, and engage in holy wars, or "jihads," against each other. Barber argues that globalism is at best indifferent to democracy, while militant tribalism is deeply antithetical. He argues in favor of seeking a confederal solution, based on democratic civil societies, which could provide human beings with a nonmilitant, parochial communitarianism as well as a framework that suits the global market economy fairly well.

Looking Ahead: Challenge Questions

What is meant by the first, second, and third waves of democratization? Describe the reversals that followed the first two.

Where are most of the countries affected by the third wave located? What factors appear to have contributed to their democratization? What are the signs that the "third wave" may be over?

What are some main problems and dilemmas of old and new democracies, according to Diamond?

In what ways can market capitalism and liberal democracy be said to be mutually supportive? How can they undermine each other?

Why is it so difficult to resolve political conflicts that arise from the political assertion of an exclusive religious or ethnic identity?

What does Benjamin Barber mean when he warns that democracy is threatened by globalism and tribalism?

IS THE THIRD WAVE OVER?

Larry Diamond

Larry Diamond is coeditor of the Journal of Democracy, *codirector of the National Endowment for Democracy's International Forum for Democratic Studies, and a senior research fellow at the Hoover Institution. Various portions of this essay will appear in his forthcoming book* Developing Democracy: Toward Consolidation, *to be published by Johns Hopkins University Press.*

Since the overthrow of Portugal's dictatorial regime in April 1974, the number of democracies in the world has multiplied dramatically. Before the start of this global trend toward democracy, there were roughly 40 countries that could be classified as more or less democratic. The number increased moderately through the late 1970s and early 1980s as a number of states experienced transitions from authoritarian (predominantly military) to democratic rule. in the mid-1980s, however, the pace of global democratic expansion accelerated markedly, and today there are between 76 and 117 democracies, depending on how one counts. *How* one counts is crucial, however, to thinking about *whether* democracy will continue to expand in the world, or even hold steady at its cur-rent level. In fact, it raises the fundamental question of what we mean by democracy.

In a seminal formulation, Samuel Huntington has dubbed this post–1974 period the "third wave" of global democratic expansion. He defines a "wave of democratization" simply as "a group of transitions from nondemocratic to democratic regimes that occur within a specified period of time and that significantly outnumber transitions in the opposite direction during that period."[1] He identifies two previous waves of democratization: a long, slow wave from 1828 to 1926 and a second wave from 1943 to 1964. Significantly, each of these ended with what he calls a "reverse wave" of democratic breakdowns (the first lasting from 1922 to 1942, the second from 1961 to 1975), in which some of the newly established (or reestablished) democracies failed. Overall, each reverse wave reduced the number of democracies in the world significantly but still left more democracies in place than had existed prior to the start of the preceding democratic wave. Reverse waves do great harm to political freedom, human rights, and peace. Thus, as I will argue, preventing a reverse wave should be paramount among the policy goals of democratic actors and institutions around the world.

Conceptualizing Democracy

Essential to tracking the progress of democracy and understanding both its causes and its consequences is a high degree of conceptual clarity about the term "democracy." Unfortunately, what prevails instead in the burgeoning empirical and theoretical literature on democracy is conceptual confusion and disarray so serious that David Collier and Steven Levitsky have identified more than 550 "subtypes" of democracy.[2] Some of these nominal subtypes merely identify specific institutional features or types of full democracy, but many denote "diminished" forms of democracy that overlap with one another in a variety of ways. Fortunately, most conceptions of democracy today (in contrast with the 1960s and 1970s, for example) do converge in defining democracy as a system of political authority, separate from any social and economic features. Where conceptions still diverge fundamentally (but not always very explicitly) is in the

From *Journal of Democracy*, July 1996, pp. 20-37. © 1996 by the National Endowment for Democracy and the Johns Hopkins University Press. Reprinted by permission.

range and extent of political attributes encompassed by democracy.

Minimalist definitions descend from Joseph Schumpeter, who defined democracy as a system "for arriving at political decisions in which individuals acquire the power to decide by means of a competitive struggle for the people's vote."[3] Huntington, among others, explicitly embraces Schumpeter's emphasis on electoral competition as the essence of democracy.[4] Over time, however, Schumpeter's appealingly concise definition has required periodic elaboration (or what Collier and Levitsky call "precising") to avoid inclusion of cases that do not fit the implicit meaning. The most influential elaboration has been Robert Dahl's concept of "polyarchy," which requires not only extensive political competition and participation but also substantial levels of freedom (of speech, press, and the like) and pluralism that enable people to form and express their political preferences in a meaningful way.[5]

Contemporary minimalist conceptions of democracy—what I term here *electoral democracy*, as opposed to *liberal democracy*,—commonly acknowledge the need for minimal levels of civil freedom in order for competition and participation to be meaningful. Typically, however, they do not devote much attention to the basic freedoms involved, nor do they attempt to incorporate them into actual measures of democracy. Such Schumpeterian conceptions—particularly common among Western policy makers who track and celebrate the expansion of democracy—risk exemplifying what Terry Karl has called the "fallacy of electoralism." That mistake consists of privileging electoral contestation over other dimensions of democracy and ignoring the degree to which multiparty elections, even if genuinely competitive, may effectively deny significant sections of the population the opportunity to contest for power or advance and defend their interests, or may leave

significant arenas of decision-making power beyond the reach or control of elected officials.[6] As Philippe Schmitter and Terry Karl emphasize, "However central to democracy, elections occur intermittently and only allow citizens to choose between the highly aggregated alternatives offered by political parties."[7]

As Collier and Levitsky note, minimalist definitions of democracy have been refined in recent years to exclude regimes with substantial "reserved domains" of military (or bureaucratic, or oligarchic) power that are not accountable to elected officials.[8] On such grounds, Guatemala in particular has often been classified as a "pseudo" or quasi democracy. But such refined definitions of democracy can still fail to acknowledge political repression that marginalizes significant segments of the population—typically the poor or ethnic and regional minorities. While conceptual "precising" has been constructive, it has left behind a welter of what Collier and Levitsky term "expanded procedural" conceptions that occupy various intermediate locations on the continuum between electoral and liberal democracy.

This conceptual disorder is not surprising given that scholars are trying to impose categories on a phenomenon—political freedom—that in fact varies only by degree. Whereas the presence or absence of competitive elections is relatively clear-cut, individual and group rights of expression, organization, and assembly can vary considerably even across countries that meet the criteria for electoral democracy.

How large and overtly repressed or marginalized must a minority be for the political system to be disqualified as a polyarchy, or, in my terms, a liberal democracy?[9] Is Turkey disqualified by the indiscriminate violence it has used to suppress a ruthless Kurdish insurgency, and its historical constraints (recently relaxed) on the peaceful expression of Kurdish political and cultural identity? Is India disqualified by the hu-

man rights violations its security forces have committed in secessionist Kashmir; or Sri Lanka by the brutal excesses on both sides in the secessionist war of Tamil guerrillas; or Russia by its savage war against Chechen secessionists; or Colombia by its internal war against drug traffickers and left-wing guerrillas, and its exceptionally high rates of political assassination and other human rights abuses? Do these polities not have a right to defend themselves against violent insurgency and secessionist terror? Or does democracy fall short—despite the presence in all five countries of highly competitive elections that in recent years have produced party alternation in power? As indicated below, this problem affects a growing group of countries that are commonly considered "democracies" today.

By a minimalist, electoral definition, all five of the above-mentioned countries qualify as democracies. But by a stricter conception of liberal democracy, all fall short. All suffer sufficiently serious abridgments of political rights and civil liberties that they failed to attain a rating of "free" in the most recent "Comparative Survey of Freedom," the annual global survey of political rights and civil liberties conducted by Freedom House. This gap between electoral democracy and liberal democracy, which has become one of the most striking features of the "third wave," has serious consequences for theory, policy, and comparative analysis.

Liberal Democracy and Pseudodemocracy

How does *liberal* democracy extend beyond the minimalist (or formal) and intermediate conceptions of democracy described above? In addition to regular, free, and fair electoral competition and universal suffrage, it requires the absence of "reserved domains" of power for the military or other social and political forces that are not either directly or indirectly accountable to the electorate. Second, in addition to the "vertical" accountability of rulers to the ruled (which is secured most reliably through regular, free, and fair elections), it requires "horizontal" accountability of officeholders to one another; this constrains executive power and so helps protect constitutionalism, the rule of law, and the deliberative process.[10] Third, it encompasses extensive provisions for political and civic pluralism, as well as for individual and group freedoms. Specifically, liberal democracy has the following features:

1) Real power lies—in fact as well as in constitutional theory—with elected officials and their appointees, rather than with unaccountable internal actors (e.g., the military) or foreign powers.

2) Executive power is constrained constitutionally and held accountable by other government institutions (such as an independent judiciary, parliament, ombudsman, and auditor general).

3) Not only are electoral outcomes uncertain, with a significant opposition vote and the presumption of party alternation in government over time, but no group that adheres to constitutional principles is denied the right to form a party and contest elections (even if electoral thresholds and other rules prevent smaller parties from winning representation in parliament).

4) Cultural, ethnic, religious, and other minority groups, as well as traditionally disadvantaged or unempowered majorities, are not prohibited (legally or in practice) from expressing their interests in the political process, and from using their language and culture.

5) Beyond parties and intermittent elections, citizens have multiple, ongoing channels and means for the expression and representation of their interests and values, including a diverse array of autonomous associations, movements, and groups that they are free to form and join.

6) In addition to associational freedom and pluralism, there exist alternative sources of information, including independent media, to which citizens have (politically) unfettered access.

7) Individuals have substantial freedom of belief, opinion, discussion, speech, publication, assembly, demonstration, and petition.

8) Citizens are politically equal under the law (even though they are invariably unequal in their political resources), and the above-mentioned individual and group liberties are effectively protected by an independent, impartial judiciary whose decisions are enforced and respected by other centers of power.

9) The rule of law protects citizens from unjustified detention, exile, terror, torture, and undue interference in their personal lives not only by the state but also by organized antistate forces.

These elements of liberal democracy constitute most of the criteria used by Freedom House in its annual survey of freedom around the world. Two dimensions of freedom—political rights (of contestation, opposition, and participation) and civil liberties—are measured on a seven-point scale, with a rating of 1 indicating the most free and 7 the least free. Countries whose two scores average 2.5 or below are considered "free"; those scoring 3 to 5.5, "partly free"; and those scoring 5.5 and above, "not free," with the determination for countries with the borderline score of 5.5 made on the basis of a more discriminating raw-point score.[11]

The "free" rating in the Freedom House survey is the best available empirical indicator of "liberal democracy." Of course, as with any multipoint scale, there is inevitably an element of arbitrariness in the thresholds used for each category. Yet there is a significant difference even between average scores of 2.5 and 3. In the 1995—96 survey, all nine countries with a score of 2.5— the highest score a country could attain and still be rated "free"—received a rating of 2 on political rights and 3 on civil liberties. The difference between a 2 and a 3 on political rights is substantial, with the latter typically indicating significantly more military influence in politics, electoral and political violence, or electoral irregularities, and thus political contestation that is appreciably less free, fair, inclusive, and meaningful. For example, El Salvador and Honduras each scored 3 on political rights and 3 on civil liberties, as did Venezuela, where military autonomy and impunity and political intimidation have eroded the quality of democracy in recent years. The difference between a 2 and a 3 on civil liberties is also significant, with the higher-scoring countries having at least one area— such as freedom of speech or the press, personal security from terror and arbitrary arrest, or associational freedom and autonomy—where liberty is significantly constrained.

The intermediate conceptions of democracy, which fall somewhere in between "electoral" and "liberal" democracy, explicitly incorporate basic civil freedoms of expression and association, yet still allow for considerable restriction of citizenship rights. The crucial distinction turns on whether political and civil freedoms are seen as relevant mainly to the extent that they ensure meaningful electoral competition and participation, or are instead viewed as necessary to ensure a wider range of democratic functions.

To appreciate the dynamics of regime change and the evolution of democracy, we must also allow for a third class of regimes that are less than even minimally democratic but still distinct from purely authoritarian regimes. Such regimes—which I call here *pseudodemocracies*—have legal opposition parties and perhaps many other constitutional features of electoral democracy, but fail to meet one of its crucial requirements: a sufficiently fair arena of contestation to allow the ruling party to be turned out of power.

There is wide variation among pseudodemocracies as I use the term here. They include "semidemocracies," which approach electoral democracies in their pluralism, competitiveness, and civil liberties, as well as "hegemonic party systems," such as Mexico before 1988, in which an institutionalized ruling party makes extensive use of coercion, patronage, media control, and other tools to reduce opposition parties to decidedly "second-class" status.[12] But they also encompass multiparty electoral systems in which the undemocratic dominance of the ruling party may be weak and contested (as in Kenya), or in the process of decomposing into a more competitive system (as in Mexico today), or highly personalistic and poorly institutionalized (as in Kazakhstan).

What distinguishes pseudodemocracies from the residual category of "authoritarian" regimes is that they tolerate the existence of independent opposition parties. This distinction is important theoretically. If we view democracy in *developmental* terms, as emerging in fragments or parts, by no fixed sequence or timetable, then the presence of legal opposition parties that may compete for power and win some seats in parliament, and of the greater space for civil society that tends to exist in such systems, provides important foundations for future democratic development.[13] In Mexico, Jordan, Morocco, and a number of states in subSaharan Africa where former one-party dictators engineered their reelection under pseudodemocratic conditions, these democratic fragments are pressing out the boundaries of what is politically possible, and may eventually generate breakthroughs to electoral democracy.

Empirical Trends During the Third Wave

By any measure, democracy has expanded dramatically since the beginning of the third wave. Using a minimalist or formal conception of democracy that emphasizes electoral competition, both the number and the proportion of the world's democracies have risen sharply. In

Table 1 — Number of Formal Democracies, 1974, 1990–95

Year	Number of Democracies	Number of Countries	Democracies as a % of All Countries
1974	39	142	27.5%
1990	76	165	46.1%
1991	91	183	49.7%
1992	99	186	53.2%
1993	108	190	56.8%
1994	114	191	59.7%
1995	117	191	61.3%

Sources: Data from Freedom House, *Freedom in the World: The Annual Survey of Political Rights and Civil Liberties, 1990–91, 1991–92, 1992–93, 1993–94, 1994–95* (New York: Freedom House, 1991 and years following); and *Freedom Review* 27 (January–February 1996).

Note: Figures for 1990–95 are for the end of the calendar year. Figures for 1974 reflect my estimate of the number of democracies in the world in April 1974, at the inception of the third wave.

1974 there were only 39 democracies in the world, 28 of which had populations over one million (or so close to one million that they would exceed that mark by 1995). Only about 23 percent of countries with populations over one million and about 27 percent of all countries were formally democratic. The difference between these proportions illustrates an interesting relationship between country size and regime type that has held continuously throughout the third wave: very small countries (those with populations under one million) are significantly more likely than larger countries to be democracies (especially liberal democracies). In fact, two-thirds of states with populations under one million are liberal democracies today, compared with only about one-third of states with populations over one million.

By the beginning of 1996, the number of countries meeting at least the requirements for electoral democracy had increased to 117. Moreover, even though the number of independent states has steadily grown throughout the third wave (by more than a third), the proportion of countries that are at least formally democratic has more than doubled, to over 60 percent. More striking still is how much of this increase has occurred in the 1990s, with the collapse of Soviet and East European communism and the diffusion of the third wave to sub-Saharan Africa. As Table I shows, the number and percentage of democracies in the world have increased *every year* since 1990. This can only be described as an unprecedented democratic breakthrough. As recently as 1990, when he was writing *The Third Wave*, Huntington found only 45 percent of the world's states (with populations over one million) to be democratic, a proportion virtually identical to that in 1922 at the peak of the first wave.[14] Even if we similarly restrict our view to countries with populations over one million, the proportion of formal democracies in the world now stands at 57 percent.

What has been the trend with respect to *liberal* democracy? As one would expect, both the number of countries and the proportion of countries in the world rated "free" by Freedom House have also increased significantly, albeit not as dramatically. From the survey's inception in 1972 until 1980, the number of free states increased by only ten (and the proportion of free states in the world rose only slightly, from 29 to 32 percent). Moreover, change was not in one direction. During the first six years of the third wave, five states suffered breakdowns or erosions of democracy that cost them their free ratings. In fact, although the overall global trend of regime change during the third wave has been toward democracy and free-

Table 2 — Freedom Status of Independent States, 1972–95

Year	Free	Partly Free	Not Free	Total
1972	42 (29.0%)	36 (24.8%)	67 (46.2%)	145 (100%)
1980	52 (31.9%)	52 (31.9%)	59 (36.2%)	163 (100%)
1985	56 (33.5%)	56 (33.5%)	55 (32.9%)	167 (100%)
1991	76 (41.5%)	65 (35.5%)	42 (22.9%)	183 (100%)
1992	75 (40.3%)	73 (39.2%)	38 (20.4%)	186 (100%)
1993	72 (37.9%)	63 (33.2%)	55 (28.9%)	190 (100%)
1994	76 (39.8%)	61 (31.9%)	54 (28.3%)	191 (100%)
1995	76 (39.8%)	62 (32.5%)	53 (27.7%)	191 (100%)

Sources: For 1972, 1980, and 1985: Raymond D. Gastil, ed., *Freedom in the World: Political Rights and Civil Liberties, 1988–89* (New York: Freedom House, 1989). For 1991–95: See Table 1.

Note: Ratings refer to the status of the countries at the end of the calendar year. See text for an explanation of the basis of the ratings.

dom, 22 countries suffered breakdowns of democracy between 1974 and 1991, and further deterioration has occurred since then.

During the third wave, freedom took its biggest jump in the latter half of the 1980s and the early 1990s. As Table 2 shows, between 1985 and 1991 (a crucial year, which witnessed the demise of Soviet communism), the number of free states jumped from 56 to 76 and the proportion of free states in the world increased from a third to over 40 percent. Moreover, the proportion of blatantly authoritarian ("not free") states declined to a historic low of 23 percent in 1991, falling further to just over 20 percent in 1992. By contrast, in 1972 almost half the independent states in the world were rated "not free."

The 1991–92 period seems to have been the high-water mark for freedom in the world. Since 1991, the proportion of free states has declined slightly, and since 1992, the proportion of "not free" states has jumped sharply. Despite the steady growth in the number of electoral democracies, the number of free states has stagnated in the first half of this decade, with gains in freedom offset by losses. In 1993, 43 countries registered a decline in their freedom score, while 18 posted a gain. In 1994, eight countries improved their freedom category (e.g., from partly free to free) and four declined in category; overall, however,

freedom scores increased in 22 countries while declining in 23.15. In 1995, the trend was slightly more positive, with four category upgrades and three downgrades and a total of 29 increases in freedom scores and 11 decreases. Yet the total number of free states did not change at all.

Juxtaposing the two divergent trends of the 1990s—continued growth of electoral democracy, but stagnation of liberal democracy—demonstrates the increasing shallowness of democratization in the latter part of the third wave. During the 1990s, the gap between electoral and liberal democracy has steadily grown. As a proportion of all the world's democracies, free states (liberal democracies) have declined from 85 percent in 1990 to 65 percent today (Table 3). During this period, the quality of democracy (as measured by the extent of political rights and civil liberties) has eroded in many of the most important and influential new third-wave democracies—including Russia, Turkey, Brazil, and Pakistan—while an expected transition to democracy in Africa's most populous country, Nigeria, imploded. At the same time, political freedom has deteriorated in several of the longest-surviving democracies in the developing world, including India, Sri Lanka, Colombia, and Venezuela. In fact, with a few notable exceptions (including South Korea, Poland, and South Africa), the overall

trend of the past decade among regionally influential countries that are electoral democracies today has been toward a decline in freedom. This is particularly disturbing given that, as Huntington has argued in *The Third Wave,* the "demonstration effects" that are so important in the wavelike diffusion or recession of democracy emanate disproportionately from the more powerful countries within a region and internationally.

The undertow in the third wave has been particularly striking in Latin America. Of the 22 countries below the Rio Grande with populations over one million, 10 have experienced significant declines in freedom since 1987, while 6 have seen increases. While five countries made transitions to formal democracy (Chile, Nicaragua, Haiti, Panama, and Paraguay), only Chile became a free state, and six countries lost their free status. Even in some free states (such as Argentina, Ecuador, and Jamaica), Freedom House has observed a downward trend in recent years. Although it is commonly assumed that Latin America today is overwhelmingly democratic, only 8 of the 22 principal countries in the region were rated free at the end of 1995, compared with 13 in 1987. While blatantly authoritarian rule has receded in the hemisphere, so has liberal democracy, as the region has experienced a "convergence" toward "more mixed kinds of semi-democratic regimes."[16]

Some consider it remarkable that Latin American democracies have survived at all considering the enormous stresses they have experienced over the past decade: dramatic economic downturns and increases in poverty (only recently reversed in some countries), the mushrooming drug trade, and the violence and corruption that have flourished in its wake. Since the redemocratization of Latin America began in the early 1980s, the response to severe adversity and political crisis—including scandals that have forced presidential resignations in several countries—has primarily been ad-

Table 3 — Formal and Liberal Democracies, 1990–95

Year	Number of Formal Democracies	Number of Free States (Liberal Democracies)	Free States as a % of Formal Democracies	Total
1990	76 (46.1%)	65 (39.4%)	85.5%	165
1991	91 (49.7%)	76 (41.5%)	83.5%	183
1992	99 (53.2%)	75 (40.3%)	75.8%	186
1993	108 (56.8%)	72 (37.9%)	66.7%	190
1994	114 (59.7%)	76 (39.8%)	66.7%	191
1995	117 (61.3%)	76 (39.8%)	65.0%	191

Sources: See Table 1.

herence to constitutional process and electoral alternation in office (although the military did nearly overthrow democracy in Venezuela in 1992, and has rattled its sabers loudly elsewhere). In the practice of "voting the bums out" rather than mobilizing against democracy itself, Latin American publics have given many observers cause to discern a normalization and maturation of democratic politics not seen in previous eras. Indeed, a number of democratic governments (in Southern and Eastern Europe as well as in Latin America) have been able to make considerable progress in economic reform during the third wave, and in one sizeable sample of such reform experiences, "the party that initiated cuts in working-class income has been defeated in less than half the cases."[17]

This persistence of constitutional procedures gives grounds for hope about the future of democracy in Latin America, as do recent reforms that have decentralized power and opened up the electoral process in Venezuela and Colombia, instituted an independent electoral commission in Panama, and improved judicial functioning in several countries. But these positive steps have been outweighed by conditions that render electoral democracy in the region increasingly hollow, illiberal, delegative, and afflicted. These trends, evident in the resurgence of authoritarian practices under elected civilian presidents in countries such as Peru and Venezuela, and in a general erosion of the rule of law under

pressure from the drug trade, reflect the growing gap between electoral and liberal democracy in the region.

As mentioned above, the trends of increasing (or persisting) disorder, human rights violations, legislative and judicial inefficacy, corruption, and military impunity and prerogatives have been evident in other third-wave democracies around the world—not only major countries like Turkey and Pakistan but smaller ones such as Zambia and most of the electoral regimes of the former Soviet Union. Indeed, in the former Soviet Union, Africa, parts of Asia, and the Middle East, elections themselves are increasingly hollow and uncompetitive, a thin disguise for the authoritarian hegemony of despots and ruling parties: "As recognition grows of the right freely to elect one's governmental representatives, more governments [feel] compelled to hold elections in order to gain [international] legitimacy."[18] In 1995 these contests degenerated into "an electoral charade" in Kazakhstan, Turkmenistan, Tajikistan, Armenia, and Azerbaijan (not to mention Iraq, Iran, Egypt, and Algeria) because of intimidation, rigging, and constriction (or, in extreme cases, utter obliteration) of the right of opposition forces to organize and contest. Since the most recent wave of democratization began its sweep through Africa in early 1991, at least ten civilian regimes have held multiparty elections so flawed that they do not meet the minimal criteria for electoral democracy.[19] All of these regimes are "pseudodemocracies."

Perhaps the most stunning feature of the third wave is how few regimes are left in the world (only slightly over 20 percent) that do not exhibit some degree of multiparty competition, whether that level corresponds with liberal democracy, electoral democracy, or pseudo-democracy. This broad diffusion signals the ideological hegemony of "democracy" in the post–Cold War world, but also the superficial nature of that hegemony. In Latin America and the Caribbean, the United States and the international community demand electoral democracy in exchange for recognition and economic rewards, but are not too insistent about human rights and the rule of law. For Africa, a lower standard is set by the major Western powers: there, all that is required is the presence of opposition parties that can contest for office, even if they are manipulated, hounded, and robbed of victory at election time.

A Period of Stasis

With the number of liberal democracies now stagnating, with the quality of many third-wave and Third World democracies sharply deteriorating, and with the world's most powerful and influential authoritarian states—China, Indonesia, Iran, and Saudi Arabia—showing little or no prospect of democratization in the near term, the question arises: Is the third wave over?

The evidence in the affirmative appears to be mounting. If we look beyond the form of democracy—a form that is increasingly expected by world culture and organizations—we see erosion and stagnation offsetting liberalization and consolidation. *Liberal* democracy has stopped expanding in the world, and so has political freedom more generally. If we take the liberal content of democracy seriously, it seems that the third wave of democratic expansion has come to a halt, and probably to an end. We may or may not see in the coming years the emergence of a few new electoral democracies, but a further sizeable increase seems unlikely, given that democratization has already occurred in the countries where conditions are most favorable. Movement to electoral democracy also seems likely to be offset by movement away from it, as some fledgling electoral democracies in Africa and elsewhere are either blatantly overthrown (as in Gambia and Niger), squelched just before birth (as in Nigeria) or strangled by deterioration in the fairness of contestation and the toleration of opposition (as in Peru, Cambodia, and some of the former communist states). In these circumstances, more and more countries may seek to satisfy the expectation of "democracy" with its most hollow form, pseudo-democracy.

Does this mean that we are on the edge of a third "reverse wave" of democracy? This more frightening prospect is not yet apparent; indeed, a reverse wave may well be avoidable. It is theoretically possible for a wave of democratic expansion to be followed for some time not by a reverse wave but rather by equilibrium, in which the overall number of democracies in the world neither increases nor decreases significantly. It is precisely such a period of stasis that we seem to have entered.

Many of the new democracies of the third wave are in serious trouble today, and it could be argued that the erosion of democratic substance is a precursor to the actual suspension or overthrow of democracy, whether by executive or military coup. The *autogolpe* of President Alberto Fujimori of Peru was preceded by years of steady deterioration in political rights and civil liberties. Historically, the path to military coups and other forms of democratic breakdown has been paved with the accumulation of unsolvable problems, the gross corruption and malfunctioning of democratic institutions, the gradual aggrandizement of executive power, and the broad popular disaffection with politics and

politicians that is evident today in many third-wave democracies (and a few of longer standing).

Yet three things are different today:

1) Military establishments are extremely reluctant to seize power overtly, for several reasons: the lack of popular support for a coup (due in part to the discredit many militaries suffered during their previous periods of brutal and inept rule); their sharply diminished confidence in their ability to tackle formidable economic and social problems; the "disastrous effects on the coherence, efficiency, and discipline of the army" that they have perceived during previous periods of military rule;[20] and, not least, the instant and powerful sanctions that the established democracies have shown an increasing resolve to impose against such democratic overthrows. In addition, many third-wave democracies have made great progress toward establishing the conditions of "objective civilian control" that prevail in the industrialized democracies: high levels of military professionalism, constrained military roles, subordination of the military to civilian decision makers, autonomy for the military in its limited area of professional competence, and thus "the minimization of military intervention in politics and of political intervention in the military."[21]

2) Even where, as in Turkey, the Philippines, Brazil, Pakistan, and Bangladesh, progress toward democratic consolidation has been partial and slow, and the quality of democracy has deteriorated in some respects, publics have shown no appetite for a return to authoritarian rule of any kind; culturally, democracy remains a valued goal.

3) Finally, no antidemocratic ideology with global appeal has emerged to challenge the continued global ideological hegemony of democracy as a principle and a formal structure of government.

Together, these factors have so far prevented a new wave of democratic breakdowns. Instead of expiring altogether, democracy has gradually

been "hollowed out" in many countries, leaving a shell of multiparty electoralism—often with genuine competition and uncertainty over outcomes—adequate for the attainment of international legitimacy and economic rewards. Rather than mobilize against the constitutional system, political leaders and groups that have no use for democracy, or are (to use Juan Linz's term) "semi-loyal" to the system, are more likely to choose and condone oblique and partial assaults on democracy, such as the repression of particularly troublesome oppositions and minorities. Instead of seizing power through a coup, the military may gradually reclaim more operational autonomy and control over matters of internal security and counterinsurgency, as they have done in Guatemala, Nicaragua, Colombia, Pakistan, Turkey, and probably India and Sri Lanka. Instead of terminating multiparty electoral competition and declaring a one-party (or no-party) dictatorship, as they did during the first and second reverse waves, frustrated chief executives (like Alberto Fujimori in Peru) may temporarily suspend the constitution, dismiss and reorganize the legislature, and reshape to their advantage a constitutional system that will subsequently retain the formal structure or appearance of democracy. Or they may engage in a cat-and-mouse game with international donors, liberalizing politically in response to pressure while repressing as much as they can get away with in order to hang on to power—as the former one-party regimes of Daniel arap Moi in Kenya, Omar Bongo in Gabon, and Paul Biya in Cameroon have done in Africa.

Is this, then, the way the third wave of democratization ends: death by a thousand subtractions?

The Imperative of Consolidation

If the historical pattern is to be defied and a third reverse wave avoided, the overriding imperative in the coming years is to consolidate those democracies that have come into being during the third wave. In essence, consolidation is the process of achieving broad and deep legitimation, such that all significant political actors, at both the elite and mass levels, believe that the democratic regime is better for their society than any other realistic alternative they can imagine. As Juan Linz and Alfred Stepan, among others, have stressed, this legitimation must be more than a commitment to democracy in the abstract; it must also involve a shared normative and behavioral commitment to the specific rules and practices of the country's constitutional system.[22] It is this unquestioning embrace of democratic procedures that produces a crucial element of consolidation: a reduction in the uncertainty of democracy, regarding not so much the outcomes as the rules and methods of political competition. As consolidation advances, "there is a widening of the range of political actors who come to assume democratic conduct [and democratic loyalty] on the part of their adversaries," a transition from "instrumental" to "principled" commitments to the democratic framework, a growth in trust and cooperation among political competitors, and a socialization of the general population (through both deliberate efforts and the practice of democracy in politics and civil society).[23] Although many contemporary theorists are strangely determined to avoid the term, I believe that these elements of the consolidation process encompass a shift in *political culture*.

Democratic consolidation is fostered by a number of institutional, policy, and behavioral changes. Many of these changes improve governance directly by strengthening state capacity, liberalizing and rationalizing economic structures, securing social and political order while maintaining basic freedoms, improving horizontal accountability and the rule of law, and controlling corruption. Others improve the representative functions of democratic governance by strengthening political parties and their linkages to social groups, reducing fragmentation in the party system, strengthening the autonomous capacity and public accountability of legislatures and local governments, and invigorating civil society. Most new democracies need these types of institutional reform and strengthening. Some also require a steady program of reforms to reduce military involvement in nonmilitary issues and subject the military and intelligence establishments to oversight and control by elected civilian leaders. And some require legal and institutional innovations to foster accommodation and mutual security among different ethnic and national groups.

Underlying all of these specific challenges, however, is an intimate connection between the deepening of democracy and its consolidation. Some new democracies have become consolidated during the third wave, but none of the "nonliberal" electoral democracies that have emerged during the third wave has yet achieved consolidation. And those electoral democracies that predate the third wave and that have declined from liberal to nonliberal status during it (India, Sri Lanka, Venezuela, Colombia, Fiji) have become less stable and consolidated.

The less respectful of political rights, civil liberties, and constitutional constraints on state power are the behaviors of key state, incumbent-party, and other political actors, the weaker will be the procedural consensus underpinning democracy. Consolidation is then obstructed, by definition. Furthermore, the more shallow, exclusive, unaccountable, and abusive of individual and group rights is the electoral regime, the more difficult it will be for that regime to become deeply legitimated at the mans level (or to retain such legitimacy), and thus the lower will be the perceived costs for the elected president or the military to overthrow the system or to reduce it to pseudodemocracy. Consolidation is then obstructed or destroyed caus-

ally, by the effects of institutional shallowness and decay. If they are to become consolidated, therefore, electoral democracies must become deeper and more liberal. This will require greater executive (and military) accountability to both the law and the scrutiny of other branches of the government, as well as the public; the reduction of barriers to political participation and mobilization by marginalized groups; and more effective protection for the political and civil rights of all citizens. Deepening will also be facilitated by the institutionalization of a political-party system that stimulates mass participation, incorporates marginalized groups, and forges vibrant linkages with civil society organizations and party branches and officials at the local level.

Holding Democratic Ground

None of this should be seen as ruling out the possibility of democratic progress in the world's autocratic and pseudodemocratic states. Indeed, a developmental perspective should sensitize us to the real scope for partial gains and sudden breakthroughs that no theory of the "preconditions for democracy" could anticipate. However, if we think strategically about democracy's future, the key question must be, to borrow Huntington's analogy to a military campaign, how the democratic idea can hold the vast new territory it has conquered.[24]

The overriding imperative for the long-term global advance of democracy is to prevent its near-term recession into a new reverse wave. That encompasses three challenges. First, the new liberal democracies of the third wave must become consolidated (only a few of them have so far). Since consolidation is partly a process of habituation, time is on their side, but only if they can avoid major crises, sink institutional roots, and provide some degree of effective governance. Second, the merely electoral democracies must be deepened and liberalized politically so that their institutions will become more broadly and intrinsically valued by their populations.

Finally, the established, industrialized democracies must show their own continued capacity for democratic vitality, reform, and good governance. The ideological hegemony of democracy in the world has flourished on two foundations: the clear moral and practical superiority of the political systems of the established democracies; and their increasing use of pressure and conditional assistance to promote democratic development around the world. If the world's wealthy, established democracies have the wisdom and energy to preserve those two foundations, more democracies will become "established" in the coming decade, even if the overall expansion of (electoral) democracy draws to a halt. As the universe of stable liberal democracies expands, new points of democratic diffusion, pressure, and assistance will emerge, and cultural arguments that liberal democracy is a Western, ethnocentric concept will become increasingly perverse and untenable.

At some point in the first two decades of the twenty-first century—as economic development transforms the societies of East Asia in particular—the world will then be poised for a "fourth wave" of democratization, and quite possibly a boon to international peace and security far more profound and enduring than we have seen with the end of the Cold War.

Notes

1. Samuel P. Huntington, *The Third Wave: Democratization in the Late Twentieth Century* (Nonnan: University of Oklahoma Press, 1991), 15.
2. David Collier and Steven Levitsky, "Democracy 'With Adjectives': Conceptual Innovation in Comparative Research" (unpubl. ms., Department of Political Science, University of California at Berkeley, 8 April 1996).
3. Joseph Schumpeter, *Capitalism, Socialism and Democracy*, 2nd ed. (New York: Harper, 1947), 269.
4. Huntington, *The Third Wave*, 5–13.
5. Robert A. Dahl, *Polyarchy: Participation and Opposition* (New Haven: Yale University Press, 1971), 3.
6. See Terry Lynn Karl, "Imposing Consent? Electoralism versus Democratization in El Salvador," in Paul Drake and Eduardo Silva, eds., *Elections and Democratization in Latin America, 1980–1985* (San Diego: Center for Iberian and Latin American Studies and Center for U.S.-Mexican Studies, University of California at San Diego, 1986), 9–36; "Dilemmas of Democratization in Latin America," *Comparative Politics* 23 (October 1990): 14–15; and "The Hybrid Regimes of Central America," *Journal of Democracy* 6 (July 1995): 72–86.
7. Philippe C. Schmitter and Terry Lynn Karl, "What Democracy Is . . . and Is Not," *Journal of Democracy* 2 (Summer 1991): 78.
8. An important discussion of reserved domains appears in J. Samuel Valenzuela, "Democratic Consolidation in Post–Transitional Settings: Notion, Process and Facilitating Conditions," in Scott Mainwaring, Guillermo O'Donnell, and J. Samuel Valenzuela, eds., *Issues in Democratic Consolidation: The New South American Democracies in Comparative Perspective* (Notre Dame, Ind.: University of Notre Dame Press, 1992), 64–66.
9. I use the term "liberal" to refer not to an economic regime featuring a limited state and an open economy but to a political regime in which individual and group liberties are particularly strong and well protected. There is obviously some affinity between economic and political liberty in these senses, but there are tensions and complexities as well that are beyond the scope of this discussion. Moreover, the term "liberal" should be construed here very broadly, even in the political sense. It requires sufficient civil liberties and pluralism to allow for free and meaningful competition of interests and the rule of law between elections as well as during them. But this still leaves substantial scope for variation in the balance a society places on individual rights versus responsibilities—or, to put it another way, in the emphasis on the individual versus the community.
10. Richard L. Sklar, "Developmental Democracy," *Comparative Studies in Society and History* 29 (October 1987): 686–714, and "Towards a Theory of Developmental Democracy," in Adrian Leftwich, ed., *Democracy and Development: Theory and Practice* (Cambridge, England: Polity Press, 1996), 26–27; and Guillermo O'Donnell, "Delegative Democracy," *Journal of Democracy* 5 (January 1994): 60–62. Sklar terms the lateral form "constitutional democracy" and emphasizes its mutually reinforcing relationship to vertical accountability.
11. Raw-point scores are determined by assigning from 0 to 4 points to each country on each of 8 checklist items for political rights and each of 13 checklist items for civil liberties. For a full explanation of the survey methodology, see Freedom House, *Freedom in the World: The Annual Survey of Political Rights and Civil Liberties, 1994–1995* (New York: Freedom House, 1995), 672–77, or *Freedom Review* 27 (January–February 1996): 11–15.
12. Giovanni Sartori, *Parties and Party Systems: A Framework for Analysis* (Cambridge: Cambridge University Press, 1976), 230–38.
13. Both my use of the term "developmental" and my emphasis on the continuous and open-ended nature of change in the character, degree, and depth of democratic institutions owe much to the work of Richard L. Sklar ("Developmental Democracy" and "Towards a Theory of Developmental Democracy"). Readers will nevertheless note important differences in our perspectives.
14. Huntington, *The Third Wave*, 25–26.
15. Freedom House, *Freedom in the World 1994–1995*, 5–7.
16. Jonathan Hartlyn, "Democracies in Contemporary South America: Convergences and Diversities," in Joseph Tulchin, ed., *Argentina: The Challenges of Modernization* (forthcoming). Quotations are from page 14 of a draft manuscript written in November 1995.
17. Barbara Gpeddes, "Challenging the Conventional Wisdom," in Larry Diamond and Marc F. Plattner, eds., *Economic Reform and Democracy* (Baltimore: Johns Hopkins University Press, 1995), 67.
18. Human Rights Watch, *Human Rights Watch World Report 1996* (New York: Human Rights Watch, 1995), xxv.
19. These ten are Senegal, Côte d'Ivoire, Burkina Faso, Ghana, Togo, Cameroon, Gabon, Zimbabwe, Kenya, and Ethiopia.
20. Samuel P. Huntington, "Armed Forces and Democracy: Reforming Civil-Military Relations," *Journal of Democracy* 6 (October 1995): 13.
21. Ibid., 9–10.
22. Juan J. Linz and Alfred Stepan, *Problems of Democratic Transition and Consolidation: Southern Europe, South America, and Post–Communist Europe* (Baltimore: Johns Hopkins University Press, forthcoming), ch. 2, and "Toward Consolidated Democracies," *Journal of Democracy* 7 (April 1996): 14–33; and Richard Gunther, Hans-Jürgen Puhle, and P. Nikiforos Diamandouros, "Introduction," in Gunther, Diamandouros, and Puhle, eds., *The Politics of Democratic Consolidation: Southern Europe in Comparative Perspective* (Baltimore: Johns Hopkins University Press, 1995), 7–10.
23. Laurence Whitehead, "The Consolidation of Fragile Democracies: A Discussion with Illustrations," in Robert A. Pastor, ed., *Democracy in the Americas: Stopping the Pendulum* (New York: Holmes and Meier, 1989), 79.
24. Samuel P. Huntington, "Democracy for the Lang Haul," *Journal of Democracy* 7 (April 1996): 5.

Capitalism
and
Democracy*

Gabriel A. Almond

Gabriel A. Almond, professor of political science emeritus at Stanford University, is a former president of the American Political Science Association.

Joseph Schumpeter, a great economist and social scientist of the last generation, whose career was almost equally divided between Central European and American universities, and who lived close to the crises of the 1930s and '40s, published a book in 1942 under the title, *Capitalism, Socialism, and Democracy.* The book has had great influence, and can be read today with profit. It was written in the aftergloom of the great depression, during the early triumphs of Fascism and Nazism in 1940 and 1941, when the future of capitalism, socialism, and democracy all were in doubt. Schumpeter projected a future of declining capitalism, and rising socialism. He thought that democracy under socialism might be no more impaired and problematic than it was under capitalism.

He wrote a concluding chapter in

*Lecture presented at Seminar on the Market, sponsored by The Ford Foundation and the Research Institute on International Change of Columbia University, Moscow, October 29–November 2.

the second edition which appeared in 1946, and which took into account the political-economic situation at the end of the war, with the Soviet Union then astride a devastated Europe. In this last chapter he argues that we should not identify the future of socialism with that of the Soviet Union, that what we had observed and were observing in the first three decades of Soviet existence was not a necessary expression of socialism. There was a lot of Czarist Russia in the mix. If Schumpeter were writing today, I don't believe he would argue that socialism has a brighter future than capitalism. The relationship between the two has turned out to be a good deal more complex and intertwined than Schumpeter anticipated. But I am sure that he would still urge us to separate the future of socialism from that of Soviet and Eastern European Communism.

Unlike Schumpeter I do not include Socialism in my title, since its future as a distinct ideology and program of action is unclear at best. Western Marxism and the moderate socialist movements seem to have settled for social democratic solutions, for adaptations of both capitalism and democracy producing acceptable mixes of market competition, political pluralism, participation, and welfare. I deal with these modifications

of capitalism, as a consequence of the impact of democracy on capitalism in the last half century.

At the time that Adam Smith wrote *The Wealth of Nations,* the world of government, politics and the state that he knew—pre-Reform Act England, the French government of Louis XV and XVI—was riddled with special privileges, monopolies, interferences with trade. With my tongue only half way in my cheek I believe the discipline of economics may have been traumatized by this condition of political life at its birth. Typically, economists speak of the state and government instrumentally, as a kind of secondary service mechanism.

I do not believe that politics can be treated in this purely instrumental and reductive way without losing our analytic grip on the social and historical process. The economy and the polity are the main problem solving mechanisms of human society. They each have their distinctive means, and they each have their "goods" or ends. They necessarily interact with each other, and transform each other in the process. Democracy in particular generates goals and programs. You cannot give people the suffrage, and let them form organizations, run for office, and the like, without their developing all kinds of ideas as to

From *PS: Political Science and Politics,* September 1991, pp. 467-474. © 1991 by The American Political Science Association. Reprinted by permission.

how to improve things. And sometimes some of these ideas are adopted, implemented and are productive, and improve our lives, although many economists are reluctant to concede this much to the state.

My lecture deals with this interaction of politics and economics in the Western World in the course of the last couple of centuries, in the era during which capitalism and democracy emerged as the dominant problem solving institutions of modern civilization. I am going to discuss some of the theoretical and empirical literature dealing with the themes of the positive and negative interaction between capitalism and democracy. There are those who say that capitalism supports democracy, and those who say that capitalism subverts democracy. And there are those who say that democracy subverts capitalism, and those who say that it supports it.

The relation between capitalism and democracy dominates the political theory of the last two centuries. All the logically possible points of view are represented in a rich literature. It is this ambivalence and dialectic, this tension between the two major problem solving sectors of modern society—the political and the economic—that is the topic of my lecture.

Capitalism Supports Democracy

Let me begin with the argument that capitalism is positively linked with democracy, shares its values and culture, and facilitates its development. This case has been made in historical, logical, and statistical terms.

Albert Hirschman in his *Rival Views of Market Society* (1986) examines the values, manners and morals of capitalism, and their effects on the larger society and culture as these have been described by the philosophers of the 17th, 18th, and 19th centuries. He shows how the interpretation of the impact of capitalism has changed from the enlightenment view of Montesquieu, Condorcet, Adam Smith and others, who stressed the *douceur* of commerce, its "gentling," civilizing effect

on behavior and interpersonal relations, to that of the 19th and 20th century conservative and radical writers who described the culture of capitalism as crassly materialistic, destructively competitive, corrosive of morality, and hence self-destructive. This sharp almost 180-degree shift in point of view among political theorists is partly explained by the transformation from the commerce and small-scale industry of early capitalism, to the smoke blackened industrial districts, the demonic and exploitive entrepreneurs, and exploited laboring classes of the second half of the nineteenth century. Unfortunately for our purposes, Hirschman doesn't deal explicitly with the capitalism–democracy connection, but rather with culture and with manners. His argument, however, implies an early positive connection and a later negative one.

Joseph Schumpeter in *Capitalism, Socialism, and Democracy* (1942) states flatly, "History clearly confirms . . . [that] . . . modern democracy rose along with capitalism, and in causal connection with it . . . modern democracy is a product of the capitalist process." He has a whole chapter entitled "The Civilization of Capitalism," democracy being a part of that civilization. Schumpeter also makes the point that democracy was historically supportive of capitalism. He states, ". . . the bourgeoisie reshaped, and from its own point of view rationalized, the social and political structure that preceded its ascendancy. . ." (that is to say, feudalism). "The democratic method was the political tool of that reconstruction." According to Schumpeter capitalism and democracy were mutually causal historically, mutually supportive parts of a rising modern civilization, although as we shall show below, he also recognized their antagonisms.

Barrington Moore's historical investigation (1966) with its long title, *The Social Origins of Dictatorship and Democracy; Lord and Peasant in the Making of the Modern World,* argues that there have been three historical routes to industrial modernization. The first of these followed by Britain, France, and the United States, involved the subordination and transformation of the

agricultural sector by the rising commercial bourgeoisie, producing the democratic capitalism of the 19th and 20th centuries. The second route followed by Germany and Japan, where the landed aristocracy was able

---

The relation between capitalism and democracy dominates the political theory of the last two centuries.

---

to contain and dominate the rising commercial classes, produced an authoritarian and fascist version of industrial modernization, a system of capitalism encased in a feudal authoritarian framework, dominated by a military aristocracy, and an authoritarian monarchy. The third route, followed in Russia where the commercial bourgeoisie was too weak to give content and direction to the modernizing process, took the form of a revolutionary process drawing on the frustration and resources of the peasantry, and created a mobilized authoritarian Communist regime along with a state-controlled industrialized economy. Successful capitalism dominating and transforming the rural agricultural sector, according to Barrington Moore, is the creator and sustainer of the emerging democracies of the nineteenth century.

Robert A. Dahl, the leading American democratic theorist, in the new edition of his book (1990) *After the Revolution? Authority in a Good Society,* has included a new chapter entitled "Democracy and Markets." In the opening paragraph of that chapter, he says:

It is an historical fact that modern democratic institutions . . . have existed only in countries with predominantly privately owned, market-oriented economies, or capitalism if you prefer that name. It is also a fact that all "socialist" countries with predominantly state-owned centrally directed economic orders—command economies—have not enjoyed democratic governments, but have in fact been ruled by authoritarian dictatorships. It is also an historical fact that some "capitalist" countries have also been, and are, ruled by authoritarian dictatorships.

To put it more formally, it looks to be the case that market-oriented economies are necessary (in the logical sense) to democratic institutions, though they are certainly not sufficient. And it looks to be the case that state-owned centrally directed economic orders are strictly associated with authoritarian regimes, though authoritarianism definitely does not require them. We have something very much like an historical experiment, so it would appear, that leaves these conclusions in no great doubt. (Dahl 1990)

Peter Berger in his book *The Capitalist Revolution* (1986) presents four propositions on the relations between capitalism and democracy:

Capitalism is a necessary but not sufficient condition of democracy under modern conditions.

If a capitalist economy is subjected to increasing degrees of state control, a point (not precisely specifiable at this time) will be reached at which democratic governance becomes impossible.

If a socialist economy is opened up to increasing degrees of market forces, a point (not precisely specifiable at this time) will be reached at which democratic governance becomes a possibility.

If capitalist development is successful in generating economic growth from which a sizable proportion of the population benefits, pressures toward democracy are likely to appear.

This positive relationship between capitalism and democracy has also been sustained by statistical studies. The "Social Mobilization" theorists of the 1950s and 1960s which included Daniel Lerner (1958), Karl Deutsch (1961), S. M. Lipset (1959) among others, demonstrated a strong statistical association between GNP per capita and democratic political institutions. This is more than simple statistical association. There is a logic in the relation between level of economic development and democratic institutions. Level of economic development has been shown to be associated with education and literacy, exposure to mass media, and democratic psychological propensities such as subjective efficacy, participatory

aspirations and skills. In a major investigation of the social psychology of industrialization and modernization, a research team led by the sociologist Alex Inkeles (1974) interviewed several thousand workers in the modern industrial and the traditional economic sectors of six countries of differing culture. Inkeles found empathetic, efficacious, participatory and activist propensities much more frequently among the modern industrial workers, and to a much lesser extent in the traditional sector in each one of these countries regardless of cultural differences.

The historical, the logical, and the statistical evidence for this positive relation between capitalism and democracy is quite persuasive.

Capitalism Subverts Democracy

But the opposite case is also made, that capitalism subverts or undermines democracy. Already in John Stuart Mill (1848) we encounter a view of existing systems of private property as unjust, and of the free market as destructively competitive—aesthetically and morally repugnant. The case he was making was a normative rather than a political one. He wanted a less competitive society, ultimately socialist, which would still respect individuality. He advocated limitations on the inheritance of property and the improvement of the property system so that everyone shared in its benefits, the limitation of population growth, and the improvement of the quality of the labor force through the provision of high quality education for all by the state. On the eve of the emergence of the modern democratic capitalist order John Stuart Mill wanted to control the excesses of both the market economy and the majoritarian polity, by the education of consumers and producers, citizens and politicians, in the interest of producing morally improved free market and democratic orders. But in contrast to Marx, he did not thoroughly discount the possibilities of improving the capitalist and democratic order.

Marx argued that as long as capitalism and private property existed there could be no genuine democracy, that democracy under capitalism was bourgeois democracy,

which is to say not democracy at all. While it would be in the interest of the working classes to enter a coalition with the bourgeoisie in supporting this form of democracy in order

There is a logic in the relation between level of economic development and democratic institutions.

to eliminate feudalism, this would be a tactical maneuver. Capitalist democracy could only result in the increasing exploitation of the working classes. Only the elimination of capitalism and private property could result in the emancipation of the working classes and the attainment of true democracy. Once socialism was attained the basic political problems of humanity would have been solved through the elimination of classes. Under socialism there would be no distinctive democratic organization, no need for institutions to resolve conflicts, since there would be no conflicts. There is not much democratic or political theory to be found in Marx's writings. The basic reality is the mode of economic production and the consequent class structure from which other institutions follow.

For the followers of Marx up to the present day there continues to be a negative tension between capitalism, however reformed, and democracy. But the integral Marxist and Leninist rejection of the possibility of an autonomous, bourgeois democratic state has been left behind for most Western Marxists. In the thinking of Poulantzas, Offe, Bobbio, Habermas and others, the bourgeois democratic state is now viewed as a class struggle state, rather than an unambiguously bourgeois state. The working class has access to it; it can struggle for its interests, and can attain partial benefits from it. The state is now viewed as autonomous, or as relatively autonomous, and it can be reformed in a progressive direction by working class and other popular movements. The bourgeois democratic state can be moved in the direction of a socialist state by political action short of violence and institutional destruction.

Schumpeter (1942) appreciated the tension between capitalism and democracy. While he saw a causal connection between competition in the economic and the political order, he points out "... that there are some deviations from the principle of democracy which link up with the presence of organized capitalist interests.... [T]he statement is true both from the standpoint of the classical and from the standpoint of our own theory of democracy. From the first standpoint, the result reads that the means at the disposal of private interests are often used in order to thwart the will of the people. From the second standpoint, the result reads that those private means are often used in order to interfere with the working of the mechanism of competitive leadership." He refers to some countries and situations in which "... political life all but resolved itself into a struggle of pressure groups and in many cases practices that failed to conform to the spirit of the democratic method." But he rejects the notion that there cannot be political democracy in a capitalist society. For Schumpeter full democracy in the sense of the informed participation of all adults in the selection of political leaders and consequently the making of public policy, was an impossibility because of the number and complexity of the issues confronting modern electorates. The democracy which was realistically possible was one in which people could choose among competing leaders, and consequently exercise some direction over political decisions. This kind of democracy was possible in a capitalist society, though some of its propensities impaired its performance. Writing in the early years of World War II, when the future of democracy and of capitalism were uncertain, he leaves unresolved the questions of "... Whether or not democracy is one of those products of capitalism which are to die out with it..." or "... how well or ill capitalist society qualifies for the task of working the democratic method it evolved."

Non-Marxist political theorists

have contributed to this questioning of the reconcilability of capitalism and democracy. Robert A. Dahl, who makes the point that capitalism historically has been a necessary precondition of democracy, views contemporary democracy in the United States as seriously compromised, impaired by the inequality in resources among the citizens. But Dahl stresses the variety in distributive patterns, and in politico-economic relations among contemporary democracies. "The category of capitalist democracies" he writes, "includes an extraordinary variety ... from nineteenth century, laissez faire, early industrial systems to twentieth century, highly regulated, social welfare, late or postindustrial systems. Even late twentieth century 'welfare state' orders vary all the way from the Scandinavian systems, which are redistributive, heavily taxed, comprehensive in their social security, and neocorporatist in their collective bargaining arrangements to the faintly redistributive, moderately taxed, limited social security, weak collective bargaining systems of the United States and Japan" (1989).

In *Democracy and Its Critics* (1989) Dahl argues that the normative growth of democracy to what he calls its "third transformation" (the first being the direct city-state democracy of classic times, and the second, the indirect, representative inegalitarian democracy of the contemporary world) will require democratization of the economic order. In other words, modern corporate capitalism needs to be transformed. Since government control and/or ownership of the economy would be destructive of the pluralism which is an essential requirement of democracy, his preferred solution to the problem of the mega-corporation is employee control of corporate industry. An economy so organized, according to Dahl, would improve the distribution of political resources without at the same time destroying the pluralism which democratic competition requires. To those who question the realism of Dahl's solution to the problem of inequality, he replies that history is full of surprises.

Charles E. Lindblom in his book, *Politics and Markets* (1977), concludes his comparative analysis of the

political economy of modern capitalism and socialism, with an essentially pessimistic conclusion about contemporary market-oriented democracy. He says

> We therefore come back to the corporation. It is possible that the rise of the corporation has offset or more than offset the decline of class as an instrument of indoctrination.... That it creates a new core of wealth and power for a newly constructed upper class, as well as an overpowering loud voice, is also reasonably clear. The executive of the large corporation is, on many counts, the contemporary counterpart of the landed gentry of an earlier era, his voice amplified by the technology of mass communication.... [T]he major institutional barrier to fuller democracy may therefore be the autonomy of the private corporation.

Lindblom concludes, "The large private corporation fits oddly into democratic theory and vision. Indeed it does not fit."

There is then a widely shared agreement, from the Marxists and neo-Marxists, to Schumpeter, Dahl, Lindblom, and other liberal political theorists, that modern capitalism with the dominance of the large corporation, produces a defective or an impaired form of democracy.

Democracy Subverts Capitalism

If we change our perspective now and look at the way democracy is said to affect capitalism, one of the dominant traditions of economics from Adam Smith until the present day stresses the importance for productivity and welfare of an economy that is relatively free of intervention by the state. In this doctrine of minimal government there is still a place for a framework of rules and services essential to the productive and efficient performance of the economy. In part the government has to protect the market from itself. Left to their own devices, according to Smith, businessmen were prone to corner the market in order to exact the highest possible price. And according to Smith businessmen were prone to bribe public officials in order to gain special privileges, and legal monopolies. For Smith good capitalism was competitive capitalism, and good government provided just those goods and services which the market needed to flourish, could not itself provide, or would not provide. A good government according to Adam Smith was a minimal government, providing for the national defense, and domestic order. Particularly important for the economy were the rules pertaining to commercial life such as the regulation of weights and measures, setting and enforcing building standards, providing for the protection of persons and property, and the like.

For Milton Friedman (1961, 1981), the leading contemporary advocate of the free market and free government, and of the interdependence of the two, the principal threat to the survival of capitalism and democracy is the assumption of the responsibility for welfare on the part of the modern democratic state. He lays down a set of functions appropriate to government in the positive inter-

---

. . . one of the dominant traditions of economics from Adam Smith until the present day stresses the importance for productivity and welfare of an economy that is relatively free of intervention by the state.

---

play between economy and polity, and then enumerates many of the ways in which the modern welfare, regulatory state has deviated from these criteria.

A good Friedmanesque, democratic government would be one ". . . which maintained law and order, defended property rights, served as a means whereby we could modify property rights and other rules of the economic game, adjudicated disputes about the interpretation of the rules, enforced contracts, promoted competition, provided a monetary framework, engaged in activities to counter technical monopolies and to overcome neighborhood

effects widely regarded as sufficiently important to justify government intervention, and which supplemented private charity and the private family in protecting the irresponsible, whether madman or child. . . ." Against this list of proper activities for a free government, Friedman pinpointed more than a dozen activities of contemporary democratic governments which might better be performed through the private sector, or not at all. These included setting and maintaining price supports, tariffs, import and export quotas and controls, rents, interest rates, wage rates, and the like, regulating industries and banking, radio and television, licensing professions and occupations, providing social security and medical care programs, providing public housing, national parks, guaranteeing mortgages, and much else.

Friedman concludes that this steady encroachment on the private sector has been slowly but surely converting our free government and market system into a collective monster, compromising both freedom and productivity in the outcome. The tax and expenditure revolts and regulatory rebellions of the 1980s have temporarily stemmed this trend, but the threat continues. "It is the internal threat coming from men of good intentions and good will who wish to reform us. Impatient with the slowness of persuasion and example to achieve the great social changes they envision, they are anxious to use the power of the state to achieve their ends, and confident of their own ability to do so." The threat to political and economic freedom, according to Milton Friedman and others who argue the same position, arises out of democratic politics. It may only be defeated by political action.

In the last decades a school, or rather several schools, of economists and political scientists have turned the theoretical models of economics to use in analyzing political processes. Variously called public choice theorists, rational choice theorists, or positive political theorists, and employing such models as market exchange and bargaining, rational self interest, game theory, and the like, these theorists have produced a substantial literature throwing new and often controversial light on dem-

ocratic political phenomena such as elections, decisions of political party leaders, interest group behavior, legislative and committee decisions, bureaucratic, and judicial behavior, lobbying activity, and substantive public policy areas such as constitutional arrangements, health and environment policy, regulatory policy, national security and foreign policy, and the like. Hardly a field of politics and public policy has been left untouched by this inventive and productive group of scholars.

The institutions and names with which this movement is associated in the United States include Virginia State University, the University of Virginia, the George Mason University, the University of Rochester, the University of Chicago, the California Institute of Technology, the Carnegie Mellon University, among others. And the most prominent names are those of the leaders of the two principal schools: James Buchanan, the Nobel Laureate leader of the Virginia "Public Choice" school, and William Riker, the leader of the Rochester "Positive Theory" school. Other prominent scholars associated with this work are Gary Becker of the University of Chicago, Kenneth Shepsle and Morris Fiorina of Harvard, John Ferejohn of Stanford, Charles Plott of the California Institute of Technology, and many others.

One writer summarizing the ideological bent of much of this work, but by no means all of it (William Mitchell of the University of Washington), describes it as fiscally conservative, sharing a conviction that the ". . . private economy is far more robust, efficient, and perhaps, equitable than other economies, and much more successful than political processes in efficiently allocating resources. . . ." Much of what has been produced ". . . by James Buchanan and the leaders of this school can best be described as contributions to a theory of the failure of political processes." These failures of political performance are said to be inherent properties of the democratic political process. "Inequity, inefficiency, and coercion are the most general results of democratic policy formation." In a democracy the demand for publicly provided services seems to be insatiable. It ultimately turns into a special interest, "rent seeking" society. Their remedies take the form of proposed constitutional limits on spending power and checks and balances to limit legislative majorities.

One of the most visible products of this pessimistic economic analysis of democratic politics is the book by Mancur Olson, *The Rise and Decline of Nations* (1982). He makes a strong argument for the negative democracy–capitalism connection. His thesis is that the behavior of individuals and firms in stable societies inevitably leads to the formation of dense networks of collusive, cartelistic, and lobbying organizations that make economies less efficient and dynamic and polities less governable. "The longer a society goes without an upheaval, the more powerful such organizations become and the more they slow down economic expansion. Societies in which these narrow interest groups have been destroyed, by war or revolution, for example, enjoy the greatest gains in growth." His prize cases are Britain on the one hand and Germany and Japan on the other.

> The logic of the argument implies that countries that have had democratic freedom of organization without upheaval or invasion the longest will suffer the most from growth-repressing organizations and combinations. This helps explain why Great Britain, the major nation with the longest immunity from dictatorship, invasion, and revolution, has had in this century a lower rate of growth than other large, developed democracies. Britain has precisely the powerful network of special interest organization that the argument developed here would lead us to expect in a country with its record of military security and democratic stability. The number and power of its trade unions need no description. The venerability and power of its professional associations is also striking. . . . In short, with age British society has acquired so many strong organizations and collusions that it suffers from an institutional sclerosis that slows its adaptation to changing circumstances and technologies. (Olson 1982)

By contrast, post-World War II Germany and Japan started organizationally from scratch. The organizations that led them to defeat were all

dissolved, and under the occupation inclusive organizations like the general trade union movement and general organizations of the industrial and commercial community were first formed. These inclusive organizations had more regard for the general national interest and exercised some discipline on the narrower interest organizations. And both countries in the post-war decades experienced "miracles" of economic growth under democratic conditions.

The Olson theory of the subversion of capitalism through the propensities of democratic societies to foster special interest groups has not gone without challenge. There can be little question that there is logic in his argument. But empirical research testing this pressure group hypothesis thus far has produced mixed findings. Olson has hopes that a public educated to the harmful consequences of special interests to economic growth, full employment, coherent government, equal opportunity, and social mobility will resist special interest behavior, and enact legislation imposing anti-trust, and anti-monopoly controls to mitigate and contain these threats. It is somewhat of an irony that the solution to this special interest disease of democracy, according to Olson, is a democratic state with sufficient regulatory authority to control the growth of special interest organizations.

Democracy Fosters Capitalism

My fourth theme, democracy as fostering and sustaining capitalism, is not as straightforward as the first three. Historically there can be little doubt that as the suffrage was extended in the last century, and as mass political parties developed, democratic development impinged significantly on capitalist institutions and practices. Since successful capitalism requires risk-taking entrepreneurs with access to investment capital, the democratic propensity for redistributive and regulative policy tends to reduce the incentives and the resources available for risk-taking and creativity. Thus it can be argued that propensities inevitably resulting from democratic politics, as Friedman, Olson and many others argue, tend to reduce productivity, and hence welfare.

But precisely the opposite argument can be made on the basis of the historical experience of literally all of the advanced capitalist democracies in existence. All of them without exception are now welfare states with some form and degree of social insurance, health and welfare nets, and regulatory frameworks designed to mitigate the harmful impacts and shortfalls of capitalism. Indeed, the welfare state is accepted all across the political spectrum. Controversy takes place around the edges. One might make the argument that had capitalism not been modified in this welfare direction, it is doubtful that it would have survived.

This history of the interplay between democracy and capitalism is clearly laid out in a major study involving European and American scholars, entitled *The Development of Welfare States in Western Europe and America* (Flora and Heidenheimer 1981). The book lays out the relationship between the development and spread of capitalist industry, democratization in the sense of an expanding suffrage and the emergence of trade unions and left-wing political parties, and the gradual introduction of the institutions and practices of the welfare state. The early adoption of the institutions of the welfare state in Bismarck Germany, Sweden, and Great Britain were all associated with the rise of trade unions and socialist parties in those countries. The decisions made by the upper and middle class leaders and political movements to introduce welfare measures such as accident, old age, and unemployment insurance, were strategic decisions. They were increasingly confronted by trade union movements with the capacity of bringing industrial production to a halt, and by political parties with growing parliamentary representation favoring fundamental modifications in, or the abolition of capitalism. As the calculations of the upper and middle class leaders led them to conclude that the costs of suppression exceeded the costs of concession, the various parts of the welfare state began to be put in place—accident, sickness, unemployment insurance, old age insurance, and the like. The problem of maintaining the loyalty of the working classes through two world wars resulted in additional concessions to working class demands: the filling out of the social security system, free public education to higher levels, family allowances, housing benefits, and the like.

Social conditions, historical factors, political processes and decisions produced different versions of the welfare state. In the United States, manhood suffrage came quite early, the later bargaining process emphasized free land and free education to the secondary level, an equality of opportunity version of the welfare state. The Disraeli bargain in Britain resulted in relatively early manhood suffrage and the full attainment of parliamentary government, while the Lloyd George bargain on the eve of World War I brought the beginnings of a welfare system to Britain. The Bismarck bargain in Germany produced an early welfare state, a postponement of electoral equality and parliamentary government. While there were all of these differences in historical encounters with democratization and "welfarization," the important outcome was that little more than a century after the process began all of the advanced capitalist democracies had similar versions of the welfare state, smaller in scale in the case of the United States and Japan, more substantial in Britain and the continental European countries.

We can consequently make out a strong case for the argument that democracy has been supportive of capitalism in this strategic sense. Without this welfare adaptation it is doubtful that capitalism would have survived, or rather, its survival, "unwelfarized," would have required a substantial repressive apparatus. The choice then would seem to have been between democratic welfare capitalism, and repressive undemocratic capitalism. I am inclined to believe that capitalism as such thrives more with the democratic welfare adaptation than with the repressive one. It is in that sense that we can argue that there is a clear positive impact of democracy on capitalism.

* * *

We have to recognize, in conclusion, that democracy and capitalism are both positively and negatively related, that they both support and subvert each other. My colleague, Moses Abramovitz, described this dialectic more surely than most in his presidential address to the American Economic Association in 1980, on the eve of the "Reagan Revolution." Noting the decline in productivity in the American economy during the latter 1960s and '70s, and recognizing that this decline might in part be attributable to the "tax, transfer, and regulatory" tendencies of the welfare state, he observes,

> The rationale supporting the development of our mixed economy sees it as a pragmatic compromise between the competing virtues and defects of decentralized market capitalism and encompassing socialism. Its goal is to obtain a measure of distributive justice, security, and social guidance of economic life without losing too much of the allocative efficiency and dynamism of private enterprise and market organization. And it is a pragmatic compromise in another sense. It seeks to retain for most people that measure of personal protection from the state which private property and a private job market confer, while obtaining for the disadvantaged minority of people through the state that measure of support without which their lack of property or personal endowment would amount to a denial of individual freedom and capacity to function as full members of the community. (Abramovitz, 1981)

Democratic welfare capitalism produces that reconciliation of opposing and complementary elements which makes possible the survival, even enhancement of both of these sets of institutions. It is not a static accommodation, but rather one which fluctuates over time, with capitalism being compromised by the tax-transfer-regulatory action of the state at one point, and then correcting in the direction of the reduction of the intervention of the state at another point, and with a learning process over time that may reduce the amplitude of the curves.

The case for this resolution of the capitalism-democracy quandary is made quite movingly by Jacob Viner who is quoted in the concluding paragraph of Abramovitz's paper, "... If ... I nevertheless conclude that I believe that the welfare state, like old Siwash, is really worth fighting for and even dying for as compared to any rival system, it is because, despite its imperfection in theory and practice, in the aggregate it provides more promise of preserving and enlarging human freedoms, temporal prosperity, the extinction of mass misery, and the dignity of man and his moral improvement than any other social system which has previously prevailed, which prevails elsewhere today or which outside Utopia, the mind of man has been able to provide a blueprint for" (Abramovitz, 1981).

References

Abramovitz, Moses. 1981. "Welfare Quandaries and Productivity Concerns." *American Economic Review,* March.

Berger, Peter. 1986. *The Capitalist Revolution.* New York: Basic Books.

Dahl, Robert A. 1989. *Democracy and Its Critics.* New Haven: Yale University Press.

———. 1990. *After the Revolution: Authority in a Good Society.* New Haven: Yale University Press.

Deutsch, Karl. 1961. "Social Mobilization and Political Development." *American Political Science Review,* 55 (Sept.).

Flora, Peter, and Arnold Heidenheimer. 1981. *The Development of Welfare States in Western Europe and America.* New Brunswick, NJ: Transaction Press.

Friedman, Milton. 1981. *Capitalism and Freedom.* Chicago: University of Chicago Press.

Hirschman, Albert. 1986. *Rival Views of Market Society.* New York: Viking.

Inkeles, Alex, and David Smith. 1974. *Becoming Modern: Individual Change in Six Developing Countries.* Cambridge, MA: Harvard University Press.

Lerner, Daniel. *The Passing of Traditional Society.* New York: Free Press.

Lindblom, Charles E. 1977. *Politics and Markets.* New York: Basic Books.

Lipset, Seymour M. 1959. "Some Social Requisites of Democracy." *American Political Science Review,* 53 (September).

Mill, John Stuart. 1848, 1965. *Principles of Political Economy,* 2 vols. Toronto: University of Toronto Press.

Mitchell, William. 1988. "Virginia, Rochester, and Bloomington: Twenty-Five Years of Public Choice and Political Science." *Public Choice,* 56: 101-119.

Moore, Barrington. 1966. *The Social Origins of Dictatorship and Democracy.* New York: Beacon Press.

Olson, Mancur. 1982. *The Rise and Decline of Nations.* New Haven: Yale University Press.

Schumpeter, Joseph. 1946. *Capitalism, Socialism, and Democracy.* New York: Harper.

For Democracy,
the Next Revolution
Is Devolution

■ **Politics:** *Central governments yield cash, control to states and towns.*

Working out details can be troublesome.

ROBIN WRIGHT

TIMES STAFF WRITER

TIAHUANACO, Bolivia—This dusty hamlet, home to one of the greatest and longest-reigning cultures in all the Americas, is making a comeback.

It began in 1995 when the town high in the Andean plateau finally got its first library—more than two millenniums after an early, pre-Incan civilization produced hieroglyphics so sophisticated that they are still largely undeciphered.

Last year, Mayor Pablo Peralta Patti dug new wells to give the town near the shores of Lake Titicaca running water for more than half an hour a day. And this year, he hopes to bring back the outside world by building a tourist inn close to nearby stone monoliths, a sun gate and

temple ruins that were once covered with thin layers of gold.

Progress is returning to Tiahuanaco courtesy of the most radical democratic experiment in Latin America. After an era of instability that averaged a coup d'etat every 10 months for 162 years, Bolivia is trying to stabilize its young democracy by transferring power and resources to its 311 municipalities.

"What we're doing is revolutionary and irreversible," said Bolivian President Gonzalo Sanchez de Lozada. "We're giving power to people who are better able to solve their own problems. No other society has undergone the level of change we have. We think this is a new model for Latin America."

And beyond.

Bolivia's "Popular Participation Law" reflects the single most dynamic political

trend in democracies worldwide in the mid-1990s: devolution of power from national capitals to regions and even municipalities. Devolution has become the front line of democratization in Latin America, Central Europe, Africa and Asia—and is taking off in the United States as well.

"Devolution is a prerequisite of democracy today," said Janusz Onyszkiewicz, a Polish member of Parliament who was a political prisoner during the Communist regime. "How far it goes differs from country to country, but there is an eruption of different initiatives and in all of them the state is being stripped of functions. If I am optimistic about the future, it is because devolution encourages an emerging sense of community that is the key to strengthening democracy."

Tiahuanaco typifies the transformation. In 1993, an appointed administra-

 From the *Los Angeles Times*, February 19, 1997, pp. A1, A12. © 1997 by the Los Angeles Times. Reprinted by permission.

tion received less than $100 from the national government to provide for 13,000 people. Last year, the local government received $340,000.

"This democracy stuff is marvelous," Peralta said.

Tiahuanaco has used the windfall to improve streets so deeply rutted that they were swimmable, to add classrooms for 200 children, to buy a computer for the town hall and to develop farm irrigation plans. The town's hopes are reflected in the small library's wall-size mural: bold colors depict an Aymara Indian breaking from chains with a book in his hands.

"Now we're determining our own future," said Peralta, a former plumber and Tiahuanaco's first elected mayor, who favors a black leather jacket to ward off the perpetual morning chill at 15,000 feet.

Shifting the Burdens of Democracy

Worldwide, devolution has produced an array of imaginative experiments. The West African nation of Mali, so poor that a block of the capital's open air market is for used underwear and rural travel is done by camel, leads the way on a continent of many centralized regimes. Its first democratic government transferred administrative and financial autonomy over education, health and development to 500 rural and urban communities.

Each community sets tax rates and spends revenues as it sees fit. Each is also empowered to negotiate with foreign aid groups, a move designed to allow local direction and limit corruption.

The goal in Mali, roughly twice the size of Texas, is to prevent the democratic setbacks witnessed nearby. Armies have undone democracies in Niger and Gambia and voided Nigeria's first democratic elections. Benin and Burkina Faso have popularly elected former dictators. And elections in Mauritania, Guinea-Bissau and Equatorial Guinea have been marred by irregularities. Decentralization helps impede the usurpation of power at the center.

It also forces the citizenry to become engaged. "In new democracies like ours, the only way to make people feel they are part of what's going on is to put administration in the hands of people who can decide what is good for them and what will work," said Malian Prime Minister Ibrahima Boubacar Keita. "It's our No. 1 project."

In a country with 75% illiteracy, the government is so intent on devolution that the Cabinet has held all-day sessions on Mali TV and toured the country—from the southern savannah to a northern desert so dry that mud mosques in towns such as Timbuktu have survived centuries—to answer questions. During a stop in the capital of Bamako in October, then-U.S. Secretary of State Warren Christopher heralded Mali as "a democracy that listens to its people."

In Latin America and Eastern Europe, devolution is also designed to shift burdens beyond central governments no longer willing or able to provide services or solutions.

Democratic Poland is now devolving power to *gaminas*, local communities run by elected councils. "The *gamina* is outside anyone's control. Its decisions are final as long as they are taken by law. No one can change them unless the local population reverses them," Onyszkiewicz said.

Last year the national government began to cede control of schools to many *gaminas*, which receive about 10% of national revenues to pay for services. As *gamina* councils feel their way, they are also passing statutes to address local needs and concerns.

"This is still a system in the making, but *gaminas* are becoming stronger. They have the highest public support and trust of all institutions—more than Parliament or the central government," said Lena Kolarska-Bobinska, sociologist and executive director of CBOS, a public opinion research center in Warsaw.

Devolution is also a device to defuse ethnic or sectarian differences.

After divisive ethnic wars undermined an ancient monarchy and then Marxist rule, Ethiopia's new democracy is trying to hold together its 80 ethnic groups—with a dozen languages and three alphabets—by devolving power on the basis of ethnicity.

Its radical decentralization program divides 55 million people into nine states, redrawn on ethnic lines, and bestows powers of self-administration as well as the right to secede.

"Ethnicity is a profound feature of society which African states have tried too long to ignore or overlook. But in a democracy it has to be given due recognition," said Ato Kifle Wadojo, chairman of the constitutional commission. "This is the way to prevent further dismemberment of the country."

In 1993, after a 31-year struggle for independence, the province of Eritrea successfully broke away.

In practice, devolution has not been without major glitches. High on a long list are poorly prepared mayors and local councils whose first actions often have little to do with pressing problems. In Bolivia, many municipalities first improved central plazas, symbols of civic pride, before repairing school roofs.

On the premise "build it and they will come," a Bolivian mayor constructed a bus station to lure more traffic on a route where only one bus stopped a week. Another bought furniture for the public defender's office, which later turned up in his home.

Narco-Democracy and Other Glitches

Mayors and council members are also coming from unusual quarters. Guido Tarqui, a portly Bolivian Quechua Indian whose wife still wears traditional dress, finished only the second grade. He could read the label on the Sprite bottle from which he was drinking only because of skills learned while in prison during military rule.

But in January he took over as mayor of 47,000 constituents with a budget of $701,000 in the Bolivian municipality of Puerto Villarröel, a muddy tropical gateway to the Amazon lowlands.

Tarqui also happens to be a coca-grower whose crop he admits almost certainly ends up as cocaine, making him one of a handful of a new "narco-democrats" in the Chapare—a region that produces the second-largest amount of coca on the continent. Tarqui's constituency is predominantly illiterate coca-growers, the poorest community in South America's poorest state.

"We were tired of the traditional parties. We couldn't continue being just an object for them to get our votes. They offer everything but never follow through," Tarqui said. "So we decided the first step would be elections at the local level and then for parliament so the *campesino's* voice can be heard."

In a five-way contest, he won 59% of the vote. His priorities are schools and roads to link his remote area in the rain forest with urban centers, the closest of which is six hours away.

Western officials now fear narco-democrats will contaminate democracy. "As the political system here opens up, the danger grows as it did in Colombia that drug producers, processors and dealers could acquire political power through people who are beholden to them," said a prominent Western envoy.

Bolivians think otherwise. "It should not worry us that they elect their own people to solve their problems. They're not criminals. They're simple people. It's a survival strategy," said President Sanchez de Lozada.

"We think it's better to have them in rather than to have them out. Their representatives will now have to become more connected to the country's organization and move further away from the fringe subcultures."

For the first time, "popular participation" has brought in the country's majority—the 65% indigenous population long excluded by descendants of Spanish colonials.

It has also expedited democracy. Towns and villages no longer have to appeal to regional or national authorities for everything from electricity to school desks. "Before, the process of getting potable water might take a year or two. Now decisions can be made in a day," said Evaristo Maido, director of Project Concern International in the Chapare.

'Vigilance Committees': The New Watchdogs

One danger, however, has already developed. As power is spreading, so is corruption; it too is being democratized.

As a check on local management, Bolivia instituted "vigilance committees." Members rotate annually to ensure they are not corrupted too. But ever a year can be too long. "Vigilance committees don't get paid, so big landowners and other interest groups, even mayors, try to buy them off by giving them food," charged Jose Pinelo, a Bolivian sociologist.

In Tiahuanaco, Mayor Peralta's vigilance committee accused him of absconding with school funds. He countercharged that the committee was paid off by a rival who fled with the town's books.

Elsewhere, nations have transferred the burden of power without providing adequate resources.

Last year, the Leszno *gamina* outside Warsaw was granted control of local schools—but only half the funds allocated by the Polish government to run them. As a result, Stefan Batory Elementary School, named for a famed Polish king, now runs double shifts. Its chipped walls were finally repainted by parents.

The biggest question mark, however, is how devolution will ultimately alter the role of the national government.

"We're finding we didn't think much about what happens to the state," said Fernando Ruiz, former national secretary for social policy at Bolivia's Ministry of Human Development. "We've opened the gate and the horses are out. Now we're running after them to figure out where they're going."

CULTURAL EXPLANATIONS

The man in the Baghdad café

Which "civilisation" you belong to matters less than you might think

GOERING, it was said, growled that every time he heard the word culture he reached for his revolver. His hand would ache today. Since the end of the cold war, "culture" has been everywhere—not the opera-house or gallery kind, but the sort that claims to be the basic driving force behind human behaviour. All over the world, scholars and politicians seek to explain economics, politics and diplomacy in terms of "culture-areas" rather than, say, policies or ideas, economic interests, personalities or plain cock-ups.

Perhaps the best-known example is the notion that "Asian values" explain the success of the tiger economies of South-East Asia. Other accounts have it that international conflict is—or will be—caused by a clash of civilisations; or that different sorts of business organisation can be explained by how much people in different countries trust one other. These four pages review the varying types of cultural explanation. They conclude that culture is so imprecise and changeable a phenomenon that it explains less than most people realise.

To see how complex the issue is, begin by considering the telling image with which Bernard Lewis opens his history of the Middle East. A man sits at a table in a coffee house in some Middle Eastern city, "drinking a cup of coffee or tea, perhaps smoking a cigarette, reading a news-paper, playing a board game, and listening with half an ear to whatever is coming out of the radio or the television installed in the corner." Undoubtedly Arab, almost certainly Muslim, the man would clearly identify himself as a member of these cultural groups. He would also, if asked, be likely to say that "western culture" was alien, even hostile to them.

Look closer, though, and the cultural contrasts blur. This coffee-house man probably wears western-style clothes—sneakers, jeans, a T-shirt. The chair and table at which he sits, the coffee he drinks, the tobacco he smokes, the newspaper he reads, all are western imports. The radio and television are western inventions. If our relaxing friend is a member of his nation's army, he probably operates western or Soviet weapons and trains according to western standards; if he belongs to the government, both his bureaucratic surroundings and the constitutional trappings of his regime may owe their origins to western influence.

The upshot, for Mr Lewis, is clear enough. "In modern times," he writes, "the dominating factor in the consciousness of most Middle Easterners has been the impact of Europe, later of the West more generally, and the transformation—some would say dislocation—which it has brought." Mr Lewis has put his finger on the most important and least studied aspect of cultural identity: how it changes. It would be wise to keep that in mind during the upsurge of debate about culture that is likely to follow the publication of Samuel Huntington's new book, "The Clash of Civilisations and the Remaking of World Order".

The clash of civilisations

A professor of international politics at Harvard and the chairman of Harvard's Institute for Strategic Planning, Mr Huntington published in 1993, in *Foreign Affairs*, an essay which that quarterly's editors said generated more discussion than any since George Kennan's article (under the by-line "x") which argued in July 1947 for the need to contain the Soviet threat. Henry Kissinger, a former secretary of state, called Mr Huntington's book-length version of the article "one of the most important books ... since the end of the cold war."

The article, "The Clash of Civilisations?", belied the question-mark in its title by predicting wars of culture. "It is my hypothesis", Mr Huntington wrote, "that the fundamental source of conflict in this new world will not be primarily ideological or primarily economic. The great division among humankind and the dominating source of conflict will be cultural."

After the cold war, ideology seemed less important as an organising principle of foreign policy. Culture seemed a plausible candidate to fill the gap. So future wars, Mr Huntington claimed, would oc-

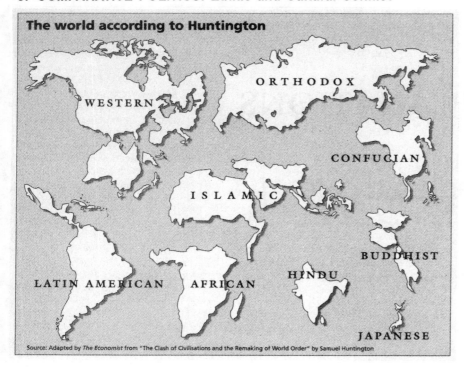

The world according to Huntington

WESTERN

ORTHODOX

CONFUCIAN

ISLAMIC

LATIN AMERICAN   AFRICAN   HINDU

BUDDHIST

JAPANESE

Source: Adapted by *The Economist* from "The Clash of Civilisations and the Remaking of World Order" by Samuel Huntington

cur "between nations and groups of different civilisations"—western, Confucian, Japanese, Islamic, Hindu, Orthodox and Latin American, perhaps African and Buddhist. Their disputes would "dominate global politics" and the battle-lines of the future would follow the fault-lines between these cultures.

No mincing words there, and equally few in his new book:

> Culture and cultural identities...are shaping the patterns of cohesion, disintegration and conflict in the post-cold war world...Global politics is being reconfigured along cultural lines.

Mr Huntington is only one of an increasing number of writers placing stress on the importance of cultural values and institutions in the confusion left in the wake of the cold war. He looked at the influence of culture on international conflict. Three other schools of thought find cultural influences at work in different ways.

• **Culture and the economy.** Perhaps the oldest school holds that cultural values and norms equip people—and, by extension, countries—either poorly or well for economic success. The archetypal modern pronouncement of this view was Max Weber's investigation of the Protestant work ethic. This, he claimed, was the reason why the Protestant parts of Germany and Switzerland were more successful economically than the Catholic areas. In the recent upsurge of interest in issues cultural, a handful of writers have returned to the theme.

It is "values and attitudes—culture", claims Lawrence Harrison, that are

"mainly responsible for such phenomena as Latin America's persistent instability and inequity, Taiwan's and Korea's economic 'miracles', and the achievements of the Japanese." Thomas Sowell offers other examples in "Race and Culture: A World View". "A disdain for commerce and industry", he argues, "has...been common for centuries among the Hispanic elite, both in Spain and in Latin America." Academics, though, have played a relatively small part in this debate: the best-known exponent of the thesis that "Asian values"—a kind of Confucian work ethic—aid economic development has been Singapore's former prime minister, Lee Kuan Yew.

• **Culture as social blueprint.** A second group of analysts has looked at the connections between cultural factors and political systems. Robert Putnam, another Harvard professor, traced Italy's social and political institutions to its "civic culture", or lack thereof. He claimed that, even today, the parts of Italy where democratic institutions are most fully developed are similar to the areas which first began to generate these institutions in the 14th century. His conclusion is that democracy is not something that can be put on like a coat; it is part of a country's social fabric and takes decades, even centuries, to develop.

Francis Fukuyama, of George Mason University, takes a slightly different approach. In a recent book which is not about the end of history, he focuses on one particular social trait, "trust". "A nation's well-being, as well as its ability to compete, is conditioned by a single, pervasive cultural

characteristic: the level of trust inherent in the society," he says. Mr Fukuyama argues that "low-trust" societies such as China, France and Italy—where close relations between people do not extend much beyond the family—are poor at generating large, complex social institutions like multinational corporations; so they are at a competitive disadvantage compared with "high-trust" nations such as Germany, Japan and the United States.

• **Culture and decision-making.** The final group of scholars has looked at the way in which cultural assumptions act like blinkers. Politicians from different countries see the same issue in different ways because of their differing cultural backgrounds. Their electorates or nations do, too. As a result, they claim, culture acts as an international barrier. As Ole Elgstrom puts it: "When a Japanese prime minister says that he will 'do his best' to implement a certain policy," Americans applaud a victory but "what the prime minister really meant was 'no'." There are dozens of examples of misperception in international relations, ranging from Japanese-American trade disputes to the misreading of Saddam Hussein's intentions in the weeks before he attacked Kuwait.

What are they talking about?

All of this is intriguing, and much of it is provocative. It has certainly provoked a host of arguments. For example, is Mr Huntington right to lump together all European countries into one culture, though they speak different languages, while separating Spain and Mexico, which speak the same one? Is the Catholic Philippines western or Asian? Or: if it is true (as Mr Fukuyama claims) that the ability to produce multinational firms is vital to economic success, why has "low-trust" China, which has few such companies, grown so fast? And why has yet-more successful "low-trust" South Korea been able to create big firms?

This is nit-picking, of course. But such questions of detail matter because behind them lurks the first of two fundamental doubts that plague all these cultural explanations: how do you define what a culture is?

In their attempts to define what cultures are (and hence what they are talking about), most "culture" writers rely partly on self definition: cultures are what people think of themselves as part of. In Mr Huntington's words, a civilisation "is the broadest level of identification with which [a person] intensely identifies."

The trouble is that relatively few people identify "intensely" with broad cultural groups. They tend to identify with something narrower: nations or ethnic groups. Europe is a case in point. A poll done last year for the European Commission found that half the people of Britain, Portugal and

Greece thought of themselves in purely national terms; so did a third of the Germans, Spaniards and Dutch. And this was in a part of the world where there is an institution—the EU itself—explicitly devoted to the encouragement of "Europeanness".

The same poll found that in every EU country, 70% or more thought of themselves either purely in national terms, or primarily as part of a nation and only secondly as Europeans. Clearly, national loyalty can coexist with wider cultural identification. But, even then, the narrower loyalty can blunt the wider one because national characteristics often are—or at least are often thought to be—peculiar or unique. Seymour Martin Lipset, a sociologist who recently published a book about national characteristics in the United States, called it "American Exceptionalism". David Willetts, a British Conservative member of Parliament, recently claimed that the policies espoused by the opposition Labour Party would go against the grain of "English exceptionalism". And these are the two components of western culture supposedly most like one another.

In Islamic countries, the balance between cultural and national identification may be tilted towards the culture. But even here the sense of, say, Egyptian or Iraqi or Palestinian nationhood remains strong. (Consider the competing national feelings unleashed during the Iran-Iraq war.) In other cultures, national loyalty seems pre-eminent: in Mr Huntington's classification, Thailand, Tibet and Mongolia all count as 'Buddhist'. It is hard to imagine that a Thai, a Tibetan and a Mongolian really have that much in common.

So the test of subjective identification is hard to apply. That apart, the writers define a culture in the usual terms: language, religion, history, customs and institutions and so on. Such multiple definitions ring true. As Bernard Lewis's man in the Levantine café suggests, cultures are not singular things: they are bundles of characteristics.

The trouble is that such characteristics are highly ambiguous. Some push one way, some another.

Culture as muddle

Islamic values, for instance, are routinely assumed to be the antithesis of modernising western ones. In Islam, tradition is good; departure from tradition is presumed to be bad until proven otherwise. Yet, at the same time, Islam is also a monotheistic religion which encourages rationalism and science. Some historians have plausibly argued that it was the Islamic universities of medieval Spain that kept science and rationalism alive during Europe's Dark Ages, and that Islam was a vital medieval link between the ancient world of Greece and Rome and the Renaissance. The scientific-rationalist aspect of Islam could

well come to the fore again.

If you doubt it, consider the case of China and the "Confucian tradition" (a sort of proxy for Asian values). China has been at various times the world's most prosperous country and also one of its poorest. It has had periods of great scientific innovation and times of technological backwardness and isolation. Accounts of the Confucian tradition have tracked this path. Nowadays, what seems important about the tradition is its encouragement of hard work, savings and investment for the future, plus its emphasis on co-operation towards a single end. All these features have been adduced to explain why the tradition has helped Asian growth.

To Max Weber, however, the same tradition seemed entirely different. He argued that the Confucian insistence on obedience to parental authority discouraged competition and innovation and hence inhibited economic success. And China is not the only country to have been systematically misdiagnosed in this way. In countries as varied as Japan, India, Ghana and South Korea, notions of cultural determination of economic performance have been proved routinely wrong (in 1945, India and Ghana were expected to do best of the four—partly because of their supposed cultural inheritance).

If you take an extreme position, you could argue from this that cultures are so complicated that they can never be used to explain behaviour accurately. Even if you do not go that far, the lesson must be that the same culture embraces such conflicting features that it can produce wholly different effects at different times.

That is hard enough for the schools of culture to get to grips with. But there is worse to come. For cultures never operate in isolation. When affecting how people behave, they are always part of a wider mix. That mix includes government policies, personal leadership, technological or economic change and so on. For any one effect, there are always multiple causes. Which raises the second fundamental doubt about cultural explanations: how do you know whether it is culture—and not something else—that has caused some effect? You cannot. The problem of causation seems insoluble. The best you can do is work out whether, within the mix, culture is becoming more or less important.

Culture as passenger

Of the many alternative explanations for events, three stand out: the influence of ideas, of government and what might be called the "knowledge era" (shorthand for globalisation, the growth of service-based industries and so forth). Of these, the influence of ideas as a giant organising principle is clearly not what it was when the cold war divided the world between commu-

nists and capitalists. We are all capitalists now. To that extent, it is fair to say that the ideological part of the mix has become somewhat less important—though not, as a few people have suggested, insignificant.

As for the government, it is a central thesis of the cultural writers that its influence is falling while that of culture is rising: cultures are in some ways replacing states. To quote Mr Huntington again "peoples and countries with similar cultures are coming together. Peoples and countries with different cultures are coming apart."

In several respects, it is counter-intuitive. Governments still control what is usually the single most powerful force in any country, the army. And, in all but the poorest places, governments tax and spend a large chunk of GDP—indeed, a larger chunk, in most places, than 50 years ago.

Hardly surprising, then, that governments influence cultures as much as the other way around. To take a couple of examples. Why does South Korea (a low-trust culture, remember) have so many internationally competitive large firms? The answer is that the government decided that it should. Or another case: since 1945 German politicians of every stripe have been insisting that they want to "save Germany from itself"—an attempt to assert political control over cultural identity.

South Korea and Germany are examples of governments acting positively to create something new. But governments can act upon cultures negatively: ie, they can destroy a culture when they collapse. Robert Kaplan, of an American magazine *Atlantic Monthly*, begins his book, "The Ends of the Earth", in Sierra Leone: "I had assumed that the random crime and social chaos of West Africa were the result of an already-fragile cultural base." Yet by the time he reaches Cambodia at the end of what he calls "a journey at the dawn of the 21st century" he is forced to reconsider that assumption:

> Here I was . . . in a land where the written script was one thousand two hundred years old, and every surrounding country was in some stage of impressive economic growth. Yet Cambodia was eerily similar to Sierra Leone: with random crime, mosquito-borne disease, a government army that was more like a mob and a countryside that was ungovernable.

His conclusion is that "The effect of culture was more a mystery to me near the end of my planetary journey than at its beginning." He might have gone further: the collapse of governments causes cultural turbulence just as much as cultural turbulence causes the collapse of governments.

Culture as processed data

Then there is the "knowledge era". Here is a powerful and growing phenomenon. The culture writers do not claim anything different. Like the Industrial Revolution before it, the knowledge era—in which the creation, storage and use of knowledge becomes the basic economic activity—is generating huge change. Emphasising as it does rapid, even chaotic, transformation, it is anti-traditional and anti-authoritarian.

Yet the cultural exponents still claim that, even in the knowledge era, culture remains a primary engine of change. They do so for two quite different reasons. Some claim that the new era has the makings of a world culture. There is a universal language, English. There are the beginnings of an international professional class that cuts across cultural and national boundaries: increasingly, bankers, computer programmers, executives, even military officers are said to have as much in common with their opposite numbers in other countries as with their next-door neighbors. As Mr Fukuyama wrote in his more famous book: the "unfolding of modern natural science . . . guarantees an increasing homogenisation of all human societies." Others doubt that technology and the rest of it are producing a genuinely new world order. To them, all this is just modern western culture.

Either way, the notion that modernity is set on a collision course with culture lies near the heart of several of the culture writers' books. Summing them up is the title of Benjamin Barber's "Jihad versus McWorld". In other words, he argues that the main conflicts now and in future will be between tribal, local "cultural" values (Jihad) and a McWorld of technology and democracy.

It would be pointless to deny that globalisation is causing large changes in every society. It is also clear that such influences act on different cultures differently, enforcing a kind of natural selection between those cultures which rise to the challenge and those which do not.

But it is more doubtful that these powerful forces are primarily cultural or even western. Of course, they have a cultural component: the artefacts of American culture are usually the first things to come along in the wake of a new road, or new television networks. But the disruptive force itself is primarily economic and has been adopted as enthusiastically in Japan, Singapore and China as in America. The world market is not a cultural concept.

Moreover, to suggest that trade, globalisation and the rest of it tend to cause conflict, and then leave the argument there, is not enough. When you boil the argument down, much of it seems to be saying that the more countries trade with each other, the more likely they are to go to war. That seems implausible. Trade—indeed, any sort of link—is just as likely to reduce the potential for violent conflict as to increase it. The same goes for the spread of democracy, another feature which is supposed to encourage civilisations to clash with each other. This might well cause ructions within countries. It might well provoke complaints from dictators about "outside interference". But serious international conflict is a different matter. And if democracy really did spread round the world, it might tend to reduce violence; wealthy democracies, at any rate, are usually reluctant to go to war (though poor or angrily nationalist ones may, as history has shown, be much less reluctant).

In short, the "knowledge era" is spreading economic ideas. And these ideas have three cultural effects, not one. They make cultures rub against each other, causing international friction. They also tie different cultures closer together, which offsets the first effect. And they may well increase tension within a culture-area as some groups accommodate themselves to the new world while others turn their back on it. And all

this can be true at the same time because cultures are so varied and ambiguous that they are capable of virtually any transformation.

The conclusion must be that while culture will continue to exercise an important influence on both countries and individuals, it has not suddenly become more important than, say, governments or impersonal economic forces. Nor does it play the all-embracing defining role that ideology played during the cold war. Much of its influence is secondary, ie, it comes about partly as a reaction to the "knowledge era". And within the overall mix of what influences people's behaviour, culture's role may well be declining, rather than rising, squeezed between the greedy expansion of the government on one side, and globalisation on the other.

....
The books mentioned in this article are:

Benjamin Barber. Jihad versus McWorld (Random House; 1995; 400 pages; $12.95).

Francis Fukuyama. The End of History and the Last Man (Free Press; 1992; 419 pages; $24.95. Hamish Hamilton; £20.) and Trust: The Social Virtues and the Creation of Prosperity (Free Press; 1995; 480 pages; $25. Hamish Hamilton; £25).

Lawrence E. Harrison. Who Prospers? How Cultural Values Shape Economic and Political Success (Basic Books; 1992; 288 pages; $14.).

Samuel Huntington. The Clash of Civilisations? *Foreign Affairs* Vol. 72 (Summer 1993) and The Clash of Civilisations and the Remaking of World Order (Simon & Schuster; 1996; 367 pages; $26).

Robert Kaplan. The Ends of the Earth (Random House; 1996; 475 pages; $27.50. Papermac; £10).

Bernard Lewis. The Middle East (Wiedenfeld & Nicolson; 1995; 433 pages; £20. Simon & Schuster; $29.50).

Seymour Martin Lipset. American Exceptionalism (Norton; 1996; 352 pages; $27.50 and £19.95).

Robert Putnam. Making Democracy Work: Civic Traditions in Modern Italy (Princeton, 1993, 288 pages, $24.95 and £18.95).

Thomas Sowell. Race and Culture: A World View (Basic Books, 1994, 331 pages, $14).

A Debate on Cultural Conflicts

The Coming Clash of Civilizations—Or, the West Against the Rest

Samuel P. Huntington

Samuel P. Huntington is professor of government and director of the Olin Institute for Strategic Studies at Harvard. This article is adapted from the lead essay in the summer issue of Foreign Affairs.

World politics is entering a new phase in which the fundamental source of conflict will be neither ideological or economic. The great divisions among mankind and the dominating source of conflict will be cultural. The principal conflicts of global politics will occur between nations and groups of different civilizations. The clash of civilizations will dominate global politics.

During the cold war, the world was divided into the first, second and third worlds. Those divisions are no longer relevant. It is far more meaningful to group countries not in terms of their political or economic systems or their level of economic development but in terms of their culture and civilization.

A civilization is the highest cultural grouping of people and the broadest level of cultural identity people have short of that which distinguishes humans from other species.

Civilizations obviously blend and overlap and may include sub-civilizations. Western civilization has two major variants, European and North American, and Islam has its Arab, Turkic and Malay subdivisions. But while the lines between them are seldom sharp, civilizations are real. They rise and fall; they divide and merge. And as any student of history knows, civilizations disappear.

Westerners tend to think of nation-states as the principal actors in global affairs. They have been that for only a few centuries. The broader reaches of history have been the history of civilizations. It is to this pattern that the world returns.

Global conflict will be cultural.

Civilization identity will be increasingly important and the world will be shaped in large measure by the interactions among seven or eight major civilizations. These include the Western, Confucian, Japanese, Islamic, Hindu, Slavic-Orthodox, Latin American and possibly African civilizations.

The most important and bloody conflicts will occur along the borders separating these cultures. The fault lines between civilizations will be the battle lines of the future.

Why? First, differences among civilizations are basic, involving history, language, culture, tradition and, most importantly, religion. Different civilizations have different views on the relations between God and man, the citizen and the state, parents and children, liberty and authority, equality and hierarchy. These differences are the product of centuries. They will not soon disappear.

Second, the world is becoming smaller. The interactions between peoples of different civilizations are increasing. These interactions intensify civilization consciousness: awareness of differences between civilizations and commonalities within civilizations. For example, Americans react far more negatively to Japanese investment than to larger investments from Canada and European countries.

Third, economic and social changes are separating people from long-standing local identities. In much of the world, religion has moved in to fill this gap, often in the form of movements labeled fundamentalist.

Such movements are found in Western Christianity, Judaism, Buddhism, Hinduism and Islam. The "unsecularization of the world," . . . George Weigel has remarked, "is one of the dominant social facts of life in the late 20th century." ·

Fourth, the growth of civilization consciousness is enhanced by the fact that at the moment that the West is at the peak of its power a return-to-the-roots phenomenon is occurring among non-Western civilizations—the "Asianization" in Japan, the end of the Nehru legacy and the "Hinduization" of India, the failure of Western ideas of socialism and nationalism and, hence, the "re-Islamization" of the Middle East, and now a debate over Westernization versus Russianization in Boris Yeltsin's country.

More importantly, the efforts of the West to promote its values of democracy and liberalism as universal values, to maintain its military predominance and to advance its economic interests engender countering responses from other civilizations.

The central axis of world politics is likely to be the conflict between "the West and the rest" and the responses of non-Western civilizations to Western power and values. The most prominent example of anti-Western cooperation is the connection between Confucian and Islamic states that are challenging Western values and power.

Fifth, cultural characteristics and differences are less mutable and hence less easily compromised and resolved than political and economic ones. In the former Soviet Union, Communists can become democrats, the rich can become poor and the poor rich, but Russians cannot become Estonians. A person can be half-French and half-Arab and even a citizen of two countries. It is more difficult to be half Catholic and half Muslim.

Finally, economic regionalism is increasing. Successful economic regionalism will reinforce civilization consciousness. On the other hand, economic regionalism may succeed only when it is rooted in common civilization. The European Community rests on the shared foundation of European culture and Western Christianity. Japan, in contrast, faces difficulties in creating a comparable economic entity in East Asia because it is a society and civilization unique to itself.

As the ideological division of Europe has disappeared, the cultural division of Europe between Western Christianity and Orthodox Christianity and Islam has re-emerged. Conflict along the fault line between Western and Islamic civilizations has been going on for 1,300 years. This centuries-old military interaction is unlikely to decline. Historically, the other great antagonistic interaction of Arab Islamic civilization has been with the pagan, animist and now, increasingly, Christian black peoples to the south. On the northern border of Islam, conflict has increasingly erupted between Orthodox and Muslim peoples, including the carnage of Bosnia and Sarajevo, the simmering violence between Serbs and Albanians, the tenuous relations between Bulgarians and their Turkish minority, the violence between Ossetians and Ingush, the unremitting slaughter of each other by Armenians and Azeris and the tense relations between Russians and Muslims in Central Asia.

The historic clash between Muslims and Hindus in the Subcontinent manifests itself not only in the rivalry between Pakistan and India but also in intensifying religious strife in India between increasingly militant Hindu groups and the substantial Muslim minority.

Groups or states belonging to one civilization that become involved in war with people from a different civilization naturally try to rally support from other members of their own civilization. Decreasingly able to mobilize support and form coalitions on the basis of ideology, governments and groups will increasingly attempt to mobilize support by appealing to common religion and civilization identity. As the conflicts in the Persian Gulf, the Caucasus and Bosnia continued, the positions of nations and the cleavages between them increasingly were along civilizational lines. Populist politicians, religious leaders and the media have found it a potent means of arousing mass support and of pressuring hesitant governments. In the coming years, the local conflicts most likely to escalate into major wars will be those, as in Bosnia and the Caucasus, along the fault lines between civilizations. The next world war, if there is one, will be a war between civilizations.

Only Japan is non-Western and modern.

If these hypotheses are plausible, it is necessary to consider their implications for Western policy. These implications should be divided between short-term advantage and long-term accommodation. In the short term, it is clearly in the interest of the West to promote greater cooperation and unity in its own civilization, particularly between its European and North American components; to incorporate into the West those societies in Eastern Europe and Latin America whose cultures are close to those of the West; to maintain close relations with Russia and Japan; to support in other civilizations groups sympathetic to Western values and interests; and to strengthen international institutions that reflect and legitimate Western interests and values. The West must also limit the expansion of the military strength of potentially hostile civilizations, principally Confucian and Islamic civilizations, and exploit differences and conflicts among Confucian and Islamic states. This will require a moderation in the reduction of Western military capabilities, and, in particular, the maintenance of American military superiority in East and Southwest Asia.

In the longer term, other measures would be called for. Western civilization is modern. Non-Western civilizations have attempted to become modern without becoming Western. To date, only Japan has fully succeeded in this quest. Non-Western civilizations will continue to attempt to acquire the wealth, technology, skills, machines and weapons that are part of being modern. They will ✳ attempt to reconcile this modernity with their traditional culture and values. Their economic and military strength relative to the West will increase.

Hence, the West will increasingly have to accommodate to these non-Western modern civilizations, whose power approaches that of the West but whose values and interests differ significantly from those of the West. This will require the West to develop a ✳ much more profound understanding of the basic religious and philosophical assumptions underlying other civilizations and the ways in which people in those civilizations see their interests. It will require an effort to identify elements of commonality among Western and other civilizations. For the relevant future, there will be no universal civilization but instead a world of different civilizations, each of which will have to learn to co-exist with others.

Global debate on a controversial thesis

A Clash Between Civilizations —or Within Them?

SüddeutscheZeitung

■ *A recent essay by Harvard professor Samuel P. Huntington in "Foreign Affairs" magazine—"The Clash of Civilizations?"—has attracted a good deal of attention not only in the U.S. but abroad, as well. Huntington is attempting to establish a new model for examining the post-cold-war world, a central theme around which events will turn, as the ideological clash of the cold war governed the past 40 years. He finds it in cultures. "Faith and family, blood and belief," he has written, "are what people identify with and what they will fight and die for." But in the following article, Josef Joffe, foreign-affairs specialist at the independent "Süddeutsche Zeitung" of Munich, argues that "kultur-kampf"—cultural warfare—is not a primary threat to world security. And in a more radical view, Malaysian political scientist Chandra Muzaffar writes for the Third World Network Features agency of Penang, Malaysia, that Western dominance—economic and otherwise—continues to be the overriding factor in world politics.*

A ghost is walking in the West: cultural warfare, total and international. Scarcely had we banished the 40-year-long cold war to history's shelves, scarcely had we begun to deal with the seductive phrase "the end of history," when violence broke out on all sides. But this time it was not nations that were behind the savagery but peoples and ethnic groups, religions and races—from the Serbs and Bosnians in the Balkans to the Tiv and Jukun in Nigeria.

Working from such observations, one of the best brains in America, Harvard professor Samuel Huntington, produced a prophecy, perhaps even a philosophy of history. His essay "The Clash of Civilizations?" has caused a furor. For centuries, it was the nations that made history; then, in the 20th century, it was the totalitarian ideologies. Today, at the threshold of the 21st century, "the clash of civilizations will dominate global politics." No longer will "Which side are you on?" be the fateful question but "What are you?" Identity will no longer be defined by passport or party membership card but by faith and history, language and customs—culture, in short. Huntington argues that "conflicts between cultures" will push the old disputes between nations and ideologies off center stage. Or put more apocalyptically: "The next world war, if there is one, will be a war between civilizations."

Between which? Huntington has made a list of more than half a dozen civilizations, including the West (the U.S. plus Europe), the Slavic-Orthodox, the Islamic, the Confucian (China), the Japanese, and the Hindu. At first glance, he seems to be right. Are not Catholic Croats fighting Orthodox Serbs—and both of them opposing Muslim Bosnians? And recently, the ruthless struggle between the Hindus and Muslims of India has re-erupted. Even such a darling of the West as King Hussein of Jordan announced during the Persian Gulf war: "This is a war against all Arabs and all Muslims and not against Iraq alone." The long trade conflict pitting Japan against the United States (and against Europe) has been called a "war"—and not only by the chauvinists. Russian Orthodox nationalists see themselves in a two-front struggle: against the Islamic Turkic peoples in the south and the soulless modernists of the West. And even worse: The future could mean "the West against the rest."

But this first look is deceptive; after a closer look, the apocalypse dissolves, to be replaced by a more complex tableau. This second look shows us a world that is neither new nor simple. First of all, conflicts between civilizations are as old as history itself. Look at the struggle of the Jews against Rome in the first century, or the revolt of the Greeks against the Turks in the 19th century. The Occident and Orient have been in conflict, off and on, for the last 1,300 years. Second, the disputes with China, Japan, or North Korea are not really nourished by conflicts among civilizations. They are the results of palpable national interests at work. Third, if we look only at the conflicts between cultures, we will miss the more important truth: Within each camp, divisions and rivalries are far more significant than unifying forces.

The idea of cultural war seems to work best when we examine Islam. The demonization of the West is a part of the standard rhetoric of Islamic fundamentalists. The Arab-Islamic world is one of the major sources of terrorism, and most armed conflicts since World War II have involved Western states against Muslim countries. But if we look more closely, the Islamic monolith fractures into many pieces that cannot be reassembled. There is the history of internecine conflicts, coups, and rebellions: a 15-year-long civil war of each against all in Lebanon (not simply Muslims against Maronite Christians), the Palestine Liberation Organization against Jordan, and Syria against the PLO. Then consider the wars among states in the Arab world: Egypt versus Yemen, Syria against Jordan, Egypt versus Libya, and finally Iraq versus Kuwait. Then the wars of ideologies and finally, the religiously tinted struggles for dominance within the faith—between Sunnis and Shiites, Iraq and Iran.

But most important: What does the term "Islam" really mean? What does a Malay Muslim have in common with a Bosnian? Or an Indonesian with a Saudi? And what are we to understand by "fundamentalism"? The Saudi variety is passive and inward-looking, while the expansive Iranian variety arouses fear. It is true that, from Gaza to Giza, fundamentalists are shedding innocent blood. But most of the Arab world sided with the West during the Gulf war. And, beyond this, only 10 percent of the trade of the Middle East takes place within the region; most of it flows westward. Economic interdependence, a good index of a common civilization, is virtually nonexistent in the Islamic world.

The real issue is not a cultural war but actually another twofold problem. Several Islamic nations are importing too many weapons, and some are exporting too many people. The first demands containment and denial, calling for continued military strength and readiness in the West. And what of the "human exports"? They are not just a product of the Islamic world but of the entire poor and overpopulated world—no matter what culture they are part of. Along with the spread of nuclear weapons and missiles, this is the major challenge of the coming century, because massive migrations of people will inevitably bring cultural, territorial, and political struggles in their wake. No one has an answer to this. But a narrow vision produced by the "West-against-the-rest" notion is surely the worst way to look for answers.

—*Josef Joffe*

The West's Hidden Agenda

Third World Network
FEATURES

Like Francis Fukuyama's essay "The End of History?" published in 1989, Samuel Huntington's "The Clash of Civilizations?" has received a lot of publicity in the mainstream Western media. The reason is not difficult to fathom. Both articles serve U.S. and Western foreign-policy goals. Huntington's thesis is simple enough: "The clash of civilizations will dominate global politics. The fault lines between civilizations will be the battle lines of the future."

The truth, however, is that cultural, religious, or other civilizational differences are only some of the many factors responsible for conflict. Territory and resources, wealth and property, power and status, and individual personalities and group interests are others. Indeed, religion, culture, and other elements and symbols of what Huntington would regard as "civilization identity" are sometimes manipulated to camouflage the naked pursuit of wealth or power—the real source of many conflicts.

Reprinted with permission from *World Press Review*, February 1994, pp. 25-26. Originally from *Third World Network Features*.

But the problem is even more serious. By overplaying the "clash of civilizations" dimension, Huntington has ignored the creative, constructive interaction and engagement between civilizations. This is a much more constant feature of civilization than conflict per se. Islam, for instance, through centuries of exchange with the West, laid the foundation for the growth of mathematics, science, medicine, agriculture, industry, and architecture in medieval Europe. Today, some of the leading ideas and institutions that have gained currency within the Muslim world, whether in politics or in economics, are imports from the West.

That different civilizations are not inherently prone to conflict is borne out by another salient feature that Huntington fails to highlight. Civilizations embody many similar values and ideals. At the philosophical level at least, Buddhism, Christianity, Hinduism, Islam, Judaism, Sikhism, and Taoism, among other world religions, share certain common perspectives on the relationship between the human being and his environment, the integrity of the community, the importance of the family, the significance of moral leadership, and, indeed, the meaning and purpose of life. Civilizations, however different in certain respects, are quite capable of forging common interests and aspirations. For example, the Association of Southeast Asian Nations encompasses at least four "civilization identities," to use Huntington's term—Buddhist (Thailand), Confucian (Singapore), Christian (the Philippines), and Muslim (Brunei, Indonesia, and Malaysia). Yet it has been able to evolve an identity of its own through 25 years of trials.

It is U.S. and Western dominance, not the clash of civilizations, that is at the root of global conflict. By magnifying the so-called clash of civilizations, Huntington tries to divert attention from Western dominance and control even as he strives to preserve, protect, and perpetuate that dominance. He sees a compelling reason for embarking on this mission. Western dominance is under threat from a "Confucian-Islamic connection that has emerged to challenge Western interests, values, and power," he writes. This is the most mischievous—and most dangerous—implication of his "clash of civilizations."

By evoking this fear of a Confucian-Islamic connection, he hopes to persuade the Western public, buffeted by unemployment and recession, to acquiesce to huge military budgets in the post-cold-war era. He argues that China and some Islamic nations are acquiring weapons on a massive scale. Generally, it is the Islamic states that are buying weapons from China, which in turn "is rapidly increasing its military spending." Huntington observes that "a Confucian-Islamic military connection has thus come into being, designed to promote acquisition by its members of the weapons and weapons technologies needed to counter the military power of the West." This is why the West, and the U.S. in particular, should not, in Huntington's view, be "reducing its own military capabilities."

There are serious flaws in this argument. One, it is not true that the U.S. has reduced its military capability; in fact, it has enhanced its range of sophisticated weaponry. Two, though China is an important producer and exporter of arms, it is the only major power whose military expenditures consistently declined throughout the 1980s. Three, most Muslim countries buy their weapons not from China but from the U.S. Four, China has failed to endorse the Muslim position on many global issues. Therefore, the Confucian-Islamic connection is a myth propagated to justify increased U.S. military spending.

It is conceivable that Huntington has chosen to target the Confucian and Islamic civilizations for reasons that are not explicitly stated in his article. Like many other Western academics, commentators, and policy analysts, Huntington, it appears, is also concerned about the economic ascendancy of so-called Confucian communities such as China, Hong Kong, Taiwan, Singapore, and overseas Chinese communities in other Asian countries. He is of the view that "if cultural commonality is a prerequisite for economic integration, the principal East Asian economic bloc of the future is likely to be centered on China." The dynamism and future potential of these "Confucian" economies have already set alarm bells ringing in various Western capitals. Huntington's warning to the West about the threat that China poses should be seen in that context—as yet another attempt to curb the rise of yet another non-Western economic competitor.

"U.S. and Western dominance is at the root of global conflict."

As far as the "Islamic threat" is concerned, it is something that Huntington and his kind have no difficulty selling in the West. Antagonism toward Islam and Muslims is deeply embedded in the psyche of mainstream Western society. The rise of Islamic movements has provoked a new, powerful wave of negative emotions against the religion and its practitioners. Most Western academics and journalists, in concert with Western policy makers, grant no legitimacy to the Muslim resistance to Western domination and control. When Huntington says, "Islam has bloody borders," the implication is that Islam and Muslims are responsible for the spilling of blood. Yet anyone who has an elementary knowledge of many current conflicts will readily admit that, more often than not, it is the Muslims who have been bullied, bludgeoned, and butchered.

The truth, however, means very little to Huntington. The title of his article "The Clash of Civilizations?" is quoted from [British educator] Bernard Lewis's "The Roots of Muslim Rage," an essay that depicts the Islamic resurgence as an irrational threat to Western heritage. Both Huntington and Lewis are "Islam baiters" whose role is to camouflage the suffering of and the injustice done to the victims of U.S. and Western domination by concocting theories about the conflict of cultures and the clash of civilizations. Huntington's "The Clash of Civilizations?" will not conceal the real nature of the conflict: The victims—or at least some of them—know the truth.

—*Chandra Muzaffar*

THE MYTH OF GLOBAL ETHNIC CONFLICT

John R. Bowen

John R. Bowen is professor of anthropology and chair of the Program in Social Thought and Analysis at Washington University in St. Louis. His most recent books are Muslims Through Discourse: Religion and Ritual in Gayo Society *(1993) and a forthcoming coedited book on comparisons in political science and anthropology. He is now completing a study of changes in religious and civil law in Indonesia.*

Much recent discussion of international affairs has been based on the misleading assumption that the world is fraught with primordial ethnic conflict. According to this notion, ethnic groups lie in wait for one another, nourishing age-old hatreds and restrained only by powerful states. Remove the lid, and the cauldron boils over. Analysts who advance this idea differ in their predictions for the future: some see the fragmentation of the world into small tribal groups; others, a face-off among several vast civilizational coalitions. They all share, however, the idea that the world's current conflicts are fueled by age-old ethnic loyalties and cultural differences.[1]

This notion misrepresents the genesis of conflict and ignores the ability of diverse people to coexist. The very phrase "ethnic conflict" misguides us. It has become a shorthand way to speak about any and all violent confrontations between groups of people living in the same country. Some of these conflicts involve ethnic or cultural identity, but most are about getting more power, land, or other resources. They do not result from ethnic diversity; thinking that they do sends us off in pursuit of the wrong policies, tolerating rulers who incite riots and suppress ethnic differences.

In speaking about local group conflicts we tend to make three assumptions: first, that ethnic identities are ancient and unchanging; second, that these identities motivate people to persecute and kill; and third, that ethnic diversity itself inevitably leads to violence. All three are mistaken.

Contrary to the first assumption, ethnicity is a product of modern politics. Although people have had identities—deriving from religion, birthplace, language, and so on—for as long as humans have had culture, they have begun to see themselves as members of vast ethnic groups, opposed to other such groups, only during the modern period of colonization and state-building.

The view that ethnicity is ancient and unchanging emerges these days in the potent images of the cauldron and the tribe. Out of the violence in Eastern Europe came images of the region as a bubbling cauldron of ethnonationalist sentiments that were sure to boil over unless suppressed by strong states. The cauldron image contrasts with the American "melting pot," suggesting that Western ethnicities may melt, but Eastern ones must be suppressed by the region's unlikable, but perhaps necessary, Titos and Stalins.

Serbs, Croats, and Bosnians all speak the same language (Italy has greater linguistic diversity) and have lived side by side, most often in peace, for centuries.

Nowhere does this notion seem more apt than in the former Yugoslavia. Surely the Serbs, Croats, and Bosnians are distinct ethnic groups destined to clash throughout history, are they not? Yet it is often forgotten how small the differences are among the currently warring factions in the Balkans. Serbs, Croats, and Bosnians all speak the same language (Italy has greater linguistic diversity) and have lived side by side, most often in peace, for centuries. Although it is common to say that they are separated by religion—Croats being Roman Catholic, Serbs Orthodox Christian, and Bosnians Muslim—in fact each population includes sizeable numbers of the other two religions. The three religions have indeed become symbols of group differences, but religious differences have not, by themselves, caused intergroup conflict. Rising rates of intermarriage (as high as 30 percent in Bosnia) would have led to the gradual blurring of contrasts across these lines.

As knowledgeable long-term observers such as Misha Glenny have pointed out, the roots of the current Balkan violence lie not in primordial ethnic and religious differences but rather in modern attempts to rally people around nationalist ideas. "Ethnicity" becomes "nationalism" when it includes aspirations to gain a monopoly of land, resources, and power. But nationalism, too, is a learned and frequently manipulated

From *Journal of Democracy*, October 1996, pp. 3-14. © 1996 by the National Endowment for Democracy and the Johns Hopkins University Press. Reprinted by permission.

set of ideas, and not a primordial sentiment. In the nineteenth century, Serb and Croat intellectuals joined other Europeans in championing the rights of peoples to rule themselves in "nation-states": states to be composed of one nationality. For their part, Serbs drew on memories of short-lived Serb national states to claim their right to expand outward to encompass other peoples, just as other countries in Europe (most notably France) had done earlier. That Balkan peoples spoke the same language made these expansionist claims all the more plausible to many Serbs.[2]

At the same time, Croats were developing their own nationalist ideology, with a twist: rather than claiming the right to overrun nonCroats, it promised to exclude them. Nationalism among the Croats naturally was directed against their strong Serb neighbors. When Serbs dominated the state of Yugoslavia that was created after the First World War, Croat resentment of Serbs grew. The most militant of Croat nationalists formed an underground organization called Ustashe ("Uprising"), and it was this group, to which the Nazis gave control of Croatia, that carried out the forced conversions, expulsions, and massacres of Serbs during the Second World War. The later calls to war of the Serb leader Slobodan Milošević worked upon the still fresh memories of these tragedies.

But the events of the Second World War did not automatically lead to the slaughters of the 1990s; wartime memories could have been overcome had Yugoslavia's new leaders set out to create the social basis for a multiethnic society. But Marshal Tito chose to preserve his rule by forbidding Yugoslavs from forming independent civic groups and developing a sense of shared political values. Political opposition, whether in Croatia, Serbia, or Slovenia, coalesced instead around the only available symbols, the nationalisms of each region. Tito further fanned nationalist flames by giving Serbs and Croats privileges in each other's territories—Serbs held positions of power in Croatia, and Croats in Belgrade. In the countryside these minority presences added to nationalist resentments. Tito's short-term political cleverness—nostalgically remembered by some in the West—in fact set the stage for later slaughter. Resentments and fears generated by modern state warfare and the absence of a civil society—not ethnic differences—made possible the success of the nationalist politicians Milošević and Franjo Tudjman.

The Legacy of Colonialism

But what about Africa? Surely there we find raw ethnic conflict, do we not? Our understandings of African violence have been clouded by visions, not of boiling cauldrons, but of ancient tribal warfare. I recall a National Public Radio reporter interviewing an African UN official about Rwanda. Throughout the discussion the reporter pressed the official to discuss the "ancient tribal hatreds" that were fueling the slaughter. The official ever so politely demurred, repeatedly reminding the reporter that mass conflict began when Belgian colonial rulers gave Tutsis a monopoly of state power. But, as happens so often, the image of ancient tribalism was too deeply ingrained

in the reporter's mind for him to hear the UN official's message.

What the African official had to say was right: ethnic thinking in political life is a product of modern conflicts over power and resources, and not an ancient impediment to political modernity. True, before the modern era some Africans did consider themselves Hutu or Tutsi, Nuer or Zande, but these labels were not the main sources of everyday identity. A woman living in central Africa drew her identity from where she was born, from her lineage and in-laws, and from her wealth. Tribal or ethnic identity was rarely important in everyday life and could change as people moved over vast areas in pursuit of trade or new lands. Conflicts were more often within tribal categories than between them, as people fought over sources of water, farmland, or grazing rights.

It was the colonial powers, and the independent states succeeding them, which declared that each and every person had an "ethnic identity" that determined his or her place within the colony or the postcolonial system. Even such a seemingly small event as the taking of a census created the idea of a colony-wide ethnic category to which one belonged and had loyalties. (And this was not the case just in Africa: some historians of India attribute the birth of Hindu nationalism to the first British census, when people began to think of themselves as members of Hindu, Muslim, or Sikh populations.) The colonial powers—Belgians, Germans, French, British, and Dutch—also realized that, given their small numbers in their dominions, they could effectively govern and exploit only by seeking out "partners" from among local people, sometimes from minority or Christianized groups. But then the state had to separate its partners from all others, thereby creating firmly bounded "ethnic groups."

In Rwanda and Burundi, German and Belgian colonizers admired the taller people called Tutsis, who formed a small minority in both colonies. The Belgians gave the Tutsis privileged access to education and jobs, and even instituted a minimum height requirement for entrance to college. So that colonial officials could tell who was Tutsi, they required everyone to carry identity cards with tribal labels.

But people cannot be forced into the neat compartments that this requirement suggests. Many Tutsis are tall and many Hutus short, but Hutus and Tutsis had intermarried to a such an extent that they were not easily distinguished physically (nor are they today). They spoke the same language and carried out the same religious practices. In most regions of the colonies the categories became economic labels: poor Tutsis became Hutus, and economically successful Hutus became Tutsis. Where the labels "Hutu" and "Tutsi" had not been much used, lineages with lots of cattle were simply labeled Tutsi; poorer lineages, Hutu. Colonial discrimination against Hutus created what had not existed before: a sense of collective Hutu identity, a Hutu cause. In the late 1950s Hutus began to rebel against Tutsi rule (encouraged by Europeans on their way out) and then created an independent and Hutu-dominated state in Rwanda; this state then gave rise to Tutsi resentments and to the creation of a Tutsi rebel army, the Rwandan Patriotic Front.

The logic of rule through ethnic division worked elsewhere, too. The case of Sri Lanka (formerly Ceylon) shows how, even when colonizers did not favor a single group, colonial rule could foster interethnic violence. The Sinhalese and Tamils of Sri Lanka have a common origin and, contrary to stereotypes of dark Tamils and light-skinned Sinhalese, they cannot easily be distinguished by their physical characteristics. The distinction between them is based mainly on the language spoken. Before this century there was little conflict between them; indeed, they did not think of themselves as two distinct kinds of people. Then came British rule. As they did throughout their empire, the British ruled Ceylon by creating an English-speaking elite, and, here as elsewhere, their favoritism engendered an opposition. In Ceylon this opposition took on racial and religious overtones. The majority of those who had been left out of the elite spoke Sinhalese and were Buddhists, and they began to promote a racist notion of Sinhalese superiority as an "Aryan race." After independence it was this Sinhalese-speaking group that gained control of the new state of Sri Lanka, and began to exclude Tamils from the best schools and jobs, mainly by requiring competence in Sinhalese. Not surprisingly, Tamils resented this discrimination, and some—initially only a few—launched violent protests in the 1970s. These riots led to massive state repression and, by a logic similar to that shaping Tutsi rebellions in Rwanda, to the creation of the Tamil Tigers (the Liberation Tigers of Tamil Eelam) and their demands for an autonomous Tamil region. As the anthropologist Stanley Tambiah has argued, the island's violence is a late-twentieth-century response to colonial and postcolonial policies that relied on a hardened and artificial notion of ethnic boundaries.[3]

It is fear and hate generated from the top, and not ethnic differences, that finally push people to commit acts of violence.

In these cases and many others—Sikhs in India, Maronites in Lebanon, Copts in Egypt, Moluccans in the Dutch East Indies, Karens in Burma—colonial and postcolonial states created new social groups and identified them by ethnic, religious, or regional categories. Only in living memory have the people who were sorted into these categories begun to act in concert, as political groups with common interests. Moreover, their shared interests have been those of political autonomy, access to education and jobs, and control of local resources. Far from reflecting ancient ethnic or tribal loyalties, their cohesion and action are products of the modern state's demand that people make themselves heard as powerful groups, or else risk suffering severe disadvantages.

Fear from the Top

A reader might say at this point: Fine, ethnic identities are modern and created, but today people surely do target members of other ethnic groups for violence, do they not? The answer is: Less than we usually think, and when they do, it is only after a long period of being prepared, pushed, and threatened by leaders who control the army and the airwaves. It is fear and hate generated from the top, and not ethnic differences, that finally push people to commit acts of violence. People may come to fear or resent another group for a variety of reasons, especially when social and economic change seems to favor the other group. And yet such competition and resentment "at the ground level" usually does not lead to intergroup violence without an intervening push from the top.

Let us return to those two most unsettling cases, Rwanda and the Balkans. In Rwanda the continuing slaughter of the past few years stemmed from efforts by the dictator-president Juvenal Habyarimana to wipe out his political opposition, Hutu as well as Tutsi. In 1990–91 Habyarimana began to assemble armed gangs into a militia called Interahamwe. This militia carried out its first massacre of a village in March 1992, and in 1993 began systematically to kill Hutu moderates and Tutsis. Throughout 1993 the country's three major radio stations were broadcasting messages of hate against Tutsis, against the opposition parties, and against specific politicians, setting the stage for what followed. Immediately after the still unexplained plane crash that killed President Habyarimana in April 1994, the presidential guard began killing Hutu opposition leaders, human rights activists, journalists, and others critical of the state, most of them Hutus. Only then, after the first wave of killings, were the militia and soldiers sent out to organize mass killings in the countryside, focusing on Tutsis.

Why did people obey the orders to kill? Incessant radio broadcasts over the previous year had surely prepared them for it; the broadcasts portrayed the Tutsi-led Rwandan Patriotic Front as bloodthirsty killers. During the massacres, radio broadcasts promised the land of the dead to the killers. Town mayors, the militia, the regular army, and the police organized Hutus into killing squads, and killed those Hutus who would not join in. The acting president toured the country to thank those villagers who had taken part in the massacres. Some people settled personal scores under cover of the massacre, and many were carried away with what observers have described as a "killing frenzy." The killings of 1994 were not random mob violence, although they were influenced by mob psychology.[4]

In reading accounts of the Rwanda killings, I was struck by how closely they matched, point by point, the ways Indonesians have described to me their participation in the mass slaughters of 1965–66. In Indonesia the supposed target was "communists," but there, too, it was a desire to settle personal scores, greed, willingness to follow the army's orders, and fear of retaliation that drove people to do things they can even now barely admit to themselves, even though many of them, like many Hutus, were convinced that the killings stopped the takeover of the country by an evil power. In both countries, people were told to kill the children and not to spare pregnant women, lest children grow up to take revenge on their killers. Americans continue to refer to those massacres in Indonesia as an instance of "ethnic violence" and to assume that Chinese residents were major targets, but they were not: the killings by and large pitted Javanese against Javanese, Acehnese against Acehnese, and so forth.

The two massacres have their differences: Rwanda in 1993–94 was a one-party state that had carried out mass indoctrination through absolute control of the mass media; Indonesia in 1965–66 was a politically fragmented state in which certain factions of the armed forces only gradually took control. But in both cases leaders were able to carry out a plan, conceived at the top, to wipe out an opposition group. They succeeded because they persuaded people that they could survive only by killing those who were, or could become, their killers.

The same task of persuasion faced Serb and Croat nationalist politicians, in particular Croatia's Franjo Tudjman and Serbia's Slobodan Milošević, who warned their ethnic brethren elsewhere—Serbs in Croatia, Croats in Bosnia—that their rights were about to be trampled unless they rebelled. Milošević played on the modern Serb nationalist rhetoric of expansion, claiming the right of Serbs everywhere to be united. Tudjman, for his part, used modern Croat rhetoric of exclusionary nationalism to build his following. Once in power in Croatia, he moved quickly to define Serbs as second-class citizens, fired Serbs from the police and military, and placed the red-and-white "checkerboard" of the Nazi-era Ustashe flag in the new Croatian banner.

Both leaders used historical memories for their own purposes, but they also had to erase recent memories of new Yugoslav identities, tentatively forged by men and women who married across ethnic boundaries or who lived in the cosmopolitan cities. The new constitutions recognized only ethnic identity, not civil identity, and people were forced, sometimes at gunpoint, to choose who they "really" were.[5]

Contrary to the "explanations" of the war frequently offered by Western journalists, ordinary Serbs do not live in the fourteenth century, fuming over the Battle of Kosovo; nor is the current fighting merely a playing out of some kind of inevitable logic of the past, as some have written. It took hard work by unscrupulous politicians to convince ordinary people that the other side consisted not of the friends and neighbors they had known for years but of genocidal people who would kill them if they were not killed first. For Milošević this meant persuading Serbs that Croats were all crypto-Nazi Ustashe; for Tudjman it meant convincing Croats that Serbs were all Chetnik assassins. Both, but particularly Milošević, declared Bosnian Muslims to be the front wave of a new Islamic threat. Each government indirectly helped the other: Milošević's expansionist talk confirmed Croat fears that Serbs intended to control the Balkans; Tudjman's politics revived Serbs' still remembered fears of the Ustashe. Serb media played up these fears, giving extensive coverage in 1990–91 to the exhumation of mass graves from the Second World War and to stories of Ustashe terror. This "nationalism from the top down," as Warren Zimmerman, the last U.S. ambassador to Yugoslavia, has characterized it, was also a battle of nationalisms, with each side's actions confirming the other's fears.

If Rwanda and the Balkans do not conform to the images of bubbling cauldrons and ancient tribal hatreds, even less do other ongoing local-level conflicts. Most are drives for political autonomy, most spectacularly in the former Soviet Union, where the collapse of Soviet power allowed long-suppressed peoples to reassert their claims to practice their own languages and religions, and to control their own territory and resources—a rejection of foreign rule much like anti-imperial rebellions in the Americas, Europe, Asia, and Africa. Elsewhere various rebellions, each with its own history and motivations, have typically—and erroneously—been lumped together as "ethnic conflict." Resistance in East Timor to Indonesian control is a 20-year struggle against invasion by a foreign power, not an expression of ethnic or cultural identity. People fighting in the southern Philippines under the banner of a "Moro nation" by and large joined up to regain control of their homelands from Manila-appointed politicians. Zapatista rebels in Chiapas demand jobs, political reform, and, above all, land. They do not mention issues of ethnic or cultural identity in their statements—indeed, their leader is from northern Mexico and until recently spoke no Mayan. Other current conflicts are raw struggles for power among rival factions, particularly in several African countries (Liberia, Somalia, Angola) where rival forces often recruit heavily from one region or clan (giving rise to the notion that these are "ethnic conflicts") in order to make use of local leaders and loyalties to control their followers.[6]

Ethnic Diversity and Social Conflict

This brings us to the third mistaken assumption: that ethnic diversity brings with it political instability and the likelihood of violence. To the contrary, greater ethnic diversity is not associated with greater interethnic conflict. Some of the world's most ethnically diverse states, such as Indonesia, Malaysia, and Pakistan, though not without internal conflict and political repression, have suffered little interethnic violence, while countries with very slight differences in language or culture (the former Yugoslavia, Somalia, Rwanda) have had the bloodiest such conflicts. It is the number of ethnic groups and their relationships to power, not diversity per se, that strongly affect political stability. As shown in recent studies by political scientist Ted Gurr, and contrary to popular thinking, local conflicts have not sharply increased in frequency or severity during the last ten years. The greatest increase in local conflicts occurred during the Cold War, and resulted from the superpowers efforts to arm their client states. (The sense that everything exploded after 1989, Gurr argues, comes from the reassertions of national identity in Eastern Europe and the former Soviet Union.)[7]

By and large, the news media focus on countries racked by violence and ignore the many more cases of peaceful relations among different peoples. Take Indonesia, where I have carried out fieldwork since the late 1970s. If people know of Indonesia, it is probably because of its occupation of East Timor and its suppression of political freedoms. But these are not matters of ethnic conflict, of which there is remarkably little in a country composed of more than three hundred peoples, each with its own distinct language and culture. Although throughout the 1950s and 1960s there were rebellions against Jakarta in many parts of the country, these concerned control over local resources, schooling, and religion. An on-again, off-again rebellion where I work, on the northern tip of Sumatra, has been about control over the region's vast oil and gas resources (although the Western press continues to stereotype it as "ethnic conflict").

Cultural diversity does, of course, present challenges to national integration and social peace. Why do some countries succeed at meeting those challenges while others fail? Two sets of reasons seem most important, and they swamp the mere fact of ethnic and cultural diversity.

First there are the "raw materials" for social peace that countries possess at the time of independence. Countries in which one group has been exploiting all others (such as Rwanda and Burundi) start off with scores to settle, while countries with no such clearly dominating group (such as Indonesia) have an initial advantage in building political consensus. So-called centralized polities, with two or three large groups that continually polarize national politics, are less stable than "dispersed" systems, in which each of many smaller groups is forced to seek out allies to achieve its goals. And if the major ethnic groups share a language or religion, or if they have worked together in a revolutionary struggle, they have a bridge already in place that they can use to build political cooperation.[8]

Take, again, the case of Indonesia. In colonial Indonesia (the Dutch East Indies) the Javanese were, as they are today, the most numerous people. But they were concentrated on Java and held positions of power only there. Peoples of Java, Sumatra, and the eastern islands, along with Malays and many in the southern Philippines, had used Malay as a *lingua franca* for centuries, and Malay became the basis for the language of independent Indonesia. Islam also cut across regions and ethnicities, uniting people on Sumatra, Java, and Sulawesi. Dominance was "dispersed," in that prominent figures in literature, religion, and the nationalist movement tended as often as not to be from someplace other than Java, notably Sumatra. Moreover, people from throughout the country had spent five years fighting Dutch efforts to regain control after the Second World War, and could draw on the shared experience of that common struggle.[9]

One can see the difference each of these features makes by looking next door at culturally similar Malaysia. Malays and Chinese, the largest ethnic groups, shared neither language nor religion, and had no shared memory of struggle to draw on. Malays had held all political power during British rule. On the eve of independence there was a clear fault line running between the Malay and Chinese communities.

The Importance of Political Choices

But these initial conditions do not tell the whole story, and here enters the second set of reasons for social peace or social conflict. States do make choices, particularly about political processes, that ease or exacerbate intergroup tensions. As political scientist Donald Horowitz has pointed out, if we consider only their starting conditions, Malaysia ought to have experienced considerable interethnic violence (for the reasons given above), whereas Sri Lanka, where Tamils and Sinhalese had mingled in the British-trained elite, should have been spared such violence. And yet Malaysia has largely managed to avoid it while Sri Lanka has not. The crucial difference, writes Horowitz, was in the emerging political systems in the two countries. Malaysian politicians constructed a multiethnic political coalition, which fostered ties between Chinese and Malay leaders and forced political candidates to seek the large middle electoral ground. In Sri Lanka, as we saw earlier, Sinhalese-speakers formed a chauvinist nationalist movement, and after early cooperation Tamils and Sinhalese split apart to form ethnically based political parties. Extreme factions appeared on the wings of each party, forcing party leaders to drift in their directions.

But political systems can be changed. Nigeria is a good example. Prior to 1967 it consisted of three regions—North, South, and East—each with its own party supported by ethnic allegiances. The intensity of this three-way division drove the southeast region of Biafra to attempt to break away from Nigeria in 1967, and the trauma of the civil war that followed led politicians to try a new system. They carved the country into 19 states, the boundaries of which cut through the territories of the three largest ethnic groups (Hausa, Yoruba, and Igbo), encouraging a new federalist politics based on multiethnic coalitions. The new system, for all its other problems, prevented another Biafra. Subsequent leaders, however, continued to add to the number of states for their own political reasons. The current leader, General Sani Abacha, is now adding to an already expanded list of 30 states; this excessive fragmentation has broken up the multiethnic coalitions and encouraged ethnic politics anew. A similar direction has been pursued by Kenya's Daniel arap Moi, who has created an ethnic electoral base that excludes most Kikuyus, increasing the relevance of ethnicity in politics and therefore the level of intergroup tensions.

What the myth of ethnic conflict would say are ever-present tensions are in fact the products of political choices. Negative stereotyping, fear of another group, killing lest one be killed—these are the doings of so-called leaders, and can be undone by them as well. Believing otherwise, and assuming that such conflicts are the natural consequences of human depravity in some quarters of the world, leads to perverse thinking and perverse policy. It makes violence seem characteristic of a people or region, rather than the consequence of specific political acts. Thinking this way excuses inaction, as when U.S. president Bill Clinton, seeking to retreat from the hard-line Balkan policy of candidate Clinton, began to claim that Bosnians and Serbs were killing each other because of their ethnic and religious differences. Because it paints all sides as less rational and less modern (more tribal, more ethnic) than "we" are, it makes it easier to tolerate their suffering. Because it assumes that "those people" would naturally follow their leaders' call to kill, it distracts us from the central and difficult question of just how and why people are sometimes led to commit such horrifying deeds.

Notes

1. Two of the most widely read proponents of the view I am contesting are Robert Kaplan, in his dispatches for *The Atlantic* and in his *Balkan Ghosts: A Journey Through History* (New York: St. Martin's, 1993), and (writing mainly on large-scale conflict) Samuel P. Huntington, in "The Clash of Civilizations?" *Foreign Affairs* 72 (Summer 1993): 22–49. My concern is less with the particular difficulties of these writers' arguments, about which others have written, than with the general notion, which, as with all myths, survives the death of any one of its versions.

2. See Misha Glenny, *The Fall of Yugoslavia* (New York: Penguin, 1992), for a balanced and ethnographically rich account of the Balkan wars. On recent tendencies in European nationalisms, see especially Rogers Brubaker, *Nationalism Reframed: Nationhood and the National Question in the New Europe* (Cambridge: Cambridge University Press, 1996). Brubaker makes the important point that "nationalism" should be treated as a category of social and political ideology, and not a pre-ideological "thing."

3. S. J. Tambiah, *Sri Lanka: Ethnic Fratricide and the Dismantling of Democracy* (Chicago: University of Chicago Press, 1986). For a different view on the culture of violence in Sri Lanka, see Bruce Kapferer, *Legends of People, Myths of State* (Washington, D.C.: Smithsonian Institution Press, 1988).

4. Among recent overviews of massacres in Rwanda and Burundi, see Philip Gourevitch, "The Poisoned Country," *New York Review of Books*, 6 June 1996, 58–64, and René Lemarchand, *Burundi: Ethnic Conflict and Genocide* (Cambridge: Cambridge University Press, 1995).

5. That there were memories, fears, and hatreds to exploit is important to bear in mind, lest we go to the other extreme and argue that these conflicts are entirely produced from the top, an extreme toward which an overreliance on rational-choice models may lead some analysts. Russell Hardin's otherwise excellent *One for All: The Logic of Group Conflict* (Princeton: Princeton University Press, 1995) errs, I believe, in attributing nothing but rational, self-aggrandizing motives to those leaders who stir up ethnic passions, ignoring that they, too, can be caught up in these passions. The cold rationality of leaders is itself a variable: probably Milošević fits Hardin's rational-actor model better than Tudjman, and Suharto better than Sukarno. In each case, it is an empirical question.

6. The same points could be made concerning the religious version of "ancient hatreds," such as Muslim-Hindu elations in India. However peaceful or conflictual "ancient" relations may have been (and on this issue there continues to be a great deal of controversy among historians of South Asia), the often bloody conflicts of the past ten years in India have been fueled by ambitious politicians who have seen boundless electoral opportunity in middle-class Hindu resentment toward 1) lower castes' claims that they deserve employment and education quotas, and 2) the recent prosperity of some middle-class Muslims. See the penetrating political analyses by Susanne Hoeber Rudolph and Lloyd I. Rudolph in the *New Republic*, 22 March 1993 and 14 February 1994, and a historical and ethnographic study by Peter van der Veer, *Religious Nationalism: Hindus and Muslims in India* (Berkeley: University of California Press, 1994).

7. See Ted Gurr, *Ethnic Conflict in World Politics* (Boulder, Colo.: Westview, 1994).

8. See Donald L. Horowitz, *Ethnic Groups in Conflict* (Berkeley: University of California Press, 1985), 291–364.

9. I would propose "dispersed dominance" (a situation in which each of several groups considers itself to dominate on some social or political dimension) as a second important mechanism for reducing intergroup conflict alongside the well-known "cross-cutting cleavages" (a situation in which one or more important dimensions of diversity cut across others, as religion cuts across ethnicity in many countries). "Dispersed dominance" takes into account social and cultural dimensions, such as literary preeminence or a sense of social worth stemming from putative indigenous status. It is thus broader than, but similar to, political mechanisms such as federalism, when these mechanisms are aimed at (in Donald Horowitz's phrase) "proliferating the points of power." It is the empirical correlate to the normative position articulated by Michael Walzer in *Spheres of Justice* (New York: Basic Books, 1983) that dominance in one sphere (or dimension) ought not to automatically confer dominance in others.

Jihad vs. McWorld

*The two axial principles of our age—tribalism and globalism—clash at every point
except one: they may both be threatening to democracy*

Benjamin R. Barber

*Benjamin R. Barber is the Whitman Pro-
fessor of Political Science at Rutgers
University. Barber's most recent books
are* Strong Democracy *(1984),* The Con-
quest of Politics *(1988), and* An Aristocracy of Everyone.

Just beyond the horizon of current
events lie two possible political figures—both bleak, neither democratic.
The first is a retribalization of large
swaths of humankind by war and blood-
shed: a threatened Lebanonization of national states in which culture is pitted
against culture, people against people,
tribe against tribe—a Jihad in the name of
a hundred narrowly conceived faiths
against every kind of interdependence,
every kind of artificial social cooperation and civic mutuality. The second is
being borne in on us by the onrush of
economic and ecological forces that demand integration and uniformity and that
mesmerize the world with fast music, fast
computers, and fast food—with MTV,
Macintosh, and McDonald's, pressing
nations into one commercially homoge-
nous global network: one McWorld tied
together by technology, ecology, communications, and commerce. The planet
is falling precipitately apart and coming
reluctantly together at the very same
moment.

These two tendencies are sometimes
visible in the same countries at the same
instant: thus Yugoslavia, clamoring just
recently to join the New Europe, is ex-
ploding into fragments; India is trying to
live up to its reputation as the world's
largest integral democracy while powerful new fundamentalist parties like the
Hindu nationalist Bharatiya Janata Party,
along with nationalist assassins, are im-

periling its hard-won unity. States are
breaking up or joining up: the Soviet
Union has disappeared almost overnight,
its parts forming new unions with one
another or with like-minded nationalities
in neighboring states. The old interwar
national state based on territory and political sovereignty looks to be a mere
transitional development.

The tendencies of what I am here
calling the forces of Jihad and the forces
of McWorld operate with equal strength
in opposite directions, the one driven by
parochial hatreds, the other by universalizing markets, the one re-creating ancient subnational and ethnic borders
from within, the other making national
borders porous from without. They have
one thing in common: neither offers
much hope to citizens looking for practical ways to govern themselves democratically. If the global future is to put
Jihad's centrifugal whirlwind against
McWorld's centripetal black hole, the
outcome is unlikely to be democratic—or
so I will argue.

MCWORLD, OR THE
GLOBALIZATION OF POLITICS

Four imperatives make up the dynamic
of McWorld: a market imperative, a resource imperative, an information-technology imperative, and an ecological
imperative. By shrinking the world and
diminishing the salience of national borders, these imperatives have in combination achieved a considerable victory over
factiousness and particularism, and not
least of all over their most virulent traditional form—nationalism. It is the real-
ists who are now Europeans, the utopians
who dream nostalgically of a resurgent
England or Germany, perhaps even a
resurgent Wales or Saxony. Yesterday's

wishful cry for one world has yielded to
the reality of McWorld.

The market imperative. Marxist and
Leninist theories of imperialism assumed
that the quest for ever-expanding markets
would in time compel nation-based capitalist economies to push against national
boundaries in search of an international
economic imperium. Whatever else has
happened to the scientistic predictions of
Marxism, in this domain they have proved
farsighted. All national economies are
now vulnerable to the inroads of larger,
transnational markets within which trade
is free, currencies are convertible, access
to banking is open, and contracts are
enforceable under law. In Europe, Asia,
Africa, the South Pacific, and the Americas such markets are eroding national
sovereignty and giving rise to entities—
international banks, trade associations,
transnational lobbies like OPEC and
Greenpeace, world news services like
CNN and the BBC, and multinational
corporations that increasingly lack a
meaningful national identity—that neither reflect nor respect nationhood as an
organizing or regulative principle.

The market imperative has also reinforced the quest for international peace
and stability, requisites of an efficient
international economy. Markets are enemies of parochialism, isolation, fractiousness, war. Market psychology attenuates
the psychology of ideological and religious cleavages and assumes a concord
among producers and consumers—categories that ill fit narrowly conceived
national or religious cultures. Shopping
has little tolerance for blue laws, whether
dictated by pub-closing British paternalism, Sabbath-observing Jewish Orthodox
fundamentalism, or no-Sunday-liquor-sales
Massachusetts puritanism. In the context
of common markets, international law
ceases to be a vision of justice and be-

comes a workaday framework for getting things done—enforcing contracts, ensuring that governments abide by deals, regulating trade and currency relations, and so forth.

Common markets demand a common language, as well as a common currency, and they produce common behaviors of the kind bred by cosmopolitan city life everywhere. Commercial pilots, computer programmers, international bankers, media specialists, oil riggers, entertainment celebrities, ecology experts, demographers, accountants, professors, athletes—these compose a new breed of men and women for whom religion, culture, and nationality can seem only marginal elements in a working identity. Although sociologists of everyday life will no doubt continue to distinguish a Japanese from an American mode, shopping has a common signature throughout the world. Cynics might even say that some of the recent revolutions in Eastern Europe have had as their true goal not liberty and the right to vote but well-paying jobs and the right to shop (although the vote is proving easier to acquire than consumer goods). The market imperative is, then, plenty powerful; but, notwithstanding some of the claims made for "democratic capitalism," it is not identical with the democratic imperative.

The resource imperative. Democrats once dreamed of societies whose political autonomy rested firmly on economic independence. The Athenians idealized what they called autarky, and tried for a while to create a way of life simple and austere enough to make the polis genuinely self-sufficient. To be free meant to be independent of any other community or polis. Not even the Athenians were able to achieve autarky, however: human nature, it turns out, is dependency. By the time of Pericles, Athenian politics was inextricably bound up with a flowering empire held together by naval power and commerce—an empire that, even as it appeared to enhance Athenian might, ate away at Athenian independence and autarky. Master and slave, it turned out, were bound together by mutual insufficiency.

The dream of autarky briefly engrossed nineteenth-century America as well, for the underpopulated, endlessly bountiful land, the cornucopia of natural resources, and the natural barriers of a continent walled in by two great seas led many to believe that America could be a world unto itself. Given this past, it has been harder for Americans than for most to accept the inevitability of interdependence. But the rapid depletion of resources even in a country like ours, where they once seemed inexhaustible, and the maldistribution of arable soil and mineral resources on the planet, leave even the wealthiest societies ever more resource-dependent and many other nations in permanently desperate straits.

Every nation, it turns out, needs something another nation has; some nations have almost nothing they need.

The information-technology imperative. Enlightenment science and the technologies derived from it are inherently universalizing. They entail a quest for descriptive principles of general application, a search for universal solutions to particular problems, and an unswerving embrace of objectivity and impartiality.

Scientific progress embodies and depends on open communication, a common discourse rooted in rationality, collaboration, and an easy and regular flow and exchange of information. Such ideals can be hypocritical covers for power-mongering by elites, and they may be shown to be wanting in many other ways, but they are entailed by the very idea of science and they make science and globalization practical allies.

Business, banking, and commerce all depend on information flow and are facilitated by new communication technologies. The hardware of these technologies tends to be systemic and integrated—computer, television, cable, satellite, laser, fiber-optic, and microchip technologies combining to create a vast interactive communications and information network that can potentially give every person on earth access to every other person, and make every datum, every byte, available to every set of eyes. If the automobile was, as George Ball once said (when he gave his blessing to a Fiat factory in the Soviet Union during the Cold War), "an ideology on four wheels," then electronic telecommunication and information systems are an ideology at 186,000 miles per second—which makes for a very small planet in a very big hurry. Individual cultures speak particular languages; commerce and science increasingly speak English; the whole world speaks logarithms and binary mathematics.

Moreover, the pursuit of science and technology asks for, even compels, open societies. Satellite footprints do not respect national borders; telephone wires penetrate the most closed societies. With photocopying and then fax machines having infiltrated Soviet universities and *samizdat* literary circles in the eighties, and computer modems having multiplied like rabbits in communism's bureaucratic warrens thereafter, *glasnost* could not be far behind. In their social requisites, secrecy and science are enemies.

The new technology's software is perhaps even more globalizing than its hardware. The information arm of international commerce's sprawling body reaches out and touches distinct nations and parochial cultures, and gives them a common face chiseled in Hollywood, on Madison Avenue, and in Silicon Valley. Throughout the 1980s one of the most-watched television programs in South Africa was *The Cosby Show.* The demise of apartheid was already in production. Exhibitors at the 1991 Cannes film festival expressed growing anxiety over the "homogenization" and "Americanization" of the global film industry when, for the third year running, American films dominated the awards ceremonies. America has dominated the world's popular culture for much longer, and much more decisively. In November of 1991 Switzerland's once insular culture boasted best-seller lists featuring *Terminator 2* as the No. 1 movie, *Scarlett* as the No. 1 book, and Prince's *Diamonds and Pearls* as the No. 1 record album. No wonder the Japanese are buying Hollywood film studios even faster than Americans are buying Japanese television sets. This kind of software supremacy may in the long term be far more important than hardware superiority, because culture has become more potent than armaments. What is the power of the Pentagon compared with Disneyland? Can the Sixth Fleet keep up with CNN? McDonald's in Moscow and Coke in China will do more to create a global culture than military colonization ever could. It is less the goods than the brand names that do the work, for they convey life-style images that alter perception and challenge behavior. They make up the seductive software of McWorld's common (at times much too common) soul.

Yet in all this high-tech commercial world there is nothing that looks particularly democratic. It lends itself to surveillance as well as liberty, to new forms of manipulation and covert control as well as new kinds of participation, to skewed, unjust market outcomes as well as greater productivity. The consumer society and the open society are not quite synonymous. Capitalism and democracy have a relationship, but it is something less than a marriage. An efficient free market after all requires that consumers be free to vote their dollars on competing goods, not that citizens be free to vote their values and beliefs on competing political candidates and programs. The free market flourished in junta-run Chile, in military-governed Taiwan and Korea, and, earlier, in a variety of autocratic European empires as well as their colonial possessions.

The ecological imperative. The impact of globalization on ecology is a cliché even to world leaders who ignore it. We know well enough that the German forests can be destroyed by Swiss and Italians driving gas-guzzlers fueled by leaded gas. We also know that the planet can be asphyxiated by greenhouse gases because Brazilian farmers want to be part of the twentieth century and are burning down tropical rain forests to clear a little land to plough, and because Indonesians make a living out of converting their lush jungle into toothpicks for fastidious Japanese diners, upsetting the delicate oxygen balance and in effect puncturing our global lungs. Yet this ecological consciousness has meant not only greater awareness but also greater inequality, as modernized nations try to slam the door behind them, saying to developing nations, "The world cannot afford *your* modernization; ours has wrung it dry!"

Each of the four imperatives just cited is transnational, transideological, and transcultural. Each applies impartially to Catholics, Jews, Muslims, Hindus, and Buddhists; to democrats and totalitarians; to capitalists and socialists. The Enlightenment dream of a universal rational society has to a remarkable degree been realized—but in a form that is commercialized, homogenized, depoliticized, bureaucratized, and, of course, radically incomplete, for the movement toward McWorld is in competition with forces of global breakdown, national dissolution, and centrifugal corruption. These forces, working in the opposite direction, are the essence of what I call Jihad.

JIHAD, OR THE LEBANONIZATION OF THE WORLD

OPEC, the World Bank, the United Nations, the International Red Cross, the multinational corporation . . . there are scores of institutions that reflect globalization. But they often appear as ineffective reactors to the world's real actors: national states and, to an ever greater degree, subnational factions in permanent rebellion against uniformity and integration—even the kind represented by universal law and justice. The headlines feature these players regularly: they are cultures, not countries; parts, not wholes; sects, not religions; rebellious factions and dissenting minorities at war not just with globalism but with the traditional nation-state. Kurds, Basques, Puerto Ricans, Ossetians, East Timoreans, Quebecois, the Catholics of Northern Ireland, Abkhasians, Kurile Islander Japanese, the Zulus of Inkatha, Catalonians, Tamils, and, of course, Palestinians—people without countries, inhabiting nations not their own, seeking smaller worlds within borders that will seal them off from modernity.

A powerful irony is at work here. Nationalism was once a force of integration and unification, a movement aimed at bringing together disparate clans, tribes, and cultural fragments under new, assimilationist flags. But as Ortega y Gasset noted more than sixty years ago, having won its victories, nationalism changed its strategy. In the 1920s, and again today, it is more often a reactionary and divisive force, pulverizing the very nations it once helped cement together. The force that creates nations is "inclusive," Ortega wrote in *The Revolt of the Masses.* "In periods of consolidation, nationalism has a positive value, and is a lofty standard. But in Europe everything is more than consolidated, and nationalism is nothing but a mania. . . ."

This mania has left the post-Cold War world smoldering with hot wars; the international scene is little more unified than it was at the end of the Great War, in Ortega's own time. There were more than thirty wars in progress last year, most of them ethnic, racial, tribal, or religious in character, and the list of unsafe regions doesn't seem to be getting any shorter. Some new world order!

The aim of many of these small-scale wars is to redraw boundaries, to implode states and resecure parochial identities: to escape McWorld's dully insistent imperatives. The mood is that of Jihad: war not as an instrument of policy but as an emblem of identity, an expression of community, an end in itself. Even where there is no shooting war, there is fractiousness, secession, and the quest for ever smaller communities. Add to the list

of dangerous countries those at risk: In Switzerland and Spain, Jurassian and Basque separatists still argue the virtues of ancient identities, sometimes in the language of bombs. Hyperdisintegration in the former Soviet Union may well continue unabated—not just a Ukraine independent from the Soviet Union but a Bessarabian Ukraine independent from the Ukrainian republic; not just Russia severed from the defunct union but Tatarstan severed from Russia. Yugoslavia makes even the disunited, ex-Soviet, nonsocialist republics that were once the Soviet Union look integrated, its sectarian fatherlands springing up within factional motherlands like weeds within weeds within weeds. Kurdish independence would threaten the territorial integrity of four Middle Eastern nations. Well before the current cataclysm Soviet Georgia made a claim for autonomy from the Soviet Union, only to be faced with its Ossetians (164,000 in a republic of 5.5 million) demanding their own self-determination within Georgia. The Abkhasian minority in Georgia has followed suit. Even the good will established by Canada's once promising Meech Lake protocols is in danger, with Francophone Quebec again threatening the dissolution of the federation. In South Africa the emergence from apartheid was hardly achieved when friction between Inkatha's Zulus and the African National Congress's tribally identified members threatened to replace Europeans' racism with an indigenous tribal war after thirty years of attempted integration using the colonial language (English) as a unifier, Nigeria is now playing with the idea of linguistic multiculturalism—which could mean the cultural breakup of the nation into hundreds of tribal fragments. Even Saddam Hussein has benefited from the threat of internal Jihad, having used renewed tribal and religious warfare to turn last season's mortal enemies into reluctant allies of an Iraqi nationhood that he nearly destroyed.

The passing of communism has torn away the thin veneer of internationalism (workers of the world unite!) to reveal ethnic prejudices that are not only ugly and deep-seated but increasingly murderous. Europe's old scourge, anti-Semitism, is back with a vengeance, but it is only one of many antagonisms. It appears all too easy to throw the historical gears into reverse and pass from a Communist dictatorship back into a tribal state.

Among the tribes, religion is also a battlefield. ("Jihad" is a rich word whose generic meaning is "struggle"—usually the struggle of the soul to avert evil. Strictly applied to religious war, it is used only in reference to battles where the faith is under assault, or battles against a government that denies the practice of Islam. My use here is rhetorical, but does follow both journalistic practice and history.) Remember the Thirty Years War? Whatever forms of Enlightenment universalism might once have come to grace such historically related forms of monotheism as Judaism, Christianity, and Islam, in many of their modern incarnations they are parochial rather than cosmopolitan, angry rather than loving, proselytizing rather than ecumenical, zealous rather than rationalist, sectarian rather than deistic, ethnocentric rather than universalizing. As a result, like the new forms of hypernationalism, the new expressions of religious fundamentalism are fractious and pulverizing, never integrating. This is religion as the Crusaders knew it: a battle to the death for souls that if not saved will be forever lost.

The atmospherics of Jihad have resulted in a breakdown of civility in the name of identity, of comity in the name of community. International relations have sometimes taken on the aspect of gang war—cultural turf battles featuring tribal factions that were supposed to be sublimated as integral parts of large national, economic, postcolonial, and constitutional entities.

THE DARKENING FUTURE OF DEMOCRACY

These rather melodramatic tableaux vivants do not tell the whole story, however. For all their defects, Jihad and McWorld have their attractions. Yet, to repeat and insist, the attractions are unrelated to democracy. Neither McWorld nor Jihad is remotely democratic in impulse. Neither needs democracy; neither promotes democracy.

McWorld does manage to look pretty seductive in a world obsessed with Jihad. It delivers peace, prosperity, and relative unity—if at the cost of independence, community, and identity (which is generally based on difference). The primary political values required by the global market are order and tranquillity, and freedom—as in the phrases "free trade," "free press," and "free love." Human rights are needed to a degree, but not citizenship or participation—and no more social justice and equality than are necessary to promote efficient economic production and consumption. Multinational corporations sometimes seem to prefer doing business with local oligarchs, inasmuch as they can take confidence from dealing with the boss on all crucial matters. Despots who slaughter their own populations are no problem, so long as they leave markets in place and refrain from making war on their neighbors (Saddam Hussein's fatal mistake). In trading partners, predictability is of more value than justice.

The Eastern European revolutions that seemed to arise out of concern for global democratic values quickly deteriorated into a stampede in the general direction of free markets and their ubiquitous, television-promoted shopping malls. East Germany's Neues Forum, that courageous gathering of intellectuals, students, and workers which overturned the Stalinist regime in Berlin in 1989, lasted only six months in Germany's mini-version of McWorld. Then it gave way to money and markets and monopolies from the West. By the time of the first all-German elections, it could scarcely manage to secure three percent of the vote. Elsewhere there is growing evidence that *glasnost* will go and *perestroika*—defined as privatization and an opening of markets to Western bidders—will stay. So understandably anxious are the new rulers of Eastern Europe and whatever entities are forged from the residues of the Soviet Union to gain access to credit and markets and technology—McWorld's flourishing new currencies—that they have shown themselves willing to trade away democratic prospects in pursuit of them: not just old totalitarian ideologies and command-economy production models but some possible indigenous experiments with a third way between capitalism and socialism, such as economic cooperatives and employee stock-ownership plans, both of which have their ardent supporters in the East.

Jihad delivers a different set of virtues: a vibrant local identity, a sense of community, solidarity among kinsmen, neighbors, and countrymen, narrowly conceived. But it also guarantees parochialism and is grounded in exclusion. Solidarity is secured through war against outsiders. And solidarity often means obedience to a hierarchy in governance, fanaticism in beliefs, and the obliteration of individual selves in the name of the group. Deference to leaders and intolerance toward outsiders (and toward "enemies within") are hallmarks of tribalism—hardly the attitudes required for the cultivation of new democratic women and men capable of governing themselves. Where new democratic experiments have been conducted in retribalizing societies, in both Europe and the Third World, the result has often been anarchy, repression, persecution, and the coming of new, noncommunist forms of very old kinds of despotism. During the past year, Havel's velvet revolution in Czechoslovakia was imperiled by partisans of "Czechland" and of Slovakia as independent entities. India seemed little less rent by Sikh, Hindu, Muslim, and Tamil infighting than it was immediately after the British pulled out, more than forty years ago.

To the extent that either McWorld or Jihad has a *natural* politics, it has turned out to be more of an antipolitics. For McWorld, it is the antipolitics of globalism: bureaucratic, technocratic, and meritocratic, focused (as Marx predicted it would be) on the administration of things—with people, however, among the chief things to be administered. In its politico-economic imperatives McWorld has been guided by laissez-faire market principles that privilege efficiency, productivity, and beneficence at the expense of civic liberty and self-government.

For Jihad, the antipolitics of tribalization has been explicitly antidemocratic: one-party dictatorship, government by military junta, theocratic fundamentalism—often associated with a version of the *Führerprinzip* that empowers an individual to rule on behalf of a people. Even the government of India, struggling for decades to model democracy for a people who will soon number a billion, longs for great leaders; and for every Mahatma Gandhi, Indira Gandhi, or Rajiv Gandhi taken from them by zealous assassins, the Indians appear to seek a replacement who will deliver them from the lengthy travail of their freedom.

THE CONFEDERAL OPTION

How can democracy be secured and spread in a world whose primary tendencies are at best indifferent to it (McWorld) and at worst deeply antithetical to it (Jihad)? My guess is that globalization will eventually vanquish retribalization.

The ethos of material "civilization" has not yet encountered an obstacle it has been unable to thrust aside. Ortega may have grasped in the 1920s a clue to our own future in the coming millennium.

Everyone sees the need of a new principle of life. But as always happens in similar crises—some people attempt to save the situation by an artificial intensification of the very principle which has led to decay. This is the meaning of the "nationalist" outburst of recent years . . . things have always gone that way. The last flare, the longest; the last sigh, the deepest. On the very eve of their disappearance there is an intensification of frontiers—military and economic.

Jihad may be a last deep sigh before the eternal yawn of McWorld. On the other hand, Ortega was not exactly prescient; his prophecy of peace and internationalism came just before blitzkrieg, world war, and the Holocaust tore the old order to bits. Yet democracy is how we remonstrate with reality, the rebuke our aspirations offer to history. And if retribalization is inhospitable to democracy, there is nonetheless a form of democratic government that can accommodate parochialism and communitarianism, one that can even save them from their defects and make them more tolerant and participatory: decentralized participatory democracy. And if McWorld is indifferent to democracy, there is nonetheless a form of democratic government that suits global markets passably well—representative government in its federal or, better still, confederal variation.

With its concern for accountability, the protection of minorities, and the universal rule of law, a confederalized representative system would serve the political needs of McWorld as well as oligarchic bureaucratism or meritocratic elitism is currently doing. As we are already beginning to see, many nations may survive in the long term only as confederations that afford local regions smaller than "nations" extensive jurisdiction. Recommended reading for democrats of the twenty-first century is not the U.S. Constitution or the French Declaration of Rights of Man and Citizen but the Articles of Confederation, that suddenly pertinent document that stitched together the thirteen American colonies into what then seemed a too loose confederation of

independent states but now appears a new form of political realism, as veterans of Yeltsin's new Russia and the new Europe created at Maastricht will attest.

By the same token, the participatory and direct form of democracy that engages citizens in civic activity and civic judgment and goes well beyond just voting and accountability—the system I have called "strong democracy"—suits the political needs of decentralized communities as well as theocratic and nationalist party dictatorships have done. Local neighborhoods need not be democratic, but they can be. Real democracy has flourished in diminutive settings: the spirit of liberty, Tocqueville said, is local. Participatory democracy, if not naturally apposite to tribalism, has an undeniable attractiveness under conditions of parochialism.

Democracy in any of these variations will, however, continue to be obstructed by the undemocratic and antidemocratic trends toward uniformitarian globalism and intolerant retribalization which I have portrayed here. For democracy to persist in our brave new McWorld, we will have to commit acts of conscious political will—a possibility, but hardly a probability, under these conditions. Political will requires much more than the quick fix of the transfer of institutions. Like technology transfer, institution transfer rests on foolish assumptions about a uniform world of the kind that once fired the imagination of colonial administrators. Spread English justice to the colonies by exporting wigs. Let an East Indian trading company act as the vanguard to Britain's free parliamentary institutions. Today's well-intentioned quick-fixers in the National Endowment for Democracy and the Kennedy School of Government, in the unions and foundations and universities zealously nurturing contacts in Eastern Europe and the Third World, are hoping to democratize by long distance. Post Bulgaria a parliament by first-class mail. Fed Ex the Bill of Rights to Sri Lanka. Cable Cambodia some common law.

Yet Eastern Europe has already demonstrated that importing free political parties, parliaments, and presses cannot establish a democratic civil society; imposing a free market may even have the opposite effect. Democracy grows from the bottom up and cannot be imposed

from the top down. Civil society has to be built from the inside out. The institutional superstructure comes last. Poland may become democratic, but then again it may heed the Pope, and prefer to found its politics on its Catholicism, with uncertain consequences for democracy. Bulgaria may become democratic, but it may prefer tribal war. The former Soviet Union may become a democratic confederation, or it may just grow into an anarchic and weak conglomeration of markets for other nations' goods and services.

Democrats need to seek out indigenous democratic impulses. There is always a desire for self-government, always some expression of participation, accountability, consent, and representation, even in traditional hierarchical societies. These need to be identified, tapped, modified, and incorporated into new democratic practices with an indigenous flavor. The tortoises among the democratizers may ultimately outlive or outpace the hares, for they will have the time and patience to explore conditions along the way, and to adapt their gait to changing circumstances. Tragically, democracy in a hurry often looks something like France in 1794 or China in 1989.

It certainly seems possible that the most attractive democratic ideal in the face of the brutal realities of Jihad and the dull realities of McWorld will be a confederal union of semi-autonomous communities smaller than nation-states, tied together into regional economic associations and markets larger than nation-states—participatory and self-determining in local matters at the bottom, representative and accountable at the top. The nation-state would play a diminished role, and sovereignty would lose some of its political potency. The Green movement adage "Think globally, act locally" would actually come to describe the conduct of politics.

This vision reflects only an ideal, however—one that is not terribly likely to be realized. Freedom, Jean-Jacques Rousseau once wrote, is a food easy to eat but hard to digest. Still, democracy has always played itself out against the odds. And democracy remains both a form of coherence as binding as McWorld and a secular faith potentially as inspiriting as Jihad.

Index

Credits/Acknowledgments

Cover design by Charles Vitelli

1. Pluralist Democracies: Country Studies
Facing overview—*The Christian Science Monitor* photo by R. Norman Matheny.

2. Pluralist Democracies: Factors in the Political Process
Facing overview—AP/Wide World Photo by Michel Euler.

3. Europe—West, Center, and East
Facing overview—United Nations photo.

4. Political Diversity in the Developing World
Facing overview—United Nations photo by P. Jambor. 205—*The Christian Science Monitor* map by Dave Herring. © 1996 by The Christian Science Publishing Society. All rights reserved. Reprinted by permission.

5. Comparative Politics
Facing overview—Aramco photo.

ANNUAL EDITIONS ARTICLE REVIEW FORM

■ NAME: _____ DATE: _____

■ TITLE AND NUMBER OF ARTICLE: _____

■ BRIEFLY STATE THE MAIN IDEA OF THIS ARTICLE: _____

_____

■ LIST THREE IMPORTANT FACTS THAT THE AUTHOR USES TO SUPPORT THE MAIN IDEA:

_____

_____

_____

_____

■ WHAT INFORMATION OR IDEAS DISCUSSED IN THIS ARTICLE ARE ALSO DISCUSSED IN YOUR TEXTBOOK OR OTHER READINGS THAT YOU HAVE DONE? LIST THE TEXTBOOK CHAPTERS AND PAGE NUMBERS:

_____

_____

_____

_____

_____

■ LIST ANY EXAMPLES OF BIAS OR FAULTY REASONING THAT YOU FOUND IN THE ARTICLE:

_____

_____

_____

_____

■ LIST ANY NEW TERMS/CONCEPTS THAT WERE DISCUSSED IN THE ARTICLE, AND WRITE A SHORT DEFINITION:

_____

_____

_____

_____

We Want Your Advice

ANNUAL EDITIONS revisions depend on two major opinion sources: one is our Advisory Board, listed in the front of this volume, which works with us in scanning the thousands of articles published in the public press each year; the other is you—the person actually using the book. Please help us and the users of the next edition by completing the prepaid article rating form on this page and returning it to us. Thank you for your help!

ANNUAL EDITIONS: COMPARATIVE POLITICS 97/98
Article Rating Form

Here is an opportunity for you to have direct input into the next revision of this volume. We would like you to rate each of the 60 articles listed below, using the following scale:

1. **Excellent: should definitely be retained**
2. **Above average: should probably be retained**
3. **Below average: should probably be deleted**
4. **Poor: should definitely be deleted**

Your ratings will play a vital part in the next revision. So please mail this prepaid form to us just as soon as you complete it.
Thanks for your help!

Rating	Article	Rating	Article
	1. The Politics of Power		31. Campaign and Party Finance: What Americans Might Learn from Abroad
	2. Tony Blair and the New Left		32. Electoral Reform: Good Government? Fairness? Or Vice Versa. Or Both?
	3. Britain's 1997 General Election		33. Presidents and Prime Ministers
	4. Revamping Britain's Constitution		34. An American Perspective on the European Experiment
	5. Blair on the Constitution: Democracy's Second Age		35. The Politics of European Monetary Union
	6. What Is Scotland's Future?		36. Sweden: A Model Crisis
	7. After the Talking Stopped		37. Rising Health Costs Threaten Generous Benefits in Europe
	8. Helmut Kohl: Extra Extra Large		38. Europe and the Underclass: The Slippery Slope
	9. United Germany in an Integrating Europe		39. Inequalities in Europe: Affirmative Laissez Faire
	10. The Shadow of Weimar		40. The Return of the Habsburgs
	11. Perspectives on the German Model		41. Witness to the Fall
	12. Germany's New Foreign Policy: Looking Both East & West		42. A Transition Leading to Tragedy
	13. Chirac and France: Prisoners of the Past?		43. Can Russia Change?
	14. For France, Sagging Self-Image and Esprit		44. Let's Abolish the Third World
	15. Is Le Pen Mightier than the Sword?		45. The 'Third World' Is Dead, but Spirits Linger
	16. Tocqueville in Italy		46. The Backlash in Latin America: Gestures against Reform
	17. Italy's General Election of 1996		47. Mexico: Uneasy, Uncertain, Unpredictable
	18. Italy Experiments with Stability		48. Democracy, of a Sort, Sweeps Africa
	19. Italy at a Turning Point		49. Why Is Africa Eating Asia's Dust?
	20. Hashimoto's Headache		50. Deng Xiaoping, Architect of Modern Chi Dies at 92
	21. Reforming Japan: The Third Opening		51. India: Between Turmoil and Hope
	22. The Left's New Start		52. Miracles beyond the Free Market
	23. Guide to the West European Left		53. Confucius Says: Go East, Young M
	24. Europe's Far Right: Something Nasty in the Woodshed		54. Is the Third Wave Over?
	25. The Impacts of Postwar Migration to Western Europe		55. Capitalism and Democracy
	26. Cherchez la Femme		56. For Democracy, the Next Re
	27. Women, Power, and Politics: The Norwegian Experience		57. Cultural Explanations: The
	28. Where Women's Work Is Job No. 1		58. A Debate on Cultural C
	29. What Democracy Is . . . and Is Not		59. The Myth of Global Et'
	30. Parliament and Congress: Is the Grass Greener on the Other Side?		60. Jihad vs. McWorld

ABOUT YOU

Name _____ Date _____

Are you a teacher? ❑ Or a student? ❑

Your school name _____

Department _____

Address _____

City _____ State _____ Zip _____

School telephone # _____

YOUR COMMENTS ARE IMPORTANT TO US !

Please fill in the following information:

For which course did you use this book? _____

Did you use a text with this *ANNUAL EDITION*? ❑ yes ❑ no

What was the title of the text? _____

What are your general reactions to the *Annual Editions* concept?

Have you read any particular articles recently that you think should be included in the next edition?

Are there any articles you feel should be replaced in the next edition? Why?

Are there any World Wide Web sites you feel should be included in the next edition? Please annotate.

May we contact you for editorial input?

May we quote your comments?